MW00390676

6. Can a local account be used in a trust relation-ship? Explain.

7. In a complete trust domain model that uses 4 different domains, what is the total number of trust relationships required to use a complete trust domain model?

Exam Questions

The following questions are similar to those you will face on the Microsoft exam. Answers to these questions can be found in section Answers and Explanations, later in the chapter. At the end of each of those answers, you will be informed of where (that is, in what section of the chapter) to find more information..

1. ABC Corporation has locations in Toronto, New York, and San Francisco. It wants to install Windows NT Server 4 to encompass all its locations in a single WAN environment. The head office is located in New York. What is the best domain model for ABC's directory services implementation?

   A. Single-domain model

   B. Single-master domain model

   C. Multiple-master domain model

   D. Complete-trust domain model

2. JPS Printing has a single location with 1,000 users spread across the LAN. It has special printers and applications installed on the servers in its environment. It needs to be able to centrally manage the user accounts and the resources. Which domain model would best fit its needs?

   A. Single-domain model

   B. Single-master domain model

   C. Multiple-master domain model

   D. Complete-trust domain model

5. What must be created to allow a user account from one domain to access resources in a different domain?

   A. Complete Trust Domain Model

   B. One Way Trust Relationship

   C. Two Way Trust Relationship

   D. Master-Domain Model

Answers to Review Questions

1. Single domain, master domain, multiple-master domain, complete-trust domain. See section, Windows NT Server 4 Domain Models, in this chapter for more information. (This question deals with objective Planning 1.)

2. One user, one account, centralized administration, universal resource access, synchronization. See section, Windows NT Server 4 Directory Services, in this chapter for more information. (This question deals with objective Planning 1.)

6. Local accounts cannot be given permissions across trusts. See section, Accounts in Trust Relationships, in this chapter for more information. (This question deals with Planning 1.)

Answers and Explanations: For each of the Review and Exam questions, you will find thorough explanations located at the end of the section.

Exam Questions: These questions reflect the kinds of multiple-choice questions that appear on the exams. Use them to become familiar with the exam question formats and to help you determine what you know and what you need to review or study more.

Suggested Readings and Resources

The following are some recommended readings on the subject of installing and configuring NT Workstation:

1. Microsoft Official Curriculum course 770: *Installing and Configuring Microsoft Windows NT Workstation 4.0*

   • Module 1: Overview of Windows NT Workstation 4.0

   • Module 2: Installing Windows NT Workstation 4.0

2. Microsoft Official Curriculum course 922: *Supporting Microsoft Windows NT 4.0 Core Technologies*

   • Module 2: Installing Windows NT

   • Module 3: Configuring the Windows NT Environment

3. *Microsoft Windows NT Workstation Resource Kit Version 4.0* (Microsoft Press)

   • Chapter 2: Customizing Setup

   • Chapter 4: Planning for a Mixed Environment

4. Microsoft TechNet CD-ROM

   • *MS Windows NT Workstation Technical Notes*

     • MS Windows NT Workstation Deployment Guide – Automating Windows NT Setup

     • An Unattended Windows NT Workstation Deployment

5. Web Sites

   • www.microsoft.com/train_cert

Suggested Readings and Resources: The very last element in each chapter is a list of additional resources you can use if you wish to go above and beyond certification-level material or if you need to spend more time on a particular subject that you are having trouble understanding.

CISCO CERTIFIED NETWORK ASSOCIATE
EXAM #640-407

OSI REFERENCE

OBJECTIVE	PAGE REFERENCE
Identify and describe the functions of each of the seven layers of the OSI Reference Model.	Chapter 1, "The Seven Layers," page 16.
Describe connection-oriented network service and connectionless network service and identify the key differences between them.	Chapter 1, "Connection-oriented and Connectionless Services," page 23.
Describe data link addresses and network addresses and identify the key differences between them.	Chapter 1, "Data Link and Network Addresses," page 21.
Identify at least 3 reasons why the industry uses a layered model.	Chapter 1, "OSI Reference Model Communication," page 18.
Define and explain the 5 conversion steps of data encapsulation.	Chapter 1, "Encapsulation," page 19.
Define flow control and describe the three basic methods used in networking.	Chapter 1, "Flow Control," page 24.
List the key internetworking functions of the OSI Network layer and how they are performed in a router.	Chapter 1, "Network Layer," page 17.

WAN PROTOCOLS

OBJECTIVE	PAGE REFERENCE
Differentiate between the following WAN services: Frame Relay, ISDN/LAPD, HDLC, & PPP.	Chapter 5, "How Routers Communicate via Serial Links," page 186 and "Frame Relay," page 189.
Recognize key Frame Relay terms and features.	Chapter 5, "Frame Relay," page 189.
List commands to configure Frame Relay LMIs, maps, and subinterfaces.	Chapter 5, "Configuring Frame Relay," page 195.
List commands to monitor Frame Relay operation of the router.	Chapter 5, "Monitoring Frame Relay," page 198.
Identify PPP operations to encapsulate WAN data on Cisco routers.	Chapter 5, "Configuring Point-to-Point Frame Relay," page 197.
State a relevant use and context for ISDN networking.	Chapter 5, "Integrated Services Digital Network," page 180.

OBJECTIVE	PAGE REFERENCE
Identify ISDN protocols, function groups, reference points, and channels.	Chapter 5, "Integrated Services Digital Network," page 180.
Describe Cisco's implementation of ISDN BRI.	Chapter 5, "Integrated Services Digital Network," page 180.

INTERNETWORKING OPERATING SYSTEM

OBJECTIVE	PAGE REFERENCE
Log in to a router in both user and privileged modes.	Chapter 2, "Logging in to a Router in Both User and Privileged Modes," page 44.
Use the context-sensitive help facility.	Chapter 2, "Context-Sensitive Help," page 48.
Use the command history and editing features.	Chapter 2, "Using the Command History and Editing Features," page 55.
Examine router elements (RAM, ROM, CDP, show).	Chapter 2, "Understanding Router Elements," page 60.
Manage configuration files from the privileged exec mode.	Chapter 2, "Managing Configuration Files from the Privileged Exec Mode," page 72.
Control router passwords, identification, and banner.	Chapter 2, "Configuring the Router," page 49.
Identify the main Cisco IOS commands for router startup.	Chapter 2, "Cisco IOS Commands for Router Startup," page 73.
Enter an initial configuration using the setup command.	Chapter 2, "Configuring a Router with the Setup Command," page 74
Copy and manipulate configuration files.	Chapter 2, "Managing Configuration Files from the Privileged Exec Mode," page 72.
List the commands to load Cisco IOS software from flash memory, a TFTP server, or ROM.	Chapter 2, "Flash Memory," page 60 and "Cisco IOS Commands for Router Startup," page 73.
Prepare to back up, upgrade, and load a back up Cisco IOS software image.	Chapter 2, "Back Up and Upgrade IOS," page 78.
Prepare the initial configuration of your router and enable IP.	Chapter 2, "Configuring the Router," page 49.

CCNA

Cisco Certified
Network Associate

New
Riders

Kevin Mahler, CCNA, CCNP

CCNA Training Guide

International Standard Book Number: 0-7357-0051-6

Library of Congress Catalog Card Number: 99-63017

Printed in the United States of America

First Printing: September, 1999

03   02   01   00   99   7   6   5   4   3   2   1

Interpretation of the printing code: The rightmost double-digit number is the year of the book's printing; the rightmost single-digit number is the number of the book's printing. For example, the printing code 99-1 shows that the first printing of the book occurred in 1999.

Trademarks

Warning and Disclaimer

EXECUTIVE EDITOR
Mary Foote

ACQUISITIONS EDITOR
Stacey Beheler

DEVELOPMENT EDITOR
Ami Frank

MANAGING EDITOR
Sarah Kearns

PROJECT EDITOR
Alissa Cayton

COPY EDITOR
Daryl Kessler

INDEXER
Lisa Stumpf

TECHNICAL EDITORS
Joel Barrett
Michael Keele

SOFTWARE DEVELOPMENT SPECIALIST
Craig Atkins

PRODUCTION
Cheryl Lynch

Contents at a Glance

Table of Contents

PART II

Study and Exam Prep Tips   299

Fast Facts   305

PART III Appendixes

About the Author

Kevin Mahler, CCNA, CCNP lives in Duluth, Georgia with his beautiful wife Wendy and the two best dogs in the world: Khayman, a Sheltie, and Keyser Söze, a German Shepherd. Kevin grew up in Newport News, Virginia, where most of his family still lives. He is currently working as the Wide Area Network Manager for The American Cancer Society. He is also actively seeking his fortune starting an Internet company to provide e-commerce and Web hosting services. During the seventeen years Kevin has been working with computers, he has earned a living as a salesman, technician, programmer, database administrator, and network administrator. He spent 10 years self-employed as a computer seller, installer, programmer, and consultant. In addition to living on the bleeding edge of computing, Kevin's hobbies include SCUBA diving, snow skiing, water skiing, photography, and flying.

In the short time between his many projects, hobbies, and yard work, Kevin is training his dog, Keyser Söze, for Schutzhund. If you've never experienced the love of a dog, please do. Your local human society has wonderful friends that will appreciate you beyond belief. If you have experienced the love of a dog, why not get another?

There are a few thoughts Kevin would like to share with as many people as possible. Cherish your family. Love a dog. Read. Don't smoke. Don't litter. If you don't like what you're doing for a living, do something else. Dance. Above all, be true to yourself.

You can find Kevin on the Internet at `http://www.kmahler.com`. You can email him comments, complaints, jokes, or just say "Hi" at `kmahler@kmahler.com`.

About the Technical Editors

Joel Barrett is an internetworking consultant and manager with over 13 years of experience in project management and network engineering, design, and analysis. Joel is a CCNA, MCNE, MCSE, MCP+Internet, IMB PSE, and NPA CNP. He is also the facilitator for the Atlanta Cisco Certification Study Group.

Michael Keele holds Master CNE, Master CNI, and CCNA certifications, as well as a BSEE from the University of Colorado. He has over 10 years of experience as a networking professional, including administration of various internetworks. He is currently an instructor at CCTI in Denver and is certified to teach NetWare, Intel, and Cisco courses.

Dedication

This book is dedicated to two people who left this world during the time I was writing it.

Karen Newby, who left this world way too soon due to lung cancer. Karen's greatest accomplishment in life was raising the woman who is my wonderful wife, Wendy.

Samuel Mahler Sr., who left this world old and wise. My grandfather taught me many lessons, but the most valuable one was "You can accomplish anything you put your mind to."

The world is a lesser place without you.

Acknowledgments

So many people supported me in this endeavor and I have learned so much from each of you.

I must first thank the woman who brings me happiness. Wendy, thank you for tolerating the long evenings and for your undying support of me and all of my antics. You are truly the love of my life. My only hope in life is that I grow old with you as my lover and best friend.

I must thank all the staff at New Riders. Sean Angus, thank you for believing in me and giving me my break into writing. Ami Frank, what can I say? Thanks for putting up with me. Thanks for your guidance through writing this book. But most of all, thanks for putting up with me. Stacey Beheler, thanks for all of your support.

My parents gave me the greatest gift of all, encouraging me throughout my life. I have learned so much good from you. The evil, I picked up on my own.

Keyser and Khayman, thanks for bringing me the Frisbee and insisting I go play when I worked too long.

Thanks to my friends at Cisco who help me out from time to time: Todd Burgess, Mike Lundy, Michael Slate and all the staff at the Atlanta, Georgia branch.

Taurus Bones and Robert Williams, thanks for playing my little quiz games and helping me see another perspective on the day-to-day responsibilities of an internetworking engineer.

Joel Barrett and Michael Keele: thanks for all your words of encouragement and help with explaining tough topics.

Tell Us What You Think!

As the reader of this book, *you* are our most important critic and commentator. We value your opinion and want to know what we're doing right, what we could do better, what areas you'd like to see us publish in, and any other words of wisdom you're willing to pass our way.

As the Executive Editor for the Certification team at New Riders Publishing, I welcome your comments. You can fax, email, or write me directly to let me know what you did or didn't like about this book—as well as what we can do to make our books stronger.

Please note that I cannot help you with technical problems related to the topic of this book, and that due to the high volume of mail I receive, I might not be able to reply to every message.

When you write, please be sure to include this book's title and author, as well as your name and phone or fax number. I will carefully review your comments and share them with the author and editors who worked on the book.

Fax: 317-581-4663

Email: certification@mcp.com

Mail: Mary Foote
          Executive Editor
          Certification
          New Riders Publishing
          201 West 103rd Street
          Indianapolis, IN 46290 USA

How to Use This Book

New Riders Publishing has made an effort in its Training Guide series to make the information as accessible as possible for the purposes of learning the certification material. Here, you have an opportunity to view the many instructional features that have been incorporated into the books to achieve that goal.

CHAPTER OPENER

Each chapter begins with a set of features designed to allow you to maximize study time for that material.

List of Objectives: Each chapter begins with a list of the objectives as stated by Cisco Systems.

Objective Explanations: Immediately following each objective is an explanation of it, providing context that defines it more meaningfully in relation to the exam. The objective explanations are designed to clarify any vagueness by relying on the author's test-taking experience.

OBJECTIVES

Microsoft provides the following objectives for "Connectivity":

Add and configure the network components of Windows NT Workstation.

▶ This objective is necessary because someone certified in the use of Windows NT Workstation technology must understand how it fits into a networked environment and how to configure the components that enable it to do so.

Use various methods to access network resources.

▶ This objective is necessary because someone certified in the use of Windows NT Workstation technology must understand how resources available on a network can be accessed from NT Workstation.

Implement Windows NT Workstation as a client in a NetWare environment.

▶ This objective is necessary because someone certified in the use of Windows NT Workstation technology must understand how NT Workstation can be used as a client in a NetWare environment and how to configure the services and protocols that make this possible.

Use various configurations to install Windows NT Workstation as a TCP/IP client.

▶ This objective is necessary because someone certified in the use of Windows NT Workstation technology must understand how TCP/IP is important in a network environment and how Workstation can be configured to use it.

CHAPTER 4

Connectivity

OUTLINE

Chapter Outline: Learning always gets a boost when you can see both the forest and the trees. To give you a visual image of how the topics in a chapter fit together, you will find a chapter outline at the beginning of each chapter. You will also be able to use this for easy reference when looking for a particular topic.

STUDY STRATEGIES

▶ Disk configurations are a part of both the planning and the configuration of NT Server computers. To study for Planning Objective 1, you will need to look at both the following section and the material in Chapter 2, "Installation Part 1." As with many concepts, you should have a good handle on the terminology and know the best applications for different disk configurations. For the objectives of the NT Server exam, you will need to know only general disk configuration concepts—at a high level, not the nitty gritty. Make sure you memorize the concepts relating to partitioning and know the difference between the system and the boot partitions in an NT system (and the fact that the definitions of these are counter-intuitive). You should know that NT supports both FAT and NTFS partitions, as well as some of the advantages and disadvantages of each. You will also need to know about the fault-tolerance methods available in NT—stripe sets with parity and disk mirroring—including their definitions, hardware requirements, and advantages and disadvantages.

Of course, nothing substitutes for working with the concepts explained in this objective. If possible, get an NT system with some free disk space and play around with the Disk Administrator just to see how partitions are created and what they look like.

You might also want to look at some of the supplementary readings and scan TechNet for white papers on disk configuration.

▶ The best way to study for Planning Objective 2 is to read, memorize, and understand the use of each protocol. You should know what the protocols are, what they are used for, and what systems they are compatible with.

As with disk configuration, installing protocols on your NT Server is something that you plan for, not something you do just because it feels good to you at the time. Although it is much easier to add or remove a protocol than it is to reconfigure your hard drives, choosing a protocol is still an essential part of the planning process because specific protocols, like spoken languages, are designed to be used in certain circumstances. There is no point in learning to speak Mandarin Chinese if you are never around anyone who can understand you. Similarly, the NWLink protocol is used to interact with NetWare systems; therefore, if you do not have Novell servers on your network, you might want to rethink your plan to install it on your servers. We will discuss the uses of the major protocols in Chapter 7, "Connectivity." However, it is important that you have a good understanding of their uses here in the planning stage.

Study Strategies: Each topic presents its own learning challenge. To support you through this, New Riders has included strategies for how to best approach studying in order to retain the material in the chapter, particularly as it is addressed on the exam.

INSTRUCTIONAL FEATURES WITHIN THE CHAPTER

These books include a large amount and different kinds of information. The many different elements are designed to help you identify information by its purpose and importance to the exam and also to provide you with varied ways to learn the material. You will be able to determine how much attention to devote to certain elements, depending on what your goals are. By becoming familiar with the different presentations of information, you will know what information will be important to you as a test-taker and which information will be important to you as a practitioner.

EXAM TIP

Only One NTVDM Supports Multiple 16-bit Applications Expect at least one question about running Win16 applications in separate memory spaces. The key concept is that you can load multiple Win16 applications into the same memory space only if it is the initial Win16 NTVDM. It is not possible, for example, to run Word for Windows 6.0 and Excel for Windows 5.0 in one shared memory space and also run PowerPoint 4.0 and Access 2.0 in another shared memory space.

Exam Tip: Exam Tips appear in the margins to provide specific exam-related advice. Such tips may address what material is covered (or not covered) on the exam, how it is covered, mnemonic devices, or particular quirks of that exam.

Note: Notes appear in the margins and contain various kinds of useful information, such as tips on the technology or administrative practices, historical background on terms and technologies, or side commentary on industry issues.

Warning: When using sophisticated information technology, there is always potential for mistakes or even catastrophes that can occur through improper application of the technology. Warnings appear in the margins to alert you to such potential problems.

8   Chapter 1   PLANNING

INTRODUCTION

Microsoft grew up around the personal computer industry and established itself as the preeminent maker of software products for personal computers. Microsoft has a vast portfolio of software products, but it is best known for its operating systems.

Microsoft's current operating system products, listed here, are undoubtedly well-known to anyone studying for the MCSE exams:

◆ Windows 95
◆ Windows NT Workstation
◆ Windows NT Server

NOTE **Strange But True** Although it sounds backward, it is true: Windows NT boots from the system partition and then loads the system from the boot partition.

Some older operating system products—namely MS-DOS, Windows 3.1, and Windows for Workgroups—are still important to the operability of Windows NT Server, so don't be surprised if you hear them mentioned from time to time in this book.

Windows NT is the most powerful, the most secure, and perhaps the most elegant operating system Microsoft has yet produced. It languished for a while after it first appeared (in part because no one was sure why they needed it or what to do with it), but Microsoft has persisted with improving interoperability and performance. With the release of Windows NT 4 which offers a new Windows 95-like user interface, Windows NT has assumed a prominent place in today's world of network-based computing.

WINDOWS NT SERVER AMONG MICROSOFT OPERATING SYSTEMS

▶ As we already mentioned, Microsoft has three operating system products now competing in the marketplace: Windows 95, Windows NT Workstation, and Windows NT Server. Each of these operating systems has its advantages and disadvantages.

Looking at the presentation of the desktop, the three look very much alike—so much so that you might have to click the Start button and read the banner on the left side of the menu to determine which operating system you are looking at. Each offers the familiar Windows 95 user interface featuring the Start button, the Recycling

WARNING **Don't Overextend Your Partitions and Wraps** It is not necessary to create an extended partition on a disk; primary partitions might be all that you need. However, if you do create one, remember that you can never have more than one extended partition on a physical disk.

STEP BY STEP

5.1 Configuring an Extension to Trigger an Application to Always Run in a Separate Memory Space

1. Start the Windows NT Explorer.

2. From the View menu, choose Options.

3. Click the File Types tab.

4. In the Registered File Types list box, select the desired file type.

5. Click the Edit button to display the Edit File Type dialog box. Then select Open from the Actions list and click the Edit button below it.

6. In the Editing Action for Type dialog box, adjust the application name by typing **cmd.exe /c start /separate** in front of the existing contents of the field (see Figure 5.15).

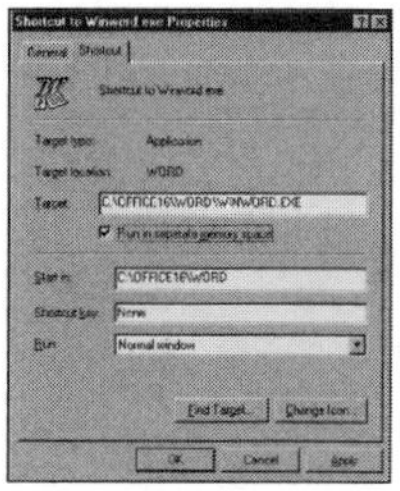

FIGURE 5.15
Configuring a shortcut to run a Win16 application in a separate memory space.

Step by Step: Step by Steps are hands-on tutorial instructions that walk you through a particular task or function relevant to the exam objectives.

Figure: To improve readability, most figures have been placed in the margins so they do not interrupt the main flow of text.

14   Chapter 1   PLANNING

You must use NTFS if you want to preserve existing permissions when you migrate files and directories from a NetWare server to a Windows NT Server system.

Windows 95 is Microsoft's everyday workhorse operating system. It provides a 32-bit platform and is designed to operate with a variety of peripherals. See Table 1.1 for the minimum hardware requirements for the installation and operation of Windows 95. Also, if you want to allow Macintosh computers to access files on the partition through Windows NT's Services for Macintosh, you must format the partition for NTFS.

MAKING REGISTRY CHANGES

To make Registry changes, run the REGEDT32.EXE program. The Registry in Windows NT is a complex database of configuration settings for your computer. If you want to configure the Workstation service, open the HKEY_LOCAL_MACHINE hive, as shown in Figure 3.22.

The exact location for configuring your Workstation service is

HKEY_LOCAL_MACHINE\System\CurrentControlSet\Services\
LanmanWorkstation\Parameters

To find additional information regarding this Registry item and others, refer to the Windows NT Server resource kit.

This summary table offers an overview of the differences between the FAT and NTFS file systems.

In-Depth Sidebar: These more extensive discussions cover material that perhaps is not as directly relevant to the exam, but which is useful as reference material or in everyday practice. In-Depths may also provide useful background or contextual information necessary for understanding the larger topic under consideration.

REVIEW BREAK

Choosing a File System

But if the system is designed to store data, mirroring might produce disk bottlenecks. You might only know whether these changes are significant by setting up two identical computers, implementing mirroring on one but not on the other, and then running Performance Monitor on both under a simulated load to see the performance differences.

This summary table offers an overview of the differences between the FAT and NTFS file systems.

Review Break: Crucial information is summarized at various points in the book in lists or tables. At the end of a particularly long section, you might come across a Review Break that is there just to wrap up one long objective and reinforce the key points before you shift your focus to the next section.

CASE STUDIES

Case Studies are presented throughout the book to provide you with additional, more conceptual opportunities to apply the knowledge you are developing. They also reflect the "real-world" experiences of the authors in ways that prepare you not only for the exam but for actual network administration as well. In each Case Study, you will find similar elements: a description of a Scenario, the Essence of the Case, and an extended Analysis section.

CASE STUDY: REALLY GOOD GUITARS

ESSENCE OF THE CASE

Here are the essential elements in this case:

- need for centralized administration
- the need for WAN connectivity nation-wide
- a requirement for Internet access and e-mail
- the need for Security on network shares and local files
- an implementation of Fault-tolerant systems

SCENARIO

Really Good Guitars is a national company specializing in the design and manufacturer of custom acoustic guitars. Having grown up out of an informal network of artisans across Canada, the company has many locations but very few employees (300 at this time) and a Head Office in Churchill, Manitoba. Although they follow the best traditions of hand-making guitars, they are not without technological savvy and all the 25 locations have computers on-site which are used to do accounting, run MS Office applications, and run their custom made guitar design software. The leadership team has recently begun to realize that a networked solution is essential to maintain consistency and to provide security on what are becoming some very innovative designs and to provide their employees with e-mail and Internet access.

RGG desires a centralized administration of its

continues

Essence of the Case: A bulleted list of the key problems or issues that need to be addressed in the Scenario.

Scenario: A few paragraphs describing a situation that professional practitioners in the field might face. A Scenario will deal with an issue relating to the objectives covered in the chapter, and it includes the kinds of details that make a difference.

Analysis: This is a lengthy description of the best way to handle the problems listed in the Essence of the Case. In this section, you might find a table summarizing the solutions, a worded example, or both.

CASE STUDY: PRINT IT DRAFTING INC.

continued

too, which is unacceptable. You are to find a solution to this problem if one exists.

ANALYSIS

The fixes for both of these problems are relatively straightforward. In the first case, it is likely that all the programs on the draftspeople's workstations are being started at normal priority. This means that they have a priority of 8. But the default says that anything running in the foreground is getting a 2-point boost from the base priority, bringing it to 10. As a result, when sent to the background, AutoCAD is not getting as much attention from the processor as it did when it was the foreground application. Because multiple applications need to be run at once without significant degradation of the performance of AutoCAD, you implement the following solution:

1. On the Performance tab of the System Properties dialog box for each workstation, set the Application Performance slider to None to prevent a boost for foreground applications.

2. Recommend that users keep the additional programs running alongside AutoCAD at a minimum (because all programs will now get equal processor time).

The fix to the second problem is to run each 16-bit application in its own NTVDM. This ensures that the crashing of one application will not adversely affect the others, but it still enables interoperability between the applications because they use OLE (and not shared memory) to transfer data. To make the fix as transparent as possible to the users, you suggested that two things be done:

1. Make sure that for each shortcut a user has created to the office applications, the Run in Separate Memory Space option is selected on the Shortcut tab.

2. Change the properties for the extensions associated with the applications (for example, .XLS and .DOC) so that they start using the /separate switch. Then any file that is double-clicked invokes the associated program to run in its own NTVDM.

CHAPTER SUMMARY

KEY TERMS

Before you take the exam, make sure you are comfortable with the definitions and concepts for each of the following key terms:

- FAT
- NTFS
- workgroup
- domain

This chapter discussed the main planning topics you will encounter on the Windows NT Server exam. Distilled down, these topics revolve around two main goals: understanding the planning of disk configuration and understanding the planning of network protocols.

◆ Windows NT Server supports an unlimited number of inbound sessions; Windows NT Workstation supports no more than 10 active sessions at the same time.

◆ Windows NT Server accommodates an unlimited number of remote access connections (although Microsoft only supports up to 256); Windows NT Workstation supports only a single remote access connection.

Key Terms: A list of key terms appears at the end of each chapter. These are terms that you should be sure you know and are comfortable defining and understanding when you go in to take the exam.

Chapter Summary: Before the Apply Your Learning section, you will find a chapter summary that wraps up the chapter and reviews what you should have learned.

EXTENSIVE REVIEW AND SELF-TEST OPTIONS

At the end of each chapter, along with some summary elements, you will find a section called "Apply Your Knowledge" that gives you several different methods with which to test your understanding of the material and review what you have learned.

Chapter 1 PLANNING   23

APPLY YOUR KNOWLEDGE

This section allows you to assess how well you understood the material in the chapter. Review and Exam questions test your knowledge of the tasks and concepts specified in the objectives. The Exercises provide you with opportunities to engage in the sorts of tasks that comprise the skill sets the objectives reflect.

Exercises

1.1   Synchronizing the Domain Controllerys

The following steps show you how to manually synchronize a backup domain controller within your domain. (This objective deals with Objective Planning 1.)

Estimated Time: Less than 10 minutes.

1. Click Start, Programs, Administrative Tools, and select the Server Manager icon.

2. Highlight the BDC (Backup Domain Controller) in your computer list.

3. Select the Computer menu, then select Synchronize with Primary Domain Controller.

12.2   Establishing a Trust Relationship between Domains

The following steps show you how to establish a trust relationship between multiple domains. To complete this exercise, you must have two Windows NT Server computers, each installed in their own domain. (This objective deals with objective Planning 1.)

Estimated Time: 10 minutes

1. From the trusted domain select Start, Programs, Administrative Tools, and click User Manager for Domains. The User Manager.

FIGURE 1.2
The login process on a local machine.

2. Select the Policies menu and click Trust Relationships. The Trust Relationships dialog box appears.

4. When the trusting domain information has been entered, click OK and close the Trust Relationships dialog box.

Review Questions

1. List the four domain models that can be used for directory services in Windows NT Server 4.

2. List the goals of a directory services architecture.

3. What is the maximum size of the SAM database in Windows NT Server 4.0?

4. What are the two different types of domains in a trust relationship?

5. In a trust relationship which domain would contain the user accounts?

Exercises: These activities provide an opportunity for you to master specific hands-on tasks. Our goal is to increase your proficiency with the product or technology. You must be able to conduct these tasks in order to pass the exam.

Review Questions: These open-ended, short-answer questions allow you to quickly assess your comprehension of what you just read in the chapter. Instead of asking you to choose from a list of options, these questions require you to state the correct answers in your own words. Although you will not experience these kinds of questions on the exam, these questions will indeed test your level of comprehension of key concepts.

6. Can a local account be used in a trust relationship? Explain.

7. In a complete trust domain model that uses 4 different domains, what is the total number of trust relationships required to use a complete trust domain model?

Exam Questions

The following questions are similar to those you will face on the Microsoft exam. Answers to these questions can be found in section Answers and Explanations, later in the chapter. At the end of each of those answers, you will be informed of where (that is, in what section of the chapter) to find more information..

1. ABC Corporation has locations in Toronto, New York, and San Francisco. It wants to install Windows NT Server 4 to encompass all its locations in a single WAN environment. The head office is located in New York. What is the best domain model for ABC's directory services implementation?

   A. Single-domain model

   B. Single-master domain model

   C. Multiple-master domain model

   D. Complete-trust domain model

2. JPS Printing has a single location with 1,000 users spread across the LAN. It has special printers and applications installed on the servers in its environment. It needs to be able to centrally manage the user accounts and the resources. Which domain model would best fit its needs?

   A. Single-domain model

   B. Single-master domain model

   C. Multiple-master domain model

   D. Complete-trust domain model

5. What must be created to allow a user account from one domain to access resources in a different domain?

   A. Complete Trust Domain Model

   B. One Way Trust Relationship

   C. Two Way Trust Relationship

   D. Master-Domain Model

Answers to Review Questions

1. Single domain, master domain, multiple-master domain, complete-trust domain. See section, Windows NT Server 4 Domain Models, in this chapter for more information. (This question deals with objective Planning 1.)

2. One user, one account, centralized administration, universal resource access, synchronization. See section, Windows NT Server 4 Directory Services, in this chapter for more information. (This question deals with objective Planning 1.)

6. Local accounts cannot be given permissions across trusts. See section, Accounts in Trust Relationships, in this chapter for more information. (This question deals with Planning 1.)

Exam Questions: These questions reflect the kinds of multiple-choice questions that appear on the Cisco exams. Use them to become familiar with the exam question formats and to help you determine what you know and what you need to review or study more.

Answers and Explanations: For each of the Review and Exam questions, you will find thorough explanations located at the end of the section.

Suggested Readings and Resources

The following are some recommended readings on the subject of installing and configuring NT Workstation:

1. Microsoft Official Curriculum course 770: *Installing and Configuring Microsoft Windows NT Workstation 4.0*

   • Module 1: Overview of Windows NT Workstation 4.0

   • Module 2: Installing Windows NT Workstation 4.0

2. Microsoft Official Curriculum course 922: *Supporting Microsoft Windows NT 4.0 Core Technologies*

   • Module 2: Installing Windows NT

   • Module 3: Configuring the Windows NT Environment

3. *Microsoft Windows NT Workstation Resource Kit Version 4.0* (Microsoft Press)

   • Chapter 2: Customizing Setup

   • Chapter 4: Planning for a Mixed Environment

4. Microsoft TechNet CD-ROM

   • *MS Windows NT Workstation Technical Notes*

     • MS Windows NT Workstation Deployment Guide – Automating Windows NT Setup

     • An Unattended Windows NT Workstation Deployment

5. Web Sites

   • www.microsoft.com/train_cert

   • www.prometric.com/testingcandidates/assessment/chosetest.html (take online

Suggested Readings and Resources: The very last element in every chapter is a list of additional resources you can use if you want to go above and beyond certification-level material or if you need to spend more time on a particular subject that you are having trouble understanding.

Introduction

CCNA Training Guide is designed for advanced end-users, service technicians, and network administrators with the goal of certification as a Cisco Certified Network Associate. The CCNA exam measures your ability to install and configure Cisco routers and switches in an internetwork in order to improve performance, bandwidth, security, and connectivity.

This book is your one-stop shop. Everything you need to know to prepare for the exam is in here. You do not have to take a class in addition to buying this book to pass the exam. However, depending on your personal study habits or learning style, you may benefit from buying this book *and* taking a class.

HOW THIS BOOK HELPS YOU

This book conducts a tour of all the areas covered by the CCNA exam and teaches you the specific skills you need to achieve your Network Associate certification. You'll also find helpful hints, tips, real-world examples, exercises, and references to additional study materials. Specifically, this book is set up to help you in the following ways:

◆ **Organization.** This book is organized by major exam topics and individual exam objectives. Every objective you need to know for the CCNA exam is covered in this book. The objectives are not covered in exactly the same order as they are listed by Cisco. However, we have attempted to organize the topics in the most logical and accessible fashion to make it as easy as possible for you to learn the information. We have also attempted to make the information accessible in the following ways:

- The full list of exam topics and objectives is included in this introduction.

- Each chapter begins with a list of the objectives to be covered.

- Following the list of objectives, you'll find an outline that provides you an overview of the material and the page numbers where particular topics can be found.

- The objectives are repeated in the text directly under a heading where the material most directly relevant to it is covered (unless the whole chapter addresses a single objective).

- Information about where the objectives are covered is also conveniently condensed in the tear card at the front of this book.

◆ **Instructional Features**. This book has been designed to provide you with multiple ways to learn and reinforce the exam material. Following are some of the helpful methods:

- *Objective explanations.* As mentioned previously, each chapter begins with a list of the objectives covered in the chapter. In addition, immediately following each objective is an explanation of it in a context that defines it more meaningfully.

- *Study strategies.* Following the chapter outline, you'll find strategies for how to approach studying and retaining the material in the chapter, particularly as it is addressed on the exam.

- *Exam tips.* Exam tips appear in the margins to provide specific exam-related advice. Such tips might address what material is covered (or not covered) on the exam, how it is covered, mnemonic devices, or particular quirks of that exam.

- *Review breaks and summaries.* Crucial information is summarized at various points in the book in lists or tables. Each chapter includes a summary section, as well.

- *Key terms.* A list of key terms appears near the end of each chapter.

- *Notes.* These appear in the margins and contain various kinds of useful information, such as tips on technology or administrative practices, historical background on terms and technologies, or side commentary on industry issues.

- *Warnings.* When using sophisticated information technology, there is always the potential for mistakes or even catastrophes that can occur because of improper application of the technology. Warnings appear in the margins to alert you to such potential problems.

- *In-depths.* These more extensive discussions cover material that may not be directly relevant to the exam, but which is useful as reference material or in everyday practice. In-depth sidebars may also provide useful background or contextual information necessary for understanding the larger topic under consideration.

- *Step by Steps.* These are hands-on, tutorial instructions that lead you through a particular task or function relevant to the exam objectives.

- *Exercises.* Found near the end of each chapter in the "Apply Your Knowledge" section, exercises may include additional tutorial material as well as other types of problems and questions.

- *Case studies.* Presented throughout the book, case studies provide you with a more conceptual opportunity to apply and reinforce the knowledge you are developing. Case studies include a description of a scenario, the essence of the case, and an extended analysis section. They also reflect the real-world experiences of the authors in ways that prepare you not only for the exam but for actual network administration as well.

◆ **Extensive practice test options.** This book provides numerous opportunities for you to assess your knowledge and practice for the exam. The practice options include the following:

- *Review questions.* These open-ended questions appear in the "Apply Your Knowledge" section that appears at the end of each chapter. These questions allow you to quickly assess your comprehension of what you just read in the chapter. Answers to the questions are provided later in the section.

- *Exam questions.* These questions also appear in the "Apply Your Knowledge" section. They reflect the kinds of multiple-choice questions that appear on the Cisco Certification exams. Use them to practice for the exam and to help you determine what you know and what you need to review or study further. Answers and explanations for them are provided.

- *Practice exam.* A practice exam is included in the "Final Review" section of the book. The "Final Review" section and the practice exam are discussed later in this Introduction.

- *Top Score software.* The Top Score Test Simulation Software Suite included on the CD-ROM provides further self-evaluation opportunities, in the form of practice exams, study cards, flash cards, and product simulations.

◆ **Final Review.** This part of the book provides you
with three valuable tools for preparing for the exam.

- *Fast Facts.* This condensed version of the
information contained in the book will prove
extremely useful for last-minute review.

- *Study and Exam Tips.* Read this section early
on to help you develop study strategies. It
also provides you with valuable exam-day tips
and information on new exam and question
formats, such as adaptive tests and simulation-
based questions.

- *Practice Exam.* A full practice exam is
included. Questions are written in the styles
used on the actual exam. Use it to assess your
readiness for the real thing.

The book includes other features, such as sections
titled "Suggested Reading and Resources," which direct
you toward further information that could aid you in
your exam preparation or your actual work. There are
several valuable appendices as well, including a glossary
(Appendix A), an overview of the Cisco certification
program (Appendix B), and a description of what is on
the CD-ROM (Appendix C). These and all the other
book features mentioned previously will provide you
with thorough preparation for the exam.

For more information about the exam or the certification
process, contact Cisco:

Cisco Education: (800) 829-NETS (6387) or (408)
525-NETS (6387)

World Wide Web:
http://www.cisco.com/training

Email: ciscotraining@cisco.com

WHAT THE CCNA EXAM COVERS

The CCNA exam covers the 640-407 main topic areas
represented by the conceptual groupings of the test
objectives: OSI Reference, WAN Protocols, IOS,
Network Protocols, Routing, Network Security, and
LAN Switching. Each chapter represents one or more of
these main topic areas. The exam objectives are listed by
topic area in the following sections.

OSI Reference Model

◆ Identify and describe the functions of each of the
seven layers of the OSI reference model.

◆ Describe connection-oriented network service and
connectionless network service, and identify the
key differences between them.

◆ Describe data link addresses and network
addresses, and identify the key differences
between them.

◆ Identify at least three reasons why the industry
uses a layered model.

◆ Define and explain the five conversion steps of
data encapsulation.

◆ Define flow control and describe the three basic
methods used in networking.

◆ List the key internetworking functions of the OSI
Network layer and how they are performed in a
router.

WAN Protocols

◆ Differentiate between the following WAN services:
Frame Relay, ISDN/LAPD, HDLC, and PPP.

◆ Recognize key Frame Relay terms and features.

◆ List commands to configure Frame Relay LMIs, maps, and subinterfaces.

◆ List commands to monitor Frame Relay operation in the router.

◆ Identify PPP operations to encapsulate WAN data on Cisco routers.

◆ State a relevant use and context for ISDN networking.

◆ Identify ISDN protocols, function groups, reference points, and channels.

◆ Describe Cisco's implementation of ISDN BRI.

Internetworking Operating Systems (IOS)

◆ Log in to a router in both user and privileged modes.

◆ Use the context-sensitive help facility.

◆ Use the command history and editing features.

◆ Examine router elements (RAM, ROM, CDP, and show).

◆ Manage configuration files from the privileged exec mode.

◆ Control router passwords, identification, and banner.

◆ Identify the main Cisco IOS commands for router startup.

◆ Enter an initial configuration using the setup command.

◆ Copy and manipulate configuration files.

◆ List the commands to load Cisco IOS software from flash memory, a TFTP server, or ROM.

◆ Prepare to back up, upgrade, and load a backup Cisco IOS software image.

◆ Prepare the initial configuration of your router and enable IP.

Network Protocols

◆ Monitor Novell IPX operation on the router.

◆ Describe the two parts of network addressing; then identify the parts in specific protocol address examples.

◆ Create the different classes of IP addresses (and subnetting).

◆ Configure IP addresses.

◆ Verify IP addresses.

◆ List the required IPX address and encapsulation type.

◆ Enable the Novell IPX protocol and configure interfaces.

◆ Identify the functions of the TCP/IP Transport layer protocols.

◆ Identify the functions of the TCP/IP Network layer protocols.

◆ Identify the functions performed by ICMP.

◆ Configure IPX access lists and SAP filters to control basic Novell traffic.

Routing

◆ Add the RIP routing protocol to your configuration.

◆ Add the IGRP routing protocol to your configuration.

◆ Explain the services of separate and integrated multiprotocol routing.

◆ List problems that each routing type encounters when dealing with topology changes and describe techniques to reduce the number of these problems.

◆ Describe the benefits of network segmentation with routers.

Network Security

◆ Configure standard and extended access lists to filter IP traffic.

◆ Monitor and verify selected access list operations on the router.

LAN Switching

◆ Describe the advantages of LAN segmentation.

◆ Describe LAN segmentation using bridges.

◆ Describe LAN segmentation using routers.

◆ Describe LAN segmentation using switches.

◆ Name and describe two switching methods.

◆ Describe full- and half-duplex Ethernet operation.

◆ Describe network congestion problems in Ethernet networks.

◆ Describe the benefits of network segmentation with bridges.

◆ Describe the benefits of network segmentation with switches.

◆ Describe the features and benefits of Fast Ethernet.

◆ Describe the guidelines and distance limitations of Fast Ethernet.

◆ Distinguish between cut-through and store-and-forward LAN switching.

◆ Describe the operation of the Spanning Tree protocol and its benefits.

◆ Describe the benefits of virtual LANs.

◆ Define and describe the function of a MAC address.

HARDWARE AND SOFTWARE YOU'LL NEED

A self-paced study guide, this book was designed with the expectation that you will use Windows 95 or later with Hyperterm as you follow along through the exercises while you learn. However, the theory covered in *CCNA Training Guide* is applicable to a wide range of network systems in a wide range of actual situations, and the exercises in this book encompass that range.

Your computer should meet the following criteria:

◆ 486DX2 66Mhz (or better) processor

◆ 3.5-inch 1.44MB floppy drive

◆ VGA (or Super VGA) video adapter

◆ VGA (or Super VGA) monitor

◆ Mouse or equivalent pointing device

◆ Double-speed (or faster) CD-ROM drive (optional)

◆ Network Interface Card (NIC) (optional)

◆ Presence on an existing network, or use of a two-port (or more) miniport hub to create a test network (optional)

◆ Hyperterm or other terminal emulation software for connection to console ports

It is also recommended that you have one or more Cisco routers available in order to become familiar with Cisco's Internetwork Operating System and Command Line Interface. Used Cisco 2500 series routers can be obtained through many used equipment dealers.

It is easier to access the necessary computer hardware and software in a corporate business environment. It can be difficult, however, to allocate enough time within the busy workday to complete a self-study program. Most of your study time will necessarily occur after normal working hours, away from the everyday interruptions and pressures of your regular job.

ADVICE ON TAKING THE EXAM

Extensive tips can be found in "Study and Exam Prep Tips," located in the "Final Review" section of this book, but keep this advice in mind as you study:

◆ **Read all the material.** This book has included additional information not reflected in the objectives in an effort to give you the best possible preparation for the examination—and for the real-world network experiences to come.

◆ **Do the Step by Steps and complete the exercises in each chapter.** They will help you gain experience using the product and/or carrying out the tasks you need to be familiar with in order to pass the exam.

◆ **Use the questions to assess your knowledge.** Don't just read the chapter content; use the review and exam questions to find out what you know and what you don't. Study some more, review, then assess your knowledge again.

◆ **Review the exam objectives.** Develop your own questions and examples for each topic listed. If you can make and answer several questions for each topic, you should not find it difficult to pass the exam.

N O T E   **Exam-Taking Advice**   Although this book is designed to prepare you to take and pass the CCNA exam, there are no guarantees. Read this book, work through the questions and exercises, and when you feel confident, take the practice exam and additional exams using the test engine located on the CD included at the back of this book. Your results should indicate whether you are ready for the real thing.

When taking the actual certification exam, make sure you answer all the questions before your time limit expires. Don't spend too much time on any one question. If you are unsure about a question, answer it to the best of your ability; then mark it and review it when you have finished the rest of the questions.

Remember that the primary object is not to pass the exam—it is to understand the material. After you understand the material, passing the exam should be simple. Knowledge is a pyramid; to build upward, you need a solid foundation. This book is designed to ensure that you have that solid foundation.

Good luck!

NEW RIDERS PUBLISHING

The staff of New Riders Publishing is committed to bringing you the very best in computer reference material. Each New Riders book is the result of months of work by authors and staff who research and refine the information contained within its covers.

As part of this commitment to you, the NRP reader, New Riders invites your input. Please let us know if you enjoy this book, if you have trouble with the information or examples presented, or if you have a suggestion for the next edition.

Please note, however, that New Riders staff cannot serve as a technical resource during your preparation for the Cisco certification exams or for questions about software- or hardware-related problems. Please refer instead to the documentation that accompanies the Cisco products or to the applications' Help systems.

If you have a question or comment about any New Riders book, there are several ways to contact New Riders Publishing. We will respond to as many readers as we can. Your name, address, or phone number will never become part of a mailing list or be used for any purpose other than to help us continue to bring you the best books possible. You can write to us at the following address:

New Riders Publishing
Attn: Mary Foote, Executive Editor
201 W. 103rd Street
Indianapolis, IN 46290

If you prefer, you can fax New Riders Publishing at 317-581-4663.

You also can send email to New Riders at the following Internet address:

certification@mcp.com

Thank you for selecting *CCNA Training Guide!*

PART

I

EXAM PREPARATION

Cisco provides the following objectives for the OSI Reference portion of the CCNA exam:

Identify and describe the functions of each of the seven layers of the OSI Reference Model.

▶ Understanding the seven layers of the OSI Reference Model is fundamental to understanding network functions and how they operate in routers, bridges, and network stations.

Describe connection-oriented network service and connectionless network service and identify the key differences between them.

▶ An understanding of connection-oriented and connectionless services is required to diagnose and maintain internetworking systems.

Describe data link addresses and network addresses and identify the key differences between them.

▶ Data link and network addresses work together in internetworking systems. An understanding of the differences between these addresses and how they are used is necessary for maintaining internetworking systems.

Identify at least three reasons why the industry uses a layered model.

▶ The layered model is the foundation for networking and internetworking systems. It is important to have a thorough understanding of why the layered model is used.

CHAPTER 1

The OSI Reference Model

Define and explain the five conversion steps of data encapsulation.

▶ Data encapsulation is the process by which data passes from the source application through the OSI Reference Model to the network and back up the model at the receiving station to the receiving application.

Define flow control and describe the three basic methods used in networking.

▶ Flow control techniques are used by networking stations to avoid data congestion. A thorough understanding of how flow control works is necessary for the maintenance of internetworking systems.

▶ Memorize the seven layers of the OSI Reference Model. Make sure you fully understand the functions of each and know common examples of each layer. Not only will this ensure that you will be able to answer these questions on the CCNA exam, but it will also help you with daily design and diagnostics of internetworking systems.

▶ Understand how data link addresses and network addresses work together to deliver network traffic.

▶ Have a good understanding of the common networking technologies and how they work. A good way to do this might be to set up a study lab. In doing so, it is useful to connect two Cisco routers to each other via the serial ports.

You can do this by using a DCE cable on one router and a DTE cable on the other and connecting the two cables. Cisco's part numbers for the cables to accomplish this are CAB-V35MT (DTE, male) and CAB-V35FC (DCE, female).

▶ As you read this chapter, keep in mind the practical application of this knowledge. One good exercise for you to test yourself is to review networking systems in your company and identify each of the layers used. This exercise will help you understand where different functions fit into the scheme.

INTRODUCTION

This chapter covers the building blocks that make up internetworking systems. These blocks include the OSI Reference Model, types of network connections, data link and networking addresses, and flow control. These concepts are the building blocks of networking systems.

The importance of understanding these basics and building on this knowledge cannot be overemphasized. Internetworking systems are complex. They involve hardware, protocols, and designs from many different vendors that must work together for successful communication. To design, maintain, or diagnose these systems, it is imperative to understand the basics around which these complex systems were built.

Many examples in this chapter that illustrate working protocols use TCP/IP. Thanks to the Internet, this is one of the most prevalent protocols in use today. This makes it a natural choice for examples. An important fact to remember in these discussions is that TCP/IP is not one protocol but a group of protocols covering many networking functions.

Internetworking systems is a term used to describe an environment where different networks are connected. This could be as basic as two simple networks with a bridge between them, or it could be a complex enterprise network with frame relay, Ethernet, token ring, and a FDDI backbone.

UNDERSTANDING THE OSI REFERENCE MODEL

The Open Systems Interconnection (OSI) Reference Model provides the basis for almost everything in networking. The OSI Reference Model is conceptual rather than factual since it doesn't really describe one particular protocol. Developers of networking products use the OSI Reference Model as a loose guide for design and implementation.

In 1984, the International Organization for Standardization (ISO) created the Open Systems Interconnection (OSI) Reference Model.

This model divides the functions of networking into small, mostly self-contained functions called layers. Since the layers are modular, one layer can be changed or updated, and the remaining layers should still function properly. For example, you could replace the Physical layer with another network topology and expect the rest of the networking pieces to function as they did before.

The Institute of Electrical and Electronic Engineers (IEEE) defines many of the standards used in today's networking systems. The IEEE formed the 802 committee in February of 1980 (where 80 represents the year 1980 and 2 represents the second month of the year). The 802 committee standardizes many networking technologies. Its committee numbers represent these standards:

◆ 802.1 defines issues common to all LANs, such as the spanning tree protocol defined in 802.1D.

◆ 802.2 defines the logical link control (LLC) sublayer.

◆ 802.3 defines LANs based on Carrier Sense Multiple Access/Collision Detection (CSMA/CD) such as Ethernet.

◆ 802.4 defines token bus networks. This networking topology isn't used much anymore.

◆ 802.5 defines token ring networks. IBM's TokenRing and IEEE 802.5 are functionally the same.

The Internet Engineering Task Force (IETF) maintains these standards on its Web site at www.ietf.org. Another good starting point for references is InterNIC's Web site at www.internic.net.

Networking functions are divided into layers for several reasons:

◆ It divides complex network operations into less-complex pieces.

◆ It keeps changes in one area from adversely affecting other layers. This facilitates the evolution of networking components, since companies can focus on improving one area without worrying about the functions handled at other layers.

◆ It allows different vendors to create products that will work together.

◆ It makes understanding the complex concepts of networking easier by dividing the concepts into smaller, easier-to-understand pieces.

EXAM TIP

The OSI Reference Model Is a Basic Concept A strong grasp of the OSI Reference Model for networking will make life much easier when you are diagnosing complex internetworks. Cisco expects anyone certified to have a strong understanding of the OSI Reference Model and how it relates to the different aspects of internetworking.

The Seven Layers

The seven layers of the OSI Reference Model are Application, Presentation, Session, Transport, Network, Data Link, and Physical, as shown in Figure 1.1. The following sections describe each in detail.

FIGURE 1.1

The Network layers define where networking functionality exists.

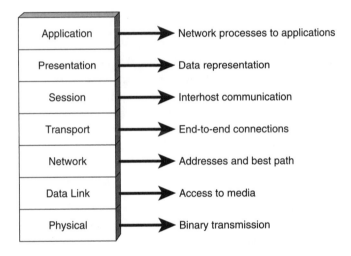

Application	Network processes to applications
Presentation	Data representation
Session	Interhost communication
Transport	End-to-end connections
Network	Addresses and best path
Data Link	Access to media
Physical	Binary transmission

> **EXAM TIP**
>
> **A Useful Mnemonic Device** A good way to remember the seven layers and the order in which they occur is to create a sentence from the layers' first letters. One common sentence is **A**ll **P**eople **S**eem **T**o **N**eed **D**ata **P**rocessing. This represents **A**pplication, **P**resentation, **S**ession, **T**ransport, **N**etwork, **D**ata Link, and **P**hysical.

Application Layer

The Application layer provides the interface from the OSI Reference Model to the end user's application. Some examples of Application-layer implementations include File Transfer Protocol (FTP), Simple Mail Transport Protocol (SMTP), and telnet.

Presentation Layer

The Presentation layer defines how the data will be presented to the Application layer. Some examples of Presentation-layer implementations include MIDI, JPEG, EBCDIC, ASCII, MPEG, and encryption.

Session Layer

Communication sessions between network stations are established, managed, and terminated at the Session layer. Sessions handle the requests and responses between applications on the network stations.

Transport Layer

The Transport layer accepts data from the Session layer and puts it in segments to pass down to the Network layer. It is responsible for making sure packets are delivered error-free, in sequence, and without any losses or duplications.

Acknowledgments, a technique used for flow control, are generally sent from the Transport layer.

Network Layer

The Network layer defines the network address, which is different from the media access control (MAC) address. An Internet Protocol (IP) address is an example of a Network layer address. Segments of data passed down from the Transport layer are put into packets and are passed down to the Data Link layer.

The Network layer determines the path to the destination and forwards packets that are destined for remote networks. The Network layer evaluates the network address of the destination system and determines whether it is on the same network as the source system. If so, it obtains the destination system's MAC address either from a table or through a resolution technique such as IP's Address Resolution Protocol (ARP). Once it has addressed the packet with the source and destination addresses, it passes the packet down to the Data Link layer for delivery. If the Network layer determines that the destination system is not on the same network as the source system, it addresses the packet with the MAC address of the router that can deliver the packet. It determines this by referencing routing tables that can be built either statically or dynamically. Once it addresses the packet with the source address and the address of the router that can deliver the packet, it passes the packet down to the Data Link layer for delivery to the router.

Data Link Layer

The Data Link layer provides an error-free link between two network devices. Packets passed down from the Network layer are packaged into frames compatible with the networking topology and are passed down to the Physical layer. Error checking and correction information is added to the frame. One error-correction technique that is used is cyclic redundancy check (CRC).

It is important to realize that there are areas of redundancy in some networking standards. Error checking and correction can actually take place at multiple layers of the OSI Reference Model.

The IEEE 802 committee has further subdivided the Data Link layer into two sublayers: logical link control (LLC) and media access control (MAC). This separation of functionality allows upper-layer protocols to operate without relying on the physical media.

◆ **LLC sublayer.** The LLC sublayer provides the functionality required for connection-oriented or connectionless services at the Data Link layer. It provides the resources for multiple upper-layer protocols to share the physical media. This is performed via Destination Service Access Point (DSAP) and Source Service Access Point (SSAP). It is beneficial to know that these services exist. However, further exploration of these functions is not required to pass the CCNA.

◆ **MAC sublayer.** The MAC sublayer provides the functions necessary for network media access. On any network, stations must be addressed individually so that data can be delivered to the desired station. The MAC address provides this individuality.

Physical Layer

The Physical layer is responsible for placing the data on the network media. The Physical layer defines such things as voltage levels, wire specifications, maximum distances, and connector types.

The layers of the OSI Reference Model communicate with each other and with remote stations. A key concept within this communication is the encapsulation of data. The process of encapsulation takes the user's data and prepares it for travel across the network and then places it on the network media.

OSI Reference Model Communication

Within the OSI Reference Model, each layer communicates with three other layers: the layer directly above, the layer directly below, and its peer layer on the other end of the communication link (see Figure 1.2).

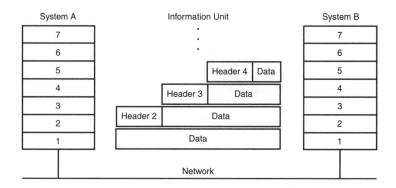

FIGURE 1.2
As the data passes down the protocol stack, headers are added and the data is passed down to the next layer.

Encapsulation

Each layer uses control information to communicate with the corresponding layer at the other end of the link. This control data is added to the packet as it moves down the stack. This process is called encapsulation.

As a packet travels down through the seven layers, each layer adds control data and then passes the data down to the next layer until the data reaches the network. Once the packet is delivered to the receiving station, the process is reversed. Each layer strips off its control data and passes the packet up to the next layer until the packet reaches the application.

Encapsulation consists of five steps, beginning at the Transport layer:

1. Build the data.

2. Package the data for end-to-end transport.

3. Append the network address in the header.

4. Append the local address in the data link header.

5. Convert to bits for transmission.

For an example, follow some data through the process. When you visit Cisco's Web page at http://www.cisco.com, the process goes something like what is shown in Figure 1.3.

FIGURE 1.3
Data flowing through the OSI layers when a
user makes an HTTP request.

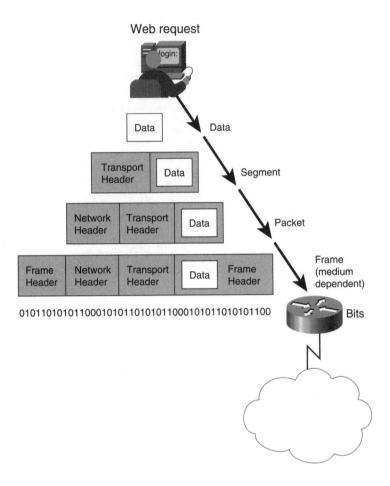

◆ **Build the data.** You enter the URL for Cisco's Web site in
your browser. The Web address you are requesting is converted
to data that can travel over the Internet.

◆ **Package the data for end-to-end transport.** The data is
packaged for the Transport layer. A Transport layer header is
added to the data. In this example, the header will be a TCP
header. This header will include information specifying that
this request is destined for an HTTP service.

◆ **Append the network address in the header.** The data is
now put in a packet or datagram so that it can be transmitted
over the network. The source and destination network
addresses are included in the packet header. In this example,
these addresses would be IP addresses.

◆ **Append the local address in the data link header.** The packet is now put in a frame compatible with the network media. The data link addresses of the source and destination stations are placed in the frame header. Since our packet will be traveling through a router, the destination data link address is that of our default gateway router. (This will be explained more in later chapters.)

◆ **Convert to bits for transmission.** The frame is converted to ones and zeros and placed on the network media.

This process is repeated many times during the connection to the Web site. The process is reversed on the receiving side: The data travels back up the process until it reaches the application and is presented to the user. Networking functions generally happen so fast that most people never consider what happens after they press Enter. As an internetworking expert, it is important that you consider what is happening at each level of the process and how it occurs.

EXAM TIP

Start at the Bottom When internetworking systems break, the first thing you must figure out is where in the process the problem is occurring. You can waste much time trying to diagnose a routing problem when the problem actually exists at the physical or Data Link layer. Generally, when you're trying to resolve a problem, it's a good idea to start at the bottom and work your way up the model.

DATA LINK AND NETWORK ADDRESSES

Networking requires that each device have a unique address so that data can be delivered reliably. Within the OSI Reference Model are two definitions for station addresses—the network address and the data link address. Understanding the use of each of these addresses is crucial to following how data is delivered in an internetworking system.

MAC Addresses

The Media Access Control (MAC) address from the Data Link layer uniquely identifies each station on the network media. MAC addresses are 48 bits long and are usually represented as three groups of four hexadecimal digits:

```
00e0.a38d.0800
```

N O T E **A Useful Reason to Alter the MAC Address** Changing the MAC address is used in Hot Standby Router Protocol (HSRP), a method of using two routers in fail-safe mode. Both routers are connected to the network and configured similarly. One is the primary router, and the other is the secondary. The primary router services the network, and the secondary constantly makes sure that the primary is still operational. If the secondary router detects that the primary router has failed, the secondary router changes its interface's MAC address to that of the primary router. This allows the stations on the network to still forward their data to the same MAC address even though the data is now handled by the secondary router.

The first 24 bits of the MAC address make up the Organizational Unique Identifier (OUI). The OUI is a number assigned to each vendor by the IEEE. In the example, the OUI is 00e0.a3.

The second 24 bits make up the unique address that the manufacturer assigned to this network interface. In the example, the unique address is 8d.0800.

The MAC address is usually burned into a ROM on the device when it is made. When the device is powered on, the address is copied from the ROM to RAM, where it identifies the network device on the network media. Some devices allow you to change the MAC address of a networking device. In this case, the MAC address would be obtained from the driver for the device and copied to RAM. This is not very common in Ethernet installations but is quite common on token ring networks where mainframes are involved.

The data link address identifies the network station on the physical network media. MAC addresses are generally flat, meaning that there is no structure to how they are assigned. In contrast, network addresses are usually hierarchical in structure.

Network Addresses

The network address identifies the station at the network level (layer 3) of the OSI Reference Model. In TCP/IP, the network address is the device's IP address. Under Novell's IPX, the network address is dynamically assigned as a combination of the IPX network number and the station's MAC address. Network addresses are usually hierarchical, like the mailing address of a business or home.

The sorting of mail is hierarchical since the sorting equipment can separate mail first by the ZIP code to which it is addressed, then the state, then the city, then the street, and finally the house number. This lets the sorting equipment worry about only a piece of the address as the letter makes its way through the post office. Each time the letter is sorted, the piece of the address used is more specific. Networking addresses can be structured the same way. Routers can look at part of the network address and forward the packet. Each router along the path looks at more specific information in the network address until the packet is delivered to the end network station.

This concept becomes more important later when you look at IP addresses and how they are structured. A well-designed network addressing scheme can reduce the burden placed on routers by making use of this hierarchical address structure.

Since routing occurs at the Network layer, you will be looking at network addresses and how they function in more depth in Chapter 6, "Routing."

For an internetworking system to operate, it must have a way to map network addresses to data link addresses. In the TCP/IP protocol suite, this is performed by Address Resolution Protocol (ARP).

Address Resolution Protocol (ARP)

Address Resolution Protocol is responsible for mapping IP addresses to MAC addresses. ARP builds a table of IP addresses and their corresponding MAC addresses. If the network device needs to communicate with a station not in the ARP table, ARP sends out a data link broadcast with the IP address it is looking for. The desired station will see the broadcast and will reply with a directed response that includes its MAC address. This new entry is added to the ARP table, and a timer is set. This timer is called the ARP cache timer. It is updated each time the entry is referenced. Once this timer expires, the entry will be removed from the table. This way, the ARP entry is available in the local cache during an entire network conversation. After the two stations have not communicated for a period of time, the entry is removed from the cache. This keeps the table from growing too large and requiring large amounts of memory.

CONNECTION-ORIENTED AND CONNECTIONLESS SERVICES

Network protocols can generally be classified as either connection-oriented or connectionless.

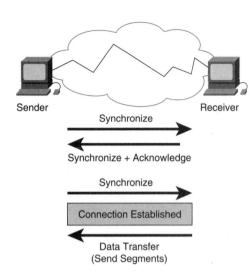

FIGURE 1.4

A connection must be established before data can be exchanged.

Connection-oriented protocols establish a connection with the other end before they begin sending data. The protocol makes a request to the station it wants to exchange data with. This request must be accepted before the exchange can occur (see Figure 1.4).

During the exchange of data, the two stations verify that the data was received error-free. After the data exchange is complete, the connection between the two stations is terminated.

One protocol that uses connection-oriented network services is Transmission Control Protocol (TCP). TCP is one of the Transport layer protocols of the TCP/IP protocol suite.

In a connectionless exchange, the two stations don't need to establish a connection. One station can just send data to the other. Connectionless exchanges don't verify that the data was received or that it is error-free. Generally in a connectionless exchange, layers above the Transport layer are responsible for making sure that all the data is exchanged completely and free of errors.

User Datagram Protocol (UDP) is an example of connectionless protocol from the TCP/IP protocol suite. UDP exchanges datagrams without acknowledgments or guaranteed delivery.

File Transfer Protocol (FTP) is an application to copy files across a network to another station. FTP makes use of TCP exchanges. This puts the burden of error correction and reliable delivery on the Transport layer of the OSI Reference Model. FTP can pass the data it wants to send to the Transport layer protocol, TCP, and know that the data will arrive at the destination station error-free. There is a similar application called Trivial File Transfer Protocol (TFTP). TFTP uses UDP for its exchanges. This places the burden of reliable delivery on the application, not on the Transport layer of the OSI Reference Model. TFTP becomes more important when maintaining routers since it is used to copy software and configurations to and from Cisco routers.

Flow Control

Flow control techniques prevent network congestion, which can be caused by several different factors. A high-speed server might be sending data faster than a workstation can process it. Many different workstations might be trying to send data through a router simultaneously, overflowing the router's capability to deal with the traffic.

Traffic from a high-speed network might need to be transferred over a slower serial link to a remote office. Whatever the case, flow control paces data transmission to meet the capabilities of the network and receiving station.

There are three common methods of flow control: using source-quench messages, buffering, and windowing. These techniques are often used together to pace the flow of data.

Source-Quench Messages

Source-quench messages are used to signal the sending station to slow down. When packets are arriving at a receiving station faster than it can process them, it starts by dropping packets. It then sends a source-quench message for every packet dropped. The sending station receives the source-quench messages and slows sending until it stops getting source-quench messages. The sending station then gradually increases the sending rate as long as no source-quench messages are received. One of the problems with source-quench messages is if the network is overburdened, there is no guarantee that the source-quench packet will arrive at the sending station.

Windowing

Windowing relies on the receiving station's acknowledging receipt of packets. This acknowledgment is commonly called an ACK. It would create a great deal of overhead if the receiving station had to acknowledge every packet individually, so a window is used. The sending and receiving stations agree on a window size. This window defines the number of packets they will exchange before an acknowledgment is required. If the window size is five packets, the sending station will send five packets and then wait for an acknowledgment from the receiving station. If the acknowledgment comes, the sending station sends the next five packets and waits again. If the sending station does not receive the acknowledgment within a set period of time, it resends all the packets in the window at a reduced speed.

Buffering

Buffering allows the receiving station to temporarily store packets received until it can process them. As long as the bursts are short and don't overflow the buffer, this technique works well. However, if bursts overrun the available memory for buffering, the station must drop packets. Buffering is commonly used in conjunction with source-quench messages and windowing.

NETWORKING TOPOLOGIES

A good understanding of different networking topologies is required for Cisco certification. A description of Ethernet, token ring, FDDI, and Cisco serial ports is included here. Chapter 5, "WAN Protocols," discusses other internetworking topologies, such as frame relay and ISDN.

Ethernet

Ethernet is by far the most popular networking topology in use today. Its ease of use, simplicity, and reliability have established it as the mainstream networking topology.

Ethernet operates at 10Mbps (megabits per second) and uses Carrier Sense Multiple Access/Collision Detection (CSMA/CD) to access the media. Contention for the network media is handled by collision detection. When a network interface has data to place on the wire, it first listens to the network to see if another station is currently transmitting. If the network isn't busy, it begins transmitting its data. After the transmission, it listens again. If it detects another station transmitting right after it finishes, it assumes a collision occurred. When this occurs, both network stations involved in the collision must retransmit their packets. Each backs off for a random amount of time and then retries its transmission.

Ethernet is a broadcast-based network, meaning that every station sees all the packets on the media. The individual stations look at the destination address in the packet and determine whether the packet is intended for them. If it is, they copy the packet off the media and process it. If not, they simply ignore the packet. This is true of non-switched networks. In networks where layer 2 switches are used, this process is much more complex. Layer 2 switches are discussed in more depth in Chapter 8, "LAN Switching."

NOTE

Ethernet History Xerox Corporation originally developed Ethernet in the 1970s. Ethernet was later modified and specified in the IEEE 802.3 specification. Ethernet is actually slightly different from the IEEE 802.3 specification, but it is common to refer to all CSMA/CD network topologies as Ethernet.

Ethernet can be implemented several different ways. The most common are 10Base5, 10Base2, 10BaseT, 100BaseTX, and 100BaseFX.

Each implementation has different characteristics. 10Base5 is implemented on a thick coaxial cable with an impedance of 50 ohms. 10Base5 is commonly called ThickNet. Since 10Base5 uses low-loss coaxial cable, it has a maximum segment length of 500 meters.

10Base2 is implemented on a thin 50-ohm coaxial cable. 10Base2 is commonly called ThinNet. ThinNet is easier to work with and cheaper to implement than ThickNet. However, it has some problems that make it unsuitable for large installations. Since the network is made up of one string of coaxial that runs from one end of the network to the other, if a user unplugs one of the wires from the back of his workstation, the entire network fails. The maximum segment length for 10Base2 is 185 meters.

10BaseT is an implementation of Ethernet on unshielded twisted pair wire. It is the most reliable method of implementing Ethernet since it doesn't suffer from the frailty of ThinNet. 10BaseT is wired differently than 10Base5 or 10Base2. 10BaseT is still one wire in a logical networking sense, but the workstations are connected to hubs that are connected to each other. Since each station is wired to the hub separately, it is less likely that a problem at a workstation will cause the entire network to fail. More-advanced hubs include features to isolate stations that are transmitting garbage so that they don't affect the rest of the network. 10BaseT has a maximum segment length of 100 meters.

Token Ring

IBM developed Token Ring in the 1970s. The IEEE 802.5 specification is almost identical to IBM's Token Ring. Token Ring is arranged in a ring, where each station is a node on the ring. These stations pass traffic around the ring. A network station accepts a packet from its downstream neighbor and sends it to its upstream neighbor. Token Ring supports multiple speeds; 4Mbps and 16Mbps are the most common. Newer token ring equipment is starting to support 100Mbps.

In token ring, contention for the media is handled via a token. The token is a special packet that is passed around the ring.

If a station has traffic to place on the network, it must wait until it gets the token. It then changes the token into a regular packet header by changing one of the bits. The data it must transmit is added to the packet, and the packet is sent to the upstream neighbor. As each station on the network gets this packet, it checks the packet to see if it was destined for this station. If so, it processes the packet, marks it as read, and then sends it back onto the network. The originating station waits for the packet it sent out to come back around the ring. Once it arrives back at the sending station, the sending station checks to make sure the packet it received matches the packet it sent. If not, a network error must have occurred. Once the packet is received back at the originating station, the originating station releases the token so that other stations can use the network. Some token ring networks support a feature called early token release. This allows the originating station to release the token after putting its traffic on the network and before seeing it return. This allows multiple packets to traverse the network simultaneously. For a network to support early token release, every station on the network must support it and be configured for it.

Active Monitor

Token ring networks require someone to watch over the network. The station that does this is called the active monitor. A station becomes the active monitor through a negotiation process. All other stations on the network monitor the active monitor, and if it exits the network, a new active monitor is elected.

The active monitor is responsible for making sure packets don't circle the ring more than once. When a packet traveling around the ring reaches the active monitor, it sets a special bit in the packet called the monitor bit. If the active monitor sees this packet again, it means that the station that originated the packet must have exited the ring and couldn't remove it. The active monitor removes this packet and releases a new token on the network.

If the token somehow becomes lost, the active monitor creates a new token and releases it on the network.

FDDI

Fiber Distributed Data Interface (FDDI) is an American National Standards Institute (ANSI) standard. FDDI operates a dual token ring LAN at 100Mbps. Its most common use is for campus and backbone installations. An implementation of FDDI that operates over twisted pair wire is called Copper Distributed Data Interface (CDDI).

FDDI is immune to the electromagnetic interference that plagues wire-based networks. This makes it very useful in hostile environments such as factories and Navy ships. It supports networks that are spread out physically.

FDDI has the following limitations:

◆ 500 nodes per FDDI LAN

◆ 100 kilometer maximum ring circumference

◆ 2 kilometer distance between nodes using multimode fiber

Serial Ports

Cisco routers use serial ports to connect to many devices, including Channel Service Unit/Data Service Unit (CSU/DSU). CSU/DSUs are similar to modems but are used for digital circuits such as 64K leased lines and T1s.

These serial ports are very versatile. They support several different standards from one port. The port configures itself for the different standards based on the cable that is plugged in.

The end of the cable that plugs into the router includes pins for configuration. When the cable is made, certain combinations of these configuration pins are connected. When this cable is plugged into the router's serial port, the serial port detects the type of cable and configures itself accordingly.

Here are some of the types of interfaces supported by Cisco serial ports:

◆ V.35

◆ EIA-232 (RS-232)

◆ EIA-449

◆ X.21

◆ EIA-530

Serial devices are divided into two categories: Data Terminal Equipment (DTE) and Data Communications Equipment (DCE). The main difference between these two types of equipment is that DCE devices supply the clock signal that synchronizes the communication. DTE devices use the clock signal generated by the DCE.

The serial ports built into Cisco routers support high speeds compared to PC serial ports. Most PC serial ports only support up to 115Kbps. Cisco's serial ports can support varying speeds. Some serial interfaces can support up to 8Mbps. The platform and serial card determine the speed. Cisco's documentation for your platform should be referenced.

Serial communication can be divided into two categories: synchronous and asynchronous. Asynchronous serial communication relies on start and stop bits in the data stream to signal clocking information. Synchronous serial communication relies on a clocking source outside the data stream.

CASE STUDY: THE SCHUTZHUND CLUB

ESSENCE OF THE CASE

▶ Diagnosing network problems using the layered approach

▶ Layer 3 routing problems

▶ Ping as a diagnostic tool

SCENARIO

The Schutzhund Dog Club has automated its event registration process. It had custom software developed that allows handlers to register their dogs over the Web. The software also lets show workers access a secured Web site during the Schutzhund trials to update scores and show information.

The automated system consists of several servers connected via 100Mbps Ethernet to a layer 2 switch. Also connected to this switch is a Cisco 2501 router. The router is connected to the Internet via a T1.

CASE STUDY: THE SCHUTZHUND CLUB

One of the older servers is replaced with a new Pentium II server running Windows NT. After installing the server, it finds that although the server has no problem talking with other servers on the local network, it can't communicate with the Internet.

The club president spends days trying to resolve the problem but can't. A major trial is coming, and it needs a solution quickly. You are called in to find the problem and provide a fix.

ANALYSIS

The club president explains the problem and what he has tried. He asks you to correct the problem as quickly as possible. The trial is in one week, and handlers are trying to register their dogs over the Web but can't.

You start by identifying the troubled server and following its network patch cable to the switch. You remember that when diagnosing a networking problem it is best to start at the bottom of the OSI Reference Model and work your way up.

You find that the server is plugged into port 3 of the switch. The server is up and running,

but the link light on the switch is not on. You remember the club president telling you that he could ping the other servers at first, but after working with it for a few days, he couldn't ping any computers. He mentioned that he had tried different cables and ports in his diagnostics. After looking around, you find another patch cord and replace the one on the server. The link light on the switch is now active. You have resolved a layer 1 (Physical) networking problem.

You try pinging the other servers on the network and find that your pings are successful. This confirms that the OSI Reference Model is working up to layer 3 (Network)—at least locally. You ping the router's Ethernet port and get successful replies. You now try to ping an outside Internet address, and the pings fail.

On the server, you open a command window and type `route print`. This displays the server's routing table. You notice that the table doesn't have a default route. The default route would be shown by a network address of 0.0.0.0 and a netmask of 0.0.0.0. In the following example, this entry is missing:

```
C:>route print
Active Routes:

      Network Address          Netmask    Gateway Address         Interface    Metric
          127.0.0.0          255.0.0.0          127.0.0.1          127.0.0.1         1
      192.168.137.0      255.255.255.0     192.168.137.37     192.168.137.37         1
     192.168.137.37    255.255.255.255          127.0.0.1          127.0.0.1         1
     192.168.137.38    255.255.255.255          127.0.0.1          127.0.0.1         1
     192.168.137.39    255.255.255.255          127.0.0.1          127.0.0.1         1
     192.168.137.41    255.255.255.255          127.0.0.1          127.0.0.1         1
     192.168.137.42    255.255.255.255          127.0.0.1          127.0.0.1         1
     192.168.137.51    255.255.255.255          127.0.0.1          127.0.0.1         1
    192.168.137.255    255.255.255.255     192.168.137.37     192.168.137.37         1
          224.0.0.0          224.0.0.0     192.168.137.37     192.168.137.37         1
    255.255.255.255    255.255.255.255     192.168.137.37     192.168.137.37         1
```

continues

CASE STUDY: THE SCHUTZHUND CLUB

continued

In opening the network configuration dialog box, you discover there is no entry for the default gateway. That explains it. The server can communicate with the local computers since they are all on the same network and the packets never need to travel through a layer 3 router. When you try to reach an IP address on a remote network, however, the server doesn't know where to send the packets for forwarding.

You enter the IP address of the router's Ethernet port in the default gateway dialog box and reboot the server. You now can successfully ping remote stations on the Internet.

You check the routing tables again and find a route representing the default gateway as 0.0.0.0 subnet 0.0.0.0. This is shown in the first line of the following routing table. This is a common way to represent a route to any unknown route. This is discussed in more detail in Chapter 6, "Routing."

```
C:>route print
Active Routes:
```

Network Address	Netmask	Gateway Address	Interface	Metric
0.0.0.0	0.0.0.0	192.168.137.1	192.168.137.37	1
127.0.0.0	255.0.0.0	127.0.0.1	127.0.0.1	1
192.168.137.0	255.255.255.0	192.168.137.37	192.168.137.37	1
192.168.137.37	255.255.255.255	127.0.0.1	127.0.0.1	1
192.168.137.38	255.255.255.255	127.0.0.1	127.0.0.1	1
192.168.137.39	255.255.255.255	127.0.0.1	127.0.0.1	1
192.168.137.41	255.255.255.255	127.0.0.1	127.0.0.1	1
192.168.137.42	255.255.255.255	127.0.0.1	127.0.0.1	1
192.168.137.51	255.255.255.255	127.0.0.1	127.0.0.1	1
192.168.137.255	255.255.255.255	192.168.137.37	192.168.137.37	1
224.0.0.0	224.0.0.0	192.168.137.37	192.168.137.37	1
255.255.255.255	255.255.255.255	192.168.137.37	192.168.137.37	1

The moment you get this working, the server becomes active with HTTP requests, and the database starts filling with registration information for the upcoming trial.

CHAPTER SUMMARY

This chapter covered some of the building blocks that make up networking systems. The layers of the OSI Reference Model were explained, as well as the reasons the OSI Reference Model is used. Understanding this model is imperative. Networking protocols and equipment use the model to build complex systems from relatively simple tasks.

You looked at each layer of the model and saw examples of each. The types of network conversations were covered. Connection-oriented conversations require that the two stations establish a communication link before exchanging data. In a connectionless conversation, none of this preliminary setup is required.

These pieces of networking help make up complex enterprise networks. If you start with a strong foundation, it will be easier to understand more complex concepts later.

KEY TERMS

- OSI Reference Model
- MAC address
- Network address
- Connection-oriented service
- Connectionless service
- Flow control
- Windowing
- CSMA/CD
- Encapsulation
- Source-quench message
- Address Resolution Protocol (ARP)

Review Questions

1. What are the seven layers of the OSI Reference Model, listed in order from layer 7 to layer 1?

2. What are some examples of Presentation layer implementations?

3. What are some examples of network addresses?

4. How are data link addresses mapped to network addresses?

5. Which layer of the OSI Reference Model is responsible for routing?

6. What does CSMA/CD stand for, and which networking technology does it represent?

7. What is an active monitor, and with which networking topology is it associated?

8. List the five steps of data encapsulation.

9. List three reasons why the industry uses the OSI Reference Model.

10. What are the differences between connection-oriented and connectionless network conversations?

Exam Questions

1. Which of the following is an example of a function handled at the Physical layer of the OSI Reference Model?

   A. Application data is encrypted for secure transport over the network.

   B. A route for the packet is determined.

   C. A CRC is calculated and added to the packet to ensure that it is delivered error-free.

   D. The data is converted to voltage levels defined by the network standard and is placed on the network media.

2. List the levels of the OSI Reference Model in the correct order.

   A. Application, Session, Presentation, Transport, Network, Data Link, Physical

   B. Application, Presentation, Session, Transport, Network, Data Link, Physical

   C. Application, Presentation, Session, Transfer, Network, Data Link, Physical

   D. Application, Physical, Session, Transport, Network

3. A computer using TCP/IP can ping computers on the local network but is unable to ping computers on remote networks. Other computers on the same network have no problem reaching remote computers. At which layer of the OSI Reference Model is this computer likely experiencing problems?

   A. Network

   B. Data Link

   C. Physical

   D. Transport

4. Which of the following statements is false regarding network addresses and data link addresses?

   A. Data link addresses are usually burned into ROM and are copied to RAM during initialization.

   B. Data link addresses are made up of 48 bits, with 24 bits as the OUI and 24 bits as the station number.

C. Under TCP/IP, network addresses are mapped to data link addresses using a protocol called RAP.

D. Network addresses are used to route packets.

5. The OSI Reference Model is used for the following reason(s):

   A. It allows different layers of the protocol stack to be upgraded without adversely affecting the operation of the rest of the stack.

   B. It divides complex network operations into less-complex pieces.

   C. It defines a rigid standard for specific protocols that all networking manufacturers must design for.

   D. It makes understanding the complex nature of networking easier by dividing the complex pieces into smaller, easier-to-understand subcomponents.

6. A LAN engineer comes to you and says he is seeing many acknowledgments (ACKs) on the network and wants you to correct the problem. What do you do?

   A. You adjust the number of buffers in the router to reduce the number of ACKs.

   B. You ask the LAN engineer to provide you with a LAN diagram so that you can determine where the problem lies.

   C. You tell the LAN engineer there is no problem with the network. ACKs are normal for protocols using windowing flow control.

   D. You ask for the MAC address of the station sending the ACKs so that you can replace the Network Interface Card (NIC).

7. Which of the following is/are example(s) of the Presentation layer of the OSI Reference Model?

   A. MPEG

   B. FTP

   C. Telnet

   D. MIDI

8. Which of the following is/are example(s) of the Application layer of the OSI Reference Model?

   A. MPEG

   B. FTP

   C. Telnet

   D. MIDI

9. Which of the following is an example of flow control?

   A. Buffering

   B. Active monitor

   C. Cyclic Redundancy Check (CRC)

   D. Packet header

10. Which of the following is/are example(s) of network address(es)?

    A. IPX address

    B. IP address

    C. MAC address

    D. ARP

11. The routing of packets occurs at which layer?

    A. Data Link

    B. Network

    C. Session

    D. Transport

APPLY YOUR KNOWLEDGE

12. Which of the following is/are associated with CSMA/CD networks such as IEEE 802.3 and Ethernet?

    A. Token passing

    B. Collisions

    C. Active monitor

    D. ThinNet

13. Which of the following is/are example(s) of the Transport layer?

    A. TCP

    B. UDP

    C. ARP

    D. IP

Answers to Review Questions

1. The seven layers of the OSI Reference Model are Application, Presentation, Session, Transport, Network, Data Link, and Physical. For more information, see "The Seven Layers."

2. MIDI, MPEG, JPEG, and GIF are examples of Presentation layer implementations. There are many others. For more information, see "Presentation Layer."

3. IP and IPX addresses are examples of network addresses. For more information, see "Network Addresses."

4. Data link addresses are mapped to network addresses using Address Resolution Protocol (ARP). ARP uses data link broadcasts to resolve an IP address and then places the addresses in a table for future reference. After a timer expires, the ARP entry is deleted to keep required resources to a minimum.

For more information, see "Data Link and Network Addresses."

5. Layer 3, the Network layer, is responsible for routing. This will be examined in more detail later in this book. For more information, see "Network Layer."

6. CSMA/CD stands for Carrier Sense Multiple Access/Collision Detection. It is associated with IEEE 802.3 and Ethernet networks. For more information, see "Networking Topologies."

7. An active monitor is a network station responsible for making sure the token doesn't get lost. It is associated with token ring and IEEE 802.5 networks. For more information, see "Active Monitor."

8. The five steps of data encapsulation are build the data, package the data, append the network address, append the data link address, and convert to bits for transmission. For more information, see "Encapsulation."

9. The OSI Reference Model divides complex network operations into less-complex pieces, keeps changes in one area from adversely affecting other layers, and makes complex concepts easier to understand by dividing them into smaller, more comprehensible pieces. For more information, see "Understanding the OSI Reference Model."

10. A connection-oriented conversation must initially establish a connection with the network station with which it wants to exchange data. After data exchange, the connection is closed. In a connectionless conversation, this initial connection is not established. For more information, see "Connection-Oriented and Connectionless Services."

Answers to Exam Questions

1. **D.** The Physical layer (layer 1) of the OSI Reference Model is responsible for the network's physical characteristics. Such things as connector type, voltage levels, and clocking rates are defined at the Physical layer. For more information, see "Physical Layer."

2. **B.** Remember the sentence All People Seem To Need Data Processing. This is something you just need to memorize. Take the time to do so; it will save you a lot of headaches later. For more information, see "Understanding the OSI Reference Model."

3. **A.** Routing is handled by the Network layer. Since this computer can ping local computers, the Physical and Data Link layers must be working properly. The Network layer is functioning properly for the local network where route determination is simple. However, when the computer tries to communicate with a remote computer, it fails. This is most likely a configuration problem with the IP address or default gateway on this computer since other computers on the same network are not experiencing this problem. For more information, see "Network Layer."

4. **C.** Although this answer is almost correct, the protocol used to map network addresses to data link addresses is Address Resolution Protocol (ARP). For more information, see "Address Resolution Protocol (ARP)."

5. **A, B, D.** Although the OSI Reference Model is a guide for networking, it is not a rigid standard for specific protocols. For more information, see "Understanding the OSI Reference Model."

6. **C.** Acknowledgments are normal for protocols that use windowing flow control. For more information, see "Windowing."

7. **A, D.** MPEG and MIDI are Presentation layer examples. FTP and telnet are Application layer examples. For more information, see "Understanding the OSI Reference Model."

8. **B, C.** FTP and telnet are examples of Application layer implementations. MPEG and MIDI are Presentation layer examples. For more information, see "Understanding the OSI Reference Model."

9. **A.** Buffering is used in flow control to temporarily store packets until the network station can process them. For more information, see "Buffering."

10. **A, B.** IPX and IP addresses are examples of network addresses. The MAC address is a data link address. ARP is the protocol that maps between IP addresses and MAC addresses. For more information, see "Network Addresses."

11. **B.** The Network layer is responsible for routing packets. We will discuss this in more depth when we discuss how the Network layer is implemented in a router. For more information, see "Network Layer."

12. **B, D.** Collisions and ThinNet are associated with Ethernet. Token passing and active monitor are associated with token ring. For more information, see "Networking Topologies."

13. **A, B.** TCP and UDP are implementations of transport protocols in the TCP/IP suite. For more information, see "Transport Layer."

APPLY YOUR KNOWLEDGE

Suggested Readings and Resources

1. Chappell, Laura. *Introduction to Cisco Router Configuration.* Cisco Press, 1998.

2. Ford, Merilee, H. Kim Lew, Steve Spanier, and Tim Stevenson. *Internetworking Technologies Handbook.* Cisco Press, 1997.

Cisco provides the following objectives for the Internetworking Operating System (IOS) portion of the CCNA exam.

Log in to a router in both user and privileged modes.

▶ To be able to maintain and diagnose routers and switches, you will need to be able to access the routers' different modes.

Use the context-sensitive help facility.

▶ There are so many commands available for configuring routers that it is impossible to remember them all. By using the context-sensitive help, it is easier to continue working without having to reference a manual.

Use the command history and editing features.

▶ Cisco routers and switches offer some advanced editing and command history features that can save time. These features can also aid in reducing errors.

Examine router elements (RAM, ROM, CDP, show)

▶ It is important to be able to examine the elements of the router to diagnose internetworking problems.

Manage configuration files from the privileged exec mode.

▶ The configuration files tell the router what to do and how to do it. Managing these files is imperative.

CHAPTER 2

Internetworking Operating System

Control router passwords, identification, and banner.

▶ Maintaining the router passwords, identification, and banners is important to the daily maintenance of routers and switches.

Identify the main Cisco IOS commands for router startup.

▶ Understanding Cisco startup commands is important to maintain routers.

Enter an initial configuration using the setup command.

▶ Cisco routers provide a setup routine that you need to be familiar with.

Copy and manipulate configuration files.

▶ Copying and manipulating router configuration files is important for maintaining routers.

List the commands to load Cisco IOS software from flash memory, a TFTP server, or ROM.

▶ The IOS software can be loaded from several sources. Being able to perform these techniques is important.

Prepare to back up, upgrade, and load a backup Cisco IOS software image.

▶ Upgrading IOS software is a common occurrence. The skills required to perform this are necessary.

Prepare the initial configuration of your router and enable IP.

▶ Preparing an initial configuration with IP enabled is essential for an internetworking professional.

▶ It is important to have actual hands-on experience with Cisco router configuration and maintenance. Cisco certification tests are structured to require hands-on experience. Without this, it is difficult to pass the test. While studying for any Cisco certification, it is a good idea to build a small router lab for practice. The investment in used routers can be recouped after you have completed your certification by selling them. There is always a market for used 2500-series routers.

▶ This lab can be as small as one Cisco 2501 hooked to an Ethernet LAN. A more useful lab environment would consist of two Cisco 2500-series routers that are connected via their serial ports and a small LAN. In order to connect two routers back-to-back via the serial ports, you will need a DTE cable on one router and a DCE cable on the other. The router with the DCE cable must have the `clockrate` command added to it's configuration. This provides the clocking signal a CSU/DSU would normally provide. More details on DCE and DTE devices are covered in Chapter 5, "WAN Protocols."

▶ There are two choices for connecting the routers via the serial ports. One choice is to use two Cisco cables—one DCE female and one DTE male. The other choice is to purchase a cable specifically made to connect two routers. Cisco doesn't make a cable of this type but there are vendors that do. However, be prepared to do some homework because the cables are not always available from any one vendor.

▶ Some of the procedures that should be practiced will cause connectivity outages and other problems on production networks. Having a router lab allows you to work the exercises and try different configurations without causing problems for an existing network.

▶ After you have your routers in place, play with them. Create different configurations. Try variations of the commands and explore. Reference the context-sensitive help and Cisco's documentation for explanations of the commands and their options. Documentation for Cisco routers is available to everyone from its Web site at `http://www.cisco.com`. At first, it is difficult to learn to traverse the Web site and find what you are seeking, but in searching you will inevitably run across something else that may come in handy. Spend a good deal of time researching different subjects on Cisco's Web site. It has a great deal of information available for free to those willing to take the time searching. Cisco also includes a documentation CD with each router and switch. This CD is helpful for reading up on the documentation when you do not have Internet access.

▶ Practice working with a Cisco router. Practice using the editing commands. They will save you lots of time. Above all, practice. Experience with different configurations and commands will make the difference when it comes time for the test. Although you can learn by reading, you gain superior knowledge and understanding through experience.

INTRODUCTION

This chapter discusses Cisco's Internetworking Operating System (IOS). The IOS is what makes the router work. An internetworking engineer interfaces with the IOS through a command line much like old interactive BASIC programming or the DOS operating system. With most applications today using graphical user interfaces, it is hard to imagine using such a seemingly archaic interface. However, it is arguably the best way to configure and maintain the complex systems that make up our networks. Cisco has developed a program with a graphical interface for creating simple configurations and downloading to a router. This software is called *ConfigMaker* and is available from Cisco's Web site. However, it is difficult to create complex configurations and use advanced features of the IOS with this program.

This chapter introduces you to the following:

◆ The Command Line Interface (CLI). This chapter will cover some features for making life easier. The CLI includes advanced tools for editing. It also includes context-sensitive help for quick reference.

◆ The basic components of a router and how they are used in configurations and daily operation. The procedures for updating the IOS and maintaining configuration files are also explained.

◆ Configuration commands for basic configuration of the router.

◆ Managing configuration files using a TFTP server.

◆ Upgrading and managing the IOS using a TFTP server.

◆ Cisco Discovery Protocol (CDP). A protocol used to discover neighboring devices and exchange capability information with them.

There are some tools you will need to gather to perform some of the exercises in this chapter. You will need a Trivial File Transfer Protocol (TFTP) server and your router lab. A good TFTP server can be obtained from Cisco's Web site at `http://www.cisco.com/public/sw-center/sw-other.shtml`.

LOGGING IN TO A ROUTER IN BOTH USER AND PRIVILEGED MODES

Cisco routers and switches provide password protection to prevent unauthorized access and administration. Several different methods are supported for authenticating users. Only one of these methods—normal passwords—is addressed on the CCNA exam. However, it is useful to know about the other methods of authentication.

◆ Normal passwords stored in the router's configuration

◆ TACACS+ (Terminal Access Controller Access Control System)

◆ RADIUS (Remote Access Dial-In User Service)

Authentication Servers

Authentication servers are applications that provide an authentication service to the router, switch, or access server. An authentication server can run under most operating systems including UNIX, Linux, and Windows NT. There are two main protocols for authentication: RADIUS and TACACS+. Cisco routers support both. Authentication servers store a database of usernames and levels of security these users are assigned. When a user tries to access a router, it accepts a username and password. It then sends this information to the authentication server where it is verified and usually logged. The server will respond with either an authorization or rejection for the user. Depending on the implementation, the authentication packets can be encrypted so network sniffers cannot capture clear text passwords traversing the network. Some advanced features of authentication servers and Cisco's IOS allow an administrator to control on a granular level what commands users have access to.

Normal Password Authentication

The type of user authentication that is addressed on the CCNA exam is password login authentication. This method of authentication simply uses a password stored in the configuration file of the router.

When a user tries to access the router, a password is requested. This password is compared to the one stored in the configuration file and if they match, the user is granted access. There are two types of passwords: login and enable. The login password grants the user access to the router's user exec mode. The user exec mode allows you to view some of the components of the router that will be helpful for diagnosing problems. Configuration changes are not allowed in the user exec mode. More advanced diagnostic methods and configuration of the router are available from the privileged exec mode. The privileged exec mode is accessed with the enable password. When you attempt to access a router, either through the console port or telnet, the initial login will appear as follows:

```
User Access Verification

Password:
Router>
```

The router displays either the standard message "User Access Verification" or a Message of the Day (MOTD). The MOTD comes from multiuser days where a system presents a message to each person logging in. This message can provide any information the administrator wants to tell the user. Sometimes this message is used for warnings, scheduled outages, or any other information the administrator would like users or potential hackers to have before logging in.

After the initial message, the router prompts you to enter your password. If the password you enter matches the router's configuration, you are granted access. The normal user exec prompt of the router includes the router's hostname and a prompt character. In our example, the router's hostname is the default Router.

The prompt character is >. The > character (prompt character) indicates you are now in the user exec mode. In this mode, you have access to commands for monitoring the router and its interfaces. What can be performed at this level is restricted. To configure the router or perform advanced diagnostics, you will need to access the privileged exec mode. To access the privileged exec mode, enter the command enable. Then, enter the enable password.

```
User Access Verification

Password:
Router>enable
Password:
Router#
```

From the user exec mode, you enter the command enable. This command enables the privileged exec mode. The router then prompts you to enter the enable password. After this is entered successfully, the router grants you access to the privileged exec mode. The new command prompt character (#) indicates you are now in privileged exec mode.

If you want to return to user exec mode from privileged exec, enter the command disable.

```
User Access Verification

Password:
Router>enable
Password:
Router#disable
Router>
```

Entering Commands

You interface with the router's IOS through the command line interface (CLI). This CLI accepts commands from the user and executes them. When entering commands, you only need to enter enough of the command so the CLI can determine which command you want.

You could enter the following command:

```
c2511r1#show interface serial0
Serial0 is administratively down, line protocol is down
  Hardware is HD64570
  MTU 1500 bytes, BW 1544 Kbit, DLY 20000 usec, rely
➡255/255, load 1/255
  Encapsulation HDLC, loopback not set, keepalive set
➡(10 sec)
  Last input never, output never, output hang never
  Last clearing of "show interface" counters 00:07:03
  Queueing strategy: fifo
  Output queue 0/40, 0 drops; input queue 0/75, 0 drops
  5 minute input rate 0 bits/sec, 0 packets/sec
  5 minute output rate 0 bits/sec, 0 packets/sec
     0 packets input, 0 bytes, 0 no buffer
     Received 0 broadcasts, 0 runts, 0 giants, 0 throttles
     0 input errors, 0 CRC, 0 frame, 0 overrun, 0 ignored,
➡0 abort
     0 packets output, 0 bytes, 0 underruns
     0 output errors, 0 collisions, 0 interface resets
     0 output buffer failures, 0 output buffers swapped out
     0 carrier transitions
     DCD=down  DSR=down  DTR=down  RTS=down  CTS=down
c2511r1#
```

But the same results can be obtained by entering this abbreviated
command:

```
c2511r1#sh int s0
Serial0 is administratively down, line protocol is down
  Hardware is HD64570
  MTU 1500 bytes, BW 1544 Kbit, DLY 20000 usec, rely
➥255/255, load 1/255
  Encapsulation HDLC, loopback not set, keepalive set (10
➥sec)
  Last input never, output never, output hang never
  Last clearing of "show interface" counters 00:07:55
  Queueing strategy: fifo
  Output queue 0/40, 0 drops; input queue 0/75, 0 drops
  5 minute input rate 0 bits/sec, 0 packets/sec
  5 minute output rate 0 bits/sec, 0 packets/sec
     0 packets input, 0 bytes, 0 no buffer
     Received 0 broadcasts, 0 runts, 0 giants, 0 throttles
     0 input errors, 0 CRC, 0 frame, 0 overrun, 0 ignored,
➥0 abort
     0 packets output, 0 bytes, 0 underruns
     0 output errors, 0 collisions, 0 interface resets
     0 output buffer failures, 0 output buffers swapped out
     0 carrier transitions
     DCD=down  DSR=down  DTR=down  RTS=down  CTS=down
c2511r1#
```

If you abbreviate a command too much, the CLI will not be able to
uniquely identify which command you are trying to execute.
Instead, it will respond as follows:

```
c2511r1#te
% Ambiguous command:  "te"
c2511r1#
```

To find out which commands begin with "te", type the following lines:

```
c2511r1#te?
telnet  terminal  test

c2511r1#te
```

If you add one more letter to the command, the CLI will be able to
determine which of these three commands you intended.

```
c2511r1#tel
Host: 192.168.137.33
Trying 192.168.137.33 ... Open


User Access Verification

Password:
```

The CLI will complete a command for you. By typing the unique portion of the command and then pressing the Tab key, the IOS will complete the command for you.

```
c2511r1#tel<Tab>
c2511r1#telnet
```

With all the different versions of IOS deployed, you will find that what works in one router may not in another. Cisco is constantly upgrading the IOS and adding new features. The context-sensitive help can be handy for discovering what commands are available with the version of IOS you are currently configuring.

It is difficult to remember all of the commands and the parameters for each. Cisco added context-sensitive help to the CLI for this reason.

Context-Sensitive Help

Cisco's IOS provides help for command syntax and options. This help system is available from the user exec or privileged exec mode command prompts.

To see a list of commands available at any time, simply type a question mark at the prompt. This list provides the commands available from the current mode and a brief description of each command.

```
c2511r1>?
Exec commands:
  <1-99>           Session number to resume
  access-enable    Create a temporary Access-List entry
  clear            Reset functions
  connect          Open a terminal connection
  disable          Turn off privileged commands
  disconnect       Disconnect an existing network connection
  enable           Turn on privileged commands
  exit             Exit from the EXEC
  help             Description of the interactive help system
  lock             Lock the terminal
  login            Log in as a particular user
  logout           Exit from the EXEC
  mrinfo           Request neighbor and version information from a multicastrouter
  mstat            Show statistics after multiple multicast traceroutes
  mtrace           Trace reverse multicast path from destination to source
  name-connection  Name an existing network connection
  pad              Open a X.29 PAD connection
  ping             Send echo messages
  ppp              Start IETF Point-to-Point Protocol (PPP)
  resume           Resume an active network connection
 —More—
```

Notice that the last line listed is —More—. This is the IOS' way of
indicating that there is more information to display. To see the next
line of text, press the Enter key. To display the entire next screen of
information, press the spacebar key. The line-by-line display key will
come in very handy when you start looking at interface parameters.
If the information for which you were searching is displayed on the
screen and you want to end the listing and return to the exec
prompt, press the Esc key.

During command entry, you can get more information about the
command by entering a question mark after the command. Entering
a command followed by a space and then the question mark will list
the options for the command.

```
c1604>show ?
  WORD          Flash device information - format <dev:>[partition]
  clock         Display the system clock
  dialer        Dialer parameters and statistics
  history       Display the session command history
  hosts         IP domain-name, lookup style, nameservers, and host table
  isdn          ISDN information
  location      Display the system location
  modemcap      Show Modem Capabilities database
  ppp           PPP parameters and statistics
  rmon          rmon statistics
  sessions      Information about Telnet connections
  snmp          snmp statistics
  tacacs        Shows tacacs+ server statistics
  terminal      Display terminal configuration parameters
  traffic-shape traffic rate shaping configuration
  users         Display information about terminal lines
  version       System hardware and software status c1604>show
```

CONFIGURING THE ROUTER

To configure the router, you must enter the configuration mode. The
configuration can be set from several different sources: terminal,
memory, or network. When you configure from the terminal, you are
entering commands directly into the routers running configuration.
When you make a change, it takes effect immediately. When you configure from memory, the startup configuration is copied to the running configuration. When you configure from network, the router
copies a new running configuration from a TFTP server. This section
will address the interactive configuration mode first. This is where you
enter configuration commands from a terminal. This mode is accessed
using the configuration command.

```
Router#configure terminal
Enter configuration commands, one per line.  End with CNTL/Z.
Router(config)#
```

Notice that the prompt changes to Router(config)#. This indicates that the config mode has been entered. A new set of commands is available. In this mode, you are configuring global settings. These are settings affecting the entire router. The first thing you might want to do is assign a hostname to the router.

Hostname

The hostname of a router is set by using the global config command.

```
c2513r1(config)#hostname Keyser
Keyser(config)#
```

Notice that, after setting the hostname, the prompt changes immediately. The hostname is used to identify the router. It should represent something about the router. Some examples of router hostnames might be the city in which the router is located: Atlanta, Chicago, or Boston. Another feature of the IOS that can be used for identification is the Message of the Day (MOTD).

Message of the Day (MOTD)

The Message of the Day (MOTD) is displayed when someone accesses the router. The MOTD can be used to inform network personnel about network changes, planned outages, or upcoming upgrades. The MOTD is displayed prior to prompting for a password.

To enter a MOTD, use the following command from the global config mode:

```
c2511r1(config)#banner motd #This router was replaced 1/09/99#
c2511r1(config)#
```

The # before and after the message is simply a delimiter character and can be any character not included in the message. It simply identifies the beginning and end of the message. The preceding command will display the following lines the next time someone connects to the router.

```
This router was replaced 1/09/99

User Access Verification

Password:
```

Beginning Configuration Review

▶ The IOS has two levels of access: user exec mode and privileged exec mode. Logging in to a router puts you in user exec mode. Privileged exec mode is accessed by entering the command `enable` and then entering the enable password.

▶ Commands are entered at the Command Line Interface (CLI) and are executed immediately. Configuration changes take effect when the change is made.

▶ Commands can be abbreviated. As long as you enter enough of the command for the CLI to determine which command you intended, it will execute the command.

▶ Configuration changes are made in the config mode, which is entered by executing the command `config` from the privileged exec mode.

▶ Context-sensitive help is available by typing `?` at any prompt. If you have started a command and then press `?`, the CLI will show you a list of parameters for that command.

▶ Configuration changes can come from a terminal, network, or memory. Usually, you will make all changes from a terminal.

▶ The hostname identifies the router. Choose a sensible one that describes something about the router's location or function. When your network grows to hundreds of routers, you will be thankful you did this.

▶ The Message of the Day (MOTD) is displayed when a user accesses the router before the password prompt is displayed. It can be used to identify information about the router or any other information you might want someone to know before entering the router.

Configuring Interfaces

When configuring interface parameters such as bandwidth, IP address, media type, and most anything else specific to an interface, you use the interface configuration mode. To enter the interface configuration mode, enter the following command:

```
Router(config)#interface ethernet0/0
Router(config-if)#
```

This places you in the interface configuration mode for Ethernet0/0. Parameters specific to the interface are entered here. IP addresses and ring numbers are just two examples of interface-specific parameters.

Cisco routers represent interfaces differently depending on the platform. Cisco 2500-series routers simply list the interfaces by type and number. The first serial port on a Cisco 2501 is called Serial0; the second is called Serial1. Each interface type starts at number 0 and if there are multiples of that type, they increment. In routers supporting plug-in modules such as the 3600 series, the interfaces are identified by interface type, then by slot/port. In a 3600 with a dual Ethernet module in slot 0, the first interface is identified as Ethernet0/0, and the second is Ethernet0/1. The 4000 series is an exception to this rule. It simply identifies the ports by type/number. Larger routers like the 7500 series have slots, modules, and ports. Their interfaces are addressed as type slot/module/port, such as Ethernet4/0/1. As with commands, IOS will accept abbreviated references to interfaces as long as it is able to uniquely identify which interface you are referring to. The same results can be obtained using the abbreviated command:

```
c3620r1(config)#in e0/0
c3620r1(config-if)#
```

To return to the global config mode after configuring the interface, enter the command exit or use the command sequence Ctrl+Z to return to the privileged exec command prompt.

When you make changes to a router's configuration, you are changing the running config. This is the config file currently used by the router for operation. After you make a change, it takes effect immediately. If you shut down the port you are using to access the router, you will immediately lose connectivity. Some config changes require forethought as to how to effectively make the necessary changes without losing connectivity.

Saving Config Changes

When changes are made to the running configuration, they must be saved to the startup configuration or the changes will be lost the next time the router is rebooted. To save the changes, use the following command:

```
c3620r1#copy running-config startup-config
Building configuration...
[OK]
c3620r1#
```

This is commonly abbreviated `copy run start`.

A legacy command that is still used often (`write memory`) is commonly abbreviated `wr`. It is unclear whether this command will still be available in future versions of IOS.

The `copy run start` and `wr` commands both copy the running configuration file to the NVRAM of the router so that the next time it is booted, this configuration will be used.

Managing Passwords

Cisco routers store passwords for login access in the configuration file. There are two types of passwords used in this manner for accessing a router: the login password and the enable password. The *login password* is used to gain access to the router's user exec mode. The *enable password* is used to enter the privileged exec mode where configuration changes can be made.

In the configuration file, the entries for passwords appear as follows:

```
c2513r1#sh run
Building configuration...

Current configuration:
!
! Last configuration change at 00:17:36 EST Tue Dec 22 1998
!
version 11.2
.
.
hostname c2513r1
!
enable password khayman
!
partition flash 2 8 8
.
.
.
line con 0
 password cisco
 login
line aux 0
 password cisco
 login
line vty 0 4
 password cisco
 login
.
.
end

c2513r1#
```

Choosing Passwords Although some testing situations use cisco as a password, as an administrator, it is never a good idea to use cisco as the password for one of your routers. This book uses it as an example in some places, but in a real life situation, you don't want to use simple or obvious passwords. Strong passwords include both upper- and lowercase letters and numbers or special characters. A good example of a strong password is jst4u2GuEs.

The preceding example shows the enable password set to khayman. Lines console 0, auxiliary 0, and vty 0 through 4 all have a login password of cisco.

In this example, when an attempt is made to access this router via any of the available terminals, the router will prompt for a password. After the password is entered, it is compared to the password for the line the request is coming from. In our example, the password for all lines is cisco. It is important to note that passwords for Cisco routers are case-sensitive. (cisco is not the same as Cisco.)

To enter the privileged exec mode, we would enter the password khayman at the enable prompt.

Because it is possible that your configuration may be viewed by people who you do not want to have access to the passwords, a method to encrypt the passwords is built into Cisco's IOS. This service is enabled by entering the global configuration command:

```
c2513r1(config)#service password-encryption
c2513r1(config)#
```

This service encrypts the passwords stored in the configuration file. Now when the configuration is viewed, the passwords appear as follows:

```
c2513r1#sh run
Building configuration...

Current configuration:
!
! Last configuration change at 00:28:43 EST Tue Dec 22 1998
! NVRAM config last updated at 00:21:21 EST Tue Dec 22 1998
!
version 11.2
.
.
service password-encryption
no service udp-small-servers
no service tcp-small-servers
!
hostname c2513r1
!
enable password 7 110211040E1F0A02
!
partition flash 2 8 8
.
.
.
line con 0
 password 7 094F471A1A0A
 login
line aux 0
```

```
 password 7 094F471A1A0A
 login
line vty 0 4
 password 7 094F471A1A0A
 login
 .
 .

c2513r1#
```

Someone viewing the configuration of this router will not be able to immediately identify the passwords. However, the algorithm used for encrypting these passwords is relatively easy to break. There are several programs available on the Internet that will reverse the encryption used by Cisco's password-encryption service.

A more robust method of encryption is available for the enable password by using the enable secret command instead of enable password. The enable secret command encrypts the password using the MD5 algorithm. The config for an enable secret appears as follows:

```
!
enable secret 5 $1$er0I$Qe0nMh/.7T73WsTq31r0l1
!
```

enable secret always shows the password encrypted even if the password-encryption service is not enabled. There is no reason to use the enable password command if you are using enable secret.

USING THE COMMAND HISTORY AND EDITING FEATURES

Cisco's IOS provides some advanced features to make your job easier, such as command history and editing features. The following sections will discuss the command history as well as cursor movement, deletion, pasting buffers, and other miscellaneous commands.

Command History

The IOS exec keeps a number of the commands you type in a buffer called the *command history buffer*. The default size of this buffer is ten command lines. This command history buffer allows you to recall a previously typed command and execute it again.

This is very helpful when trying to diagnose problems and you have to keep trying to ping a remote location. It is also not uncommon to have to enter the same line many times with just a small change, such as the last digit of the IP address. The command history used in conjunction with the advanced editing commands can be a real typing saver.

Viewing the Contents of the Command History Buffer

The contents of the command history buffer can be viewed by entering the command show history.

```
c2511r1#show history
  en
  sh interfaces
  sh log
  sh clock detail
  sh run
  clear counters
  sh history
c2511r1#
```

Scroll through the commands by pressing the up-arrow or down-arrow key. After the command you want to execute is displayed, you can press Enter to execute it or you can modify it and then press Enter. Alternatives to the up and down arrows are Ctrl+P for previous and Ctrl+N for next. For the special editing keys such as up arrow or down arrow to work, your terminal program must support VT100 emulation.

Changing the Size of the History Buffer

The default size of the command history buffer is ten commands. The history buffer size can be changed. The change can be for the current session or for every session connecting on a particular line. To change the size of the buffer for the current session, enter the following command, which would change the size of the history buffer to 25 lines:

```
c2511r1#terminal history size 25
c2511r1#
```

The size of the history buffer can be changed for every connection via a particular line by adding the following commands to the line configuration:

```
c2511r1#config terminal
Enter configuration commands, one per line.  End with
➥CNTL/Z.
```

```
c2511r1(config)#line vty 1
c2511r1(config-line)#history size 25
c2511r1(config-line)#
```

Editing Features

The editing features built into Cisco's IOS can make your job much easier. Often, you will be entering the same command multiple times with just one slight change. By using the command history to bring up the last entered command and then using the editing features, you can save yourself much typing. Another benefit is that, with less typing to do, there is less of a chance to make a typographical error.

Cursor Movement

Even though the IOS supports the entry of only one line of text at a time, it is very helpful to be able to move the cursor around on this line. The cursor can be moved around by using the following keys:

◆ Ctrl+A. Move the cursor to the beginning of the line.

◆ Ctrl+E. Move the cursor to the end of the line.

◆ Esc+B. Move to the beginning of the previous word.

◆ Ctrl+F. Move forward one character.

◆ Ctrl+B. Move back one character.

◆ Esc+F. Move forward one word.

If the line you are typing extends beyond the width of your terminal, the CLI will scroll the line left ten characters and display a dollar sign at the beginning of the line to indicate that there is more to the left.

```
c2511r1(config)#$estamps debug datetime localtime msec
➥show-timezone
```

Deleting

When you type, you must delete. It's a law that seems unbreakable. The IOS provides some sophisticated deletion commands for a CLI. The following are the deletion commands available to the user:

◆ Delete or Backspace. Erase the character to the left of the cursor.

◆ Ctrl+D. Delete the character at the cursor.

◆ Ctrl+K. Delete all characters from the cursor to the end of the command line.

◆ Ctrl+U or Crtl+X. Delete all characters from the cursor to the beginning of the command line.

◆ Ctrl+W. Delete the word to the left of the cursor.

◆ Esc+D. Delete from the cursor to the end of the word.

Each of these deletion commands places the deleted text in a buffer. IOS keeps the last ten deletions in buffers. These buffers can be recalled and pasted back into a line.

Pasting Buffers

There are ten buffers holding the last ten deletions. These deletions can be recalled and pasted in the line at the cursor using the recall paste keys. To paste the buffer in the line at the cursor, type one of the following commands:

◆ Ctrl+Y. Recall and paste the most recent deletion at the cursor.

◆ Esc+Y. Recall the next buffer entry and paste at the cursor.

Miscellaneous Editing Commands

There are some miscellaneous commands that can also come in handy:

◆ Esc+C. Capitalize the letter at the cursor.

◆ Esc+L. Change the word at the cursor to lowercase.

◆ Esc+U. Capitalize letters from the cursor to the end of the word.

◆ Ctrl+T. Transpose the character to the left of the cursor with the character at the cursor.

◆ Ctrl+R. Redisplay the current command line.

Turning Off Editing Features

The editing features are on by default. They can be turned off for the current session by entering the following command:

```
c2511r1#terminal no editing
c2511r1#
```

The editing features can also be turned off for all sessions on a
particular line with the following configuration command:

```
c2511r1#config terminal
Enter configuration commands, one per line.  End with
➥CNTL/Z.
c2511r1(config)#line vty 1
c2511r1(config-line)#no editing
```

This will disable the editing features for any connection via this line.

Terminal Settings

Editing features, command history, and several other options are
known as terminal settings. *Terminal settings* define some
parameters about how the CLI interfaces with your terminal.
This includes the type of terminal, screen length and width, and
more. The current values of these parameters can be viewed using
the IOS command.

```
c2511r1#show terminal
Line 18, Location: "", Type: "ANSISYS"
Length: 24 lines, Width: 80 columns
Baud rate (TX/RX) is 9600/9600
Status: Ready, Active, No Exit Banner
Capabilities: none
Modem state: Ready
Special Chars: Escape  Hold  Stop  Start  Disconnect  Activation
               ^^x     none   -     -        none
Timeouts:      Idle EXEC    Idle Session   Modem Answer  Session    Dispatch
               00:10:00       never                        none     not set
                            Idle Session Disconnect Warning
                              never
Modem type is unknown.
Session limit is not set.
Time since activation: 00:17:41
Editing is disabled.
History is enabled, history size is 25.
DNS resolution in show commands is enabled
Full user help is disabled
Allowed transports are pad v120 telnet rlogin.  Preferred is telnet.
No output characters are padded
No special data dispatching characters
c2511r1#
```

Here, you see that editing has been disabled and the history buffer
has been set to 25 commands.

UNDERSTANDING ROUTER ELEMENTS

A router contains many of the same components as a computer. There is a processor for executing the operating system and random access memory (RAM) for storing programs and storing data. There is read-only memory (ROM), where Cisco stores the self test program and the initial IOS that will get the router running, and Non-Volatile RAM—memory that maintains its contents when power is lost. Cisco routers also include a type of memory not commonly found in computers. Flash memory (discussed later) is used for storing the IOS the router will execute. The router also includes network interfaces for connecting to the networks it will be handling traffic for.

Random Access Memory (RAM)

Like a computer, the router needs RAM to store data, execute programs, and buffer data. Packets of data can be buffered in RAM until the router has time to process them. In some models of Cisco routers (3600, 7200, 7500, and more), the IOS runs in RAM. Routers that run the IOS from RAM need enough RAM to store the version of IOS they are running plus enough to store routing tables, ARP tables, buffer packets, and more. Some routers, like the 2500 series, run the IOS from flash memory.

Read-Only Memory (ROM)

Cisco routers use read-only memory in much the same way a computer does. The instructions for performing a self-test of the device are stored in ROM. The ROM also contains a subset (some routers contain a full version) of the IOS. This subset is used to get the router up and running in case the normal version of IOS in the router becomes corrupt or missing.

Flash Memory

Flash memory is like ROM that can be erased and rewritten electronically. Cisco routers use flash memory much like personal computers use disk storage. The copy of IOS the router runs is stored in flash memory.

In larger routers, when the router boots, this copy of IOS is copied to RAM where it is executed. The smaller routers like the 2500 series run the IOS directly from flash. This creates a challenge when you need to upgrade the IOS in the router. Because the router is actually running the copy of IOS in flash memory, you cannot copy a new version over it while it is running.

In routers in which the IOS is copied to RAM during the boot process, the IOS can be upgraded by copying a new version of IOS to flash while the router runs the copy stored in RAM. After the new version of IOS is stored in flash memory, the router can be rebooted and the new version will be loaded and executed.

This does not work when the router is running the IOS from flash. In this case you have two options:

◆ You can partition the flash memory into multiple areas. Then, copy a new version of the IOS to the currently unused partition. After the IOS is stored there, change the router's config to boot from the partition with the new version of IOS. Reboot the router and the new version is executed. This method requires the router to have enough flash memory for two full copies of the IOS to be stored simultaneously.

◆ You can also use the flash load helper built into the IOS. The flash load helper will prompt you for the information needed to update the router's IOS. It will then proceed to download the new version of IOS. After completing the download, it will reboot. After it reboots, it will be running the new version of IOS.

Network Interfaces

Serving as a network interface is secondary to a computer's primary function. A desktop PC is used primarily for word processing, spreadsheets, and games. Its network interface is secondary to those functions. It simply provides connectivity for storing data, printing to shared printers, or joining in a multiuser game of Quake II.

The network interfaces are primary to a router. It does not do word processing or spreadsheets, and it only provides connectivity for the multiuser game of Quake II. The router's primary function is to connect networks. Therefore, the network interfaces are very important for the router.

Unlike desktop PCs, which usually have only one network interface, the router can have many network interfaces. These interfaces can be for different types of networks such as Ethernet, token ring, or FDDI. They can also be for Wide Area Network connections via serial ports.

Within the router, these interfaces are connected and pass data between each other based on the configuration of the router. The components of a router work together to function as a network connection for many different networks.

Examining the Components of a Router

The router can provide much information about the components within. Information on the amount of memory, version of IOS, and interfaces installed can be viewed with the show version command.

```
c2511r1#show version
Cisco Internetwork Operating System Software
IOS (tm) 2500 Software (C2500-IS-L), Version 11.2(9),
➡RELEASE SOFTWARE (fc1)
Copyright (c) 1986-1997 by cisco Systems, Inc.
Compiled Mon 22-Sep-97 21:31 by ckralik
Image text-base: 0x0302EB70, data-base: 0x00001000

ROM: System Bootstrap, Version 5.2(8a), RELEASE SOFTWARE
BOOTFLASH: 3000 Bootstrap Software (IGS-RXBOOT), Version
➡10.2(8a), RELEASE SOFTW
ARE (fc1)

c2511r1 uptime is 5 days, 1 hour, 49 minutes
System restarted by power-on at 21:31:57 EST Wed Dec 9 1998
System image file is "flash:25ipp12.bin", booted via flash

cisco 2511 (68030) processor (revision D) with 16384K/2048K
➡bytes of memory.
Processor board ID 02313574, with hardware revision
➡00000000
Bridging software.
X.25 software, Version 2.0, NET2, BFE and GOSIP compliant.
1 Ethernet/IEEE 802.3 interface(s)
2 Serial network interface(s)
16 terminal line(s)
32K bytes of non-volatile configuration memory.
8192K bytes of processor board System flash (read-only)

Configuration register is 0x2102

c2511r1#
```

This information tells us quite a bit about this router. The router is running IOS version 11.2(9). The ROM bootstrap, the subset of IOS stored in ROM, is version 10.2(8a). The router's hostname is c2511r1 and it has been running for five days, one hour, and 49 minutes. The last time the router was restarted, it was due to a power-on. This occurred at 21:31:57 EST on Wednesday, December 9, 1998. The IOS file the router is executing is flash:25ippl2.bin. This router is a model 2511 and has 1,6384KB of RAM. There is one Ethernet/ IEEE 802.3 interface, as well as two serial interfaces and 16 terminal lines. There are 32KB of Non-Volatile RAM. The router has 8,192KB of ROM. Finally, the router's configuration register is set to 0x2102. The 0x indicates that the following number is represented in the hexadecimal numbering system. This numbering system is explained in more detail in Chapter 4, "Understanding and Configuring IPX/SPX and Other Network Protocols."

Configuration Register

The last line in the show version information tells us the configuration register's value. The configuration register is 16 bits wide and defines some important characteristics of the router.

The lowest four bits of the configuration register (bits 0–3), make up the boot field. The *boot field* tells the router how to start up the IOS. For more information on the hexadecimal numbering system, see Chapter 4. The following list shows the values and the function they perform for the first four bits.

◆ 00 – Stay at the boot prompt.

◆ 01 – Boot the system image stored in ROM.

◆ 02-0F – Specifies the default netboot filename.

Processor

The processor does much of the work in the router. It keeps routing tables updated by calculating paths, moving packets, and performing many other tasks. When diagnosing problems, it is often important to check on the load of the processor. To view statistics on the processor, enter the command show processes.

```
CPU utilization for five seconds: 15%/7%; one minute: 20%; five minutes: 24%
 PID QTy       PC Runtime (ms)     Invoked   uSecs    Stacks TTY Process
   1 Csp  316BB12       16540      157074     105   736/1000   0 Load Meter
   2 M*         0        3768         178   21168  2216/4000  18 Virtual Exec
   3 Lst  3159C24     1253740       13415   93458  1724/2000   0 Check heaps
   4 Cwe  315F7A6           0           1       0  1728/2000   0 Pool Manager
   5 Mst  30FF97C           8           2    4000  1692/2000   0 Timers
   6 Lwe  31860BE       23996       29013     827  1292/2000   0 ARP Input
   7 Mwe  30B959E           0           1       0  1740/2000   0 SERIAL A'detect
   8 Hwe  31A575C      231024      226402    1020  3016/4000   0 IP Input
   9 Mwe  3206206       55356       91643     604  1504/2000   0 CDP Protocol
  10 Hwe  324F448           4           1    4000  1816/2000   0 Asy FS Helper
  11 Mwe  3191136        9936      160567      61  1300/2000   0 TCP Timer
  12 Lwe  3195CAC         104          34    3058  3176/4000   0 TCP Protocols
  13 Lwe  31D0878           0           1       0  1724/2000   0 Probe Input
  14 Mwe  31D1792           0           1       0  1736/2000   0 RARP Input
  15 Mwe  318AB40           4           1    4000  1612/2000   0 BOOTP Server
  16 Mwe  31DE68C     1116072      797761    1399  2496/3000   0 IP Background
  17 Lsi  32007E2        1140       13080      87  1724/2000   0 IP Cache Ager
  18 Cwe  3162C1E           0           1       0  1748/2000   0 Critical Bkgnd
  19 Mwe  3144E58          28           7    4000  1168/2000   0 Net Background
  20 Lwe  30F6F12           8          32     250  1644/2000   0 Logger
  21 Msp  30EE7EE      927644      784718    1182  1512/2000   0 TTY Background
—More—
```

Here, we see that the processor of this router is running at an average load of 24% over the past five minutes. Over the last minute the processor averaged 20% utilization, and for the last five seconds it averaged 15%, and 7% of this time was spent at the interrupt level.

Following the statistics for the CPU is a table of information about processes the CPU is executing. Each process list details how the process is being executed.

Interfaces

The interfaces of a router connect it to the networks for which it will be handling traffic. These interfaces provide a great deal of information about the network and how the interface is performing.

To view information about an interface, use the command show interfaces.

```
c2511r1#show interfaces
Ethernet0 is up, line protocol is up
  Hardware is Lance, address is 0000.0c75.9d72
➡(bia 0000.0c75.9d72)
  Internet address is 192.168.137.50/24
  MTU 1500 bytes, BW 10000 Kbit, DLY 1000 usec, rely 255/
➡255, load 1/255
  Encapsulation ARPA, loopback not set, keepalive set
➡(10 sec)
  ARP type: ARPA, ARP Timeout 04:00:00
  Last input 00:00:00, output 00:00:00, output hang never
```

```
 Last clearing of "show interface" counters 1w0d
 Queueing strategy: fifo
 Output queue 0/40, 0 drops; input queue 0/75, 0 drops
 5 minute input rate 0 bits/sec, 1 packets/sec
 5 minute output rate 0 bits/sec, 1 packets/sec
    312235 packets input, 25029135 bytes, 0 no buffer
    Received 289017 broadcasts, 0 runts, 0 giants, 0
➥throttles
    0 input errors, 0 CRC, 0 frame, 0 overrun, 0 ignored,
➥0 abort
       0 input packets with dribble condition detected
       233453 packets output, 19662124 bytes, 0 underruns
       0 output errors, 1 collisions, 1 interface resets
       0 babbles, 0 late collision, 10 deferred
       0 lost carrier, 0 no carrier
       0 output buffer failures, 0 output buffers swapped out
Serial0 is administratively down, line protocol is down
 Hardware is HD64570
 MTU 1500 bytes, BW 1544 Kbit, DLY 20000 usec, rely
➥255/255, load 1/255
 Encapsulation HDLC, loopback not set, keepalive set
➥(10 sec)
 Last input never, output never, output hang never
 Last clearing of "show interface" counters 1w0d
 Queueing strategy: fifo
 Output queue 0/40, 0 drops; input queue 0/75, 0 drops
 5 minute input rate 0 bits/sec, 0 packets/sec
 5 minute output rate 0 bits/sec, 0 packets/sec
    0 packets input, 0 bytes, 0 no buffer
    Received 0 broadcasts, 0 runts, 0 giants, 0 throttles
    0 input errors, 0 CRC, 0 frame, 0 overrun, 0 ignored,
➥0 abort
       0 packets output, 0 bytes, 0 underruns
       0 output errors, 0 collisions, 0 interface resets
       0 output buffer failures, 0 output buffers swapped out
       0 carrier transitions
       DCD=down  DSR=down  DTR=down  RTS=down  CTS=down
Serial1 is administratively down, line protocol is down
 Hardware is HD64570
 MTU 1500 bytes, BW 1544 Kbit, DLY 20000 usec, rely 255/
➥255, load 1/255
 Encapsulation HDLC, loopback not set, keepalive set
➥(10 sec)
 Last input never, output never, output hang never
 Last clearing of "show interface" counters 1w0d
 Input queue: 0/75/0 (size/max/drops); Total output drops:
➥0
 Queueing strategy: weighted fair
 Output queue: 0/64/0 (size/threshold/drops)
    Conversations  0/0 (active/max active)
    Reserved Conversations 0/0 (allocated/max allocated)
 5 minute input rate 0 bits/sec, 0 packets/sec
 5 minute output rate 0 bits/sec, 0 packets/sec
    0 packets input, 0 bytes, 0 no buffer
    Received 0 broadcasts, 0 runts, 0 giants, 0 throttles
```

continues

continued

```
        0 input errors, 0 CRC, 0 frame, 0 overrun, 0 ignored,
→0 abort
        0 packets output, 0 bytes, 0 underruns
        0 output errors, 0 collisions, 0 interface resets
        0 output buffer failures, 0 output buffers swapped out
        0 carrier transitions
        DCD=down  DSR=down  DTR=down  RTS=down  CTS=down
c2511r1#
```

In the preceding command, you see the output from show interfaces
on a Cisco 2511 router. The 2511 has one Ethernet port, two serial
ports, and 16 RS/EIA-232 serial lines.

You can also view this information for a specific interface by specifying
the interface as follows:

```
c2511r1>show interfaces e0
Ethernet0 is up, line protocol is up
  Hardware is Lance, address is 0000.0c75.9d72
→(bia 0000.0c75.9d72)
  Internet address is 199.250.137.50/27
  MTU 1500 bytes, BW 10000 Kbit, DLY 1000 usec, rely
255/255, load 1/255
  Encapsulation ARPA, loopback not set, keepalive set
→(10 sec)
  ARP type: ARPA, ARP Timeout 04:00:00
  Last input 00:00:00, output 00:00:00, output hang never
  Last clearing of "show interface" counters never
  Queueing strategy: fifo
  Output queue 0/40, 0 drops; input queue 1/75, 0 drops
  5 minute input rate 3000 bits/sec, 4 packets/sec
  5 minute output rate 2000 bits/sec, 4 packets/sec
     1272652 packets input, 99574686 bytes, 0 no buffer
     Received 1210186 broadcasts, 0 runts, 0 giants, 0
→throttles
     0 input errors, 0 CRC, 0 frame, 0 overrun, 0 ignored,
→0 abort
     0 input packets with dribble condition detected
     913831 packets output, 74071677 bytes, 0 underruns
     0 output errors, 4 collisions, 3 interface resets
     0 babbles, 0 late collision, 35 deferred
     0 lost carrier, 0 no carrier
     0 output buffer failures, 0 output buffers swapped out
c2511r1>
```

In reviewing the output from show interfaces, we can see that
Ethernet0 is "up and up." This is a term used when talking about
an interface on a Cisco router. There are two parts to an interface
being considered "up." First, the interface must be administratively up.
To set an interface administratively down, the command shutdown is
placed in the configuration for the interface. To set the interface in
an administratively up state, the command no shutdown is added to
the configuration for the interface.

In looking at Ethernet0, it is administratively up and the line protocol is up. The line protocol reports if the interface is receiving link status. On an Ethernet port, this would be the carrier signal. On a serial port, it means the router is receiving hello packets. When the line protocol is up, it means the port is able to pass packets to and from the network attached to this interface. A common state for an interface experiencing problems is "up and down." The interface is administratively up, yet the link protocol is down. An Ethernet interface would display this state if the cable were unplugged from the hub. The port would still be administratively up, but would no longer be receiving a carrier signal from the hub, and thus, the link protocol would be down. In this state, the interface cannot pass traffic.

In the following lines, you see the MAC address for this interface is 0000.0c75.9d72.

```
Hardware is Lance, address is 0000.0c75.9d72
➥(bia 0000.0c75.9d72)
  Internet address is 192.168.137.50/24
  MTU 1500 bytes, BW 10000 Kbit, DLY 1000 usec, rely 255/
➥255, load 1/255
```

The *burned-in address (bia)* is also 0000.0c75.9d72. If we set the MAC address on an interface different than the bia, these would be different. The first would be the MAC address the router is using to talk on the network, and the bia would simply be the address the interface was assigned when it was manufactured.

The Internet address for this interface is 192.168.137.50/24. This is the IP address assigned to the interface. It is represented somewhat differently than most people are accustomed to seeing with an IP address. The number after the IP address /24 is the number of subnet bits assigned to the IP address. You will learn more about this in Chapter 4. This is equivalent to a subnet mask of 255.255.255.0.

The maximum *transmission unit (MTU)* for this interface is 1,500 bytes. This is the largest packet size this interface can transmit. This information is important when the router must move data from dissimilar networks. Token ring has a much higher MTU than Ethernet. Therefore, when a router is routing data from a token ring network to an Ethernet network, it will need to fragment packets larger than the MTU for Ethernet so the data can be transmitted over the media. *Fragmenting* is the process of taking a large packet and dividing it into smaller packets. The smaller packets are marked as fragments and the last packet in the fragmented packet is marked as such. When the end station receives fragmented packets, it reassembles them as they are passed up the OSI model. The application never knows the data was separated during transmission.

The bandwidth of this interface is 10,000 kilobits and the delay is 1,000 milliseconds. The reliability of this network is 255/255. This information is represented as a fraction. In this case the reliability is 100%, 255 of 255 parts. A 50% reliable network would be 127/255. The current load on this network is 1/255. Again, this is a fraction showing a very light load on the network. This information is used by advanced routing protocols to determine the fastest and most reliable path between two end stations.

```
Encapsulation ARPA, loopback not set, keepalive set
➥(10 sec)
  ARP type: ARPA, ARP Timeout 04:00:00
  Last input 00:00:00, output 00:00:00, output hang never
  Last clearing of "show interface" counters 1w0d
  Queueing strategy: fifo
  Output queue 0/40, 0 drops; input queue 0/75, 0 drops
```

The preceding lines of the output provide more information about the interfaces. We see the encapsulation used for this interface is ARPA, there is not a loopback set, and keepalive packets are sent and expected every ten seconds. The address resolution protocol (ARP) used on this network is ARPA and the timeout for ARP data is four hours. The last packet coming in this interface was zero seconds ago and the last packet sent out this interface was zero seconds ago. There has never been an output hang on this interface. The last time the statistic counters for this interface were reset was one week, zero days ago.

The queuing strategy for this interface is first in first out (fifo). The *queuing strategy* is how the router decides which packets to send first, in the event the network interface becomes backed up with data.

The output queue for this interface currently has zero packets in it and has room for 40 packets. The input queue currently has zero packets in it and has room for 75 packets. There have been no packets dropped by this interface

```
5 minute input rate 0 bits/sec, 1 packets/sec
  5 minute output rate 0 bits/sec, 1 packets/sec
    312235 packets input, 25029135 bytes, 0 no buffer
    Received 289017 broadcasts, 0 runts, 0 giants, 0
➥throttles
    0 input errors, 0 CRC, 0 frame, 0 overrun, 0 ignored,
➥0 abort
      0 input packets with dribble condition detected
      233453 packets output, 19662124 bytes, 0 underruns
      0 output errors, 1 collisions, 1 interface resets
      0 babbles, 0 late collision, 10 deferred
      0 lost carrier, 0 no carrier
      0 output buffer failures, 0 output buffers swapped out
```

This information gives us statistics about the interface. In the past five minutes, the average input and output rates have been zero bits per second and one packet per second. Because the counters were reset, the interface has had 312,235 packets input, which total 25,029,135 bytes. None of the input packets were dropped, due to no buffers being available. The interface has sent 233,453 packets, totaling 19,662,124 bytes. There has been one collision and one interface reset. TEN packets were deferred.

The 16 serial lines do not show up in the show interfaces because they are considered lines to the router. The command show line displays information about these lines along with the console and auxiliary line.

```
c2511r1#show line
  Tty Typ    Tx/Rx      A Modem  Roty AccO AccI  Uses    Noise   Overruns
    0 CTY                -  -      -    -    -     0       0       1/7983
    1 TTY    9600/9600   - inout   -    -    -     1       285833  0/2
    2 TTY    9600/9600   - inout   -    -    -     0       7870839 0/2
    3 TTY    9600/9600   - inout   -    -    -     0       2484165 0/0
    4 TTY    9600/9600   - inout   -    -    -     0       0       0/0
    5 TTY    9600/9600   -  -      -    -    -     0       0       0/0
    6 TTY    9600/9600   -  -      -    -    -     0       0       0/0
    7 TTY    9600/9600   -  -      -    -    -     0       0       0/0
    8 TTY    9600/9600   -  -      -    -    -     0       0       0/0
    9 TTY    9600/9600   -  -      -    -    -     0       0       0/0
   10 TTY    9600/9600   -  -      -    -    -     0       0       0/0
   11 TTY    9600/9600   -  -      -    -    -     0       0       0/0
   12 TTY    9600/9600   -  -      -    -    -     0       0       0/0
   13 TTY    9600/9600   -  -      -    -    -     0       0       0/0
   14 TTY    9600/9600   -  -      -    -    -     0       0       0/0
   15 TTY    9600/9600   -  -      -    -    -     0       0       0/0
   16 TTY    9600/9600   -  -      -    -    -     0       0       0/0
   17 AUX    9600/9600   -  -      -    -    -     0       0       0/0
*  18 VTY                -  -      -    -    -     28      0       0/0
   19 VTY                -  -      -    -    -     0       0       0/0
   20 VTY                -  -      -    -    -     0       0       0/0
   21 VTY                -  -      -    -    -     0       0       0/0
  Tty Typ    Tx/Rx      A Modem  Roty AccO AccI  Uses    Noise   Overruns

   22 VTY                -  -      -    -    -     0       0       0/0

c2511r1#
```

The console port is displayed as CTY and the auxiliary port as AUX. The 16 lines between these two are the 16 RS/EIA-232 lines of the 2511. The last five entries are the virtual terminal connections for telnet sessions. Notice the asterisk next to number 18. This indicates this is the line via which we are currently accessing the router.

CISCO DISCOVERY PROTOCOL (CDP)

Cisco discovery protocol runs on Cisco-manufactured devices including routers, access servers, and workgroup switches. It starts automatically when the device is booted. CDP operates at the Data Link layer. Because it runs at the Data Link layer, it is not necessary for the devices to be in common network address domains to exchange CDP data.

CDP provides a method for a Cisco device to discover its neighbor Cisco devices and exchange information about the devices.

Enabling and Disabling CDP

CDP is enabled by default; it can be disabled on a router by entering the following global command:

```
c2511r1(config)#no cdp run
```

You can also disable CDP on a particular interface by entering the following command:

```
c2511r1(config-if)#no cdp enable
```

Seeing CDP Neighbors

You can view a router's CDP neighbors by entering the following command:

```
c3620r1#sh cdp neighbors
Capability Codes: R - Router, T - Trans Bridge, B - Source Route Bridge
                  S - Switch, H - Host, I - IGMP, r - Repeater

Device ID          Local Intrfce    Holdtme    Capability  Platform  Port ID
GSD0090F28CE000     Eth 0/0          167          T S       1900      24
c2513r1             Tok 0/0          155          R         2500      Tok 0
c1604               BRI1/0           147          R         1604      BRI0
c3620r1#
```

This router has three neighbors. The first is a Cisco 1900 switch attached to local interface Ethernet0/0. It is attached via port 24 in the 1900. This neighbor has transparent bridging and switching capability. Next, we have a Cisco 2500 attached via local interface TokenRing0/0 and remote interface TokenRing0. The first two devices support routing across the link. There is also a Cisco 1604 router attached to local interface BRI1/0 and remote interface BRI0 supporting routing.

More detailed information about the neighbors can be viewed with
the following command:

```
c3620r1#sh cdp neighbors detail
-------------------------
Device ID: GSD0090F28CE000
Entry address(es):
  IP address: 192.168.137.40
Platform: cisco 1900,  Capabilities: Trans-Bridge Switch
Interface: Ethernet0/0,  Port ID (outgoing port): 24
Holdtime : 132 sec

Version :
V8.00

-------------------------
Device ID: c2513r1
Entry address(es):
  IP address: 192.168.200.3
Platform: cisco 2500,  Capabilities: Router
Interface: TokenRing0/0,  Port ID (outgoing port):
➥TokenRing0
Holdtime : 123 sec

Version :
Cisco Internetwork Operating System Software
IOS (tm) 2500 Software (C2500-J-L), Version 11.2(14),
➥RELEASE SOFTWARE (fc1)
Copyright (c) 1986-1998 by cisco Systems, Inc.
Compiled Mon 18-May-98 12:57 by tlane

-------------------------
Device ID: c1604
Entry address(es):
  IP address: 192.168.99.1
Platform: cisco 1604,  Capabilities: Router
Interface: BRI1/0,  Port ID (outgoing port): BRI0
Holdtime : 139 sec

Version :
Cisco Internetwork Operating System Software
IOS (tm) 1600 Software (C1600-Y-L), Version 11.2(16)P,
➥RELEASE SOFTWARE (fc1)
Copyright (c) 1986-1998 by cisco Systems, Inc.
Compiled Mon 19-Oct-98 13:49 by pwade

c3620r1#
```

This information lists each neighbor and the version of IOS it is
running. This is very helpful when trying to diagnose why a feature
is not working. If the neighbor router is running an older version of
IOS, it may not support some newer features. In an environment
where different groups support different routers, this can be helpful
in finding information about the routers with which you may need
to communicate.

CDP Parameters

CDP has two timers you can adjust. The first determines how often the router sends a CDP packet. The default for this timer is every 60 seconds. The second timer is the holdtime—how long the device will wait for a CDP packet before removing the neighboring device from the CDP table. The default holdtime is 180 seconds.

The values of these timers can be viewed using the following command:

```
c3620r1#sh cdp interface
Ethernet0/0 is up, line protocol is up
  Encapsulation ARPA
  Sending CDP packets every 60 seconds
  Holdtime is 180 seconds
```

To alter how often the router sends a CDP packet, use the following global command:

```
c3620r1(config)#cdp timer 90
```

This sets the time between CDP packets to 90 seconds. We can change the holdtimer to 120 seconds by using the following global command:

```
c3620r1(config)#cdp holdtime 120
```

MANAGING CONFIGURATION FILES FROM THE PRIVILEGED EXEC MODE

The configuration file defines how the router will interact with the connected networks and the data on those networks. Network addresses, bridge numbers, and routing protocols are just some of the parameters stored in the configuration file. As with any important information, this should be backed up so it can be retrieved if the device should fail.

Earlier you used the command copy running-config startup-config. This is much like copying files on a computer using DOS or a DOS window on a Windows 95 computer. You are copying the file running-config to the file startup-config. The only difference is that in a router, these files have special meaning. The running-config specifies how the router will behave with the networks attached. The startup-config will become the running-config the next time the router is rebooted either by power-on or by a software reload.

These files can be copied to and from a TFTP server. To copy the running-config to a TFTP server, use the following command:

```
c2511r1#copy running-config tftp
Remote host []? 192.169.169.140
Name of configuration file to write [c2511r1-confg]?
Write file c2511r1-confg on host 192.168.169.140? [confirm]y
Building configuration...

Writing c2511r1-confg !! [OK]
c2511r1#
```

Each exclamation point (!) indicates that one packet has been successfully transferred.

The running-config file is copied via the TFTP protocol to the TFTP server at IP address 129.168.169.140. The filename used on the TFTP server is c2511r1-config. Finally, the file is transferred to the server. The startup-config can be copied using the same technique.

To reverse the process, simply reverse the order of the devices. Copy from the TFTP server to the filename running-config.

```
c2511r1#copy tftp running-config
Host or network configuration file [host]?
Address of remote host [255.255.255.255]? 192.168.169.140
Name of configuration file [c2511r1-confg]?
Configure using c2511r1-confg from 192.168.169.140?
➥[confirm]y
Loading c2511r1-confg from 192.168.169.140 (via Ethernet0):
➥!
[OK - 1260/32723 bytes]

c2511r1#
```

CISCO IOS COMMANDS FOR ROUTER STARTUP

As with any other computer, a Cisco router must boot an operating system to function fully. For a Cisco router, this operating system is Internetworking Operating System (IOS). The IOS exists as a file that can be stored in Flash RAM, in ROM, or on a TFTP server.

The configuration file of the router can dictate from where the router loads the IOS. The commands to do this are referred to as *boot commands*.

Normally, the router will boot the first image of IOS found in flash memory. If there are multiple copies of IOS stored in flash, you can specify which copy to load using the following command:

```
boot system flash ios.new
```

This tells the router to load the image ios.new from flash memory. Multiple boot statements can be placed in the config file. They are executed in the order they appear in the config file.

To make your router config as robust as possible, it is a good idea to give your router other methods of booting should the flash memory become corrupt.

This can be achieved by adding the boot command for a TFTP server and finally telling the router to boot from ROM if the first two options fail.

The following command will instruct the router to boot from a TFTP server:

```
c2511r1(config)#boot system tftp ios.net 192.168.1.9
```

The router will boot the system file named ios.net from the TFTP server at IP address 192.168.1.9.

In the event of both the flash being corrupt and the TFTP server being unreachable, the router can finally boot from the system ROM. In most of Cisco's routers, the copy of IOS stored in ROM is not complete. It contains just enough features to start the router. It is, however, better than the router not booting at all. To instruct the router to boot from ROM, use the following command:

```
c3620r1(config)#boot system rom
```

Note that not all router platforms support the command
`boot system rom`.

CONFIGURING A ROUTER WITH THE SETUP COMMAND

Cisco provides a script-like setup method for routers. This script will set up the basics of a configuration. The setup script can be entered two ways. A new router without a configuration stored in NVRAM will boot and prompt you to ask if you would like to enter the initial setup as follows:

```
System Bootstrap, Version 5.2(5), RELEASE SOFTWARE
Copyright (c) 1986-1994 by cisco Systems
2500 processor with 4096 Kbytes of main memory

F3: 5292020+130664+266752 at 0x3000060

             Restricted Rights Legend

Use, duplication, or disclosure by the Government is
subject to restrictions as set forth in subparagraph
(c) of the Commercial Computer Software - Restricted
Rights clause at FAR sec. 52.227-19 and subparagraph
(c) (1) (ii) of the Rights in Technical Data and Computer
Software clause at DFARS sec. 252.227-7013.

             cisco Systems, Inc.
             170 West Tasman Drive
             San Jose, California 95134-1706

Cisco Internetwork Operating System Software
IOS (tm) 3000 Software (IGS-J-L), Version 10.3(3), RELEASE
➥SOFTWARE (fc4)
Copyright (c) 1986-1995 by cisco Systems, Inc.
Compiled Sat 20-May-95 01:17 by nitin
Image text-base: 0x0302D220, data-base: 0x00001000


cisco 2500 (68030) processor (revision D) with 4092K/2048K
➥bytes of memory.
Processor board serial number 02336429
SuperLAT software copyright 1990 by Meridian Technology
➥Corp).
TN3270 Emulation software (copyright 1994 by TGV Inc).
X.25 software, Version 2.0, NET2, BFE and GOSIP compliant.
Bridging software.
Authorized for Enterprise software set.  (0x0)
1 Ethernet/IEEE 802.3 interface.
1 Token Ring/IEEE 802.5 interface.
2 Serial network interfaces.
32K bytes of non-volatile configuration memory.
8192K bytes of processor board System flash (read-only)

Notice: NVRAM invalid, possibly due to write erase.
        —- System Configuration Dialog —-

At any point you may enter a question mark '?' for help.
Refer to the 'Getting Started' Guide for additional help.
Use ctrl-c to abort configuration dialog at any prompt.
Default settings are in square brackets '[]'.
Would you like to enter the initial configuration dialog?
➥[yes]:
```

In the preceding example, the router states that the NVRAM is
invalid, possibly due to write erase.

N
O
T
E

**Clearing the Configuration from a
Router** Write erase is an IOS command that can be used to wipe out
the NVRAM. This is useful if you are
taking a router out of service. You
could erase the configuration. The
router would then be ready to configure for a future implementation.

The router then prompts Would you like to enter the initial
configuration dialog? [yes]:. The answer between the brackets ([ ])
is the default answer. Simply pressing Enter will enter the setup dialog.
It will then guide you through building a configuration for the router.

The following example demonstrates building a configuration with
the setup dialog:

```
Router#setup

          — · System Configuration Dialog  — ·

At any point you may enter a question mark '?' for help.
Refer to the 'Getting Started' Guide for additional help.
Use ctrl-c to abort configuration dialog at any prompt.
Default settings are in square brackets '[]'.
```

```
Continue with configuration dialog? [yes]:

First, would you like to see the current interface summary? [yes]:

Interface    IP-Address    OK?  Method   Status                   Protocol
Ethernet0    unassigned    YES  not set  administratively down    down
Serial0      unassigned    YES  not set  administratively down    down
Serial1      unassigned    YES  not set  administratively down    down
TokenRing0   unassigned    YES  not set  administratively down    down
```

Prior to actually configuring the router, the setup dialog will ask if
you would like to see the current interface summary. If you answer
yes it will show you a table of the router's interfaces.

```
Configuring global parameters:

  Enter host name [Router]: c2513r4

The enable secret is a one-way cryptographic secret used
instead of the enable password when it exists.

  Enter enable secret: cisco

The enable password is used when there is no enable secret
and when using older software and some boot images.

  Enter enable password: cisco1
  Enter virtual terminal password: cisco
  Configure SNMP Network Management? [no]:
  Configure IP? [yes]:
    Configure IGRP routing? [yes]: n
    Configure RIP routing? [no]:
  Configure Vines? [no]:
  Configure IPX? [no]:
  Configure AppleTalk? [no]:
  Configure Apollo? [no]:
  Configure DECnet? [no]:
  Configure XNS? [no]:
```

```
  Configure CLNS? [no]:
  Configure bridging? [no]:
  Configure LAT? [no]:

Configuring interface parameters:

Configuring interface Ethernet0:
  Is this interface in use? [no]: y
  Configure IP on this interface? [no]: y
    IP address for this interface: 192.168.28.9
    Number of bits in subnet field [0]:
    Class C network is 192.168.28.0, 0 subnet bits; mask is
➥255.255.255.0
```

Notice that Cisco's setup dialog refers to subnet bits in a non-intuitive
way. Most people think of the number of subnet bits as the total
number of bits in the subnet mask. In a Class C address, this would
be 24 bits (255.255.255.0). In contrast, Cisco's setup dialog refers to
subnet bits from the normal boundary for the class of address. In the
above example, a Class C address was entered and zero subnet bits
were specified. This resulted in an IP address of 192.168.28.9 with a
subnet mask of 255.255.255.0, which is normal for a Class C address.

```
Configuring interface Serial0:
  Is this interface in use? [no]:

Configuring interface Serial1:
  Is this interface in use? [no]:

Configuring interface TokenRing0:
  Is this interface in use? [no]:
```

After completing settings for all of the interfaces, the setup dialog
displays the configuration created.

```
The following configuration command script was created:

hostname c2513r4
enable secret 5 $1$DkrH$hY5W7HTq/epbwshCPwhPf.
enable password cisco1
line vty 0 4
password cisco
no snmp-server
!
ip routing
no vines routing
no ipx routing
no appletalk routing
no apollo routing
no decnet routing
no xns routing
no clns routing
no bridge 1
!
```

continues

continued

```
interface Ethernet0
no shutdown
ip address 192.168.28.9 255.255.255.0
no mop enabled
!
interface Serial0
shutdown
no ip address
!
interface Serial1
shutdown
no ip address
!
interface TokenRing0
shutdown
no ip address
!
end

Use this configuration? [yes/no]: y
#######
%LINK-3-UPDOWN: Interface Ethernet0, changed state to
↪up[OK]
Use the enabled mode 'configure' command to modify this
↪configuration.
```

```
c2513r4#
```

After displaying the configuration created, the router asks if you want to Use this configuration? [yes/no]: If you answer yes, the configuration is saved and the router enters the enable mode.

For some reason, the setup dialog creates both an enable secret and an enable password. Both of these are not needed. Because the enable password uses a weak encryption algorithm, it is generally best to use enable secret instead of enable password. After using the setup dialog to create the configuration, the enable password statement can be removed by typing no enable password in configuration mode.

BACK UP AND UPGRADE IOS

The IOS image resides in the router as a file stored in flash memory. This file can become corrupt due to a power problem or hardware failure. This file may also need to be upgraded to a newer version to support new features or correct problems due to software bugs. The TFTP server is used for this process.

Some of Cisco's routers run IOS directly from flash memory
and some copy the IOS from flash to RAM and execute it there.
Generally, lower-end routers like the 1600s and 2500s run from
flash. Higher-end routers like the 3600s, 4700s, 7200s, and 7500s
run from RAM. Copying a new version of IOS to a run from flash
router presents some challenges because you cannot overwrite the
version currently executing from flash. There are two options available. If the router is equipped with enough flash memory, you can
partition the flash memory. This divides the flash memory into logical partitions much like can be done to a hard disk in a PC. After
the flash is partitioned, the router can execute a copy of IOS in one
partition while another partition can be erased and a new copy of
IOS can be copied. After this is complete, the router's configuration
is changed to boot from the partition with the new IOS, and the
router is rebooted.

If the router does not have enough flash memory to partition and
hold two copies of IOS, you must upgrade it another way. Run
from flash routers have a *flash load helper* that can help. The flash
load helper will accept the copy command. It will then verify that
the TFTP server can be reached and the file requested is available.
After this has been confirmed, the flash load helper will reboot the
router using the ROM-based IOS and copy the new IOS into flash.
During this time, the router will not perform routing functions.

The following example demonstrates copying an IOS file from the
TFTP server to the router's flash using the flash load helper:

```
c2511r1#copy tftp flash
 ****NOTICE****
Flash load helper v1.0
This process will accept the copy options and then
➥terminate
the current system image to use the ROM based image for the
➥copy.
Routing functionality will not be available during that
➥time.
If you are logged in via telnet, this connection will
➥terminate.
Users with console access can see the results of the copy
➥operation.
 .... ******** ....
Proceed? [confirm]y

System flash directory:
FileLength Name/status
1 580636425ipp12.bin
[5806428 bytes used, 2582180 available, 8388608 total]
```

continues

continued

```
Address or name of remote host [255.255.255.255]?
↳199.250.137.37
Source file name? c2500-js-l_112-16.bin
Destination file name [c2500-js-l_112-16.bin]?
Accessing file 'c2500-js-l_112-16.bin' on 199.250.137.37...
Loading c2500-js-l_112-16.bin from 199.250.137.37
↳(via Ethernet0): ! [OK]

Erase flash device before writing? [confirm]y
Flash contains files. Are you sure you want to erase?
↳[confirm]y

Copy 'c2500-js-l_112-16.bin' from server
as 'c2500-js-l_112-16.bin' into Flash WITH erase? [yes/no]y
```

To make a copy of the IOS stored in flash on the TFTP server, use the copy command with the source and destination reversed.

```
c3620r1#copy flash tftp

System flash directory:
File   Length    Name/status
  1    4201072   c3620-js-mz_112-16_P.bin
[4201136 bytes used, 4187472 available, 8388608 total]
Address or name of remote host [255.255.255.255]?
↳199.250.137.37
Source file name? c3620-js-mz_112-16_P.bin
Destination file name [c3620-js-mz_112-16_P.bin]?
Verifying checksum for 'c3620-js-mz_112-16_P.bin'
↳(file # 1)...  OK
Copy 'c3620-js-mz_112-16_P.bin' from Flash to server
  as 'c3620-js-mz_112-16_P.bin'? [yes/no]y
!!!!!!!!!!!!!!!!!!!!!!!!!!!!!!!!!!!!!!!!!!!!!!!!!!!!!!!!!!!!!!
↳!!!!!!!!!!!!!!!!!!!!!!
!!!!!!!!!!!!!!!!!!!!!!!!!!!!!!!!!!!!!!!!!!!!!!!!!!!!!!!!!!!!!!
↳!!!!!!!!!!!!!!!!!!!!!!
!!!!!!!!!!!!!!!!!!!!!!!!!!!!!!!!!!!!!!!!!!!!!!!!!!!!!!!!!!!!!!
↳!!!!!!!!!!!!!!!!!!!!!!
!!!!!!!!!!!!!!!!!!!!!!!!!!!!!!!!!!!!!!!!!!!!!!!!!!!!!!!!!!!!!!
↳!!!!!!!!!!!!!!!!!!!!!!
!!!!!!!!!!!!!!!!!!!!!!!!!!!!!!!!!!!!!!!!!!!!!!!!!!!!!!!!!!!!!!
↳!!!!!!!!!!!!!!!!!!!!!!
!!!!!!!!!!!!!!!!!!!!!!!!!!!!!!!!!!!!!!!!!!!!!!!!!!!!!!!!!!!!!!
↳!!!!!!!!!!!!!!!!!!!!!!
!!!!!!!!!!!!!!!!!!!!!!!!!!!!!!!!!!!!!!!!!!!!!!!!!!!!!!!!!!!!!!
↳!!!!!!!!!!!!!!!!!!!!!!
!!!!!!!!!!!!!!!!!!!!!!!!!!!!!!!!!!!!!!!!!!!!!!!!!!!!!!!!!!!!!!
↳!!!!!!!!!!!!!!!!!!!!!!
!!!!!!!!!!!!!!!!!!!!!!!!!!!!!!!!!!!!!!!!!!!!!!!!!!!!!!!!!!!!!!
↳!!!!!!!!!!!!!!!!!!!!!!
!!!!!!!!!!!!!!!!!!!!!!
Upload to server done
Flash device copy took 00:01:23 [hh:mm:ss]
c3620r1#
```

CASE STUDY: PUTTING A ROUTER IN SERVICE

ESSENCE OF THE CASE

▶ Erase the configuration from a router.

▶ Upgrade the IOS.

▶ Create a simple configuration.

This case study reviews some of the techniques you learned in this chapter. It deals with taking a previously used router and implementing it in a new environment.

SCENARIO

You have been asked to take a 2513 router that was once in service in a branch office and configure it for use as an Internet gateway router. The router was taken out of the office when the office was closed. The version of IOS is very old and will need to be upgraded. You will need to create a simple configuration for an Internet gateway.

In this case study, you are taking a router that has previously been in service and configuring it for a new use. The router has an older version of IOS that you need to upgrade and the configuration in the router is for the old installation. That must be cleared before configuring it for the new use. After you have completed the upgrade of IOS and clearing of the config, you must configure the router for the new use as an Internet gateway.

ANALYSIS

The Cisco 2513 you have been given for this task was previously installed in a branch office for its connection to the corporate Frame Relay WAN. Your Internet provider has given you the following instructions for configuring the router:

The serial port IP address should be 155.175.34.35 255.255.255.0.

The subnet assigned to your office is 155.175.35.0.

continues

CASE STUDY: PUTTING A ROUTER IN SERVICE

First, you should power up the router and erase the configuration stored in the NVRAM. Connect your laptop to the console port with a Cisco cable and launch Hyperterminal. Then, configure Hyperterminal for 9600 baud, No Parity.

In powering up the router you see the following:

```
System Bootstrap, Version 11.0(10c)XB1,
➥PLATFORM SPECIFIC RELEASE SOFTWARE (fc1)
Copyright (c) 1986-1997 by cisco Systems
2500 processor with 14336 Kbytes of main
➥memory

F3: 3522860+70900+216864 at 0x3000060

            Restricted Rights Legend

Use, duplication, or disclosure by the
➥Government is
subject to restrictions as set forth in
➥subparagraph
(c) of the Commercial Computer Software -
➥Restricted
Rights clause at FAR sec. 52.227-19 and
➥subparagraph
(c) (1) (ii) of the Rights in Technical Data
➥and Computer
Software clause at DFARS sec. 252.227-7013.

            cisco Systems, Inc.
            170 West Tasman Drive
            San Jose, California 95134-1706

Cisco Internetwork Operating System Software
IOS (tm) 3000 Software (IGS-IN-L), Version
➥10.3(19a), RELEASE SOFTWARE (fc1)
Copyright (c) 1986-1997 by cisco Systems, Inc.
Compiled Thu 04-Sep-97 20:00 by phester
Image text-base: 0x0301EB58, data-base:
➥0x00001000

cisco 2500 (68030) processor (revision M)
➥with 14336K/2048K bytes of memory.
Processor board serial number 10187811
Bridging software.
X.25 software, Version 2.0, NET2, BFE and
➥GOSIP compliant.
1 Ethernet/IEEE 802.3 interface.
1 Token Ring/IEEE 802.5 interface.
```

```
2 Serial network interfaces.
32K bytes of non-volatile configuration memory.
16384K bytes of processor board System flash
➥(read-only)

Press RETURN to get started!

0:00:07: %LINEPROTO-5-UPDOWN: Line protocol
➥on Interface Ethernet0, changed state to up
0:00:07: %LINEPROTO-5-UPDOWN: Line protocol
➥on Interface Serial0, changed state to down
0:00:07: %LINEPROTO-5-UPDOWN: Line protocol
➥on Interface Serial1, changed state to down
0:00:07: %LINEPROTO-5-UPDOWN: Line protocol on
➥Interface TokenRing0, changed state to down
0:00:07: %LINK-3-UPDOWN: Interface Ethernet0,
➥changed state to up
0:00:07: %LINK-3-UPDOWN: Interface Serial0,
➥changed state to up
0:00:07: %LINK-3-UPDOWN: Interface Serial1,
➥changed state to up
0:00:07: %LINEPROTO-5-UPDOWN: Line protocol
➥on Interface Loopback0, changed state to up
0:00:07: %LINEPROTO-5-UPDOWN: Line protocol
➥on Interface Loopback1, changed state to up
0:00:07: %LINEPROTO-5-UPDOWN: Line protocol
➥on Interface Serial0, changed state to up
0:00:07: %LINEPROTO-5-UPDOWN: Line protocol
➥on Interface Serial1, changed state to up
0:00:08: %LINEPROTO-5-UPDOWN: Line protocol
➥on Interface Serial0, changed state to down
0:00:09: %SYS-5-CONFIG_I: Configured from
➥memory by console
0:00:09: %SYS-5-RESTART: System restarted —
Cisco Internetwork Operating System Software
IOS (tm) 3000 Software (IGS-IN-L), Version
➥10.3(19a), RELEASE SOFTWARE (fc1)
Copyright (c) 1986-1997 by cisco Systems, Inc.
Compiled Thu 04-Sep-97 20:00 by phester
0:00:10: %LINK-5-CHANGED: Interface Serial0,
➥changed state to administratively down
0:00:10: %LINK-5-CHANGED: Interface
➥TokenRing0, changed state to administrativel
y down
```

Log in to the router and perform a show run.

```
c2513r1#sh run
Building configuration...

Current configuration:
!
```

CASE STUDY: PUTTING A ROUTER IN SERVICE

```
version 10.3
service timestamps debug uptime
service timestamps log uptime
service password-encryption
service udp-small-servers
service tcp-small-servers
!
hostname c2513r1
!
enable secret 5
$1$wEaA$FeD7UevtNmlnInde.YQUC1
!
!
interface Loopback0
 ip address 10.10.43.1 255.255.255.0
!
interface Loopback1
 ip address 10.10.70.109 255.255.255.0
!
interface Ethernet0
 ip address 199.250.137.59 255.255.255.224
 no cdp enable
!
interface Serial0
 ip address 192.168.220.2 255.255.255.0
 ip access-group 1 out
 shutdown
!
interface Serial1
 ip address 192.168.42.1 255.255.255.0
 ip access-group 1 out
 no cdp enable
!
interface TokenRing0
 no ip address
 shutdown
 no cdp enable
!
router eigrp 100
 network 192.168.220.0
!
router rip
 network 10.0.0.0
 network 192.168.42.0
!
access-list 1 permit 10.10.42.0
access-list 1 permit 192.168.200.0 0.0.0.255
!
line con 0
 exec-timeout 0 0
 password 7 0822455D0A16
```

```
 login
line aux 0
 password 7 0822455D0A16
 login
 transport input all
line vty 0 4
 password 7 0822455D0A16
 login
!
end

c2513r1#
```

You see that the router already has a configuration stored in the NVRAM. To clear this configuration and prepare the router for a new configuration you perform a write erase.

```
c2513r1#write erase
[OK]
c2513r1#sh run
Building configuration...

Current configuration:
!
version 10.3
service timestamps debug uptime
service timestamps log uptime
service password-encryption
service udp-small-servers
service tcp-small-servers
!
hostname c2513r1
!
enable secret 5
$1$wEaA$FeD7UevtNmlnInde.YQUC1
!
!
interface Loopback0
 ip address 10.10.43.1 255.255.255.0
!
interface Loopback1
 ip address 10.10.70.109 255.255.255.0
!
interface Ethernet0
 ip address 199.250.137.59 255.255.255.224
 no cdp enable
!
interface Serial0
 ip address 192.168.220.2 255.255.255.0
```

continues

Case Study: Putting a Router in Service

continued

```
  ip access-group 1 out
  shutdown
 !
 interface Serial1
  ip address 192.168.42.1 255.255.255.0
  ip access-group 1 out
  no cdp enable
 !
 interface TokenRing0
  no ip address
  shutdown
  no cdp enable
 !
 router eigrp 100
  network 192.168.220.0
 !
 router rip
  network 10.0.0.0
  network 192.168.42.0
 !
 access-list 1 permit 10.10.42.0
 access-list 1 permit 192.168.200.0 0.0.0.255
 !
 line con 0
  exec-timeout 0 0
  password 7 0822455D0A16
  login
 line aux 0
  password 7 0822455D0A16
  login
  transport input all
 line vty 0 4
  password 7 0822455D0A16
  login
 !
 end

 c2513r1#sh startup
 %% Non-volatile configuration memory has not
 ➥been set up
 c2513r1#
```

As you can see in the preceding example, the running config has been unaffected by the write erase. However, when you try to show startup-config, the router reports %% Non-volatile configuration memory has not been set up.

Reboot the router. It states that the NVRAM is empty, possibly due to a write erase—do you want to enter the setup dialog? You still need to upgrade the IOS, so answer "no" to the query about using the setup dialog. The router then proceeds to boot and presents you with the user exec prompt. Typing enable places you in the privileged exec mode where you can configure the Ethernet port with an IP address so you can access your TFTP server on the network to download the new version of IOS.

```
System Bootstrap, Version 11.0(10c)XB1,
➥PLATFORM SPECIFIC RELEASE SOFTWARE (fc1)
Copyright (c) 1986-1997 by cisco Systems
2500 processor with 14336 Kbytes of main
➥memory

Notice: NVRAM invalid, possibly due to write
erase.

F3: 3522860+70900+216864 at 0x3000060

             Restricted Rights Legend

Use, duplication, or disclosure by the
➥Government is
subject to restrictions as set forth in
➥subparagraph
(c) of the Commercial Computer Software -
➥Restricted
Rights clause at FAR sec. 52.227-19 and
➥subparagraph
(c) (1) (ii) of the Rights in Technical Data
➥and Computer
Software clause at DFARS sec. 252.227-7013.

        cisco Systems, Inc.
        170 West Tasman Drive
        San Jose, California 95134-1706

Cisco Internetwork Operating System Software
IOS (tm) 3000 Software (IGS-IN-L), Version
➥10.3(19a), RELEASE SOFTWARE (fc1)
Copyright (c) 1986-1997 by cisco Systems,
➥Inc.
```

CASE STUDY: PUTTING A ROUTER IN SERVICE

```
Compiled Thu 04-Sep-97 20:00 by phester
Image text-base: 0x0301EB58, data-base:
➥0x00001000

cisco 2500 (68030) processor (revision M)
➥with 14336K/2048K bytes of memory.
Processor board serial number 10187811
Bridging software.
X.25 software, Version 2.0, NET2, BFE and
➥GOSIP compliant.
1 Ethernet/IEEE 802.3 interface.
1 Token Ring/IEEE 802.5 interface.
2 Serial network interfaces.
32K bytes of non-volatile configuration
➥memory.
16384K bytes of processor board System flash
➥(read-only)

Notice: NVRAM invalid, possibly due to ➥write
erase.
        —- System Configuration Dialog —-

At any point you may enter a question mark
➥'?' for help.
Use ctrl-c to abort configuration dialog at
➥any prompt.
Default settings are in square brackets '[]'.
➥Would you like to enter the initial
➥configuration dialog? [yes]: n


Press RETURN to get started!


%LINEPROTO-5-UPDOWN: Line protocol on
➥Interface Ethernet0, changed state to up
%LINEPROTO-5-UPDOWN: Line protocol on
➥Interface Serial0, changed state to down
%LINEPROTO-5-UPDOWN: Line protocol on
➥Interface Serial1, changed state to down
%LINEPROTO-5-UPDOWN: Line protocol on
➥Interface TokenRing0, changed state to down
%LINK-3-UPDOWN: Interface Ethernet0, changed
➥state to up
%LINK-3-UPDOWN: Interface Serial0, changed
➥state to down
%LINK-3-UPDOWN: Interface Serial1, changed
➥state to down
%LINEPROTO-5-UPDOWN: Line protocol on
➥Interface Ethernet0, changed state to down
```

```
%LINK-5-CHANGED: Interface Ethernet0, changed
➥state to administratively down
%LINK-5-CHANGED: Interface Serial0, changed
➥state to administratively down
%LINK-5-CHANGED: Interface Serial1, changed
➥state to administratively down
%LINK-5-CHANGED: Interface TokenRing0,
➥changed state to administratively down
%SYS-5-RESTART: System restarted —
Cisco Internetwork Operating System Software
IOS (tm) 3000 Software (IGS-IN-L), Version
➥10.3(19a), RELEASE SOFTWARE (fc1)
Copyright (c) 1986-1997 by cisco Systems, Inc.
Compiled Thu 04-Sep-97 20:00 by phester
Router>en
Router#
```

After answering "no," you are presented with the router's prompt. You enter the privileged exec mode with the command enable.

You now need to configure the Ethernet port with an IP address so you can download the new version of IOS to the router's flash

```
Router>en
Router#config t
Enter configuration commands, one per line.
➥End with CNTL/Z.
Router(config)#int e0
Router(config-if)#ip address 199.250.137.59
➥255.255.255.224
Router(config-if)#no shut
Router(config-if)#exit
%LINEPROTO-5-UPDOWN: Line protocol on
➥Interface Ethernet0, changed state to up
%LINK-3-UPDOWN: Interface Ethernet0, changed
➥state to up
Router(config)#exit
Router#
```

Now, confirm that you can reach your TFTP server with a ping.

```
Router#ping 54.250.137.37
Type escape sequence to abort.
Sending 5, 100-byte ICMP Echos to
➥199.250.137.37, timeout is 2 seconds:
.!!!!
```

continues

continued

```
Success rate is 80 percent (4/5), round-trip
➥min/avg/max = 1/2/4 ms
Router#
```

You can now upgrade the IOS stored in flash memory. Use the flash load helper to perform this task.

```
Router#copy tftp flash
                    **** NOTICE ****
Flash load helper v1.0
This process will accept the copy options and
➥then terminate
the current system image to use the ROM based
➥image for the copy.
Routing functionality will not be available
➥during that time.
If you are logged in via telnet, this
➥connection will terminate.
Users with console access can see the results
➥of the copy operation.
                    — — ******** — —
➥Proceed? [confirm]y

System flash directory:
File  Length   Name/status
  1   3593792  igs-in-l_103-19a.bin
[3593856 bytes used, 13183360 available,
➥16777216 total]
Address or name of remote host
➥[255.255.255.255]? 199.250.137.37
Source file name? c2500-js-l_112-16.bin
Destination file name [c2500-js-l_112-16.bin]?
Accessing file 'c2500-js-l_112-16.bin' on
➥www.kmahler.com...
Loading c2500-js-l_112-16.bin from
➥199.250.137.37 (via Ethernet0): ! [OK]

Erase flash device before writing? [confirm]y
Flash contains files. Are you sure you want to
➥erase? [confirm]y

System configuration has been modified. Save?
➥[yes/no]: y
Building configuration...
[OK]

Copy 'c2500-js-l_112-16.bin' from server
  as 'c2500-js-l_112-16.bin' into Flash WITH
➥erase? [yes/no]y
```

```
%SYS-5-RELOAD: Reload requested
%FLH: c2500-js-l_112-16.bin from
➥199.250.137.37 to flash ...

System flash directory:
File  Length   Name/status
  1   3593792  igs-in-l_103-19a.bin
[3593856 bytes used, 13183360 available,
➥16777216 total]Domain server mapped ip
address 199.250.137.37 to www.kmahler.com
Accessing file 'c2500-js-l_112-16.bin' on
➥www.kmahler.com...
Loading c2500-js-l_112-16.bin from
➥199.250.137.37 (via Ethernet0): ! [OK]

Erasing device...
➥eeeeeeeeeeeeeeeeeeeeeeeeeeeeeeeeeeeeeeeeeeee
➥eeeeeeeeeeeeeeeeee
ee ...erased
Loading c2500-js-l_112-16.bin from
➥199.250.137.37 (via Ethernet0):
➥!!!!!!!!!!!!!
!!!!!!!!!!!!!!!!!!!!!!!!!!!!!!!!!!!!!!!!!!!!!
➥!!!!!!!!!!!!!!!!!!!!!!!!!!!!!!!!!!!!
!!!!!!!!!!!!!!!!!!!!!!!!!!!!!!!!!!!!!!!
➥!!!!!!!!!!!!!!!!!!!!!!!!!!!!!!!!!!
!!!!!!!!!!!!!!!!!!!!!!!!!!!!!!!!!!!!!!
➥!!!!!!!!!!!!!!!!!!!!!!!!!!!!!!!!
!!!!!!!!!!!!!!!!!!!!!!!!!!!!!!!!!!!!!!!!!!
➥!!!!!!!!!!!!!!!!!!!!!!!!!!!!!!!!!
!!!!!!!!!!!!!!!!!!!!!!!!!!!!!!!!!!!!!!!
➥!!!!!!!!!!!!!!!!!!!!!!!!!!!!!!
!!!!!!!!!!!!!!!!!!!!!!!!!!!!!!!!!!!!!
➥!!!!!!!!!!!!!!!!!!!!!!!!!!!!!
!!!!!!!!!!!!!!!!!!!!!!!!!!!!!!!!!!!!!!!!!!
➥!!!!!!!!!!!!!!!!!!!!!!!!!!!!!
!!!!!!!!!!!!!!!!!!!!!!!!!!!!!!!!!!!!!!
➥!!!!!!!!!!!!!!!!!!!!!!!!!!!!
!!!!!!!!!!!!!!!!!!!!!!!!!!!!!!!!!!!!!!!!!!!
➥!!!!!!!!!!!!!!!!!!!!!!!!!!!!
!!!!!!!!!!!!!!!!!!!!!!!!!!!!!!!!!!!!!!!
➥!!!!!!!!!!!!!!!!!!!!!!!!!!!
!!!!!!!!!!!!!!!!!!!!!!!!!!!!!!!!!!!!
➥!!!!!!!!!!!!!!!!!!!!!!!!!!!!!!!!!
!!!!!!!!!!!!!!!!!!!!!!!!!!!!!!!!!!!!!!!!!!!!
➥!!!!!!!!!!!!!!!!!!!!!!!!!!!!!!!!!
```

CASE STUDY: PUTTING A ROUTER IN SERVICE

```
!!!!!!!!!!!!!!!!!!!!!!!!!!!!!!!!!!!!!!!!!!!!!
➥!!!!!!!!!!!!!!!!!!!!!!!!!!!!!!!!!!!!!!
!!!!!!!!!!!!!!!!!!!!!!!!!!!!!!!!!!!!!!!!!!!!!
➥!!!!!!!!!!!!!!!!!!!!!!!!!!!!!!!!!!!!
!!!!!!!!!!!!!!!!!!!!!!!!!!!!!!!!!!!!!!!!!!!!!!!
➥!!!!!!!!!!!!!!!!!!!!!!!!!!!!!!!!!!!!
!!!!!!!!!!!!!!!!!!!!!!!!!!!!!!!!!!!!!!!!!!!!!!
➥!!!!!!!!!!!!!!!!!!!!!!!!!!!!!!!!!!!!
!!!!!!!!!!!!!!!!!!!!!!!!!!!!!!!!!!!!!!!!!!!!!!
➥!!!!!!!!!!!!!!!!!!!!!!!!!!!!!!!!!!!!
!!!!!!!!!!!!!!!!!!!!!!!!!!!!!!!!!!!!!!!!!!!!!!!
➥!!!!!!!!!!!!!!!!!!!!!!!!!!!!!!!!!!!!
!!!!!!!!!!!!!!!!!!!!!!!!!!!!!!!!!!!!!!!!!!!!!!
➥!!!!!!!!!!!!!!!!!!!!!!!!!!!!!!!!!!!!
[OK - 8102652/16777216 bytes]

Verifying checksum... OK (0x8DCB)
Flash copy took 0:04:01 [hh:mm:ss]
%FLH: Re-booting system after download
%SYS-3-CPUHOG: Task ran for 2912 msec (4/0),
Process = Boot Load, PC = 1117942
-Traceback= 10E781A 10E7E24 10E5F80 1010080
➥10005DE
F3: 8004052+98568+315656 at 0x3000060


                 Restricted Rights Legend

Use, duplication, or disclosure by the
➥Government is
subject to restrictions as set forth in
➥subparagraph
(c) of the Commercial Computer Software -
➥Restricted
Rights clause at FAR sec. 52.227-19 and
➥subparagraph
(c) (1) (ii) of the Rights in Technical Data
➥and Computer
Software clause at DFARS sec. 252.227-7013.

                 cisco Systems, Inc.
                 170 West Tasman Drive
                 San Jose, California 95134-1706



Cisco Internetwork Operating System Software
IOS (tm) 2500 Software (C2500-JS-L), Version
➥11.2(16), RELEASE SOFTWARE (fc1)
Copyright (c) 1986-1998 by cisco Systems, Inc.
Compiled Tue 06-Oct-98 11:54 by ashah
```

```
Image text-base: 0x030400AC, data-base:
➥0x00001000

cisco 2500 (68030) processor (revision M)
➥with 14336K/2048K bytes of memory.
Processor board ID 10187811, with hardware
➥revision 00000000
Bridging software.
SuperLAT software copyright 1990 by Meridian
Technology Corp).
X.25 software, Version 2.0, NET2, BFE and
➥GOSIP compliant.
TN3270 Emulation software.
1 Ethernet/IEEE 802.3 interface(s)
1 Token Ring/IEEE 802.5 interface(s)
2 Serial network interface(s)
32K bytes of non-volatile configuration
➥memory.
16384K bytes of processor board System flash
➥(read-only)



Press RETURN to get started!


%LINK-3-UPDOWN: Interface Ethernet0, changed
➥state to up
%LINK-3-UPDOWN: Interface Serial0, changed
➥state to down
%LINK-3-UPDOWN: Interface Serial1, changed
➥state to down
%LINEPROTO-5-UPDOWN: Line protocol on
➥Interface Ethernet0, changed state to up
%LINEPROTO-5-UPDOWN: Line protocol on
➥Interface Serial0, changed state to down
%LINEPROTO-5-UPDOWN: Line protocol on
➥Interface Serial1, changed state to down
%LINEPROTO-5-UPDOWN: Line protocol on
➥Interface TokenRing0, changed state to down
%SYS-5-CONFIG_I: Configured from memory by
➥console
%SYS-5-RESTART: System restarted —
Cisco Internetwork Operating System Software
IOS (tm) 2500 Software (C2500-JS-L), Version
➥11.2(16), RELEASE SOFTWARE (fc1)
Copyright (c) 1986-1998 by cisco Systems, Inc.
➥Compiled Tue 06-Oct-98 11:54 by ashah
%LINK-5-CHANGED: Interface Serial0, changed
➥state to administratively down
```

continues

CASE STUDY: PUTTING A ROUTER IN SERVICE

continued

```
%LINK-5-CHANGED: Interface Serial1, changed
➥state to administratively down
%LINK-5-CHANGED: Interface TokenRing0,
➥changed state to administratively down
Router>sh ver
Cisco Internetwork Operating System Software
IOS (tm) 2500 Software (C2500-JS-L), Version
➥11.2(16), RELEASE SOFTWARE (fc1)
Copyright (c) 1986-1998 by cisco Systems, Inc.
➥Compiled Tue 06-Oct-98 11:54 by ashah
Image text-base: 0x030400AC, data-base:
➥0x00001000

ROM: System Bootstrap, Version 11.0(10c)XB1,
➥PLATFORM SPECIFIC RELEASE SOFTWARE
(fc1)
BOOTFLASH: 3000 Bootstrap Software
➥(IGS-BOOT-R), Version 11.0(10c)XB1, PLATFORM
➥SPECIFIC RELEASE SOFTWARE (fc1)

Router uptime is 0 minutes
System restarted by reload
System image file is "flash:c2500-js-l_112-
➥16.bin", booted via flash

cisco 2500 (68030) processor (revision M)
➥with 14336K/2048K bytes of memory.
Processor board ID 10187811, with hardware
➥revision 00000000
Bridging software.
SuperLAT software copyright 1990 by Meridian
➥Technology Corp).
X.25 software, Version 2.0, NET2, BFE and
➥GOSIP compliant.
TN3270 Emulation software.
1 Ethernet/IEEE 802.3 interface(s)
1 Token Ring/IEEE 802.5 interface(s)
2 Serial network interface(s)
```

```
32K bytes of non-volatile configuration
➥memory.
16384K bytes of processor board System flash
➥(read-only)

Configuration register is 0x2102

Router>
```

Now proceed to enter the configuration for the router.

```
Router#config terminal
Router(config)#interface serial0
Router(config-if)#ip address 155.175.34.35
➥255.255.255.0
Router(config-if)#no shutdown
Router(config-if)#exit
Router(config)#interface ethernet0
Router(config-if)#ip address 155.175.35.1
➥255.255.255.0
Router(config-if)#no shutdown
Router(config-if)#exit
Router(config)#ip route 0.0.0.0 0.0.0.0
➥155.175.34.1
Router(config)#exit
Router#copy running-config startup-config
```

You have now successfully cleared the configuration of a router's NVRAM, upgraded the IOS, and configured it to be the Internet gateway for your company.

After installing the router, test the Internet connection by visiting Cisco's Web site to register for your CCNA test.

CHAPTER SUMMARY

This chapter covered a substantial amount of information. You were introduced to logging in to a router and interacting with the CLI. You saw how the context-sensitive help aids when configuring a router. The elements of a router and the methods used to monitor them were introduced. You saw how the password encryption service can make the configuration files less vulnerable to wandering eyes. You also learned how to use a TFTP server to perform several tasks such as backing up configuration files and IOS images.

In preparation for your CCNA exam, it is important to practice the tasks of configuring a router often. The repetition of performing these tasks will firmly implant them in your mind.

KEY TERMS

- Internetworking Operating System
- Context-sensitive help
- TFTP server
- RAM
- ROM
- Flash memory
- CDP
- IOS image file

APPLY YOUR KNOWLEDGE	

Exercises

2.1 Viewing Neighboring Cisco Devices

Use CDP to view neighboring Cisco devices.

Estimated Time: 10 minutes

1. Log in to your router.

2. At the Router> prompt, type **show CDP neighbor**.

3. View the neighboring device information and make note of the versions of IOS that each neighboring device is running.

4. View the neighboring device information and make note of what capabilities each device provides. These can include routing, switching, bridging, and more.

5. Choose one of the neighbors and use the command show CDP neighbor detail Router1 to view more information about the device.

2.2 Using show version to Discover Information About a Router

Use the show command to see information about the router's components.

Estimated Time: 10 minutes

1. Log in to your router and enter the privileged exec mode with the enable command.

2. At the Router# prompt, type **show version**.

3. View the version information and make note of the version of IOS the router is running.

4. View the version information and make note of how long the router has been running.

5. View the version information and make note of what interfaces are installed in the router.

2.3 Using show interfaces to Discover Information About Interfaces

Use the show command to see information about the interfaces in a router.

Estimated Time: 15 minutes

1. Log in to your router and enter the privileged exec mode with the enable command.

2. At the Router# prompt, type **show interfaces**.

3. View the interface information and make note of which interfaces are up and which are down. Of the interfaces that are down, note which ones are administratively down.

4. View the interface information and make note of the interface's details such as bandwidth, Maximum Transmission Unit (MTU) size, and the current load on the interface. The load on the interface is shown as a fraction of 255. (For example, 128/255 is 50% utilization, and 25/255 would be 10% utilization.)

Review Questions

1. Where are passwords stored, and what services does IOS provide for encrypting them?

2. List some of the prompts the CLI presents and what they indicate.

3. How is the running config saved to the startup config? Explain the function of each.

4. List the types of memory in a router and describe how each type is used by the router.

5. What does the command history feature of IOS do?

6. How can you find out how long a router has been up and running?

APPLY YOUR KNOWLEDGE

7. What is CDP and what does it do?

8. What are boot commands?

9. How do you view statistics on a router interface?

10. What is a TFTP server, and how can it be useful when configuring and maintaining Cisco routers?

Exam Questions

1. What does the router prompt Router> indicate?

    A. You are logged in to the router at the privileged exec level.

    B. You are logged in to the router at the user exec level.

    C. The router is prompting you to log in.

    D. You have entered the global configuration mode of the router.

2. What is the proper way to copy the IOS image from flash to a TFTP server?

    A. Router(config)#copy tftp flash

    B. Router#copy tftp flash

    C. Router#(config)#copy flash tftp

    D. Router#copy flash tftp

3. What is the proper method for creating a banner message for a router?

    A. Router#banner motd "This router replaced 1/3/99"

    B. Router>motd "This router replaced 1/3/99"

    C. Router(config)#motd "This router replaced 1/3/99"

    D. Router(config)#banner motd "This router replaced 1/3/99"

4. How would you view the contents of the configuration register?

    A. Router#show config-register

    B. Router>show config-register

    C. Router#show version

    D. Router#show running-config

5. How do you enter the privileged exec mode?

    A. Router>enable

    B. Enter the enable password at the password prompt.

    C. Router>privileged-mode

    D. Router>config

6. How is the router's name set?

    A. Router(config)#hostname ParrotHead

    B. Router(config)>hostname ParrotHead

    C. Router#hostname ParrotHead

    D. Router#set hostname ParrotHead

7. Which command will give you statistics on network interfaces?

    A. Router#show interface statistics

    B. Router#show statistics

    C. Router#show interfaces

    D. Router#list interfaces

APPLY YOUR KNOWLEDGE

8. What does changing the CDP timer to 90 do?

    A. Changes the Collision Detection Protocol backoff timer to 90 seconds

    B. Causes the router to wait 90 clock ticks between routing updates

    C. Causes the router to send CDP packets every 90 seconds

    D. Changes the Congestion Detection Protocol update timer to 90 seconds

9. How would you find out whether an interface is up or down?

    A. `Router#show interfaces`

    B. `Router#show running-config`

    C. `Router#show startup-config`

    D. `Router#show cdp neighbors`

Answers to Review Questions

1. Passwords are stored in the router's configuration file. IOS has a password encryption service that will encrypt the passwords, making them fairly secure from wondering eyes. For more information, see "Normal Password Authentication."

2. `Router>` indicates we are logged in, in user exec mode.

    `Router#` indicates we are logged in, in privileged exec mode.

    `Router(config)#` indicates we are in global config mode.

    `Router(conifg-if)#` indicates we are in interface config mode.

For more information, see "Logging in to a Router in Both User and Privileged Modes" and "Configuring the Router."

3. `copy running-config startup-config`

    The `running-config` is the configuration the router is currently executing. When changes are made to the `running-config`, they take effect immediately. The `startup-config` is stored in NVRAM and is the config that the router copies to the `running-config` when it boots up. For more information, see "Saving Config Changes."

4. RAM is used by the router to store packets, data, and routing tables. Flash memory is used much like a disk drive in a PC to store the IOS. Some routers execute the IOS directly from flash and some copy the IOS to RAM before executing. NVRAM is Non-Volatile RAM and is used to store the startup configuration file. ROM is read-only memory and is used to store self test programs and a minimal version of IOS. For more information, see "Understanding Router Elements."

5. The command history feature of IOS keeps a number of commands you have used in a buffer. These commands can be recalled by using the up arrow. After being recalled to the command line, the command can be edited and executed, or executed as is. For more information, see "Using the Command History and Editing Features."

6. The `Router#show version` command lists how long it has been since the router has been rebooted. It also lists the reason for the reboot. For more information, see "Examining the Components of a Router."

APPLY YOUR KNOWLEDGE

7. CDP is Cisco Discovery Protocol. It runs on Cisco equipment at the Data Link layer. It is used to discover neighbor devices and exchange capability information. For more information, see "Cisco Discovery Protocol (CDP)."

8. Boot commands are IOS configuration commands that instruct the router how to load the IOS. Some boot commands can instruct the router to load IOS from Flash, TFTP server, or ROM. A fault-tolerant configuration includes several boot commands, so the router can fall back to another source for the IOS image should the primary source become corrupt or unreachable. For more information, see "Cisco IOS Commands for Router Startup."

9. Statistics for an interface can be viewed using the `show interfaces` command. This will list statistics including errors, utilization, and interface parameters. For more information, see "Examining the Components of a Router."

10. A TFTP server is a computer running Trivial File Transfer Protocol server software. A free copy of TFTP server software for Windows NT can be downloaded from Cisco's Web site. The TFTP server is useful for copying files to and from a router. These files can be IOS images and configuration files. This is a good way to back up the configurations of a router and update IOS images. For more information, see "Backup and Upgrade IOS."

Answers to Exam Questions

1. **B.** The > prompt indicates you are currently at the user exec mode. For more information, see "Logging in to a Router in Both User and Privileged Modes."

2. **D.** The copy command uses syntax much like DOS's copy command. `Copy <source> <destination>`. The copy command is executed from the normal privileged exec prompt, not from the config mode. For more information, see "Managing Configuration File from the Privileged Exec Mode."

3. **D.** The MOTD is set from the config mode. This is a good example of why hands-on experience is important when studying for the CCNA exam. The proper syntax is as follows:

```
Router(config)#banner motd "This router replaced 1/3/99"
```

For more information, see "Message of the Day (MOTD)."

4. **C.** The `show version` command displays the contents of the configuration register. For more information, see "Examining the Components of a Router."

5. **A.** The `enable` command enters privileged exec mode. For more information, see "Logging in to a Router in Both User and Privileged Modes."

6. **A.** The hostname is part of the configuration file. You must be in global configuration mode to set the hostname. For more information, see "Configuring the Router."

7. **C.** `show interfaces` gives you much information about the network interfaces. Become familiar with the information provided by this command. You will use this command a great deal when diagnosing problems. For more information, see "Examining the Components of a Router."

8. **C.** The CDP timer sets how often the router will send out Cisco Discovery Protocol packets. For more information, see "Cisco Discovery Protocol."

Apply Your Knowledge

9. **A.** The show interfaces command includes information about the state of an interface, including whether it is up or down. For more information, see "Examining the Components of a Router."

Suggested Readings and Resources

1. Chappell, Laura. *Introduction to Cisco Router Configuration.* Cisco Press, 1998.

This chapter covers the following objectives from the Network Protocols portion of the CCNA exam. (Chapter 4, "Understanding and Configuring IPX/SPX and Other Network Protocols," will cover the remainder of the objectives for the Network Protocols section.)

Describe the two parts of network addressing, then identify the parts in specific protocol address examples.

▶ To successfully maintain internetworking systems, you must understand the two parts of network addressing. This chapter addresses the IP addressing; Chapter 4 addresses this in relation to IPX.

Create the different classes of IP addresses and subnetting.

▶ Understanding IP addresses and subnetting is an absolute must to design, install, and maintain Cisco routers.

Configure IP addresses.

▶ To maintain internetworking systems, you must be able to configure IP addresses.

Verify IP addresses.

▶ To maintain internetworking systems, you must be able to verify IP addresses.

Identify the functions of the TCP/IP Transport-layer protocols.

▶ A strong understanding of the TCP/IP protocol suite is necessary for internetworking engineers.

CHAPTER 3

Understanding and Configuring TCP/IP

Identify the functions of the TCP/IP Network-layer protocols.

▶ A strong understanding of the TCP/IP protocol suite is necessary for internetworking engineers.

Identify the functions performed by ICMP.

▶ ICMP can provide some very useful diagnostics. Understanding these functions is imperative for an internetworking engineer, in relation to troubleshooting.

STUDY STRATEGIES

▶ You should spend a good deal of time studying for the TCP/IP portion of the CCNA exam. TCP/IP is the foundation on which many of the other concepts and objectives are based. TCP/IP is quickly becoming the standard of many companies; it scales well. This is proven by the success of the largest WAN to date, the Internet.

Be sure you can subnet IP addresses. Being able to properly subnet IP address ranges and verify that ranges are valid is extremely important in the day-to-day tasks as an internetworking engineer. You must learn to properly subnet IP addresses and know what IP addresses are valid and invalid.

Understand how each of these network protocols is configured on the router and how to perform simple diagnostics.

Spend time working with the protocols on real networks. Learn to solve real problems with TCP/IP networks.

INTRODUCTION

This is what it's all about. Internetworking engineering is about making networks communicate properly. Network protocols create the platform for making it all work together.

Network protocols are born, evolve, and die. Understanding a networking protocol today does not ensure your understanding of it tomorrow. The key to staying current and keeping sharp is reading. Read everything you can get your hands on about networking. Visit Cisco's Web site regularly. Read RFCs regularly. Even reading computer magazines and newspapers can offer a great deal of insight into what is happening in the industry. The computer industry is unlike any other. In six months, more advances can be made in the computer industry than other industries make in years.

As an internetworking engineer, you are responsible for creating ways to deliver network traffic. This network traffic is delivered by networking protocols. Understanding these protocols is absolutely necessary for success. It's also necessary to pass the CCNA test.

NETWORKING ADDRESS OVERVIEW

Network addresses are the addresses used at Layer 3 of the OSI reference model. The network address is used by routers to determine where to send the data. Routable network addresses differ from the MAC addresses in that routable network addresses contain a hierarchical portion of the address, whereas MAC addresses are flat in structure.

Network Addresses

There are two network address types you need to understand for the CCNA exam: IP addresses and IPX addresses (Novell). Each address type includes two parts a network number and a host address. The network number portion of the address is used by routers to determine how to forward traffic. The router compares the network number to its routing table and determines how to forward the traffic. After the traffic reaches the destination network, the second part of the address, the host address, is used to deliver the data to the end station.

You must be able to recognize IPX and IP addresses, and be able to determine which part of the address is the network and which part is the host address.

For IPX addresses it is relatively simple to determine the network and host portion of the address. The following is an example IPX address:

A31B3AF5.0000.0000.0001

In this example "A31B3AF5" is the network address portion. The host portion is "0000.0000.0001". IPX addresses are represented in hexadecimal notation. The network address is up to 8 hexadecimal digits long and the host address is always three groups of 4 hexadecimal digits.

IP addresses are recognizable by their dotted decimal notation. IP addresses are represented as four decimal numbers no larger than 255 separated by periods. The following is an example IP address:

199.250.138.99 netmask 255.255.255.0

With IP addresses, the separation of the network address and the host address is determined by the *netmask*. Because this topic is more complex, it will be explained in full later in this chapter.

MAC Address

The MAC address identifies a device on the local network. A MAC address is 48 bits long and is usually represented as three groups of four hexadecimal digits, such as in the following example:

00e0.a38d.0800

It is mapped in some way to the network address. For Novell's IPX protocol, the MAC address is used to create the network address. Because it is made part of the network address, there is no need to create a map between the two addresses. TCP/IP, however, requires a method of mapping an IP address to a MAC address. Address Resolution Protocol (ARP) performs this mapping. MAC addresses are discussed in more detail in Chapter 1, "The OSI Reference Model."

BINARY MATH

To work with IP addresses, you must be able to convert binary numbers to decimal and back again. Most of this math is performed with a single byte of data and thus is rather simple. You learned the decimal system in school. The decimal system represents numbers as a power of 10. Each numbering system works the same way, only with different values for each position. The binary numbering system uses powers of 2 for each digit position.

How Numbers Are Represented in Binary

Computers use the byte as a unit of storage. A byte holds 8 bits. The largest number that can be stored in a byte is 11111111 in binary, FF in hexadecimal, and 255 in decimal.

The following table shows how this is so.

128	64	32	16	8	4	2	1
Bit8	7	6	5	4	3	2	1

In the previous table, you see the value of each bit position. Notice that each bit position from the left to right is reduced by half. Starting at 128, each position halves until it reaches 1. You can convert a binary number to decimal by assigning the decimal value to each bit position and then adding the numbers. The following example shows how a binary number is converted to decimal.

Take the binary number, in this instance: 1 0 1 1 0 1 1 0

Now, place that number in the table:

128	64	32	16	8	4	2	1
1	0	1	1	0	1	1	0
128		32	16		4	2	

Every number that corresponds with a one is valid, shown in row three.

Next, add the decimal numbers in the third row together:

128 + 32 + 16 + 4 + 2 = 182

182 is the correct answer.

This converts a byte from binary to decimal. Learn to do this well. It is a necessary skill later for subnetting IP addresses.

Decimal Numbers

In the decimal system, the number 249 is familiar to you. You know it is as "two-hundred forty-nine." What you probably don't think about is why. Each position of the number represents a number of the units that position represents. In the number 249, the nine represents how many ones are in the number. The number four represents how many tens are in the number, and the number two represents how many hundreds are in the number. Figure 3.1 shows how this breaks down.

In the decimal numbering system, each digit position represents 10 raised to a power (see the table):

10^5	10^4	10^3	10^2	10^1	10^0
100000	10000	1000	100	10	1

Each position is ten, raised to the power of the position-1.

Binary Numbers

The binary numbering system works exactly the same way, except that each position is two raised to the power of some number (see the following table). Because there are only two digits in the binary numbering system, it takes many more digits to represent the same number as in the decimal system.

2^7	2^6	2^5	2^4	2^3	2^2	2^1	2^0
128	64	32	16	8	4	2	1

Each position is two, raised to the power of the position-1.

In the binary numbering system, the number 11111001 is the same as the previous example. This is 249 (decimal). To determine why, you must first know the value of each position of a binary number.

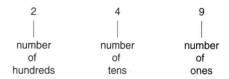

FIGURE 3.1
How decimal numbers represent the values of base 10 numbers.

Converting Numbers From Binary to Decimal

To convert the previous binary number, 11111001, to decimal, place the number below the chart as shown in the following example.

128	64	32	16	8	4	2	1
1	1	1	1	1	0	0	1
128	64	32	16	8			1

Again, every number that corresponds with a one is valid, as shown in the third row.

Add up the decimal numbers for each position with a binary one.

128 + 64 + 32 + 16 + 8 + 1 = 249

You have just converted a binary octet to decimal.

Converting Numbers from Decimal to Binary

While working with IP addresses, you will need to convert numbers from decimal to binary. To perform this function, you start by finding the largest binary position that will go into the number you are converting.

For the decimal number 249, the largest binary position that will go into it is 128, the highest bit position of an octet. Place a 1 in that bit position.

128	64	32	16	8	4	2	1
1							

Subtract 128 from 249:

249 − 128 = 121

Now perform the same over again. What is the largest bit position that will go into 121? 64 is the largest bit position that will go into 121. Place a 1 in that bit position and continue from there:

128	64	32	16	8	4	2	1
1	1						

$$121 - 64 = 57$$

128	64	32	16	8	4	2	1
1	1	1					

$$57 - 32 = 25$$

128	64	32	16	8	4	2	1
1	1	1	1				

$$25 - 16 = 9$$

128	64	32	16	8	4	2	1
1	1	1	1	1			

$$9 - 8 = 1$$

128	64	32	16	8	4	2	1
1	1	1	1	1	0	0	1

Decimal number 249 is binary number 1111001. You have now converted from decimal to binary. This is a skill you will need often when working with IP addresses. Remember the simple method of creating the decimal equivalent chart for converting from one system to the other. Start with the number 1 on the right, and double each number moving left until you reach 128 (8 bits).

IP ADDRESSES

You will often hear people describe the IP address as a TCP/IP address. Technically this is incorrect. TCP/IP describes an entire suite of protocols. IP is the Layer 3 protocol that TCP uses. The IP address is used by the Layer 3 protocol, Internet Protocol (IP), to uniquely identify the station on the IP network.

An IP address defines two things: the network and the host address on the network. The network portion of the IP address is used for determining routing information. Routers look at the network portion of an IP address to determine the proper path for forwarding packets. After the packet arrives at the proper network, the host address is used to deliver the packet to the proper networking station.

The *network mask*, sometimes called the *subnet mask*, determines which part of the IP address represents the network and which part represents the host. The network mask is described in the next section.

IP addresses are currently 32 bits long. (There is a new version of IP being developed that uses 128 bits.) This represents 4 bytes of data called *octets*. Figure 3.2 shows what an IP address looks like.

FIGURE 3.2▶
An IP address in dotted decimal format.

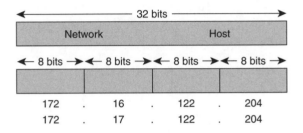

Computers perform their functions in binary, humans don't. If an IP address is to be used by human users, it is represented in decimal numbers, which are easier to understand. Each octet of the IP address is separately converted to decimal. The four octets are shown separated by periods or dots. This is called *dotted decimal notation*. Figure 3.3 shows why it is easier to read IP addresses in dotted decimal form instead of binary.

Convert each octet to a decimal number, then separate the numbers by periods. This creates a representation of the IP address that is much easier to remember and to enter without mistakes. Life would not be easy if you had to enter IP addresses in binary format.

As nice as representing IP addresses in dotted decimal makes life, this format does create some headaches.

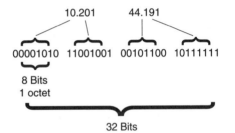

FIGURE 3.3▲
An IP address in both dotted decimal form and binary.

Network Mask

An IP address is really made up of two parts: the IP address and the network mask. The *network mask* defines the portion of the 32 bit IP address that represents the network. The remaining portion represents the host address. The network portion of the address is used for routing packets. Routers build tables of the networks in an internetwork. When packets enter a router, the router uses the subnet mask to determine how much of the address represents the network.

After this is determined, the router compares the network to the routing tables and determines whether it can forward the packet. If it is able, the router forwards the packet to the next hop along its trip to the destination. After the packet arrives on the destination network, the host portion of the IP address is used to determine which device ultimately takes delivery of the packet.

This may sound complex, but it's really not.

Consider an IP address that looks like this:

Network = 192.168.2 Computer = 26

That is pretty straightforward. The network the packet belongs on is 192.168.2. The computer on that network the packet should be delivered to is 26.

The network mask is just a shorthand method of representing this same concept. The previous example would look like the following with a network mask:

IP Address = 192.168.2.26 Network Mask = 255.255.255.0

Computing devices take these two numbers in their binary form and perform a binary *AND* on them. A binary AND says "compare the two binary numbers; if both bits in a position are 1, the result is 1. If either bit is 0, the result is 0."

The rules of the binary AND are as follows:

1 + 1 = 1

1 + 0 = 0

0 + 0 = 0

Apply the binary AND to the IP address and the subnet mask:

IP Address	192.168.2.26
Network Mask	255.255.255.0
Binary IP Address	11000000.10101000.00000010.00011010
Binary Network Mask	11111111.11111111.11111111.00000000
Results of AND	11000000.10101000.00000010.00000000
Results in Decimal	192.168.2.0 ← *This is the network.*

The IP address together with the network mask computers and routers can determine how to forward or route packets.

An example of how a TCP/IP computer determines how to forward a packet is outlined in the following numbered list.

1. A user enters a Web site name in his browser.

2. The TCP/IP stack does a Domain Name Server lookup of the name to determine the IP address of the site. (DNS is how TCP/IP resolves a computer name to an IP address. An explanation of DNS is beyond the scope of this book. (See the Suggested Readings and Resources section at the end of the chapter.)

3. After the computer has the IP address of the system with which it needs to communicate, it compares whether the IP address is on the same IP network. The computer's IP address is 192.168.86.58 with a netmask of 255.255.255.0; the computer with which it wants to talk has an IP address of 10.137.88.19.

4. Based on the netmask, the network portion of the originating computer is 192.168.86. This is compared to the same region of the destination IP address. If they match, the packet is placed on the network. The destination system will see it. However, if the network portions of the IP address do not match, the computer first checks its own routing tables. (Unless the computer has multiple network interfaces to different networks, this usually doesn't apply.) The packet is then sent to a router—either one specified in the computer's routing tables, or (if there is not a specific entry for this network in the routing tables) the packet is sent to the default gateway.

5. The router receives the packet. It compares the network portion of the IP address to its routing tables. If it finds a match, it forwards the packet to the next hop along the way. If the router does not have a specific route to this network, it may have a default gateway of its own. This may be a router connected to the Internet or an internal router with more complete routing tables.

The network mask simply designates what part of the IP address represents the network and what part represents the host.

A network mask must be a continuous run of binary ones from left to right. This allows for another method of IP address notation. Because an IP address is really useful only with its netmask, you usually find IP addresses listed as such. An example Class C address would be 192.168.1.32 netmask 255.255.255.0. There is a shorter way to represent the same thing, however. The same IP address can be written as 192.168.1.32/24. This representation lists the number of netmask bits after the IP address. The following are some other IP addresses in both notations to help you grasp the different notations.

10.100.243.76 netmask 255.255.128.0	10.100.243.76/17
172.16.99.128 netmask 255.255.0.0	172.16.99.128/16
192.168.31.22 netmask 255.255.255.240	192.168.31.22/28

Following is a valid netmask:

11111111.11111111.11111111.00000000 255.255.255.0

Following is an invalid netmask:

11111111.11111110.11111111.00000000 255.254.255.0

Because subnet masks are broken into bytes or octets, there are a few numbers you should learn, remember, and learn again. These are the decimal equivalents of an octet being filled from the left to right with bits. When a subnet is split within an octet, these are the decimal equivalents of the binary representations:

10000000	128
11000000	192
11100000	224
11110000	240
11111000	248
11111100	252
11111110	254
11111111	255

Understanding IP Address Classes

IP addresses are divided into classes. For each class, there is an assumed network mask. The most common IP address classes are shown in the following table:

Class	Range of First Octet	Maximum Networks	Maximum Hosts	First Bits
A	1–126	126	16,777,214	0
B	128–191	16,384	65,534	10
C	192–223	2,097,152	254	110

The class of an IP address is actually defined by the first few bits.

◆ If the first bit of an IP address is 0, it is a Class A address. By definition, a Class A IP address has 8 bits of network address and 24 bits of host address. The subnet mask for a Class A address is 255.0.0.0, or /8.

◆ If the first two bits are 10, it is a Class B address. By definition, a Class B IP address has 16 bits of network address and 16 bits of host address. The subnet mask for a Class B address is 255.255.0.0, or /16.

◆ If the first three bits are 110, it is a Class C address. By definition, a Class C IP address has 24 bits of network address and 8 bits of host address. The subnet mask for a Class C address is 255.255.255.0, or /24.

It is important that you learn the classes of IP addresses and their default subnet masks. Most people think of subnet bits in terms of the entire subnet. For example, a Class A address 10.201.44.1 that has a subnet mask of 255.255.255.0 is generally thought of as a Class A address with 24 bits of subnet mask. Cisco has decided to confuse this subject: This is actually a Class A address with 16 bits of subnet mask. The first 8 bits are assumed because it is a Class A IP address. Thinking this way, an IP address of 10.201.44.1 with a subnet mask of 255.0.0.0 is a Class A IP address with 0 bits of subnet mask even though there are 8 bits in the subnet mask. Be sure to remember this distinction when dealing with Cisco equipment and information. The following table shows how IP addresses are broken down by class.

Class A: N.H.H.H

Class B: N.N.H.H

Class C: N.N.N.H

Class D: multicast

Class E: experimental

N = Network portion of address
H = Host portion of address

Understanding Networks and Broadcasts

IP addresses represent many things. An IP address with all of the host bits set to 0 represents the network itself. Network IP addresses are used by routers to represent the path to a network. The following is part of an IP routing table that shows how the network address is used to identify each network.

```
Router#sh ip route
Codes: C - connected, S - static, I - IGRP, R - RIP, M -
➥mobile, B - BGP
       D - EIGRP, EX - EIGRP external, O - OSPF, IA - OSPF
➥inter area
       E1 - OSPF external type 1, E2 - OSPF external type
➥2, E - EGP
       i - IS-IS, L1 - IS-IS level-1, L2 - IS-IS level-2, *
➥- candidate default
       U - per-user static route

Gateway of last resort is 192.250.152.1 to network 0.0.0.0

D    192.168.104.0/24 [90/11151872] via 10.1.1.90,
➥02:06:36, Serial5/0.10
D    192.168.106.0/24 [90/11151872] via 10.1.1.90,
➥02:06:36, Serial5/0.10
D    192.168.107.0/24 [90/11151872] via 10.1.1.90,
➥02:06:36, Serial5/0.10
D    192.168.108.0/24 [90/11151872] via 10.1.1.14,
➥02:06:36, Serial5/0.4
D    192.168.109.0/24 [90/2809856] via 10.1.1.2, 02:06:36,
➥Serial5/0.1
D    192.168.110.0/24 [90/11151872] via 10.1.1.18,
➥02:06:36, Serial5/0.5
D    192.168.111.0/24 [90/11151872] via 10.1.2.122,
➥02:06:36, Serial5/0.133
     10.0.0.0/8 is variably subnetted, 270 subnets, 5 masks
D       10.1.3.8/30 [90/7690496] via 10.1.1.26, 02:06:36,
➥Serial5/0.7
D       10.1.2.8/30 [90/11023872] via 10.1.1.10, 02:06:36,
➥Serial5/0.3
C       10.1.1.8/30 is directly connected, Serial5/0.3

Router#
```

In the preceding routing table you can see the first entry 192.168.104.0/24 as being accessible via interface Serial5/0.10. Because 192.168.104.0 has 24 bits of network mask, the host portion of the address consists of the last 8 bits. The representation here has all 8 of these bits set at 0.

The *broadcast address* is just the opposite of the network address. The broadcast address for a network has all of the host bits set to one. The broadcast address is used to send a packet to every host on a network. One reason to send broadcasts is to resolve a host name to an IP address. Some name-to-IP address mapping schemes use broadcast addresses to send out a query looking for a host name. Every computer on the network receives the query, and most ignore it. The computer with the name the query is looking for replies with its IP address in the source field of the packet. The name-to-IP address mapping scheme can then add that host name and IP address combination to its cache. For the network 192.168.104.0/24, the broadcast address is 192.168.104.255—the same as the network but with all of the host bits set to one. A broadcast of this type is called a *directed broadcast* because it specifies the network for the broadcast. Broadcasts that originate on the network for which the broadcast is intended can use the broadcast address 255.255.255.255, which will be translated into the Layer 2 broadcast address for the network topology in use.

Special IP Address Ranges

There are two other classes of IP addresses that are not used in the same way as Class A, B, and C addresses: multicast and experimental.

Multicast addresses fall in the range of 224–239 in the first octet. Multicast IP addresses are classified as Class D addresses. A multicast address represents a multicast group. Multicast groups are used to send large amounts of data to a group of computers rather than sending the same information to each one individually. *Multicasting* requires special configurations in the routers and switches to work properly. However, when used for such things as RealAudio or Video Streaming, multicasting can reduce network traffic significantly. Multicasting is beyond the scope of the CCNA exam and is not covered in detail in this book.

The second type of IP address is the *experimental* class. These IP addresses are rarely used. Experimental IP addresses fall in the range of 240–254 in the first octet. Experimental IP addresses are classified as Class E addresses.

There are some other special ranges of IP addresses. There are several regions of IP addresses that are reserved for private networks. These IP addresses are not used for the Internet and will be dropped by Internet routers if they enter the Internet.

The first reserved IP range offers flexibility in network design to individual companies. The Class A IP network 10.0.0.0 is reserved for private use. This IP range allows companies to build elaborate internal networks. By subnetting the IP range, a company can create networks for a large number of offices without problem. Most companies are moving their internal networks to this range. This reserved IP range is commonly referred to as *Ten Net* or *Ten Net Addresses*.

There also is a reserved IP range in the Class B IP range. This range consists of IP networks from 172.16.0.0–172.31.0.0. This Class B range is not routed on the Internet and can be used by companies for use on private networks.

Another area of reserved IP addresses consists of IP networks 192.168.0.0–192.168.255.0. These Class C IP addresses are not routed on the Internet and thus are good for use on private networks. Because the Ten Net range offers more flexibility in network design, most organizations use it for network stations. It is common to use addresses from each range in an enterprise for different purposes.

SUBNETTING IP ADDRESS RANGES

It would be rare for any organization to have sixteen million workstations on one network. In fact, it would make for one very slow network. To use their address space more efficiently, the organization could subnet a class A address.

Subnetting is the process of dividing a network range into smaller subnetworks. Subnetting allows a network designer more flexibility when allocating IP address ranges. It does not make sense to use an entire range of 254 Class C addresses for an office with only 15 computers. Network designers can create "subnets" of a Class C range and assign parts of the range to different offices. Subnetting allows network designers to make more efficient use of the IP network ranges assigned to them.

Subnetting a Class A Address

A Class A IP address can support 16,777,212 hosts with the default subnet mask of 255.0.0.0. To make better use of this IP address range, an organization could divide it up into smaller networks. To subnet a larger IP range into more networks with fewer hosts per network, you add subnet mask bits. For this example, use the private network Class A address of 10.0.0.0 netmask 255.0.0.0. This private Class A network can support one network with 16,777,212 hosts.

Most organizations don't have quite this many computers on one network, so they subnet the Class A into many networks with fewer computers per network. By adding subnet mask bits to the default subnet of 255.0.0.0 divides the Class A into multiple networks. For example, the Class A IP address 10.110.2.1 could use a subnet mask of 255.255.255.0. Now the IP address scheme will support 65,534 networks with 254 hosts per network. This is much more useful. You can distribute IP addresses to division offices and each office can have 254 hosts. To determine how many networks a subnet creates and how many hosts per subnet there can be, use the equation 2^n-2, where n is the number of bits. This works for both networks and hosts per network. In the previous example, 16 bits of subnet were added to a Class A address. Using the equation $2^{16} = 65536 - 2 = 65,534$ networks. In the previous example, 8 bits were used for hosts. Using the equation $2^8 = 256 - 2 = 254$ hosts. Table 3.1 lists the Class A subnets.

TABLE 3.1

CLASS A SUBNETS

# bits	Subnet Mask	# Subnets	# Hosts
2	255.192.0.0	2	4194302
3	255.224.0.0	6	2097150
4	255.240.0.0	14	1048574
5	255.248.0.0	30	524286
6	255.252.0.0	62	262142
7	255.254.0.0	126	131070
8	255.255.0.0	254	65534
9	255.255.128.0	510	32766
10	255.255.192.0	1022	16382

# bits	Subnet Mask	# Subnets	# Hosts
11	255.255.224.0	2046	8190
12	255.255.240.0	4094	4094
13	255.255.248.0	8190	2046
14	255.255.252.0	16382	1022
15	255.255.254.0	32766	510
16	255.255.255.0	65534	254
17	255.255.255.128	131070	126
18	255.255.255.192	262142	62
19	255.255.255.224	524286	30
20	255.255.255.240	1048574	14
21	255.255.255.248	2097150	6
22	255.255.255.252	4194302	2

Subnetting a Class B Address

Class B IP addresses have a default subnet mask of 255.255.0.0, or /16. Class B address space provides you with a great deal of flexibility in designing your network.

Suppose you have been given the IP address space 130.214.0.0. With this address space, you must subnet it to accommodate 487 offices with no more than 100 hosts per office. Look to the table of Class B subnets (see Table 3.2) and find the number of subnet bits required. You find that 9 bits of subnet mask allows for 510 subnets with 126 hosts per subnet. You can now divide the IP address space into the networks and assign them to different offices.

TABLE 3.2

CLASS B SUBNETS

# bits	Subnet Mask	# Subnets	# Hosts
2	255.255.192.0	2	16382
3	255.255.224.0	6	8190
4	255.255.240.0	14	4094

continues

TABLE 3.2

CLASS B SUBNETS

# bits	Subnet Mask	# Subnets	# Hosts
5	255.255.248.0	30	2046
6	255.255.252.0	62	1022
7	255.255.254.0	126	510
8	255.255.255.0	254	254
9	255.255.255.128	510	126
10	255.255.255.192	1022	62
11	255.255.255.224	2046	30
12	255.255.255.240	4094	14
13	255.255.255.248	8190	6
14	255.255.255.252	16382	2

Subnetting a Class C Address

By now, you should be getting the hang of this. This section takes you through the process of subnetting a Class C address.

Suppose your ISP (Internet service provider) has assigned a Class C IP address (199.250.155.0) for your office. However, you have five offices needing IP addresses reachable from the Internet. Each of the offices has 25 computers that will need IP addresses from this range. How do you subnet this? See Step by Step 3.1.

STEP BY STEP

3.1 Subnetting a Class C Address

1. You have a Class C IP address range. You must divide it into five subnets that allow for 25 hosts on each subnet. Can this be done? Look ahead to Table 3.3 to find a subnet mask that will support at least five networks and at least 25 hosts per network.

2. 255.255.255.224 allows for six networks with 30 hosts each. That will work. Now what are the six networks this subnet creates? You have subnetted using 3 bits. Write out the chart from converting binary to decimal and place the three bits in beneath the chart.

128	64	32	16	8	4	2	1
1	1	1	0	0	0	0	0

3. The last bit of subnet mask falls under the 32. Your first valid network will be 199.250.155.32. Because the network is represented by 199.250.155.32, the first valid IP address you can assign to a host is 199.250.155.33. Each network is 32 more. The number of hosts is equal to 32 minus 2.

4. Add 32 to 199.250.155.32 and you find the next network starts at 199.250.155.64. The following is a list of all the networks created by this subnet and the host addresses for each.

Subnet	Hosts	Broadcast
32	33–62	63
64	65–94	95
96	97–126	127
128	129–158	159
160	161–190	191
192	193–222	223

5. Now look at this octet of the address in binary. Notice the underlined bits in the following table. These bits are the three bits of a subnet. In the subnet column, notice each subnet is a unique combination of bits. In the hosts column, notice how when the subnet bits are discarded each range goes from 00001-11110. In the broadcast column, notice when the subnet bits are discarded, each broadcast address is 11111. It is much easier to see how subnetting works when you look at it in binary. However, we use IP addresses represented in decimal.

continues

continued

Subnet	Hosts	Broadcast
00100000	00100001–00111110	00111111
01000000	01000001–01011110	01011111
01100000	01100001–01111110	01111111
10000000	10000001–10011110	10011111
11000000	11000001–11011110	11011111

6. From the previous table, notice the underlined bits. These bits are the three bits of subnet. In the Subnet column, notice that each subnet is a unique combination of bits. In the Hosts column, notice how when the subnet bits are discarded, each range goes from 00001–11110. In the Broadcast column, notice that when the subnet bits are discarded, each broadcast address is 11111. It is much easier to see how subnetting works when you look at it in binary. However, we use IP addresses represented in decimal.

In looking at the two previous tables, you may wonder why 0–31 and 224–254 are not valid address ranges. To understand why, look at these two ranges in the following table.

Subnet	Hosts	Broadcast
0	1–30	31
00000000	00000001–00011110	00011111
224	225–254	255
11100000	11100001–11111110	11111111

Subnetting on byte boundaries is easy. However, when your subnet mask splits a byte boundary, as the previous example does, there are some rules. When a subnet splits an octet, the subnet bits in the partial octet cannot be all 1s or all 0s. This is why the two previous subnets are not valid.

TABLE 3.3

CLASS C SUBNETS

# bits	Subnet Mask	# Subnets	# Hosts
2	255.255.255.192	2	62
3	255.255.255.224	6	30
4	255.255.255.240	14	14
5	255.255.255.248	30	6
6	255.255.255.252	62	2

Subnet masks can be represented in a shorthand method. It is somewhat cumbersome to write out 199.250.155.35 255.255.255.0. Another way to represent the same subnet mask is 199.250.155.35/24. The /24 means 24 bits of network mask. Thus, if you added 3 bits of subnet mask to this address, it would be written 199.250.155.35/27. This shorthand method is used when Cisco routers display routing, as shown in the following example:

```
c3620r1#sh ip route
Codes: C - connected, S - static, I - IGRP, R - RIP, M -
➥mobile, B - BGP
       D - EIGRP, EX - EIGRP external, O - OSPF, IA - OSPF
➥inter area
       N1 - OSPF NSSA external type 1, N2 - OSPF NSSA
➥external type 2
       E1 - OSPF external type 1, E2 - OSPF external type
➥2, E - EGP
       i - IS-IS, L1 - IS-IS level-1, L2 - IS-IS level-2, *
➥- candidate default
       U - per-user static route, o - ODR

Gateway of last resort is 10.1.99.1 to network 0.0.0.0

D    192.168.104.0/24 [90/41689600] via 10.1.99.1, 1d20h,
➥BRI1/0
D    192.168.105.0/24 [90/41689600] via 10.1.99.1, 1d20h,
➥BRI1/0
D    192.168.106.0/24 [90/41689600] via 10.1.99.1, 1d20h,
➥BRI1/0
D    192.168.107.0/24 [90/41689600] via 10.1.99.1, 1d20h,
➥BRI1/0
D    192.168.108.0/24 [90/41689600] via 10.1.99.1,
➥07:26:06, BRI1/0
```

continues

continued

```
D    192.168.109.0/24 [90/41689600] via 10.1.99.1, 1w0d,
➥BRI1/0
D    192.168.110.0/24 [90/41689600] via 10.1.99.1, 1d11h,
➥BRI1/0
D    192.168.111.0/24 [90/41689600] via ➥10.1.99.1, 1w0d,
➥BRI1/0
```

Notice how in the preceding example the router shows the network mask in the /bits format.

Good Design Principles When Assigning IP Addresses

When you create IP subnets and assign them to offices, there are some principles you should follow to make life easier for your routers. When a router learns of a network, it places an entry for that network in its routing table with a pointer to the next hop to reach that network. If your network is hierarchical in design, you can help your router reduce the size of its routing tables.

Variable-Length Subnet Masking (VLSM)

Sometimes you may have a limited amount of address space and an odd combination of networks to use it on. Suppose that when you subnet a Class C address with a subnet mask of 255.255.255.240, you get 14 networks that can accommodate 14 hosts each. However, one of your locations has 15 hosts.

By creating different subnets using different subnet masks, you can make better use of address space—but at a cost. The price is complexity. Creating a VLSM network requires a great deal of planning and a strong understanding of subnetting and routing. Figure 3.4 shows how VLSM can be used in a network.

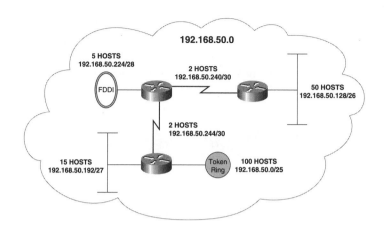

FIGURE 3.4
An example of how VLSM can be use to create different size networks from one Class C address space.

Classless InterDomain Routing (CIDR)

When the Internet began its explosion of growth, IP addresses became very scarce. To help keep from running out of IP addresses, and to make good use of the IP addresses available, *Classless InterDomain Routing (CIDR)* was created. CIDR allows multiple Class C addresses to be combined by supernetting the subnet mask.

Supernetting is accomplished by changing the network mask in the opposite direction of subnetting. Supernetting removes bits from the default subnet mask to create a larger network containing multiple Class C addresses.

For an organization that needs more than 254 IP addresses, a CIDR block can be assigned. By removing two subnet mask bits from the normal Class C subnet mask of 255.255.255.0, you get a subnet mask of 255.255.252.0. The list below shows the IP ranges that fall under this scheme.

192.34.128.0	Class C address
192.34.129.0	Class C address
192.34.130.0	Class C address
192.34.131.0	Class C address

192.34.128.0	Supernetted address
255.255.252.0	Subnet Mask for Supernet
192.34.131.255	Broadcast address for Supernet

By making use of Supernetting, Internet routers can be more efficient with routing table entries. Rather than having four entries for four different Class C IP address spaces, the routers can have one entry for the Supernet or CIDR block. More information on CIDR can be found in RFC1519.

Configuring IP Addresses

Now that you understand IP address classes and how to subnet, you need to apply these addresses to router interfaces.

To configure a router interface with an IP address, you use the interface configuration command IP address. The following is an example of how you would place an IP address on an interface:

```
c2513r1#config t
Enter configuration commands, one per line.  End with
➥CNTL/Z.
c2513r1(config)#int ethernet 0
c2513r1(config-if)#ip address 192.168.31.1 255.255.255.0
c2513r1(config-if)#exit
c2513r1(config)#exit
c2513r1#
```

This assigns the IP address 192.168.31.1 255.255.255.0 to interface Ethernet0 on the router.

In large enterprises where networks grow quickly, it is sometimes necessary to place more than one IP network on the same physical network. You can configure this by using secondary IP addresses on an interface. When a router interface is configured with multiple IP addresses, the router will forward traffic from one IP network to the other on the interface. Essentially, it will route traffic from one IP network to the other on the same physical network. To configure a secondary IP address on an interface, you add the secondary keyword to the IP address as shown following:

```
c2513r1#config t
Enter configuration commands, one per line.  End with
➥CNTL/Z.
c2513r1(config)#int ethernet 0
c2513r1(config-if)#ip address 192.168.32.1 255.255.255.0
➥secondary
c2513r1(config-if)#exit
c2513r1(config)#exit
c2513r1#wr
```

If you view a router configuration file with multiple IP addresses assigned to an interface, the interface configuration will resemble the following:

```
interface Ethernet0
  ip address 192.168.32.1 255.255.255.0 secondary
  ip address 192.168.31.1 255.255.255.0
```

Now that you understand IP addresses and how to subnet and verify that the IP subnets are valid, it is time to move on to some of the functions Cisco's IOS has for TCP/IP services.

TCP/IP OVERVIEW

Transmission Control Protocol/Internet Protocol (TCP/IP) delivers more data every day than any other protocol. TCP/IP was originally developed for use on the fledgling Internet by the United States Department of Defense. The design criteria for TCP/IP included the requirement for interoperability between different platforms. TCP/IP is the most widely supported protocol today. Almost every computer manufacturer, has implemented TCP/IP to some degree on their equipment. TCP/IP is not the fastest protocol. It's not the most efficient protocol. It's not even the easiest protocol to use. TCP/IP quite simply is the most widely available protocol for interconnecting different systems. The protocol is simple enough to be implemented in embedded systems like factory control devices. It is also complex enough to be the foundation of the largest network in the world, the Internet. One of TCP/IP's greatest assets is that it belongs to no one organization. Other protocols are driven by the needs and desires of companies. The development of SNA is almost exclusively in the hands of IBM. IPX is in the hands of Novell, and DecNET is now in the hands of Compaq since the company's acquisition of Digital Equipment Corporation.

TCP/IP is a suite of protocols that supports a vast array of services. In the suite, there are elements to support Layer 3 network connectivity and IP. TCP and UDP are Transport protocols (Layer 4). There are even Layer 7 application implementations such as Telnet. TCP/IP's greatest strength is its widespread availability and its ability to connect dissimilar computing systems in a manner that they can exchange data effectively.

At the Application layer, TCP/IP supports such services as file transfers (FTP), email delivery (SMTP and POP), remote login (Telnet and rlogin), network management (SNMP), and name resolution (DNS). These applications define a methodology for working together no matter on what platform they are implemented. This allows an IBM mainframe to exchange email with an Alpha-based Linux computer using SMTP. Figure 3.5 shows how the Application layer protocols fit into the OSI model.

FIGURE 3.5

Some of the application layer implementations of TCP/IP.

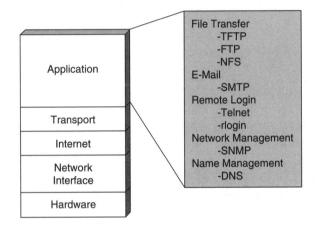

The Transport protocols (OSI Layer 4) of TCP/IP include TCP and UDP. Functions supported at the Transport layer include flow control and acknowledgments for data delivery. Figure 3.6 shows how the Transport protocols fit into the OSI model.

FIGURE 3.6

How the transport protocols fit into the OSI model.

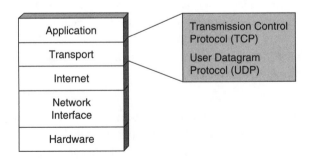

The following list describes the different transport protocols of the TCP/IP suite:

◆ TCP is a connection-oriented protocol that guarantees packet delivery using acknowledgments. When a packet is dropped, TCP is responsible for making sure it is re-sent. TCP is responsible for breaking messages into segments for transmission. After the segments arrive at the destination, TCP reassembles them. TCP creates a connection between networking stations before transferring data.

◆ UDP is a connectionless protocol that makes no guarantees about data delivery. UDP can transmit data faster than TCP because it does use acknowledgments. UDP does not break messages into segments—that function is handled by a different layer. Reliability is also the responsibility of another layer. Reliability can be handled by an Application layer protocol or by a reliable lower-layer protocol.

TCP connections include several steps. First the TCP protocol creates a connection. Then data is delivered. While data is being delivered, reliability information in the form of acknowledgments is sent. After all of the data is delivered, the connection is torn down. The process of creating a connection, using acknowledgments, and tearing down the connection makes TCP slower than UPD. However, TCP provides a quick, efficient, reliable connection.

UDP data transfer does not include the creation of a connection. UDP can start sending data immediately. However, there is no method for UDP to ensure that data makes it to the destination. UDP sends the data and assumes it arrives at the destination intact. For UDP transfers, another layer of the protocol must handle the function of reliable data delivery whether it be a lower layer or a higher layer.

TCP Segment Format

The TCP segment format supports several functions of the protocol. Figure 3.7 shows the format of a TCP segment.

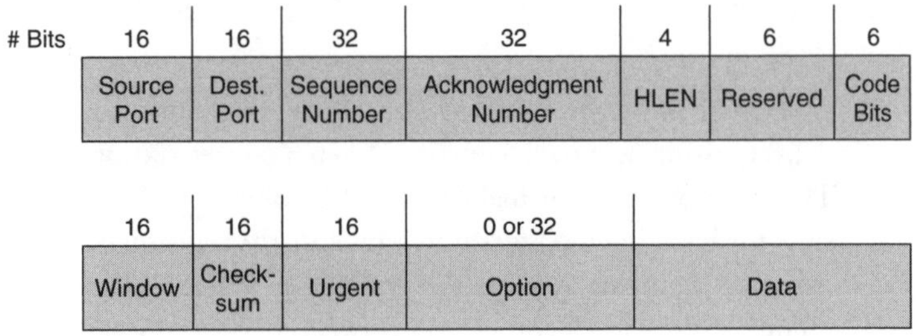

FIGURE 3.7
The TCP segment format.

Descriptions of the TCP segment are as follows:

◆ **Source Port.** The source port is the port number of the originating upper-layer protocol.

◆ **Destination Port.** The destination port is the port number of the destination upper-layer protocol port.

◆ **Sequence Number.** The sequence number is this segments position in the data stream.

◆ **Acknowledgment Number.** The acknowledgment number is the next expected TCP octet. This is used to guarantee reliable transfer of data.

◆ **HLEN.** The HLEN is the number of 32-bit words in the header of the segment. The HLEN indicates where the data begins.

◆ **Reserved.** This position is set to zero. This position is not used currently.

◆ **Code Bits.** The code bits are used for signaling. The code bits are used to indicate the creation of a connection and the termination of a connection.

◆ **Window.** The window defines the number of bytes or octets the receiver will accept before acknowledging.

◆ **Checksum.** The checksum is a calculated checksum of the header and data fields. It is used to determine whether the data sent is the data received.

◆ **Urgent Pointer.** The urgent pointer indicates the end of urgent data.

◆ **Option.** The option field currently has one use: to define the maximum TCP segment size.

◆ **Data.** The data field is filled with the data of the transmission. This data will be passed up to the layer above TCP at the destination network workstation.

Because TCP services many upper-level protocols, it must have some way to indicate which upper-layer protocol for which a message is intended. TCP uses port numbers for this purpose. *Port numbers* define which upper-layer protocol and perhaps even which session of an upper-layer protocol for which a message is intended. Some common port numbers are listed in the following table:

Port Number	Function
21	FTP
23	Telnet
25	SMTP
53	DNS
69	TFTP
80	HTTP
161	SNMP

TCP/IP Services

TCP/IP is an elegant protocol. After the basics are mastered, it is a very simple protocol to understand and configure. The TCP/IP protocol includes many different implementations of protocols to solve the problem of connecting computers. The following are of some of the protocols and their functions:

◆ **Internet Protocol (IP).** The Layer 3 (Network) protocol of the suite. Used for communication at the network layer of the OSI model.

◆ **Address Resolution Protocol (ARP).** Used to map IP addresses to MAC addresses.

◆ **Transmission Control Protocol (TCP).** A Layer 4 protocol. TCP provides guaranteed data delivery.

◆ **User Datagram Protocol (UDP).** A Layer 4 protocol. UDP does not guarantee data delivery.

◆ **Internet Control Message Protocol (ICMP).** Provides diagnostic information about the protocol suite. Most people are familiar with the diagnostic utility ping. *Ping* provides a means of confirming network connectivity between two stations. Ping is an implementation of ICMP. (Today it is best to specify an ICMP ping because many other protocols now support ping in their implementations. Novell has added ping to IPX. IBM has even added some ping-like functions to SNA.)

◆ **Telnet.** An Application layer implementation of a program that allows remote terminal access to a device. For internetworking engineers, Telnet is often used to log in to routers.

◆ **File Transfer Protocol (FTP).** Allows stations to transfer files from one to another. FTP used TCP packets to guarantee data delivery.

◆ **Trivial File Transfer Protocol (TFTP).** A file transfer implementation. It differs from FTP in that it uses UDP packets to deliver its data; hence, it does not guarantee delivery of data.

◆ **Simple Mail Transfer Protocol (SMTP).** An email implementation that delivers mail from network to network or from user to user within one domain. SMTP is used throughout the Internet for delivery of millions of emails daily.

◆ **Post Office Protocol (POP3).** An email implementation that allows users to connect with the system that receives their email and download that email to their computers. POP is used by millions of users everyday to get email from their ISP. Programs that can use POP include Eudora Pro, Outlook, Pegasus Mail, and the email portion of most browsers.

◆ **Network Time Protocol (NTP).** Used to synchronize the clocks of networking computers. NTP is typically used to synchronize your system's clock with one of the very accurate time sources available on the Internet. Cisco routers support NTP and can be configured to synchronize their clocks. This can be very helpful when diagnosing problems.

◆ **HyperText Transfer Protocol (HTTP).** The protocol that Netscape Navigator uses to talk with Web servers. Your browser uses HTTP to download HTML from Web servers and display the information on your screen.

◆ **Domain Name System (DNS).** Used to map domain names like www.cisco.com to IP addresses. When you type the name of a site you want to visit in your browser, the first thing the computer does is resolve that name to an IP address using DNS. After the IP address is found, it is passed to the IP stack, and HTTP is used to communicate with the Web server. Without DNS, you would have to remember IP addresses instead of domain names. DNS makes life much easier.

◆ **Simple Network Managment Protocol (SNMP).** Used to gather statistics from networking devices for monitoring and reporting. Most networking monitoring software, such as Cisco Works, use SNMP to gather information.

Each of these protocols serves a purpose in the overall data communication between networking stations. As new needs arise, protocols are updated or expanded to accommodate these new needs. Therefore, it is very important to stay abreast of changes in networking technologies.

Host Name-to-IP Address Mapping

Computers are content using IP addresses to communicate. Names really mean very little to a computer. However, human users prefer to address network stations by names that indicate something about the stations. For instance, would you rather remember 192.31.7.130 or www.cisco.com? www.cisco.com is much more meaningful to you isn't it? For networking to function well for both human users and computers, there must be a way to map names like www.cisco.com to IP addresses like 192.31.7.130. On the Internet, this is done with *Domain Name Server (DNS)*.

Domain Name Server (DNS)

The inner workings of DNS are beyond the scope of this book. However, using DNS is something you will need to do often in internetworking. In most places in which you are required to enter a network station address, either the IP address or the name is acceptable. For instance, ping 192.31.7.130 is equivalent to ping www.cisco.com.

The latter requires the router to resolve the name www.cisco.com to the IP address 192.31.7.130 before performing the ping. If everything is configured properly, this resolution of the name happens very quickly.

If you have not configured any name to IP address mapping and you attempt to use a hostname in place of an IP address the following will occur:

```
ACS-2500#ping www.cisco.com
Translating "www.cisco.com"
% Unrecognized host or address, or protocol not running.

ACS-2500#
```

Cisco's IOS has different ways to map names to IP addresses. If your organization makes use of DNS, you can configure your routers to use this DNS to resolve names to IP addresses. To turn this on in the router, you use the ip name-server command to identify the DNS machine to the router. This is the machine that provides the DNS service. You must also turn on domain lookup in the router. This is done with the command ip domain-lookup.

The following example shows how to configure the DNS server in the router's configuration:

```
ACS-2500#config t
Enter configuration commands, one per line.  End with
➥CNTL/Z.
ACS-2500(config)#ip name-server 155.229.1.69
ACS-2500(config)#ip domain-lookup
ACS-2500(config)#exit
```

Now that the name server is configured and domain lookup is enabled, the same command that failed before will work:

```
ACS-2500#ping www.cisco.com

Type escape sequence to abort.
Sending 5, 100-byte ICMP Echoes to 192.31.7.130, timeout is
➥2 seconds:
!!!!!
Success rate is 100 percent (5/5), round-trip min/avg/max =
➥92/99/108 ms
ACS-2500#
```

When the router performs a DNS lookup, it caches the information for future use. You can view the contents of the cache with the show hosts command.

```
ACS-2500#sh hosts
Default domain is not set
Name/address lookup uses domain service
Name servers are 155.229.1.5, 155.229.1.69
```

```
Host                    Flags      Age Type   Address(es)
www.kmahler.com         (temp, OK)  0  IP     199.250.137.37
cio-sys.cisco.com       (temp, OK)  0  IP     192.31.7.130
  www.cisco.com
ACS-2500#
```

This shows each of the domain names cached in the router. Notice that the router reports that the Default domain is not set. The default domain is the domain in which the router resides. The router can provide a shortcut to accessing stations within its domain. If you set the default domain in the router, it will then append this default domain to any name that is not fully entered. If you wanted to ping `kestrel.kmahler.com` and the default domain name `kmahler.com` was defined in the router with the name server set along with domain name lookup on, the router will be able to identify that station with just `kestrel`.

This router has been configured with a name server and IP domain lookup has been turned on.

```
c3620r1#ping kestrel.kmahler.com
Translating "kestrel.kmahler.com"...domain server
➥(199.250.137.37) [OK]

Type escape sequence to abort.
Sending 5, 100-byte ICMP Echos to 199.250.137.34, timeout
➥is 2 seconds:
!!!!!
Success rate is 100 percent (5/5), round-trip min/avg/max =
➥1/4/8 ms
c3620r1#
```

Now try it without the full name. Try pinging just `kestrel`":

```
c3620r1#ping kestrel
Translating "kestrel"...domain server (199.250.137.37)
% Unrecognized host or address, or protocol not running.

c3620r1#
```

Now turn set the default domain name in the router:

```
c3620r1#config t
Enter configuration commands, one per line.  End with
➥CNTL/Z.
c3620r1(config)#ip domain-name kmahler.com
c3620r1(config)#exit
c3620r1#
```

Now try pinging `kestrel` again:

```
c3620r1#ping kestrel
```

continues

continued

```
Type escape sequence to abort.
Sending 5, 100-byte ICMP Echos to 199.250.137.34, timeout
➥is 2 seconds:
!!!!!
Success rate is 100 percent (5/5), round-trip min/avg/max =
➥1/2/4 ms
c3620r1#
```

The router automatically added .kmahler.com to the name. This produced kestrel.kmahler.com, which was then resolved with DNS to the IP address 199.250.137.34 and the ping was successful.

Because the router keeps prior name resolutions cached for some time, it is possible that the IP address of a network station can change and the router will have the wrong IP address cached. You can force the router to clear its name cache with the clear host command. With this command, you can specify a specific host to clear, or you can use the wildcard (*) to clear all name-to-IP address mappings:

```
c3620r1#sh host
Default domain is kmahler.com
Name/address lookup uses domain service
Name servers are 199.250.137.37
```

```
Host                    Flags      Age Type  Address(es)
www.kmahler.com         (temp, OK)  0   IP    199.250.137.37
linux.kmahler.com       (temp, OK)  0   IP    199.250.137.55
kestrel.kmahler.com     (temp, OK)  0   IP    199.250.137.34
c3620r1#
```

To clear an individual host mapping, use the clear host with the host name specified:

```
c3620r1#clear host kestrel.kmahler.com
c3620r1#sh host
Default domain is kmahler.com
Name/address lookup uses domain service
Name servers are 199.250.137.37
```

```
Host                    Flags      Age Type  Address(es)
www.kmahler.com         (temp, OK)  0   IP    199.250.137.37
linux.kmahler.com       (temp, OK)  0   IP    199.250.137.55
c3620r1#
```

Now if you attempt to ping kestrel.kmahler.com again, the router will resolve the name instead of using the cache. If the DNS has been updated with the new IP address, the ping will be successful.

To clear all name to IP address mappings use the wildcard "(*)":

```
c3620r1#sh host
Default domain is kmahler.com
Name/address lookup uses domain service
Name servers are 199.250.137.37
```

```
Host                    Flags       Age Type  Address(es)
kestrel.kmahler.com     (temp, OK)  0   IP    199.250.137.34
www.kmahler.com         (temp, OK)  0   IP    199.250.137.37
linux.kmahler.com       (temp, OK)  0   IP    199.250.137.55
c3620r1#clear host *
c3620r1#sh host
```

```
Default domain is kmahler.com
Name/address lookup uses domain service
Name servers are 199.250.137.37
```

```
Host                    Flags       Age Type  Address(es)
c3620r1#
```

Because there is not always a DNS available, Cisco has provided another method of mapping host names to IP addresses. *Static name mappings* can be made part of the router's configuration.

Static Name Mappings

Not every organization is connected to the Internet or is running DNS. Cisco has provided a method for mapping your host names to IP addresses as well. IOS provides a way to enter host names and IP mappings directly in the router's configuration. Using these static mappings, you can enter commonly used network hosts and reference them by the name you assign. In a router without an IP name server configured and IP domain lookup disabled, try to ping the hostname kestrel.

```
c3620r1#ping kestrel
Translating "kestrel"
% Unrecognized host or address, or protocol not running.

c3620r1#
```

The router has no way to resolve the name to an IP address. To create a static host mapping in the router's configuration, use the command ip host. The following is an example to map the name kestrel to the IP address 199.250.137.34:

```
c3620r1#config t
Enter configuration commands, one per line.  End with
➡CNTL/Z.
c3620r1(config)#ip host kestrel 199.250.137.34
c3620r1(config)#exit
```

After assigning this hostname to the IP address, try to ping the host again.

```
c3620r1#ping kestrel

Type escape sequence to abort.
Sending 5, 100-byte ICMP Echos to 199.250.137.34, timeout
➡is 2 seconds:
!!!!!
Success rate is 100 percent (5/5), round-trip min/avg/max =
4/4/4 ms
c3620r1#
```

The router can now resolve the name kestrel to the IP address 199.250.137.34. Performing the show host command displays the following:

```
c3620r1#sh host
Default domain is not set
Name/address lookup uses static mappings
```

Host	Flags	Age	Type	Address(es)
kestrel	(perm, OK)	0	IP	199.250.137.34
c3620r1#				

REVIEW BREAK

Host Name-to-IP Address Mapping Review

▶ To make life easier for human users, computers provide a method of mapping meaningful names to IP addresses.

▶ One very common way to do this is with Domain Name Servers (DNS).

▶ Cisco's IOS supports DNS by configuring the name server's IP address with the command ip name-server and turning on domain lookup with the command ip domain-lookup.

▶ You can provide a default domain name with the ip domain-name command. The router will append this default domain name to any abbreviated name entered. If the entire name is entered, the router does not append the default domain name.

- ▶ Name resolutions are cached in the router.

- ▶ You can view the cached names with the command `show host`.

- ▶ If you have a need to clear a cached name resolution, you can use the command `clear host`.

- ▶ In the event that you are not running DNS, you can statically map names to IP addresses in the router's configuration file. The command `ip host` is used to create these mappings.

Internet Control Message Protocol (ICMP)

Internet Control Message Protocol (ICMP) is responsible for reporting messages and errors at the Network layer of the TCP/IP protocol suite. Many people use ICMP every day when they perform the most basic IP diagnostic tool: Ping.

Using the `ping` Command

Ping is actually an acronym for Packet INternet Groper. Ping provides a very basic diagnostic to confirm that one network station can communicate on a Network level with another network station. Ping sends an ICMP echo packet to the destination network station. If it arrives at the destination, the destination echoes the packet back to the sender. In reporting this information, Ping also supplies information about how long it took for a packet to make a round trip from the source station to the destination station.

Cisco routers support Ping from the IOS Command Line Interface (CLI). Cisco's implementation of Ping supports some unusual options.

At its basic level, Ping allows you to specify a network station to ping and then it reports its success or failure. Following is an example of a ping from a Cisco router:

```
c3620r1#ping 199.250.136.10

Type escape sequence to abort.
Sending 5, 100-byte ICMP Echos to 199.250.136.10, timeout
➥is 2 seconds:
```

continues

continued

```
!!!!!
Success rate is 100 percent (5/5), round-trip min/avg/max =
36/70/196 ms
c3620r1#
```

In the previous example, the ping command was entered with an IP address to attempt Layer 3 communication with the destination device. The router then sent five (the default number) pings to the destination station. With each ping, the router reports the success or failure of the ping.

◆ An exclamation point (!) indicates a successful ping.

◆ A period (.) indicates a failure.

◆ The letter "U" indicates that the destination is unreachable.

◆ The ampersand (&) indicates that the Time To Live (TTL) was exceeded.

The router then reports the success rate in percentage and fraction. It also reports the minimum, average, and maximum times it took for a ping packet to make the round trip from the source station to the destination and back.

As mentioned before, Cisco's implementation of Ping supports some options not available in many other implementations. A ping packet contains a source IP address and a destination IP address. Because two stations communicating properly is often a function of the source address, and routers generally have many IP addresses, Cisco's Ping allows you to specify the source address.

Cisco calls this the *extended ping*. The extended ping is available only in the privileged exec mode. Entering the ping command without an address accesses options for the extended ping. The CLI will then prompt you for several options including the target IP address. One of the prompts will ask if you would like Extended Commands. Answer Yes to this question to enter other options. One of these options is the source IP address. After you complete the options, the router will attempt to ping the destination IP address using the source IP address you specified.

```
c3620r1#ping
Protocol [ip]:
Target IP address: 19.250.138.1
Repeat count [5]:
```

```
Datagram size [100]:
Timeout in seconds [2]:
Extended commands [n]: y
Source address or interface: 65.64.176.1
Type of service [0]:
Set DF bit in IP header? [no]:
Validate reply data? [no]:
Data pattern [0xABCD]:
Loose, Strict, Record, Timestamp, Verbose[none]:
Sweep range of sizes [n]:
Type escape sequence to abort.
Sending 5, 100-byte ICMP Echos to 19.250.138.1, timeout is
➥2 seconds:
!!!!!
Success rate is 100 percent (5/5), round-trip min/avg/max =
➥32/32/36 ms
c3620r1#
```

Again, the `ping` command reports the success or failure of the ping and the round-trip times for the ping packets.

> **NOTE**
>
> **Ping is limited** IP Ping is very useful for determining whether two network stations can successfully communicate at the Layer 3 protocol. Do not attempt to use the information provided by Ping to make other assessments of the network. Trying to use ping times to determine bandwidth or some other aspect of the network is fruitless.
>
> Ping determines if two stations can communicate at the Network layer—that is all.

Using the `traceroute` Command

Traceroute shows the path from one end of the connection to the other, listing each hop along the way. *Hop* is a term used to describe each router a packet passes thorough to reach its destination. The following example shows a traceroute from a router to Cisco's Web site. Notice that the actual URL is used rather than the IP address. This can be done because this router has an IP domain-server defined in the configuration.

```
Router#traceroute www.cisco.com

Type escape sequence to abort.
Tracing the route to cio-sys.cisco.com (192.31.7.130)

  1 cisco_2500_t1.cancer.org (199.250.136.10) 0 msec 0 msec 4 msec
  2 s0.atl514.gw.eni.net (155.229.99.229) 8 msec 4 msec 4 msec
  3 fe1-0.atl100.gw.eni.net (155.229.0.1) 4 msec 4 msec 4 msec
  4 H3-1-0.dca100.gw.eni.net (155.229.120.130) 180 msec 76 msec 16 msec
  5 f1-0.maeeast.BBNPLANET.net (192.41.177.2) 20 msec 20 msec 24 msec
  6 p2-2.vienna1-nbr2.BBNPLANET.net (4.0.1.93) 24 msec 20 msec 20 msec
  7 p1-0.vienna1-nbr3.BBNPLANET.net (4.0.5.46) 24 msec 24 msec 20 msec
  8 p3-1.paloalto-nbr2.BBNPLANET.net (4.0.3.178) 100 msec 100 msec 100 msec
  9 p0-0-0.paloalto-cr18.BBNPLANET.net (4.0.3.86) 104 msec 96 msec 104 msec
 10 h1-0.cisco.BBNPLANET.net (131.119.26.10) 100 msec 124 msec 100 msec
 11 sty.CISCO.com (192.31.7.39) 100 msec 104 msec 100 msec
 12 cio-sys.cisco.com (192.31.7.130) 100 msec *  100 msec
Router#
```

Want to find the travel path? To determine where in the United States your packets are traveling, look at the names returned. Not all Internet backbones support this, but most use the three letter abbreviation for the major airport near the area of the network facility. In the previous example, two are shown: ATL refers to Atlanta Hartsfield Airport, and DCA is National Airport in Washington, D.C. A list of these abbreviations can be found at gopher://wiretap.spies.com/00/Library/Article/Aero/airport.lis.

Each hop along the way is listed with the times required for each of three probes to return. The name for each hop is the second item listed on each line. For example, the name for the 11th hop is sty.CISCO.com. In the previous example, the router used had an IP domain-server defined in the configuration. This allows the router to use DNS to resolve names to IP addresses and IP addresses to names. For each hop in this example the name is found.

Because Traceroute shows the path between two network stations, it can be very useful for discovering routing problems. When Traceroute reaches a router and fails to go any further, the connectivity problem is usually just beyond the last router Traceroute was able to successfully reach.

Traceroute provides some other feedback as well. Responses, other than times for probes, can indicate other types of problems:

!H Indicates that the probe was received by a router but not forwarded. This is generally due to an access list filtering the packet.

P Indicates that the protocol was unreachable.

N Indicates that the network was unreachable.

U Indicates that the port was unreachable.

* Indicates that a timeout occurred.

Traceroute is a very useful tool when trying to diagnose connectivity problems. Whereas Ping only lets you know whether you have connectivity, Traceroute lets you know what path the packets are taking and where in the path a failure is occurring.

Remote Access Using Telnet

As an internetworking engineer, you will use Telnet on a regular basis. Telnet defines a protocol for remote access. After you have initially configured a router using the serial port, you will most likely access that router using Telnet for future changes and additions.

Telnet is available on most any computer system. Most every version of UNIX has a Telnet client available. Windows 95, 98, and NT all have Telnet clients. However, the Windows implementations of Telnet are very slow. Get a good Telnet client that is fast and supports large scroll back buffers and macros. You will be surprised how much typing a simple terminal macro can save you.

A very good implementation of Telnet is included with Datastorm Technologies' Procomm Plus 32.

The Telnet protocol is an Application layer implementation of a TCP/IP protocol. Because Cisco routers support Telnet from both a connection side as well as a client side, Telnet can be used to confirm network connectivity all the way to the Application layer.

Successfully telnetting from one router to another confirms that you have network connectivity on all seven layers of the OSI model. If you are unable to telnet, try to ping the remote router. If that is successful, the problem is most likely above the Network layer of the OSI model. However, if your ping is unsuccessful, try a traceroute to find where the connection is lost.

From the IOS CLI, you can telnet to a device by entering the command `telnet 192.168.1.1`.

```
c3620r1#telnet 199.250.137.50
Trying 199.250.137.50 ... Open
This router was replaced 1/09/99

User Access Verification

Password:
```

Because Telnet is such a common utility, Cisco has provided a shortcut. By entering an IP address directly on the command line without any command, the router will initiate a Telnet connection to the other device:

```
c3620r1#199.250.137.50
Trying 199.250.137.50 ... Open
This router was replaced 1/09/99

User Access Verification

Password:
```

If you mistype a command at the command prompt, the route will try to resolve it as a host name and try to telnet to it. This can actually become somewhat of a nuisance because internetworking engineers are not necessarily great typists. The following example shows the command `sh run` without a space. The router tries to resolve the name "shrun" with the DNS, which is not configured. After a lengthy delay waiting for the router to timeout looking for the DNS, the router reports that it is unable to resolve the name.

```
c3620r1#shrun
Translating "shrun"...domain server (255.255.255.255)
% Unknown command or computer name, or unable to find
computer address
c3620r1#
```

If you have DNS configured and the server is responsive, the router responds very quickly with the failure. When you are not running DNS, however, the router will take a long time to report the failure. To reduce the annoyance, you can disable domain lookup in the router.

To turn off domain name resolution in the router, use the command no ip domain-lookup. This is a global configuration command:

```
c3620r1#config terminal
c3620r1(config)#no ip domain-lookup
c3620r1(config)#exit
c3620r1#copy running-config startup-config
```

Now that domain lookup is disabled, it will no longer try to resolve the name to an IP address. The following example shows how this speeds up the router reporting back that you entered an incorrect command:

```
c3620r1#shrun
Translating "shrun"
% Unknown command or computer name, or unable to find
computer address
c3620r1#
```

The router did not try to resolve the name to an IP address and thus reported immediately that your typing skills could use some polishing.

CASE STUDY: INTERNET IP ADDRESS

ESSENCE OF THE CASE

Here are the essential elements in this case:

▶ Your job is to subnet the IP address space assigned to your company in such a way that each office will have enough IP addresses for all of their networking devices and allow for the future addition of another office.

SCENARIO

You are the network guru for Emotion Cybernetics, a robotics company that makes robots with human emotions. Your company has decided to get Internet service for the entire company. Emotion Cybernetics currently has four offices but has plans to soon open another. All of the offices are connected via a Frame Relay WAN.

CASE STUDY: INTERNET IP ADDRESS

▶ Your company currently has four offices and expects to open another soon.

▶ The largest number of network devices in an office is 25. There is little expected growth of this number.

▶ You have been assigned the IP address range 63.250.143.1–63.250.143.254.

Your building (the main office) will be getting a T1 to the Internet. You want to allow the people in your remote offices to access the Internet over the WAN and through your T1. The Internet service provider (ISP) has assigned you one Class A address with a 24-bit subnet mask (63.250.143.0/24). Your largest office has 25 networked devices installed and does not expect any substantial growth in the number of devices.

ANALYSIS

You start by writing out the bit positions for the last octet of the IP range.

128	64	32	16	8	4	2	1

Remembering the method of determining the number of workstations in a subnet, you determine that 3 bits of subnet mask will give you 30 workstations per subnet.

128	64	32	16	8	4	2	1
1	1	1					

3 subnet bits puts you in the position of the decimal number 32. This will give you 30 usable IP addresses per subnet.

Now you check whether this subnet will provide the necessary number of subnetworks. You begin by writing out the ranges of addresses for each subnet. Because your last subnet bit falls in the position of 32, your first usable network range begins at 32. Each following IP range begins at the last network + 32.

Network	First IP Address	Last IP Address
63.250.143.0	63.250.143.1	63.250.143.31 Invalid
63.250.143.32	63.250.143.33	63.250.143.62

continues

CASE STUDY: INTERNET IP ADDRESS

63.250.143.64	63.250.143.65	63.250.143.94
63.250.143.96	63.250.143.97	63.250.143.126
63.250.143.128	63.250.143.129	63.250.143.158
63.250.143.160	63.250.143.161	63.250.143.190
63.250.143.192	63.250.143.193	63.250.143.222
63.250.143.224	63.250.143.225	63.250.143.254 Invalid

Looking at the subnets this creates, you find that you have six valid ranges, each with 30 usable IP addresses. This subnetting scheme will accommodate the needs of Emotion Cybernetics.

CHAPTER SUMMARY

KEY TERMS

- IP address
- Network mask
- subnet
- Class A IP address
- Class B IP address
- Class C IP address
- multicast
- DNS
- MAC address
- secondary IP address

This chapter covers IP addressing and subnetting. Understanding how IP addresses work and how to create subnets is important in any internetworking engineer's daily tasks. Because IP is quickly becoming the standard protocol for most businesses, a thorough understanding of how this protocol's addressing works is important.

Along with IP addressing, this chapter covered some of the IP services Cisco's IOS provides. Configuring DNS on a router allows the router to perform name resolution for IP addresses. This can be helpful when diagnosing problems.

Review Questions

1. What are the classes of IP addresses?

2. What is the equation for determining the number of subnets or the number of hosts based on the number of bits in the subnet mask?

3. What are some of the functions of ICMP?

4. What does the subnet mask define?

5. How does a router use the IP address and subnet mask to determine how to forward a packet?

6. Which class of IP address allows the greatest number of hosts per network?

7. What are the numbers you should remember for subnetting IP networks?

8. What are the rules for a binary AND function?

9. Briefly describe TCP and UDP.

10. What is the function of DNS?

Exam Questions

1. What is the proper equation for finding the number of networks or hosts that a subnet mask allows?

    A. $2^n - 2$

    B. $2 - n \times 2$

    C. $255 - n\char94 2$

    D. $n*2 - 2$

2. Which of the following is a valid IP address for a host computer?

    A. 192.168.45.32 netmask 255.255.255.224

    B. 192.168.45.159 netmask 255.255.255.224

    C. 192.168.45.169 netmask 255.255.255.252

    D. 192.168.45.167 netmask 255.255.255.252

3. What command will show the host mappings in a router?

    A. `Router#show mapping`

    B. `Router(config)#show host`

    C. `Router#map host`

    D. `Router#show host`

4. How many networks and hosts will the subnet mask 255.255.255.224 allow on a Class C IP address?

    A. 30 networks with six hosts each

    B. 32 networks with eight hosts each

    C. Six networks with 30 hosts each

    D. Eight networks with 32 hosts each

5. What IOS command shows the path IP packets travel to reach a destination?

    A. `ping`

    B. `tracert`

    C. `pong`

    D. `traceroute`

6. Which of the following is valid?

    A. `Router(config-if)#ip address 199.250.137.63 255.255.255.224`

    B. `Router(config)#ip address 199.250.137.63 255.255.255.224`

    C. `Router(config-if)#ip address 199.250.137.98 255.255.255.224`

APPLY YOUR KNOWLEDGE

D. `Router(config-if)#ip address`
`199.250.137.63 255.255.255.224`

7. Which command will clear the router's host mapping table without any other input?

    A. `Router#clear host`

    B. `Router#clear host *`

    C. `Router#clear host mapping table`

    D. `Router#clear mapping`

8. Which of the following is a valid static IP hostname mapping?

    A. `Router#ip host computername 192.168.1.1`

    B. `Router(config)#ip host computername 192.168.1.1`

    C. `Router(config)#ip hostname computername 192.168.1.1`

    D. `Router(config)>ip host computername 192.168.1.1`

9. Which of the following best describes the following two IP addresses?

    192.168.1.0 netmask 255.255.255.0

    192.168.1.255 netmask 255.255.255.0

    A. Class A addresses, valid IP addresses for workstations

    B. Class A addresses, invalid IP addresses for workstations

    C. Class C addresses, valid IP addresses for workstations

    D. Class C addresses, invalid IP addresses for workstations.

10. Which of the following are private network ranges that are not routed on the Internet? Select three.

    A. 10.0.0.0

    B. 199.168.0.0

    C. 192.168.0.0

    D. 172.16.0.0

Answers to Review Questions

1. There are five classes of IP addresses. Class A, B, and C are used for assigning to computers and routers. Class D addresses are used for multicast, and Class E addresses are for experimental use. For more information, see "IP Addresses."

2. $2^n - 2$. For more information, see "IP Addresses."

3. ICMP provides echo services for the Ping diagnostic. It also sends source quench messages when a device is being overrun. ICMP is also responsible for sending host unreachable packets. For more information, see "TCP/IP Services."

4. The subnet mask separates the two parts of an IP address: the network and the host address. For more information, see "IP Addresses."

5. The router ANDs the network mask to the IP address to get the network portion of the IP address. The router then tries to find the network in its routing tables. If the network is found, the router forwards the packet. For more information, see "IP Addresses."

6. Class A IP addresses allow the greatest number of hosts per network. For more information, see "IP Addresses."

APPLY YOUR KNOWLEDGE

7. 128, 192, 224, 240, 248, 252, 254, 255. These numbers represent an octet filled from the right to left with bits. For more information, see "Subnetting IP Address Ranges."

8. 1 AND 1 = 1; 1 AND 0 = 0; 0 AND 0 = 0. For more information, see "Binary Math."

9. TCP and UDP are both Layer 4 Transport protocols. TCP provides a connection-oriented link. It also provides reliable data transmission and guaranteed delivery of data using acknowledgments. UDP provides a connectionless link and does not provide any guarantee of delivery. For more information, see "TCP/IP Services."

10. DNS is Domain Name Server. It provides a method of mapping meaningful names to IP addresses, and vice versa. For more information, see "TCP/IP Services."

Answers to Exam Questions

1. **A.** The proper equation for finding the number of subnets or the number of hosts a subnet mask will support is $2^n - 2$. For more information, see "Subnetting IP Address Ranges."

2. **C.** 192.168.45.169 netmask 255.255.255.252 is the only valid IP address. All of the others are either network addresses (all host bits set to zero) or broadcast addresses (all host bits set to one). For more information, see "IP Addresses."

3. **D.** The `show host` command displays a table of host mappings, both static and dynamic. For more information, see "TCP/IP Services."

4. **C.** The subnet mask 255.255.255.224 on a Class C IP address allows for six networks with 30 hosts each. For more information, see "Subnetting IP Address Ranges."

5. **D.** `traceroute` is the proper command for finding the path that packets take to reach a destination. For more information, see "TCP/IP Services."

6. **C.** The other answers have invalid IP addresses or the router prompts are incorrect. For more information, see "IP Addresses."

7. **B.** `clear host *` clears the host mapping tables. For more information, see "Host Name to IP Address Mapping."

8. **B.** `ip host computername 192.168.1.1` is the proper syntax for defining static hostname mappings. For more information, see "Static Name Mappings."

9. **D.** The IP addresses fall in the range of Class C IP addresses. They are also not valid IP addresses for workstations because 192.168.1.0 describes the network and 192.168.1.255 is the broadcast address for the network. For more information, see "IP Addresses."

10. **A, C, D.** 10.0.0.0, 192.168.0.0, and 172.16.0.0 are private networks that are not routed on the Internet. For more information, see "IP Addresses."

Suggested Readings and Resources

1. Chappell, Laura. *Introduction to Cisco Router Configuration,* Cisco Press, 1998.

2. Albitz, Paul, et al. *DNS and BIND*, O'Reilly, 1998.

Cisco provides the following objectives for the IPX/SPX portion of the CCNA exam:

Monitor Novell IPX operation on the router.

▶ You must be able to monitor Novell's IPX protocol on the router to successfully maintain networks using this protocol. Novell network problems can be difficult to diagnose. Making use of the monitoring tools in the router can aid in discovering what is happening and why.

Describe the two parts of network addressing, then identify the parts in specific protocol address examples.

▶ To successfully maintain internetworking systems, you must understand the two parts of network addressing so that you can effectively determine how routing of traffic will occur.

List the required IPX address and encapsulation types.

▶ Understanding IPX address and encapsulation types is necessary to maintain internetworking systems because many problems occur regarding the encapsulation types.

Enable the Novell IPX protocol and configure interfaces.

▶ In order to maintain internetworking systems, you must be able to configure and enable Novell IPX protocol on Cisco routers.

CHAPTER 4

Understanding and Configuring IPX/SPX and Other Network Protocols

Configure IPX access lists and SAP filters to control basic Novell traffic.

▶ Novell traffic can produce a large amount of network traffic. Understanding how to filter SAPs and control the protocol is essential for internetworking engineers. Novell networks generate a large number of broadcasts to advertise services. By making use of access lists, you can limit which services will be advertised. This can be beneficial for both reducing the bandwidth impact and for securing networks from unauthorized use.

OUTLINE

▶ The network protocols portion of the CCNA test is perhaps the most important for which to study. Network protocols make up the pieces of the whole. The two networking protocols you are required to understand for the CCNA exam are IPX and TCP/IP. These two are the most used in today's networks. TCP/IP is quickly becoming the standard of many companies, and many would argue it already is a standard. It scales well. This is proven by the success of the largest WAN to date, the Internet.

Learn Novell's types of encapsulation and how they relate to Cisco's encapsulation types. Learn to recognize Novell network addresses.

Understand how each of these network protocols is configured on the router and how to perform simple diagnostics.

Spend time working with the protocols on real networks. Learn to solve real problems with IPX networks.

INTRODUCTION

Novell's IPX protocol has been the foundation of many networks for years. IPX is small and fast. It has delivered much data since its introduction. Novell introduced IPX in the 1980s. IPX was based on networking technology developed at Xerox.

Novell has recognized that the world is becoming an IP-based world. In release 5.0 of Novell's networking operating system, they have included IP as a native protocol. IPX is still available for compatibility with existing systems.

Although Novell is moving toward IP-based networks, IPX is installed in many organizations and will be around for many more years.

Novell IPX/SPX Protocol

Like other protocols, Novell's IPX has portions of the protocol that fit into the OSI layers (see Figure 4.1).

FIGURE 4.1
The layers of the IPX protocol and OSI model.

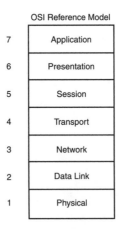
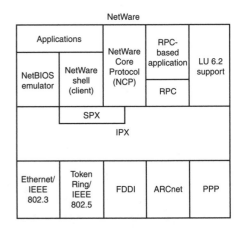

IPX includes functions at layers three and four of the OSI model. Thus it is responsible for determining the routing of network traffic. Novell's implementation includes two routing protocols: RIP and NLSP.

Internet Packet eXchange (IPX)

Internet Packet eXchange (IPX) is the Layer 3 protocol in the Novell
suite. It is a connectionless protocol like TCP/IP's IP protocol.
There are no acknowledgments and no guarantees of data delivery.
Like TCP's ports, IPX uses sockets to communicate with upper-layer
protocols and applications. An IPX network address consists of two
parts: a network number and a node number. The network administrator assigns the IPX network number. The network number is up
to eight hexadecimal digits (32 bits, or 4 bytes) long. The node
number is usually the MAC address for the network interface and is
twelve hexadecimal digits (48 bits, or 6 bytes) in length. When an
IPX network address is displayed in a Cisco router, it is displayed
with the network number first, a period, and then the MAC address
with periods every two bytes. 3485BA61.0000.0000.0001 is an
example of an IPX address. This example address is actually a server.
When the network number has leading zeros, the zeros are not displayed. In the case of network 00000121, a network address for the
server would be displayed as 121.0000.0000.0001.

Sequenced Packet eXchange (SPX)

Novell's implementation includes a connection-oriented protocol,
Sequenced Packet eXchange (SPX). SPX functions similar to TCP/IP's
TCP protocol. SPX provides a virtual circuit or connection between
network nodes and guarantees delivery of data.

NetWare Core Protocol (NCP)

NetWare Core Protocol (NCP) gives client nodes access to server
resources such as printing, file access, and security.

Routing Information Protocol (RIP)

Routing Information Protocol (RIP) is a distance-vectoring routing
protocol used to route IPX traffic in internetworks. IPX RIP uses
ticks and hop count to determine the best path for network traffic to
travel in an internetwork. It should be noted that IPX RIP functions
similarly to IP's RIP, but there are some differences. (See Chapter 6,
"Routing," for more information.)

NetWare Link Services Protocol (NLSP)

NetWare Link Services Protocol (NLSP) provides an advanced link state routing protocol to the Novell suite. Novell developed it as a replacement for both SAP and RIP. NLSP was included in release 3.12 and 4.x of NetWare.

Novell realized that IPX RIP had limitations and developed NLSP as its replacement. NLSP works similar to IP's *Open Shortest Path First (OSPF)* routing protocol. NLSP offers many advantages over IPX RIP. NLSP is more efficient, scalable, and offers better routing. NLSP is more efficient because it only sends updates when a topology change occurs or every two hours, whichever comes first. This is in contrast to RIP sending the entire routing table every 60 seconds whether or not the topology has changed. NLSP also sends service-information updates only when a service status has changed. This is in contrast to SAPs being sent every 60 seconds whether or not the service status has changed. NLSP is scalable, supporting up to 127 hops. This is in contrast to 15 hops for RIP.

NLSP also offers load balancing of traffic over parallel paths. NLSP periodically checks network paths for integrity. If a path is found unusable, NLSP selects an alternative link and updates the network topology.

Service Advertising Protocol (SAP)

Novell has an interesting way of advertising which services are available. It uses *Service Advertising Protocol (SAP)* to broadcast which services are available from which servers. SAPs present a great challenge to internetworking engineers. Each type of service uses a SAP identifier. File servers use SAP=4 and print servers use SAP=7. By default, SAP updates are sent every 60 seconds.

Routers listen to the SAP broadcasts and build a table of available services on the network the service is available on. When a client requests a network service, the router responds with the network address the requested service is on. The client then contacts the service directly.

In release 4.x of NetWare, Novell introduced *Novell Directory Services (NDS)*. NDS is a distributed directory service that reduces the need for SAPs. SAPs are still used by NetWare 4.x clients when they first boot to discover NDS servers.

Each of these protocols serves a purpose on the network. As an internetworking engineer, it's your job to understand how the protocols function so that when there is a connectivity problem, you are able to determine why the problem is occurring and find a resolution.

IPX and SPX generally carry the data around the network for applications. When a client is connected to a server, it can use either protocol during a conversation depending on what transactions are occurring between the server and workstation.

SAPs are broadcasts that file servers, access servers, print servers, and other devices with services to advertise use. Cisco routers configured for IPX routing will listen for these SAPs and build a table of the services being advertised. In an organization with many servers and offices connected through a WAN, this can create a large SAP table in the routers. Most of the time services such as print servers are used only on the local area network and do not need to be broadcast across WAN links where bandwidth is a premium. By using access lists to limit which SAPs are placed in the SAP table, you can reduce the impact of these SAPs on the WAN.

NETWORK ADDRESSES

The IPX network address consists of two parts: the network number and the node number. When an IPX address is displayed in a router, it takes the form of 4c.03cb.530c.1cd3, where 4c is the network number and 03cb.530c.1cd3 is the node number. Novell's IPX protocols have an interesting way of mapping the network address to the MAC address. The MAC address is actually used to derive the network address. Given the previous example, the node number 03cb.530c.1cd3 is also the MAC address of the node. Therefore it is simple for the IPX network to determine for which node the packet is destined.

MULTIPLE ENCAPSULATIONS

Novell's NetWare protocols support multiple protocol encapsulations. This has been a source of headaches for network administrators for quite some time. Often times, a new networking station would not be able to communicate with the server. After hours of investigation, it would be discovered that the encapsulation setting of the networking station was different than that of the server.

To add even more confusion, Novell changed the default encapsulation method used starting with NetWare Version 3.12.

Now that you will be connecting Novell networks to Cisco routers, Cisco has made this source of headaches even worse by coming up with its own names for the encapsulation methods. You not only need to remember the various methods of encapsulation Novell uses, but now, when you connect these networks to a Cisco router, you must also know what Cisco calls the different methods of encapsulation.

◆ **Novell_Ether encapsulation.** This is the equivalent of Novell's Ethernet_802.3. This frame format includes the IEEE 802.3 length field, but not an IEEE 802.2 Logical Link Control (LLC) header. This encapsulation was the default through NetWare 3.11.

◆ **SAP encapsulation.** This is the equivalent of Novell's Ethernet_802.2. This frame format is the standard IEEE frame format including an 802.2 LLC header. This encapsulation method became the default with the release of NetWare 3.12 and 4.x. For token ring use, SAP also equates to Novell's Token_Ring encapsulation.

◆ **ARPA encapsulation.** This is the equivalent of Novell's Ethernet_II or Ethernet version 2. It uses the standard Ethernet 2 header.

◆ **SNAP encapsulation.** This is the equivalent of Novell's Ethernet_SNAP or SNAP. It extends the IEEE 802.2 header by adding a *SubNetwork Access Protocol (SNAP)* header. This header provides an encapsulation type code similar to that of Ethernet version 2. Cisco's SNAP also equates to Novell's Token_Ring_SNAP.

EXAM TIP

Remembering the Encapsulation Types   It can be quite challenging to remember the encapsulation types and what their corresponding Cisco types are. The following associations might make it somewhat easier.

SNAP is a "snap" for Ethernet or token ring.

SAP is short, and 802.2 is less than 802.3 and token ring, too.

Novell_Ether is longer, and 802.3 is greater than 802.2.

ARPA doesn't really fit, but then neither does Ethernet_II.

A WARNING ABOUT BRIDGING

Cisco routers support *Concurrent Routing and Bridging (CRB)*. This is a feature by which the router can route routable protocols like IP and IPX on an interface and, at the same time, bridge non-routable protocols like SNA and NetBEUI. The danger here is that when bridging of any type is configured on an interface, it will bridge all non-routed protocols—including routable protocols that are not currently configured for routing.

To configure an interface for routing is not complex. Simply assign the interface an address for the routable protocol. Assigning an IP address to an interface configures the interface for IP routing. Assigning an IPX address to an interface configures it for IPX routing.

When an interface has any bridging configured, whether it is *Source Route Bridging (SRB)* or *Data Link Switching (DLSw)*, the interface will bridge any traffic that is not routable.

The danger occurs when an interface has bridging configured and an IP address, but no IPX network, configured. All IPX traffic will be bridged with the other bridged networks. You will know this is happening when system administrators call to complain that the Novell servers are beeping constantly and giving the warning message of a misconfigured router.

What is happening is that the IPX traffic from one network is bridged to another network without the network portion of the address being adjusted for the new network. The server sees the network address with the incorrect IPX network number and gives warning messages.

Be careful when configuring bridging on interfaces. Make sure you consider what traffic, other than the intended traffic, might end up on the destination networks.

CONFIGURING IPX ROUTING

Configuring a Cisco router for IPX routing involves multiple steps. IPX routing is turned off by default in Cisco's IOS. This is in contrast to TCP/IP routing, which is on by default.

The first step is to enable IPX routing on the router. This is done with the global configuration command ipx routing.

```
Router#config t
Enter configuration commands, one per line. End with CNTL/Z.
Router(config)#ipx routing
Router(config)#exit
Router#sh run
Building configuration...

Current configuration:
!
version 11.2
no service password-encryption
service udp-small-servers
```

continues

continued

```
service tcp-small-servers
!
hostname Router
!
!
ipx routing 0010.7b3b.d0a9
!
interface Ethernet0
 ip address 199.250.137.59 255.255.255.224
!
interface Serial0
 no ip address
 encapsulation frame-relay
 no keepalive
!
interface Serial1
 no ip address
```

Notice that after entering the ipx routing statement, a show run was executed on the router. In the configuration, the command ipx routing 0010.7b3b.d0a9 is shown. The MAC address after the ipx routing statement is necessary for the IPX protocol. As you remember, IPX uses the MAC address as part of the network address. Therefore, the router needs a MAC address to use as its node address on any IPX networks it routes. You can specify a MAC address to use in the IPX routing statement by simply entering the MAC address you wish to use after the ipx routing command. If you do not specify the MAC, the router uses the MAC address of the first Ethernet, token ring, or FDDI interface. If the router does not have any of these interfaces, then you must specify a MAC address for IPX routing to use.

The next step in configuring IPX routing is to set the IPX network number on each of the interfaces routing IPX traffic. The following example shows the network 3c being placed on the interface Ethernet0 and the network 5c being placed on the interface Serial0.

```
Router#config t
Enter configuration commands, one per line. End with CNTL/Z.
Router(config)#int Serial0
Router(config-if)#ipx network 3c
Router(config-if)#exit
Router(config)#int ethernet1
Router(config-if)#ipx network 5c
Router(config-if)#exit
Router(config)#exit
Router#
```

When configuring IPX routing over WAN links, the common interfaces of the WAN routers need to have a unique IPX network number just as LAN interfaces do. The WAN interfaces use the encapsulation type of the interface.

Now that IPX routing has been enabled and the network numbers have been assigned to the interfaces, you must ensure that the encapsulation types are correct. If you do not define an encapsulation type, the router uses the default for the media type. The following list shows the defaults as of IOS version 11.2:

- ◆ **Ethernet.** The default is Novell_Ether, known as Ethernet_802.3. This is the default encapsulation type for Novell through NetWare 3.11. Starting with Novell 3.12 the default encapsulation for Novell servers changed to Ethernet_802.2.

- ◆ **Token Ring.** The default is SAP, or Token-Ring to a Novell server.

- ◆ **FDDI.** The default is SNAP or FDDI_SNAP to a Novell server.

To specify the encapsulation type, add the encapsulation keyword to the `ipx network` configuration command. The following example shows the encapsulation types added to the configuration:

```
Router#config terminal
Enter configuration commands, one per line. End with CNTL/Z.
Router(config)#int ethernet0
Router(config-if)#ipx network 3c encapsulation sap
Router(config-if)#exit
Router(config)#int ethernet1
Router(config-if)#ipx network 5c encapsulation arpa
Router(config-if)#exit
Router(config)#exit
Router#
```

In the previous example, the encapsulation types for each of the interfaces are different. The router will exchange packets correctly from one network to the next, making the necessary changes to the packet format for each network.

In some environments, multiple Novell networks are present on one LAN; however, the different logical networks must be using different encapsulation types. To configure for this in a Cisco router requires the use of *subinterfaces*. For an interface, only one IPX network can be defined.

NOTE

Check the Version Defaults for certain items change from revision to revision of IOS, so be sure to check the defaults for the version of IOS you are running. This is true of all defaults, not just IPX encapsulation types. Many problems occur when the version of IOS is upgraded in a router and certain settings are not specified in a router's configuration. A new version of IOS may use different defaults for the setting and something that used to work no longer works.

However, if multiple encapsulation types are used on one network, the different encapsulation types can be configured using subinterfaces. You can create subinterfaces on a LAN interface and then assign a different encapsulation type to each subinterface and a different network number to each. Each subinterface must have a different encapsulation type and IPX network number. Once configured properly, the router will route traffic between the two different logical networks. Following is part of an IPX configuration that shows different IPX networks on the subinterfaces of an Ethernet port:

```
hostname Router
!
!
ipx routing 0010.7b3b.d0a9
!
interface Ethernet0
 ip address 192.168.33.1 255.255.255.0
!
interface Ethernet0.1
 arp timeout 0
 ipx network 3C encapsulation SAP
!
interface Ethernet0.2
 arp timeout 0
 ipx network 54 encapsulation ARPA
!
interface Serial0
 no ip address

Router#
```

REVIEW BREAK

Configuring Novell Routing

As you can see, configuring Novell routing is not terribly complicated. There are several things you need to remember when configuring IPX routing on a Cisco router:

▶ IPX routing is not active in a default Cisco router configuration. The first step to setting up IPX routing is to turn on IPX routing with the global command `ipx routing [mac-address]`. The MAC address can be specified or not. If it is not specified, the MAC address of the first Ethernet, token ring, or FDDI interface is used. If the router does not have any of these types of interfaces, you must specify the MAC address to use.

▶ The IPX network number must be placed on the interfaces attached to which Novell networks you wish to route data.

▶ Within the Novell protocols, there are multiple encapsulation types. To properly route IPX traffic, the encapsulation type used by the router must match the encapsulation type used by the Novell network. This is an area that can produce problems. The names of the encapsulation types used by Cisco do not match what Novell servers use.

After these settings are properly configured, the router should begin discovering Novell services by listening for SAPs on the network. The router will begin building a table of the services it detects. Because many of these services are important only to the local network and do not need to be advertised or transmitted to remote networks, it is useful to limit through the use of Access Lists which of these services will be added to the table.

NOVELL ACCESS LISTS

In the Novell environment, it is often useful to control which networks can communicate with others.

Novell access lists fall into four categories: standard, extended, SAP filtering, and NLSP route aggregation filtering.

When using IPX access lists, it is sometimes necessary to indicate all IPX networks. This is represented in an access list as ffffffff. Another way to represent all networks is by using the number –1.

> **EXAM TIP**
>
> **NLSP Filters Not on Exam** For the CCNA exam, you will need to understand the standard, extended, and SAP filtering access lists. NLSP route aggregation filtering is not covered in this book.

Standard IPX Access Lists

Standard IPX access lists are numbered 800–899. In a standard IPX access list, you can permit or deny traffic based on source address and destination address.

A standard access list can be used to limit which networks can communicate with others. Given the following example shown in Figure 4.2, you want to create an access list that will allow only networks 5c and 3b to communicate with network 21d. However, you do not want 3b to be able to communicate with 5c.

FIGURE 4.2
Novell networks connected via a router.

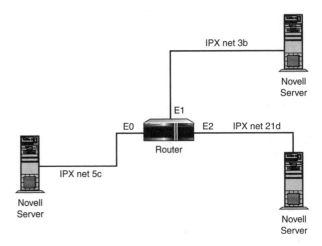

To create an access list to accomplish this type of traffic control, you must first create an access list for interface Ethernet2 that allows traffic from networks 3b and 5c. Following is an example of how to create a standard IPX access list for this purpose:

```
Router#config t
Router(config)#access-list 800 permit 3c 21d
Router(config)#access-list 800 permit 5c 21d
Router(config)#exit
Router#
```

Now that the access list 800 is created, you need to apply it to the interface Ethernet2. The default mode for an access list is to effect outgoing traffic on the interface. Thus this access list will allow IPX traffic from only networks 3c and 5c to exit interface Ethernet2:

```
Router#config t
Router#(config)#interface Ethernet2
Router(config-if)#ipx access-group 800 out
Router(config-if)#exit
Router(config)#exit
Router#
```

For interface Ethernet0 and Ethernet1, you want to limit traffic to just IPX network 21d. This is accomplished in much the same way. Following is an example that creates two additional access lists, 801 and 802, that permit traffic only from 21d to the respective networks:

```
Router#config t
Router(config)#access-list 801 permit 21d 5c
Router(config)#access-list 802 permit 21d 3b
Router(config)#exit
Router#
```

Each of these new access lists must be applied to the respective
interfaces. Following is an example of how this is accomplished:

```
Router#config t
Router#(config)#interface Ethernet0
Router(config-if)#ipx access-group 801 out
Router(config-if)#exit
Router(config)interface Ethernet1
Router(config-if)#ipx access-group 802 out
Router(config)#exit
Router#
```

With these access lists in place, only traffic from network 21d is permitted to exit interfaces Ethernet0 and Ethernet1. Traffic from both
networks 5c and 3b are allowed to exit interface Ethernet2. The goal
is accomplished.

Extended IPX Access Lists

Extended IPX access lists are numbered 900-999. In an extended
access list, you can permit or deny traffic based on source address,
destination address, protocol, source socket, and destination socket.
You can also log when access list violations occur.

SAP Filtering Access Lists

SAP filtering access lists allow you to filter the SAPs exchanged with
other routers. This is very useful because many IPX networks include
elements such as network printers that send SAP broadcasts. Generally
you do not need these SAPs to be broadcast across WAN links to
remote sites. You can filter these SAPs by using a SAP access list. For
example, if you wanted to allow only server SAPs from all networks to
be broadcast over a WAN link, you could use an access list as follows:

```
Router(config)#access-list 1000 permit ffffffff 4
Router(config)#
```

The global command access-list creates the access list. You have
assigned this access list 1000, which indicates that it is a SAP access
list. The network ffffffff indicates all networks. You could also have
used -1 here and had the same result. The number 4 indicates the
SAP type to permit. After the access list is created, it must be applied
to the WAN link as follows. SAP access lists can be applied to either
outgoing SAPs or incoming SAPs. When you apply a
SAP access list to outgoing SAPs, you are limiting the SAPs sent
from the router's table out of the interface the access list is applied.

When the access list is applied to incoming SAPs, you are limiting the SAPs the router will add to its table from the interface the access list is applied. The important difference here is that if the SAPs you are not allowing are important only to the local segment, an incoming SAP filter will reduce the size of the router's SAP table, thus requiring less router memory and processing overhead.

```
Router#config t
Router(config)#interface serial0
Router(config-if)#ipx output-sap-filter 1000
Router(config-if)#
```

This access list will allow only server SAPs to be broadcast through the interface Serial0. Table 4.1 lists the more common SAP types used in IPX networks.

TABLE 4.1

COMMON SAPs USED IN IPX NETWORKS

Service Type (Hexadecimal)	Description
1	User
2	User group
3	Print server queue
4	File server
5	Job server
7	Print server
9	Archive server
A	Queue for job servers
21	Network Application Support Systems Network Architecture (NAS SNA) gateway
2D	Time Synchronization value-added process (VAP)
2E	Dynamic SAP
47	Advertising print server
4B	Btrieve VAP 5.0
4C	SQL VAP
7A	TES—NetWare for Virtual Memory System (VMS)
98	NetWare access server
9A	Named Pipes server

Service Type (Hexadecimal)	Description
9E	Portable NetWare—UNIX
107	RCONSOLE
111	Test server
166	NetWare management (Novell's Network Management Station [NMS])
26A	NetWare management (NMS console)

DIAGNOSING IPX PROBLEMS

When diagnosing an IPX problem, you will find that it is useful to view what SAPs a router is seeing, and from what networks and interfaces they are being seen. There are several IOS commands that help in finding out where in the network the failure is occurring.

Displaying IPX Addresses

One of the first things to do when diagnosing an IPX problem is to check the IPX network numbers assigned to a router's interfaces.

The command show ipx interface displays IPX-related information about the router's interfaces. The IPX network number is displayed in full, including the node number. The command can be used without an interface description and will then display information for each interface in the router with an IPX address assigned. Following is an example output from the show ipx interface command:

```
Router#sh ipx interface
FastEthernet0/0 is up, line protocol is up
  IPX address is 11010.00e0.a38d.0800, SAP [up] line-up,
➥RIPPQ: 0, SAPPQ: 0
  Delay of this IPX network, in ticks is 1 throughput 0 link
➥delay 0
  IPXWAN processing not enabled on this interface.
  IPX SAP update interval is 1 minute(s)
  IPX type 20 propagation packet forwarding is disabled
  Incoming access list is not set
  Outgoing access list is not set
  IPX helper access list is not set
```

continues

continued

```
SAP GNS processing enabled, delay 0 ms, output filter list
➥is not set
SAP Input filter list is not set
SAP Output filter list is not set
SAP Router filter list is not set
Input filter list is not set
Output filter list is not set
Router filter list is not set
Netbios Input host access list is not set
Netbios Input bytes access list is not set
Netbios Output host access list is not set
Netbios Output bytes access list is not set
Updates each 60 seconds, aging multiples RIP: 3 SAP: 3
SAP interpacket delay is 55 ms, maximum size is 480 bytes
RIP interpacket delay is 55 ms, maximum size is 432 bytes
IPX accounting is disabled
IPX fast switching is configured (enabled)
RIP packets received 9229358, RIP packets sent 846238
SAP packets received 35260817, SAP packets sent 1498927
Token Ring1/0 is administratively down, line protocol is
➥down
IPX address is 88888888.0007.c5b1.1010, SAP [up] line-
➥down, RIPPQ: 0, SAPPQ: 0
Delay of this IPX network, in ticks is 1 throughput 0 link
➥delay 0
IPXWAN processing not enabled on this interface.
IPX SAP update interval is 1 minute(s)
IPX type 20 propagation packet forwarding is disabled
Incoming access list is not set
Outgoing access list is not set
IPX helper access list is not set
SAP GNS processing enabled, delay 0 ms, output filter list
➥is not set
SAP Input filter list is not set
SAP Output filter list is not set
SAP Router filter list is not set
Input filter list is not set
Output filter list is not set
Router filter list is not set
Netbios Input host access list is not set
Netbios Input bytes access list is not set
Netbios Output host access list is not set
Netbios Output bytes access list is not set
Updates each 60 seconds, aging multiples RIP: 3 SAP: 3
SAP interpacket delay is 55 ms, maximum size is 480 bytes
RIP interpacket delay is 55 ms, maximum size is 432 bytes
IPX accounting is disabled
IPX fast switching is configured (enabled)
RIP packets received 0, RIP packets sent 0
SAP packets received 0, SAP packets sent 0

Router#
```

If you are diagnosing a problem specific to one interface in the
router, you can limit the information shown to just that interface.
The interface about which you are seeking information can also be
specified and then only IPX information about that interface will be
displayed. Following is an example of how to specify the interface
about which you wish to see IPX information.

```
Router#sh ipx interface token ring1/1
TokenRing1/1 is up, line protocol is up
 IPX address is 33333333.0007.c5b1.1090, SAP [up] line-up,
➡RIPPQ: 0, SAPPQ: 0
 Delay of this IPX network, in ticks is 1 throughput 0 link
➡delay 0
 IPXWAN processing not enabled on this interface.
 IPX SAP update interval is 1 minute(s)
 IPX type 20 propagation packet forwarding is disabled
 Incoming access list is not set
 Outgoing access list is not set
 IPX helper access list is not set
 SAP GNS processing enabled, delay 0 ms, output filter list
➡is not set
 SAP Input filter list is not set
 SAP Output filter list is not set
 SAP Router filter list is not set
 Input filter list is not set
 Output filter list is not set
 Router filter list is not set
 Netbios Input host access list is not set
 Netbios Input bytes access list is not set
 Netbios Output host access list is not set
 Netbios Output bytes access list is not set
 Updates each 60 seconds, aging multiples RIP: 3 SAP: 3
 SAP interpacket delay is 55 ms, maximum size is 480 bytes
 RIP interpacket delay is 55 ms, maximum size is 432 bytes
 IPX accounting is disabled
 IPX fast switching is configured (enabled)
 RIP packets received 136, RIP packets sent 246974
 SAP packets received 101, SAP packets sent 7493686
Router#
```

If you want to see a brief description of the IPX information for the
interfaces in a router, you can use the variation of the previous command, show ipx interface brief. This command simply lists each
interface in the router, the IPX network number assigned, the encapsulation type, the interface status, and the IPX state. Following is an
example of the output from the show ipx interface brief command:

```
Router#sh ipx interface brief
Interface        IPX Network   Encapsulation   Status                    IPX State
FastEthernet0/0  11010         SAP             up                        [up]
TokenRing1/0     88888888      SAP             administratively down     [up]
TokenRing1/1     33333333      SAP             up                        [up]
TokenRing1/2     11111111      SAP             up                        [up]
TokenRing1/3     unassigned    not config'd    administratively down     n/a
Ethernet2/0      011019        NOVELL_ETHER    administratively down     [up]
Ethernet2/1      unassigned    not config'd    up                        n/a
Ethernet2/2      unassigned    not config'd    administratively down     n/a
Ethernet2/3      unassigned    not config'd    administratively down     n/a
Serial5/0        unassigned    not config'd    up                        n/a
Serial5/0.1      unassigned    not config'd    up                        n/a
Serial5/0.2      112233        FRAME-RELAY-I   up                        [up]
Serial5/0.3      unassigned    not config'd    up                        n/a
Serial5/0.4      unassigned    not config'd    up                        n/a
Serial5/0.5      unassigned    not config'd    up                        n/a
Serial5/0.6      unassigned    not config'd    up                        n/a
Serial5/0.7      unassigned    not config'd    up                        n/a
Serial5/0.8      1174          FRAME-RELAY-I   up                        [up]
Serial5/0.9      unassigned    not config'd    up                        n/a
Serial5/0.10     unassigned    not config'd    up                        n/a
Serial5/0.11     unassigned    not config'd    up                        n/a
Serial5/0.12     unassigned    not config'd    up                        n/a
Serial5/0.122    unassigned    not config'd    up                        n/a
Serial5/0.123    unassigned    not config'd    up                        n/a
Serial5/0.133    unassigned    not config'd    up                        n/a
Serial5/0.138    unassigned    not config'd    down                      n/a
Serial5/0.146    unassigned    not config'd    up                        n/a
Serial5/0.147    unassigned    not config'd    up                        n/a
Serial5/0.148    unassigned    not config'd    up                        n/a
Serial5/0.149    unassigned    not config'd    up                        n/a
Serial5/0.150    unassigned    not config'd    up                        n/a
Serial5/1        1011088F      HDLC            up                        [up]
Serial5/2        unassigned    not config'd    administratively down     n/a
Serial5/3        unassigned    not config'd    administratively down     n/a
Loopback1        unassigned    not config'd    up                        n/a
Router#
```

Displaying Servers

The command show ipx servers is a very useful command when diagnosing an IPX problem. When the router receives SAP broadcasts from servers, it places them in its server table. When two routers are exchanging IPX information, the server tables are exchanged so that each then knows about the servers available through the other router. For the router to be able to route traffic to a server, it must first see that server's SAP broadcasts. When the router receives SAP broadcasts for a server, certain information from that SAP is placed in the router's SAP table. The command show ipx servers allows you to view this table.

The following is an example of the output of this command:

```
Router#sh ipx ser

   Codes: S - Static, P - Periodic, E - EIGRP, N - NLSP, H -
   Holddown, + = detail
   221 Total IPX Servers
```

```
   Table ordering is based on routing and server info

      Type Name              Net      Address    Port      Route Hops   Itf
   P    4 RESEARCH                  A5.0000.0000.0001:0451   2185984/00   1   Fa0/0
   P    4 BENEFIT           36B08649.0000.0000.0001:0451        2/01     1   Fa0/0
   P    4 EPI                       A6.0000.0000.0001:0451        2/01     1   Fa0/0
   P    4 FINANCE           3634E2C8.0000.0000.0001:0451        2/01     1   Fa0/0
   P    4 NACSS01           351F5D27.0000.0000.0001:0451        2/01     1   Fa0/0
   P    4 NAPPD01           36B71C16.0000.0000.0001:0451        2/01     1   Fa0/0
   P    4 NATIONAL                  B3.0000.0000.0001:0451        2/01     1   Fa0/0
   P    4 NHOFSE01          34197AED.0000.0000.0001:0451        2/01     1   Fa0/0
   P    4 NHO_CSS_5          ADF0FCF.0000.0000.0001:0451        2/01     1   Fa0/0
   P    4 NOV1                   12497.0000.0000.0001:0451        2/01     1   Fa0/0
   E    4 APC_NOVELL        3485BA61.0000.0000.0001:0451 269824000/02   2   Se5/0.2
   P    4 NAGOV01           3238529B.0000.0000.0001:0451        8/02     2   Se5/0.8


   Router#
```

The table lists the SAP type, server name, network address and port,
route to the network, hops to the network, and the interface on which
the SAP was seen. Earlier you learned that the node address of an IPX
networking station is the MAC address of the node. However, in the
preceding table, the node addresses of the different Novell servers
shows 0000.0000.0001. This is due to an operating characteristic of
Novell servers. A Novell server using the IPX protocol has two node
addresses. The first is the MAC address of the node and the second is
0000.0000.0001, which represents an internal network number in the
server.

It is not unlikely that you would need to search for a server name in
a large table of servers. The command show ipx servers has several
options to make this easier. You can sort the table by server name,
network number, or SAP type. However, starting in Release 11.2,
Cisco added the option to search for a specific server using the
option regexp. The following example shows how the regexp option
is used to find a server named NOV1:

```
Router#sh ipx server regexp NOV1
Codes: S - Static, P - Periodic, E - EIGRP, N - NLSP,
H - Holddown, + = detail
208 Total IPX Servers
```

continues

continued

```
Table ordering is based on routing and server info

    Type Name                 Net      Address    Port   Route Hops Itf
P     4 NOV1                  12497.0000.0000.0001:0451    8/02   2  Se0/0.1
P   107 NOV1                  12497.0000.0000.0001:8104    8/02   3  Se0/0.1
Router#
```

Working with IPX Routing Tables

When a router is routing IPX traffic, it builds a routing table to determine the proper path to forward traffic. Although this topic is discussed in more detail in Chapter 6, "Routing," a few commands specific to IPX are covered here.

To view the IPX routing table, use the command show ipx route. This will display all of the networks the router has determined paths for and certain information about those paths. Following is an example IPX routing table:

```
Router#sh ipx route
Codes: C - Connected primary network,    c - Connected secondary network
       S - Static, F - Floating static, L - Local (internal), W - IPXWAN
       R - RIP, E - EIGRP, N - NLSP, X - External, A - Aggregate
       s - seconds, u - uses

34 Total IPX routes. Up to 1 parallel paths and 16 hops allowed.

No default route known.

C      1174 (FRAME-RELAY-IETF),                                      Se5/0.8
C     11010 (SAP),                                                   Fa0/0
C    112233 (FRAME-RELAY-IETF),                                      Se5/0.2
C 1011088F (HDLC),                                                   Se5/1
C 11111111 (SAP),                                                    To1/2
C 33333333 (SAP),                                                    To1/1
R         1 [02/01]      via    11010.0060.0803.8c4d,           54s, Fa0/0
R        58 [02/01]      via    11010.0080.2968.af0c,           21s, Fa0/0
E        A3 [2185984/0]  via    112233.4145.0000.0003, age 17:39:14,1267u, Se5/0.2
E        A4 [2185984/0]  via    112233.4145.0000.0003,   age 3d04h,1311u, Se5/0.2
E        A5 [2185984/0]  via    112233.4145.0000.0003,   age 3d04h,25742u, Se5/0.2
R        A6 [02/01]      via    11010.0060.979b.61a4,           54s, Fa0/0
R        B3 [02/01]      via    11010.0060.979b.6218,           37s, Fa0/0
E        F0 [269824000/2] via   112233.4145.0000.0003,   age 3d04h,317u, Se5/0.2
E        FD [269824000/2] via   112233.4145.0000.0003,   age 3d04h,317u, Se5/0.2
R       100 [07/01]      via    1174.00e0.1e89.5841,            29s, Se5/0.8
R       101 [07/01]      via    1174.00e0.1e89.5841,            29s, Se5/0.8
```

```
R      444 [02/01]    via     11010.0060.b01a.3678,           47s,  Fa0/0
R     FFFF [02/01]    via     11010.0060.b067.b81d,            0s,  Fa0/0
R    11011 [02/01]    via     11010.0060.979b.6218,           37s,  Fa0/0
R    12497 [02/01]    via     11010.0080.2968.af0c,           22s,  Fa0/0
R  ADF0FCF [02/01]    via     11010.0010.4bd2.0977,           38s,  Fa0/0
R 1011088A [07/01]    via 1011088F.00e0.1ea9.ce78,            48s,  Se5/1
R 3238529B [08/02]    via     1174.00e0.1e89.5841,            29s,  Se5/0.8
R 34197AED [02/01]    via     11010.0060.08a4.e896,           45s,  Fa0/0
E 3485BA61 [269824000/2] via  112233.4145.0000.0003, age 17:38:43,1097u,  Se5/0.2
R 351F5D27 [02/01]    via     11010.0060.979b.6180,           16s,  Fa0/0
R 3634E2C8 [02/01]    via     11010.0060.083a.93be,           56s,  Fa0/0
R 36B08649 [02/01]    via     11010.0060.97d1.9a35,           43s,  Fa0/0
R 36B71C16 [02/01]    via     11010.0090.2728.3699,            1s,  Fa0/0
R 75757657 [02/01]    via     11010.00c0.490e.703d,           27s,  Fa0/0
R A31B0596 [08/02]    via 1011088F.00e0.1ea9.ce78,            50s,  Se5/1
R A31B3AF5 [08/02]    via 1011088F.00e0.1ea9.ce78,            50s,  Se5/1
R B067B81D [21/01]    via     11010.0060.b067.b81d,            2s,  Fa0/0
Router#
```

The routing table lists each of the IPX networks in the table. The letter to the left of each network represents how the router learned of the network. Some networks are connected directly to this router, which are represented by a "C." An "R" represents networks learned through the RIP routing protocol. Networks learned through the routing protocol EIGRP are represented by an "E."

The routing table can sometimes become unstable because of network topology changes or software bugs. You can force the router to rebuild the routing table by clearing it. The command clear ipx route * will clear all routes in the table:

```
Router#clear ipx route *
Router#
```

You can clear a specific network route by specifying the route in the command, such as clear ipx route 3c. This will cause the router to clear this route and relearn the route if possible.

```
Router#clear ipx route 3c
Router#
```

Load Sharing with IPX

Cisco routers routing IPX traffic can perform load sharing across equal cost paths. When two paths of equal cost or delay exist from one network to another, the router can distribute the data across those paths.

This is called *load sharing*. Using load sharing can increase the usable bandwidth between the networks. To allow a Cisco router to make use of multiple equal cost paths, you must set the parameter `ipx maximum-paths`. The default value is 1. You can allow a Cisco router to use up to 512 equal cost paths for IPX traffic, but a more realistic limit would be two or three paths. Following is an example of how to set the maximum number of paths the router will use for load sharing to 3:

```
Router(config)#ipx maximum-paths 3
Router(config)#
```

CASE STUDY: ACME PAINT COMPANY

ESSENCE OF THE CASE

▶ You must configure the two Cisco routers for IPX networking and create an IPX link across the Wide Area Network.

▶ The router at your office is named Acme and is connected to the accounting department on interface Ethernet1/2.

▶ The router at the remote office is named PPlace and is connected to the accounting department on interface Ethernet0/1.

▶ The two routers are connected via a leased line. This line is connected to interface Serial0/0 on each router. You must configure an IPX network on these interfaces also.

▶ The routers are currently configured to route IP traffic from one office to the other.

▶ The IPX network for the accounting department at Acme is 00001b0c and is using 802.3. The IPX network for the accounting department at Paint'n Place is 00002f43 and is using Ethernet_802.2 encapsulation.

SCENARIO

You are the network guru for Acme Paint Company. Your company just purchased its largest competitor, Paint'n Place. During the merger of the two companies, you are responsible for ensuring that the accounting department of your company can access the financial data of the purchased company. Both your accounting department and the accounting department of Paint'n Place use Novell Networks. As part of the merger, your company has installed a leased line between the two offices and you are responsible for the routers on each end.

Your office has a Cisco 7206 router named Acme with four Ethernet interfaces installed. Your accounting department has its own LAN and is connected to interface Ethernet1/2 of Acme.

Paint'n Place has a Cisco 3640 router named PPlace with two Ethernet interfaces installed. The accounting department at Paint'n Place is connected to Ethernet0/1.

The two routers are connected using a point-to-point leased line connected at each end to Serial0/0.

CASE STUDY: ACME PAINT COMPANY

ANALYSIS

You log in to the router at Paint'n Place and make the necessary changes:

```
PPlace(config)#interface Ethnernet0/1
PPlace(config-if)#ipx network 2f43
encapsulation sap
PPlace(conifg-if)#exit
PPlace(config)#interface serial0/0
PPlace(config-if)#ipx network 7700
PPlace(config-if)#exit
PPlace(config)#exit
PPlace#copy running-config startup-config
```

You then log in to the router at Acme and make the necessary changes:

```
Acme(config)#interface Ethnernet1/2
Acme(config-if)#ipx network 1b0c encapsulation
Novell_Ether
Acme(config-if)#exit
Acme(config)#interface Serial0/0
Acme(config-if)#ipx network 7700
Acme(config-if)#exit
Acme(config)#exit
Acme#copy running-config startup-config
```

You have successfully configured the routers and find that the accounting department at Acme is now able to access the data stored on the server at Paint'n Place.

CHAPTER SUMMARY

This chapter covered the aspects of Novell Networking. You have learned to configure Novell networking on Cisco routers and have been exposed to some of the techniques for diagnosing problems. Although Novell networking is relatively simple to implement on Cisco routers, problems with Novell routing can prove to be elusive. There is no better teacher than experience.

Unlike IP routing, IPX routing is not turned on by default in Cisco routers. For a Cisco router to route IPX traffic, IPX routing must first be enabled. This is done with the `ipx routing` command at the global configuration. Follow that by configuring the IPX network numbers for each segment on the interfaces connected to the segments. If an encapsulation type other than Cisco's default is being used, make sure you configure the encapsulation also.

IPX access lists offer a means of enforcing security policies as well as reducing the overhead of excessive SAPs traveling over slow WAN links.

KEY TERMS

- IPX dncapsulation
- IPX network
- Internet Packet eXchange (IPX)
- Sequenced Packet eXchange (SPX)
- Service Advertising Protocol (SAP)
- Novell Directory Service (NDS)
- NetWare Core Protocol (NCP)
- NetWare Link Services Protocol (NLSP)

APPLY YOUR KNOWLEDGE

Review Questions

1. What is the purpose of the SAP protocol within an IPX network?

2. What must you do prior to configuring an IPX network on an interface of a router?

3. What is significant about the IPX address 5c.0000.0000.0001?

4. How can you configure multiple IPX encapsulation types on one interface of a router?

5. What does network ffffffff represent?

6. How could you determine if a router is receiving SAPs for a particular server?

7. What does IPX load sharing do?

8. List some of the useful information displayed with the command show ipx interface.

9. What are some of the advantages of NLSP over RIP?

10. On which protocol was IPX based?

Exam Questions

1. Describe the parts of this IPX address: 76c.03cd.feed.beef

   A. 76c is the network and 03cd.feed.beef is the node address.

   B. 76c.03cd is the network and feed.beef is the node address.

   C. You need a subnet mask to determine the network portion of the address.

   D. 76c is the node address and 03cd.feed.beef is the network.

2. Which of the following encapsulation types are properly matched? Select two.

   A. Ethernet_802.3 - SAP

   B. Ethernet_802.2 - Novell_Ether

   C. Ethernet_II - ARPA

   D. TokenRing_SNAP - SNAP

3. What is the affect of the following partial configuration?

```
Ethernet0
       Ipx network 7d
       Ipx access-group 800

Access-list 800 permit 55fd
```

   A. Any network including network 55fd will be allowed to talk to network 7d.

   B. Only network 55fd will be allowed to talk to network 7d.

   C. Only network 800 will be allowed to talk to network 7d.

   D. No network will be able to talk to 7d because the access list is improper.

4. What is the proper configuration for IPX network 1fd using Ethernet_II encapsulation?

   A. Router(config-if)#ipx network 1fd encapsulation Ethernet_II

   B. Router(config-if)#ipx network 1fd encapsulation ARPA

   C. Router(config)#ipx network 1fd encapsulation Ethernet_II

   D. Router(config)#ipx network 1fd encapsulation ARPA

APPLY YOUR KNOWLEDGE

5. What command limits how many equal-cost parallel paths will be used to load share?

   A. `ipx load-sharing-paths`

   B. `ipx maximum-paths`

   C. `ipx equal-costs`

   D. `ipx parallel-paths`

6. Which of the following commands will display the IPX address of an interface? Select two.

   A. `show interface`

   B. `show ipx interface`

   C. `show ipx interface brief`

   D. `show interface ipx`

7. Which command will fully clear the router's IPX routing table?

   A. `Router#clear ipx route`

   B. `Router#clear ipx route *`

   C. `Router#clear ipx route ffffffff`

   D. `Router#clear ipx routing table`

8. Which of the following statements are true of the IPX protocol? Select two.

   A. IPX is a connection-oriented protocol.

   B. IPX uses subnet masks to differentiate the network from the node.

   C. IPX uses the MAC address of the network station as the node address in the network address.

   D. IPX is a connectionless protocol.

Answers to Review Questions

1. SAP broadcasts announce the availability of a service on the network. For more information, see "Service Advertising Protocol (SAP)."

2. By default IPX routing is not on. It must be turned on with the global configuration command `ipx routing`. For more information, see "Configuring IPX Routing."

3. The IPX address 5c.0000.0000.0001 is a server's internal network address. For more information, see "Network Addresses."

4. By using subinterfaces, you can configure an interface with multiple IPX encapsulation types. For more information, see "Configuring IPX Routing."

5. ffffffff is a wildcard address representing all IPX networks. For more information, see "Novell Access Lists."

6. The command `show ipx servers` shows a list of services including servers for which the router has received SAPs. For more information, see "Diagnosing IPX Problems."

7. IPX load sharing allows a router to use equal-cost parallel paths to increase the bandwidth between networks. For more information, see "Configuring IPX Routing."

8. The command `show ipx interface` displays a great deal of useful information, including IPX address, IPX SAP update interval, input and output access list status, IPX accounting status, RIP packets received and sent, and SAP packets received and sent. For more information, see "Diagnosing IPX Problems."

APPLY YOUR KNOWLEDGE

9. NLSP is a link state routing protocol that is scalable. It reduces bandwidth overhead by sending only topology changes rather than entire routing tables. For more information, see "NetWare Link Services Protocol (NLSP)."

10. IPX is based on XNS. XNS was developed by Xerox. For more information, see "Novell IPX/SPX Protocol."

Answers to Exam Questions

1. **A.** The network portion of an IPX address is the first group of hexadecimal digits. The rest of the address is the node address. For more information, see "Network Addresses."

2. **C, D.** The first two answers are reversed. For more information, see "Multiple Encapsulations."

3. **B.** Only network 55fd will be allowed to talk to network 7d. For more information, see "Novell Access Lists."

4. **B.** B represents the proper configuration statement. For more information, see "Configuring IPX Routing."

5. **B.** The command `ipx maximum-paths` limits how many equal-cost parallel paths will be used for load sharing of IPX traffic. For more information, see "Configuring IPX Routing."

6. **B, C.** `show ipx interface` and `show ipx interface brief` will display the IPX address of interfaces in the router. For more information, see "Diagnosing IPX Problems."

7. **B.** `clear ipx route *` is the proper syntax to clear the entire IPX routing table. The `*` indicates all routes. For more information, see "Working with IPX Routing Tables."

8. **C, D.** IPX does use the MAC address as the node address and IPX is a connectionless protocol. For more information, see "Novell IPX/SPX Protocol."

Suggested Readings and Resources

1. Chappell, Laura. *Introduction to Cisco Router Configuration*, Cisco Press, 1998.

Cisco provides the following objectives for the WAN Protocols portion of the CCNA exam:

Differentiate between the following WAN services: Frame Relay, ISDN/LAPD, HDLC, and PPP.

▶ To be an internetworking professional, you must be able to differentiate between these services.

Recognize key Frame Relay terms and features.

▶ Because Frame Relay is a very popular WAN technology, you must be well-versed in the terms and features of this very flexible technology.

List commands to configure Frame Relay LMIs, maps, and subinterfaces.

▶ To be able to maintain Frame Relay systems, you must be familiar with the commands used to configure its features.

List commands to monitor Frame Relay operation of the router.

▶ To diagnose problems with Frame Relay systems, you must be familiar with the monitoring commands.

Identify PPP operations to encapsulate WAN data on Cisco routers.

▶ As an internetworking professional, you must be familiar with PPP operations and technologies.

CHAPTER 5

WAN Protocols

State a relevant use and context for ISDN networking.

▶ As an internetworking professional, you must know when to use such technologies as ISDN.

Identify ISDN protocols, function groups, reference points, and channels.

▶ ISDN is another popular WAN technology. You must be able to identify its protocols, function groups, reference points, and channels.

Describe Cisco's implementation of ISDN BRI.

▶ You must be able to relate ISDN technologies to Cisco's implementation.

STUDY STRATEGIES

▶ Wide Area Networking protocols, configuration, troubleshooting, and design are the areas in which most internetworking professionals spend the majority of their time. Most companies have some sort of connection between offices or a connection to the Internet. As an internetworking professional, you will be expected to be knowledgeable about these technologies. You must know not only how to configure connections and troubleshoot problems, but also when each type of connection should be used.

Become proficient and knowledgeable about the products offered by your communications company. Not all products are available everywhere in the United States. If your company is international, you will need to become proficient with the offerings of companies in other countries. Knowing what is available and how cost effective your options are will make you more valuable to your company. You will be able to make informed recommendations and decisions about the best technologies to utilize when connecting your company. Spend time with a representative of your communication company to learn what they offer.

INTRODUCTION

Wide Area Networks (WANs) require their own set of protocols for communication. Wide Area Networking generally defines connecting geographically separated locations together for network communication. The methods used to do this vary from normal dialup phone lines to high-speed fiber connects, even satellite communication can be used to build a WAN.

WANs are implemented in a variety of ways. Not too long ago, most companies connected remote offices using leased point-to-point lines. This was expensive and not an effective use of bandwidth. From this grew technologies for sharing bandwidth such as Frame Relay. This chapter explains different WAN technologies and how they are implemented using Cisco routers.

WAN TERMS

When building or maintaining WANs, you must understand a few new terms and technologies. You will be interfacing with equipment and services from telephone companies. Following are some terms with descriptions.

Central Office

A *Central Office (CO)* is the local telephone office serving your location. The CO houses the switching equipment for Voice and Data circuits. Figure 5.1 shows how your office and remote offices are connected to COs and then to each other.

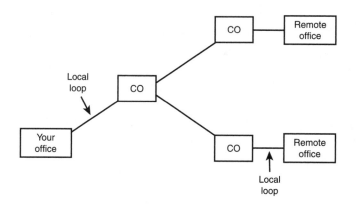

Plain Old Telephone Service (POTS)

It's amazing how something that never had a name needs a name when a new technology comes along. *Plain Old Telephone Service (POTS)* is one of those things. POTS describes the normal telephone service most people have installed in their homes. It's a normal telephone line capable of connecting to a modem and providing connections to other telephone numbers. POTS never really had a name until newer technologies such as ISDN and ATM came about.

Local Loop

The *local loop* is the part of the telephone network that runs from your local CO to your office. It connects you to the telephone network where your data can then be placed on shared services like Frame Relay. The local loop is commonly referred to as the "last mile." Figure 5.1 shows where the local loop falls in the network.

Demarcation Point

Before the telephone companies were split from AT&T, the telephone company was responsible for everything connected to its network, including your telephone equipment. In fact, it was illegal to connect any of your own equipment to the telephone network. When AT&T was broken apart from the local Bell companies, this changed. Now you can purchase your own equipment and connect it to the network.

With this change came the need for a *point of demarcation* that defined where the telephone company's responsibility ended and the customer's began. This means if there is a problem with wiring on the customer side of the demarcation point, the customer is responsible for repairing it. The customer can contract the local Bell company to perform this work, but at the customer's expense. If a problem develops on the Bell side of the demarcation point, it is the Bell company's responsibility to repair the problem at their expense.

The demarcation point is not always well defined and has become more vague than telephone companies would like. Generally speaking, the demarcation point is where the telephone company terminates its lines in your building. However, when ordering data lines, it is common to request an extended demarcation point. When requesting an extended demarcation point, you tell the telephone company where to terminate the line and they will extend your circuit to that point, generally at an additional cost.

Customer Premises Equipment (CPE)

Customer Premises Equipment (CPE) is equipment that resides at the customer site. This equipment interfaces with the telephone company's network. A CSU/DSU is a good example of Customer Premise Equipment.

T1 Service

A *T1* is a digital telephone line that provides a bandwidth of 1.54 million bits per second. This bandwidth is delivered as 24 channels of 64Kbps data channels. Thus $24 \times 64 = 1536$Kbps, or a rounded 1.54 million bits per second. T1s are often used for data connections between offices, local loop connections to Frame Relay networks, or connections to the Internet.

In many areas of the country, T1s can be ordered as fractional circuits. If you need 512Kbps of bandwidth, you can order a fractional T1 with eight channels. These eight 64Kbps channels make up the 512Kbps bandwidth you needed. When a T1 is connected to a CSU/DSU, one parameter that must be set is the number of active channels.

Typically this is all 24 channels; however, in the case of a fractional T1 this must be set per circuit. When diagnosing installation problems in which fractional T1s are involved, always confirm that the CSU/DSUs are configured properly for the number of channels used.

Channel Service Unit/Data Service Unit (CSU/DSU)

A *Channel Service Unit/Data Service Unit (CSU/DSU)* (also often called just a *CSU*) interfaces with digital telephone lines. A CSU provides an interface for the router to connect to the digital line delivered by the telephone company. There are generally two types of CSUs: 56Kbps CSUs connect to 56Kbps lines and provide one channel of data over the line. T1 CSUs connect to fractional T1s and full T1s. A T1 CSU can usually be configured to use any number of channels on the line. This allows the use of fractional T1s.

A special type of CSU, called an *add/drop CSU*, can actually split the use of the channels between devices or even types of equipment. This feature can make better use of resources. Suppose a company has two offices with sophisticated phone switches. These two phone systems are connected together with a PRI line. (A *PRI* is an ISDN line packaged in a T1 span. This provides 23 channels for voice or data and one channel for signaling. The PRI line is described in more detail in the later section "Primary Rate Interface (PRI).") This PRI allows calls to be transferred and connected throughout the company as if it were all in one building. This company has purchased a full PRI line with 23 channels. One channel is used for signaling. Of these 23 channels, the company never uses more than 19. The four channels that are never used can be used for data. An add/drop CSU can be installed at either end of the PRI. The CSUs are configured to split the channels, giving the first 19 channels to the telephone system. The remaining four channels are given to the router. This gives the router a bandwidth of 256Kbps. Now the company not only has voice connectivity through the PRI, but it also has data connectivity without any additional monthly cost.

Integrated Services Digital Network (ISDN)

Integrated Services Digital Network (ISDN) is a technology that has been around for many years. However, only recently has it become a commonly used technology. ISDN defines a digital communication link for voice and data communication. ISDN can be ordered in two different ways: *Basic Rate Interface (BRI)* and *Primary Rate Interface (PRI)*. With each type of ISDN, there are data channels and a signaling channel. The data channels are used for the delivery of data. This data can consist of network packets of data or digitized voice data for normal telephone conversations. Data channels usually have a bandwidth of 64Kbps each. However, there are installations of ISDN that have 56Kbps data channels. The signaling channel is used for communication with the telephone network. This signaling includes dialing and special features such as initiating conference calls or call waiting.

ISDN Layer 2 Protocols (LAPD)

The ISDN specification includes implementations of layer 2 and layer 3 protocols. The layer 2 signaling protocol is *Link Access Procedure, D channel (LAPD)*. LAPD is used across D channels to provide control and signaling information. LAPD is formally specified in ITU-T Q.920 and ITU-T Q.921.

ISDN Layer 3 Protocols

There are two layer 3 protocols defined within the ISDN framework for signaling: ITU-T Q.930 and ITU-T Q931. These two protocols work together to provide user-to-user, circuit-switched, and packet-switched connections. These protocols specify how call establishment, call termination information, and miscellaneous messages are communicated.

Network Termination

In the United States, when an ISDN BRI line is installed, it requires equipment to provide power to the line from the customer location. This is unlike a normal telephone line, where operating power is supplied from the Central Office. The equipment at the customer location that provides this power is called a *Network Termination 1 (NT1)*.

The device that interfaces with the line and provides data connectivity to the ISDN line is not a modem. A modem *mo*dulates and *demo*dulates digital data to analog signals. In ISDN, the digital data is placed on the ISDN line in digital fashion. Therefore, no modulation or demodulation is required. The device that interfaces with the ISDN line is called a *Terminal Adapter (TA)*. Some implementations of terminal adapters include an NT1. These devices can be plugged directly into the ISDN line. Other implementations do not include the NT1 and require this device for operation.

In the United States, when an ISDN line is installed, the NT1 is not provided by the telephone company. In many parts of Europe, when an ISDN line is installed, the telephone company supplies the NT1. For this reason, ISDN interfaces can commonly be purchased with or without an integrated NT1. Because Cisco 2500 routers do not have removable modules, Cisco decided not to include NT1s in the ISDN implementation of these routers. This makes the router usable in both the U.S. and Europe. It does create the need for an external NT1 for U.S. installations, however.

ISDN Reference Points

ISDN specifies several reference points that define the logical interface between functional devices such as TAs and NT1s. The ISDN reference points are as follows:

◆ **R.** This is the reference point between non-ISDN equipment and a TA.

◆ **S.** This is the reference point between user terminals and the NT2.

◆ **T.** This is the reference point between NT1 and NT2 devices.

◆ **U.** This is the reference point between NT1 devices and line-termination equipment. The U reference point is only relevant in North America where the carrier does not provide the NT1.

Basic Rate Interface (BRI)

Basic Rate Interface (BRI) ISDN consist of two communication channels, called *bearer channels* and one signaling channel called the *data channel.* BRI ISDN is often referred to as *2B+D*. This refers to the two bearer channels and one data channel. The two bearer channels are normally 64Kbps each; however, there are installations with 56Kbps channels.

Check with your local telephone company about the speed of your bearer channels. The installation information from the telephone company should tell you. Along with the two bearer channels, there is a 16Kbps data channel. This channel is used for communicating with the CO equipment. BRI bearer channels can be used together to get a data throughput of 128Kbps data transfer. Often this is mistakenly called bonding the channels. (Bonding is an actual protocol that is not often used.) Typically when the channels are used together it is done through a protocol called multilink. *Multilink* is an extension of point-to-point protocol (PPP). Figure 5.2 shows a representation of an ISDN BRI line.

FIGURE 5.2
ISDN line makeup.

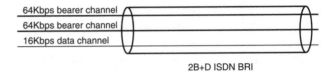

2B+D ISDN BRI

Understanding SPIDs

A *Service Profile ID (SPID)* is used between your ISDN equipment and the telephone companies switch. A SPID is usually some variation on the telephone number for your ISDN line. BRI lines normally have two telephone numbers assigned—one to each bearer channel. There are implementations of ISDN in which one SPID is used for both B channels.

Configuring BRI ISDN

There are several pieces of information you will need before attempting to configure ISDN BRI on a Cisco router. When your ISDN line is installed, the telephone company should supply you with this information. You will need to know the SPIDs of the bearer channels and the switch type that is supplying your ISDN service. There is a move toward ISDN devices autodetecting SPIDs and other necessary information. However, it is generally still necessary to configure this information manually.

The following example shows a configuration of a router with a BRI line.

```
version 11.2
service timestamps log datetime msec localtime show-
➥timezone
```

```
service password-encryption
service udp-small-servers
service tcp-small-servers
!
hostname Router1
!
boot system flash 2:
enable secret 5 $1$v5wf$t4849SbzncSTyNbE1qWOi/
!
username Router password 7 49494938292
partition flash 2 4 4
!
isdn switch-type basic-ni1
clock timezone EST -5
clock summer-time EDT recurring
!
interface Ethernet0
 ip address 10.250.1.99 255.255.255.0
 media-type 10BaseT
!
interface Serial0
 no ip address
 shutdown
!
interface BRI0
 ip address 10.1.99.1 255.255.255.0
 encapsulation ppp
 dialer map ip 10.1.99.2 broadcast 7705557435
 dialer map ip 10.1.99.2 broadcast 7705557443
 dialer load-threshold 1 either
 dialer-group 1
 isdn spid1 40455512120100 5551212
 isdn spid2 40455512130100 5551213
 no fair-queue
 ppp authentication chap
 ppp chap password 7 030B594831C79
 ppp multilink
!
router eigrp 100
 network 10.0.0.0
 no auto-summary
!
ip classless
logging buffered 4096 debugging
dialer-list 1 protocol ip permit
!
line con 0
 password 7 848473837211
 login
line vty 0 4
 password 7 382483249238
 login
!
end
```

The previous example shows a BRI configuration. The first line in the configuration having to do with ISDN is `isdn switch-type basic-ni1`. ISDN is supposed to be standardized; however, there are several different implementations. The switch type tells the router how to communicate with the CO's ISDN equipment. Basic-NI1 is the most common switch type. Many ISDN switches emulate NI1 signaling.

In one installation, the telephone company supplied the ISDN information listing the switch type as 5ESS which is one of the switch types a Bell Company might use. After hours of diagnosing, the switch type in the router was changed to Basic-NI1 and the circuit came up. This is an example of why you shouldn't blindly trust the information you are given by the telephone company. This BRI interface has an IP address assigned and encapsulation is set to PPP. The dialup configuration is using CHAP as the authentication method.

Monitoring ISDN

Cisco's IOS has several commands for monitoring ISDN. One of these commands is `show isdn status`. Its output is shown in the following example.

```
Router#show isdn status
The current ISDN Switchtype = basic-ni1
ISDN BRI1/0 interface
    Layer 1 Status:
        ACTIVE
    Layer 2 Status:
        TEI = 72, State = MULTIPLE_FRAME_ESTABLISHED
        TEI = 81, State = MULTIPLE_FRAME_ESTABLISHED
    Spid Status:
        TEI 72, ces = 1, state = 5(init)
            spid1 configured, spid1 sent, spid1 valid
            Endpoint ID Info: epsf = 0, usid = 0, tid = 1
        TEI 81, ces = 2, state = 5(init)
            spid2 configured, spid2 sent, spid2 valid
            Endpoint ID Info: epsf = 0, usid = 1, tid = 1
    Layer 3 Status:
        2 Active Layer 3 Call(s)
    Activated dsl 0 CCBs = 3
        CCB: callid=0x0, sapi=0, ces=1, B-chan=0
        CCB: callid=0x19, sapi=0, ces=2, B-chan=1
        CCB: callid=0x1A, sapi=0, ces=1, B-chan=2
    Total Allocated ISDN CCBs = 3
Router#
```

Primary Rate Interface (PRI)

Primary Rate Interface (PRI) ISDN is implemented over the same type line as a T1. This gives the PRI line 24 channels of 64Kbps data. Of these 24 channels, one must be used for signaling. This gives a PRI line 23 bearer channels of 64Kbps, or in some cases 56Kbps, data. These channels can be used independently or used together in a multilink configuration. In some installations where multiple PRI lines are used together, one signaling channel can be used for multiple lines. This gives one PRI line use of all 24 channels and the second PRI use of 23 channels. The signaling channel of the second PRI provides signaling for both lines. Special configuration from the CO is required to do this. Work with your local telephone company when you order PRIs if you would like to use multiple PRIs in this way.

A PRI is a versatile type of data circuit. Many modern telephone systems use PRI lines to connect with the COs. Telephone conversations (voice traffic) is digitized by the telephone system and transmitted over the digital telephone line. The digital data can be transmitted through the telephone network until it reaches its destination where it is converted back into analog signals.

ISDN Review

▶ ISDN comes in two packages: BRI and PRI.

▶ BRI ISDN has two bearer channels of 64Kbps (or 56Kbps) bandwidth and one signaling channel of 16Kbps.

▶ PRI ISDN is delivered on the same type circuit as a T1 and has 23 bearer channels and one signaling channel.

▶ A SPID is a Service Profile ID and is usually a variation of the telephone number for the bearer channels in your ISDN line.

▶ To configure a BRI line, you set the switch type and set up the SPIDS and the encapsulation type.

▶ ISDN lines do not provide power like normal POTS lines. ISDN lines require an NT1 at the customer site. Some ISDN devices have an NT1 built into them and some do not. Cisco 2500s with BRI require an external NT1 to work with ISDN.

▶ The command `show isdn status` provides information about an ISDN line and the status of the channels.

Remote Access Server (RAS)

Remote Access Servers (RAS) can be as simple as a few modems connected to a computer running Windows NT or as complex as a Cisco AS5300. However it's implemented, a RAS provides remote network connectivity through dialup services. RAS can be used to dial into the company network to retrieve email and access network resources such as shared storage. RAS is also used for dialup access to the Internet. Most ISPs use RAS to provide their dialup access. More sophisticated RAS systems can make use of PRI lines to provide both analog mode access and digital ISDN access. It is the use of digital PRI lines for RAS systems that made 56Kbps modems possible. 56Kbps modems take advantage of the digital connection between the RAS and the CO to increase the potential bandwidth for analog modems.

How Routers Communicate via Serial Links

Routers communicate over serial lines when connected to dedicated circuits, Frame Relay, dialup lines, and other types of WAN links. When two routers communicate over the serial ports, they must use a protocol to encapsulate the data they are transferring. These protocols include Synchronous Data-Link Control (SDLC), High-Level Data Link Control (HDLC) and Point-to-Point Protocol (PPP).

Synchronous Data-Link Control (SDLC)

Synchronous Data-Link Control (SDLC) was developed by IBM for use with its SNA protocol. Cisco routers support SDLC on their serial ports. A common use of SDLC is when an automated teller machine (ATM) is attached to a router. The router can communicate with the ATM using SDLC protocol. The traffic can then be encapsulated in TCP/IP and sent to a bank's mainframe. The following example shows the output from a show interfaces on a serial port using SDLC encapsulation.

```
Router#show interfaces serial0
Serial0 is up, line protocol is up
  Hardware is HD64570
```

```
     MTU 1500 bytes, BW 1544 Kbit, DLY 20000 usec, rely
➡255/255, load 1/255
     Encapsulation SDLC, loopback not set
       Router link station role: NONE (DTE)
       Router link station metrics:
         group poll not enabled
         poll-wait 40000 seconds
         N1 (max frame size)  12016 bits
         modulo 8
         sdlc vmac: 0000.0000.00—
     Last input 00:00:31, output 00:00:30, output hang never
     Last clearing of "show interface" counters 00:06:41
     Queueing strategy: fifo
     Output queue 0/40, 0 drops; input queue 0/75, 0 drops
     5 minute input rate 0 bits/sec, 0 packets/sec
     5 minute output rate 0 bits/sec, 0 packets/sec
        137 packets input, 8110 bytes, 0 no buffer
        Received 90 broadcasts, 0 runts, 0 giants, 0 throttles
        0 input errors, 0 CRC, 0 frame, 0 overrun, 0 ignored,
➡0 abort
        63 packets output, 3302 bytes, 0 underruns
        0 output errors, 0 collisions, 5 interface resets
        0 output buffer failures, 0 output buffers swapped out
        8 carrier transitions
        DCD=up  DSR=up  DTR=up  RTS=up  CTS=up
Router#
```

High-Level Data-Link Control (HDLC)

The *High-Level Data-Link Control (HDLC)* protocol grew from SDLC. HDLC is a Data Link layer protocol. It encapsulates data for transmission on synchronous serial connections. Although most vendors support HDLC, many implementations are slightly different. This creates some confusion for those new to internetworking. If you are connecting a Cisco router to a Bay Networks router, for example, and try to use HDLC as the protocol on the serial link, you will find that they will not communicate. This is due to the differences in the implementations. HDLC is the default encapsulation type for serial ports on Cisco routers and is often used when connecting Cisco to Cisco routers. The following example shows the output from a show interfaces command on a serial port using HDLC encapsulation.

```
Router#show interfaces seriial0
Serial0 is up, line protocol is up
  Hardware is HD64570
  Internet address is 192.168.220.2/24
  MTU 1500 bytes, BW 1544 Kbit, DLY 20000 usec, rely
➡255/255, load 1/255
```

continues

continued

```
  Encapsulation HDLC, loopback not set, keepalive set
➥(10 ➥sec)
  Last input 00:00:00, output 00:00:07, output hang never
  Last clearing of "show interface" counters 00:02:58
  Input queue: 0/75/0 (size/max/drops); Total output drops:
0
  Queueing strategy: weighted fair
  Output queue: 0/1000/64/0 (size/max total/threshold/
➥drops)
    Conversations  0/1/256 (active/max active/max total)
    Reserved Conversations 0/0 (allocated/max allocated)
  5 minute input rate 0 bits/sec, 0 packets/sec
  5 minute output rate 0 bits/sec, 0 packets/sec
    70 packets input, 3582 bytes, 0 no buffer
    Received 64 broadcasts, 0 runts, 0 giants, 0 throttles
    0 input errors, 0 CRC, 0 frame, 0 overrun, 0 ignored,
➥0 abort
    40 packets output, 1998 bytes, 0 underruns
    0 output errors, 0 collisions, 4 interface resets
    0 output buffer failures, 0 output buffers swapped out
    4 carrier transitions
    DCD=up  DSR=up  DTR=up  RTS=up  CTS=up
Router#
```

Point-to-Point Protocol (PPP)

Point-to-Point Protocol (PPP) is a Data Link layer protocol that will work over synchronous or asynchronous serial connections. PPP uses *Link Control Protocol (LCP)* to build and monitor connections. PPP provides a non-vendor-specific standard for serial link communication. PPP is often used when routers from two different manufactures must communicate with each other. PPP is the protocol used by most all dial-up Internet connections.

Because PPP is often used over dial-up lines, the LCP portion supports authentication using two protocols: *Password Authentication Protocol (PAP)* and *Challenge-Handshake Authentication Protocol (CHAP)*. PAP provides a simple authentication technique. Its biggest disadvantage is that passwords are transmitted over the link in clear text. CHAP provides a more secure authentication technique using a "magic" number. CHAP authentication never transmits the password over the link.

PPP supports many different network protocols, including TCP/IP, IPX/SPX, AppleTalk, Transparent Bridging, DECnet, and OSI/CLNS.

To configure PPP on a serial port, use the command encapsulation
ppp, as shown in the following example.

```
Router#configure terminal
Enter configuration commands, one per line.  End with
➡CNTL/Z.
Router(config)#interface serial1
Router(config-if)#encapsulation ppp
Router(config-if)#
```

The following example shows the output from a show interfaces
for a serial port using PPP encapsulation.

```
Router#
Router#show interfaces serial0
Serial0 is up, line protocol is up
  Hardware is HD64570
  Internet address is 192.168.220.2/24
  MTU 1500 bytes, BW 1544 Kbit, DLY 20000 usec, rely
➡255/255, load 1/255
  Encapsulation PPP, loopback not set, keepalive set (10
➡sec)
  LCP Open
  Open: IPCP, CDPCP
  Last input 00:00:01, output 00:00:01, output hang never
  Last clearing of "show interface" counters 00:00:02
  Input queue: 0/75/0 (size/max/drops); Total output drops:
➡0
  Queueing strategy: weighted fair
  Output queue: 0/1000/64/0 (size/max total/threshold/
➡drops)
     Conversations  0/1/256 (active/max active/max total)
     Reserved Conversations 0/0 (allocated/max allocated)
  5 minute input rate 0 bits/sec, 0 packets/sec
  5 minute output rate 0 bits/sec, 0 packets/sec
     3 packets input, 96 bytes, 0 no buffer
     Received 3 broadcasts, 0 runts, 0 giants, 0 throttles
     0 input errors, 0 CRC, 0 frame, 0 overrun, 0 ignored,
➡0 abort
     2 packets output, 32 bytes, 0 underruns
     0 output errors, 0 collisions, 0 interface resets
     0 output buffer failures, 0 output buffers swapped out
     0 carrier transitions
     DCD=up  DSR=up  DTR=up  RTS=up  CTS=up
Router#
```

FRAME RELAY

Frame Relay is a packet-switching network. This type of network
shares expensive resources among subscribers. By sharing the
expensive resources such as long distance digital connections, the
Frame Relay provider can offer a more cost-effective solution than
dedicated lines. Dedicated lines are charged on a per-mile basis.

When dedicated lines cross state lines, costs and complexity of problem solving are increased. Because different areas are handled by different Bell Operating Companies (BOCs) it is difficult to get one BOC to take responsibility for a line crossing several states. This creates problems when a line is having problems. Many times, vendors will point fingers at one another rather than try to resolve the problem.

Frame Relay circuits save the customer money because the only mileage charge is from the customer site to the Frame Relay provider's local Point Of Presence (POP). Once in the provider's POP, the traffic can travel throughout the Frame Relay network without regard to distance. A business can save a tremendous amount of money by switching from dedicated lines to Frame Relay. Frame Relay allows the telephone companies to make more efficient use of their networks, therefore costing the customer less. Frame Relay is an enhancement of the X.25 packet-switching network.

In a Frame Relay network, customer data is fed into the Frame Relay network by a local loop. After the data enters the Frame Relay network, it can travel over circuits with data from other companies. The data travels within the Frame Relay network until it reaches the local Frame Relay switch for the destination. It then exits the network on the destination's local loop and arrives at the destination network. During the time the data is in the Frame Relay network, it can be sent over different paths based on network load and availability of circuits. In a Frame Relay network, if a circuit is cut, data can be rerouted automatically to other circuits. This gives Frame Relay very high reliability.

Frame Relay Cloud

Frame Relay cloud, or just *cloud*, is used to describe the multitude of Frame Relay switches and circuits that make up the Frame Relay network. It describes most everything after the local loop of the source network to the local loop of the destination network.

Committed Information Rate (CIR)

When you order a Frame Relay circuit, you request a *Committed Information Rate (CIR)*. The CIR is how much bandwidth the Frame Relay vendor guarantees you. Because Frame Relay networks are shared, this number can be very important. What you are charged for a Frame Relay circuit is directly related to the CIR. If you order a circuit with 384Kbps of bandwidth and a CIR of 256Kbps, then your Frame Relay vendor guarantees delivery of 256Kbps of data. Some Frame Relay providers allow you to burst up to the full speed of your circuit, thus exceeding your CIR. Some vendors do not. This is something you should consider when choosing a Frame Relay provider. If your provider allows you to burst above the CIR, data in excess of the CIR is marked Discard Eligible (DE), which is explained later in this chapter.

Data-Link Connection Identifier (DLCI)

In a Frame Relay network, one physical circuit can support multiple virtual circuits The router needs some way to identify for which virtual circuit a packet of data is destined. The *Data-Link Connection Identifier* (*DLCI*, pronounced "del-see") is used to identify this virtual circuit. After the packet of data is received by the Frame Relay switch, the router is attached, and the Frame Relay switch makes a determination as to how to forward the packet. The Frame Relay switch has been programmed by the Frame Relay vendor to know where to forward packets containing particular DLCI numbers. The programming is specific to the local Frame Relay switch with which the router is connected. After the packet of data exits the local Frame Relay switch and starts, it travels through the Frame Relay cloud, the local DLCI number is no longer significant. The local DLCI number is used only between the router and the Frame Relay switch with which the router is connected.

To review, the DLCI represents a virtual circuit to the Frame Relay switch attached to the router. Beyond that point in the Frame Relay cloud, the DLCI has no significance. This is what people mean when they state that a DLCI has "local significance" only.

This topic can be very confusing. A DLCI does not identify the connection between two routers, it identifies the virtual circuit only between the Frame Relay switch and the locally connected router.

Figure 5.3 shows a typical Frame Relay network. Tampa, Fl. is connected to a Frame Relay switch through its local loop. This Frame Relay switch identifies this connection as DLCI 100. The Frame Relay provider created a connection between this Frame Relay switch and the Frame Relay switch connected to Atlanta, Ga.. This connection is called a Permanent Virtual Circuit (PVC). (PVCs are explained in more detail later in this chapter.) The Frame Relay switch connected to Atlanta, Ga. communicates with the destination router through its local loop. This connection is identified as DLCI 101. To the router in Tampa, Fl., it communicates with the Frame Relay switch using DLCI 100. The router in Atlanta, Ga. communicates with it's Frame Relay switch using DLCI 101. Each of the DLCIs has local significance because the router on the other end of the connection does not know of the use at the other Frame Relay switch.

Frame Relay providers have begun to configure the DLCIs in such a way that they seem more logical. The providers will assign the same DLCI for each connection back to one location to make it appear as if the DLCI refers to a location rather than only being locally significant. Figure 5.3 shows how this might look.

FIGURE 5.3

A method of assigning DLCIs to simplify the network.

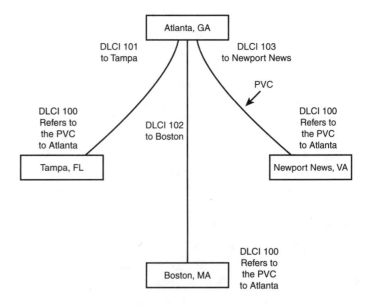

Configurations from the routers in Figure 5.3 would look like the ones shown in the following four examples.

Atlanta, GA

```
interface Serial0
 no ip address
 no ip directed-broadcast
 encapsulation frame-relay IETF
!
interface Serial0.101 point-to-point
 description Tampa, FL
 ip address 10.1.1.5 255.255.255.252
 frame-relay interface-dlci 101
!
interface Serial0.102 point-to-point
 description Boston, MA
 ip address 10.1.1.9 255.255.255.252
 frame-relay interface-dlci 102
!
interface Serial0.103 point-to-point
 description Newport News, VA
 ip address 10.1.1.13 255.255.255.252
 frame-relay interface-dlci 103
!
```

Tampa, FL

```
interface Serial0
 no ip address
 no ip directed-broadcast
 encapsulation frame-relay IETF
!
interface Serial0.100 point-to-point
 description Atlanta, GA
 ip address 10.1.1.6 255.255.255.252
 frame-relay interface-dlci 100
```

Boston, MA

```
interface Serial0
 no ip address
 no ip directed-broadcast
 encapsulation frame-relay IETF
!
interface Serial0.100 point-to-point
 description Atlanta, GA
 ip address 10.1.1.10 255.255.255.252
 frame-relay interface-dlci 100
```

Newport News, VA

```
interface Serial0
 no ip address
 no ip directed-broadcast
 encapsulation frame-relay IETF
!
interface Serial0.100 point-to-point
 description Atlanta, GA
 ip address 10.1.1.14 255.255.255.252
 frame-relay interface-dlci 100
```

In the previous four examples, it appears that the DLCI for Atlanta is 100, and each of the other routers reference its DLCI. Actually, the DLCI 100 is unknown to the Atlanta router. DLCI 100 is defined in each of the other router's local Frame Relay switches and it refers to the PVC that connects to Atlanta. This means the DLCI numbers are locally significant to the Frame Relay switch at which they are defined.

When you are bringing up a new Frame Relay site and it does not appear to be working properly, try reversing the DLCI numbers at the two ends. It is not uncommon for a Frame Relay provider to accidentally program the Frame Relay switches with the DLCI numbers opposite of what your documentation says. Trying this first can save you days of headaches.

Permanent Virtual Circuit (PVC)

A *Permanent Virtual Circuit (PVC)* is a connection created within the Frame Relay cloud by the Frame Relay provider. The PVC is created as a virtual connection between two locations. A PVC can seem like a dedicated connection between two different locations.

The Frame Relay provider programs PVCs into the Frame Relay switches. When data enters the Frame Relay cloud, it is identified by a DLCI. This DLCI relates to a PVC within the network. The data is switched through the network to the destination for that PVC.

It is important to realize that one Frame Relay circuit can support multiple PVCs. This is one of the cost-saving advantages of Frame Relay. By supporting multiple connections on one local loop, a company can save money on the recurring circuit costs and on the hardware required to support another circuit.

Switched Virtual Circuit (SVC)

A *Switched Virtual Circuit (SVC)* works much like a Permanent Virtual Circuit. However, an SVC is created and deleted by the customer's equipment. This allows greater flexibility in the network. An SVC is much like making a telephone call: You pick up the telephone and dial a phone number. The telephone switch translates this number and switches the lines required to connect your telephone to the telephone you are calling. When your call is complete, you hang up the telephone and the switch terminates all of the connections it created for your telephone call.

An SVC works much like this. When your router needs to communicate with another router, it sends the signals to the Frame Relay switch to connect it to the other router. The Frame Relay switch dynamically creates a path between the two routers. The routers communicate and when they are finished the router tells the Frame Relay switch to terminate the connection. The Frame Relay switch then removes the dynamic connection it created. SVCs are not used very much but do serve a useful purpose.

Local Management Interface (LMI)

Local Management Interface (LMI) is a protocol used between the Frame Relay switch and your router. In 1990 Cisco Systems, StrataCom, Northern Telecom, and Digital Equipment worked together to create what is known as "Gang-of-Four LMI," or "Cisco LMI." They took the original Frame Relay protocol and added extensions that make supporting larger internetworks easier.

The extensions that were added include the following:

◆ **Virtual Circuit Status Messages.** This extension provides synchronization between the network and the user device. It periodically reports the existence of net PVCs and the deletion of already existing ones. It provides basic information about the integrity of PVCs.

◆ **Multicasting.** This extension allows a sender to transmit a single frame and have it delivered to multiple recipients.

◆ **Global Addressesing.** This extension gives connection identifiers global rather than local significance.

◆ **Simple Flow Control.** This extension offers a flow control mechanism that applies to the entire Frame Relay interface.

CONFIGURING FRAME RELAY

Configuring Frame Relay on a Cisco router involves configuring the interface for each of the protocols that will be used such as IP or IPX, and relating the interface to the DLCI for the connection.

There are two different ways to configure Frame Relay on a router supporting multiple connections: multipoint and point-to-point.

Configuring Multipoint Frame Relay

In Figure 5.4, you see a Frame Relay network with multiple sites connecting to the Atlanta office. This Frame Relay network is set up in a multipoint configuration. In a *multipoint* configuration, all of the routers are on one network.

FIGURE 5.4
Frame Relay network using multipoint interfaces.

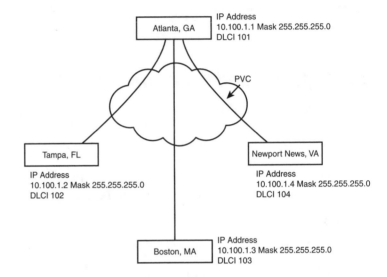

In a multipoint Frame Relay configuration, each of the DLCIs are listed under one subinterface. The following example shows how the serial port would be configured in the Atlanta router in Figure 5.4.

```
interface Serial0/0.1 multipoint
 ip address 10.100.1.1 255.255.255.0
 frame-relay interface-dlci 102
 frame-relay interface-dlci 103
 frame-relay interface-dlci 104
```

Multipoint Frame Relay networks present a challenge for network designers. Note that in Figure 5.3 each of the routers has a direct connection back to Atlanta. However, none of the routers have connections to the other branch routers. This means that if the router in Tampa needs to communicate with the router in Newport News, it must send the data to Atlanta first. The way the IP protocol works is different. Because Tampa and Newport News are in the same subnet, the routers would try to communicate directly. This is why most Frame Relay networks are configured in a point-to-point configuration.

Configuring Point-to-Point Frame Relay

The opposite of multipoint is point-to-point. In a point-to-point
Frame Relay network, each PVC is represented by a separate interface
connection within the router. Since Frame Relay can support multiple connections on one physical circuit, there needs to be a way of
separating these connections within the router. Cisco supports this
logical separation of a physical connection through the use of subinterfaces. To configure Frame Relay on a serial port, use the command
encapsulation frame-relay, as shown in the following example.

```
Router#configure terminal
Enter configuration commands, one per line.  End with
➥CNTL/Z.
Router(config)#interface serial0
Router(config-if)#encapsulation frame-relay
Router(config-if)#
```

Separating Logical Connections with Subinterfaces

Subinterfaces provide a method of separating one physical network
connection into multiple logical connections. This is useful for
Frame Relay because one physical local loop can support many
PVCs. This creates the appearance of many different physical connections to other sites on one interface. The router must have some
means of separating these logical connections so it can properly
deliver the traffic destined to them. Subinterfaces provide this
means. Subinterfaces have uses beyond just Frame Relay, but this
section focuses on how subinterfaces are used with Frame Relay.

To create a subinterface, use the interface command in the configure
mode of the router. Enter the interface description to which you want to
add a subinterface, with an added period and a number following to
identify the subinterface. When configuring Frame Relay, it is a good
idea to use the DLCI number for the subinterface number. This makes
it easier to identify items in the config later. The following example
shows how DLCI 199 is configured as a subinterface of interface Serial0.

```
Router#config terminal
Router(config)#interface Serial0.199
Router(config-if)#ip address 10.199.2.1 255.255.255.0
Router(config-if)#frame-relay interface DLCI 199
Router(config-if)#exit
Router(config)#
```

Figure 5.5 shows how subinterfaces connect with the router. Serial0 is connected to the local loop that connects the office with the Frame Relay cloud. Serial0 is subinterfaced to three interfaces. Serial0.1 has an IP address of 10.100.2.1 and connects to the PVC for Boston. Serial0.2 has an IP address of 10.200.2.1 and connects to the PVC for Newport News. Serial0.3 has an IP address of 10.1.2.1 and connects to Atlanta. Each of these interfaces works logically as a separate network interface although they all exist on one physical interface. Each subinterface can be shut down independently of the others and can support different protocols. For example, Serial0.2 might support IPX traffic as well as TCP/IP, although the other two subinterfaces only support TCP/IP.

FIGURE 5.5
An example of how subinterfaces can be used in a Frame Relay network.

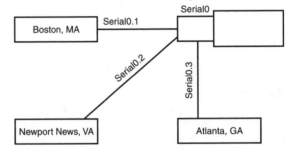

Monitoring Frame Relay

There are several commands specific to Frame Relay monitoring. These commands allow you to see specific data on Frame Relay networks.

Monitoring the Serial Port of a Frame Relay Connection

The show interfaces command lists some Frame Relay specific information for interfaces connected to Frame Relay networks. The following example shows the output from show interfaces for a Frame Relay network.

```
Router#sh int s5/0
Serial5/0 is up, line protocol is up
  Hardware is M4T
  MTU 1500 bytes, BW 1544 Kbit, DLY 20000 usec, rely
➡255/255, load 3/255
  Encapsulation FRAME-RELAY IETF, loopback not set,
➡keepalive set (10 sec)
```

```
   LMI enq sent  18350, LMI stat recvd 18350, LMI upd recvd
➥6, DTE LMI up
   LMI enq recvd 0, LMI stat sent  0, LMI upd sent  0
   LMI DLCI 1023  LMI type is CISCO  frame relay DTE
   Broadcast queue 0/64, broadcasts sent/dropped 0/0,
➥interface broadcasts 102718
0
   Last input 00:00:00, output 00:00:00, output hang never
   Last clearing of "show interface" counters 2d02h
   Input queue: 0/75/0 (size/max/drops); Total output drops:
0
   Queueing strategy: weighted fair
   Output queue: 0/64/0 (size/threshold/drops)
      Conversations  0/163 (active/max active)
      Reserved Conversations 0/0 (allocated/max allocated)
   5 minute input rate 24000 bits/sec, 24 packets/sec
   5 minute output rate 23000 bits/sec, 21 packets/sec
      5397749 packets input, 1050654351 bytes, 0 no buffer
      Received 0 broadcasts, 0 runts, 0 giants
      0 input errors, 0 CRC, 0 frame, 0 overrun, 0 ignored,
➥0 abort
      5045209 packets output, 1227209722 bytes, 0 underruns
      0 output errors, 0 collisions, 0 interface resets
      0 output buffer failures, 0 output buffers swapped out
      0 carrier transitions    DCD=up  DSR=up  DTR=up
➥RTS=up  CTS=up
Router#
```

The show interfaces command shows a subset of this information
for each of the subinterfaces. Because a subinterface is a logical separation of networks, it is not necessary for it to display all of the physical information about the interface. The following example shows
the output from show interfaces for a Frame Relay subinterface.

```
Router#show interfaces serial5/0.1
Serial5/0.1 is up, line protocol is up
  Hardware is M4T
  Description: Boston
  Internet address is 10.110.17.1/24
  MTU 1500 bytes, BW 1544 Kbit, DLY 20000 usec, rely
➥255/255, load 4/255
  Encapsulation FRAME-RELAY IETF
Router#
```

Seeing Active PVCs

To view the PVCs your router can see, use the show frame-relay
pvc. The following example shows the output from this command.

```
Tampa_FL#show frame-relay pvc

PVC Statistics for interface Serial0/0 (Frame Relay DTE)
```

continues

continued

```
DLCI = 100, DLCI USAGE = LOCAL, PVC STATUS = ACTIVE,
➥INTERFACE = Serial0/0.100

  input pkts 26318755        output pkts 33295916       in
➥bytes 2677624387
  out bytes 3218704665       dropped pkts 46            in
➥FECN pkts 312
  in BECN pkts 0             out FECN pkts 0            out
➥BECN pkts 0
  in DE pkts 170015          out DE pkts 0
  out bcast pkts 5016413     out bcast bytes 402198896
  pvc create time 35w4d, last time pvc status changed 2d18h

DLCI = 101, DLCI USAGE = LOCAL, PVC STATUS = ACTIVE,
➥INTERFACE = Serial0/0.101

  input pkts 13540113        output pkts 12640482       in
➥bytes 476157705
  out bytes 1523146301       dropped pkts 42            in FECN
➥pkts 30858
  in BECN pkts 0             out FECN pkts 0            out
➥BECN pkts 0
  in DE pkts 1998143         out DE pkts 0
  out bcast pkts 4981728     out bcast bytes 399422790
  pvc create time 35w4d, last time pvc status changed 1d03h

DLCI = 161, DLCI USAGE = LOCAL, PVC STATUS = ACTIVE,
➥INTERFACE = Serial0/0.161

  input pkts 5229620         output pkts 5285702        in
➥bytes 525271058
  out bytes 1180706730       dropped pkts 63            in FECN
➥pkts 7
  in BECN pkts 22057         out FECN pkts 0            out
➥BECN pkts 0
  in DE pkts 85329           out DE pkts 0
  out bcast pkts 3266531     out bcast bytes 261916791
  pvc create time 26w1d, last time pvc status changed 2d18h
Tampa_FL#
```

In the preceding example you see the statistics shown with the command `show frame-relay pvc`. Each of the DLCIs assigned is listed with statistics about each. The input/output packets and bytes are self-explanatory. They represent the amount of data that has been passed using this DLCI. The number of dropped packets represents the number of packets that were dropped at the Frame Relay level because an active outbound DLCI was not found. The next two statistics are FECN and BECN. These are methods of informing the network devices of congestion in the Frame Relay network.

◆ **Forward Explicit Congestion Notification (FECN).** A method used in Frame Relay to inform the routers of congestion on the network. When a Frame Relay switch detects congestion, it can set a bit in the frame to notify the receiving network device that the packet experienced congestion in the network. This is called FECN (pronounced feck-in).

◆ **Backward Explicit Congestion Notification (BECN).** Often used in conjunction with FECN. When a packet is passing back to the sending station, the Frame Relay switch can set the BECN bit to tell the sending station its traffic is experiencing congestion. The sending station can then reduce the speed at which it is sending data. This is called BECN (pronounced beck-in).

Because Frame Relay is a shared network, there are times when your traffic may not be delivered due to network congestion. When a Frame Relay switch experiences congestion, it will first start discarding traffic. One way it decides what traffic to discard is to look at the Discard Eligible (DE) bit. Your router can set this bit when the traffic enters the Frame Relay network, indicating that this packet can be dropped if necessary. A common use of the DE bit is when bandwidth utilization exceeds the Committed Information Rate (CIR). Traffic in excess of the CIR can be set as Discard Eligible (DE). Because many networking protocols such as TCP guarantee delivery of packets, if the Frame Relay network drops a packet, the TCP protocol will resend the data.

Viewing the Frame Relay Map

Cisco routers create an internal map of frame relay DLCIs and the ports they are mapped with. This map can be viewed using the command show frame-relay map, as shown in the following example.

```
Router#sh frame-relay map
Serial5/0.123 (up): point-to-point dlci, dlci
➥123(0x7B,0x1CB0), broadcast, BW =
64000
          status defined, active
Serial5/0.149 (up): point-to-point dlci, dlci
➥141(0x8D,0x20D0), broadcast, BW =
16000
```

continues

continued

```
        status defined, active
Serial5/0.133 (up): point-to-point dlci, dlci
➥168(0xA8,0x2880), broadcast, BW =
16000
        status defined, active
Serial5/0.148 (up): point-to-point dlci, dlci
➥164(0xA4,0x2840), broadcast, BW =
16000
        status defined, active
Serial5/0.7 (up): point-to-point dlci, dlci
➥102(0x66,0x1860), broadcast, BW = 16
000
        status defined, active
Serial5/0.9 (up): point-to-point dlci, dlci 16(0x10,0x400),
➥broadcast, BW = 1600
0
        status defined, active
Serial5/0.5 (up): point-to-point dlci, dlci
➥106(0x6A,0x18A0), broadcast, BW = 16
000
        status defined, active
Serial5/0.8 (up): point-to-point dlci, dlci
➥111(0x6F,0x18F0), broadcast, BW = 16
000
        status defined, active
Serial5/0.122 (up): point-to-point dlci, dlci
➥122(0x7A,0x1CA0), broadcast, BW =
64000
        status defined, active
Serial5/0.2 (up): point-to-point dlci, dlci
➥100(0x64,0x1840), broadcast, BW = 16
000
        status defined, active
Serial5/0.146 (up): point-to-point dlci, dlci
➥146(0x92,0x2420), broadcast, BW =
16000
        status defined, active
Serial5/0.10 (up): point-to-point dlci, dlci
➥113(0x71,0x1C10), broadcast, BW = 1
6000
        status defined, active
Serial5/0.11 (up): point-to-point dlci, dlci
➥134(0x86,0x2060), broadcast, BW = 1
6000
        status defined, active
Serial5/0.6 (up): point-to-point dlci, dlci
➥105(0x69,0x1890), broadcast, BW = 16
000
        status defined, active
Serial5/0.4 (up): point-to-point dlci, dlci
➥108(0x6C,0x18C0), broadcast, BW = 16
000
```

```
              status defined, active
Serial5/0.138 (up): point-to-point dlci, dlci
→138(0x8A,0x20A0), broadcast, BW =
16000
              status defined, active
Serial5/0.147 (up): point-to-point dlci, dlci
→157(0x9D,0x24D0), broadcast, BW =
16000
              status defined, active
Serial5/0.3 (up): point-to-point dlci, dlci
→107(0x6B,0x18B0), broadcast, BW = 16
000
              status defined, active
Serial5/0.150 (up): point-to-point dlci, dlci
→206(0xCE,0x30E0), broadcast, BW =
16000
              status defined, active
Serial5/0.12 (up): point-to-point dlci, dlci
→114(0x72,0x1C20), broadcast, BW = 1
6000
              status defined, active
Serial5/0.1 (up): point-to-point dlci, dlci
→109(0x6D,0x18D0), broadcast, BW = 16
000
              status defined, active
Router#
```

In the previous example you see that each interface that has been set
for frame relay encapsulation is listed along with other information
about the DLCI. Listed as BW is the bandwidth of the circuit's CIR.

Frame Relay Review

REVIEW BREAK

▶ Frame Relay is a packet-switching network that provides low
cost connections due to the sharing of resources.

▶ The entire Frame Relay network is called the cloud.

▶ The Committed Information Rate (CIR) is how much bandwidth your Frame Relay provider guarantees you will have
available.

▶ A Data-Link Connection Identifier (DLCI) is a number
assigned to map an IP address to a PVC. DLCIs have local significance. This means they can be different on either end of a
PVC and can be reused within the network.

▶ A Permanent Virtual Circuit (PVC) is a path created in the
Frame Relay network between two points. The Frame Relay
provider creates PVCs.

▶ A Switched Virtual Circuit (SVC) is a path created dynamically in the Frame Relay network in much the same way a telephone call is placed. When one router needs to communicate with another, it requests that the Frame Relay switch create an SVC. The switch creates the SVC dynamically. When the routers no longer need to communicate, the SVC is deleted.

▶ Local Management Interface (LMI) is the protocol used between the router and the Frame Relay switch to add management functions for large internetworks.

▶ To configure Frame Relay on an interface, use the command `encapsulation frame-relay`.

▶ To separate a physical interface into subinterfaces, use the configuration command `interface serial0.100`, where `.100` is the subinterface you want to create. Add the `frame-relay interface DLCI 100` command, where 100 is the DLCI number for the PVC.

▶ To diagnose Frame Relay problems, the commands `show interfaces` and `show frame-relay pvc` offer much information.

WAN Technologies—When to Use What

Wide Area Network (WAN) technologies are tricky. One of the variables that can greatly affect the decision of one technology over another is cost. Cost varies greatly across the United States and ever more so in other countries. This creates quite a challenge when trying to determine which WAN technology to use.

There are several factors to consider when choosing a WAN technology for a remote site. What facilities do you have at the site to which you are connecting? If you are connecting an office in Boston to an office in Atlanta, and the office in Atlanta can only support Frame Relay, that pretty much makes the decision for you.

The most wisely designed WANs use a variety of technologies, each used where it is strong in both cost and versatility. It wouldn't make sense to use ISDN to connect two offices when the long distance charges between the offices would exceed the cost of a point-to-point fractional T1. It also wouldn't make sense to use a full T1 point-to-point connection to connect an office of three light email users to the company's network, unless the cost of a full T1 in that part of the country was cheaper than an ISDN line.

With every decision of how to connect offices, weigh all the factors. Consider the options and make a wise decision. Too many companies set a standard and live by that standard no matter what. In short, use common sense.

There are parts of the country where you can get a dedicated 56Kbps line for under $100 a month. This is an excellent deal. There are also parts of the country where ISDN lines are very inexpensive. In these parts of the country it might make sense to connect smaller offices to a larger one via ISDN and then connect the larger office to the company's Frame Relay network with a T1 or fractional T1.

Use your company's money wisely. In the case of the American Cancer Society, for example, the money you save could save lives. In the case of an automotive manufacturer, on the other hand, the money you save may mean a bigger bonus.

It is difficult to set standards for how large a circuit is required for what size office. It depends greatly on the network traffic that office will generate. An office of salespeople who mainly use email and browse the Web will generate far less traffic than a data center that constantly queries database servers distributed around your WAN. Find a way to monitor the traffic on your circuits and adjust the bandwidths based on this information. An excellent product for monitoring circuit utilization is Multi Router Traffic Graphic (MRTG). MRTG is a freeware product that will run on Linux/UNIX or Windows NT. (It runs much better on Linux/UNIX than it does on Windows NT. It tends to bog down a Windows NT server.) It is available at no cost from its creator at
`http://ee-staff.ethz.ch/~oetiker/webtools/mrtg/mrtg.html`.

CASE STUDY: RAPTOR RESCUE ORGANIZATION

ESSENCE OF THE CASE

▶ You need to install a T1 line with very little information. The sales representative who sold the circuit no longer works for the ISP so you cannot question him about what he told the Raptor Rescue. The person from the Raptor Rescue who ordered the circuit is out of the country for a month, so you are unable to find out any information from him. You must use your background in WAN technologies to help you figure out how things work together.

SCENARIO

You have been hired to install and connect a T1 line for the Raptor Rescue organization. This organization takes in birds of prey that have been injured. Birds that can recover are rehabilitated and released back into the wild. Birds that have sustained more serious injuries are kept well and used for educational programs to teach people about the benefits of Raptors. The Raptor Rescue has ordered a T1 connection for the Internet and the ISP was supposed to provide installation. Unfortunately, at the last minute the Raptor Rescue found out they would have to hire someone for the installation. You are that lucky person.

The Raptor Rescue knows very little about what they have ordered. They simply listened to the sales representative that sold them the T1. They purchased a Cisco 2501 router and a Kentrox D-Serv 56/64 DSU.

ANALYSIS

You have been told that the Raptor Rescue ordered a T1 line from the ISP. You take the equipment to the telephone room and evaluate the situation. You notice the Kentrox D-Serv 56/64 DSU and think to yourself, "If they truly get a T1, this DSU won't work because it's only for 56/64Kbps lines." A CSU/DSU capable of handling 24 channels would be required for a full T1 line. The Kentrox 56/64Kbps DSU handles only one channel of either 56Kbps or 64Kbps.

In the telephone room you find a work order on the floor. The work order is from the telephone company. It says they were to install a 56Kbps line to Acme Internet. Finally, some clue as to what is happening here! They are not getting a T1 as was described to you; they are getting a 56Kbps line.

CASE STUDY: RAPTOR RESCUE ORGANIZATION

You have found that it is not uncommon to find people not familiar with WAN technologies referring to any dedicated circuit as a T1.

You contact the ISP and get the IP address that has been assigned to the Raptor Rescue. You configure the router with that IP address and set the bandwidth on the interface for 56Kbps. You remove the DSU from its box and refer to the configuration guide.

The DSU has two connectors on the back: one is an RS-232 and the other a V.35. You have a Cisco V.35 cable in the box with the router.

In the manual, you find how to set the DSU to use the V.35 connector. You also find how to set the data rate to 56Kbps. After completing this configuration, you plug the DSU into the jack marked by the telephone company. You connect the V.35 cable from the DSU to the router and turn on all of the equipment. The DSU starts to light up and the router is now up and running.

You plug the router into the local network and configure your laptop with the IP address of the router as your default gateway. After you have connected your laptop to the network, you try and connect to the Cisco Web site. Success!

CHAPTER SUMMARY

KEY TERMS

- Integrated Services Digital Network (ISDN)
- Basic Rate Interface (BRI)
- Primary Rate Interface (PRI)
- Service Profile ID (SPID)
- Central Office (CO)
- Plain Old Telephone Service (POTS)
- Local loop
- Demarcation point
- Customer Premises Equipment (CPE)
- T1
- Channel Service Unit/Data Service Unit (CSU/DSU)
- Synchronous Data-Link Control (SDLC)
- High-Level Data-Link Control (HDLC)
- Point-to-Point Protocol (PPP)
- Frame Relay
- Committed Information Rate (CIR)
- Data-Link Connection Identifier (DLCI)
- Permanent Virtual Circuit (PVC)
- Switched Virtual Circuit (SVC)
- Local Management Interface (LMI)

This chapter covered WAN protocols, terms, and technologies. In any internetwork, you will find connections to the outside world in one or more of these fashions. T1s are commonly used for connections to the Internet. Frame Relay is often used for connecting branch offices of a company together. ISDN is a good solution for backup circuits and intermittent connections for branch offices. ISDN is also a good solution for small office Internet connectivity.

Knowing and understanding these technologies will make your life as an internetworking engineer much easier. There are many nuances in dealing with local telephone companies that you will simply have to learn through experience.

APPLY YOUR KNOWLEDGE

Review Questions

1. Describe the channel makeup of a T1 circuit.

2. Describe a CO and some of the services it can provide.

3. Describe an ISDN BRI line and PRI line.

4. Describe HDLC as a protocol and how it interoperates with different vendors' equipment.

5. How do you know how much bandwidth will be guaranteed by your Frame Relay provider?

6. What are two ways that Frame Relay can be configured within a router?

7. How are DLCIs assigned?

8. What techniques do Frame Relay switches use to inform routers of congestion in the network?

9. How is a subinterface created? What is its purpose?

10. What is an NT1? What is its function?

Exam Questions

1. Which of the following are related to Frame Relay? Select two.

   A. SPID

   B. LMI

   C. CIR

   D. 2B+D

2. An ISDN BRI line can be described as which of the following?

   A. 23B+D

   B. 2B+D

   C. 23D+B

   D. 2D+B

3. What does CIR represent?

   A. A CIR is the number used to represent the connection between a router and the Frame Relay switch.

   B. A CIR connects two Frame Relay sites through Frame Relay switch programming.

   C. The CIR is the amount of bandwidth your Frame Relay provider guarantees you will have available.

   D. CIR is the protocol used between a router and a Frame Relay switch.

4. To configure ISDN, you must set which of the following?

   A. ISDN switch-type; SPIDs; encapsulation

   B. SPIDs; encapsulation; NT1

   C. cir; ISDN switch-type; encapsulation

   D. ISDN switch-type; LMI; SPIDs

5. Why is Frame Relay more cost effective than leased lines?

   A. Smaller connections are cheaper than leased lines.

   B. Frame Relay connections are cheaper because of competition between providers.

   C. Because Frame Relay providers can share resources between many companies, they can charge less for the service.

   D. Frame Relay uses bearer channels to increase the bandwidth available.

APPLY YOUR KNOWLEDGE

6. Which answer best describes DLCIs?

   A. DLCIs are global throughout the network.

   B. DLCIs are locally significant.

   C. DLCIs set the amount of bandwidth allocated to your circuit.

   D. DLCIs prioritize traffic so that more important traffic is delivered first.

7. Which of the following commands shows the status of PVCs?

   A. `Router#show frame-relay pvc`

   B. `Router#list frame-relay pvc`

   C. `Router#show frame-relay dlci`

   D. `Router#list frame-relay dlci`

8. Which of the following commands shows the status of an ISDN line?

   A. `Router#show isdn status`

   B. `Router(config)#show isdn status`

   C. `Router#show spid status`

   D. `Router(config)#show spid status`

9. How do you create a subinterface?

   A. `Router(config)#interface serial0`
      `subinterface 100`

   B. `Router(config)#subinterface serial0.100`

   C. `Router(config)#create subinterface 100`

   D. `Router(config)#interface serial0.100`

10. What method do Frame Relay switches use to inform routers of congestion within the Frame Relay network?

    A. Forward Error Congestion Notification (FECN) and Backward Error Congestion Notification (BECN)

    B. Congestion Control Protocol (CCP)

    C. Data-Link Connection Identifier (DLCI)

    D. Latency Algorithm, Traffic Errors (LATE)

Answers to Review Questions

1. A T1 circuit contains 24 channels, each having a bandwidth of 64Kbps, giving the T1 a bandwidth of 1.54Mbps. For more information, see "T1 Service."

2. A CO is a Central Office and can provide POTS, ISDN, Drame Relay, and local loop connections. For more information, see "Central Office."

3. An ISDN BRI line has two bearer channels with a bandwidth of 64Kbps or 56Kbps each, and a signaling channel with a bandwidth of 16Kbps. A PRI line is delivered on the same type of circuit as a T1 and contains 23 64Kbps bearer channels with one channel used for signaling. For more information, see "Basic Rate Interface (BRI)" and "Primary Rate Interface (PRI)."

4. HDLC is used for serial communication and is generally vendor specific. Being vendor specific, routers from different manufacturers cannot use HDLC for communication with one another. For more information, see "High-Level Data-Link Control (HDLC)."

APPLY YOUR KNOWLEDGE

5. When you order a circuit, you specify a Committed Information Rate (CIR). This CIR is how much bandwidth the provider guarantees. The higher the CIR, the higher the price. For more information, see "Committed Information Rate (CIR)."

6. Frame Relay can be configured as either multipoint or point-to-point. In multipoint, all of the DLCIs are listed under one subinterface. In point-to-point, each DLCI is separated under its own subinterface with a separate network. For more information, see "Configuring Frame Relay."

7. DLCIs are assigned by the Frame Relay vendor and are only significant in the local connection between the Frame Relay switch and the router. Although in some implementations they may appear to be global, they are not. For more information, see "Data-Link Connection Identifier (DLCI)."

8. Frame Relay switches use FECN and BECN to let routers know there is congestion within the frame relay network. For more information, see "Seeing Active PVCs."

9. A subinterface is created in the config mode by typing the command `interface serial 0.100`, where the number `100` is the subinterface you want to create. It is generally a good idea to match the subinterface number with the DLCI number to make the config easier to read. For more information, see "Separating Logical Connections with Subinterfaces."

10. An NT1 provides termination of an ISDN line and provides power to the line. In the U.S., an NT1 is not provided with an ISDN line.

In some parts of Europe, the telephone company supplies an NT1 with the ISDN line. This creates the need for ISDN interfaces with and without integrated NT1. Cisco 2500 routers, not being modular, do not have an integrated NT1. When ordering equipment for other routers, be sure to order the correct module. For more information, see "Integrated Services Digital Network (ISDN)."

Answers to Exam Questions

1. **B, C.** LMI and CIR are related to Frame Relay. SPID and 2B+D relate to ISDN. For more information, see "Frame Relay."

2. **B.** An ISDN BRI line has two bearer channels and one data channel for signaling. It is sometimes called a 2B+D. For more information, see "Basic Rate Interface (BRI)."

3. **C.** The CIR is the Committed Information Rate. This is the amount of bandwidth a Frame Relay provider guarantees will be available for you. For more information, see "Committed Information Rate (CIR)."

4. **A.** Configuring ISDN requires you set the switch type, SPIDs, and encapsulation. For more information, see "Configuring BRI ISDN."

5. **C.** By sharing resources, Frame Relay providers can reduce the cost to customers. For more information, see "Frame Relay."

6. **B.** DLCIs are locally significant, even if they seem otherwise. For more information, see "Data-Link Connection Identifier (DLCI)."

APPLY YOUR KNOWLEDGE

7. **A.** `show frame-relay pvc` gives information and statistics for PVCs. For more information, see "Monitoring Frame Relay."

8. **A.** `show isdn status` from the exec prompt, not the config, gives information about an ISDN line and its status. For more information, see "Monitoring ISDN."

9. **D.** Simply use the `interface serial0.100` command from the config prompt, where `100` is the subinterface you wish to create. Remember that it's a good idea to match the subinterface with the DLCI number for readability of the configuration. For more information, see "Separating Logical Connections with Subinterfaces."

10. **A.** FECN and BECN are used to inform routers of congestion in the Frame Relay network. For more information, see "Monitoring Frame Relay."

Suggested Readings and Resources

1. Chappell, Laura. *Introduction to Cisco Router Configuration,* Cisco Press, 1998

2. Ford, Merilee; Lew, H. Kim; Spanier, Steve; Stevenson, Tim. *Internetworking Technologies Handbook,* Cisco Press, 1997

Cisco provides the following objectives for the Routing Protocols portion of the CCNA exam:

Add the RIP routing protocol to your configuration.

▶ RIP is a routing protocol that is used in many legacy systems. It is often used to communicate between different manufactures' routers. Being able to configure a router for RIP is necessary because it is often the common routing protocol between different brands of routers. RIP is also implemented in many operating systems such as Windows NT and UNIX.

Add the IGRP routing protocol to your configuration.

▶ IGRP is a popular routing protocol. Being able to configure a router for IGRP is important because many organizations are using more advanced routing protocols like IGRP.

Explain the services of separate and integrated multiprotocol routing.

▶ Because many organizations have a variety of equipment and often interface with outside organizations, it is likely that you will need to understand how different routing protocols can be integrated together. There are two ways to have multiple protocols on a router: separate or integrated. Cisco uses a combination. Each protocol has its own routing table, but different routing protocols in the same stack can share the same table.

CHAPTER 6

Routing

List problems that each routing type encounters when dealing with topology changes and describe techniques to reduce the number of these problems.

▶ Understanding what happens when a routing protocol experiences a change in network topology is important when designing and maintaining networks. Different routing protocols handle network changes differently. One routing protocol that reconverges quickly for a small simple network may take an unreasonably long time to reconverge a larger network.

> **NOTE**
>
> **One more objective** The objective "Describe the benefits of network segmentation with routers" is covered in detail in Chapter 8, "LAN Switching."

STUDY STRATEGIES

▶ Studying for the routing protocols section of the CCNA exam can be challenging. Routing protocols exchange network information between routers. Understanding how these routing protocols perform this operation and the problems that can occur will help you diagnose problems when they occur.

Try configuring RIP and IGRP on Cisco routers. Experiment with how different settings can affect the operation of the routing protocol. Experience is the best teacher.

INTRODUCTION

Routing traffic is the process of getting a packet of data from the originating station to the destination station. This could be as simple as putting the packet on the network where the local destination station can receive the packet. It can also be as complex as sending the packet to a default gateway (a router) where the packet is compared to a routing table and then forwarded to the next router that can help the packet along its path. The next router then compares the packet to its routing tables and forwards it to the next hop along its journey. This continues until the packet reaches a router directly attached to the network of the destination station. The packet is then delivered to the destination station.

TCP/IP traffic is routed based on the Network portion of the address. If the network node generating the packet is on the same network as the destination node, then the packet is simply placed on the network where the destination node will see it. If however, the destination node is on a remote network, the source node must make a decision. In most cases, network nodes are attached to only one network. A desktop PC in an office for instance is usually connected to one network—the office network. In the case of a network node that is attached to only one network, there is usually a "default gateway" IP address defined in the routing table. This default gateway IP address is usually a router.

When the network node generates an IP packet for a destination node that is on a remote network, the source node compares the network portion of the IP address to its own network. The two will not match and thus the source node sends the packet to the default gateway IP address for forwarding. The default gateway can be a router attached to many networks like a router connected to the Internet. After the packet is received at the default gateway, it is compared to the routing tables to determine how to forward it. In some cases, the router itself may be attached to the destination network, in which case the packet is simply placed on the destination network for the destination node to receive. However, if the router is not attached to the destination network, the routing tables are searched for the destination network. If a match is found in the routing tables, the packet is sent to the next hop defined in the table. If a match is not found and there is not a default gateway, the packet is dropped and a "network unreachable" message is sent to the originator of the packet.

What this chapter covers is how the routing tables of the router are built and maintained. Routing protocols are used to exchange information about the networks to which they are directly connected. Routing exchanges also include information about routes they have learned from other routers. This allows a router to build a table of paths to each network in an internetworking system. There are several challenges that must be overcome for a routing protocol to be successful.

People often confuse routing protocols with routable protocols. There is a big difference. A *routable protocol* is a network protocol that transports data across a network and includes some sort of structure that allows the traffic to be routed to the proper network. A *routing protocol* is a method by which routers exchange information about the networks they can reach. This exchange of information allows the routers to build tables of how to reach each network. This is relatively simple until changes start happening in the network. These changes could include a WAN link failing because a construction crew cut a fiber, or a power outage at an office location. Just about anything that causes a portion of the network to become unreachable can be called a network outage. Basically, any change in the network that would affect a router's ability to reach a network would create a topology change. When a topology change occurs, routers update each other with new information. This information may simply say that the network is no longer reachable. In the case where there are multiple paths to a network, the information may provide an alternate path to the network. This process of updating routing tables is called *convergence*. When a network change occurs the routers reconverge.

Routing protocols are responsible for determining the path by which to send data between networks. When there is only one path from one network to another, the decision is rather easy. However, when multiple paths exist, the task becomes more complex. A routing protocol uses information it has gathered to determine which is the best path for the transport of data. This information is commonly referred to as *metrics*, or *distance*. Metrics may include information such as bandwidth of the path, delay of the path, number of hops to the destination, reliability of a path, and current load on an interface.

There are two main types of routing protocols: distance vector and link state.

Although there are many routing protocols, this chapter covers the routing protocols you are required to know for the CCNA exam.

The dynamic routing protocols include RIP and IGRP. In addition to these you need to understand static routes. *Static routes* are simply routes that you pre-select. You can specify in a router that to reach a certain network, take this path. Static routes can be used for many things. The following sections will elaborate on these topics for you.

ROUTING PROTOCOL BASICS

A *routing protocol* is responsible for exchanging valid routing information between routers so that routers can find the best path for traffic between two networks. There are several elements that might make one routing protocol a better choice than another. Some routing protocols are available on most vendors' equipment. In cases where multiple types of routers will be exchanging routing information, you must choose a routing protocol common to the routers involved. In the case of Bay Router talking to Cisco routers, for example, you might choose RIP or OSPF as a routing protocol because both of these routing protocols are supported by both Bay and Cisco. In other cases, you may be forced to use a certain routing protocol because your network is interfacing with another that is already using a particular routing protocol. Whatever the variables, choosing a routing protocol can be an enlightening experience. Each has its advantages and disadvantages. Each also has a following with a faith stronger than some religions.

There are some terms relating to routing protocols with which you must be familiar:

◆ **Topology change.** Any change in the layout of a network that will affect routing of traffic. This could include an interface being shut down by an administrator or a link failing due to a line being cut. It could also include the addition of a new circuit to a network. Any occurrence that causes a path to be unusable or unreliable can cause a topology change.

◆ **Convergence.** The processes of all routers on a network updating their routing tables when a topology change occurs.

◆ **Metric.** Any piece of data that a routing protocol uses to make a routing decision. Metrics can include hop count, bandwidth, reliability, ticks, cost, delay, load, and MTU.

Path Selection

The elements used to determine the best path vary with the routing protocol. Some simple protocols use the number of hops between networks. This is not necessarily the most accurate method of deciding the best path. Consider the network shown in Figure 6.1.

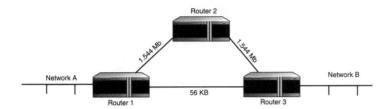

FIGURE 6.1
A network where number of hops is not the best method of choosing a path.

If Network A has traffic for Network B, the fastest path would be through Router 2 because the bandwidth is much higher than the direct route from Router 1 to Router 3. However, a routing protocol that only considers the number of hops between two points when choosing a path would take the direct route between Router 1 and Router 3. A more "intelligent" routing protocol would consider the bandwidth of the links and then would choose the faster link. An even more intelligent routing protocol would consider the reliability of the link and the load already on the link when making a routing decision. This is an example of how different routing protocols choose a path. An important consideration when designing a network is how the routing protocol you choose will work within the design. If the network you are designing does not include redundant paths, then a routing protocol that considers link speed and link load is not as important as it would be in a network with redundant paths.

Static and Dynamic Routing

Routers can obtain routing information multiple ways. When a network is configured, you can place static routes in the router's configuration. A *static route* is a route statement that you place in the router's configuration. You, the network designer, determine the path to a network and use a configuration command to tell the router how to reach that network. These routes tell the router where to forward traffic destined for a remote network. Static routes are useful in many cases.

However, the biggest disadvantage to static routes is they cannot adapt to a changing network. Not too many networks fall in the category of "never changing." Most networks are in a state of constant growth and change. Static routes do have uses, however; they are generally used in conjunction with a dynamic routing protocol.

Static routes are routes that you enter in the configuration of the router. They do not change dynamically with the changes in network topology. Static routes have specific uses within a network. Most Internet connections for organizations use a static route to the ISP. It would be useless for an organization with one connection to the Internet to maintain routing tables for the Internet. By using a static route to the default gateway, the router can be configured to send any traffic for which it doesn't specifically have a routing entry to the Internet.

Dynamic routing is when the router uses some sort of routing protocol to learn about the network and create routing tables based on this information. In a network using dynamic routing, when changes occur in the network, the changes are reflected in the routing tables soon after.

A common way that static and dynamic routing are combined is by creating a static default gateway entry and letting everything else be learned dynamically. This way, the router will reference its routing tables for a path to a remote network. If the remote network is not found in the routing tables, the packet is then forwarded to the default gateway, which would normally be a router with more complete routing tables.

In most cases in which a company has a connection to the Internet, the default gateway approach is used to forward Internet traffic to the ISP. This is helpful because maintaining complete routing tables for the Internet is a large task for a router and is also not necessary when there is only one path to the Internet.

MULTIPROTOCOL ROUTING

Cisco routers can run and use multiple routing protocols simultaneously. This makes it important to understand what they do when they receive routes for the same network from two different routing protocols.

The router assigns an administrative distance to each routing protocol that it runs. This distance is used to weigh routes to the same network that were learned on two different routing protocols.

Administrative Distance

When a Cisco router receives routing information, this information is evaluated and valid routes are placed in the routing tables of the router. It is possible for a router to be running multiple routing protocols and to receive valid routing information for the same route via two different routing protocols. How does the router decide which route to use? Just as routes within a routing protocol are weighted with metrics, different routing protocols are weighted using a metric called administrative distance. To determine which routing protocol to select over the other, the router uses the administrative distance. The default values for administrative distance are as follows:

Network directly connected to the router	0
Static route	1
EIGRP summary route	5
External BGP	20
Internal EIGRP	90
IGRP	100
OSPF	110
IS-IS	115
RIP	120
EGP	140
Internal BGP	200
Unknown	255

When a route is received from two different routing protocols, the route from the protocol with the lowest administrative distance is the one placed in the routing tables.

For instance, a route to 10.110.33.0 is received via the RIP routing protocol. A route to 10.110.33.0 is also received via the IGRP routing protocol. The router compares the administrative distances for the two routing protocols: RIP is 120 and IGRP is 100. Therefore, the route from the IGRP routing protocol is placed in the routing tables.

Why are some routing protocols preferred over others? IGRP uses more meaningful metrics than RIP. RIP simply uses hop count to select the most efficient path between two networks. IGRP uses bandwidth, reliability, and load in calculating the most efficient path. These metrics are far more meaningful than those used by RIP. Therefore a route selected by IGRP is preferred over a route selected by RIP.

Autonomous Systems (AS)

An *autonomous system (AS)* is a group of routers under one administrative control that shares a routing strategy. The routers in an autonomous system can freely exchange routing information. Routing protocols used within an AS are commonly called *interior routing protocols*.

When networks that have different administrators are connected, there is more concern about the routing information that is being exchanged. A common example of this type of environment is the Internet. The Internet consists of many networks administered by different groups that must exchange routing information with one another. By using a border gateway routing protocol, these networks can exchange routing information without concern that routing errors in one AS will adversely affect another AS. Figure 6.2 shows an example of this.

FIGURE 6.2
Two autonomous networks connected together.

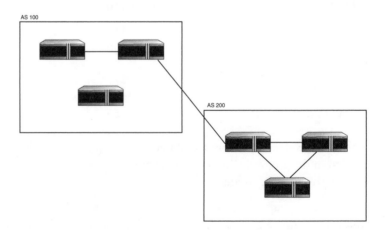

ROUTING PROBLEMS

The biggest challenge for a routing protocol is a topology change. A topology change could be a new network path or the loss of an existing one. When a topology change occurs, one of the problems that can occur is a routing loop. A *routing loop* is a situation that occurs when two routers have routing entries that point to the same network where each route sends the data to the other router. Figure 6.3 shows an example network.

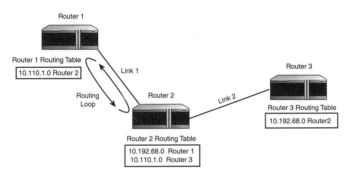

FIGURE 6.3
Example network with routing tables.

In Figure 6.3, you see that Router 2 has routes to two networks. If Link2 goes down, Router 2 loses its path to network 10.110.1.0. If this happens, Router 1 sends a routing update to Router 2, indicating that it has a path to network 10.110.1.0. Now Router 2 thinks it can reach network 10.110.1.0 through Router 1. In reality this is not true. However, if Router 1 forwards a packet for network 10.110.1.0 to Router 2, Router 2 will forward the packet back to Router 1, which will forward the packet back to Router 2. This will continue until the packet's *Time To Live (TTL)* expires.

TTL is a field in the packet header of an IP packet that is set to a number when the packet is generated. Every time the packet passes through a router, the TTL is decremented. If this number reaches zero, the packet is discarded. This keeps packets from endlessly being caught in a routing loop.

Different routing protocols have different ways of trying to avoid routing loops. Two such techniques are the split horizon rule and the poison reverse update.

Split Horizon

Split horizon is a rule that states "do not send routing updates back out of the interface they were learned on." This keeps a router from sending routing updates back to the router from which they were learned. If you refer to Figure 6.3, you will see that if Router 1 did not advertise the route for network 10.110.1.0 back out of the interface from which it learned the path, Router 2 would not have been able to create a routing loop. Another method to avoid routing updates is the poison reverse update.

Poison Reverse Update

A *poison reverse update* is a routing update that contains a route that is no longer reachable. The hop count for the route is set to infinity (as defined by the routing protocol) so the route will be marked as invalid. A poison reverse update allows a router that knows a path is no longer reachable to update other routers in the network with this information.

REVIEW BREAK

Routing Recap

▶ *Routed protocols* are protocols that carry data for applications. These protocols include an addressing scheme that contains some hierarchical information that allows the packets to be routed. Examples of routed protocols include IP and IPX.

▶ *Routing protocols* are the protocols used by routers to exchange information about connected networks. Routing protocols are used by routers to make decisions about which path to use when forwarding packets from a routed protocol. Examples of routing protocols include RIP and IGRP.

▶ A *metric* is any piece of information a routing protocol uses to decide which network path to use when forwarding packets of data. Some items that can be considered metrics are hop count, bandwidth, reliability, ticks, cost, delay, load, and MTU.

▶ *Convergence* is the process a routing protocol goes through when a topology change occurs in a network. During convergence, the routing tables of the routers in the network are updated with new information about the network.

▶ *Static routes* are determined by the network designer and are added to the configuration of the router. Static routes are static. They do not change unless you physically change them in the configuration.

▶ *Dynamic routes* are determined by a routing protocol. These routes are added to the routing table by the routing protocol after the routing protocol considers all of the metrics and determines the best path to forward data to a particular network.

▶ A *topology change* is anything that changes the connections in a network. This could be the addition of a connection, a lost connection, or even a congested connection.

▶ When a router is using multiple routing protocols, and multiple routing protocols report paths to a particular network, the router uses the *administrative distance* to determine which routing protocol's path to use. The routing protocol with the lowest administrative distance is the one used to forward packets.

▶ An autonomous number creates a group of routers that freely exchange routing information.

▶ A *routing loop* is a situation in which two routers each think the other is a path to a particular network. Router A will forward a packet to Router B. Router B will reference its routing table for a path to the network and find Router A as the path. Router B then forwards the packet to Router A. Router A again forwards the packet to router B. This continues until the *Time To Live (TTL)* of the packet expires and the packet is dropped.

▶ One of two methods used to avoid routing loops is the split horizon rule. *Split horizon* is a rule that states "do not advertise routes on interfaces they were learned from." Basically, this rule states "do not tell the router you learned a route from that you are a path to that network."

▶ The second method used to avoid routing loops is a *poison reverse update*, which is a routing update that marks a network as unreachable. When a router attached to a network determines the network is no longer reachable, the router sends out a poison reverse update to tell other routers that the network is no longer reachable.

Beyond understanding the basic workings of routing, you should be familiar with the inner workings of the different protocols at your disposal. The remainder of the chapter will go into detail regarding the two different types of routing protocols (link state and distance vector) and the different options and configurations for each, including examples.

DISTANCE VECTOR PROTOCOLS

A *distance vector* routing protocol uses the number of hops between networks. Any time a packet must be read off a network, a routing decision is made and the packet is forwarded to another network. This trip through a router is called a *hop*. A distance vector routing protocol exchanges two pieces of information in a routing exchange: distance and vector. *Distance* is defined as a metric and the *vector* is defined as next hop router.

When distance vector protocols send updates to neighboring routers, the default is to send the entire routing table. This can use up valuable bandwidth on a network with many routers. This also leads to routing loops as described previously.

Distance vector routing protocols include Routing Information Protocol (RIP) and Internetwork Gateway Routing Protocol (IGRP), which are discussed in the following sections.

Routing Information Protocol (RIP)

Routing Information Protocol (RIP) is a distance-vector routing protocol that uses hop count as the metric to determine the best path. RIP is used for routing IPX and IP traffic. For IP traffic, there are two versions of RIP currently in use: RIPv1 and RIPv2.

The biggest difference between the two versions has to do with subnet masks. RIPv1 does not include the subnet mask in the routing update. Because RIPv1 does not include subnet mask information with the update, all networks connected via RIP must use the same subnet mask. If you are designing a network where different subnet masks will be used on different networks, you must use RIPv2 if you are using RIP as a routing protocol.

RIP Routing Tables

Different routing protocols maintain different information in the routing tables. RIP maintains the following information in its routing table:

Destination	Next Hop	Distance	Timers	Flags
10.110.20.0	10.65.32.1	2	t1, t2, t3	x, y
10.44.17.0	10.65.32.1	3	t1, t2, t3	x, y
10.202.14.0	10.44.23.1	13	t1, t2, t3	x, y

The destination network is listed with the IP address of the next hop along the path to reach that network. The distance to the network in hops is the metric used to determine the best path. The timers are used to determine when a route is no longer valid and to avoid routing loops. The timers will be discussed in more detail later in this section. The flags indicate whether the route is valid and whether it is currently being held down.

The router builds its routing tables by listening to its neighbors. The neighbor routers send out updates with the networks reachable through that router and the number of hops to that network. The receiving router takes that information and builds a table like the previous one. If the router receives an update from another router with a path to a network it already has in its routing table, the hop counts are compared. If the new route is shorter in terms of hops than the one in the routing table, the routing table entry is replaced with the new path. This is an important point. RIP maintains only one path to any destination network although there may be multiple paths to the network. Some other routing protocols keep multiple paths in the routing tables and select the one of lower cost. This helps other routing protocols make quicker decisions about routing traffic when a path becomes unusable.

Regular Updates and Triggered Updates

RIP has two types of updates: *regular updates* that occur periodically based on the routing update timer, and *triggered updates* that occur anytime there is a network topology change. Regular updates are used to update routing tables and indicate a route is still available. Triggered updates make the network converge faster since routers do not wait until the regular update to report the changes to the network.

Hop Count

RIP uses the number of hops to a network as the metric for determining the best path. This is not necessarily the best way to determine the most efficient path for network traffic. There is a limit of 15 hops in a RIP network. Any network 16 or more hops away is considered unreachable. This is significant because this is the method RIP uses to report a down path. When a route becomes unreachable, the router connected to the path sends out a triggered update reporting the path as 16 hops away. Because 16 hops is considered unreachable, routers receiving this update will mark the path unreachable in their routing tables.

Routing Update Timer

RIP uses timers as methods to many of its functions. The first timer to discuss is the *routing update timer*. The routing update timer is normally set to 30 seconds. This ensures that every router sends a complete copy of its routing table every time the routing update timer counts down to zero, or 30 seconds if the default is kept.

Each time the routing update timer counts down to zero, the router sends its entire routing table out to all active interfaces. After the complete table is sent, the timer is reset.

One of the disadvantages of RIP is that it sends the entire routing table periodically even if no topology changes have occurred. This is very inefficient compared to some other routing protocols. This is one of the things that limits RIP's scalability for large networks. Also, if the routing tables are large, the routing updates can consume a large amount of bandwidth from low bandwidth WAN connections.

Route Invalid Timer

The *route invalid timer* determines the amount of time that must pass without hearing a routing update before the router considers a route invalid. The default setting for the route invalid timer is 90 seconds. This is three times the default for the routing update timer. There is a route invalid timer for each entry in the routing table. Each time an update for that entry is received, the route invalid timer is reset. If the timer counts down to zero, the route is then marked as invalid. After a route is marked invalid, neighbor routers are sent this information.

Route Flush Timer

The *route flush timer* determines the amount of time that must pass without receiving an update for a routing table entry before the entry is removed from the table. There is a route flush timer attached to each entry in the routing table. When an update is received for that entry, this timer, along with the route invalid timer, is reset. If the route flush timer counts down to zero, the route entry is completely removed from the routing table. The default for the route flush timer is 270 seconds, or nine times the update timer.

Hold-Down Timer

Hold-down timers are used to prevent a regular routing update from reinstating a route that is down. When a route goes down, the neighboring routers detect it and calculate new routes. These new routes are sent out in routing updates to inform their neighbors of the change. This change ripples through the network. Because this update does not instantly arrive at every router in the network, it is conceivable that a router that has not yet received the update could send out a regular update indicating the route that has just gone down is still good. A router that has just received the update that the route has gone bad could receive this update indicating the route is good.

A hold-down timer tells the router to hold down any changes that might have recently gone down for a period of time. This prevents a stale routing update from changing the route to an up status during this time. This allows time for the update indicating that a route has gone down to converge throughout the network.

Configuring RIP

To configure RIP in a router, you must first have your interfaces configured with the IP addresses. Configuring an IP address on an interface is covered in Chapter 3, "Understanding and Configuring TCP/IP." Then you configure the router rip as follows:

```
c2513r2#config t
Enter configuration commands, one per line.  End with
➡CNTL/Z.
c2513r2(config)#router rip
c2513r2(config-router)#network 10.0.0.0
c2513r2(config-router)#exit
c2513r2(config)#exit
c2513r2#
```

This configures RIP on all of the networks that fall under the Class A range of 10.0.0.0. It is conceivable that you may not want RIP routing updates to be broadcast out all of the interfaces on a router. Many times it is not desirable for routing updates to be broadcast on LAN interfaces if there are no routers on that segment to receive the updates. In this case, you can set the interface to passive in the router configuration. When an interface is set to passive, it will not broadcast routing updates but it will still listen for them. Following is an example of how to set the Ethernet segment as passive for this configuration:

```
c2513r2#config t
Enter configuration commands, one per line.  End with
➡CNTL/Z.
c2513r2(config)#router rip
c2513r2(config-router)#network 10.0.0.0
c2513r2(config-router)#passive-interface ethernet 0
c2513r2(config-router)#exit
c2513r2(config)#exit
c2513r2#
```

After RIP is configured, it will begin exchanging routing updates with other RIP enabled networking devices. It is helpful to view the routing tables and statistics about what RIP has learned.

Working with RIP

As with everything in life, routing protocols are not perfect. There will be times you think you have configured everything correctly but the routers just can't seem to find a path to the network you just added. In this case, it is necessary to check how the routing protocol is reacting. The first place to start looking is the routing table.

The following example shows how to check the routing tables using
the show ip route command:

```
Router#show ip route
Codes: C - connected, S - static, I - IGRP, R - RIP, M -
➥mobile, B - BGP
       D - EIGRP, EX - EIGRP external, O - OSPF, IA - OSPF
➥inter area
       N1 - OSPF NSSA external type 1, N2 - OSPF NSSA
➥external type 2
       E1 - OSPF external type 1, E2 - OSPF external type
➥2, E - EGP
       i - IS-IS, L1 - IS-IS level-1, L2 - IS-IS level-2, *
➥- candidate default
       U - per-user static route, o - ODR

Gateway of last resort is not set

     10.0.0.0/24 is subnetted, 1 subnets
C       10.245.34.0 is directly connected, TokenRing0
R    192.168.99.0/24 [120/1] via 10.245.34.2, 00:00:12,
➥TokenRing0
     199.250.137.0/27 is subnetted, 1 subnets
C       199.250.137.32 is directly connected, Ethernet0
Router#
```

The routing table includes a great deal of useful information for
diagnosing a routing problem. In the routing table above, notice the
route to 10.245.34.0 is listed as directly connected to TokenRing0.
This is information that RIP will broadcast to other routers. Network
10.245.34.0 is reachable via this router. To the left of the route
is a letter indicating how the route was learned. In the case of
10.245.34.0 it is C, which stands for connected network. The table
shown at the top of the routing table lists each letter and its meaning.

The next route in the table is to 192.168.99.0 and it was learned via
the RIP routing protocol. The numbers [120/1] indicate that it has an
administrative distance of 120 and a RIP distance of 1 hop. The first
number is the administrative distance assigned to the routing protocol. The second number is the calculated distance for the routing protocol and thus will be greatly different for different routing protocols.
The next piece of information about this route is that it was learned
via 10.245.34.2. This indicates the router that advertised this route.
The next entry is the time since the route was last updated. If this
time reaches the invalid timer, then the route will be considered
invalid and will not be used. The last piece of information about the
route indicates the interface from which the routing update was
received. In this case, it was learned on interface TokenRing0.

The following example shows how to view the settings of the majority of RIP's timers and other important information using the command `show ip protocol`:

```
c2513r2#sh ip protocol
Routing Protocol is "rip"
  Sending updates every 30 seconds, next due in 24 seconds
  Invalid after 180 seconds, hold down 180, flushed after
➡240
  Outgoing update filter list for all interfaces is not set
  Incoming update filter list for all interfaces is not set
  Redistributing: rip
  Default version control: send version 1, receive any
➡version
    Interface       Send  Recv  Key-chain
    Loopback0        1    1 2
    TokenRing0       1    1 2
  Routing for Networks:
    192.168.99.0
    192.168.42.0
    10.0.0.0
  Passive Interface(s):
    Ethernet0
  Routing Information Sources:
    Gateway        Distance      Last Update
    10.245.34.1         120      00:00:15
  Distance: (default is 120)

c2513r2#
```

The command `show ip protocol` will list each of the routing protocols the router is running and statistics on each. For RIP, the information shown includes the settings for each of the timers, which interfaces are being used to broadcast the RIP information, for which networks information is being advertised, any passive interfaces, and the sources from which routing information has been learned.

The Limitations of RIP

RIP is a useful routing protocol in small networks where compatibility is necessary with other equipment that only supports RIP. However, RIP has some serious limitations that make it unsuitable for large complicated networks.

The first limitation is that of the hop count. RIP supports no more than 15 hops from one end of a network to the other. This limits the physical size of the network on which RIP can be used.

Another limitation of RIP is the fact that RIP sends its entire routing table every 30 seconds by default. By sending the entire routing table periodically, RIP generates a fair amount of network traffic. In a large network this could become very significant.

RIP also is slow to converge, which can cause problems in large networks when topology changes occur.

The single metric of hop count creates another limitation for RIP. Because RIP considers only the number of hops when determining the best path for traffic, it will not always select the most efficient route for the traffic. More useful routing protocols consider many other factors when selecting a best path for traffic, such as bandwidth and current load.

Given the option, it is best to use a routing protocol more sophisticated than RIP. IGRP is a more robust routing protocol and is also easy to configure.

> **EXAM TIP**
>
> **Exam-related protocols** Most people use EIGRP or OSPF (BGP for ISPs). But these routing protocols are not covered on the CCNA exam. OSPF and EIGRP are on the ACRC test. BGP is touched on the ACRC test, but is mainly CCIE material.

Internet Gateway Routing Protocol (IGRP)

Internet Gateway Routing Protocol (IGRP) was developed by Cisco as a routing protocol more scalable than RIP. IGRP offers many other advantages, as well. Its main disadvantage is that it is Cisco proprietary and only works with Cisco routers. Therefore, in a network where multiple vendors' routers are used, IGRP is not an option. IGRP uses more meaningful metrics, however, when selecting a path for network traffic.

IGRP Metrics

When IGRP selects the best path for network traffic, it uses many metrics. IGRP considers bandwidth, delay, load, and reliability when deciding which path is the best to a network. Each metric in IGRP is weighted and a distance is equated. This distance is used to determine the best path to a network.

Similarities Between IGRP and RIP

In many ways, IGRP is not much different than RIP. They are both distance vector routing protocols. Both protocols periodically transmit their entire routing table, with the exception of routes suppressed by split horizon. They both use split horizon with poison reverse, triggered updates, and hold-down timers to prevent routing loops.

Differences Between IGRP and RIP

IGRP has several significant differences from RIP. IGRP uses autonomous systems to group routers in a routing domain.

IGRP broadcasts its full routing table every 90 seconds by default. RIP does this every 30 seconds.

IGRP Timers

IGRP uses timers much like RIP does. These timers ensure that certain events occur periodically—such as routing updates. They can also indicate when a route is no longer valid or when a route should be purged from the routing tables.

IGRP uses the following timers to operate properly:

◆ **Update timer.** This timer indicates when a new routing update should be sent out. The default value for this timer is 90 seconds.

◆ **Invalid timer.** An invalid timer is attached to every route in the routing tables. When an update is received for this route, the timer is reset. If the timer ever reaches zero, the route is then considered invalid and is no longer used. The default is three times the update timer, or 270 seconds.

◆ **Hold-down timer.** When a route is marked invalid, it is kept marked invalid for the duration of the hold-down timer. The default is three times the update timer plus 10 seconds.

◆ **Flush timer.** A flush timer is attached to every route in the routing table. The flush timer is reset every time a route update is received for the route. If the route flush timer counts down to zero, the route entry is completely removed from the routing table. The default time is 270 seconds.

Configuring IGRP

Configuring IGRP is very much like configuring RIP—with one caveat: IGRP requires an autonomous number. This autonomous number indicates a group of routers participating in a routing scheme.

Routers using the same autonomous number will freely exchange routing information. Some networks have multiple autonomous numbers and one or two routers will be used to exchange the routing information between the two systems. These routers will control what routing information is exchanged between the systems. The concept of exchanging information between different autonomous systems is beyond the scope of the CCNA exam and thus is not covered in this book.

IGRP, like RIP, does require that the interfaces be configured with IP addresses because it is the IP protocol that is being routed. To configure IGRP on a router, start with the `routing igrp asnumber` command where asnumber is the number representing the autonomous system in which the router will participate. It is common to use 100 as a starting number in private networks; however, you are free to use any number you prefer between 1 and 65,535 if you are in sole control of the network. If your network is participating with other networks outside of your control, you will need to coordinate with the other network administrators. After the routing command is configured, list the networks under the control of this routing protocol. Following is an example of how IGRP is configured on a router.

```
Router#config t
Enter configuration commands, one per line.  End with
➥CNTL/Z.
Router(config)#router igrp 100
Router(config-router)#network 199.250.137.0
Router(config-router)#network 10.0.0.0
Router(config-router)#exit
Router(config)#exit
Router#
```

Working with IGRP

Just as with RIP, after you have configured IGRP on a router, it is helpful to check the routing tables to see what the router has learned and placed in the routing tables. Because the routing information from all routing protocols is consolidated in one routing table, the same command is used to view this information in IGRP as it was for RIP.

The following example shows how to check the routing tables using the `show ip route` command:

```
Router#sh ip route
Codes: C - connected, S - static, I - IGRP, R - RIP, M -
➥mobile, B - BGP
```

continues

continued

```
        D - EIGRP, EX - EIGRP external, O - OSPF, IA - OSPF
➡inter area
        N1 - OSPF NSSA external type 1, N2 - OSPF NSSA
➡external type 2
        E1 - OSPF external type 1, E2 - OSPF external type
➡2, E - EGP
        i - IS-IS, L1 - IS-IS level-1, L2 - IS-IS level-2, *
➡- candidate default
        U - per-user static route, o - ODR

Gateway of last resort is not set

     10.0.0.0/24 is subnetted, 1 subnets
C       10.245.34.0 is directly connected, TokenRing0
I    192.168.99.0/24 [100/1188] via 10.245.34.2, 00:00:03,
➡TokenRing0
I    192.168.33.0/24 [100/1188] via 10.245.34.2, 00:00:03,
➡TokenRing0
     199.250.137.0/27 is subnetted, 1 subnets
C       199.250.137.32 is directly connected, Ethernet0
Router#
```

The routing table information looks much the same as RIP with one noticeable difference. Look at the route for 192.168.99.0. The distance to this route is [100/1188]. The 100 is the administrative distance for the routing protocol IGRP. The 1188 is the metric IGRP calculated for this path. The metric is based on all of the factors that IGRP uses to calculate the most efficient path.

There are times at which you may want to force the router to rebuild its routing table. When diagnosing problems, you might find that a router has an improper route for a network. If you think the router may have missed an update for some reason, you can clear the router's routing table. This will force the router to rebuild this table from current information. To clear the routing table, use the command clear ip route followed by the network for which you want to clear the route. If you want to clear the entire routing table, use the command clear ip route *. This clears the entire routing table and rebuilds it. Depending on the routing protocol being used, rebuilding the routing table may take a few minutes.

Just like RIP, the show ip protocol command will display information about the IGRP protocol.

```
Router#sh ip protocol
Routing Protocol is "igrp 100"
  Sending updates every 90 seconds, next due in 43 seconds
```

```
      Invalid after 270 seconds, hold down 280, flushed after
  ➥630
     Outgoing update filter list for all interfaces is not set
     Incoming update filter list for all interfaces is not set
     Default networks flagged in outgoing updates
     Default networks accepted from incoming updates
     IGRP metric weight K1=1, K2=0, K3=1, K4=0, K5=0
     IGRP maximum hopcount 100
     IGRP maximum metric variance 1
     Redistributing: igrp 100
     Routing for Networks:
       199.250.137.0
       10.0.0.0
     Routing Information Sources:
       Gateway         Distance       Last Update
       10.245.34.2          100       00:00:10
     Distance: (default is 100)

  Router#
```

The information displayed is similar to that of RIP. There are a few
exceptions, however. There are metric weights listed, which are parameters that allow you to change the behavior of the IGRP routing
protocol. You can adjust how much weight is given to each of the
metrics considered by IGRP. You could adjust bandwidth to have
less weight than reliability when making a routing decision. Other
information different from RIP includes the maximum hop count
that can be adjusted.

LINK STATE PROTOCOLS

Link state routing protocols were designed to make up for some of
the shortcomings of distance vector methods. Link state protocols do
not forward their entire route table, instead sending only information about networks to which the router has direct connections. This
saves bandwidth and helps avoid routing loops caused by 'second-
hand' information. These updates, called *Link State Packets (LSPs)*
are forwarded around the network so that all routers get a consistent
view of the network as a whole.

Link state protocols are also designed to handle much larger networks. Many distance vector protocols are limited in size to 15 hops,
whereas link state protocols can go much higher. This adds a scalability that is not possible with distance vector routing.

The primary disadvantages of link state routing are expense and implementation. Link state routing requires significantly more processing than distance vector protocols do, which makes it more expensive to implement in a router.

SELECTING A ROUTING PROTOCOL

When you are faced with making a decision on which routing protocol to use, there are many factors you need to consider. First, you need to ask yourself what routing protocols are supported by all of the routers that will participate in the routing domain. If there is only one common routing protocol, your choice is fairly simple. If multiple routing protocols are support by all of the routers that will participate, then you must consider the ease of configuration. The two routing protocols you are required to know for the CCNA exam are RIP and IGRP, which are both simple to configure. However, there are other routing protocols that take a great deal more time and effort to configure. This should be considered when selecting a routing protocol. For instance, the size of the network is also a consideration when selecting a routing protocol. If you are designing the next Internet, RIP is not an option because its limitation of 15 hops would not work for a worldwide network like the Internet.

CASE STUDY: THE PASSIVE INTERFACE

ESSENCE OF THE CASE

▶ A newly installed router has been configured to use the RIP routing protocol in an attempt to have it and the existing router exchange routing information. However, after installing the new router, workstations on the new network segment cannot communicate with the existing network segment.

▶ You must use the diagnostic commands to determine why you are unable to communicate between the networks.

SCENARIO

You are a network engineer for a computer training facility. Recently your company added a new network for one of the classes. The network is segmented from the main office network by a router named Classrm. In the classroom, there are 10 workstations and one server. Each of the workstations is assigned an IP address in the range 10.200.1.10–19. The server is assigned the IP address 10.200.1.5 and the router's Ethernet0 port is connected to the network in the classroom.

CASE STUDY: THE PASSIVE INTERFACE

Ethernet0 has been assigned the IP address 10.200.1.1. This network is using a subnet mask of 255.255.255.0.

The main router for the office is named Denver. Denver is connected to the main office LAN using Ethernet0. The IP address assigned to Ethernet0 of Denver is 10.100.1.1 and subnet mask 255.255.255.0. The router Classrm is connected to the main LAN using interface Ethernet1, which has been assigned the IP address 10.100.1.2 and subnet mask 255.255.255.0. After installing the router Classrm, you find that the workstations in the classroom can communicate among themselves and the server in the classroom but none of the computers can communicate with the computers on the main office network. You need to fix this so the computers can access the testing software that is on a server on the main network. Router Denver has already been configured to use the RIP routing protocol, so the person who installed the new router configured Classrm to use it as well.

ANALYSIS

You begin by checking the routing tables of the router Classrm. You find that the route to network 10.100.1.0 is in the routing table as a connected network. You also find a route to network 10.200.1.0 as a connected network. From the router, you ping the server on the main network that houses the testing software. The ping is successful.

You then log in to the router Denver and check the routing tables. You find that the network 10.100.1.0 is listed in the routing table as a connected network. However, you do not see the network 10.200.1.0. You check the routing statements in the router and they appear as follows:

```
Router rip
Network 10.0.0.0
```

You then log back into the router Classrm and check the routing statements in that router. They appear as follows:

```
Router rip
Network 10.0.0.0
Passive-interface Ethernet1
```

This does not appear correct to you. You check your reference material and find that the passive-interface command is telling the router not to advertise RIP on the network attached to Ethernet1. This could be the problem. You remove the passive-interface command from the configuration and save the changes.

You wait a couple of minutes to allow the routing broadcasts to update the routing tables.

Again you check the routing tables in the router Denver and find that now network 10.200.1.0 is appearing in the table and is listed as being learned through RIP.

You go to the workstations in the classroom and ping the server on the main network where the testing software is housed. The ping is successful. You then attempt to run the testing software and it works. Congratulations!

CHAPTER SUMMARY

KEY TERMS

- routing protocol
- RIP
- IGRP
- metric
- hop
- update timer
- hold-down timer
- invalid timer
- flush timer
- routing loop
- split horizon
- poison reverse update
- autonomous system
- administrative distance

Routing protocols are used by routers to exchange information about the networks with which they are connected. By exchanging this information, other routers in the network can learn what path to take to reach a destination network. Routing protocols use *metrics* to determine the most efficient path between to routers. These metrics can include such items as the number of hops between the networks, the bandwidth of the links between the networks, the reliability of the link, and the load on the link. The routing protocol being used determines how the metrics are used in calculations to determine the best path. Know how to configure both RIP and IGRP, as well as the strengths and weaknesses of both.

APPLY YOUR KNOWLEDGE

Review Questions

1. What metrics are considered by the RIP routing protocol?

2. What is considered unreachable by the RIP routing protocol?

3. What situation could be true that would make RIP select a path that is not the most efficient?

4. What are some of the metrics considered by the IGRP routing protocol?

5. What timers are used in RIP and IGRP to maintain the routing tables and prevent routing loops?

6. Describe split horizon.

7. Describe a poison reverse update.

8. What is an autonomous system?

9. What is the function of the flush timer?

10. Describe how a router uses administrative distance when making a routing decision.

Exam Questions

1. What is the proper way to configure RIP in a router?

   A. `Router(config)#router rip`

   B. `Router(config)#router rip 100`

   C. `Router(config)#routing rip`

   D. `Router(config)#routing rip 100`

2. After RIP is configured, how do you specify which networks to distribute information about?

   A. `Router(config-router)#distribute 10.0.0.0`

   B. `Router(config)#network 10.0.0.0`

   C. `Router(config-router)#network 10.0.0.0`

   D. `Router(config)#distribute 10.0.0.0`

3. What is special about a hop count of 16 in the RIP protocol?

   A. It indicates that the network is directly connected to the router.

   B. It indicates a network 16 hops away.

   C. It indicates that the route was received 16 seconds ago.

   D. It indicates that the network is unreachable.

4. Which timer limits how long a route that has been marked invalid will be kept in the routing tables?

   A. Update timer

   B. Invalid timer

   C. Flush timer

   D. Hold-down timer

5. What does the statement "Routing information is not sent back out of the interface from which it was learned" describe?

   A. The split horizon rule

   B. Poison reverse updates

   C. A routing loop

   D. The divided parallel rule

APPLY YOUR KNOWLEDGE

6. Suppose a router is running two routing protocols and a valid route is received from both protocols to one remote network. How does the router choose which route to place in its routing table?

   A. The first routing protocol to report the route is used.

   B. The first routing protocol configured is preferred over the next.

   C. The administrative distance of the routing protocols are used to select which route to add.

   D. The route with the lowest metric is used.

7. What command will display statistics about the routing protocols running and their timers?

   A. `Router#show ip interface`

   B. `Router#show routing protocols`

   C. `Router#show ip protocol`

   D. `Router#sh ip stats`

8. What command will clear the entire routing table and force the router to rebuild them?

   A. `Router#clear routing table`

   B. `Router#clear ip route`

   C. `Router#clear ip route *`

   D. `Router#rebuild routing table`

9. Given the following line from a routing table, what does the [120/12] indicate?

   ```
   R    192.168.99.0/24 [120/12] via
   ➥10.245.34.2, 00:00:06, TokenRing0
   ```

   A. The administrative distance of RIP is 120 and the network is 12 hops away.

   B. The administrative distance of RIP is 12 and the network is 120 hops away.

   C. The route was received 120 seconds ago and is 12 hops away.

   D. The route was received 12 seconds ago and is 120 hops away.

Answers to Review Questions

1. RIP considers only the number of hops between networks when making routing decisions. For more information, see "Routing Information Protocol (RIP)."

2. RIP considers any network more than 15 hops away unreachable. For more information, see "Routing Information Protocol (RIP)."

3. Because RIP considers only the number of hops, it is possible that RIP could select a slow link of only one hop rather than a much faster link that is two hops away. This would cause RIP to select a less efficient path for network traffic. For more information, see "Routing Information Protocol (RIP)."

4. IGRP considers bandwidth, delay, reliability, and load on the link when making a routing decision. For more information, see "Internet Gateway Routing Protocol (IGRP)."

5. RIP and IGRP use the update timer, invalid timer, hold-down timer, and flush timer. For more information, see "Routing Information Protocol (RIP)" and "Internet Gateway Routing Protocol (IGRP)."

APPLY YOUR KNOWLEDGE

6. Split horizon is a rule that states "routes are not sent back out of the interface from which they were learned." For more information, see "Split Horizon."

7. A poison reverse update is a routing update with a metric that makes the network unreachable. This is a method for a router to force other routers to update their routing tables with information about a down network. For more information, see "Poison Reverse Update."

8. An autonomous system is a group of routers freely exchanging routing information. For more information, see "Autonomous Systems (AS)."

9. The flush timer specifies how long a route is kept in the routing table after it has been marked invalid. For more information, see "Route Flush Timer."

10. A router uses the administrative distance to select the route to add to the routing table when a path to a network is learned from two different routing protocols. For more information, see "Routing Information From Multiple Protocols."

Answers to Exam Questions

1. **A.** The proper way to configure RIP on a router is `router rip`. For more information, see "Routing Information Protocol (RIP)."

2. **C.** The proper way to list a network for RIP to distribute is `Router(config-router)#network 10.0.0.0`. For more information, see "Routing Information Protocol (RIP)."

3. **D.** In RIP, a hop count of 16 is considered unreachable. For more information, see "Routing Information Protocol (RIP)."

4. **C.** The flush timer limits how long a route that has been marked invalid will be kept in the routing table. For more information, see "Flush Timer."

5. **A.** The statement describes the split horizon rule. For more information, see "Split Horizon."

6. **C.** The administrative distance is used to select which routing protocol to use. For more information, see "Administrative Distance."

7. **C.** `show ip protocol` lists a great deal of information about the routing protocols running on a router and the timers associated with those routing protocols. For more information, see "Working with IGRP."

8. **C.** `clear ip route *` will clear the routing tables and force the router to rebuild them. For more information, see "Working with IGRP."

9. **A.** The [120/12] indicates that the administrative distance of RIP is 120 and the network is 12 hops away. For more information, see "Working with RIP."

Suggested Readings and Resources

1. Chappell, Laura. *Introduction to Cisco Router Configuration*, Cisco Press, 1998.

2. Doyle, Jeff. *Routing TCP/IP Volume I,* Cisco Press 1998.

Cisco provides the following objectives for the Network Security portion of the CCNA exam:

Configure standard and extended access lists to filter IP traffic.

▶ In order to secure complex networks, you must be able to configure standard and extended access lists for filtering IP traffic.

Monitor and verify selected access list operations on the router.

▶ To maintain the security of complex networks where access lists are implemented, you must be able to monitor and verify these access lists.

CHAPTER 7

Network Security

STUDY STRATEGIES

▶ The key to studying for the security objectives is to practice using access lists. Create access lists and test them to be sure they are working as you expect. Experiment with different ways of creating access lists to find the most efficient method of arranging the tests. Access lists can be tricky. When you create a new access list, check to be sure it does what you want it to do.

INTRODUCTION

When designing networks that will interface with other networks beyond your control, you need methods to secure your network. With the rush for companies to connect their networks to the Internet, there is a real need to secure local networks from distrusted network attacks, configuration errors, and failures. One way to secure a local network is through the use of access lists within the router's configuration.

An access list can filter the type of network traffic that will be allowed to pass through the router. Cisco's IOS provides a means to identify traffic in many of the protocols it supports. This chapter focuses on how to create and apply TCP/IP access lists.

UNDERSTANDING ACCESS LISTS

Access lists are basically a set of tests that packets must pass before being allowed to enter. In an outgoing access list, the packet must be allowed by the access list before being forwarded out of an interface. An incoming access list tests each packet entering the router from an interface. If the packet is allowed by the access list, it may enter. If it is not allowed, the packet is dropped.

When a packet is being evaluated with an access list, the router checks to see if a packet matches the test in each line of the access list and then either allows or denies the packet. If the packet doesn't match any of the lines in an access list, it is discarded. This is called the implicit *deny all.* If a packet is not explicitly allowed by an access list, it will be dropped.

An access list is created in the router configuration with parameters identifying the traffic for special handling. This access list is identified by a number or, starting with release 11.2 of Cisco's IOS, a name. This access list is then applied to an interface of the router or to some other part of the configuration for special handling.

Uses of Access Lists

An access list can be used to identify network traffic for priority handling. Traffic matching the access list can be given higher priority when the network is congested and traffic is queued for an interface.

Access lists identify interesting traffic for dial-up links. Interesting traffic is network traffic you have determined can initiate dialing on a dial-up link. This can be very important when you're facing the high cost of some ISDN links.

An access list can be used to limit routing updates or to limit certain SAPs for bridging. Access lists have many uses. As you climb the Cisco Certification ladder, the uses you are required to understand become more complex.

The most common use of an access list is as a filter. In the access list, you identify certain types of traffic that will not be allowed to exit an interface. This creates a filter for network traffic and is often used to secure networks from other networks, such as the Internet. If you have a router that attaches a private network to the Internet, it is common to create access lists to limit the types of traffic that can come from the Internet to your private network.

The Parts of an Access List

An access list has two elements: the list itself, and the statement that assigns a router interface to the access list. The statement assigning an interface to an access list is called the *access group statement*.

You can assign only one access list per protocol to an interface. You can have one IP access list and one IPX access list.

Access lists are identified by number. Starting with IOS 11.2, named access lists are supported for some protocols. By carefully selecting a name, you can provide a clue as to what the access list is doing. This can be very helpful when you're looking at a config that hasn't been touched for a year and you're trying to determine the access list's goal.

Here is a list of the types of access lists available under Cisco's IOS 11.2:

Protocol	Range
IP	1-99
Extended IP	100-199
Ethernet type code	200-299
DECnet	300-399
XNS	400-499

Protocol	Range
Extended XNS	500-599
AppleTalk	600-699
Ethernet address	700-799
Novell	800-899
Extended Novell	900-999
Novell SAP	1000-1099

How an Access List Works

An access list can be applied to traffic entering or exiting an interface. These two ways of implementing an access list are called *inbound* and *outbound*. Inbound access lists create more of a load on the router's processor, and thus, are not recommended unless absolutely necessary. In most cases, you should be able to enforce network traffic or routing polices using outbound access lists. The discussions in this chapter focus on outbound access lists.

Figure 7.1 shows how the router evaluates a packet for forwarding with an access list.

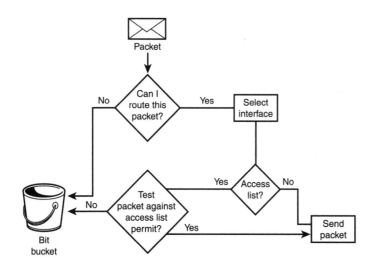

FIGURE 7.1
The flow of an access list.

Each statement in the access list is evaluated. The packet is either permitted to pass, denied passage and tossed in the bit bucket, or falls through to the next statement in the access list because it doesn't match that statement. If a packet reaches the end of the access list and it hasn't matched any statements, it is discarded. This is because access lists have an implicit "deny all" added to the end. This is an important concept to understand. If you don't explicitly permit some traffic in your access list, all traffic will be denied.

When the router receives a packet for routing, it first checks the routing tables to determine how to forward the packet. If it determines that it doesn't have a way to forward the packet, the packet is dropped. However, if the router determines it can forward the packet and knows which interface the packet should be sent to, it then checks to see if the interface is grouped to an access list. If not, the packet is copied to the interface's output buffer, and the packet is forwarded.

If the router determines that the exiting interface is grouped to an access list, the packet is subjected to the test of the access list before it is forwarded. Only if the packet is specifically allowed in the access list is it forwarded.

> **NOTE**
>
> **Network Traffic Must Be Explicitly Allowed**   When an access list is applied to an interface, all traffic is disallowed except that which is explicitly allowed in the access list.
>
> When you're creating an access list, remember that the router adds the deny all command to the end of the access list.

How Access Lists Affect Performance

An access list adds much overhead to the forwarding process. The router must perform a great deal of work each time it forwards a packet. How you design an access list and apply it to an interface can help reduce some of this overhead.

When the router is evaluating a packet through an access list, it works through the list from top to bottom. Remember this when creating an access list. The router will stop processing the access list on the first match. Whenever possible, design your access lists so that the majority of traffic matches the first few statements. This will keep the processor load created by the access list to a minimum.

Types of Access Lists

You will deal with two types of access lists for the CCNA exam: the standard IP access list and the extended IP access list.

Standard IP Access Lists

A standard IP access list is a simple list of permit and deny statements based on a source IP address. The standard IP access list permits or denies the entire IP protocol suite based on the source IP address. The extended IP access list offers more granular control over network traffic.

Extended IP Access Lists

An extended IP access list gives you more granular control over traffic identification. It allows decisions based on source and destination IP addresses, particular protocols within the IP protocol suite, and port numbers. The extended IP access list offers much more flexibility in describing the type of network traffic to allow or deny.

IMPLEMENTING STANDARD IP ACCESS LISTS

The access list itself is created in the router's global configuration. Then, the access-group command is used in the interface configuration of the interface you want the access list applied to. Here is the syntax for creating a standard IP access list:

```
access-list 1-99 {permit¦deny} address mask
```

The access-list command identifies this as an access list. 1-99 identifies it as a standard access list entry. The permit or deny command tells the router what to do with traffic that matches this statement. address is the source IP address. mask is used to identify wildcard bits, which identify parts of the IP address to ignore when doing the test.

Here is the syntax for the access-group command that is applied to the interface:

```
Router(config)#ip access-group 1-99 {out¦in}
```

The ip access-group command identifies this interface as belonging to an IP access list group. 1-99 identifies which standard access list to apply to this interface. The out or in command tells the router to apply this access list to either outgoing traffic or incoming traffic. The default is outgoing traffic.

> **NOTE**
>
> **Incoming Traffic Versus Outgoing**
> Applying an access list to incoming traffic creates more of a load on the router's processor than applying it to outgoing traffic.

Restricting Traffic to One Network

For security reasons, you might want to limit the traffic allowed to pass through a router to certain networks. In the first example, you will limit traffic to only 10.0.0.0. This network might represent your company's entire network.

The following example shows a standard access list that allows only traffic from the network 10.0.0.0. You can't assign more than one access list to an interface for a particular protocol type.

```
.
.
.
interface Serial1
 ip address 192.168.42.1 255.255.255.0
 ip access-group 1 out
.
.
.
router rip
 network 10.0.0.0
 network 192.168.42.0
!
no ip classless
!
access-list 1 permit 10.0.0.0 0.255.255.255
.
.
.
```

This code shows that the `access-list` statement permits traffic from the source address 10.0.0.0 0.255.255.255, which includes any network station that has an IP address beginning with 10. Since access lists include an implicit deny all at the end, any network traffic originating from a network other than 10.0.0.0 would be denied. The access list is applied to interface Serial1. Notice that the `access-group` statement is stated as out, meaning that the access list applies to traffic exiting this interface. This access list will have no effect on traffic entering the router through Serial1.

Restricting Traffic from One Network

You just created an access list that allows only traffic from the network 10.0.0.0. Now, you will restrict traffic from only one network. You will allow traffic from any network other than 10.0.0.0 to pass. Any traffic originating from network 10.0.0.0 will be dropped into the bit bucket.

This can be useful for securing an internal network. If your company connects to another company's network, you might want to restrict which parts of your network that company's traffic travels.

```
  .
  .
  .
interface Serial1
 ip address 192.168.42.1 255.255.255.0
 ip access-group 1 out
  .
  .
  .
router rip
 network 10.0.0.0
 network 192.168.42.0
!
no ip classless
!
access-list 1 deny 10.0.0.0 0.255.255.255
access-list 1 permit any
  .
  .
  .
```

The first test for traffic exiting interface Serial1 is whether the IP address falls within the network 10.0.0.0. If it does, the packet is denied and sent off to the bit bucket. Otherwise, the packet is evaluated by the second line of the access list, which permits any traffic. Since any packet making it past the first statement would be permitted by the second, no traffic would fall to the implicit deny all statement at the end of the access list. The command permit any is shorthand for 0.0.0.0 255.255.255.255. Either of these notations will work, but permit any is more readable and makes it easier to see what the access list is doing. Access lists can become very complex. Anything you can do to make them more readable will make your life easier.

Restricting Traffic from One Network Station

In this example, you will restrict traffic from one specific network station. In the following code, the access list specifies the IP address of a station that will be denied access. Any other station on the network will be allowed to pass. You might use this to keep a machine from being accessed outside your local network. By not allowing traffic from that machine to exit the local network through the router, you ensure some security over who can access it.

```
.
.
.
interface Serial1
 ip address 192.168.42.1 255.255.255.0
 ip access-group 1 out
.
.
.
router rip
 network 10.0.0.0
 network 192.168.42.0
!
no ip classless
!
access-list 1 deny 10.99.68.102 0.0.0.0
access-list 1 permit any
.
.
.
```

The wildcard bits are all set to zero. This tells the router to evaluate all the bits of the IP address when comparing traffic to the access list. This example allows all traffic to pass except traffic originating from IP address 10.99.68.102.

Allow Only Traffic from IP Addresses Ending in .242

In this example, you will allow only traffic from IP addresses ending in .242. All other traffic will be denied. The wildcard bits are set to ignore the first three octets when comparing network traffic. If the last octet is not equal to .242, traffic is denied.

To secure data within your company, you place systems in each office that transfers customer information to the home office. In order to secure this data from possible access by other machines, you assign each of the database machines an IP address with a final octet of .242. You then set up access lists to allow only traffic from IP addresses ending in .242 to access the network where the consolidated customer database is stored.

```
.
.
.
interface Serial1
 ip address 192.168.42.1 255.255.255.0
 ip access-group 1 out
.
.
.
```

```
router rip
 network 10.0.0.0
 network 192.168.42.0
!
no ip classless
!
access-list 1 permit 0.0.0.242 255.255.255.0
access-list 1 deny any
 .
 .
 .
```

Here, the wildcard bits in the first three octets are set to one. This tells the router to ignore these bits when evaluating network traffic. If the last octet of the IP address is not equal to .242, the traffic is denied. Note that even though the access list would perform the same function without the second line of the access list, it is easier to see how this access list will perform when deny any is shown in the configuration.

Wildcards in the IP Address

When defining an IP address in an access list, it is often necessary to identify entire networks instead of a specific network station. In an access list, you can use wildcard bits to identify parts of the network address to not check. Wildcard bits work much like subnet mask bits but identify the station portion of the address instead of the network portion. Earlier, you saw how the entire network 10.0.0.0 could be denied. You also saw how these wildcard bits are applied to the IP address to identify what traffic matches this test.

The following are some examples of wildcard bits and how they might be used in access lists.

In the following example, any station on network 192.168.200.0 will be permitted. Since the wildcard bits in the last octet are all ones, any address in the last octet will be permitted:

```
permit 192.168.200.0 0.0.0.255
```

The next example denies all traffic from one IP address:

```
deny 192.168.42.109 0.0.0.0
```

The following example permits any IP address. A shortcut for this is to use the keyword any in the access list, as shown in the second line. These two lines are synonymous and can be used interchangeably.

However, using the keyword any can make it easier for someone reading the router's configuration to quickly identify what the access list is doing.

```
permit 0.0.0.0 255.255.255.255
permit any
```

Implementing Access Lists

▶ Standard IP access lists allow filtering on the source address only.

▶ When a wildcard bit is set to one, the router doesn't care what value is in that bit position.

▶ By default, access lists are applied to outgoing traffic. An access list can be applied to incoming traffic, but at the cost of performance to the router.

▶ Access lists are evaluated from the top down. Once a match is found, the router either forwards or drops the packet.

IMPLEMENTING EXTENDED IP ACCESS LISTS

An extended access list offers more detailed control over traffic. With an extended access list, you can specify the source IP address, destination IP address, protocol, and port used. You use an extended access list when you need more granular control over what traffic to filter. If you simply need to filter traffic based on the source IP address, the standard access list will work and should be used.

Here is the syntax for an extended access list:

```
Router(config)#access-list 100-199 {permit¦deny ip¦tcp¦udp¦icmp}
↪source source-mask dest dest-mask [lt¦gt¦eq¦neq dest-port]
```

The access-list command is the same as for the standard IP access list. The number of the access list, 100-199, identifies it as an extended IP access list. The commands permit and deny work as they do in standard access lists. However, in an extended access list, you can add the protocol to permit or deny. The source address and source mask work as they do in a standard access list. In the extended access list, you can also identify the destination IP address and mask.

Extended access lists also let you specify a port number. You can specify whether the port number should be less than, greater than, equal to, or not equal to the specified port.

Putting a question mark at the end of your extended access list entry will list the well-known TCP/IP port numbers and an abbreviation that can be used in place of the actual number. These abbreviations make access lists more readable and make it easier to determine their purpose. The following is an example of the router's output. The first column shows the abbreviation you can use in the router configuration. The second column describes the service. The number in parentheses is the actual port number used by that service.

```
c2513r1(config)#access-list 100 permit tcp any any eq ?
  bgp             Border Gateway Protocol (179)
  chargen         Character generator (19)
  cmd             Remote commands (rcmd, 514)
  daytime         Daytime (13)
  discard         Discard (9)
  domain          Domain Name Service (53)
  echo            Echo (7)
  exec            Exec (rsh, 512)
  finger          Finger (79)
  ftp             File Transfer Protocol (21)
  ftp-data        FTP data connections (used infrequently, 20)
  gopher          Gopher (70)
  hostname        NIC hostname server (101)
  ident           Ident Protocol (113)
  irc             Internet Relay Chat (194)
  klogin          Kerberos login (543)
  kshell          Kerberos shell (544)
  login           Login (rlogin, 513)
  lpd             Printer service (515)
  nntp            Network News Transport Protocol (119)
  pim-auto-rp     PIM Auto-RP (496)
  pop2            Post Office Protocol v2 (109)
  pop3            Post Office Protocol v3 (110)
  smtp            Simple Mail Transport Protocol (25)
  sunrpc          Sun Remote Procedure Call (111)
  syslog          Syslog (514)
  tacacs          TAC Access Control System (49)
  talk            Talk (517)
  telnet          Telnet (23)
  time            Time (37)
  uucp            Unix-to-Unix Copy Program (540)
  whois           Nicname (43)
  www             World Wide Web (HTTP, 80)
```

The ability to specify the source and destination IP address along with protocol and port number offers you greater control over your network.

Deny Telnet Requests to a Host on Your Network

This example uses an extended IP access list to deny requests to telnet to a host on your network. This could be useful if your network is attached to the Internet and you have a UNIX computer you need to protect from telnet access over the Internet. By filtering telnet requests to the UNIX computer with an access list, you ensure that the system is safe even if the administrator of the UNIX system fails to secure it from the operating system.

```
.
.
.
interface Ethernet0
 ip address 192.168.42.1 255.255.255.0
 ip access-group 101 out
.
.
.
router rip
 network 10.0.0.0
 network 192.168.42.0
!
no ip classless
!
access-list 101 deny tcp 0.0.0.0 255.255.255.255
[ic:ccc]192.168.42.231 0.0.0.0 eq telnet
access-list 101 permit ip any any
.
.
.
```

Here, the access list will deny telnet traffic from any computer to the host 192.168.42.231. Any other network traffic for 192.168.42.231 will be allowed. A common use of this type of access list is to limit network addresses that can telnet to your router. If you have a router that borders the Internet, it's a good idea to deny telnet requests from the Internet to keep hackers at bay.

MANAGING ACCESS LISTS

Once you have created your access lists, you will no doubt need to edit them. After they are edited, you will want to verify that they are operating as expected. Another topic pertaining to managing access lists is viewing access lists. As an internetworking professional,

NOTE **The Evolution of Access Lists** One area of Cisco's IOS that changes rapidly with new versions is access lists. New releases of IOS often add capabilities to traffic control with access lists. When working with access lists, you should consult the documentation to find out which version of IOS you are using.

you will often be introduced to a new network and will need to figure out the configuration objectives.

Editing Access Lists

Cisco's IOS does not provide a way to insert a statement in an access list above current lines. If you need to make changes to an access list other than adding statements to the end of the access list, you must remove the access list from the configuration and reenter it in the correct order. One method of editing an access list is to copy the configuration from the router to a TFTP server. Edit the configuration file with a text editor and then copy the modified configuration back to the router from the TFTP server.

Deleting Access Lists

To remove an access list from a configuration, use the no access list command. The following example shows how to remove an access list:

```
c2513r1#sh run
.
.
.
router eigrp 100
 network 192.168.220.0
!
router rip
 network 10.0.0.0
 network 192.168.42.0
!
no ip classless
!
access-list 1 permit 192.168.42.1
access-list 1 permit 10.0.0.0 0.255.255.255
access-list 1 permit 192.168.200.0 0.0.0.255
access-list 1 deny    any
.
.
.
c2513r1#config t
Enter configuration commands, one per line. End with CNTL/Z.
c2513r1(config)#no access-list 1
c2513r1(config)#exit
```

This code shows how the access list looks in the configuration before its removal. There are four tests in the access list. The command no access-list 1 removes all four lines from the router's configuration.

Verifying Access Lists

To determine whether an interface is grouped to an access list, you can use the command show ip interface:

```
c2513r2#sh ip interface
 .
 .
 .
Serial0 is up, line protocol is up
  Internet address is 192.168.42.2/24
  Broadcast address is 255.255.255.255
  Address determined by non-volatile memory
  MTU is 1500 bytes
  Helper address is not set
  Directed broadcast forwarding is enabled
  Multicast reserved groups joined: 224.0.0.9
  Outgoing access list is 1
  Inbound  access list is not set
  Proxy ARP is enabled
  Security level is default
  Split horizon is enabled
  ICMP redirects are always sent
  ICMP unreachables are always sent
  ICMP mask replies are never sent
  IP fast switching is enabled
  IP fast switching on the same interface is enabled
  IP multicast fast switching is enabled
  Router Discovery is disabled
  IP output packet accounting is disabled
  IP access violation accounting is disabled
  TCP/IP header compression is disabled
  Probe proxy name replies are disabled
  Gateway Discovery is disabled
  Policy routing is disabled
  Network address translation is disabled
 .
 .
 .
c2513r2#
```

Viewing Access Lists

To view access lists created in a router, you can use the show access-lists command:

```
c2513r2#sh access-lists
Standard IP access list 1
    permit 192.168.42.1
    permit 192.168.200.0, wildcard bits 0.0.0.255
    permit 10.0.0.0, wildcard bits 0.255.255.255
    deny   any
Extended IP access list 101
```

```
     permit ip 192.168.201.0 0.0.0.255 any
     deny   tcp any host 10.100.2.101 eq ftp
c2513r2#
```

You see each access list in the configuration, whether or not it is
applied to an interface. Each `permit` or `deny` statement of the access
list is shown.

NAMED ACCESS LISTS

Release 11.2 of Cisco's IOS introduced named access lists. This
feature allows you to give a standard IP or extended IP access list a
meaningful name to make reading the configuration easier.

Named access lists have the added bonus of allowing you to edit the
access list and remove lines without having to delete and reenter
the access list.

Here is how a named access list is created:

```
c2513r2#config t
Enter configuration commands, one per line. End with CNTL/Z.
c2513r2(config)#ip access-list extended warez_protect
c2513r2(config-ext-nacl)#deny tcp any host 192.168.41.23 eq
➥ftp
c2513r2(config-ext-nacl)#deny tcp any host 192.168.41.23 eq
➥ftp-data
c2513r2(config-ext-nacl)#permit ip any any
c2513r2(config-ext-nacl)#exit
c2513r2(config)#exit
c2513r2#
```

The preceding code shows you how the named access list is created.
In the global configuration, enter the command `ip access-list`
`extended` *access-list-name*. In this example, you will filter FTP
requests to a server in your building that has been compromised in
the past by pirates creating Warez FTP sites. This begins the named
access list configuration. The router will then enter the named access
list configuration mode. This is shown by the change in the router's
prompt to `c2513r2(config-ext-nacl)#`. This indicates that you're configuring an extended named access control list. Next, you enter each
of the `permit` or `deny` statements for the access list. Here is what the
access list you just created will look like in the configuration:

```
c2513r2#sh run
.
.
```

continues

continued

```
.
no ip classless
!
ip access-list extended warez_protect
 deny   tcp any host 192.168.41.23 eq ftp
 deny   tcp any host 192.168.41.23 eq ftp-data
 permit ip any any
logging buffered 1024000 debugging
access-list 1 permit 192.168.42.1
access-list 1 permit 192.168.200.0 0.0.0.255
access-list 1 permit 10.0.0.0 0.255.255.255
access-list 1 deny    any
access-list 101 permit ip 192.168.201.0 0.0.0.255 any
access-list 101 deny    tcp any host 10.100.2.101 eq ftp
 !
 !
line con 0
 exec-timeout 0 0
 password 7 094F471A1A0A
 login
line aux 0
 password 7 094F471A1A0A
 login

c2513r2#
```

You now need to apply the access list to the interface that traffic for this host will exit. The following code shows how this is done:

```
c2513r2#config t
Enter configuration commands, one per line. End with CNTL/Z.
c2513r2(config)#int e0
c2513r2(config-if)#ip access-group warez_protect
c2513r2(config-if)#exit
c2513r2(config)#exit
c2513r2#
```

When a named access list is applied to an interface, the name of the access list shows in the show ip interface command's output:

```
c2513r2#sh ip interface
Ethernet0 is up, line protocol is down
  Internet address is 192.168.41.1/24
  Broadcast address is 255.255.255.255
  Address determined by setup command
  MTU is 1500 bytes
  Helper address is not set
  Directed broadcast forwarding is enabled
  Outgoing access list is warez_protect
  Inbound  access list is not set
  Proxy ARP is enabled
  Security level is default
  Split horizon is enabled
  ICMP redirects are always sent
```

```
ICMP unreachables are always sent
ICMP mask replies are never sent
IP fast switching is enabled
IP fast switching on the same interface is disabled
IP multicast fast switching is enabled
Router Discovery is disabled
IP output packet accounting is disabled
IP access violation accounting is disabled
TCP/IP header compression is disabled
Probe proxy name replies are disabled
Gateway Discovery is disabled
Policy routing is disabled
Network address translation is disabled
```

The named access list also shows in the output of the
show access-lists command:

```
c2513r2#sh access-lists
Standard IP access list 1
    permit 192.168.42.1
    permit 192.168.200.0, wildcard bits 0.0.0.255
    permit 10.0.0.0, wildcard bits 0.255.255.255
    deny   any
Extended IP access list 101
    permit ip 192.168.201.0 0.0.0.255 any
    deny   tcp any host 10.100.2.101 eq ftp
Extended IP access list warez_protect
    deny   tcp any host 192.168.41.23 eq ftp
    deny   tcp any host 192.168.41.23 eq ftp-data
    permit ip any any
c2513r2#
```

CASE STUDY: SECURING THE SCHUTZHUND CLUB NETWORK

ESSENCE OF THE CASE

The facts of the case are as follows:

▶ The LAN has been compromised by
  hackers on the Internet.

▶ You must provide a method of securing
  the network while still allowing use of
  the Web server.

▶ You must secure the router so that it
  isn't susceptible to login attempts from
  the Internet.

SCENARIO

The Schutzhund club whose Internet connection
you set-up calls and says it is experiencing significant delays in Internet traffic. Users of its Web
site are complaining that it is slow and that
sometimes requests fail.

You arrive at its office and place your laptop with
sniffer software on the network. You notice a large
amount of traffic from Internet IP addresses to the
NT server running the Web site. Further investigation shows that most of this traffic is FTP data.

continues

CASE STUDY: SECURING THE SCHUTZHUND CLUB NETWORK

You investigate the server and find that the FTP portion of the server was left available for anyone to use and has been compromised. You find a directory on the server called Warez with several subdirectories underneath containing commercial software. You ask if the Schutzhund Club uses the FTP server to upload updates to its Web site. It does use the FTP server for this purpose but always loads updates from computers in its office. It never uses the FTP server from the Internet.

You shut down the FTP service on the server and check the sniffer again. The traffic has stopped. You try accessing Internet sites and find that the speed has increased significantly. It obviously was unknowingly hosting a pirate Warez site. It's your job to secure the network so that this can't happen again.

The Schutzhund Club needs its Web server to be accessible so that handlers can register their dogs in events. Pirates are using the club's network for illegal activities, which is keeping the network from being available for its intended purpose. You must secure the network in such a way as to allow the desired network traffic but not allow the unwanted use of the network by pirates.

ANALYSIS

You explain that the router can be used to keep this from happening again by filtering FTP requests that come to the network from the Internet. The FTP server will still be accessible from the local network, but no one coming across the router from the Internet will be able to access the FTP server. The president of the Schutzhund Club likes the idea of securing his network and asks if there are any other safeguards you should put in place. You explain that you can secure the router to not accept telnet requests from the Internet either.

By limiting telnet access from the local network, no one on the Internet will be able to make changes to the router to reverse the filters you will put in place for the FTP server.

You begin by copying the current configuration from the router to the TFTP server on your laptop. You do this because it is always a good idea to have a copy of the configuration from where you started.

You create an access list to deny any host talking with any other host using the TCP and the FTP data ports. You also add the access list to the router's Ethernet port since this is the interface you don't want the traffic to exit. Here is the access list you create:

```
c2513r2(config)#access-list 101 deny tcp any
➥any eq ftp
c2513r2(config)#access-list 101 deny tcp any
➥any eq ftp-data
c2513r2(config)#interface e0
c2513r2(config-if)#ip access-group 101
c2513r2(config-if)#exit
c2513r2(config)#exit
c2513r2#
```

You create another access list that denies any address except one on the local network:

```
c2513r2(config)#access-list 102 permit tcp
➥192.168.41.0 0.0.0.255 eq telnet
```

You then apply this access list to incoming traffic to the VTY lines of the router:

```
c2513r2#config t
Enter configuration commands, one per line.
➥End with CNTL/Z.
c2513r2(config)#line vty 0 4
c2513r2(config-line)#access-class 102 in
c2513r2(config-line)#exit
c2513r2(config)#exit
c2513r2#
```

You connect to the Internet with your dial-up account and attempt to connect to the FTP server.

CASE STUDY: SECURING THE SCHUTZHUND CLUB NETWORK

The connection is refused. You then try to telnet to the router, and that connection is refused also.

The Schutzhund Club president thanks you for helping. He invites you to a Schutzhund trial the following weekend, where you can see the famous Keyser Soze vom Wardlaw try for his Schutzhund III title. He assures you it will be a fascinating show. Keyser's grandsire is Quando von Arminius, who was Weltsieger in 1986 and 1987. This brave dog will surely be the star of the show.

CHAPTER SUMMARY

This chapter showed you how to use access lists to restrict network traffic that passes through a router. By using access lists wisely, you can enforce policies and secure your network from attacks. Because many companies are connecting their internal networks to the Internet, private networks can be open to numerous attacks. By making use of access lists, you can restrict the type of attack.

Standard access lists allow you to restrict data based on the source IP address only. They permit or deny the entire IP protocol suite based solely on the source IP address. By using the wildcard bits, you can identify entire networks from which to restrict network traffic.

Extended access lists provide greater flexibility in identifying the types of traffic to restrict. An extended IP access list lets you specify the source and destination IP addresses. It also lets you identify the protocol and port number.

Access lists can be applied to traffic either entering or exiting an interface. Access lists that are applied to traffic entering an interface are called *inbound access lists*. Inbound access lists create a great deal of load on the router's processor. *Outbound access lists* create less of a load on the processor, and thus, are the preferred method. Either way, access lists do create a load on the router's processor, and thus, should be well-designed. The router processes the access list from the top down. When a match is found, the router either forwards or drops the packet. Design your access lists so that, for the majority of traffic, the router processes the fewest lines of the access list possible while still enforcing the traffic policy.

How access lists are implemented in the IOS changes often and rapidly. Always check the documentation for the current version of the IOS you are running for the correct way to create an access list.

KEY TERMS

- access list
- destination IP address
- destination IP access list
- octet
- packet
- port number
- wildcard bits

APPLY YOUR KNOWLEDGE

Review Questions

1. How many types of IP access lists are there, and what are their capabilities?

2. What is added to the end of every access list?

3. What performance considerations should you take into account when creating an access list?

4. What are wildcard bits?

5. What are some uses for access lists?

6. What version of IOS introduced named access lists?

7. When you apply an access list to an interface, does it filter incoming or outgoing traffic or both?

8. How can you edit an access list?

9. Why is it important to pay attention to the order of statements in an access list?

10. What is the purpose of named access lists and the use of built-in abbreviations for well-known TCP port numbers?

Exam Questions

1. An access list applied to an interface affects traffic going in which direction?

   A. Network traffic coming into the interface is filtered.

   B. Network traffic exiting the interface is filtered.

   C. Both incoming and outgoing traffic is filtered.

   D. The access list filters traffic in the direction specified when the access-group command is applied to the interface.

2. Which range of numbers indicates an extended IP access list?

   A. 0-99

   B. 100-199

   C. 1-99

   D. 101-199

3. What is the proper syntax for applying a standard IP access list to an interface?

   A. `Router(config-if)#access-list 101`

   B. `Router(config-if)#access-group 22 in`

   C. `Router(config-if)#access-group 101 out`

   D. `Router(config-if)#access-list 22 out`

4. Which command will show which IP access lists are applied to which interfaces?

   A. `Router#show ip interface`

   B. `Router#show interface`

   C. `Router#show access-lists`

   D. `Router#show traffic-filters`

5. What is the proper syntax for an access list to allow all traffic from network 192.168.42.0?

   A. `Router(config)#access-list 1 permit 192.168.42.0 255.255.255.0`

   B. `Router(config-if)#access-list 1 permit 192.168.42.0 255.255.255.0`

   C. `Router(config)#access-list 1 permit 192.168.42.0 0.0.0.255`

   D. `Router(config)#access-list 1 permit 192.168.42.0 0.0.0.255 out`

APPLY YOUR KNOWLEDGE

6. How many access lists can be applied to an interface for one protocol?

    A. Two

    B. One

    C. Up to 99

    D. As many as the router's processor can adequately service

7. What command will display the access lists currently defined?

    A. *Router*#show access-lists

    B. *Router*#show access lists

    C. *Router*#show traffic-filters

    D. *Router*#list access-lists

8. Which of the following is a properly formatted extended IP access list statement?

    A. *Router*(config)#access-list 99 permit tcp 192.168.41.0 0.0.0.255 any eq telnet

    B. *Router*(config)#access-list 102 permit tcp 192.168.41.0 0.0.0.255 any eq telnet

    C. *Router*(config)#access-list 102 permit 192.168.41.0 255.255.255.0 any tcp eq telnet

    D. *Router*(config)#access-list 99 permit tcp 192.168.41.0 255.255.255.0 eq telnet

9. What implied command is added to the end of every IP access list?

    A. deny any

    B. permit any

    C. deny ip traffic

    D. permit ip traffic

10. Access list statements are executed in what order?

    A. From the top down, executing every statement, even after a match is found

    B. Randomly until a match is found

    C. In order of importance

    D. From the top down until a match is found; then, the packet is either forwarded or dropped

Answers to Review Questions

1. There are two types of IP access lists—standard and extended. Standard access lists let you identify traffic based on source IP address. Extended IP access lists let you specify source and destination IP address, protocol, and port number. For more information, see "Implementing Standard IP Access Lists" and "Implementing Extended IP Access Lists."

2. An implicit deny any. You must have at least one permit statement in your access list to allow any traffic to pass the access list. For more information, see "Implementing Standard IP Access Lists" and "Implementing Extended IP Access Lists".

3. Access lists cause the router to look at each packet entering or exiting an interface. When the router evaluates an access list, it does so from the top down. When it finds an applicable command, it either forwards the permitted packet or drops the denied packet. Well-designed access lists deal with most of the traffic in the first few lines, so the router doesn't have to process the entire access list for most traffic. For more information, see "How Access Lists Affect Performance."

APPLY YOUR KNOWLEDGE

4. Wildcard bits are similar to a subnet mask, but they identify bit positions that the access list doesn't care about. When the wildcard bit is set to one, the access list algorithm doesn't evaluate that bit position. For more information, see "Wildcards in the IP Address."

5. Access lists can be used to filter traffic, identify interesting traffic to bring up a dial-up connection, filter routing updates, and limit SAPs. For more information, see "Uses of Access Lists."

6. Cisco's IOS version 11.2 introduced named access lists. For more information, see "Named Access Lists."

7. An access list filters traffic in the direction specified—either incoming or outgoing traffic. The default is outgoing traffic, since this creates the least load on the router's processor. For more information, see "Implementing Standard IP Access Lists."

8. A named access list can be edited line-by-line like most configuration commands. Numbered access lists must be deleted and reentered, or the configuration can be copied to a TFTP server and then edited with a text editor and copied back. For more information, see "Editing Access Lists."

9. Access lists are processed from the top down. Once a match is found, the router either forwards the packet or drops it. When most of the network traffic matches the first line of the access list, the load on the router's processor is lessened. For more information, see "How Access Lists Affect Performance."

10. Named access lists and abbreviations for well-known TCP ports make access lists easier to read and figure out. It's common to have to look at a configuration of a router you have never seen before and figure out what the purpose of each configuration line is. By giving access lists meaningful names and using the built-in abbreviations, you can make it easier for yourself later when you must evaluate the router's configuration. For more information, see "Implementing Extended IP Access Lists" and "Named Access Lists."

Answers to Exam Questions

1. **D.** By default, an access list applies to traffic exiting an interface. However, it applies to traffic in the direction specified when the access list is applied to the interface. For more information, see "Implementing Standard IP Access Lists" and "Implementing Extended Access Lists."

2. **B.** Extended access lists are numbered 100-199. For more information, see "The Parts of an Access List."

3. **B.** When applying an access list to an interface, the access-group command is used. Standard IP access lists fall in the range of 1-99. For more information, see "Implementing Standard IP Access Lists."

4. **A.** show ip interface lists many parameters that deal with the interface, including the IP access lists applied to it. For more information, see "Verifying Access Lists."

APPLY YOUR KNOWLEDGE

5. **C.** Wildcard bits are different from subnet masks. For more information, see "Wildcards in the IP Address."

6. **B.** Only one access list per protocol per interface is allowed. For more information, see "The Parts of an Access List."

7. **A.** show access-lists will display all the access lists in the configuration, even if they aren't applied to an interface. For more information, see "Viewing Access Lists."

8. **B.** The proper format for an extended IP access list is

```
access-list 100-199 {permit¦denyip¦tcp¦udp¦
↪icmp} source source-mask dest dest-mask
↪[lt¦gt¦eq¦neq dest-port]
```
For more information, see "Implementing Extended IP Access Lists."

9. **A.** Every access list has an implicit deny any command added. If you don't implicitly allow some IP traffic to pass, none will. For more information, see "Understanding Access Lists."

10. **D.** Access list statements are executed from the top down until a match is found. Once a match is found, the packet is either forwarded or dropped. For more information, see "How Access Lists Affect Performance."

Suggested Readings and Resources

1. Chappell, Laura. *Introduction to Cisco Router Configuration.* Cisco Press, 1998.

2. Cisco Press. *Cisco IOS Solutions for Network Protocols, Volume I.* Cisco Press, 1998.

3. Cisco Press. *Cisco IOS Solutions for Network Protocols, Volume II.* Cisco Press, 1998.

Cisco provides the following objectives for the LAN Switching portion of the CCNA exam.

Describe LAN segmentation using bridges.

▶ To be an internetworking professional, you will need to understand the benefits of network segmentation using bridges. As LANs grow in size, network segmentation becomes more important.

Describe LAN segmentation using routers.

▶ To be an internetworking professional, you must understand the benefits of network segmentation using routers. As LANs grow in size, network segmentation becomes more important.

Describe LAN segmentation using switches.

▶ To be an internetworking professional, you will need to understand the advantages of network segmentation using switches. As LANs grow in size, network segmentation becomes more important.

Name and describe two switching methods.

▶ To be an internetworking professional, you must understand the advantages and disadvantages of different methods of LAN switching.

Describe full- and half-duplex Ethernet operation.

▶ As an internetworking professional, you must be familiar with full- and half-duplex Ethernet operations.

CHAPTER 8

LAN Switching

Describe network congestion problems in Ethernet networks.

▶ As an internetworking professional, you must understand the effects of network congestion on Ethernet networks and how to overcome these problems with LAN segmentation.

Describe the benefits of network segmentation with bridges.

▶ As an internetworking professional, you must understand the benefits of network segmentation with bridges.

Describe the benefits of network segmentation with switches.

▶ As an internetworking professional, you must understand the benefits of network segmentation with switches.

Describe the features and benefits of Fast Ethernet.

▶ As an internetworking professional, you must understand the features and benefits of Fast Ethernet.

Describe the guidelines and distance limitations of Fast Ethernet.

▶ As an internetworking professional, you must be able to design networks using Fast Ethernet. To do this effectively, you must understand its limitations.

Distinguish between cut-through and store-and-forward LAN switching.

▶ As an internetworking professional, you must be able to distinguish between cut-through and store-and-forward LAN switching.

Describe the operation of Spanning Tree Protocol and its benefits.

▶ As an internetworking professional, you must understand the operation of Spanning Tree Protocol and how it works to guarantee a loop-free network.

Describe the benefits of virtual LANs.

▶ As an internetworking professional, you must understand the benefits of VLANs and where they should be used.

Define and describe the function of a MAC address.

▶ As an internetworking professional, you must understand the function of a MAC address.

OUTLINE

▶ Begin studying for the LAN switching section of the CCNA exam by making sure you understand the effects of collisions on a large LAN. Then, make sure you understand each of the methods covered in this chapter for segmenting a LAN to avoid the problems caused by excessive collisions.

Finally, be sure you can differentiate between store-and-forward and cut-through LAN switching. If you have a Cisco LAN switch available, spend some time learning how it is configured and review the statistics in the switch to see how it affects LAN traffic. This chapter begins with a review of how Ethernet functions and how segmenting a LAN can improve the performance of a LAN.

INTRODUCTION

When LANs were first created, it was inconceivable that there would be a network that connected the world like the Internet does today. In the 1980s, a large network consisted of 20 or 30 PCs. Today, many networks consist of 500 or more PCs. The sheer number of computers on the network creates new challenges to overcome.

This chapter discusses some of the techniques used to overcome the challenges of larger networks.

THE PROBLEMS WITH LARGE NETWORKS

Large networks present several problems that must be overcome. By understanding the challenges first, you will better grasp how the technology addresses these problems.

Some of the challenges large networks create are as follows:

◆ Because a large number of network stations are contending for the LAN media, a large number of collisions usually occur. These collisions seriously degrade the performance of the LAN. Each area of the LAN that competes for media time is called a *collision domain*.

◆ Most networks have groups of computers that typically communicate with each other. The computers in human resources, for example, usually communicate with the HR server. The computers in finance, on the other hand, usually communicate with the Finance server. When all of these computers share a common network, they are competing for LAN time with all the other departments. By segmenting the LAN into logical groups this can be overcome.

Fundamentals of Ethernet

Ethernet is a Carrier Sense Multiple Access/Collision Detect (CSMA/CD) network—but what does that really mean? *Carrier Sense* refers to the ability of Ethernet nodes to detect the Ethernet carrier. A *carrier* is a signal that is transmitted constantly. When data is transmitted, the carrier is modulated or slightly modified in a way that represents the data to be transmitted.

An example of a carrier signal is with your car radio. FM radio stations transmit a constant carrier signal. Your car stereo detects this signal. When your stereo is tuned to a frequency where there is no radio station carrier, you hear static. When you tune to a station that is currently not playing any music, you no longer hear the static. The radio is detecting the carrier and is decoding the information on the carrier, which, when there is no sound, is nothing. Ethernet uses this same technique to detect the Ethernet carrier. Most Ethernet cards have some sort of link light that shows when the card is detecting the carrier.

Multiple Access refers to the ability of multiple nodes to access the media simultaneously.

Collision Detection refers to the ability of Ethernet nodes to detect when two stations send data simultaneously and create a collision of data. When a collision occurs, the data sent is corrupt. When a collision occurs, all of the nodes involved in the collision wait a random amount of time before trying to send their data again.

Before an Ethernet node starts to send data, it listens for network traffic on the network. If there is no traffic, the Ethernet node starts to send its frame. After completion, it listens again to check if another station collided with the sending of its frame.

Because the number of network stations on a network greatly affects how many collisions will occur, this is a factor on network performance. At some point, the amount of traffic will increase to the point that very little traffic will be sent without experiencing a collision. When this occurs, network congestion becomes a significant problem. *Network congestion* occurs when a large number of collisions are occurring due to the shear number of nodes contending for the shared media. When a network reaches this point, the performance of the network degrades quickly.

Collision Domains

A *collision domain* is a group of network nodes on Ethernet that share the network media. By sharing the media, they can experience or cause collisions with other stations in the collision domain. In large networks you can divide the network into multiple collision domains to avoid the performance degradation associated with large collision domains. This dividing of the network is called *segmentation*, which is discussed in the following section.

NETWORK SEGMENTATION

To keep collision domains small on large networks, you can make use of network segmentation. By segmenting the network into small collision domain segments that can communicate with each other, you avoid the performance degradation that occurs with a large number of nodes in one collision domain. There are several different ways to segment a network:

◆ Bridges

◆ Routers

◆ Switches

The following sections detail each of these techniques.

The advantage of LAN segmentation is that it increases network performance by reducing the number of nodes participating in a collision domain.

LAN Segmentation Using Bridges

A *bridge* is a network device that is connected to multiple network segments. A bridge is a Layer 2 device. It operates at the Data Link layer, using MAC addresses to determine when to forward traffic. Years ago bridges were physical devices that connected to the network. Today when the functions of a bridge are needed, a router is typically used. Cisco routers can function as bridges as well as routers. Figure 8.1 shows a network segmented with a bridge.

FIGURE 8.1

Network segmented by a bridge.

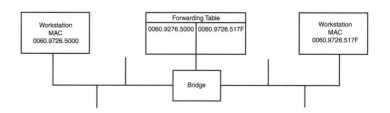

In Figure 8.1, you see a network segmented by a bridge. The bridge listens to each segment to which it is connected. When it hears network traffic, it reads the MAC address of the sending station and places that MAC address in a table. This table determines how the bridge forwards traffic. Suppose the bridge detects 0060.9726.5000 trying to reach 0060.9726.517F on segment A. Because the frame originated from 0060.9726.5000 on segment A, the bridge places this MAC address in the table for segment A. It has learned where MAC address 0060.9726.5000 resides. Because at this point the bridge does not know where 0060.9726.517F resides, the bridge reads the frame from segment A and floods it to segment B.

Node 0060.9726.517F reads the frame destined for it directly from segment A, and thus the frame forwarded to segment B goes unanswered. Node 0060.9726.517F responds to the frame. The bridge sees a frame from 0060.9726.517F destined for 0060.9726.5000 on segment A. The bridge consults its bridging table and finds that node 0060.9726.5000 is on segment A, the same segment the frame was detected on, so the bridge does nothing. The conversation between 0060.9726.517F and 0060.9726.5000 continues without causing any traffic on segment B.

Node 0060.9726.517F on segment A now sends a frame to 0060.9726.5003 on segment B.

Bridges learn MAC addresses (Layer 2) and forward traffic to other segments based on tables they build of which MAC addresses reside on which segments. Bridges have no knowledge of upper-layer protocols. All forwarding is based on MAC address.

LAN Segmentation Using Routers

A *router* can be used to segment a network into different collision domains (see Figure 8.2). Assuming that the router is routing between the networks and not bridging, this actually divides the networks into separate Layer 3 networks. Each different Layer 3 network is a separate collision domain. One of the disadvantages of separating the networks with a router is it can take a very powerful router to handle many high-speed network connections with large amounts of data.

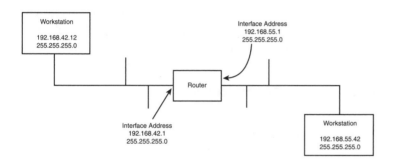

FIGURE 8.2
A network segmented using a router.

LAN Segmentation Using Switches

LAN *switches* work much like bridges with many ports. A LAN switch learns what MAC addresses are connected to which ports. After the switch learns this information, it then forwards frames only to the ports on which the destination MAC address resides. LAN switches learn on which port network nodes reside by listening to network traffic. If a LAN switch receives a frame with a destination MAC address that is not in its forwarding tables, it floods all ports with the frame. After the destination station replies to the frame, the LAN switch will learn on which port it resides and won't need to flood its traffic again.

LAN switches reduce collisions by increasing the number of collision domains. By increasing the number of collision domains, you reduce the number of network nodes contending for the media.

A LAN switch can operate in three different modes:

◆ Cut-through

◆ Fragment-free

◆ Store-and-forward

Cut-Through Switching

A switch operating in *cut-through* mode will start forwarding a frame as soon as it reads the destination address. At that point the switch looks up the MAC address in its forwarding table and starts forwarding the frame out of the destination port. Cut-through switching produces the lowest amount of latency through the switch.

Fragment-Free Switching

A switch operating in *fragment-free* mode will start forwarding a frame as soon as the first 64 bytes of the frame are received. Because most collisions occur during the first 64 bytes, this helps keep the switch from forwarding corrupt frames. It also allows the switch to read the destination MAC address and make a forwarding decision. Fragment-free mode creates the second least amount of latency or delay through the switch.

Store-and-Forward Switching

A switch operating in *store-and-forward* mode receives the entire frame before forwarding it. This ensures that corrupt frames are not forwarded. Store-and-forward mode creates more latency or delay through the switch because it must receive the entire frame before it begins to forward it. This means larger packets will have a greater latency through the switch than smaller packets.

R E V I E W   B R E A K

Bridges, Routers, and Switches in a Nutshell

▶ **Bridges.** Bridges are useful for segmenting a LAN. Cisco routers can function as bridges as well as routers. Bridges operate at Layer 2 (the MAC layer). A bridge listens to the MAC addresses on each LAN segment to which it is connected.

It builds a table of these MAC addresses along with which segment it detected the station on. When the bridge detects traffic for a MAC address that is on a remote segment, it copies the frames and forwards them to the segment on which the destination MAC address was detected. If a bridge sees traffic for a MAC address the bridge has not yet detected, it copies the frame to all LAN segments to which it is attached. It then listens for the response to the frame and then adds that station to the table. Bridges are older technology and are not used much anymore. Many of the functions of bridges have been replaced by LAN switches.

▶ **Routers.** Routers are useful for segmenting a LAN at Layer 3. A router uses the Network layer protocol to determine when to forward traffic to another network. The disadvantage to using a router to segment a high speed LAN is that the router must make routing decisions and generally will slow down the connection between two high-speed LAN segments.

▶ **LAN Switches.** LAN switches are an evolution of bridges. Basically, a LAN switch can be thought of as a bridge with many segments. LAN switches operate at Layer 2, as do bridges. It is not uncommon today to have desktops on a large LAN connected directly to switch ports.

A switch works much like a bridge in that it listens for MAC addresses and builds a table of the port on which the MAC address was detected. When traffic for that MAC address is detected on another port the frame is copied to the port the destination MAC address was detected on. This keeps the entire network from having to contend with that traffic.

LAN switches can operate in three modes. *Store-and-forward* mode receives the entire frame, stores it, looks up the destination address in the table and then forwards the frame out of the destination port. *Cut-through* mode starts forwarding the frame as soon as the destination address is read. *Fragment-free* mode begins forwarding as soon as 64 bytes are received, which is when most collisions would occur. *Store-and-forward* mode creates greater latency through the switch than the cut-through and fragment-free modes. Store-and-forward also has more latency for larger packets than smaller ones because the entire packet must be received before forwarding.

FULL-DUPLEX AND HALF-DUPLEX

To understand the differences between full- and half-duplex Ethernet, you must first have a strong grasp on the concept of full- versus half-duplex. *Full-duplex* operation allows both sides of the connection to send as well as receive data simultaneously. With *half-duplex* operation, only one side can send data at a time, and while that side is sending, it is unable to receive, or listen.

The Speakerphone

Most everyone has experienced half-duplex when talking on a speakerphone. Very few speakerphones support full-duplex. On a half-duplex speakerphone, only one person can talk at a time. In other words, you must take turns using the network media (the telephone line).

When you pick up the receiver and use the handset as opposed to the speakerphone, you are using full-duplex. Both parties can speak without blanking out the other.

The Bridge over a River

Another example that might help you fully understand the difference between full- and half-duplex is a bridge. A bridge with one lane each way allows traffic from both directions to cross a river at the same time. This is an example of full-duplex.

If a construction crew were working on the bridge and had one lane blocked, traffic would have to alternate across the bridge. A flagman at each end of the bridge would stop the traffic from one direction to allow the traffic from the other direction to pass. After some time, the traffic from that direction would have to stop to allow some of the traffic from the other direction to pass. This is an example of half-duplex.

Ethernet Full- and Half-Duplex

Ethernet can work similarly. In a shared network with no switches, the network operates at half-duplex. Only one network station can talk at a time. When you employ switches on a network, you can support full-duplex Ethernet. Full-duplex Ethernet is supported when there are only two nodes in a collision domain, or on the shared media. This could be a workstation plugged directly into a network switch. The workstation is one node and the network switch is the other node. Both devices must support full-duplex operation.

A common problem when using full-duplex-capable devices is they often do not properly auto-negotiate. Often, one device will enter full-duplex mode and the other will not. It would seem that if this occurs, traffic would not pass. However, in the experience of the author, traffic will pass, but will generate a large number of errors and cause a substantial slowdown of the network. It is best to not let devices auto-negotiate the full-duplex mode. If you want two devices to operate at full-duplex, specifically set them to do so.

Most Ethernet ports on Cisco routers do not support full-duplex mode. Before trying to interface a router with a switch in full-duplex mode, be sure that the interface on the router supports it.

Full-duplex Ethernet doubles the effective bandwidth of the link. A 10Mb link run in full-duplex mode becomes 20Mb. A 100Mb link run in full-duplex mode becomes 200Mb. Obviously, full-duplex Ethernet can help alleviate bottlenecks in networks. A common place to fully utilize full-duplex Ethernet is on network servers. These devices typically receive and send more data than any other network device. Another common use of full-duplex Ethernet is high-speed links that collapse a network backbone to one switch. Figure 8.3 shows a fully switched network with a collapsed backbone.

FIGURE 8.3
A network with a collapsed backbone to a high-speed switch.

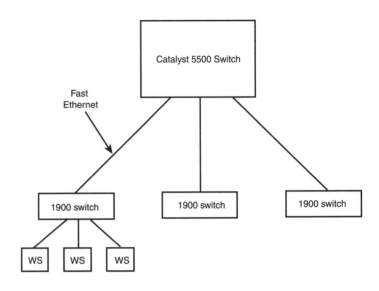

FAST ETHERNET

Over the past few years, networks have grown quickly. More demands are being placed on LANs with new technologies. Audio and video needs have created a great deal of demand for faster networks. To address these needs, manufacturers came up with *Fast Ethernet*. Fast Ethernet increases the bandwidth of Ethernet from 10Mbps to 100Mbps.

To make the transition easier, most Fast Ethernet devices can also operate at 10Mbps. However, many organizations have large numbers of 10Mbps devices installed. These organizations can benefit from Fast Ethernet by installing a Fast Ethernet switch for their servers and connect the 10Mbps devices through the switch. This way the servers have access to high-speed connections and can service more 10Mbps workstations than before. This upgrade is generally inexpensive compared to upgrading an entire network to Fast Ethernet all at once.

The Different Media Types of Fast Ethernet

Fast Ethernet supports different media types. *100BaseTX* can be used on two pairs of Category 5 copper wire like most 10BaseT installations.

This is convenient because you will not have to install new wiring in most cases.

100BaseFX is an implementation of Fast Ethernet on Fiber Optic strands. Because 100BaseFX has longer maximum distance limitations, it is commonly used to connect outlying switches with a backbone switch.

100BaseT4 is an implementation of Fast Ethernet using four pairs of Category 3, 4, or 5 wire. This implementation is good for organizations that already have a large investment of Category 3 or 4 wire in place and cannot justify upgrading the cabling to Category 5.

Distance Limitations

With Fast Ethernet advances in speed come some new limitations in distance. Because most of the Ethernet specification remained unchanged while the speed of transmission increased, there are some resulting limitations. Part of Ethernet's specification calls for devices to be able to detect a collision within the first 64 bytes. Because Fast Ethernet is now 10 times faster than 10BaseT, the time to detect a collision in 64 bytes is now 10 times shorter. Although electricity travels very quickly, it is not instantaneous. Copper Fast Ethernet has a distance limitation of 100 meters per segment. The maximum network diameter (the distance from one end of the network to the other) is 200 meters. These limitations keep the network small enough so that if nodes at each of the far ends of the network are involved in a collision, they can detect it during the first 64 bytes. Table 8.1 shows the different limitations of Fast Ethernet.

TABLE 8.1

ETHERNET DISTANCE LIMITATIONS

Characteristics	*100BaseTX*	*100BaseFX*	*100BaseT4*
Cable	Category 5 UTP, or Type 1 and 2 STP	62.5/125 micron multi-mode fiber	Category 3, 4, or 5 UTP
Number of pairs or strands	2 pairs	2 strands	4 pairs

continues

TABLE 8.1		*continued*	

ETHERNET DISTANCE LIMITATIONS

Characteristics	*100BaseTX*	*100BaseFX*	*100BaseT4*
Connector	ISO 8877 (RJ-45) connector	Duplex SCmedia-interface connector (MIC) ST	ISO 8877 (RJ-45) connector
Maximum segment length	100 meters	400 meters	100 meters
Maximum network diameter	200 meters	400 meters	200 meters

Because network switches are active devices that regenerate the frame, their use can extend the limitations of a Fast Ethernet network.

SPANNING TREE PROTOCOL

The *Spanning Tree Protocol (STP)* is a link management protocol. It manages redundant links in a network while at the same time preventing undesirable loops. To operate properly, Ethernet requires only one active path between two nodes.

Cisco switches use the Spanning Tree Protocol to maintain a loop-free network.

The Spanning Tree Protocol calculates the most efficient loop-free path through the network. To maintain this loop-free environment, the Spanning Tree Protocol defines a tree that spans all switches in the network. When a network loop exists, switches can see a node's MAC address on both sides of a port. This causes confusion for the forwarding algorithm and allows duplicate frames to be forwarded. The Spanning Tree Protocol determines where multiple paths exist and forces certain ones into *standby* (blocked) state. If a network segment in the Spanning Tree becomes unreachable or if the Spanning Tree Protocol calculates that the cost of a path has changed, the Spanning Tree algorithm reconfigures the Spanning Tree topology by activating the path that was placed in standby state.

STP operation is transparent to end stations, which do not detect whether they are connected to a single LAN segment or a switched LAN of multiple segments.

Election of a Root Switch

For a Spanning Tree to operate properly a *root switch* must be elected. This root switch becomes the logical center of the Spanning Tree topology.

When switches in a network are powered on, they begin exchanging data messages called *Bridge Protocol Data Units (BPDUs)*. By using the BPDUs, the Spanning Tree Protocol elects a root switch and designates a switch for every switched LAN segment. The Spanning Tree Protocol also detects loops in the network and places redundant switch ports in standby state.

Spanning Tree Protocol Port States

The Spanning Tree Protocol maintains a loop-free network by setting the state of switched ports. The Spanning Tree can set one of five states:

◆ Blocking

◆ Listening

◆ Learning

◆ Forwarding

◆ Disabled

Blocking State

A port placed in *blocking state* does not forward frames. When a port is placed in blocking state, it discards frames received from the attached segment. It also discards frames switched from other ports. The blocked port does not place MAC addresses in the forwarding tables.

Listening State

Listening state is the first state a port enters after the blocking state. When the Spanning Tree Protocol has determined that a port should participate in frame forwarding, it is placed in listening state. Learning is disabled while in listening state. While in listening state, a port does the following:

◆ Discards frames received from the attached segment

◆ Discards frames switched from other ports for forwarding

◆ Does not learn MAC addresses

◆ Receives BPDUs

◆ Processes BPDUs

◆ Receives and responds to network management messages

Learning State

After a port is placed in *learning state* it prepares to participate in frame forwarding. The port enters learning state from the listening state. While in learning state, the port does the following:

◆ Discards frames received from the attached segment

◆ Discards frames switched from another ports for forwarding

◆ Learns MAC address and places them in the address database

◆ Receives, processes, and transmits BPDUs

◆ Receives and responds to network management messages

Forwarding State

A port enters *forwarding state* from the learning state. While in forwarding state, the port performs the following functions:

◆ Forward frames received from the attached segment

◆ Forwards frames switched from other ports

◆ Learns MAC addresses and adds them to the forwarding database

◆ Receives BPDUs

◆ Processes BPDUs

◆ Receives and responds to network management messages

Disabled State

A port placed in *disabled state* does not participate in frame forwarding or the Spanning Tree Protocol. A port placed in disabled state is not functioning.

VIRTUAL LANS (VLANS)

Now that technology has given you Fast Ethernet and LAN switching technology, you can build very large networks. But, should you? Does it not make sense to group computers together by function? However, you don't want to have to worry about a large number of small networks. There is a happy medium: *Virtual LANs (VLANs)*. On a switched network, VLANs allow you to define logical groups. Why would you want to do this? Although switches reduce the problems with collisions occurring, broadcasts still propagate throughout a switched network. These broadcasts might be Novell SAPs or ARP requests. Either way, they are forwarded to every workstation and server on your large switched network every time a broadcast is generated. Not only do broadcasts generate network overhead, but every workstation on the network must process the broadcast. This creates processing overhead for your computers as well.

By dividing the network into logical pieces with computers grouped by function, you can reduce the overhead of broadcasts on the network and workstations. Think of switches as reducing collision domains and VLANs as reducing broadcast domains.

VLANs were designed to solve two main problems:

◆ Scalability of flat networks

◆ Simplification of network management

VLANs solve these problems by segmenting large flat networks into logically grouped VLANs. These VLANs are easier to manage because they are grouped logically. They also increase scalablity of the network because a large number of nodes can be supported as a number of smaller groups.

By adding a router in the network, you can route data from one VLAN to another just as you can route data from physically separate networks.

CASE STUDY: ACME INTERACTIVE IS GROWING TOO QUICKLY!

ESSENCE OF THE CASE

The facts of the case are as follows:

- ▶ Acme Interactive has too much traffic for a shared media network.

- ▶ The company's expected growth will only compound the problem.

- ▶ To effectively make a recommendation, you must understand the benefits of LAN segmentation and the methods of implementing it.

- ▶ You need to make sure your recommendation will be able to grow with the company as it expands.

SCENARIO

You have been hired by Acme Interactive to help improve the performance of its LAN. Chuck, the technical manager, explains that the company has recently purchased another company and added about 100 workstations to its LAN. This makes the count of workstations on the LAN now 220. Since the expansion, the LAN users have been complaining about how slow access has become.

Acme Interactive is expected to continue growing at a rapid pace and needs a solution that can grow with it.

The company is currently running 10BaseT Ethernet with Category 5 cable throughout the building. All of the servers and most of the workstations are equipped with network cards capable of running at 100Mbps as well.

The server room contains three servers. A Linux machine runs the intranet Web site and the Internet Web site for the company. A Novell server is used for file and print sharing. A Windows NT computer runs Microsoft Exchange for email and scheduling. All of the users on the network use all of these servers. There is a router installed that connects the network to the Internet.

ANALYSIS

First you need to evaluate how the company's network traffic is distributed. Do small groups of computers normally communicate among themselves, or is the traffic more distributed? With this company, it is more evenly distributed because all users make use of the three servers housed centrally in the server room.

CASE STUDY: ACME INTERACTIVE IS GROWING TOO QUICKLY!

Because you are certain that the degradation in network speed has to do with a drastic increase in collisions, you know some sort of LAN segmentation is necessary. You place a sniffer on the network to confirm your suspicions and find that you are correct. The network is experiencing an excessive amount of collisions. To segment the LAN, there are several options.

A router could be used to segment the LAN into separate networks. This would reduce the effects of collisions on each of the network segments. However, installing a router would require the network addressing scheme to change. This means the technical staff at Acme Interactive would have to make changes on each computer at the office. The router also would not be able to pass traffic from one segment to another as quickly as a LAN switch.

A bridge could be used to segment the LAN. Because a bridge operates at the Data Link layer, no changes in networking addresses would be required. The segments would be separated into different collision domains, which would reduce the effects of collisions on network traffic. However, a bridge is not necessarily the best solution. A bridge does not offer the growth potential that LAN switches would, and LAN switches could provide more segments, thus reducing the effects of collisions even more.

LAN switches are the best solution in this scenario. LAN switches would provide the best means of reducing the collision domains on the network as well as provide for future growth. Because all of the workstations on the network access the same servers, you recommend placing the servers on a Cisco 5500 switch using full-duplex Fast Ethernet. Many of the workstations can also be connected directly to the 5500 switch. Another switch is required for workstations at the far end of the building. For these workstations, you recommend installing a Cisco 5505 switch connected to the 5500 via a fiber Fast Ethernet connection. This option provides the best performance because each workstation will be placed in its own collision domain. The growth potential is very good; adding more switches allows expansion of the LAN with little to no effect from collisions. Also, because switches operate at the Data Link layer, there is no need to reconfigure the network addresses.

Chuck, the technical manager, calls you into his office and explains he is pleased with your recommendation. He contracts you to oversee the implementation project.

CHAPTER SUMMARY

KEY TERMS

- Collision domain
- Broadcast domain
- Full-duplex
- Half-duplex
- Network segmentation
- Bridge
- Network switch
- Cut-through
- Store-and-foward
- Full-duplex Ethernet
- 100BaseTX
- 100BaseFX
- 100BaseT4
- Spanning Tree Protocol
- Root switch
- Virtual LAN

This chapter covered different methods of segmenting a LAN to reduce the effects of large amounts of network traffic combined with the exponential increase in collisions large amounts of traffic create. Three devices are discussed for use in segmenting a LAN: bridges, routers, and LAN switches.

Bridges operate at Layer 2, the Data Link layer. A bridge listens to network traffic on each segment to which it is attached and builds a table of MAC addresses listing which segment they are on. When the bridge sees traffic on a segment that has a destination MAC address of a station on a different segment, the bridge copies the frame from the source segment and places it on the segment the destination address is on. The bridge determines this by referring to the MAC addresses and segments in the table it has built. When a bridge sees a frame for a MAC address that is not in its table yet, it copies the frame to all segments except the one the frame originated on. Then the bridge listens for a reply to the frame and places the MAC address with the segment it heard the reply on in its table.

Routers separate LAN segments at Layer 3, the Network layer. Routers are typically slower than LAN switches. Routers are most useful when separating a LAN at the Network layer.

LAN switches operate at Layer 2, the Data Link layer. LAN switches operate much like bridges. Switches listen to MAC addresses on each port and build a table of these MAC addresses.

APPLY YOUR KNOWLEDGE

Review Questions

1. Describe the advantages of network segmentation.

2. Describe the three methods of LAN switching.

3. Describe the purpose of the Spanning Tree Protocol.

4. Describe the difference between segmenting a LAN with a bridge and with a router.

5. Describe the features and benefits of Fast Ethernet.

6. What is an example of half-duplex?

7. What is an example of full-duplex?

8. Describe the benefits of VLANs.

9. How can different VLANs communicate with each other?

Exam Questions

1. A bridge segments a LAN at which layer?

   A. Layer 1

   B. Layer 2

   C. Layer 3

   D. Layer 5

2. A router segments a LAN at which layer?

   A. Layer 1

   B. Layer 2

   C. Layer 3

   D. Layer 5

3. A LAN switch segments a LAN at which layer?

   A. Layer 1

   B. Layer 2

   C. Layer 3

   D. Layer 5

4. A VLAN separates a network into different what?

   A. Collision domains

   B. Broadcast domains

   C. LAN segments

   D. Logical groups

5. Which of the following are characteristics of cut-through LAN switching?

   A. Lower latency than store-and-forward

   B. Higher latency than store-and-forward

   C. The same latency as store-and-forward

   D. None of the above

6. When does store-and-forward switching begin forwarding the frame?

   A. After the first 64 bytes have been received error free

   B. After the entire frame is received error free

   C. As soon as the frame is detected

   D. After the frame is received and the frame forward timer has elapsed

APPLY YOUR KNOWLEDGE

7. What function does the Spanning Tree Protocol serve?

    A. It maintains a loop-free network.

    B. It spans the entire network to determine if you have exceeded the maximum length for Fast Ethernet.

    C. It sets switches in store-and-forward or cut-through mode.

    D. It determines where routers are on the network.

8. Full-duplex Ethernet increases effective bandwidth by how much?

    A. 1.5 times.

    B. 1.75 times.

    C. 2 times.

    D. It doesn't increase bandwidth; it simply reduces collisions.

9. What is the maximum segment length for Fast Ethernet 100BaseTX?

    A. 100 feet

    B. 200 feet

    C. 100 meters

    D. 200 meters

10. What is the maximum diameter for a Fast Ethernet network?

    A. 100 feet

    B. 200 feet

C. 100 meters

D. 200 meters

Answers to Review Questions

1. Network segmentation allows larger networks because it reduces network congestion caused by a large number of network nodes contending for the shared media. For more information, see "The Problems with Large Networks."

2. The three methods of LAN switching are cut-through, fragment-free, and store-and-forward. Cut-through starts forwarding as soon as the destination address is read. Fragment-free starts forwarding the frame after the first 64 bytes are received error free. Store-and-forward receives the entire frame before beginning to forward it. Store-and-forward creates the greatest latency through the switch. For more information, see "LAN Segmentation Using Switches."

3. The Spanning Tree Protocol ensures a loop-free path on bridged and switched networks. It does this by electing a root switch and determining loops in the network. Redundant ports are placed in standby state so they do not forward frames. For more information, see "Spanning Tree Protocol."

4. Segmenting a network with a bridge segments the network at Layer 2. Using a router to segment a network segments the network at Layer 3. For more information, see "Network Segmentation."

5. Fast Ethernet is 10 times faster than 10BaseT. This increase in speed provides more bandwidth for high-demand applications such as audio and video. Fast Ethernet is good for servers and high-use workstations. For more information, see "Fast Ethernet."

APPLY YOUR KNOWLEDGE

6. A speakerphone is typically half-duplex, allowing only one person to speak at a time. For more information, see "Fast Ethernet."

7. A two-way bridge over a river is an example of full-duplex. Cars can cross in both directions simultaneously. For more information, see "Fast Ethernet."

8. VLANs allow you to separate a network into logical groups. This provides benefits of security and increased scalability. For more information, see "Virtual LANs (VLANs)."

9. A router must route data between the different VLANs. For more information, see "Virtual LANs (VLANs)."

Answers to Exam Questions

1. **B.** Bridges segment a LAN at Layer 2. For more information, see "LAN Segmentation Using Bridges."

2. **C.** Routers segment a LAN at Layer 3. For more information, see "LAN Segmentation Using Routers."

3. **B.** LAN switches segment the network at Layer 2. For more information, see "LAN Segmentation Using Switches."

4. **B.** VLANs separate a network into different broadcast domains. For more information, see "LAN Segmentation Using Switches."

5. **A.** Cut-through LAN switching has a lower latency than store-and-forward. For more information, see "LAN Segmentation Using Switches."

6. **B.** Store-and-forward LAN switching receives the entire frame error free before forwarding it. For more information, see "LAN Segmentation Using Switches."

7. **A.** The Spanning Tree Protocol maintains a loop-free network. For more information, see "Spanning Tree Protocol."

8. **C.** Full-duplex Ethernet effectively doubles the bandwidth. For more information, see "Fast Ethernet."

9. **C.** The maximum segment length for Fast Ethernet 100BaseTX is 100 meters. For more information, see "Fast Ethernet."

10. **D.** The maximum diameter for a Fast Ethernet network using copper is 200 meters. For more information, see "Fast Ethernet."

Suggested Readings and Resources

1. Ford, Merilee; Lew, H. Kim; Spanier, Steve; Stevenson, Tim. *Internetworking Technologies Handbook*, Cisco Press, 1997.

FINAL REVIEW

Study and Exam Prep Tips

Fast Facts

Practice Exam

Study and Exam Prep Tips

This chapter provides you with some general guidelines for preparing for a certification exam. It addresses your exam preparation activities, covering general study tips. To better understand the nature of preparation for the test, it is important to understand learning as a process. You probably are aware of how you best learn new material. Maybe outlining works best for you, or perhaps you are a visual learner who needs to "see" things. Whatever your learning style, test preparation takes time. Although it is obvious that you can't start studying the night before you take these exams and expect to do well, it is very important to understand that learning is a developmental process. Understanding the process helps you focus on what you know and what you need to study further.

Thinking about how you learn should help you recognize that learning takes place when we are able to match new information to old. You have some previous experience with computers and networking, and now you are preparing for this certification exam. Using this book, software, and supplementary materials will not just add incrementally to what you know. As you study, you actually change the organization of your knowledge to integrate this new information into your existing knowledge base. This leads you to a more comprehensive understanding of the tasks and concepts outlined in the objectives and related to computing in general. Again, this happens as an iterative process rather than a singular event. Keep this model of learning in mind as you prepare for the exam, and you will make better decisions about what to study and how much to study.

STUDY TIPS

There are many ways to approach studying, just as there are many different types of material to study. However, the tips that follow should work well for the type of material covered on the certification exams.

Study Strategies

Although individuals vary in the ways they best learn information, some basic principles of learning apply to everyone. You should adopt some study strategies that take advantage of these principles. One of these principles is that learning can be broken into various depths. *Recognition* (of terms, for example) exemplifies a surface level of learning: You rely on a prompt of some sort to elicit recall. *Comprehension* or *understanding* (of the concepts behind the terms, for instance) represents a deeper level of learning. The ability to *analyze* a concept and *apply* your understanding of it in a new way or to address a unique setting represents further depth of learning.

Your learning strategy should enable you to know the material a level or two deeper than mere recognition. This will help you to do well on any exam. You will know the material so thoroughly that you can easily handle the recognition-level types of questions used in multiple-choice testing. You will also be able to apply your knowledge to solve novel problems.

Macro and Micro Study Strategies

One strategy that can lead to this deeper learning involves preparing an outline that covers all the objectives and subobjectives for the particular exam you are working on. You should then delve a bit further into the material and include a level or two of detail beyond the stated objectives and subobjectives for the exam. Finally, flesh out the outline by coming up with a statement of definition or a summary for each point in the outline.

This outline provides two approaches to studying. First, you can study the outline by focusing on the organization of the material. Work your way through the points and subpoints of your outline with the goal of learning how they relate to one another. For example, be sure you understand how each of the main objective areas is similar to and different from one another. Then do the same thing with the subobjectives. Also, be sure you know which subobjectives pertain to each objective area and how they relate to one another.

Next, you can work through the outline and focus on learning the details. Memorize and understand terms and their definitions, facts, rules and strategies, advantages and disadvantages, and so on. In this pass through the outline, attempt to learn detail as opposed to the big picture (the organizational information that you worked on in the first pass through the outline).

Research shows that attempting to assimilate both types of information at the same time seems to interfere with the overall learning process. If you separate your studying into these two approaches, you will perform better on the exam than if you attempt to study the material in a more conventional manner.

Active Study Strategies

The process of writing down and defining the objectives, subobjectives, terms, facts, and definitions promotes a more active learning strategy than merely reading the material does. In human information processing terms, writing forces you to engage in more active encoding of the information. Simply reading over the material constitutes passive processing.

Next, determine whether you can apply the information you have learned by attempting to create examples and scenarios of your own. Think about how or where you could apply the concepts you are learning. Again, write down this information to process the facts and concepts in a more active fashion.

The hands-on nature of the Step by Step tutorials and the exercises at the end of the chapters provide further active learning opportunities that will reinforce concepts.

Common Sense Strategies

Finally, you should also follow common sense practices in studying: Study when you are alert, reduce or eliminate distractions, take breaks when you become fatigued, and so on.

Pre-Testing Yourself

Pre-testing allows you to assess how well you are learning. One of the most important aspects of learning is what has been called meta-learning. *Meta-learning* has to do with realizing when you know something well or when you need to study some more. In other words, you recognize how well or how poorly you have learned the material you are studying. For most people, this can be difficult to assess objectively on their own. Therefore, practice tests are useful because they reveal more objectively what you have and have not learned. You should use this information to guide review and further study. Developmental learning takes place as you cycle through studying, assessing how well you have learned, reviewing, and assessing again, until you feel you are ready to take the exam.

You may have noticed the practice exam included in this book. Use it as part of this process. In addition to the practice exam element of this book, the Top Score software on the CD-ROM also provides a variety of ways to test yourself before you take the actual exam. By using the Top Score Practice Exams, you can take an entire practice test. By using the Top Score Study Cards, you can take an entire practice exam or you can focus on a particular objective area, such as Planning, Troubleshooting, or Monitoring and Optimization. By using the Top Score Flash Cards, you can test your knowledge at a level beyond that of recognition:

You must come up with the answers in your own words. Flash Cards also enables you to test your knowledge of particular objective areas.

You should set a goal for your pre-testing. A reasonable goal would be to score consistently in the 90-percent range (or better). See Appendix D, "How to Use the Top Score Software Suite," for a more detailed explanation of this test engine.

More Exam Preparation Tips

Generic exam preparation advice is always useful. Follow these general guidelines:

- ◆ **Become familiar with the product.** Hands-on experience is one of the keys to success on any certification exam. Review the exercises and the Step by Step tutorials in the book.

- ◆ **Review the current exam preparation guide on the Cisco Certification Web site.** The documentation Cisco makes publicly available over the Web identifies the skills every exam is intended to test.

- ◆ **Memorize foundational technical detail as appropriate.** But remember: Most certification exams are generally heavier on problem solving and application of knowledge than they are on questions that require only rote memorization.

- ◆ **Take any of the available practice tests.** We recommend the one included in this book and those you can create using the Top Score software on the CD-ROM. Although these are fixed-format exams, they provide preparation that is also valuable for taking an adaptive exam. Because of the nature of adaptive testing, it is not possible for these practice exams to be offered in the adaptive format. However, fixed-format exams provide the same types of questions as adaptive exams and are the most effective way to prepare for either type of exam.

N O T E **One-of-a-kind product** New Riders Publishing has just released a new product in their certification line: ExamGear Test Simulation Software. CCNA ExamGear will be available in stores in August, 1999. This product includes 500 test questions delivered to you in random order, as well as tracking and scoring abilities that no other test simulation product has. If you want to ensure that you are prepared for the CCNA Exam, check out CCNA ExamGear.

◆ **Look on the Cisco Web site for samples and demonstration items.** These tend to be particularly valuable, if only for one significant reason: They allow you to become familiar with any new testing technologies before you encounter them on a Cisco exam.

During the Exam Session

The generic exam-taking advice you've heard for years applies when taking a Cisco exam:

◆ Take a deep breath and try to relax when you first sit down for your exam. It is very important to control the pressure you may (naturally) feel when taking exams.

◆ You will be provided scratch paper. Take a moment to write down any factual information and technical detail that you committed to short-term memory.

◆ Carefully read all information and instruction screens. These displays have been put together to give you information relevant to the exam you are taking.

◆ Accept the Non-Disclosure Agreement and preliminary survey as part of the examination process. Complete them accurately and quickly move on.

◆ Read the exam questions carefully. Reread each question to identify all relevant detail.

◆ Tackle the questions in the order they are presented. Skipping around won't build your confidence; the clock is always counting down.

◆ Don't rush, but at the same time, don't linger on difficult questions. The questions vary in degree of difficulty. Don't let yourself be flustered by a particularly difficult or verbose question.

Fixed-Form Exams

Building from this basic preparation and test-taking advice, you also need to consider the challenges presented by the different exam designs. Because a fixed-form exam is composed of a fixed, finite set of questions, add these tips to your strategy for taking a fixed-form exam:

◆ Note the time allotted and the number of questions appearing on the exam you are taking. Make a rough calculation of how many minutes you can spend on each question, and use that number to pace yourself through the exam.

◆ Take advantage of the fact that you can return to and review skipped or previously answered questions. Mark the questions you can't answer confidently, noting the relative difficulty of each question on the scratch paper provided. When you reach the end of the exam, return to the more difficult questions.

◆ If there is session time remaining when you have completed all questions (and you aren't too fatigued!), review your answers. Pay particular attention to questions that seem to have a lot of detail or that required graphics.

◆ As for changing your answers, the rule of thumb here is *don't*! If you read the question carefully and completely and you felt like you knew the right answer, you probably did. Don't second-guess yourself. If, as you check your answers, one stands out as clearly incorrect, however, of course you should change it. But if you are at all unsure, go with your first impression.

All that said, the most important thing to remember is that if you know your stuff, you should do fine. Use the self-test elements in this book, such as the practice exams and the review questions. Study where and when you are able to focus on the information, and practice with hands-on experience as much as possible. Good luck!

The "fast facts" listed in this section are designed to act as a refresher of key points and topics that are required to be successful on the Cisco CCNA exam. By using these summaries of key points, you can spend an hour prior to your exam to refresh key topics, and ensure that you have a solid understanding of the objectives and information required for you to be successful in each major area of the exam.

What follows are the main categories Cisco uses to arrange the objectives:

- ▶ OSI Reference
- ▶ WAN Protocols
- ▶ IOS
- ▶ Network Protocols
- ▶ Routing
- ▶ Network Security
- ▶ LAN Switching

For each of these main sections, or categories, the assigned objectives are reviewed, and following each objective, review material is offered. The information presented is intended as a review only. If you do not understand the summary information presented, that is a cue for you to return to the main study material in Part 1, "Exam Preparation."

Fast Facts

CCNA

OSI Reference

Objective OSI Reference: The understanding of the OSI reference model. Considerations include the following:

◆ Identify and describe the functions of each of the seven layers of the OSI reference model.

◆ Describe connection-oriented network service and connectionless network service and identify the key differences between them.

◆ Describe data link addresses and network addresses, and identify the key differences between them.

◆ Identify at least three reasons why the industry uses a layered model.

◆ Define and explain the five conversion steps of data encapsulation.

◆ Define flow control and describe the three basic methods used in networking.

◆ List the key internetworking functions of the OSI Network layer and how they are performed in a router.

Identify and describe the functions of each of the seven layers of the OSI reference model.

◆ Application
◆ Presentation
◆ Session
◆ Transport
◆ Network
◆ Data Link
◆ Physical

OSI Layers

The OSI model was developed to divide networking functions into layers that are based on functionality. The reasons for creating the OSI model are as follows:

◆ It divides the complex network operations into less complex pieces.

◆ It keeps changes in one area from adversely affecting other layers. This facilitates the evolution of networking components because, for example, companies can focus on improving one area without worrying about the functions handled at other layers.

◆ It allows different vendors to create products that will work together.

◆ It simplifies understanding the complex concepts of networking by dividing the concepts into smaller, less complex pieces.

Memorizing the sentence "All People Seem To Need Data Processing" is a good way to remember the first letters of the seven layers of the OSI model.

Each of the seven layers of the OSI model performs a function for networking systems.

Application Layer (Layer 7)

The Application layer provides the interface from the OSI model to the end user's application. Some examples of Application layer implementations include the following:

◆ Telnet
◆ FTP
◆ SMTP
◆ POP

Presentation Layer (Layer 6)

The Presentation layer defines how the data will be presented to the application layer. Some examples of Presentation layer implementations include the following:

◆ MIDI

◆ JPEG

◆ EBCDIC

◆ ASCII

◆ MPEG

Session Layer (Layer 5)

Communication sessions between network stations are established, managed, and terminated at the Session layer. Sessions handle the requests and responses between applications on the network stations. Examples of Session layer implementations include the following:

◆ SQL

◆ NFS

Transport Layer (Layer 4)

The Transport layer accepts data from the Session layer and puts it in packets to pass down to the Network layer. It is responsible for making sure packets are delivered without error, in sequence, and without any losses or duplications. Acknowledgments for packets received are generally sent from the Transport layer. Examples of Transport layer implementations include the following:

◆ TCP

◆ UDP

◆ SPX

Network Layer (Layer 3)

The Network layer defines the network address, which is different than the *media access control (MAC)* address. An *Internet Protocol (IP) address* is an example of a Network layer address.

The Network layer makes routing decisions and forwards packets that are destined for remote networks. The Network layer evaluates the network address of the destination system and determines whether it is on the same network as the source system. If the address is identical, the Network layer obtains the destination system's MAC address, either from a table or through a resolution technique such as IP's *Address Resolution Protocol (ARP)*. After the Network layer has addressed the packet with the source and destination addresses, it passes the packet down to the Data Link layer for delivery.

If the Network layer determines that the destination system is not on the same network as the source system, it addresses the packet with the MAC address of the router that can deliver the packet. It determines this by referencing routing tables that can be built either statically or dynamically. After the Networking layer addresses the packet with the source address and the address of the router that can deliver the packet, it passes the packet down to the Data Link layer for delivery to the router.

Examples of Network layer implementations include the following:

◆ IP

◆ IPX

Data Link Layer (Layer 2)

The Data Link layer provides an error-free link between two network devices. Data passed down from the Network layer is packaged into frames that will be passed down to the Physical layer. Error checking and correction information is added to the frame.

One error correction technique used is *cyclic redundancy check (CRC)*. The media access control (MAC) address is part of the Data Link layer. *Logical link control (LLC)* is also a function of the Data Link layer.

Examples of Data Link layer implementations include the following:

◆ DLC

◆ LLC

Physical Layer (Layer 1)

The Physical layer is responsible for placing the data on the network media. The Physical layer defines such things as voltage levels, wire specifications, maximum distances, and connector types. Examples of Physical layer implementations include the following:

◆ 10BaseT Ethernet

◆ 100BaseTX Ethernet

◆ Token-Ring

Encapsulation

Each layer uses control information to communicate with the corresponding layer at the other end of the link. This control data is added to the packet as it moves down the stack. This process is called *encapsulation*.

As a packet travels down through the seven layers, each layer adds control data and then passes the data down to the next layer until the data reaches the network. After the packet is delivered to the receiving station, the process is reversed. Each layer strips off its control data and passes the packet up to the next layer until the packet reaches the application.

Encapsulation consists of five steps beginning at the Transport layer:

◆ Build the data.

◆ Package the data for end-to-end transport.

◆ Append network address in the header.

◆ Append local address in the data-link header.

◆ Convert to bits for transmission.

Connection-Oriented and Connectionless Network Service

Connection-oriented protocols establish a connection with the other end before they begin sending data. The protocol makes a request to the station that it wishes to exchange data with. This request must be accepted before the exchange can occur.

During the exchange of data, the two stations verify that the data is received error free. After the data exchange is complete, the connection between the two stations is terminated.

In a *connectionless* exchange, the two stations don't need to establish a connection. One station simply sends data to the other. Connectionless exchanges do not verify that the data is received and make no attempt to ensure that the data is received error free. Generally in a connectionless exchange, layers above the Transport layer are responsible for making sure all the data is exchanged completely and error free.

MAC Address

The *Media Access Control (MAC) address* uniquely identifies each station on the network media. MAC addresses are 48 bits long and are usually represented as three groups of four hexadecimal digits. An example of a MAC address follows:

00e0.a38d.0800

Network Address

The *network address* identifies the station at the Network level (Layer 3) of the OSI model. In TCP/IP, the network address is the IP address of the device. Under Novell's IPX, the network address is dynamically assigned as a combination of the IPX network number and the MAC address of the station. Network addresses are usually hierarchical, just as is the mailing address of a business or home.

Address Resolution Protocol (ARP)

Address Resolution Protocol (ARP) is responsible for mapping IP addresses to MAC addresses. ARP builds a table of IP addresses and their corresponding MAC addresses.

Source-Quench Message

Source-quench messages are used to signal the sending station to slow down. One problem with source-quench messages is that if the network is over burdened, there is no guarantee that the source-quench packet will arrive at the sending station.

Buffering

Buffering allows the receiving station to temporarily store packets received until it can process them. As long as the bursts are short and do not overflow the buffer, this technique works well.

Windowing

The sending and receiving station agree on a window size. This *window* defines the number of packets the stations will exchange before an acknowledgment is required. If the window size is five packets, for example, the sending station will send five packets and then wait for an acknowledgment from the receiver.

Ethernet

Ethernet is by far the most popular networking topology in use today. Its ease of use, simplicity, and reliability have established it as the mainstream networking topology. Ethernet is a *Carrier Sense Multiple Access/Collision Detect (CSMA/CD)* network.

Ethernet can be implemented several different ways: 10Base5, 10Base2, 10BaseT, and 100BaseTX, and 100BaseFX are the most common.

Token Ring

The IEEE 802.5 specification is almost identical to IBM's *Token Ring*. Logically, Token Ring is arranged in a ring in which each station is a *node* on the ring. These stations pass traffic around the ring. A network station accepts a packet from its upstream neighbor and sends it to its downstream neighbor. Token Ring supports multiple speeds: 4Mbps and 16Mbps are the most common. Newer Token Ring equipment is starting to support 100Mbps.

Serial Ports

Cisco routers use *serial ports* for connection to many devices including *Channel Service Unit/Data Service Unit (CSU/DSU)*. CSU/DSUs are similar to modems but are used for digital circuits such as 64Kbps leased lines and T1s.

These serial ports are very versatile. They support several different standards from one port. The port configures itself for the different standards based on the cable that is plugged in.

Some of the types of interfaces supported by Cisco serial ports include the following:

- V.35
- EIA-232 (RS-232)
- EIA-449
- X.21
- EIA-530

WAN PROTOCOLS

Objective WAN Protocols: Understand the technologies behind WAN protcols and how to configure them within a router. The WAN protocols objective includes the following:

- Differentiate between the following WAN services: Frame Relay, ISDN/LAPD, HDLC, and PPP.
- Recognize key Frame Relay terms and features.
- List commands to configure Frame Relay LMIs, maps, and subinterfaces.
- List commands to monitor Frame Relay operation in the router.
- Identify PPP operations to encapsulate WAN data on Cisco routers.
- State a relevant use and context for ISDN networking.
- Identify ISDN protocols, function groups, reference points, and channels.
- Describe Cisco's implementation of ISDN BRI.

Following is a list of basic concepts and terms you need to be familiar with for this portion of the test.

- **Plain Old Telephone Service (POTS).** *POTS* describes the normal telephone service most people have installed in their homes.

- **Local Loop.** The *local loop* is the part of the telephone network that runs from your local CO to your office.

- **Demarcation Point.** The *demarcation point* is where the telephone company terminates its lines in your building.

- **Customer Premise Equipment (CPE).** *Customer Premise Equipment* is equipment that resides at the customer site. This equipment interfaces with the telephone company's network. A CSU/DSU is a good example of Customer Premise Equipment

- **T1 Service.** A *T1* is a digital telephone line that provides a bandwidth of 1.54 million bits per second. This bandwidth is delivered as 24 channels of 64Kbps data channels.

- **Channel Service Unit/Data Service Unit (CSU/DSU).** A *Channel Service Unit/Data Service Unit (CSU/DSU)* (also often called just a *CSU)* interfaces with digital telephone lines. A CSU provides an interface for the router to connect to the digital line delivered by the telephone company.

- **Integrated Services Digital Network (ISDN).** *ISDN* defines a digital communication link for voice and data communication. ISDN can be ordered in two different ways: *Basic Rate Interface (BRI)* and *Primary Rate Interface (PRI)*. A BRI line has two B channels and one D channel (2B+D). A PRI line has 23 B channels and one D channel (23B+D).

- **ISDN Layer 2 Protocols (LAPD).** This ISDN specification includes implementations of Layer 2 and Layer 3 protocols. The Layer 2 signaling protocol is *Link Access Procedure, D channel (LAPD).* LAPD is used across D channels to provide control and signaling information. LAPD is formally specified in ITU-T Q.920 and ITU-T Q.921.

- **ISDN Layer 3 Protocols.** There are two Layer 3 protocols defined within the ISDN framework for signaling: *ITU-T Q.930* and *ITU-T Q931.* These two protocols work together to provide *user-to-user, circuit-switched,* and *packet-switched* connections. These protocols specify how call establishment, call termination, information, and miscellaneous messages are communicated.

ISDN Reference Points

- **R.** This is the reference point between non-ISDN equipment and a TA.

- **S.** This is the reference point between user terminals and the NT2.

- **T.** This is the reference point between NT1 and NT2 devices.

- **U.** This is the reference point between NT1 devices and line-termination equipment. The U reference point is only relevant in the North America where the carrier does not provide the NT1.

Understanding SPIDs

A *Service Profile ID (SPID)* is used between your ISDN equipment and the telephone companies switch. A SPID is usually some variation on the telephone number for your ISDN line.

Monitoring ISDN

The most useful command to monitor ISDN is `show isdn status`.

ISDN in a Nutshell

ISDN comes in two packages: *BRI* and *PRI.*

BRI ISDN has two bearer channels of 64Kbps (or 56Kbps) bandwidth and one signaling channel of 16Kbps.

PRI ISDN is delivered on the same type circuit as a T1 and has 23 bearer channels and one signaling channel.

A *SPID* is a Service Profile ID and is usually a variation of the telephone number for the bearer channels in your ISDN line.

To configure a BRI line, you set the switch type, the SPIDs, and the encapsulation type.

ISDN lines do not provide power like normal POTS lines. ISDN lines require an NT1 at the customer site. Some ISDN devices have an NT1 built into them and some do not. Cisco 2500s with BRI required an external NT1 to work with ISDN.

The command `show isdn status` provides information about an ISDN line and the status of the channels.

High-Level Data-Link Control (HDLC)

HDLC is a link-layer protocol. It encapsulates data for transmission on synchronous serial connections. Although most vendors support HDLC, most implementations are slightly different. HDLC is the default encapsulation type for serial ports on Cisco routers and is often used when connecting Cisco to Cisco routers.

Point-to-Point Protocol (PPP)

Point-to-Point Protocol (PPP) is a Data Link layer protocol that will work over synchronous or asynchronous serial connections. PPP uses *Link Control Protocol (LCP)* to build and monitor connections.

Because PPP is often used over dial-up lines, the LCP portion supports authentication using two protocols: *Password Authentication Protocol (PAP)* and *Challenge-Handshake Authentication Protocol (CHAP)*. PAP provides a simple authentication technique. Its biggest disadvantage is that passwords are transmitted over the link in clear text. CHAP provides a more secure authentication technique using a magic number. CHAP authentication never transmits the password over the link.

PPP supports many different network protocols, including TCP/IP, IPX/SPX, AppleTalk, Transparent Bridging, DECnet, and OSI/CLNS.

To configure PPP on a serial port, use the command `encapsulation ppp`.

Frame Relay

Frame Relay is a packet-switching network. This type of network shares expensive resources among subscribers. By sharing the expensive resources such as long distance digital connections, the Frame Relay provider can offer a more cost-effective solution than dedicated lines.

Committed Information Rate (CIR)

When you order a Frame Relay circuit, you request a *Committed Information Rate (CIR)*. The CIR is how much bandwidth the Frame Relay vendor guarantees you.

Data-Link Connection Identifier (DLCI)

In a Frame Relay network, one physical circuit can support multiple virtual circuits. The router needs some way to identify which virtual circuit a packet of data is destine for. The *DLCI* (pronounced "del-see") is used to identify this virtual circuit. A DLCI is used to identify to which of the multiple virtual circuits a packet of data is destined. After the packet of data is received by the Frame Relay switch, the router is attached, and the Frame Relay switch makes a determination as to how to forward the packet. The Frame Relay switch has been programmed by the Frame Relay vendor for how to forward packets containing particular DLCI numbers. The programming is specific to the local Frame Relay switch with which the router is connected. After the packet of data exits the local Frame Relay switch and starts its travel through the Frame Relay *cloud*, the local DLCI number is no longer significant. The local DLCI number is only used between the router and the Frame Relay switch with which the router is connected.

To review, the DLCI represents a virtual circuit to the Frame Relay switch attached to the router. Beyond that point in the Frame Relay cloud, the DLCI had no significance. This is what people mean when they state that a DLCI has "local significance" only.

Permanent Virtual Circuit (PVC)

A *Permanent Virtual Circuit (PVC)* is a connection created within the Frame Relay cloud by the Frame Relay provider. The PVC is created as a virtual connection between two locations. A PVC can seem like a dedicated connection between two different locations.

Local Management Interface (LMI)

Local Management Interface (LMI) is a protocol used between the Frame Relay switch and your router. In 1990, Cisco Systems, StrataCom, Northern Telecom, and Digital Equipment worked together to create what is known as "Gang-of-Four LMI" or "Cisco LMI." They took the original Frame Relay protocol and added extensions that make supporting larger internetworks easier.

Configuring Multipoint Frame Relay

In a multipoint configuration, all of the routers are on one network with DLCIs listed for each connection. All connections fall under one logical port on the router.

Configuring Point-to-Point Frame Relay

Because Frame Relay can support multiple connections on one physical circuit, there must be a way of separating these connections within the router. Cisco supports this logical separation of a physical connection through the use of *subinterfaces*. Using subinterfaces, you can separate the multiple logical connections within the router.

Separating Logical Connections with Subinterfaces

Subinterfaces provide a method of separating one physical network connection into multiple logical connections. This is useful for Frame Relay because one physical local loop can support many PVCs. This creates the appearance of many different physical connections to other sites on one interface. The router must have some means of separating these logical connections so it can properly deliver the traffic destined to them. Subinterfaces provide this means. Subinterfaces have uses beyond just Frame Relay, but this discussion will focus on how subinterfaces are used with Frame Relay.

To create a subinterface, use the `interface` command in the configuration mode of the router. Enter the description of the interface to which you want to add a subinterface, with an added period and a number following it to identify the subinterface. When configuring Frame Relay, it is a good idea to use the DLCI number for the subinterface number. This makes it easier to identify items in the config later. An example for DLCI 199 would be the following:

```
interface serial0/0.199
```

Monitoring the Serial Port of a Frame Relay Connection

The `show interfaces` command lists some Frame Relay-specific information for interfaces connected to Frame Relay networks.

Seeing Active PVCs

To view the PVCs your router can see, use the `show frame-relay pvc` command.

Congestion Notification

◆ **Forward Explicit Congestion Notification (FECN).** A method used in Frame Relay to inform the routers of congestion on the network. When a Frame Relay switch detects congestion, it can set a bit in the frame to notify the receiving network device that the packet experienced congestion in the network. This is called *FECN* (pronounced "feck-in").

◆ **Backward Explicit Congestion Notification (BECN).** Often used in conjunction with FECN. When a packet is passing back to the sending station, the Frame Relay switch can set the BECN bit to tell the sending station its traffic is experiencing congestion. The sending station can then reduce the speed at which it is sending data. This is called *BECN* (pronounced "beck-in").

Viewing the Frame Relay Map

Cisco routers create an internal map of frame relay DLCIs and the ports they are mapped with. This map can be viewed using the command `show frame-relay map`.

Frame Relay in a Nutshell

Frame Relay is a packet-switching network that provides low-cost connections due to the sharing of resources.

The entire Frame Relay network is called the *cloud*.

Committed Information Rate (CIR) is how much bandwidth your Frame Relay provider guarantees you will have available.

The *Data-Link Connection Identifier (DLCI)* is a number assigned to map an IP address to a PVC. DLCIs have local significance. This means they can be different on either end of a PVC and can be reused within the network.

The *Permanent Virtual Circuit (PVC)* is a path created in the Frame Relay network between two points. The Frame Relay provider creates PVCs.

The *Switched Virtual Circuit (SVC)* is a path created dynamically in the Frame Relay network in much the same way in which a telephone call is placed. When a router needs to communicate with another, it requests that the Frame Relay switch create an SVC. The switch creates the SVC dynamically. When the routers no longer need to communicate, the SVC is deleted.

Local Management Interface (LMI) is the protocol used between the router and the Frame Relay switch to add management functions for large internetworks.

To configure Frame Relay on an interface, use the command `encapsulation frame-relay`.

To separate a physical interface into subinterfaces, use the configuration command `interface serial0.100`, in which `.100` is the subinterface you want to create. Add the `frame-relay interface DLCI 100` command, in which `100` is the DLCI number for the PVC.

To diagnose Frame Relay problems, the commands `show interfaces` and `show frame-relay pvc` offer much information.

IOS

Objective IOS: Understand how to interface with a router using Cisco's Internetworking Operating System. Considerations include the following:

- ◆ Log in to a router in both user and privileged modes.

- ◆ Examine router elements (RAM, ROM, CDP, and show).

- ◆ Control router passwords, identification, and banner.

- ◆ Identify the main Cisco IOS commands for router startup.

- ◆ Enter an initial configuration using the `setup` command.

- ◆ Copy and manipulate configuration files.

- ◆ List the commands to load Cisco IOS software from flash memory, a TFTP server, or ROM.

- ◆ Prepare to back up, upgrade, and load a backup Cisco IOS software image.

- ◆ Prepare the initial configuration of your router and enable IP.

Normal Password Authentication

This method of authentication simply uses a password stored in the configuration file of the router. When you attempt to access a router either through the console port or telnet, the initial login will look like this:

```
User Access Verification

Password:
Router>
```

The prompt character is >. The > character indicates that you are now in the user exec mode. In this mode you have access to commands for monitoring the router and its interfaces. What can be performed at this level is restricted. To configure the router or perform advanced diagnostics, you must access the privileged exec mode. To access the privileged exec mode, enter the command enable. Then enter the enable password, as follows:

```
User Access Verification

Password:
Router>enable
Password:
Router#
```

Context-Sensitive Help

Cisco's IOS provides help for command syntax and options. This help system is available from the user exec or privileged exec mode command prompts.

To see a list of commands available at any time, simply type a question mark (?) at the prompt. To see the options for a command, simply type the command followed by a question mark.

Configuring the Router

To configure the router, you must enter the configuration mode. The configuration can be changed from several different sources: terminal, memory, or network. The command configure followed by the source of the configuration change will put the router into configuration mode. To configure from the terminal, type the command configure terminal.

Hostname

The *hostname* of a router is set using the global config command:

```
c2513r1(config)#hostname Keyser
Keyser(config)#
```

Message of the Day (MOTD)

The *message of the day (MOTD)* is displayed when someone accesses the router.

To enter a MOTD, use the following command from the global config mode.

```
c2511r1(config)#banner motd #This router was
replaced 1/09/99#
c2511r1(config)#
```

The # before and after the message is simply a delimiter character and can be any character not included in the message. It simply identifies the beginning and end of the message. The preceding example will appear onscreen the next time someone connects to the router.

```
This router was replaced 1/09/99

User Access Verification

Password:
```

Configuring Interfaces

When configuring interface parameters such as bandwidth, IP address, media type, and most anything else specific to an interface, you use the interface configuration mode. To enter the interface configuration mode, type the command **interface** followed by the interface identifier. An example would be **interface ethernet0/0**.

Saving Changes

To save changes made to the config, use the command copy running-config startup-config. This copies the running configuration to NVRAM, where it is stored when the router is powered off. This command is commonly abbreviated copy run start.

Viewing the Configuration

To view the running configuration of a router, use the command show running-config or write terminal. Both commands display the running configuration on the display terminal.

Abbreviated Commands

Any router command can be abbreviated to just enough letters for the router to determine which command you are intending.

If you abbreviate a command too much, the CLI will not be able to uniquely identify which command you are trying to execute. Instead, it will respond with the following:

```
c2511r1#te
% Ambiguous command: "te"
c2511r1#
```

To find out which commands begin with te type the following:

```
c2511r1#te?
telnet  terminal  test

c2511r1#te
```

Managing Passwords

Cisco routers store passwords for login access in the configuration file. There are two types of passwords used in this manner for accessing a router: the login password and the enable password. The *login password* is used to gain access to the router's user exec mode. The *enable password* is used to enter the privileged exec mode, where configuration changes can be made.

Command History

The *command history* buffer allows you to recall a previously typed command and execute it again. Use the up arrow to scroll through the last commands executed.

Viewing the Contents of the Command History Buffer

The contents of the command history buffer can be viewed by typing the command **show history**.

Random Access Memory (RAM)

The router uses *RAM* to store data, execute programs, and buffer data. Packets of data can be buffered in RAM until the router has time to process them. In some models of Cisco routers (3600, 7200, 7500, and so on), the IOS runs in RAM. Some routers, like the 2500 series, run the IOS from *flash memory*.

Read-Only Memory (ROM)

The instructions for performing a self test of the device are stored in *ROM*. The ROM also contains a subset (some routers contain a full version) of the IOS.

Flash Memory

Flash memory is similar to ROM except that flash memory can be erased and rewritten electronically. Cisco routers use flash memory much like personal computers use disk storage.

In routers in which the IOS is copied to RAM during the boot process, the IOS can be upgraded by copying a new version of IOS to flash while the router runs the copy stored in RAM. After the new version of IOS is stored in flash memory, the router can be rebooted and the new version will be loaded and executed.

This does not work when the router is running the IOS from flash.

Examining the Components of a Router

The router can provide much information about the components within it. Information on the amount of memory, version of IOS, and interfaces installed can be viewed with the show version command.

Processor

The *processor* does most of the work in the router. It keeps routing tables updated by calculating paths, moving packets, and performing many other tasks. When you are diagnosing problems, it is often important to check on the load of the processor. To view statistics on the processor, type the command **show processes**.

Interfaces

The *interfaces* of a router connect it to the networks for which it will be handling traffic. These interfaces provide a great deal of information about the network and how the interface is performing.

To view information about an interface, type the command **show interfaces**.

You can also view this information for a specific interface by specifying the interface. An example of how to do this is as follows:

```
show interfaces ethernet0
```

Cisco Discovery Protocol (CDP)

The *Cisco discovery protocol* (CDP) runs on Cisco-manufactured devices including routers, access servers, and workgroup switches. CDP starts automatically when the device is booted. Because CDP operates at the Data Link layer, it is not necessary for the devices to be in common network address domains to exchange CDP data.

CDP provides a method for a Cisco device to discover its neighboring Cisco devices and exchange information about the devices.

CDP Enable and Disable

CDP is enabled by default; it can be disabled on a router by typing the following global command:

```
c2511r1(config)#no cdp run
```

You can also disable CDP on a particular interface by typing the following command:

```
c2511r1(config-if)#no cdp enable
```

Seeing CDP Neighbors

You can view a router's CDP neighbors by typing the **show cdp neighbors** command.

More detailed information about the neighbors can be viewed with the show cdp neighbors detail command.

This information lists each neighbor and the version of IOS it is running. This is very helpful information when you are trying to diagnose why a feature is not working. If the neighboring router is running an older version of IOS, it may not support some newer features. In an environment in which different groups support different routers, this can be helpful in finding information about the routers you may need to communicate with.

CDP Timers

CDP has two timers.

◆ **CDP timer.** Dictates how often a router sends out CDP packets. This timer is adjusted with the command cdp timer *xx*, where *xx* is the number of seconds between CDP packets.

◆ **CDP holdtime.** Sets the time a router will wait for a CDP packet from a neighbor before removing that neighbor from the routers neighbor table. This is changed with the command cdp holdtime *xxx*, where *xxx* is the number of seconds to hold information in the table before removing it.

Managing Configuration Files from the Privileged Exec Mode

The configuration file defines how the router will interact with the connected networks and the data on those networks.

To copy the running-config to a TFTP server, use the command **copy running-config tftp**, as follows:

```
c2511r1#copy running-config tftp
Remote host []? 192.169.169.140
Name of configuration file to write [c2511r1-
confg]?
Write file c2511r1-confg on host
192.168.169.140? [confirm]y
Building configuration...

Writing c2511r1-confg !! [OK]
c2511r1#
```

Each exclamation point (!) indicates one packet that has been successfully transferred.

The running-config file is copied via the TFTP protocol to the TFTP server at IP address 129.168.169.140. The filename used on the TFTP server is c2511r1-config. Finally, the file is transferred to the server. The startup-config can be copied using the same technique.

To reverse the process, simply reverse the order of the devices. Copy from the TFTP server to the filename running-config, as follows:

```
c2511r1#copy tftp running-config
Host or network configuration file [host]?
Address of remote host [255.255.255.255]?
192.168.169.140
Name of configuration file [c2511r1-confg]?
Configure using c2511r1-confg from
192.168.169.140? [confirm]y
Loading c2511r1-confg from 192.168.169.140 (via
Ethernet0): !
[OK - 1260/32723 bytes]

c2511r1#
```

Back Up and Upgrade IOS

IOS resides in the router as a file stored in flash memory. This file can become corrupt because of, for example, a power problem or hardware failure. This file may also need to be upgraded to a newer version to support new features or correct problems because of software bugs. The TFTP server is used for this process.

To copy the IOS stored in flash to the TFTP server, use the copy command with the source and destination reversed.

NETWORK PROTOCOLS

Objective Network Protocols: Understand the functions of different network protocols. Understand how to create subnets and configure network protocols on Cisco routers. Network protocols include the following:

- Monitor Novell IPX operation on the router.

- Describe the two parts of network addressing, then identify the parts in specific protocol address examples.

- Create the different classes of IP addresses (and subnetting).

- Configure IP addresses.

- Verify IP addresses.

- List the required IPX address and encapsulation type.

- Enable the Novell IPX protocol and configure interfaces.

- Identify the functions of the TCP/IP Transport layer protocols.

- Identify the functions of the TCP/IP Network layer protocols.

- Identify the functions performed by ICMP.

- Configure IPX access lists and SAP filters to control basic Novell traffic.

Network Addresses

Network addresses are the addresses used at Layer 3 of the OSI reference model. The network address differs from the MAC address in that a network address is generally routable because it includes some type of hierarchical information. A MAC address is local to the network on which it is connected. Some network addresses use the MAC address to create the network address; Novell's IPX does this. Two examples of network addresses are IPX and IP addresses.

- A Novell IPX address looks like A31B3AF5.0000.0000.0001

- An IP address looks like 192.168.19.114

MAC Address

The *MAC address* identifies a device on the local network. It is mapped in some way to the network address. For Novell's IPX protocol, the MAC address is used to create the network address. Because it is made part of the network address, there is no need to create a map between the two addresses. TCP/IP, however, requires a method of mapping IP address to a MAC address. *Address Resolution Protocol (ARP)* performs this mapping.

Converting Numbers From Binary to Decimal

To convert the binary number 11111001 to its equivalent decimal number, place the number below the chart as shown following:

128	64	32	16	8	4	2	1
1	1	1	1	1	0	0	1

Add up the decimal numbers for each position with an equivalent binary 1.

$$128 + 64 + 32 + 16 + 8 + 1 = 249$$

Converting Numbers from Decimal to Binary

While working with IP addresses, you will need to convert numbers from decimal to binary. To perform this function, you start by finding the largest binary position that will go into the number you are converting.

For the decimal number 249, for example, the largest binary position that will go into it is 128, which is the highest bit position of an octet. Place a 1 in that bit position.

128	64	32	16	8	4	2	1
1							

Subtract 128 from 249: 249 − 128 = 121. Now perform the same over again. The largest bit position that will go into 121 is 64. Place a 1 in that bit position and continue from there.

128	64	32	16	8	4	2	1
1	1						

121 − 64 = 57

128	64	32	16	8	4	2	1
1	1	1					

57 − 32 = 25

128	64	32	16	8	4	2	1
1	1	1	1				

25 − 16 = 9

128	64	32	16	8	4	2	1
1	1	1	1	1			

9 − 8 = 1

128	64	32	16	8	4	2	1
1	1	1	1	1	0	0	1

TCP/IP Overview

The key thing to understand for this objective is how the transport protocols fit into the OSI model.

◆ **TCP is a connection-oriented protocol that guarantees packet delivery using acknowledgments.** When a packet is dropped, TCP is responsible for making sure that it is resent. TCP is responsible for breaking messages into segments for transmission. After the segments arrive at the destination, TCP reassembles them. TCP creates a connection between networking stations before transferring data.

◆ **UDP is a connectionless protocol that makes no guarantees about data delivery.** UDP can transmit data faster than TCP because it does not use acknowledgments. UDP does not break messages into segments; that must be handled by a different layer. Reliability is also the responsibility of another layer. Reliability can be handled by an Application layer protocol or by a reliable lower-layer protocol.

IP Addresses

An *IP address* defines two things: the network and the host address on the network. The *network mask*, sometimes called the *subnet mask*, determines which part of the IP address represents the network and which part represents the host.

Network Mask

Consider an IP address that looks like this:

Network = 192.168.2   Computer = 26

The network mask is just a short-hand method of representing this same concept. The previous example would look like this with a network mask:

IP Address = 192.168.2.26
Network Mask = 255.255.255.0

Computing devices take these two numbers in their binary form and perform a binary *AND* on them. A binary AND says, in effect, "compare the two binary numbers; if both bits in a position are 1, the result is 1. If either bit is 0, the result is 0."

TCP/IP Services

Following is a list of some of the protocols and their functions.

◆ **Internet Protocol (IP).** The Layer 3 (Network) protocol of the suite.

◆ **Address Resolution Protocol (ARP).** Used to map IP addresses to MAC addresses.

◆ **Transmission Control Protocol (TCP).** A Layer 4 protocol. TCP provides guaranteed data delivery.

◆ **User Datagram Protocol (UDP).** A Layer 4 protocol. UDP does not guarantee data delivery.

◆ **Internet Control Message Protocol (ICMP).** Provides diagnostic information about the protocol suite. Most people are familiar with the diagnostic utility ping. *Ping* provides a means of confirming network connectivity between two stations. Ping is an implementation of ICMP. Today it is best to specify an ICMP ping because many other protocols now support ping in their implementations. Novell has added ping to IPX. IBM has even added some ping-like functions to SNA.

◆ **Telnet.** An Application layer implementation of a program that allows remote terminal access to a device. For internetworking engineers, Telnet is often used to log in to routers.

◆ **File Transfer Protocol (FTP).** Allows stations to transfer files from one to another. FTP uses TCP packets to guarantee data delivery.

◆ **Trivial File Transfer Protocol (TFTP).** A file transfer implementation. It differs from FTP in that it uses UDP packets to deliver its data; hence, it does not guarantee delivery of data.

◆ **Simple Mail Transfer Protocol (SMTP).** An email implementation that delivers mail from network to network or from user to user within one domain. SMTP is used throughout the Internet for delivery of millions of emails daily.

◆ **Post Office Protocol (POP).** An email implementation that allows users to connect with the system that receives their email and download that email to their computers. POP is used by millions of users everyday to get email from their ISPs. Programs that can use POP include Eudora Pro, Outlook, Pegasus Mail, and the email portion of most browsers.

◆ **Network Time Protocol (NTP).** Used to synchronize the clocks of networking computers. NTP is typically used to synchronize your system's clock with one of the very accurate time sources available on the Internet. Cisco routers support NTP and can be configured to synchronize their clocks. This can be very helpful when diagnosing problems.

◆ **HyperText Transfer Protocol (HTTP).** The protocol Netscape Navigator uses to talk with Web servers. Your browser uses HTTP to download HTML from Web servers and display the information on your screen.

◆ **Domain Name System (DNS).** Used to map domain names such as www.cisco.com to IP addresses. When you type the name of a site you want to visit in your browser, the computer first resolves that name to an IP address using DNS. After the IP address is found, it is passed to the IP stack and HTTP is used to communicate with the Web server. Without DNS, you would have to remember IP addresses rather than domain names. DNS makes life much easier.

◆ **Simple Network Monitor Protocol (SNMP).** Used to gather statistics from networking devices for monitoring and reporting. Most networking monitoring software, such as Cisco Works, uses SNMP to gather information.

Domain Name Server (DNS)

Cisco's IOS has different ways to map names to IP addresses. If your organization makes use of *DNS*, you can configure your routers to use DNS to resolve names to IP addresses. To turn this on in the router, you use the `ip name-server` command to identify the DNS machine to the router. This is the machine that provides the DNS service. You must also turn on domain lookup in the router, which is done with the command `ip domain-lookup`.

Use the following, for example, to configure the DNS server in the router's configuration:

```
ACS-2500#config t
Enter configuration commands, one per line.  End
with CNTL/Z.
ACS-2500(config)#ip name-server 155.229.1.69
ACS-2500(config)#ip domain-lookup
ACS-2500(config)#exit
```

When the router performs a DNS lookup, it caches the information for future use. You can view the contents of the cache with the `show hosts` command, as follows:

```
ACS-2500#sh hosts
Default domain is not set
Name/address lookup uses domain service
Name servers are 155.229.1.5, 155.229.1.69
```

Host Address(es)	Flags	Age	Type
www.kmahler.com 199.250.137.37	(temp, OK)	0	IP
cio-sys.cisco.com 192.31.7.130 www.cisco.com	(temp, OK)	0	IP

```
ACS-2500#
```

The *default domain* is the domain the router resides in. The router can provide a shortcut to accessing stations within its domain. If you set the default domain in the router, it will then append this default domain to any name that is not fully entered. If you wanted to ping `kestrel.kmahler.com` and the default domain name `kmahler.com` was defined in the router with the name server set, along with domain name lookup on, the router will be able to identify that station with just `kestrel`.

To clear an individual host mapping, use the `clear host` with the host name specified, as follows:

```
c3620r1#clear host linux.kmahler.com
c3620r1#sh host
Default domain is kmahler.com
Name/address lookup uses domain service
Name servers are 199.250.137.37
```

Host Address(es)	Flags	Age	Type
www.kmahler.com 199.250.137.37	(temp, OK)	0	IP
kestrel.kmahler.com 199.250.137.34	(temp, OK)	0	IP

```
c3620r1#
```

To clear all name to IP address mappings, use the wildcard *, as follows:

```
c3620r1#sh host
Default domain is kmahler.com
Name/address lookup uses domain service
Name servers are 199.250.137.37
```

Host Address(es)	Flags	Age	Type
kestrel.kmahler.com 199.250.137.34	(temp, OK)	0	IP
www.kmahler.com 199.250.137.37	(temp, OK)	0	IP
linux.kmahler.com 199.250.137.55	(temp, OK)	0	IP

```
c3620r1#clear host *
c3620r1#sh host
Default domain is kmahler.com
Name/address lookup uses domain service
Name servers are 199.250.137.37
```

Host Address(es)	Flags	Age	Type

```
c3620r1#
```

Because there is not always a DNS available, Cisco has provided another method of mapping host names to IP addresses. *Static* name mappings can be made part of the router's configuration.

To create a static name mapping, use the command `ip host` with the hostname and IP address. An example entry would be `ip host kestrel 199.250.137.34`.

Understanding IP Address Classes

IP addresses are divided into *classes*. For each class, there is an assumed network mask. The most common IP address classes are the following:

Class	Range of (1st octet)	Maximum Networks	Maximum Hosts
A	1–126	126	16,777,214
B	128–191	16,384	65,534
C	192–223	2,097,152	254

The class of an IP address is actually defined by the first few bits.

- If the first bit of an IP address is 0, it is a *Class A* address. By definition, a Class A IP address has eight bits of network address and 24 bits of host address. The subnet mask for a Class A address is 255.0.0.0 or /8.

- If the first two bits are 10, it is a *Class B* address. By definition, a Class B IP address has 16 bits of network address and 16 bits of host address. The subnet mask for a Class B address is 255.255.0.0 or /16.

- If the first three bits are 110, it is a *Class C* address. By definition, a Class C IP address has 24 bits of network address and eight bits of host address. The subnet mask for a Class C address is 255.255.255.0 or /24.

The IPX network address consists of two parts: the *network number* and the *node number*. When an IPX address is displayed in a router, it takes the form of 4c.03cb.530c.1cd3, where 4c is the network number and 03cb.530c.1cd3 is the node number. Novell's IPX protocol has an interesting way of mapping the network address to the MAC address. The MAC address is actually used to derive the network address.

Given the previous example, the node number 03cb.530c.1cd3 is also the MAC address of the node. Therefore, it is simple for the IPX network to determine for which node the packet is destined.

Cisco Novell encapsulation types and their Novell equivalents appear in the following list:

- **Cisco's Novell-Ether encapsulation is Novell's Ethernet_802.3.** This frame format includes the IEEE 802.3 length field, but not an IEEE 802.2 Logical Link Control (LLC) header. This encapsulation was the default for NetWare 2.x and 3.x.

- **Cisco's SAP encapsulation is Novell's Ethernet_802.2.** This frame format is the standard IEEE frame format, including an 802.2 LLC header. This encapsulation method became the default with the release of NetWare 3.12 and 4.x. For Token Ring use, SAP also equates to Novell's Token_Ring encapsulation.

- **Cisco's ARPA encapsulation is Novell's Ethernet_II or Ethernet version 2.** It uses the standard Ethernet 2 header.

- **Cisco's SNAP encapsulation is Novell's Ethernet_SNAP or SNAP.** It extends the IEEE 802.2 header by adding a *SubNetwork Access Point (SNAP)* header. This header provides an encapsulation type code similar to that of Ethernet version 2. Cisco's SNAP also equates to Novell's Token_Ring_SNAP.

Configuring IPX Routing

Configuring a Cisco router for IPX routing involves multiple steps. IPX routing is turned off by default in Cisco's IOS. This is in contrast to TCP/IP routing, which is on by default.

The first step is to enable IPX routing on the router. This is done with the global configuration command `ipx routing`.

The next step in configuring IPX routing is to set the IPX network number on each of the interfaces routing IPX traffic.

To specify the encapsulation type, add the encapsulation keyword to the `ipx network` configuration command.

In some environments, multiple Novell networks are present on one LAN although the different logical networks are using different encapsulation types. To configure for this in a Cisco router requires the use of subinterfaces. For an interface, only one IPX network can be defined. However, if multiple encapsulation types are used on one network, the different encapsulation types can be configured using subinterfaces. You can create subinterfaces on a LAN interface and then assign a different encapsulation type to each subinterface, and a different network number to each. Each subinterface must have a different encapsulation type and IPX network number. After it is configured properly, the router will route traffic between the two different logical networks.

Novell Access Lists

In the Novell environment there may be times when you need to control which networks can communicate with others. Using a *Novell access list* can accomplish this. A Novell access list can be used to limit this access.

Novell access lists fall into four categories: standard, extended, SAP filtering, and NLSP route aggregation filtering. For the CCNA exam, you will need to understand the standard, extended, and SAP filtering access lists.

When using IPX access lists, it is sometimes necessary to indicate all IPX networks. This is represented in an access list as `ffffffff` or `-1` (minus 1). This is the wildcard to indicate all IPX network numbers.

Standard IPX Access Lists

Standard IPX access lists are numbered 800–899. In a standard IPX access list, you can permit or deny traffic based on source address and destination address.

Displaying IPX Addresses

One of the first things to do when diagnosing an IPX problem is to check the IPX network numbers assigned to a router's interfaces.

The command `show ipx interface` displays IPX-related information about the router's interfaces. The IPX network number is displayed in full, including the node number. The command can be used without an interface description and will then display information for each interface in the router with an IPX address assigned.

If you are diagnosing a problem specific to one interface in the router, you can limit the information shown to just that interface.

If you wish to see a brief description of the IPX information for the interfaces in a router, you can use the variation of the previous command: `show ipx interface brief`.

Displaying IPX Servers

The command `show ipx servers` is very useful when diagnosing an IPX problem. When the router receives SAP broadcast from servers, it places them in its server table. The command `show ipx servers` allows you to view this table. Following is an example of the output of this command:

```
Router#sh ipx ser
Codes: S - Static, P - Periodic, E - EIGRP, N -
NLSP, H - Holddown, + = detail
221 Total IPX Servers

Table ordering is based on routing and server
info
```

```
    Type Name                    Net
Address    Port    Route Hops Itf
P    4 RESEARCH
A5.0000.0000.0001:0451 2185984/00   1  Fa0/0
P    4 BENEFIT
36B08649.0000.0000.0001:0451     2/01    1
Fa0/0
```

Working with IPX Routing Tables

When a router is routing IPX traffic, it builds a routing table to determine the proper path to forward traffic. To view the IPX routing table, use the command show ipx route. This will display all of the networks the router has determined paths for and certain information about those paths.

The routing table can sometimes become unstable because of network topology changes or software bugs. You can force the router to rebuild the routing table by clearing it. The command clear ipx route * will clear all routes in the table:

```
Router#clear ipx route *
Router#
```

You can clear a specific network route by specifying the route in the command, such as clear ipx route 3c. This will cause the router to clear this route and relearn the route if possible:

```
Router#clear ipx route 58
Router#
```

Load Sharing with IPX

Cisco routers routing IPX traffic can perform load sharing across equal cost paths. When two paths of equal cost or delay exist from one network to another, the router can distribute the data across those paths. This is called *load sharing*. Using load sharing can increase the usable bandwidth between the networks. To allow a Cisco router to make use of multiple equal cost paths, you must set the parameter ipx maximum-paths. The default value is 1, which means that load sharing is disabled. You can allow a Cisco router to use up to 512 equal cost paths for IPX traffic, but a more realistic number would be two or three paths.

SAP Access Lists

SAP access lists allow you to filter the SAPs exchanged with other routers. This is very useful because many IPX networks include elements such as network printers that send SAP broadcasts. Generally, you do not need these SAPs to be broadcast across WAN links to remote sites. You can filter these SAPs by using a SAP access list. For example, if you wanted to allow only server SAPs from all networks to be broadcast over a WAN link, you could use an access list.

ROUTING

Objective Routing: Understand the operations of routing protocols and how to configure them within a Cisco router. The routing objectives include the following:

The routing section of the CCNA exam includes the following objectives:

◆ Add the RIP routing protocol to your configuration.

◆ Add the IGRP routing protocol to your configuration.

◆ Explain the services of separate and integrated multiprotocol routing.

◆ List problems that each routing type encounters when dealing with topology changes and describe techniques to reduce the number of these problems.

◆ Describe the benefits of network segmentation with routers.

Routing Protocol Basics

A *routing protocol* is responsible for exchanging valid routing information between routers so that routers can find the best path for traffic between two networks.

There are some terms relating to routing protocols that you must be familiar with:

◆ **Topology Change.** Any change in the layout of a network that will affect routing of traffic. This could include an interface being shut down by an administrator or a link failing due to a line being cut. It could also include the addition of a new circuit to a network. Any occurrence that causes a path to be unusable or unreliable can cause a topology change.

◆ **Convergence.** The processes of all routers on a network updating the routing tables when a topology change occurs.

◆ **Metric.** Any piece of data that a routing protocol uses to make a routing decision. Metrics can include hop count, bandwidth, reliability, and others.

Path Selection

The elements used to determine the best path vary with the routing protocol are called *metrics*. Some simple protocols simply use the number of hops between networks. This is not necessarily the most accurate method of deciding the best path.

Dynamic routing is when the router uses some sort of routing protocol to learn about the network and create routing tables based on this information. In a network using dynamic routing, when changes occur in the network, the changes are reflected in the routing tables soon after.

It is common for static and dynamic routing to be combined. A usual configuration includes a static default gateway entry, whereas everything else is learned dynamically. In this way, the router will reference its routing tables for a path to a remote network. If the remote network is not found in the routing tables, the packet is then forwarded to the default gateway, which would normally be a router with more complete routing tables.

What to Do with Routing Information from Multiple Protocols

Cisco routers can run and use multiple routing protocols simultaneously. This makes it important to understand what they do when they receive routes for the same network from two different routing protocols.

The router assigns an administrative distance to each routing protocol that it runs. This distance is used to weigh routes to the same network that were learned on two different routing protocols.

Administrative Distance

When a Cisco router receives routing information, this information is evaluated and valid routes are placed in the routing tables of the router. To determine which routing protocol to select over another, the router uses the *administrative distance*. Make sure you are familiar with the default values for administrative distance.

Autonomous Systems (AS)

An *autonomous system (AS)* is a group of routers under one administrative control that share a routing strategy. The routers in an autonomous system can freely exchange routing information. Routing protocols used within an AS are commonly called *interior routing protocols*.

Split Horizon

Split horizon is a rule that says, in effect, "do not send routing updates back out of the interface they were learned on." This keeps a router from sending routing updates back to the router they were learned from. Another method to avoid routing updates is the poison reverse update, described next.

Poison Reverse Update

A *poison reverse update* is a routing update that contains a route that is no longer reachable. The hop count for the route is set to infinity (as defined by the routing protocol), so the route will be marked as invalid. A poison reverse update allows a router that knows a path is no longer reachable to go through that path to update neighbor routers with that information.

RIP Routing Tables

Different routing protocols maintain different information in the routing tables. RIP maintains the following in its routing table (see Table 1):

TABLE 1

RIP INFORMATION INCLUDED

Destination	Next Hop	Distance	Timers	Flags
10.110.20.0	10.65.32.1	2	t1, t2, t3	x, y
10.44.17.0	10.65.32.1	3	t1, t2, t3	x, y
10.202.14.0	10.44.23.1	13	t1, t2, t3	x, y

The *destination network* is listed with the IP address of the next *hop* along the path to reach that network. The *distance* to the network in hops is the metric used to determine the best path. The *timers* are used to determine when a route is no longer valid and to avoid routing loops. The timers will be discussed in more detail later. The *flags* indicate if the route is valid or not and whether it is currently being held down.

Regular Updates and Triggered Updates

RIP has two types of updates: *regular updates* that occur periodically based on the routing update timer and *triggered updates* that occur anytime there is a network topology change. Regular updates are used to update routing tables and indicate that a route is still available.

Triggered updates make the network converge more quickly because routers do not wait until the regular update to report the changes to the network.

Routing Update Timer

RIP uses timers as methods to many of its functions. The first timer to discuss is the routing update timer. The *routing update timer* is normally set to 30 seconds. This ensures that every router sends a complete copy of its routing table every time the routing update timer counts down to 0, or 30 seconds if the default is kept.

Each time the routing update timer counts down to 0, the router sends its entire routing table out all active interfaces. After the complete table is sent, the timer is reset.

One of the disadvantages of RIP is that it sends the entire routing table periodically even if no topology changes have occurred. This is very inefficient compared to some other routing protocols. This is one of the things that limits RIP's scalability for large networks. Also, if the routing tables are large, the routing updates can consume a large amount of bandwidth from low bandwidth WAN connections.

Route Invalid Timer

The *route invalid timer* determines the amount of time that must pass without hearing a routing update before the router considers a route invalid. The default setting for the route invalid timer is 90 seconds. This is three times the default for the routing update timer. There is a route invalid timer for each entry in the routing table. Each time an update for that entry is received, the route invalid timer is reset. If the timer counts down to 0, the route is then marked as invalid. After a route is marked invalid, neighboring routers are sent this information.

Route Flush Timer

The *route flush timer* determines the amount of time that must pass without receiving an update for a routing table entry before the entry is removed from the table.

There is a route flush timer attached to each entry in the routing table. When an update is received for that entry, this timer along with the route invalid timer is reset. If the route flush timer counts down to 0, the route entry is completely removed from the routing table. The default for the route flush timer is 270 seconds, or nine times the update timer.

Hold-Down Timer

Hold-down timers are used to prevent a regular routing update from reinstating a route that is down. When a route goes down, the neighboring routers detect it and calculate new routes. These new routes are sent out in routing updates to inform their neighbors of the change. This change ripples through the network. Because this update does not instantly arrive at every router in the network, it is conceivable that a router that has not yet received the update could send out a regular update indicating that the route that has just gone down is still good. A router that has just received the update that the route has gone bad could receive this update indicating the route is good.

A hold-down timer tells the router to hold down any changes that might have recently gone down for a period of time. This prevents a stale routing update from changing the route to an up status during this time. This allows time for the update indicating that a route has gone down to converge throughout the network.

Configuring RIP

To configure RIP in a router, you must first have your interfaces configured with the IP addresses. Then you configure the `router rip` as follows:

```
c2513r2#config t
Enter configuration commands, one per line.  End
with CNTL/Z.
c2513r2(config)#router rip
c2513r2(config-router)#network 10.0.0.0
c2513r2(config-router)#exit
c2513r2(config)#exit
c2513r2#
```

When an interface is set to `passive`, it will not broadcast routing updates but it will still listen for them. Following is an example of how to set the Ethernet segment as `passive` for this configuration:

```
c2513r2#config t
Enter configuration commands, one per line.  End
with CNTL/Z.
c2513r2(config)#router rip
c2513r2(config-router)#network 10.0.0.0
c2513r2(config-router)#passive-interface
ethernet 0
c2513r2(config-router)#exit
c2513r2(config)#exit
c2513r2#
```

Working with RIP

After RIP is configured on a router, it is helpful to check the routing tables and statistics about the RIP protocol. The following example shows how to check the routing tables using the `show ip route` command:

```
Router#show ip route
Codes: C - connected, S - static, I - IGRP, R -
RIP, M - mobile, B - BGP
       D - EIGRP, EX - EIGRP external, O -
OSPF, IA - OSPF inter area
       N1 - OSPF NSSA external type 1, N2 -
OSPF NSSA external type 2
       E1 - OSPF external type 1, E2 - OSPF
external type 2, E - EGP
       i - IS-IS, L1 - IS-IS level-1, L2 - IS-
IS level-2, * - candidate default
       U - per-user static route, o - ODR

Gateway of last resort is not set

     10.0.0.0/24 is subnetted, 1 subnets
C       10.245.34.0 is directly connected,
TokenRing0
R    192.168.99.0/24 [120/1] via 10.245.34.2,
00:00:12, TokenRing0
     199.250.137.0/27 is subnetted, 1 subnets
C       199.250.137.32 is directly connected,
Ethernet0
Router#
```

The following example shows how to view the settings of the majority of RIP's timers and other important information using the command `show ip protocol`:

```
c2513r2#sh ip protocol
Routing Protocol is "rip"
  Sending updates every 30 seconds, next due in
24 seconds
  Invalid after 180 seconds, hold down 180,
flushed after 240
  Outgoing update filter list for all interfaces
is not set
  Incoming update filter list for all interfaces
is not set
  Redistributing: rip
  Default version control: send version 1,
receive any version
    Interface       Send  Recv  Key-chain
    Loopback0        1    1 2
    TokenRing0       1    1 2
  Routing for Networks:
    192.168.99.0
    192.168.42.0
    10.0.0.0
  Passive Interface(s):
    Ethernet0
  Routing Information Sources:
    Gateway         Distance      Last Update
    10.245.34.1         120       00:00:15
  Distance: (default is 120)

c2513r2#
```

The Limitations of RIP

The first limitation of RIP is that of the hop count. RIP supports no more than 15 hops from one end of a network to the other. This limits the physical size of the network on which RIP can be used.

Another limitation of RIP is the fact that RIP sends its entire routing table every 30 seconds by default. By sending the entire routing table periodically, RIP generates a fair amount of network traffic. In a large network, this could become very significant.

RIP also is slow to converge, which can cause problems in large networks when topology changes occur.

The single metric of hop count creates another limitation for RIP. Because RIP considers the only number of hops when determining the best path for traffic, it will not always select the most efficient route for the traffic. More useful routing protocols consider many other factors when selecting a best path for traffic.

Internet Gateway Routing Protocol (IGRP)

IGRP is more scalable than RIP and offers many other advantages. Its main disadvantage is that it is Cisco proprietary and only works with Cisco routers. IGRP uses more meaningful metrics when selecting a path for network traffic.

IGRP Metrics

When IGRP selects the best path for network traffic, it uses many metrics. IGRP considers bandwidth, MTU, delay, load, and reliability when deciding which path is the best to a network. Each metric in IGRP is weighted and a distance is equated. This distance is used to determine the best path to a network.

IGRP Similarities with RIP

In many ways, IGRP is not much different than RIP. They are both distance vector routing protocols. Both protocols periodically transmit their entire routing table with the exception of routes suppressed by split horizon. They both use split horizon with poison reverse, triggered updates, and hold-down timers to prevent routing loops.

IGRP Differences from RIP

IGRP has several significant differences from RIP, however. IGRP uses autonomous systems to group routers in a routing domain.

IGRP broadcasts its full routing table every 90 seconds by default. IP RIP does this every 30 seconds.

IGRP Timers

IGRP uses timers much like RIP does. These timers ensure that certain events occur periodically, such as routing updates. These timers can also indicate when a route is no longer valid or when a route should be purged from the routing tables.

IGRP uses the following timers to operate properly:

◆ **Update timer.** This timer indicates when a new routing update should be sent out. The default value for this timer is 90 seconds.

◆ **Invalid timer.** An *invalid timer* is attached to every route in the routing tables. When an update is received for this route, the timer is reset. If the timer ever reaches 0, the route is then considered invalid and no longer used. The default is 270 seconds.

◆ **Hold-down timer.** When a route is marked invalid, it is kept marked invalid for the duration of the hold-down timer. The default is 280 seconds.

◆ **Flush timer.** A *flush timer* is attached to every route in the routing table. If a route is marked invalid and stays invalid for the duration of the flush timer, the route is completely removed from the routing table. The default is 630 seconds.

Configuring IGRP

Configuring IGRP is very much like configuring RIP, with one caveat. IGRP requires an *autonomous number*. This autonomous number indicates a group of routers participating in a routing scheme. Routers using the same autonomous number will freely exchange routing information. To configure IGRP on a router, start with the routing igrp *asnumber* command, where *asnumber* is the number representing the autonomous system the router will participate in. Following is an example of how IGRP is configured on a router:

```
Router#config t
Enter configuration commands, one per line. End
with CNTL/Z.
Router(config)#router igrp 100
Router(config-router)#network 199.250.137.0
Router(config-router)#network 10.0.0.0
Router(config-router)#exit
Router(config)#exit
Router#
```

Working with IGRP

Just like RIP, after you have configured IGRP on a router, it is helpful to check the routing tables to see what the router has learned and placed in the routing tables. Because the routing information from all routing protocols is consolidated in one routing table, the same command is used to view this information in IGRP as it was for RIP.

The following example shows how to check the routing tables using the show ip route command.

```
Router#sh ip route
Codes: C - connected, S - static, I - IGRP, R -
RIP, M - mobile, B - BGP
       D - EIGRP, EX - EIGRP external, O -
OSPF, IA - OSPF inter area
       N1 - OSPF NSSA external type 1, N2 -
OSPF NSSA external type 2
       E1 - OSPF external type 1, E2 - OSPF
external type 2, E - EGP
       i - IS-IS, L1 - IS-IS level-1, L2 - IS-
IS level-2, * - candidate default
       U - per-user static route, o - ODR

Gateway of last resort is not set

     10.0.0.0/24 is subnetted, 1 subnets
C       10.245.34.0 is directly connected,
TokenRing0
I    192.168.99.0/24 [100/1188] via
10.245.34.2, 00:00:03, TokenRing0
I    192.168.33.0/24 [100/1188] via
10.245.34.2, 00:00:03, TokenRing0
     199.250.137.0/27 is subnetted, 1 subnets
C       199.250.137.32 is directly connected,
Ethernet0
Router#
```

The routing table information looks much the same as that of RIP, with one noticeable difference. Look at the route for 192.168.99.0. The distance to this route is [100/1188]. The 100 is the administrative distance for the routing protocol IGRP. The 1188 is the metric IGRP calculated for this path. The metric is based on all of the factors that IGRP uses to calculate the most efficient path.

Just like RIP, the show ip protocol command will display information about the IGRP protocol:

```
Router#sh ip protocol
Routing Protocol is "igrp 100"
  Sending updates every 90 seconds, next due in
43 seconds
  Invalid after 270 seconds, hold down 280,
flushed after 630
  Outgoing update filter list for all interfaces
is not set
  Incoming update filter list for all interfaces
is not set
  Default networks flagged in outgoing updates
  Default networks accepted from incoming
updates
  IGRP metric weight K1=1, K2=0, K3=1, K4=0,
K5=0
  IGRP maximum hopcount 100
  IGRP maximum metric variance 1
  Redistributing: igrp 100
  Routing for Networks:
    199.250.137.0
    10.0.0.0
  Routing Information Sources:
    Gateway        Distance      Last Update
    10.245.34.2        100       00:00:10
  Distance: (default is 100)

Router#
```

NETWORK SECURITY

Objective Network security: Understand how to use access lists to secure a network. Network security objectives include the following:

◆ Configure standard and extended access lists to filter IP traffic.

◆ Monitor and verify selected access list operations on the router.

Access Lists

An *access list* is created in the router configuration with parameters identifying the traffic for special handling. This access list is identified by a number, or, starting with release 11.2 of Cisco's IOS, a name. This access list is then applied to an interface of the router or to some other part of the configuration for special handling.

An access list can be applied to traffic entering or exiting an interface. These two ways of implementing an access list are called *inbound* and *outbound*. Inbound access lists create more of a load on the router's processor and are thus not recommended unless absolutely necessary. In most cases you should be able to enforce network traffic or routing polices using outbound access lists. The following discussion focuses on outbound access lists.

Extended IP Access List

An *extended IP access list* gives more granular control to traffic identification. It allows decisions based on source and destination IP addresses, particular protocols within the IP protocol suite, and port numbers. The extended IP access list offers much more flexibility in describing the type of network traffic to allow or deny.

How an Access List Works

When the router receives a packet for routing, the router first checks the routing tables to determine how to forward the packet. If it determines that it does not have a way of forwarding the packet, the packet is dropped. However, if the router determines that it can forward the packet and to which interface the packet should be sent, it then checks to see if the interface is grouped to an access list. If not, the packet is copied to the interface's output buffer and the packet is forwarded.

If the router determines that the exiting interface is grouped to an access list, the packet is first subjected to the test of the access list before forwarding. Only if the packet is specifically allowed in the access list is it forwarded.

When defining an IP address in an access list, it is often necessary to identify entire networks instead of a specific network station. In an access list, you can use wildcard bits to identify parts of the network address to not check.

Implementing Extended Access Lists

An *extended access list* offers more detailed control over traffic. With an extended access list, you can specify the source IP address, destination IP address, the protocol, and the port used.

Following is the syntax for an extended access list:

```
access-list 100-199 {permit|deny
ip|tcp|udp|icmp} source source-mask dest dest-
mask [lt|gt|eq|neq dest-port]
```

The `access-list` command is the same as for the simple IP access list. The number of the access list 100–199 identifies it as an extended IP access list. The commands permit and deny work just as they do in simple access lists. However, in an extended access list, you can add the protocol to permit or deny. Extended access lists also allow you to specify a port number. With the port number, you can specify whether it should be less than, greater than, equal to, or not equal to the specified port.

Entering a question mark (?) at the end of your entry of the extended access list will list the well-known TCP/IP port numbers and abbreviations that can be used in place of the actual numbers.

Viewing Access Lists

To view access lists created in a router, you can use the `show access-lists` command.

LAN SWITCHING

Objective LAN switching: Understand how to access lists to secure a network. LAN switching objectives include the following:

◆ Describe the advantages of LAN segmentation.

◆ Describe LAN segmentation using bridges.

◆ Describe LAN segmentation using routers.

◆ Describe LAN segmentation using switches.

◆ Name and describe two switching methods.

◆ Describe full- and half-duplex Ethernet operation.

◆ Describe the network congestion problem in Ethernet networks.

◆ Describe the benefits of network segmentation with bridges.

◆ Describe the benefits of network segmentation with switches.

◆ Describe the features and benefits of Fast Ethernet.

◆ Describe the guidelines and distance limitations of Fast Ethernet.

◆ Distinguish between cut-through and store-and-forward LAN switching.

◆ Describe the operation of the Spanning Tree Protocol and its benefits.

◆ Describe the benefits of virtual LANs.

◆ Define and describe the function of a MAC address.

Collision Domains

A *collision domain* is a group of network nodes on Ethernet that share the network media. By sharing the media, they can experience or cause collisions with other stations in the collision domain. In large networks, you can divide the network into multiple collision domains to avoid the performance degradation associated with large collision domains. This dividing of the network is called *segmentation*.

Network Segmentation

To keep collision domains small on large networks, you can make use of network segmentation. By segmenting the network into small collision domain segments that can communicate with each other, you avoid the performance degradation that occurs with a large number of nodes in one collision domain. There are several different devices you can use to segment a network:

◆ Bridges

◆ Routers

◆ Switches

The following sections detail each of these techniques.

LAN Segmentation Using Bridges

A *bridge* is a network device that is connected to multiple network segments. A bridge is a Layer 2 device. It operates at the Data Link layer using MAC addresses to determine when to forward traffic. Years ago, bridges were physical devices that connected to the network. Today, when the functions of a bridge are needed, a router is typically used. Cisco routers can function as bridges as well as routers.

Bridges learn MAC addresses (Layer 2) and forward traffic to other segments based on tables it builds of which MAC addresses reside on which segments. Bridges have no knowledge of upper-layer protocols. All forwarding is based on MAC address.

LAN Segmentation Using Routers

A *router* can be used to segment a network into different collision domains. Assuming the router is routing between the segments and not bridging, this actually divides the segments into separate Layer 3 networks. Each different Layer 3 network is a separate collision domain. One of the disadvantages of doing this with a router is that it can take a very powerful router to handle many high-speed network connections with large amounts of data.

The advantage of LAN segmentation is that it increases network performance by reducing the number of nodes participating in a collision domain.

LAN Segmentation Using Switches

LAN *switches* work much like bridges with many ports. A LAN switch learns what MAC addresses are connected to which ports. After the switch learns this information, it then forwards frames only to the ports on which the destination MAC address resides. LAN switches learn which port network nodes reside on by listening to network traffic. If a LAN switch receives a frame with a destination MAC address that is not in its forwarding tables, it floods all ports with the frame. After the destination station replies to the frame, the LAN switch will learn on which port it resides and won't need to flood its traffic again.

LAN switches reduce collisions by increasing the number of collision domains. By increasing the number of collision domains, you reduce the number of network nodes contending for the media.

A LAN switch can operate in two different modes:

◆ Cut-through

◆ Store-and-Forward

Full-Duplex Ethernet

Full-Duplex Ethernet doubles the effective bandwidth of the link. A 10Mbit link run in Full-Duplex mode becomes 20Mbits. A 100Mbit link run in Full-Duplex mode becomes 200Mbits. Obviously, Full-Duplex Ethernet can help alleviate bottlenecks in networks. A common place to fully utilize Full-Duplex Ethernet is to network servers. These devices typically receive and send more data than any other network device. Another common use of Full-Duplex Ethernet is high-speed links that collapse a network backbone to one switch.

Fast Ethernet

Fast Ethernet increases the bandwidth of Ethernet from 10Mbits per second to 100Mbits per second—10 times faster.

Fast Ethernet supports different media types:

◆ **100BaseTX.** Can be used on two pairs of Category 5 copper wire, like most 10BaseT installations. This is convenient because you will not have to install new wiring in most cases.

◆ **100BaseFX.** An implementation of Fast Ethernet on fiber optic strands. Because 100BaseFX has longer maximum distance limitations, it is commonly used to connect outlying switches with a backbone switch.

◆ **100BaseT4.** An implementation of Fast Ethernet, using four pairs of Category 3, 4, or 5 wire. This implementation is good for organizations that already have a large investment of Category 3 or 4 wire in place and cannot justify upgrading the cabling to Category 5.

Because network switches are active devices that regenerate the frame, their use can extend the limitations of a Fast Ethernet network.

Spanning Tree Protocol

The *Spanning Tree Protocol (STP)* calculates the most efficient loop-free path through the network. To maintain this loop-free environment, the Spanning Tree Protocol defines a tree that spans all switches in the network. When a network loop exists, switches can see a node's MAC address on both sides of a port. This causes confusion for the forwarding algorithm and allows duplicate frames to be forwarded. The Spanning Tree Protocol determines where multiple paths exist and forces certain ones into standby (blocked) state.

If a network segment in the Spanning Tree becomes unreachable, or if the Spanning Tree Protocol calculates that the cost of a path has changed, the Spanning Tree algorithm reconfigures the Spanning Tree topology by activating the path that was placed in standby state.

STP operation is transparent to end stations, which do not detect whether they are connected to a single LAN segment or a switched LAN of multiple segments.

Spanning Tree Protocol Port States

Spanning Tree Protocol maintains a loop-free network by setting the state of switched ports. Spanning Tree can set any one of five states:

◆ Blocking

◆ Listening

◆ Learning

◆ Forwarding

◆ Disabled

Virtual LANs (VLANs)

On a switched network, *VLANs* allow you to define logical groups. Although switches reduce the problems with collisions occurring, broadcasts still propagate throughout a switched network. These broadcasts might be Novell SAPs or ARP requests. Either way, they are forwarded to every workstation and server on your large switched network every time a broadcast is generated. Not only do broadcasts generate network overhead, but every workstation on the network must process the broadcast. This creates processing overhead for your computers as well.

By dividing the network into logical pieces with computers grouped by function, you can reduce the overhead of broadcasts on the network and workstations.

Think of switches as reducing collision domains and VLANs as reducing broadcast domains.

VLANs were designed to solve two main problems:

◆ Scalability of flat networks

◆ Simplification of network management

VLANs solve these problems by segmenting large flat networks into logically grouped VLANs. These VLANs are easier to manage because they are grouped logically. They also increase scalability of the network; a large number of nodes can be supported as a number of smaller groups.

By adding a router in the network, you can route data from one VLAN to another just as you can route data from physically separate networks.

Practice Exam

This is an example test that is designed to resemble what you might see on your CCNA exam. You have 90 minutes to complete the test of 70 questions. Time yourself, and take your time. The test is not difficult but does require careful reading of the questions and answers. Pay attention to details in the answers such as the router prompt. You may use scratch paper and a pencil during the test. However, you will not be able to use a calculator on the real exam so don't use one here.

Cisco requires a score of 68% to pass. This would be 48 questions correct. There has been talk of Cisco raising the required score to 70%. Do not worry if this happens before you take your test. This only means you have to get one more question correct. You must correctly answer 49 of the 70 questions to score a 70%.

After completing the exam, check your answers and review any areas you missed.

EXAM QUESTIONS

1. Which terms are properly matched with their definitions? Select two.

   A. CPE—Equipment at the customer site (such as CSU/DSU)

   B. Demarc—The location where the telco switch connects to the Frame Relay network

   C. DTE—Equipment used for communication (such as a modem)

   D. CO—The telephone company's central office, where switching equipment is housed.

2. Changing the cdp timer to 90 performs what function?

   A. Sets the cdp timer to 90 seconds

   B. Sets the cdp packet size to 90 bytes

   C. Sets the priority of cdp traffic

   D. Places "90" in the header field of the cdp packet

3. Which of the following are Presentation layer implementations? Select three.

   A. PICT and JPEG

   B. ASCII and EBCDIC

   C. MIDI and MPEG

   D. NFS and SQL

4. When entering a command at the CLI, what key sequence moves the cursor to the beginning of the line?

   A. CTRL+M

   B. CTRL+A

   C. CTRL+R

   D. CTRL+T

5. Which of the following are ports of a router that will allow you to log in to the router? Select three.

   A. Console

   B. Virtual Terminal

   C. Serial0

   D. Auxiliary

6. Which of the following are characteristics of Frame Relay? Select two.

   A. PVC

   B. 2B+D

   C. DLCI

   D. SPID

7. Which of the following are Session layer implementations? Select two.

   A. MIDI—MPEG

   B. NFS—SQL

   C. ASCII—EBCIDIC

   D. RCP—NetBIOS

8. The following is from a 7500 router; which of the answers best describes its parts?

   FastEthernet2/0/1

   A. Type FastEthernet, Slot 2, Adapter 0, Interface 1

   B. Type FastEthernet, Adapter 2, Interface 0, Slot 1

   C. Type FastEthernet, Adapter 2, Slot 0, Interface 1

   D. Type FastEthernet, Slot 2, Interface 0, Adapter 1

9. Which IP address class allows the fewest number of host addresses?

    A. Class A

    B. Class B

    C. Class C

    D. Class F

10. Given the following network address, what is the protocol and what are the parts of the address?

    30020a6.0004.ac35.7e5a

    A. IP address, network 30020a6, node 0004.ac35.7e5a

    B. IP address, network 0004.ac35.7e5a, node 30020a6

    C. IPX address, network 30020a6, node 0004.ac35.7e5a

    D. IPX address, network 0004.ac35.7e5a, node 30020a6

11. What command allows a Cisco router to use multiple equal cost paths for load sharing on IPX networks?

    A. router(config)#ipx maximum-paths

    B. router(config)#ipx load-sharing

    C. router(config)#ipx multiple-paths

    D. router(config)#ipx path-sharing

12. Which serial protocol has PVCs and DLCIs?

    A. HDLC

    B. SDLC

    C. Frame Relay

    D. PLEE

13. Given the following, what is true about this interface?

    Serial5/3 is administratively down, and the line protocol is down.

    A. The port has shut down due to loss of the line protocol.

    B. The port has been shut down with the shutdown command.

    C. The port has experienced errors and is down due to excessive errors.

    D. The port is functionally operational but is currently not receiving keepalive packets.

14. Which of the following is a function of the Network layer of the OSI model?

    A. Converts data to 1s and 0s and places the data on the network media

    B. Uniquely identifies the networking station with a MAC address

    C. Uniquely identifies the networking station and is responsible for determining routing of traffic

    D. Determines how the data will be presented to the Application layer

15. What is the function of poison reverse updates?

    A. Prevents a router from exchanging LMI with a Frame Relay switch

    B. Allows a router to delete itself from another router's CDP update table

    C. Prevents routing loops by sending a routing update with a metric marking the route unreachable

    D. Prevents a router from accessing a TFTP server for its configuration file

16. Given the following network address, what is the protocol and what are the parts of the address?

    192.168.105.33 netmask 255.255.255.0

    A. IPX address, network 192.168.105.0, node 33

    B. IP address, network 192.168.105.0, node 33

    C. IPX address, network 33, node 192.168.105.0

    D. IP address, network 33, node 192.168.105.0

17. Which type of memory is used to store the startup configuration file?

    A. RAM

    B. Flash memory

    C. NVRAM

    D. SDRAM

18. ISDN supports which of the following?

    A. Voice and data traffic

    B. Data traffic only

    C. Voice traffic only

    D. PVCs and DLCIs

19. Which of the following is a valid range of IP addresses for the address 137.65.29.19 with 12 bits of subnet?

    A. 137.65.29.16 to 137.65.29.31

    B. 137.65.29.17 to 137.65.29.31

    C. 137.65.29.17 to 137.65.29.30

    D. 137.65.29.16 to 137.65.29.30

20. What is the function of the ICMP echo?

    A. To determine network connectivity

    B. To determine the noise level of a Frame Relay line

    C. To exchange routing capabilities between routers

    D. To determine the type of digital line being used to carry data

21. Which statements are true of store-and-forward switching? Select two.

    A. The entire packet is received before forwarding.

    B. Latency varies with packet length.

    C. The packet is forwarded after the first 48 bytes are received error free.

    D. Packets containing errors are forwarded.

22. Which address uniquely identifies each networking station on the network media and is usually burned into ROM?

    A. Network address

    B. DLCI

    C. PVC

    D. MAC Address

23. What is the proper method to obtain help about the show command?

    A. show help

    B. show ?

    C. show?

    D. help show

24. You have been assigned the IP network 209.168.54.0. You need to subnet it for the maximum number of networks that will support 40 hosts per network. What is the proper subnet mask?

    A. 255.255.255.192

    B. 255.255.255.224

C. 255.255.255.240

D. 255.255.255.248

25. What are the layers of the OSI reference model in order from layer 1 to layer 7?

   A. Physical, Network, Data Link, Transport, Session, Presentation, Application

   B. Physical, Data Link, Network, Transport, Presentation, Session, Application

   C. Physical, Data Link, Network, Transport, Session, Presentation, Application

   D. Physical, Data Link, Transport, Network, Session, Presentation, Application

26. What OSI layer is responsible for determining routing of data?

   A. Data Link

   B. Network

   C. Transport

   D. Application

27. Which protocol creates a connection between network stations and ensures reliable delivery of data?

   A. IP

   B. UDP

   C. TCP

   D. IPX

28. What is the proper command to back up the router's IOS to a TFTP server?

   A. `router#copy tftp flash`

   B. `router(config)#copy flash tftp`

   C. `router#backup tftp flash`

   D. `router#copy flash tftp`

29. Which command properly configures the interface for IP address 65.167.89.1 with 16 bits of subnet mask?

   A. `router(config)#ip address 65.167.89.1 255.255.255.0`

   B. `router(config-if)#ip address 65.167.89.1 255.255.255.0`

   C. `router(config-if)#ip address 65.167.89.1 255.255.0.0`

   D. `router(config)#ip address 65.167.81.1 255.255.0.0`

30. Given the IP address 126.101.29.67 255.255.255.192, what is the class, subnet, and broadcast?

   A. Class A, Subnet 126.101.29.64, Broadcast 126.101.29.127

   B. Class A, Subnet 126.101.29.0, Broadcast 126.101.29.255

   C. Class B, Subnet 126.101.29.63, Broadcast 126.101.29.128

   D. Class B, Subnet 126.101.29.64, Broadcast 126.101.29.127

31. Given the following configuration command, what are the different parts of the command?

   `Router(config)#ip route 199.250.138.0 255.255.255.0 199.250.137.1 distance 120`

   A. 199.250.138.0 is the destination network, 255.255.255.0 is the next hop subnet mask, 199.250.137.1 is the next hop, and 120 is the administrative distance you assign to this route.

   B. 199.250.138.0 is the next hop, 255.255.255.0 is the next hop subnet mask, 199.250.137.1 is the destination network, and 120 is the administrative distance you assign to this route.

C. 199.250.138.0 is the destination network, 255.255.255.0 is the destination network subnet mask, 199.250.137.1 is the next hop, and 120 is the administrative distance you assign to this route.

D. 199.250.138.0 is the destination network, 255.255.255.0 is the destination network subnet mask, 199.250.137.1 is the next hop, and 120 is the distance in hops to this network.

32. Which of the following encapsulation types are properly matched? Select two.

 A. sap—Ethernet_802.2

 B. arpa—Ethernet_802.3

 C. snap—Ethernet_II

 D. novell_ether—Ethernet_802.3

33. Which OSI layer performs the code conversion and formatting functions?

 A. Application

 B. Session

 C. Presentation

 D. Network

34. What information is displayed when you execute a show interfaces command? Select three.

 A. IP address

 B. Bandwidth

 C. IPX address

 D. Input/Output statistics

35. Where is the running configuration stored in the router?

 A. RAM

 B. Flash memory

C. NVRAM

D. ROM

36. Which command will show the IPX address of an interface?

 A. show interface

 B. show ipx networks

 C. show ipx interface

 D. show interface ipx

37. Which terms apply to ISDN? Select two.

 A. PVC

 B. SPID

 C. DLCI

 D. 2B+D

38. Which statement is true of MOTD?

 A. The MOTD protocol exchanges information with other Cisco devices.

 B. MOTD allows a router to discover faster paths through the use of bandwidth calculations.

 C. MOTD copies the configuration of the router to a backup.

 D. The MOTD is displayed prior to the login prompt.

39. What is true about access lists? Select two.

 A. Access lists can be applied to incoming traffic.

 B. Access lists have an explicit allow added to the end.

 C. Access lists can be applied to outgoing traffic.

 D. Access lists can be applied only to IP traffic.

40. Which are examples of Application layer implementations? Select the best answer.

    A. PICT and JPEG

    B. NFS and SQL

    C. ASCII and EBCIDIC

    D. Telnet and SMTP

41. How do you instruct the router to load the IOS from ROM?

    A. `router(config)#load IOS ROM`

    B. `router(config)#boot system ROM`

    C. `router(config)#boot IOS ROM`

    D. `router(config)#load system ROM`

42. Which OSI layer uses port numbers to communicate with higher layers?

    A. Network

    B. Transport

    C. Data Link

    D. Session

43. How can you deny telnet access from IP address 192.168.59.45 entering the router on serial0 ip address 192.168.99.1?

    A. `router(config)#access-list 1 deny`
       `192.168.59.45`

    B. `router(config)#access-list 1 deny`
       `192.168.99.1`

    C. `router(config)#access-list 1 deny`
       `192.168.59.45 eq 23`

    D. `router(config)#access-list 1 deny`
       `192.168.99.1 eq 23`

44. Which of the following commands will verify that you have properly configured an IP address? Select two.

    A. `testip`

    B. `verify`

    C. `traceroute`

    D. `ping`

45. What statement is true of HDLC?

    A. HDLC is a dialup protocol that can be used in place of ISDN to combine the two channels of an ISDN line for more bandwidth.

    B. HDLC is a serial protocol that varies between vendors. To use HDLC on a Cisco router, the router on the other end of the connection must also be a Cisco.

    C. HDLC is a serial protocol to connect SNA devices.

    D. HDLC provides handshaking between Cisco routers and Frame Relay switches.

46. Which of the following statements are properly matched? Select two.

    A. BRI—two B channels and one D channel

    B. BRI—23 B channels and one D channel

    C. PRI—two B channels and one D channel

    D. PRI—23 B channels and one D channel

47. What is the proper method to enter the privileged EXEC?

    A. Enter the password at the login prompt.

    B. Enter the enable password at the login prompt.

C. Enter the password at the login prompt, then enter the command `enable`, then enter the enable password.

D. Enter the password at the login prompt, then enter the command `privileged`, then enter the enable password.

48. How do you create a subinterface?

    A. `router(config)#interface serial0 sub 1`

    B. `router(config)#subinterface serial0.1`

    C. `router(config)#interface serial0.1`

    D. `router(config-if)#interface serial0.1`

49. Which OSI layer uniquely identifies the networking station on the network with an address that is usually burned into ROM?

    A. Physical

    B. Network

    C. MAC

    D. Data Link

50. What is true of the IP address 224.11.23.1?

    A. It is a Class A address.

    B. It is a Class B address.

    C. It is a multicast address.

    D. It is a loopback address.

51. Which type of routing update includes a path with a routing metric that makes the path unreachable?

    A. Poison Reverse

    B. Hold Down

    C. Unreachable Update

    D. Infinity Update

52. What is the purpose of the Novell SAP protocol?

    A. It is the core protocol used for server communication.

    B. It advertises services available.

    C. It is a tick count routing protocol.

    D. It is a link state routing protocol.

53. What statements are true of Novell's IPX protocol? Select two.

    A. IPX provides reliable transport.

    B. IPX creates a connection between two networking stations.

    C. IPX is a connectionless unreliable protocol.

    D. IPX uses the MAC address of the networking station in the network address.

54. The term *local loop* refers to what?

    A. The connection between two frame relay switches

    B. The connection from the customer's location to the local central office

    C. Creating a loop in the CSU/DSU for testing purposes

    D. A SONET ring that loops around a city

55. You entered `te` and the router responded `ambiguous command`; what should you type next to see a list of commands beginning with `te`?

    A. `router#te?`

    B. `router#te ?`

    C. `router#te[tab]`

    D. `router#te help`

56. What is the proper way to configure IPX on an interface using the Novell encapsulation Ethernet_II?

    A. `router(config-if)#ipx network 5c encapsulation sap`

    B. `router(config-if)#ipx encapsulation sap network 5c`

    C. `router(config-if)#ipx encapsulation arpa network 5c`

    D. `router(config-if)#ipx network 5c encapsulation arpa`

57. What command displays the contents of the configuration register?

    A. `show config`

    B. `show version`

    C. `show register`

    D. `show config-reg`

58. What commands will display the DLCI numbers and their status? Select two.

    A. `show frame map`

    B. `show interface`

    C. `show frame lmi`

    D. `show frame pvc`

59. What does the DE bit indicate?

    A. The destination address

    B. The sequence of the packet

    C. How many switches the packet has traversed

    D. That the packet can be discarded

60. What are FECN and BECN?

    A. Routing protocols for Frame Relay

    B. Methods for switches to prioritize traffic

    C. Congestion notification methods

    D. Frame Relay encapsulations

61. Given the following, which statements are true? Select three.

    ```
    Access-list 10 permit 10.100.10.0 0.0.0.255
    Ethernet0

    Access-group 10 in
    ```

    A. Traffic from IP address 10.100.10.153 would be allowed to enter Ethernet0.

    B. Traffic from IP address 10.100.11.45 would be allowed to enter Ethernet0.

    C. Traffic from IP address 192.168.123.56 would be allowed to exit Ethernet0.

    D. Traffic destined for 10.100.10.33 would be allowed to exit Ethernet0.

62. Which command will display a list of Novell servers?

    A. `show ipx servers`

    B. `show novell servers`

    C. `show ipx saps`

    D. `show novell saps`

63. When do configuration changes take effect?

    A. After the router is reloaded

    B. After the configuration changes are saved

    C. After the router completes all routing updates

    D. Immediately

64. What does the command `copy running-config startup-config` do?

    A. Creates an offsite backup of the router's configuration

    B. Saves configuration changes so if the router reboots, the running config will be the same

    C. Copies the running-config to flash memory

    D. Copies the startup-config to the running-config

65. Given the following address, what is the protocol and what are the portions of the address?

    192.168.33.56 netmask 255.255.0.0

    A. Protocol IP, Network 192.168.33.0, node 56

    B. Protocol IPX, Network 192.168.0.0, node 33.56

    C. Protocol IP, Network 192.168.0.0, node 33.56

    D. Protocol IPX, Network 192.168.33.0, node 56

66. A RIP routing update contains a distance of 16; which of the following statements is true?

    A. It will take 16 clock ticks to reach the destination network.

    B. The destination is 16 hops away but still reachable.

    C. The link between this router and the destination network has a bandwidth of 16 Kbits.

    D. The destination network is unreachable.

67. What is a routing loop?

    A. A ring of routers exchanging routing information

    B. A route that contains two valid paths to a destination network

    C. A situation that occurs when multiple routers think they can reach a network through each other when in reality neither has a path to the destination

    D. The loop traffic takes to get to the destination network

68. Given the following configuration command, which statement is true?

    `Router(config)#ip route 0.0.0.0 0.0.0.0 62.123.3.1`

    A. Traffic for network 62.123.3.1 has no valid path.

    B. Packets for network 62.123.3.1 will be forwarded to 0.0.0.0

    C. Packets destined for networks not explicitly listed in the routing tables will be forwarded to 62.123.3.1.

    D. Packets from network 0.0.0.0 will be forwarded to 62.123.3.1.

69. You want to know what IP address will be assigned to interface Ethernet0 when the router reboots; what is the correct command to investigate this?

    A. `sh run`

    B. `sh start`

    C. `sh int e0`

    D. `sh int e 0`

70. Given the following configuration commands, which statement is true?

    `Router eigrp 100`

    `Network 192.168.100.0`

    `Passive-interface ethernet0`

    A. Routing updates for all networks will be sent out interface Ethernet0.

B. Only routing updates for 192.168.100.0 will be sent out interface Ethernet0.

C. No routing updates will be sent out Ethernet0.

D. Routing updates for network 100 are sent out interface Ethernet0.

ANSWERS AND EXPLANATIONS

1. **A, D.**   CPE is customer premise equipment; this is equipment at the customer site, such as CSU/DSUs. CO is the central office, where the telephone company houses switching equipment. The Demarc is the location at the customer site where the telephone company's responsibility ends and the customer's begins. A modem is data communication equipment (DCE) not data terminal equipment (DTE). For more information, see the section in Chapter 5 titled "WAN Terms."

2. **A.**   The CDP timer sets how long between CDP neighbor packets are sent. For more information, see the section in Chapter 2 titled "Cisco Discovery Protocol (CDP)."

3. **A, B, C.**   PICT and JPEG, ASCII and EBCIDIC, and MIDI and MPEG are all examples of Presentation layer implementations. The Presentation layer defines how data will be presented to the Application layer. PICT and JPEG are methods of graphics representation, ASCII and EBCDIC are methods of text representation, and MIDI and MPEG are methods of multimedia representations. NFS and SQL are examples of Session layer implementations. For more information, see the section in Chapter 1 titled "Presentation Layer."

4. **B.**   Ctrl+A is the correct keystroke to return the cursor to the beginning of the line. For more information, see the section in Chapter 2 titled "Editing Features."

5. **A, B, D.**   Console, Virtual Terminal, and auxiliary ports are correct because they all allow you to access the router and log in. Although you can access a router over Serial0 and log in, you actually are accessing a Virtual Terminal session, which presents you with the login prompt. For more information, see the section in Chapter 2 titled "Logging in to a Router in Both User and Privileged Modes."

6. **A, C.**   PVC and DLCI are associated with Frame Relay networks. PVCs are Permanent Virtual Circuits and DLCIs are Data Link Connection Identifiers. 2B+D and SPID are examples of ISDN implementations. For more information, see the section in Chapter 5 titled "Frame Relay."

7. **B, D.**   NFS and SQL, and RCP and NetBIOS are examples of Session layer implementations. MIDI and MPEG, and ASCII and EBCIDIC are examples of Presentation layer implementations. For more information, see the section in Chapter 1 titled "Session Layer."

8. **A.**   In a 7000 or 7500 router with VIP cards, the interfaces are referenced as Type, Slot, Adapter, and Interface. For more information, see the section in Chapter 2 titled "Interfaces."

9. **C.**   Class C addresses allow for only 254 host addresses. Class A and B addresses allow for more hosts, and there is no class F IP address. For more information, see the section in Chapter 3 titled "Understanding IP Address Classes."

10. **C.**   This is a Novell IPX address. The first number is the network number. The following portion represents the MAC address of the station and is the node address. For more information, see the section in Chapter 4 titled "Network Addresses."

PRACTICE EXAM

11. **A.** The command `ipx maximum-paths` allows a Cisco router to use multiple paths to a network in a load sharing capacity. For more information, see the section in Chapter 4 titled "Configuring IPX Routing."

12. **C.** Frame Relay has PVCs and DLCIs. For more information, see the section in Chapter 5 titled "Frame Relay."

13. **B.** An interface that shows `administratively down` has been shut down in the configuration with the `shutdown` command. For more information, see the section in Chapter 2 titled "Interfaces."

14. **C.** The Network layer uniquely identifies the station on the network and is responsible for determining routing of traffic. For more information, see the section in Chapter 1 titled "Network Layer."

15. **C.** A poison reverse update is a routing update including a metric that indicates that the network is unreachable. For more information, see the section in Chapter 6 titled "Routing Information Protocol."

16. **B.** IP addresses are represented as four numbers separated by periods. The subnet mask 255.255.255.0 indicates that the last octet is the node. For more information, see the section in Chapter 3 titled "IP Addresses."

17. **C.** The startup configuration is stored in NVRAM. Flash memory stores the IOS image, the contents of RAM is lost when the power is lost. For more information, see the section in Chapter 2 titled "Understanding Router Elements."

18. **A.** ISDN can be used for voice and data traffic. For more information, see the section in Chapter 5 titled "Integrated Services Digital Network (ISDN)."

19. **C.** 137.65.29.17 to 137.65.29.30 are valid IP addresses for 137.65.29.19 with 12 bits of subnetting. Remember that Cisco counts subnet bits from the end of the default subnet mask.

Therefore, the default subnet mask of 8 bits is added to the 12 bits of subnetting, for a total of 20 bits of network mask. For more information, see the section in Chapter 3 titled "IP Addresses."

20. **A.** The ICMP echo confirms network connectivity between two stations. For more information, see the section in Chapter 3 titled "Internet Control Message Protocol (ICMP)."

21. **A, B.** Store-and-forward switches receive the entire packet before forwarding. This means the latency through the switch varies with the length of the packet. For more information, see the section in Chapter 8 titled "LAN Segmentation Using Switches."

22. **D.** The MAC address uniquely identifies a station on the network media and is usually burned into ROM. For more information, see the section in Chapter 1 titled "Data Link Layer."

23. **B.** `show ?` will display a list of options for the `show` command. `show?` will list all commands that begin with `show`. For more information, see the section in Chapter 2 titled "Context-Sensitive Help."

24. **A.** Two bits of subnetting will allow for 62 hosts per network. Three bits allow for only 30 hosts. For more information, see the section in Chapter 3 titled "IP Addresses."

25. **C.** Remember the sentence "*All People Seem To Need Data Processing*": Application, Presentation, Session, Transport, Network, Data Link, Physical. For more information, see the section in Chapter 1 titled "The Seven Layers."

26. **B.** The Network layer determines how packets are routed. For more information, see the section in Chapter 1 titled "Network Layer."

27. **C.** Transmission Control Protocol (TCP) is a connection-oriented transport protocol that includes error checking to ensure reliable delivery of data.

UDP is a connectionless protocol that includes no guarantee of data delivery. IP is connectionless with no guarantee of packet delivery. IPX is much like IP in this respect. For more information, see the section in Chapter 1 titled "Connection-Oriented and Connectionless Services."

28. **D.** `copy flash tftp` at the Privileged EXEC copies the flash memory to a tftp server. For more information, see the section in Chapter 2 titled "Back Up and Upgrade IOS."

29. **B.** Remember that when Cisco talks of subnet bits they are referring to bits after the default netmask for the class of address. The IP address is assigned at the Interface level of the configuration mode. This is indicated by the prompt `router(config-if)#`. For more information, see the section in Chapter 3 titled "IP Addresses."

30. **A.** This is a Class A IP address. The subnet is 64 and the broadcast is 127. For more information, see the section in Chapter 3 titled "IP Addresses."

31. **C.** A static route statement includes the destination network, subnet mask for the destination network, next hop address, and an optional administrative distance. For more information, see the section in Chapter 6 titled "Static Routes."

32. **A, D.** sap—Ethernet_802.2 and novell_ether—Ethernet_802.3 are properly matched encapsulation types. The other two should be arpa—Ethernet_II and snap—Ethernet_snap. For more information, see the section in Chapter 4 titled "Novell IPX/SPX Protocol."

33. **C.** The Presentation layer performs code conversion and formatting functions. For more information, see the section in Chapter 1 titled "Presentation Layer."

34. **A, B, D.** `show interfaces` is a very useful command. It displays the primary IP address assigned to an interface, bandwidth assigned to the interface, and Input/Output statistics.

For more information, see the section in Chapter 2 titled "Examining the Components of a Router."

35. **A.** The running configuration is stored in RAM. For more information, see the section in Chapter 2 titled "Understanding Router Elements."

36. **C.** `show ipx interface` will display information on interfaces with assigned IPX networks. For more information, see the section in Chapter 4 titled "Displaying IPX Addresses."

37. **B, D.** The terms SPID and 2B+D are related to ISDN. PVC and DLCI are related to Frame Relay. For more information, see the section in Chapter 5 titled "Integrated Services Data Network."

38. **D.** The MOTD banner is displayed before the password prompt when someone accesses the router. For more information, see the section in Chapter 2 titled "Message of the Day (MOTD)."

39. **A, C.** Access list can be applied to incoming or outgoing traffic. For more information, see the section in Chapter 7 titled "Access Lists."

40. **D.** Telnet and SMTP are examples of Application layer implementations. PICT, JPEG, ASCII, and EBCIDIC are all Presentation layer implementations. NFS and SQL are Session layer implementations. For more information, see the section in Chapter 1 titled "Application Layer."

41. **B.** The command `boot system ROM` placed in the config instructs the router to boot from system ROM. For more information, see the section in Chapter 2 titled "Cisco IOS Command for Router Startup."

42. **B.** The Transport layer uses port numbers to communicate with higher layers. For more information, see the section in Chapter 1 titled "The Seven Layers."

43. **A.** `access-list 1 deny 192.168.59.45` denies all traffic from this address. `access-list 1` is a simple access list and does not allow the specifying of a protocol as specified in answers C and D.

For more information, see the section in Chapter 7 titled "Implementing Extended Access Lists."

44. **C, D.** Both traceroute and ping can be used to verify that you have properly configured an IP address. For more information, see the section in Chapter 3 titled "Internet Control Message Protocol (ICMP)."

45. **B.** Although most vendors support HDLC, each implementation is slightly different, making it vendor specific. For more information, see the section in Chapter 5 titled "How Routers Communicate via Serial Links."

46. **A, D.** A BRI ISDN line has two B channels and one D channel. A PRI ISDN line has 23 B channels and one D channel. For more information, see the section in Chapter 5 titled "Integrated Services Data Network (ISDN)."

47. **C.** To enter a router in the privileged EXEC mode, you enter the login password. Then enter the command `enable` at the router prompt. Then enter the enable password. For more information, see the section in Chapter 2 titled "Logging In to a Router in Both User and Privileged Modes."

48. **C.** To create a subinterface, simply enter the interface command with `inteface.subinterface`. For more information, see the section in Chapter 5 titled "Configuring Frame Relay."

49. **D.** The Data Link layer uniquely identifies the networking station on the network media and is usually burned into ROM. For more information, see the section in Chapter 1 titled "The Seven Layers."

50. **C.** IP addresses beginning with 224 are multicast addresses. For more information, see the section in Chapter 3 titled "IP Addresses."

51. **A.** Poison reverse updates include a route with a metric that makes the path unreachable. For more information, see the section in Chapter 6 titled "Routing Information Protocol."

52. **B.** Novell's SAP protocol is used to broadcast services available on the network. For more information, see the section in Chapter 4 titled "Service Advertising Protocol (SAP)."

53. **C, D.** IPX is a connectionless unreliable protocol that uses the MAC address in the network address. For more information, see the section in Chapter 4 titled "Internet Packet eXchange (IPX)."

54. **B.** The local loop is the telephone line between your office and the local CO. For more information, see the section in Chapter 5 titled "Local Loop."

55. **A.** Entering `te?` will list all of the commands beginning with the letters `te`. For more information, see the section in Chapter 2 titled "Entering Commands."

56. **D.** The IPX network configuration command is `ipx network` *net* `encapsulation` *type*. The Cisco encapsulation type for Ethernet_II is arpa. For more information, see the section in Chapter 4 titled "Configuring IPX Routing."

57. **B.** The `show version` command displays the contents of the config register. For more information, see the section in Chapter 2 titled "Examining the Components of a Router."

58. **A, D.** `show frame map` and `show frame pvc` will display DLCI numbers and their status. For more information, see the section in Chapter 5 titled "Frame Relay."

59. **D.** The DE bit indicates that a packet is discard eligible. In times of congestion, frame relay switches may need to drop packets. Packets with the DE bit are dropped first. For more information, see the section in Chapter 5 titled "Frame Relay."

60. **C.** Forward Error Congestion Notification (FECN) and Backward Error Congestion Notification (BECN) are congestion notification methods used in Frame Relay.

For more information, see the section in Chapter 5 titled "Frame Relay."

61. **A, C, D.** The access list is applied only to incoming traffic on the interface. For more information, see the section in Chapter 7 titled "Implementing Simple Access Lists."

62. **A.** `show ipx servers` lists the servers found through SAP and the interface they were learned on. For more information, see the section in Chapter 4 titled "Diagnosing IPX Problems."

63. **D.** Configuration changes take effect immediately. For more information, see the section in Chapter 2 titled "Configuring the Router."

64. **B.** `copy running-config startup-config` copies the running config from RAM to the startup config stored in NVRAM, so the configuration will be used the next time the router is rebooted. A common error is making a configuration change without saving the change. The router may reboot months later and something will stop working. It can take a while to discover this type of problem. For more information, see the section in Chapter 2 titled "Managing Configuration Files from the Privileged Exec Mode."

65. **C.** Four numbers separated by periods indicates an IP address. The subnet mask separates the network from the node. For more information, see the section in Chapter 3 titled "IP Addresses."

66. **D.** In RIP, a distance of 16 is considered unreachable. For more information, see the section in Chapter 7 titled "Routing Information Protocol (RIP)."

67. **C.** A routing loop is when multiple routers think they can reach a network through each other when neither actually has a path. In some cases, a packet can be bounced back and forth between the routers until the TTL expires. For more information, see the section in Chapter 6 titled "Routing Information Protocol (RIP)."

68. **C.** A network 0.0.0.0 0.0.0.0 indicates a default gateway much like the default gateway set in your computer. The default gateway is where packets are sent when an explicit route cannot be found in the router's routing tables. For more information, see the section in Chapter 6 titled "Static Routes."

69. **B.** `show start` will show the startup configuration file. This is the configuration that will take effect when the router is rebooted. For more information, see the section in Chapter 2 titled "Managing Configuration Files from the Privileged Exec Mode."

70. **C.** Making an interface passive within a routing protocol means routing updates will not be sent out over that interface. However, the routing protocol will still listen for updates on that interface. For more information, see the section in Chapter 6 titled "Routing Information Protocol."

APPENDIXES

Glossary

PREFACE

Computer networks are quickly becoming a vital tool in the daily operations of businesses around the world. For example, employees in an accounting department can use a common database to access and share customer account information using DECnet. Using an AppleTalk network, Macintosh users in a marketing department can share product bulletins, data sheets, and slide presentations. In an engineering department, Sun workstation users can share product specifications using TCP/IP over Ethernet. And in a company's manufacturing department, IBM devices attached to a Token Ring network can process real-time data about material availability and fill orders sent over links from remote offices.

This glossary assembles and defines the terms and acronyms used in the internetworking industry. Many of the definitions have yet to be standardized, and many terms have several meanings. Multiple definitions and acronym expressions are included where they apply.

The first part of this guide lists terms and acronyms that are specific to Cisco Systems and Cisco IOS. The second part of this guide contains terms and acronyms that are commonly used in the internetworking industry.

This guide also appears on the Cisco Systems, Inc. documentation CD-ROM.

Although many product names and descriptions are included in this glossary, you are encouraged to obtain more specific information from the appropriate vendor.

For information about Cisco products, refer to the Cisco Product Catalog.

We hope that this glossary adds to your understanding of internetworking technologies and specific Cisco terms. Suggestions for new terms or acronyms and their associated definitions can be submitted by sending an email to cs-rep@cisco.com.

CISCO SYSTEMS TERMS AND ACRONYMS

A

AIP ATM Interface Processor. ATM network interface for Cisco 7000 series routers designed to minimize performance bottlenecks at the UNI. The AIP supports AAL3/4 and AAL5. See also *AAL3/4* and *AAL5*, both in the "Internetworking Terms and Acronyms" section.

APaRT Automated packet recognition/translation. Technology that allows a server to be attached to CDDI or FDDI without requiring the reconfiguration of applications or network protocols. APaRT recognizes specific Data Link layer encapsulation packet types and, when these packet types are transferred from one medium to another, translates them into the native format of the destination device.

ATG Address translation gateway. Cisco DECnet routing software function that allows a router to route multiple independent DECnet networks and to establish a user-specified address translation for selected nodes between networks.

ATM network Traditional Cisco ATM network built around BPX switches.

ATM network interface card ESP card that is used as the OC-3 interface to the BPX's BXM.

autonomous switching Feature on Cisco routers that provides faster packet processing by allowing the ciscoBus to switch packets independently without interrupting the system processor.

B

BIGA Bus Interface Gate Array. Technology that allows the Catalyst 5000 to receive and transmit frames from its packet-switching memory to its MAC local buffer memory without the intervention of the host processor.

BOBI Break-out/break-in. VNS feature that allows interworking between Euro-ISDN (ETSI) and other VNS-supported signaling variants, such as DPNSS and QSIG.

BPX Service Node Closely integrated BPX switch, AXIS interface shelf, and extended services processor designed to support ATM and Frame Relay switched virtual circuits, as well as traditional PVCs.

break-out/break-in See *BOBI.*

Bus Interface Gate Array See *BIGA.*

C

Call Detail Record See *CDR.*

CDP Cisco Discovery Protocol. Media- and protocol-independent device-discovery protocol that runs on all Cisco-manufactured equipment including routers, access servers, bridges, and switches. Using CDP, a device can advertise its existence to other devices and receive information about other devices on the same LAN or on the remote side of a WAN. Runs on all media that support SNAP, including LANs, Frame Relay, and ATM media.

CDR Call Detail Record. VNS record of voice or data SVCs, which includes calling and called numbers, local and remote node names, date and timestamp, elapsed time, and Call Failure Class fields.

CFRAD See *Cisco FRAD.*

Channel Interface Processor See *CIP.*

CIP Channel Interface Processor. Channel attachment interface for Cisco 7000 series routers. The CIP is used to connect a host mainframe to a control unit, eliminating the need for an FEP for channel attachment.

ciscoBus controller See *SP.*

Cisco Discovery Protocol See *CDP.*

Cisco FRAD Cisco Frame Relay access device. Cisco product that supports Cisco IOS Frame Relay SNA services and can be upgraded to be a full-function multiprotocol router. The Cisco FRAD connects SDLC devices to Frame Relay without requiring an existing LAN. However, the Cisco FRAD does support attached LANs and can perform conversion from SDLC to Ethernet and Token Ring. See also *FRAD*, in the "Internetworking Terms and Acronyms" section.

Cisco Frame Relay access device See *Cisco FRAD*.

CiscoFusion Cisco internetworking architecture that "fuses" together the scalability, stability, and security advantages of the latest routing technologies with the performance benefits of ATM and LAN switching, and the management benefits of VLANs. See also *Cisco IOS*.

Cisco IOS Cisco system software that provides common functionality, scalability, and security for all products under the CiscoFusion architecture. Cisco IOS allows centralized, integrated, and automated installation and management of internetworks, while ensuring support for a wide variety of protocols, media, services, and platforms. See also *CiscoFusion*.

Cisco Link Services See *CLS*.

Cisco Link Services Interface See *CLSI*.

CiscoView GUI-based device-management software application that provides dynamic status, statistics, and comprehensive configuration information for Cisco internetworking devices. In addition to displaying a physical view of Cisco device chassis, CiscoView also provides device monitoring functions and basic troubleshooting capabilities, and can be integrated with several leading SNMP-based network management platforms.

CLS Cisco Link Services. A front-end for a variety of data-link control services.

CLSI Cisco Link Services Interface. Messages that are exchanged between CLS and data-link users such as APPN, SNA service point, and DLSw+.

configuration register In Cisco routers, a 16-bit, user-configurable value that determines how the router functions during initialization. The configuration register can be stored in hardware or software. In hardware, the bit position is set using a jumper. In software, the bit position is set by specifying a hexadecimal value using configuration commands.

CPP Combinet Proprietary Protocol.

CxBus Cisco Extended Bus. Data bus for interface processors on Cisco 7000 series routers. See also *SP*.

D

Data Movement Processor See *DMP*.

Diffusing Update Algorithm See *DUAL*.

DistributedDirector Method of distributing Web traffic by taking into account Web server availability and relative client-to-server topological distances in order to determine the optimal Web server for a client. DistributedDirector uses the Director Response Protocol to query DRP server agents for BGP and IGP routing table metrics.

DLSw+ Data-link switching plus. Cisco implementation of the DLSw standard for SNA and NetBIOS traffic forwarding. DLSw+ goes beyond the standard to include the advanced features of the current Cisco RSRB implementation, and provides additional functionality to increase the overall scalability of data-link switching. See also *DLSw*, in the "Internetworking Terms and Acronyms" section.

DMP Data Movement Processor. Processor on the Catalyst 5000 that, along with the multiport packet buffer memory interface, performs the frame-switching function for the switch. The DMP also handles translational bridging between the Ethernet and FDDI interfaces, IP segmentation, and intelligent bridging with protocol-based filtering.

DRP Director Response Protocol. Protocol used by the DistributedDirector feature in IP routing.

DSPU concentration Cisco IOS feature that enables a router to function as a PU concentrator for SNA PU 2 nodes. PU concentration at the router simplifies the task of PU definition at the upstream host while providing additional flexibility and mobility for downstream PU devices.

DUAL Diffusing Update Algorithm. Convergence algorithm in Enhanced IGRP that provides loop-free operation at every instant throughout a route computation. Allows routers involved in a topology change to synchronize at the same time, while not involving routers that are unaffected by the change. See also *Enhanced IGRP*.

E

EIGRP See *Enhanced IGRP*.

EIP Ethernet Interface Processor. Interface processor card on the Cisco 7000 series routers. The EIP provides high-speed (10Mbps) AUI ports that support Ethernet Version 1 and Ethernet Version 2 or IEEE 802.3 interfaces, and a high-speed data path to other interface processors.

Enhanced IGRP Enhanced Interior Gateway Routing Protocol. Advanced version of IGRP developed by Cisco. Provides superior convergence properties and operating efficiency, and combines the advantages of link state protocols with those of distance vector protocols. Compare to *IGRP*. See also *IGP*, *OSPF*, and *RIP*, all in the "Internetworking Terms and Acronyms" section.

Enhanced Interior Gateway Routing Protocol See *Enhanced IGRP*.

Enhanced Monitoring Services Set of analysis tools on the Catalyst 5000 switch, consisting of an integrated RMON agent and the SPAN. These tools provide traffic monitoring, and network segment analysis and management. See also *RMON*, in the "Internetworking Terms and Acronyms" section, and *SPAN*.

ESP Extended Services Processor. Rack-mounted adjunct processor that is co-located with a Cisco BPX/AXIS (all three units comprise a BPX service node) and has IP connectivity to a StrataView Plus Workstation.

Ethernet Interface Processor See *EIP*.

EXEC Interactive command processor of Cisco IOS.

Extended Services Processor See *ESP*.

F

Fast Ethernet Interface Processor See *FEIP*.

Fast Sequenced Transport See *FST*.

Fast Serial Interface Processor See *FSIP*.

fast switching Cisco feature whereby a route cache is used to expedite packet switching through a router. Contrast with *process switching*.

FDDI Interface Processor See *FIP*.

FEIP Fast Ethernet Interface Processor. Interface processor on the Cisco 7000 series routers. The FEIP supports up to two 100Mbps 100BaseT ports.

FIP FDDI Interface Processor. Interface processor on the Cisco 7000 series routers. The FIP supports SASs, DASs, dual homing, and optical bypass, and contains a 16-mips processor for high-speed (100Mbps) interface rates. The FIP complies with ANSI and ISO FDDI standards.

FRAS Frame Relay access support. Cisco IOS feature that allows SDLC, Token Ring, Ethernet, and Frame Relay-attached IBM devices to connect to other IBM devices across a Frame Relay network. See also *FRAD*, in the "Internetworking Terms and Acronyms" section.

FSIP Fast Serial Interface Processor. Default serial interface processor for Cisco 7000 series routers. The FSIP provides four or eight high-speed serial ports.

FST Fast Sequenced Transport. Connectionless, sequenced transport protocol that runs on top of the IP protocol. SRB traffic is encapsulated inside of IP datagrams and is passed over an FST connection between two network devices (such as routers).

Speeds up data delivery, reduces overhead, and improves the response time of SRB traffic.

G

Gateway Discovery Protocol See *GDP*.

GDP Gateway Discovery Protocol. Cisco protocol that allows hosts to dynamically detect the arrival of new routers as well as determine when a router goes down. Based on UDP. See also *UDP*, in the "Internetworking Terms and Acronyms" section.

generic routing encapsulation See *GRE*.

GRE Generic routing encapsulation. Tunneling protocol developed by Cisco that can encapsulate a wide variety of protocol packet types inside IP tunnels, creating a virtual point-to-point link to Cisco routers at remote points over an IP internetwork. By connecting multiprotocol subnetworks in a single-protocol backbone environment, IP tunneling using GRE allows network expansion across a single-protocol backbone environment.

H

helper address Address configured on an interface to which broadcasts received on that interface will be sent.

High-Speed Communications Interface See *HSCI*.

HIP HSSI Interface Processor. Interface processor on the Cisco 7000 series routers. The HIP provides one HSSI port that supports connections to ATM, SMDS, Frame Relay, or private lines at speeds up to T3 or E3.

Hot Standby Router Protocol See *HSRP*.

HSCI High-Speed Communications Interface. Single-port interface, developed by Cisco, providing full-duplex synchronous serial communications capability at speeds up to 52Mbps.

HSRP Hot Standby Router Protocol. Provides high network availability and transparent network topology changes. HSRP creates a Hot Standby router group with a lead router that services all packets sent to the Hot Standby address. The lead router is monitored by other routers in the group, and if it fails, one of these standby routers inherits the lead position and the Hot Standby group address.

HSSI Interface Processor See *HIP*.

I

IGRP Interior Gateway Routing Protocol. IGP developed by Cisco to address the issues associated with routing in large, heterogeneous networks. Compare to *Enhanced IGRP*. See also *IGP*, *OSPF*, and *RIP*, all in the "Internetworking Terms and Acronyms" section.

interface processor Any of a number of processor modules used in the Cisco 7000 series routers. See also *AIP*, *CIP*, *EIP*, *FEIP*, *FIP*, *FSIP*, *HIP*, *MIP*, *SIP*, and *TRIP*.

Interior Gateway Routing Protocol See *IGRP*.

Inter-Switch Link See *ISL*.

IOS See *Cisco IOS*.

ISL Inter-Switch Link. Cisco-proprietary protocol that maintains VLAN information as traffic flows between switches and routers.

L

local adjacency Two VNSs that control different VSN areas, but communicate with one another through a Frame Relay PVC, are considered to be locally adjacent.

M

MICA   Multiservice IOS Channel Aggregation. Technology that enables the simultaneous support of remote-access users through both analog modems and ISDN devices.

MIP   MultiChannel Interface Processor. Interface processor on the Cisco 7000 series routers that provides up to two channelized T1 or E1 connections via serial cables to a CSU. The two controllers on the MIP can each provide up to 24 T1 or 30 E1 channel-groups, with each channel-group presented to the system as a serial interface that can be configured individually.

MultiChannel Interface Processor   See *MIP*.

N

native client interface architecture   See *NCIA*.

NCIA   Native client interface architecture. SNA applications-access architecture developed by Cisco that combines the full functionality of native SNA interfaces at both the host and client with the flexibility of leveraging TCP/IP backbones. NCIA encapsulates SNA traffic on a client PC or workstation, thereby providing direct TCP/IP access while preserving the native SNA interface at the end-user level. In many networks, this capability obviates the need for a standalone gateway and can provide flexible TCP/IP access while preserving the native SNA interface to the host.

NetFlow   Network flow. A unidirectional sequence of packets between given source and destination endpoints. Network flows are highly granular: Flow endpoints are identified by IP address as well as by Transport layer application port numbers. (NetFlow also uses IP Protocol, ToS, and the input interface port to uniquely identify flows.)

Conventional Network layer switching handles incoming packets independently, with separate serial tasks for switching, security, services, and traffic measurements applied to each packet. With NetFlow switching, this process is applied only to the first packet of a flow. Information from the first packet is used to build an entry in the NetFlow cache. Subsequent packets in the flow are handled via a single streamlined task that handles switching, services, and data collection concurrently.

NETscout   Cisco network management application that provides an easy-to-use GUI for monitoring RMON statistics and protocol analysis information. NETscout also provides extensive tools that simplify data collection, analysis, and reporting. These tools allow system administrators to monitor traffic, set thresholds, and capture data on any set of network traffic for any segment.

NMP   Network Management Processor. Processor module on the Catalyst 5000 switch used to control and monitor the switch.

NSP   Network Service Point.

P

Physical layer interface module   See *PLIM*.

PLIM   Physical layer interface module. Interface that allows the AIP to a variety of physical layers, including TAXI and SONET multimode fiber-optic cable, SDH/SONET single-mode fiber cable, and E3 coaxial cable.

process switching   Operation that provides full route evaluation and per-packet load balancing across parallel WAN links. Involves the transmission of entire frames to the router CPU, where they are repackaged for delivery to or from a WAN interface, with the router making a route selection for each packet. Process switching is the most resource-intensive switching operation that the CPU can perform. Contrast with *fast switching*.

proxy polling Technique that alleviates the load across an SDLC network by allowing routers to act as proxies for primary and secondary nodes, thus keeping polling traffic off the shared links. Proxy polling has been replaced by SDLC Transport. See *SDLC Transport.*

R

Reliable SAP Update Protocol See *RSUP.*

Route Processor See *RP.*

Route/Switch Processor See *RSP.*

RP Route Processor. Processor module in the Cisco 7000 series routers that contains the CPU, system software, and most of the memory components that are used in the router. Sometimes called a supervisory processor.

RSP Route/Switch Processor. Processor module in the Cisco 7500 series routers that integrates the functions of the RP and the SP. See also *RP* and *SP.*

RSUP Reliable SAP Update Protocol. Bandwidth-saving protocol developed by Cisco for propagating services information. RSUP allows routers to reliably send standard Novell SAP packets only when the routers detect a change in advertised services. RSUP can transport network information either in conjunction with or independently of the Enhanced IGRP routing function for IPX.

S

SDLC broadcast Feature that allows a Cisco router that receives an all-stations broadcast on a virtual multidrop line to propagate the broadcast to each SDLC line that is a member of the virtual multidrop line.

SDLC Transport Cisco router feature with which disparate environments can be integrated into a single, high-speed, enterprise-wide network. Native SDLC traffic can be passed through point-to-point serial links with other protocol traffic multiplexed over the same links. Cisco routers can also encapsulate SDLC frames inside IP datagrams for transport over arbitrary (non-SDLC) networks. Replaces proxy polling. See also *proxy polling.*

SDLLC SDLC Logical Link Control. Cisco IOS feature that performs translation between SDLC and IEEE 802.2 type 2.

serial tunnel See *STUN.*

silicon switching Switching based on the SSE, which allows the processing of packets independent of the SSP system processor. Silicon switching provides high-speed, dedicated packet switching. See also *SSE* and *SSP.*

silicon switching engine See *SSE.*

Silicon Switch Processor See *SSP.*

SIP SMDS Interface Protocol. Used in communications between CPE and SMDS network equipment. Allows the CPE to use SMDS service for high-speed WAN internetworking. Based on the IEEE 802.6 DQDB standard. See also *DQDB*, in the "Internetworking Terms and Acronyms" section.

SP Switch Processor. Cisco 7000-series processor module that acts as the administrator for all CxBus activities. Sometimes called ciscoBus controller. See also *CxBus.*

SPAN Switched Port Analyzer. Feature of the Catalyst 5000 switch that extends the monitoring abilities of existing network analyzers into a switched Ethernet environment. SPAN mirrors the traffic at one switched segment onto a predefined SPAN port. A network analyzer attached to the SPAN port can monitor traffic from any of the other Catalyst switched ports.

SPNNI connection   Frame Relay connection between two VNSs in different areas or domains. The SPNNI connection gets its name from the proprietary Network-to-Network Interface protocol that operates over this connection.

SSE   Silicon switching engine. Routing and switching mechanism that compares the Data Link or Network layer header of an incoming packet to a silicon-switching cache, determines the appropriate action (routing or bridging), and forwards the packet to the proper interface. The SSE is directly encoded in the hardware of the SSP of a Cisco 7000 series router. It can therefore perform switching independently of the system processor, making the execution of routing decisions much quicker than if they were encoded in software. See also *silicon switching* and *SSP*.

SSP   Silicon Switch Processor. High-performance silicon switch for Cisco 7000 series routers that provides distributed processing and control for interface processors. The SSP leverages the high-speed switching and routing capabilities of the SSE to dramatically increase aggregate router performance, minimizing performance bottlenecks at the interface points between the router and a high-speed backbone. See also *silicon switching* and *SSE*.

STUN   Serial tunnel. Router feature allowing two SDLC- or HDLC-compliant devices to connect to one another through an arbitrary multiprotocol topology (using Cisco routers) rather than through a direct serial link.

supervisory processor   See *RP*.

Switch Processor   See *SP*.

T

TACACS+   Terminal Access Controller Access Control System Plus. Proprietary Cisco enhancement to Terminal Access Controller Access Control System (TACACS). Provides additional support for authentication, authorization, and accounting. See also *TACACS*, in the "Internetworking Terms and Acronyms" section.

THC over X.25   Feature providing TCP/IP header compression over X.25 links, for purposes of link efficiency.

TRIP   Token Ring Interface Processor. High-speed interface processor on the Cisco 7000 series routers. The TRIP provides two or four Token Ring ports for interconnection with IEEE 802.5 and IBM Token Ring media with ports independently set to speeds of either 4 or 16Mbps.

two-way simultaneous   See *TWS*.

TWS   Two-way simultaneous. Mode that allows a router configured as a primary SDLC station to achieve better utilization of a full-duplex serial line. When TWS is enabled in a multidrop environment, the router can poll a secondary station and receive data from that station while it sends data to or receives data from a different secondary station on the same serial line.

V

Versatile Interface Processor   See *VIP*.

VIP   *1.* Versatile Interface Processor. Interface card used in Cisco 7000 and Cisco 7500 series routers. The VIP provides multilayer switching and runs Cisco IOS. The most recent version of the VIP is VIP2. *2.* Virtual IP. Function that enables the creation of logically separated switched IP workgroups across the switch ports of a Catalyst 5000 running Virtual Networking Services software. See also *Virtual Networking Services*.

virtual IP   See *VIP*.

Virtual Networking Services   Software on some Catalyst 5000 switches that enables multiple workgroups to be defined across switches and offers traffic segmentation and access control.

VNS   See *Virtual Networking Services*.

W

WorkGroup Director   Cisco SNMP-based network-management software tool. WorkGroup Director runs on UNIX workstations either as a standalone application or integrated with another SNMP-based network management platform, providing a seamless, powerful management system for Cisco workgroup products. See also *SNMP*.

INTERNETWORKING INDUSTRY TERMS AND ACRONYMS

NUMERICS

10Base2   10Mbps baseband Ethernet specification using 50-ohm thin coaxial cable. 10Base2, which is part of the IEEE 802.3 specification, has a distance limit of 606.8 feet (185 meters) per segment. See also *Cheapernet*, *Ethernet*, *IEEE 802.3*, and *Thinnet*.

10Base5   10Mbps baseband Ethernet specification using standard (thick) 50-ohm baseband coaxial cable. 10Base5, which is part of the IEEE 802.3 baseband Physical layer specification, has a distance limit of 1640 feet (500 meters) per segment. See also *Ethernet* and *IEEE 802.3*.

10BaseF   10Mbps baseband Ethernet specification that refers to the 10BaseFB, 10BaseFL, and 10BaseFP standards for Ethernet over fiber-optic cabling. See also *10BaseFB*, *10BaseFL*, *10BaseFP*, and *Ethernet*.

10BaseFB   10Mbps baseband Ethernet specification using fiber-optic cabling. 10BaseFB is part of the IEEE 10BaseF specification. It is not used to connect user stations, but rather provides a synchronous signaling backbone that allows additional segments and repeaters to be connected to the network. 10BaseFB segments can be up to 1.24 miles (2000 meters) long. See also *10BaseF* and *Ethernet*.

10BaseFL   10Mbps baseband Ethernet specification using fiber-optic cabling. 10BaseFL is part of the IEEE 10BaseF specification and, although able to interoperate with FOIRL, is designed to replace the FOIRL specification. 10BaseFL segments can be up to 3280 feet (1000 meters) long if used with FOIRL, and up to 1.24 miles (2000 meters) if 10BaseFL is used exclusively. See also *10BaseF*, *Ethernet*, and *FOIRL*.

10BaseFP   10Mbps fiber-passive baseband Ethernet specification using fiber-optic cabling. 10BaseFP is part of the IEEE 10BaseF specification. It organizes a number of computers into a star topology without the use of repeaters. 10BaseFP segments can be up to 1640 feet (500 meters) long. See also *10BaseF* and *Ethernet*.

10BaseT   10Mbps baseband Ethernet specification using two pairs of twisted-pair cabling (Category 3, 4, or 5): one pair for transmitting data and the other for receiving data. 10BaseT, which is part of the IEEE 802.3 specification, has a distance limit of approximately 328 feet (100 meters) per segment. See also *Ethernet* and *IEEE 802.3*.

10Broad36   10Mbps broadband Ethernet specification using broadband coaxial cable. 10Broad36, which is part of the IEEE 802.3 specification, has a distance limit of 2.24 miles (3600 meters) per segment. See also *Ethernet* and *IEEE 802.3*.

100BaseFX   100Mbps baseband Fast Ethernet specification using two strands of multimode fiber-optic cable per link. To guarantee proper signal timing, a 100BaseFX link cannot exceed 1312 feet (400 meters) in length. Based on the IEEE 802.3 standard. See also *100BaseX*, *Fast Ethernet*, and *IEEE 802.3*.

100BaseT   100Mbps baseband Fast Ethernet specification using UTP wiring. Like the 10BaseT technology on which it is based, 100BaseT sends link pulses over the network segment when no traffic is present.

However, these link pulses contain more information than those used in 10BaseT. Based on the IEEE 802.3 standard. See also *10BaseT*, *Fast Ethernet*, and *IEEE 802.3*.

100BaseT4   100Mbps baseband Fast Ethernet specification using four pairs of Category 3, 4, or 5 UTP wiring. To guarantee proper signal timing, a 100BaseT4 segment cannot exceed 328 feet (100 meters) in length. Based on the IEEE 802.3 standard. See also *Fast Ethernet* and *IEEE 802.3*.

100BaseTX   100Mbps baseband Fast Ethernet specification using two pairs of either UTP or STP wiring. The first pair of wires is used to receive data; the second is used to transmit. To guarantee proper signal timing, a 100BaseTX segment cannot exceed 328 feet (100 meters) in length. Based on the IEEE 802.3 standard. See also *100BaseX*, *Fast Ethernet*, and *IEEE 802.3*.

100BaseX   100Mbps baseband Fast Ethernet specification that refers to the 100BaseFX and 100BaseTX standards for Fast Ethernet over fiber-optic cabling. Based on the IEEE 802.3 standard. See also *100BaseFX*, *100BaseTX*, *Fast Ethernet*, and *IEEE 802.3*.

100VG-AnyLAN   100Mbps Fast Ethernet and Token Ring media technology using four pairs of Category 3, 4, or 5 UTP cabling. This high-speed transport technology, developed by Hewlett-Packard, can operate on existing 10BaseT Ethernet networks. Based on the IEEE 802.12 standard. See also *IEEE 802.12*.

1822   Historic term that refers to the original ARPANET host-to-IMP interface. The specifications are in BBN report 1822. See also *host* and *IMP*.

24th channel signaling   See *A&B bit signaling*.

2B1Q   2 binary 1 quaternary. Encoding scheme that provides 2 bits per baud, 80 kbaud per second, 160Kbps transfer rate. The most common signaling method on ISDN U interfaces. This protocol is defined in detail in 1988 ANSI spec T1.601.

370 block mux channel   See *block multiplexer channel*.

4B/5B local fiber   4-byte/5-byte local fiber. Fiber channel physical media used for FDDI and ATM. Supports speeds of up to 100Mbps over multimode fiber. See also *TAXI 4B/5B*.

4-byte/5-byte local fiber   See *4B/5B local fiber*.

6BONE   The Internet's experimental IPv6 network.

8-byte/10-byte local fiber   See *8B/10B local fiber*.

802.x   Set of IEEE standards for the definition of LAN protocols.

822   Short form of RFC 822. Refers to the format of Internet style email as defined in RFC 822.

8B/10B local fiber   8-byte/10-byte local fiber. Fiber channel physical media that supports speeds up to 149.76Mbps over multimode fiber.

A

A&B bit signaling   Procedure used in T1 transmission facilities in which each of the 24 T1 subchannels devotes one bit of every sixth frame to the carrying of supervisory signaling information. Also called 24th channel signaling.

AAA   Authentication, authorization, and accounting (pronounced "triple a").

AAL   ATM adaptation layer. Service-dependent sublayer of the Data Link layer. The AAL accepts data from different applications and presents it to the ATM layer in the form of 48-byte ATM payload segments. AALs consist of two sublayers: CS and SAR. AALs differ on the basis of the source-destination timing used, whether they use CBR or VBR, and whether they are used for connection-oriented or connectionless mode data transfer. At present, the four types of AAL recommended by the ITU-T are AAL1, AAL2, AAL3/4, and AAL5. See also *AAL1*, *AAL2*, *AAL3/4*, *AAL5*, *ATM*, *ATM layer*, *CS*, and *SAR*.

AAL1 ATM adaptation layer 1. One of four AALs recommended by the ITU-T. AAL1 is used for connection-oriented, delay-sensitive services requiring constant bit rates, such as uncompressed video and other isochronous traffic. See also *AAL*.

AAL2 ATM adaptation layer 2. One of four AALs recommended by the ITU-T. AAL2 is used for connection-oriented services that support a variable bit rate, such as some isochronous video and voice traffic. See also *AAL*.

AAL3/4 ATM adaptation layer 3/4. One of four AALs (merged from two initially distinct adaptation layers) recommended by the ITU-T. AAL3/4 supports both connectionless and connection-oriented links, but is primarily used for the transmission of SMDS packets over ATM networks. See also *AAL*.

AAL5 ATM adaptation layer 5. One of four AALs recommended by the ITU-T. AAL5 supports connection-oriented VBR services and is used predominantly for the transfer of classical IP over ATM and LANE traffic. AAL5 uses SEAL and is the least complex of the current AAL recommendations. It offers low bandwidth overhead and simpler processing requirements in exchange for reduced bandwidth capacity and error-recovery capability. See also *AAL* and *SEAL*.

AARP AppleTalk Address Resolution Protocol. Protocol in the AppleTalk protocol stack that maps a data-link address to a network address.

AARP probe packets Packets transmitted by AARP that determine whether a randomly selected node ID is being used by another node in a nonextended AppleTalk network. If the node ID is not being used, the sending node uses that node ID. If the node ID is being used, the sending node chooses a different ID and sends more AARP probe packets. See also *AARP*.

ABM Asynchronous Balanced Mode. HDLC (and derivative protocol) communication mode supporting peer-oriented, point-to-point communications between two stations, in which either station can initiate transmission.

ABR *1.* Available bit rate. QoS class defined by the ATM Forum for ATM networks. ABR is used for connections that do not require timing relationships between source and destination. ABR provides no guarantees in terms of cell loss or delay, providing only best-effort service. Traffic sources adjust their transmission rate in response to information they receive describing the status of the network and its capability to successfully deliver data. Compare to *CBR, UBR,* and *VBR*. *2.* Area border router. Router located on the border of one or more OSPF areas that connects those areas to the backbone network. ABRs are considered members of both the OSPF backbone and the attached areas. They therefore maintain routing tables describing both the backbone topology and the topology of the other areas.

Abstract Syntax Notation One See *ASN.1*.

access list List kept by routers to control access to or from the router for a number of services (for example, to prevent packets with a certain IP address from leaving a particular interface on the router).

access method *1.* Generally, the way in which network devices access the network medium. *2.* Software within an SNA processor that controls the flow of information through a network.

access server Communications processor that connects asynchronous devices to a LAN or WAN through network and terminal emulation software. Performs both synchronous and asynchronous routing of supported protocols. Sometimes called a network access server. See also *communication server*.

access unit See *AU*.

accounting management One of five categories of network management defined by ISO for management of OSI networks. Accounting management subsystems are responsible for collecting network data relating to resource usage. See also *configuration management, fault management, performance management,* and *security management*.

ACD   Automatic call distribution. Device or service that automatically reroutes calls to customers in geographically distributed locations served by the same CO. See also *CO*.

ACELP   Algebraic code excited linear prediction.

ACF   Advanced Communications Function. A group of SNA products that provides distributed processing and resource sharing. See also *ACF/NCP*.

ACF/NCP   Advanced Communications Function/ Network Control Program. The primary SNA NCP. ACF/NCP resides in the communications controller and interfaces with the SNA access method in the host processor to control network communications. See also *ACF* and *NCP*.

ACK   See *acknowledgment*.

acknowledgment   Notification sent from one network device to another to acknowledge that some event (for example, receipt of a message) occurred. Sometimes abbreviated ACK. Compare to *NAK*.

ACR   Allowed cell rate. Parameter defined by the ATM Forum for ATM traffic management. ACR varies between the MCR and the PCR, and is dynamically controlled using congestion control mechanisms. See also *MCR* and *PCR*.

ACSE   Association control service element. OSI convention used to establish, maintain, or terminate a connection between two applications.

active hub   Multiported device that amplifies LAN transmission signals.

active monitor   Device responsible for managing a Token Ring. A network node is selected to be the active monitor if it has the highest MAC address on the ring. The active monitor is responsible for such management tasks as ensuring that tokens are not lost, or that frames do not circulate indefinitely. See also *ring monitor* and *standby monitor*.

ActiveX   Microsoft's Windows-specific, non-Java technique for writing applets. ActiveX applets take considerably longer to download than the equivalent Java applets; however, they more fully exploit the features of Windows 95. ActiveX is sometimes said to be a superset of Java. See also *applet* and *Java*.

AD   Administrative domain. Group of hosts, routers, and networks operated and managed by a single organization.

adapter   See *NIC*.

adaptive differential pulse code modulation   See *ADPCM*.

adaptive routing   See *dynamic routing*.

ADCCP   Advanced Data Communications Control Protocol. ANSI standard bit-oriented data link control protocol.

address   Data structure or logical convention used to identify a unique entity, such as a particular process or network device.

addressed call mode   Mode that permits control signals and commands to establish and terminate calls in V.25bis. See also *V.25bis*.

address mapping   Technique that allows different protocols to interoperate by translating addresses from one format to another. For example, when routing IP over X.25, the IP addresses must be mapped to the X.25 addresses so that the IP packets can be transmitted by the X.25 network. See also *address resolution*.

address mask   Bit combination used to describe which portion of an address refers to the network or subnet and which part refers to the host. Sometimes referred to simply as mask. See also *subnet mask*.

address resolution   Generally, a method for resolving differences between computer addressing schemes. Address resolution usually specifies a method for mapping Network layer (Layer 3) addresses to Data Link layer (Layer 2) addresses. See also *address mapping*.

Address Resolution Protocol   See *ARP*.

address translation gateway   See *ATG* in the "Cisco Systems Terms and Acronyms" section.

adjacency   Relationship formed between selected neighboring routers and end nodes for the purpose of exchanging routing information. Adjacency is based upon the use of a common media segment.

adjacent nodes   *1.* In SNA, nodes that are connected to a given node with no intervening nodes. *2.* In DECnet and OSI, nodes that share a common network segment (in Ethernet, FDDI, or Token Ring networks).

ADM   Add Drop Multiplexer. In OSS, a multiplexer that allows a signal to be added into or dropped out of a SONET span. See also *SONET*.

ADMD   Administration Management Domain. An X.400 Message Handling System public carrier. The ADMDs in all countries worldwide together provide the X.400 backbone. See also *PRMD*.

administrative distance   Rating of the trustworthiness of a routing information source. Administrative distance is often expressed as a numerical value between 0 and 255. The higher the value, the lower the trustworthiness rating.

Administrative Domain   See *AD*.

administrative weight   See *AW* and *PTSP*.

admission control   See *traffic policing*.

ADPCM   Adaptive differential pulse code modulation. Process by which analog voice samples are encoded into high-quality digital signals.

ADSL   Asymmetric digital subscriber line. One of four DSL technologies. ADSL is designed to deliver more bandwidth downstream (from the central office to the customer site) than upstream. Downstream rates range from 1.5 to 9Mbps, whereas upstream bandwidth ranges from 16 to 640Kbps. ADSL transmissions work at distances up to 18,000 feet (5,488 meters) over a single copper twisted pair. See also *HDSL*, *SDSL*, and *VDSL*.

ADSU   ATM data service unit. Terminal adapter used to access an ATM network via an HSSI-compatible device. See also *DSU*.

Advanced Communications Function   See *ACF*.

Advanced Communications Function/Network Control Program   See *ACF/NCP*.

Advanced CoS Management   Advanced Class-of-Service Management. Essential for delivering the required QoS to all applications. Cisco switches contain per-VC queuing, per-VC rate scheduling, multiple CoS queuing, and egress queuing. This enables network managers to refine connections to meet specific application needs. Formerly called FairShare and OptiClass.

Advanced Data Communications Control Protocol   See *ADCCP*.

Advanced Intelligent Network   See *AIN*.

Advanced Peer-to-Peer Networking   See *APPN*.

Advanced Program-to-Program Communication   See *APPC*.

Advanced Research Projects Agency   See *ARPA*.

Advanced Research Projects Agency Network   See *ARPANET*.

advertising   Router process in which routing or service updates are sent at specified intervals so that other routers on the network can maintain lists of usable routes.

AEP   AppleTalk Echo Protocol. Used to test connectivity between two AppleTalk nodes. One node sends a packet to another node and receives a duplicate, or echo, of that packet.

AFI   Authority and format identifier. Portion of an NSAP-format ATM address that identifies the type and format of the IDI portion of an ATM address. See also *IDI* and *NSAP*.

AFP   AppleTalk Filing Protocol. Presentation-layer protocol that allows users to share data files and application programs that reside on a file server. AFP supports AppleShare and Mac OS File Sharing.

agent   *1.* Generally, software that processes queries and returns replies on behalf of an application. *2.* In NMSs, process that resides in all managed devices and reports the values of specified variables to management stations.

AIN   Advanced Intelligent Network. In SS7, an expanded set of network services made available to the user, and under user control, that requires improvement in network switch architecture, signaling capabilities, and peripherals. See also *SS7.*

AIO   Asynchronous I/O.

AIP   See *AIP*, in the "Cisco Systems Terms and Acronyms" section.

AIS   Alarm indication signal. In a T1 transmission, an all-ones signal transmitted in lieu of the normal signal to maintain transmission continuity and to indicate to the receiving terminal that there is a transmission fault that is located either at, or upstream from, the transmitting terminal. See also *T1.*

alarm   SNMP message notifying an operator or administrator of a network problem. See also *event* and *trap.*

alarm indication signal   See *AIS.*

a-law   ITU-T companding standard used in the conversion between analog and digital signals in PCM systems. A-law is used primarily in European telephone networks and is similar to the North American mu-law standard. See also *companding* and *mu-law.*

algorithm   Well-defined rule or process for arriving at a solution to a problem. In networking, algorithms are commonly used to determine the best route for traffic from a particular source to a particular destination.

alias   See *entity.*

alignment error   In IEEE 802.3 networks, an error that occurs when the total number of bits of a received frame is not divisible by eight. Alignment errors are usually caused by frame damage due to collisions.

allowed cell rate   See *ACR.*

all-rings explorer packet   See *all-routes explorer packet.*

all-routes explorer packet   Explorer packet that traverses an entire SRB network, following all possible paths to a specific destination. Sometimes called all-rings explorer packet. See also *explorer packet, local explorer packet,* and *spanning explorer packet.*

ALO transaction   At-least-once transaction. ATP transaction in which the request is repeated until a response is received by the requester or until a maximum retry count is reached. This recovery mechanism ensures that the transaction request is executed at least once. See also *ATP.*

alternate mark inversion   See *AMI.*

AM   Amplitude modulation. Modulation technique whereby information is conveyed through the amplitude of the carrier signal. Compare to *FM* and *PAM.* See also *modulation.*

AMA   Automatic Messaging Accounting. In OSS, the automatic collection, recording, and processing of information relating to calls for billing purposes.

AMADNS   AMA Data Networking System. In OSS, the next generation Bellcore system for the collection and transport of AMA data from central office switches to a billing system. See also *AMA.*

AMATPS   AMA Teleprocessing System. In OSS, the Bellcore legacy system for collecting and transporting AMA data from central office switches to a billing system. The AMATPS consists of an AMA transmitter and a collector. See also *AMA.*

American National Standards Institute   See *ANSI.*

American Standard Code for Information Interchange   See *ASCII.*

AMI   Alternate mark inversion. Line-code type used on T1 and E1 circuits. In AMI, zeros are represented by 01 during each bit cell, and ones are represented by 11 or 00, alternately, during each bit cell. AMI requires that the sending device maintain ones density. Ones density is not maintained independent of the data stream. Sometimes called binary coded alternate mark inversion. Compare to *B8ZS*. See also *ones density*.

amplitude   Maximum value of an analog or a digital waveform.

amplitude modulation   See *AM*.

analog transmission   Signal transmission over wires or through the air in which information is conveyed through variation of some combination of signal amplitude, frequency, and phase.

anonymous FTP   Allows a user to retrieve documents, files, programs, and other archived data from anywhere on the Internet without having to establish a userid and password. By using the special userid of anonymous, the network user will bypass local security checks and will have access to publicly accessible files on the remote system. See also *FTP*.

ANSI   American National Standards Institute. Voluntary organization composed of corporate, government, and other members that coordinates standards-related activities, approves U.S. national standards, and develops positions for the United States in international standards organizations. ANSI helps develop international and U.S. standards relating to, among other things, communications and networking. ANSI is a member of the IEC and the ISO. See also *IEC* and *ISO*.

ANSI X3T9.5   See *X3T9.5*.

anycast   In ATM, an address that can be shared by multiple end systems. An anycast address can be used to route a request to a node that provides a particular service.

AOW   Asia and Oceania Workshop. One of the three regional OSI Implementors Workshops. See *EWOS*.

APaRT   See *ApaRT* in the "Cisco Systems Terms and Acronyms" section.

API   Application programming interface. Specification of function-call conventions that defines an interface to a service.

APNIC   Asia Pacific Network Information Center. Nonprofit Internet registry organization for the Asia Pacific region. The other Internet registries are currently IANA, RIPE NCC, and InterNIC.

Apollo Domain   Proprietary network protocol suite developed by Apollo Computer for communication on proprietary Apollo networks.

APPC   Advanced Program-to-Program Communication. IBM SNA system software that allows high-speed communication between programs on different computers in a distributed computing environment. APPC establishes and tears down connections between communicating programs, and consists of two interfaces: programming and data-exchange. The programming interface replies to requests from programs requiring communication; the data-exchange interface establishes sessions between programs. APPC runs on LU 6.2 devices. See also *LU 6.2*.

applet   Small program, often used in the context of a Java-based program, that is compiled and embedded in an HTML page. See also *ActiveX* and *Java*.

AppleTalk   Series of communications protocols designed by Apple Computer consisting of two phases. Phase 1, the earlier version, supports a single physical network that can have only one network number and be in one zone. Phase 2, supports multiple logical networks on a single physical network and allows networks to be in more than one zone. See also *zone*.

AppleTalk Address Resolution Protocol   See *AARP*.

AppleTalk Filing Protocol   See *AFP*.

AppleTalk Echo Protocol   See *AEP*.

AppleTalk Remote Access   See *ARA*.

AppleTalk Session Protocol   See *ASP.*

AppleTalk Transaction Protocol   See *ATP.*

AppleTalk Update-Based Routing Protocol   See *AURP.*

AppleTalk zone   See *zone.*

application   Program that performs a function directly for a user. FTP and Telnet clients are examples of network applications.

Application layer   Layer 7 of the OSI reference model. This layer provides services to application processes (such as email, file transfer, and terminal emulation) that are outside of the OSI model. The Application layer identifies and establishes the availability of intended communication partners (and the resources required to connect with them), synchronizes cooperating applications, and establishes agreement on procedures for error recovery and control of data integrity. Corresponds roughly with the Transaction Services layer in the SNA model. See also *Data Link layer, Network layer, Physical layer, Presentation layer, Session layer,* and *Transport layer.*

application programming interface   See *API.*

APPN   Advanced Peer-to-Peer Networking. Enhancement to the original IBM SNA architecture. APPN handles session establishment between peer nodes, dynamic transparent route calculation, and traffic prioritization for APPC traffic. Compare to *APPN+.* See also *APPC.*

APPN+   Next-generation APPN that replaces the label-swapping routing algorithm with source routing. Also called high-performance routing. See also *APPN.*

APS   Automatic protection switching. SONET switching mechanism that routes traffic from working lines to protect them in case of a line card failure or fiber cut.

ARA   AppleTalk Remote Access. Protocol that provides Macintosh users direct access to information and resources at a remote AppleTalk site.

Archie   System that provides lists of anonymous FTP archives. See also *Gopher, WAIS,* and *WWW.*

ARCnet   Attached Resource Computer Network. 2.5Mbps token-bus LAN developed in the late 1970s and early 1980s by Datapoint Corporation.

area   Logical set of network segments (CLNS-, DECnet-, or OSPF-based) and their attached devices. Areas are usually connected to other areas via routers, making up a single autonomous system. See also *autonomous system.*

area border router   See *ABR.*

ARIN   American Registry for Internet Numbers. Nonprofit organization established for the purpose of administrating and registrating IP numbers to the geographical areas currently managed by Network Solutions (InterNIC). Those areas include, but are not limited to, North America, South America, South Africa, and the Caribbean.

ARM   Asynchronous response mode. HDLC communication mode involving one primary station and at least one secondary station, in which either the primary or one of the secondary stations can initiate transmissions. See also *primary station* and *secondary station.*

ARP   Address Resolution Protocol. Internet protocol used to map an IP address to a MAC address. Defined in RFC 826. Compare to *RARP.* See also *proxy ARP.*

ARPA   Advanced Research Projects Agency. Research and development organization that is part of DoD. ARPA is responsible for numerous technological advances in communications and networking. ARPA evolved into DARPA, and then back into ARPA again (in 1994). See also *DARPA.*

ARPANET   Advanced Research Projects Agency Network. Landmark packet-switching network established in 1969. ARPANET was developed in the 1970s by BBN and funded by ARPA (and later DARPA). It eventually evolved into the Internet. The term ARPANET was officially retired in 1990. See also *ARPA, BBN, DARPA,* and *Internet.*

ARQ   Automatic repeat request. Communication technique in which the receiving device detects errors and requests retransmissions.

AS   See *autonomous system.*

ASBR   Autonomous system boundary router. ABR located between an OSPF autonomous system and a non-OSPF network. ASBRs run both OSPF and another routing protocol, such as RIP. ASBRs must reside in a nonstub OSPF area. See also *ABR, non-stub area,* and *OSPF.*

ASCII   American Standard Code for Information Interchange. 8-bit code for character representation (7 bits plus parity).

ASI   ATM service interface.

ASN.1   Abstract Syntax Notation One. OSI language for describing data types independent of particular computer structures and representation techniques. Described by ISO International Standard 8824. See also *BER (basic encoding rules).*

ASP   AppleTalk Session Protocol. Protocol that uses ATP to provide session establishment, maintenance, and teardown, as well as request sequencing. See also *ATP.*

assigned numbers   RFC [STD2] documents the currently assigned values from several series of numbers used in network protocol implementations. This RFC is updated periodically, and current information can be obtained from the IANA. If you are developing a protocol or application that will require the use of a link, socket, port, protocol, and so forth, contact the IANA to receive a number assignment. See also *IANA* and *STD.*

association control service element   See *ACSE.*

associative memory   Memory that is accessed based on its contents rather than on its memory address. Sometimes called content addressable memory (CAM).

AST   Automatic spanning tree. Function that supports the automatic resolution of spanning trees in SRB networks, providing a single path for spanning explorer frames to traverse from a given node in the network to another. AST is based on the IEEE 802.1 standard. See also *IEEE 802.1* and *SRB.*

ASTA   Advanced Software Technology and Algorithms. Component of the HPCC program intended to develop software and algorithms for implementation on high-performance computer and communications systems. See also *HPCC.*

async   Subset of tty.

Asynchronous Balanced Mode   See *ABM.*

asynchronous response mode   See *ARM.*

asynchronous time-division multiplexing   See *ATDM.*

Asynchronous Transfer Mode   See *ATM.*

asynchronous transmission   Term describing digital signals that are transmitted without precise clocking. Such signals generally have different frequencies and phase relationships. Asynchronous transmissions usually encapsulate individual characters in control bits (called start and stop bits) that designate the beginning and end of each character. Compare to *isochronous transmission, plesiochronous transmission,* and *synchronous transmission.*

ATCP   AppleTalk Control Protocol. Protocol that establishes and configures AppleTalk over PPP, as defined in RFC 1378. See also *PPP.*

ATDM   Asynchronous time-division multiplexing. Method of sending information that resembles normal TDM, except that time slots are allocated as needed rather than preassigned to specific transmitters. Compare to *FDM, statistical multiplexing,* and *TDM.*

ATG   See *ATG* in the "Cisco Systems Terms and Acronyms" section.

at-least-once transaction   See *ALO transaction.*

ATM Asynchronous Transfer Mode. International standard for cell relay in which multiple service types (such as voice, video, or data) are conveyed in fixed-length (53-byte) cells. Fixed-length cells allow cell processing to occur in hardware, thereby reducing transit delays. ATM is designed to take advantage of high-speed transmission media such as E3, SONET, and T3.

ATM adaptation layer See *AAL*.

ATM adaptation layer 1 See *AAL1*.

ATM adaptation layer 2 See *AAL2*.

ATM adaptation layer 3/4 See *AAL3/4*.

ATM adaptation layer 5 See *AAL5*.

ATM ARP server Device that provides address-resolution services to LISs when running classical IP over ATM. See also *LIS*.

ATM data service unit See *ADSU*.

ATM endpoint Point in an ATM network at which an ATM connection is initiated or terminated. ATM endpoints include ATM-attached workstations, ATM-attached servers, ATM-to-LAN switches, and ATM routers.

ATM Forum International organization jointly founded in 1991 by Cisco Systems, NET/ADAPTIVE, Northern Telecom, and Sprint that develops and promotes standards-based implementation agreements for ATM technology. The ATM Forum expands on official standards developed by ANSI and ITU-T, and develops implementation agreements in advance of official standards.

ATM Interface Processor See *AIP* in the "Cisco Systems Terms and Acronyms" section.

ATM layer Service-independent sublayer of the Data Link layer in an ATM network. The ATM layer receives the 48-byte payload segments from the AAL and attaches a 5-byte header to each, producing standard 53-byte ATM cells. These cells are passed to the Physical layer for transmission across the physical medium. See also *AAL*.

ATMM ATM management. Process that runs on an ATM switch that controls VCI translation and rate enforcement. See also *ATM* and *VCI*.

ATM management See *ATMM*.

ATM network See *ATM network* in the "Cisco Systems Terms and Acronyms" section.

ATM NIC See *ATM network interface card* in the "Cisco Systems Terms and Acronyms" section.

ATM service interface See *ASI*.

ATM UNI See *UNI*.

ATM user-user connection Connection created by the ATM layer to provide communication between two or more ATM service users, such as ATMM processes. Such communication can be unidirectional, using one VCC, or bidirectional, using two VCCs. See also *ATM layer*, *ATMM*, and *VCC*.

ATP AppleTalk Transaction Protocol. Transport-level protocol that provides a loss-free transaction service between sockets. The service allows exchanges between two socket clients in which one client requests the other to perform a particular task and to report the results. ATP binds the request and response together to ensure the reliable exchange of request-response pairs.

Attached Resource Computer Network See *ARCnet*.

attachment unit interface See *AUI*.

attenuation Loss of communication signal energy.

attribute Form of information items provided by the X.500 Directory Service. The directory information base consists of entries, each containing one or more attributes. Each attribute consists of a type identifier together with one or more values.

AU Access unit. Device that provides ISDN access to PSNs. See also *PSN*.

AUI Attachment unit interface. IEEE 802.3 interface between an MAU and a NIC. The term AUI can also refer to the rear panel port to which an AUI cable might attach. Also called transceiver cable. See also *IEEE 802.3*, *MAU*, and *NIC*.

AUP   Acceptable use policy. Many transit networks have policies that restrict the use to which the network may be put. Enforcement of AUPs varies with the network.

AURP   AppleTalk Update-Based Routing Protocol. Method of encapsulating AppleTalk traffic in the header of a foreign protocol, allowing the connection of two or more discontiguous AppleTalk internetworks through a foreign network (such as TCP/IP) to form an AppleTalk WAN. This connection is called an AURP tunnel. In addition to its encapsulation function, AURP maintains routing tables for the entire AppleTalk WAN by exchanging routing information between exterior routers. See also *AURP tunnel* and *exterior router*.

AURP tunnel   Connection created in an AURP WAN that functions as a single, virtual data link between AppleTalk internetworks physically separated by a foreign network (a TCP/IP network, for example). See also *AURP*.

AUSM   ATM user service module.

authentication   In security, the verification of the identity of a person or process.

authority zone   Associated with DNS, an authority zone is a section of the domain-name tree for which one name server is the authority. See also *DNS*.

Automated Packet Recognition/Translation   See *APaRT* in the "Cisco Systems Terms and Acronyms" section.

automatic call distribution   See *ACD*.

automatic call reconnect   Feature permitting automatic call rerouting away from a failed trunk line.

automatic protection switching   See *APS*.

automatic repeat request   See *ARQ*.

Automatic Routing Management   Formerly AutoRoute. Cisco WAN switches use a connection-oriented mechanism to provide connectivity across the network. The switches perform a connection admission control (CAC) function on all types of connections in the network. Distributed network intelligence enables the CAC function to automatically route and reroute connections over optimal paths, while guaranteeing the required QoS.

automatic spanning tree   See *AST*.

autonomous confederation   Group of autonomous systems that rely on their own network reachability and routing information more than they rely on that received from other autonomous systems or confederations.

autonomous switching   See *autonomous switching* in the "Cisco Systems Terms and Acronyms" section.

autonomous system   Collection of networks under a common administration sharing a common routing strategy. Autonomous systems are subdivided by areas. An autonomous system must be assigned a unique 16-bit number by the IANA. Sometimes abbreviated as AS. See also *area* and *IANA*.

autonomous system boundary router   See *ASBR*.

autoreconfiguration   Process performed by nodes within the failure domain of a Token Ring network. Nodes automatically perform diagnostics in an attempt to reconfigure the network around the failed areas. See also *failure domain*.

available bit rate   See *ABR*.

average rate   Average rate, in kilobits per second (Kbps), at which a given virtual circuit will transmit

AW   Administrative weight. Value set by the network administrator to indicate the desirability of a network link. One of four link metrics exchanged by PTSPs to determine the available resources of an ATM network.

B

B8ZS   Binary 8-zero substitution. Line-code type, used on T1 and E1 circuits, in which a special code is substituted whenever 8 consecutive zeros are sent over the link. This code is then interpreted at the remote end of the connection. This technique guarantees ones density independent of the data stream. Sometimes called bipolar 8-zero substitution. Compare to *AMI*. See also *ones density*.

backbone   Part of a network that acts as the primary path for traffic that is most often sourced from, and destined for, other networks.

back end   Node or software program that provides services to a front end. See also *client, front end*, and *server*.

backoff   The (usually random) retransmission delay enforced by contentious MAC protocols after a network node with data to transmit determines that the physical medium is already in use.

backplane   Physical connection between an interface processor or card and the data buses and the power distribution buses inside a chassis.

back pressure   Propagation of network congestion information upstream through an internetwork.

backward explicit congestion notification   See *BECN*.

backward learning   Algorithmic process used for routing traffic that surmises information by assuming symmetrical network conditions. For example, if node A receives a packet from node B through intermediate node C, the backward-learning routing algorithm will assume that A can optimally reach B through C.

balanced configuration   In HDLC, a point-to-point network configuration with two combined stations.

balanced, unbalanced   See *balun*.

balun   Balanced, unbalanced. Device used for matching impedance between a balanced and an unbalanced line, usually twisted-pair and coaxial cable.

bandwidth   Difference between the highest and lowest frequencies available for network signals. The term is also used to describe the rated throughput capacity of a given network medium or protocol.

bandwidth allocation   See *bandwidth reservation*.

bandwidth reservation   Process of assigning bandwidth to users and applications served by a network. Involves assigning priority to different flows of traffic based on how critical and delay-sensitive they are. This makes the best use of available bandwidth, and if the network becomes congested, lower-priority traffic can be dropped. Sometimes called bandwidth allocation. See also *call priority*.

Banyan VINES   See *VINES*.

BARRNet   Bay Area Regional Research Network. Regional network serving the San Francisco Bay Area. The BARRNet backbone is composed of four University of California campuses (Berkeley, Davis, Santa Cruz, and San Francisco), Stanford University, Lawrence Livermore National Laboratory, and NASA Ames Research Center. BARRNET is now part of BBN Planet. See also *BBN Planet*.

baseband   Characteristic of a network technology in which only one carrier frequency is used. Ethernet is an example of a baseband network. Also called narrowband. Contrast with *broadband*.

bash   Bourne-again shell. Interactive UNIX shell based on the traditional Bourne shell, but with increased functionality. See also *root account*.

basic encoding rules   See *BER*.

Basic Rate Interface   See *BRI*.

Basic Research and Human Resources   See *BRHR*.

baud   Unit of signaling speed equal to the number of discrete signal elements transmitted per second. Baud is synonymous with bits per second (bps) if each signal element represents exactly 1 bit.

Bay Area Regional Research Network   See *BARRNet.*

BBN   Bolt, Beranek, and Newman, Inc. High-technology company located in Massachusetts that developed and maintained the ARPANET (and later, the Internet) core gateway system. See also *BBN Planet.*

BBN Planet   Subsidiary company of BBN that operates a nationwide Internet access network composed in part by the former regional networks BARRNET, NEARNET, and SURAnet. See also *BARRNet, BBN, NEARNET,* and *SURAnet.*

Bc   Committed Burst. Negotiated tariff metric in Frame Relay internetworks. The maximum amount of data (in bits) that a Frame Relay internetwork is committed to accept and transmit at the CIR. See also *Be* and *CIR.*

B channel   Bearer channel. In ISDN, a full-duplex, 64Kbps channel used to send user data. Compare to *D channel, E channel,* and *H channel.*

BCP   Best Current Practices. The newest subseries of RFCs that are written to describe BCPs in the Internet. Rather than specifying a protocol, these documents specify the best ways to use the protocols and the best ways to configure options to ensure interoperability between various vendors' products.

BDCS   Broadband Digital Cross-Connect System. SONET DCS capable of cross-connecting DS-3, STS-1 and STS-3c signals. See also *DCS.*

Be   Excess Burst. Negotiated tariff metric in Frame Relay internetworks. The number of bits that a Frame Relay internetwork will attempt to transmit after Bc is accommodated. Be data is, in general, delivered with a lower probability than Bc data because Be data can be marked as DE by the network. See also *Bc* and *DE.*

beacon   Frame from a Token Ring or FDDI device indicating a serious problem with the ring, such as a broken cable. A beacon frame contains the address of the station assumed to be down. See also *failure domain.*

bearer channel   See *B channel.*

Because It's Time Networking Services   See *BITNET.*

BECN   Backward explicit congestion notification. Bit set by a Frame Relay network in frames traveling in the opposite direction of frames encountering a congested path. DTE receiving frames with the BECN bit set can request that higher-level protocols take flow control action as appropriate. Compare to *FECN.*

Bell Communications Research   See *Bellcore.*

Bellcore   Bell Communications Research. Organization that performs research and development on behalf of the RBOCs.

Bellman-Ford routing algorithm   See *distance vector routing algorithm.*

Bell operating company   See *BOC.*

BER   *1.* Bit error rate. Ratio of received bits that contain errors. *2.* Basic encoding rules. Rules for encoding data units described in the ISO ASN.1 standard. See also *ASN.1.*

Berkeley Internet Name Domain   See *BIND.*

Berkeley Standard Distribution   See *BSD.*

BERT   Bit error rate tester. Device that determines the BER on a given communications channel. See also *BER (bit error rate).*

best-effort delivery   Describes a network system that does not use a sophisticated acknowledgment system to guarantee reliable delivery of information.

BGP   Border Gateway Protocol. Interdomain routing protocol that replaces EGP. BGP exchanges reachability information with other BGP systems. It is defined by RFC 1163. See also *BGP4* and *EGP.*

BGP4   BGP Version 4. Version 4 of the predominant interdomain routing protocol used on the Internet. BGP4 supports CIDR and uses route aggregation mechanisms to reduce the size of routing tables. See also *BGP* and *CIDR*.

BICI   Broadband Inter-Carrier Interface. ITU-T standard that defines the protocols and procedures needed for establishing, maintaining, and terminating broadband switched virtual connections between public networks.

BIGA   See *BIGA* in the "Cisco Systems Terms and Acronyms" section.

big-endian   Method of storing or transmitting data in which the most significant bit or byte is presented first. Compare to *little-endian*.

binary   Numbering system characterized by ones and zeros (1 = on, 0 = off).

binary 8-zero substitution   See *B8ZS*.

binary coded alternate mark inversion   See *AMI*.

binary synchronous communication   See *BSC*.

binary synchronous communications protocol   See *bisync*.

BIND   Berkeley Internet Name Domain. Implementation of DNS developed and distributed by the University of California at Berkeley (United States). Many Internet hosts run BIND, and it is the ancestor of many commercial BIND implementations.

BinHex   Binary Hexadecimal. Method for converting binary files into ASCII for transmission by applications, such as email, that can only handle ASCII.

BIP   Bit interleaved parity. In ATM, a method used to monitor errors on a link. A check bit or word is sent in the link overhead for the previous block or frame. Bit errors in the payload can then be detected and reported as maintenance information.

biphase coding   Bipolar coding scheme originally developed for use in Ethernet. Clocking information is embedded into and recovered from the synchronous data stream without the need for separate clocking leads. The biphase signal contains no direct current energy.

bipolar   Electrical characteristic denoting a circuit with both negative and positive polarity. Contrast with *unipolar*.

bipolar 8-zero substitution   See *B8ZS*.

BISDN   Broadband ISDN. ITU-T communication standards designed to handle high-bandwidth applications such as video. BISDN currently uses ATM technology over SONET-based transmission circuits to provide data rates from 155 to 622 Mbps and beyond. Contrast with *N-ISDN*. See also *BRI, ISDN,* and *PRI*.

bisync   Binary Synchronous Communications Protocol. Character-oriented data-link protocol for applications.

bit   Binary digit used in the binary numbering system. Can be 0 or 1.

bit error rate   See *BER*.

bit error rate tester   See *BERT*.

bit interleaved parity   See *BIP*.

BITNET   "Because It's Time" Networking Services. Low-cost, low-speed academic network consisting primarily of IBM mainframes and 9600-bps leased lines. BITNET is now part of CREN. See also *CREN*.

BITNET III   Dial-up service providing connectivity for members of CREN. See also *CREN*.

bit-oriented protocol   Class of data link layer communication protocols that can transmit frames regardless of frame content. Compared with byte-oriented protocols, bit-oriented protocols provide full-duplex operation and are more efficient and reliable. Compare to *byte-oriented protocol*.

bit rate   Speed at which bits are transmitted, usually expressed in bits per second.

bits per second   Abbreviated bps.

black hole   Routing term for an area of the internetwork where packets enter, but do not emerge, due to adverse conditions or poor system configuration within a portion of the network.

blocking   In a switching system, a condition in which no paths are available to complete a circuit. The term is also used to describe a situation in which one activity cannot begin until another has been completed.

block multiplexer channel   IBM-style channel that implements the FIPS-60 channel, a U.S. channel standard. This channel is also referred to as OEMI channel and 370 block mux channel.

blower   Internal cooling fan used in larger router and switch chassis.

BLSR   Bidirectional Line Switch Ring. SONET ring architecture that provides working and protection fibers between nodes. If the working fiber between nodes is cut, traffic is automatically routed onto the protection fiber. See also *SONET*.

BNC connector   Standard connector used to connect IEEE 802.3 10Base2 coaxial cable to an MAU.

BNI   Broadband Network Interface.

BNM   Broadband Network Module.

BNN   Boundary network node. In SNA terminology, a subarea node that provides boundary function support for adjacent peripheral nodes. This support includes sequencing, pacing, and address translation. Also called boundary node.

BOC   Bell operating company. 22 local phone companies formed by the breakup of AT&T. See *RBOC*.

Bolt, Beranek, and Newman, Inc.   See *BBN*.

BOOTP   Bootstrap Protocol. Protocol used by a network node to determine the IP address of its Ethernet interfaces, in order to affect network booting.

boot programmable read-only memory   See *boot PROM*.

boot PROM   Boot programmable read-only memory. Chip mounted on a printed circuit board used to provide executable boot instructions to a computer device.

Bootstrap Protocol   See *BOOTP*.

border gateway   Router that communicates with routers in other autonomous systems.

Border Gateway Protocol   See *BGP*.

boundary function   Capability of SNA subarea nodes to provide protocol support for attached peripheral nodes. Typically found in IBM 3745 devices.

boundary network node   See *BNN*.

boundary node   See *BNN*.

BPDU   Bridge Protocol Data Unit. Spanning-Tree Protocol hello packet that is sent out at configurable intervals to exchange information among bridges in the network. See also *PDU*.

bps   Bits per second.

BPV   Bipolar violation.

BPX Service Node   See *BPX Service Node* in the "Cisco Systems Terms and Acronyms" section.

break-out/break-in   See *BOBI* in the "Cisco Systems Terms and Acronyms" section.

BRHR   Basic Research and Human Resources. Component of the HPCC program designed to support research, training, and education in computer science, computer engineering, and computational science. See also *HPCC*.

BRI Basic Rate Interface. ISDN interface composed of two B channels and one D channel for circuit-switched communication of voice, video, and data. Compare to *PRI*. See also *BISDN, ISDN,* and *N-ISDN*.

bridge Device that connects and passes packets between two network segments that use the same communications protocol. Bridges operate at the Data Link layer (Layer 2) of the OSI reference model. In general, a bridge will filter, forward, or flood an incoming frame based on the MAC address of that frame. See also *relay*.

bridge forwarding Process that uses entries in a filtering database to determine whether frames with a given MAC destination address can be forwarded to a given port or ports. Described in the IEEE 802.1 standard. See also *IEEE 802.1*.

bridge group Bridging feature that assigns network interfaces to a particular spanning-tree group. Bridge groups can be compatible with the IEEE 802.1 or the DEC specification.

bridge number Number that identifies each bridge in an SRB LAN. Parallel bridges must have different bridge numbers.

Bridge Protocol Data Unit See *BPDU*.

bridge static filtering Process in which a bridge maintains a filtering database consisting of static entries. Each static entry equates a MAC destination address with a port that can receive frames with this MAC destination address and a set of ports on which the frames can be transmitted. Defined in the IEEE 802.1 standard. See also *IEEE 802.1*.

broadband Transmission system that multiplexes multiple independent signals onto one cable. In telecommunications terminology, any channel having a bandwidth greater than a voice-grade channel (4 kHz). In LAN terminology, a coaxial cable on which analog signaling is used. Also called wideband. Contrast with *baseband*.

Broadband ISDN See *BISDN*.

broadcast Data packet that will be sent to all nodes on a network. Broadcasts are identified by a broadcast address. Compare to *multicast* and *unicast*. See also *broadcast address*.

broadcast address Special address reserved for sending a message to all stations. Generally, a broadcast address is a MAC destination address of all ones. Compare to *multicast address* and *unicast address*. See also *broadcast*.

broadcast and unknown server See *BUS*.

broadcast domain Set of all devices that will receive broadcast frames originating from any device within the set. Broadcast domains are typically bounded by routers because routers do not forward broadcast frames.

broadcast search Propagation of a search request to all network nodes if the location of a resource is unknown to the requester. See also *directed search*.

broadcast storm Undesirable network event in which many broadcasts are sent simultaneously across all network segments. A broadcast storm uses substantial network bandwidth and, typically, causes network time-outs.

brouter Concatenation of "bridge" and "router." Used to refer to devices that perform both bridging and routing functions.

browser GUI-based hypertext client application, such as Internet Explorer, Mosaic, and Netscape Navigator, used to access hypertext documents and other services located on innumerable remote servers throughout the WWW and Internet. See also *hypertext, Internet, Mosaic,* and *WWW*.

BSC Binary synchronous communication. Character-oriented Data Link layer protocol for half-duplex applications. Often referred to simply as bisync.

BSD Berkeley Standard Distribution. Term used to describe any of a variety of UNIX-type operating systems based on the UC Berkeley BSD operating system.

BT Burst tolerance. Parameter defined by the ATM Forum for ATM traffic management. For VBR connections, BT determines the size of the maximum burst of contiguous cells that can be transmitted. See also *VBR*.

BTW "By the way." One of many short-hand phrases used in chat sessions and email conversations. See *IMHO*.

buffer Storage area used for handling data in transit. Buffers are used in internetworking to compensate for differences in processing speed between network devices. Bursts of data can be stored in buffers until they can be handled by slower processing devices. Sometimes referred to as a packet buffer.

burst tolerance See *BT*.

BUS Broadcast and unknown server. Multicast server used in ELANs that is used to flood traffic addressed to an unknown destination and to forward multicast and broadcast traffic to the appropriate clients. See also *ELAN*.

bus *1.* Common physical signal path composed of wires or other media across which signals can be sent from one part of a computer to another. Sometimes called highway. *2.* See *bus topology*.

bus and tag channel IBM channel developed in the 1960s incorporating copper multiwire technology. Replaced by the ESCON channel. See also *ESCON channel* and *parallel channel*.

Bus Interface Gate Array See *BIGA* in the "Cisco Systems Terms and Acronyms" section.

bus topology Linear LAN architecture in which transmissions from network stations propagate the length of the medium and are received by all other stations. Compare to *ring topology*, *star topology*, and *tree topology*.

BX.25 An AT&T implementation of X.25. See also *X.25*.

BXM Broadband Switch Module.

bypass mode Operating mode on FDDI and Token Ring networks in which an interface has been removed from the ring.

bypass relay Allows a particular Token Ring interface to be shut down and thus effectively removed from the ring.

byte Term used to refer to a series of consecutive binary digits that are operated upon as a unit (for example, an 8-bit byte).

byte-oriented protocol Class of data-link communications protocols that uses a specific character from the user character set to delimit frames. These protocols have largely been replaced by bit-oriented protocols. Compare to *bit-oriented protocol*.

byte reversal Process of storing numeric data with the least-significant byte first. Used for integers and addresses on devices with Intel microprocessors.

C

cable Transmission medium of copper wire or optical fiber wrapped in a protective cover.

cable range Range of network numbers that is valid for use by nodes on an extended AppleTalk network. The cable range value can be a single network number or a contiguous sequence of several network numbers. Node addresses are assigned based on the cable range value.

cable television See *CATV*.

CAC Connection admission control. Set of actions taken by each ATM switch during connection setup in order to determine whether a connection's requested QoS will violate the QoS guarantees for established connections. CAC is also used when routing a connection request through an ATM network.

caching   Form of replication in which information learned during a previous transaction is used to process later transactions.

California Education and Research Federation Network   See *CERFnet*.

Call Detail Record   See *CDR* in the "Cisco Systems Terms and Acronyms" section.

call priority   Priority assigned to each origination port in circuit-switched systems. This priority defines the order in which calls are reconnected. Call priority also defines which calls can or cannot be placed during a bandwidth reservation. See also *bandwidth reservation*.

call reference value   See *CRV*.

call setup time   Time required to establish a switched call between DTE devices.

CAM   Content-addressable memory. See *associative memory*.

Canadian Standards Association   See *CSA*.

CAP   Competitive access provider. Independent company providing local telecommunications services mainly to business customers in competition with an area's BOC or IOC. Teleport and MFS are the two major CAPs operating in major metropolitan areas in the U.S. See also *BOC* and *IOC*.

carrier   Electromagnetic wave or alternating current of a single frequency, suitable for modulation by another, data-bearing signal. See also *modulation*.

Carrier Detect   See *CD*.

carrier sense multiple access collision detect   See *CSMA/CD*.

CAS   Channel associated signaling.

Category 1 cabling   One of five grades of UTP cabling described in the EIA/TIA-586 standard. Category 1 cabling is used for telephone communications and is not suitable for transmitting data.

Compare to *Category 2 cabling*, *Category 3 cabling*, *Category 4 cabling*, and *Category 5 cabling*. See also *EIA/TIA-586* and *UTP*.

Category 2 cabling   One of five grades of UTP cabling described in the EIA/TIA-586 standard. Category 2 cabling is capable of transmitting data at speeds up to 4Mbps. Compare to *Category 1 cabling*, *Category 3 cabling*, *Category 4 cabling*, and *Category 5 cabling*. See also *EIA/TIA-586* and *UTP*.

Category 3 cabling   One of five grades of UTP cabling described in the EIA/TIA-586 standard. Category 3 cabling is used in 10BaseT networks and can transmit data at speeds up to 10Mbps. Compare to *Category 1 cabling*, *Category 2 cabling*, *Category 4 cabling*, and *Category 5 cabling*. See also *EIA/TIA-586* and *UTP*.

Category 4 cabling   One of five grades of UTP cabling described in the EIA/TIA-586 standard. Category 4 cabling is used in Token Ring networks and can transmit data at speeds up to 16Mbps. Compare to *Category 1 cabling*, *Category 2 cabling*, *Category 3 cabling*, and *Category 5 cabling*. See also *EIA/TIA-586* and *UTP*.

Category 5 cabling   One of five grades of UTP cabling described in the EIA/TIA-586 standard. Category 5 cabling can transmit data at speeds up to 100Mbps. Compare to *Category 1 cabling*, *Category 2 cabling*, *Category 3 cabling*, and *Category 4 cabling*. See also *EIA/TIA-586* and *UTP*.

catenet   Network in which hosts are connected to diverse networks, which themselves are connected with routers. The Internet is a prominent example of a catenet.

CATV   Cable television. Communication system in which multiple channels of programming material are transmitted to homes using broadband coaxial cable. Formerly called Community Antenna Television.

CBAC   Context-Based Access Control. Protocol that provides internal users with secure access control for each application and for all traffic across network perimeters.

CBAC enhances security by scrutinizing both source and destination addresses and by tracking each application's connection status.

CBDS Connectionless Broadband Data Service. European high-speed, packet-switched, datagram-based WAN networking technology. Similar to SMDS. See also *SMDS*.

CBR Constant bit rate. QoS class defined by the ATM Forum for ATM networks. CBR is used for connections that depend on precise clocking to ensure undistorted delivery. Compare to *ABR (available bit rate)*, *UBR*, and *VBR*.

CCITT Consultative Committee for International Telegraph and Telephone. International organization responsible for the development of communications standards. Now called the ITU-T. See *ITU-T*.

CCR Commitment, Concurrency, and Recovery. OSI application service element used to create atomic operations across distributed systems. Used primarily to implement two-phase commit for transactions and nonstop operations.

CCS Common channel signaling. Signaling system used in telephone networks that separates signaling information from user data. A specified channel is exclusively designated to carry signaling information for all other channels in the system. See also *SS7*.

CD Carrier Detect. *1.* Signal that indicates whether an interface is active. *2.* Signal generated by a modem indicating that a call has been connected.

CDDI Copper Distributed Data Interface. Implementation of FDDI protocols over STP and UTP cabling. CDDI transmits over relatively short distances (about 100 meters), providing data rates of 100 Mbps using a dual-ring architecture to provide redundancy. Based on the ANSI TPPMD standard. Compare to *FDDI*.

CDF Channel Definition Format. Technology for "push" applications on the World Wide Web. CDF is an application of XML. See *XML*.

CDP See *CDP* in the "Cisco Systems Terms and Acronyms" section.

CDPD Cellular Digital Packet Data. Open standard for two-way wireless data communication over high-frequency cellular telephone channels. Allows data transmissions between a remote cellular link and a NAP. Operates at 19.2Kbps.

CDV Cell delay variation. Component of cell transfer delay, which is induced by buffering and cell scheduling. CDV is a QoS delay parameter associated with CBR and VBR service. See also *CBR* and *VBR*.

CDVT Cell delay variation tolerance. In ATM, a QoS parameter for managing traffic that is specified when a connection is set up. In CBR transmissions, CDVT determines the level of jitter that is tolerable for the data samples taken by the PCR. See also *CBR* and *PCR*.

CFRAD See *Cisco FRAD* in the "Cisco Systems Terms and Acronyms" section.

cell Basic data unit for ATM switching and multiplexing. Cells contain identifiers that specify the data stream to which they belong. Each cell consists of a 5-byte header and 48 bytes of payload. See also *cell relay*.

cell delay variation See *CDV*.

cell delay variation tolerance See *CDVT*.

cell loss priority See *CLP*.

cell loss ratio See *CLR*.

cell payload scrambling Technique using an ATM switch to maintain framing on some medium-speed edge and trunk interfaces.

cell relay Network technology based on the use of small, fixed-size packets, or cells. Because cells are fixed-length, they can be processed and switched in hardware at high speeds. Cell relay is the basis for many high-speed network protocols, including ATM, IEEE 802.6, and SMDS. See also *cell*.

cells per second Abbreviated cps.

cell transfer delay   See *CTD*.

Cellular Digital Packet Data   See *CDPD*.

cellular radio   Technology that uses radio transmissions to access telephone-company networks. Service is provided in a particular area by a low-power transmitter.

CELP   Code Excited Linear Prediction Compression. Algorithm used in low bit-rate voice encoding. Used in ITU-T Recommendations G.728, G.729, G.723.1.

central office   See *CO*.

Centrex   LEC service that provides local switching applications similar to those provided by an on-site PBX. With Centrex, there is no onsite switching; all customer connections go back to the CO. See also *CO* and *LEC (local exchange carrier)*.

CEPT   Conference Europenne des Postes et des Telecommunications. Association of the 26 European PTTs that recommends communication specifications to the ITU-T.

CER   Cell error ratio. In ATM, the ratio of transmitted cells that have errors to the total cells sent in a transmission for a specific period of time.

CERFnet   California Education and Research Federation Network. TCP/IP network, based in Southern California, that connects hundreds of higher-education centers internationally while also providing Internet access to subscribers. CERFnet was founded in 1988 by the San Diego Supercomputer Center and General Atomics, and is funded by the NSF.

CERN   European Laboratory for Particle Physics. Birthplace of the World Wide Web.

CERT   Computer Emergency Response Team. Chartered to work with the Internet community to facilitate its response to computer security events involving Internet hosts, to take proactive steps to raise the community's awareness of computer security issues, and to conduct research targeted at improving the security of existing systems. The U.S. CERT is based at Carnegie Mellon University in Pittsburgh (United States), Regional CERTs are, like NICs, springing up in different parts of the world.

CES   Circuit emulation service. Enables users to multiplex or concentrate multiple circuit emulation streams for voice and video with packet data on a single high-speed ATM link without a separate ATM access multiplexer.

CGI   Common Gateway Interface. Set of rules that describes how a Web server communicates with another application running on the same computer and how the application (called a CGI program) communicates with the Web server. Any application can be a CGI program if it handles input and output according to the CGI standard.

chaining   SNA concept in which RUs are grouped together for the purpose of error recovery.

Challenge Handshake Authentication Protocol   See *CHAP*.

channel   *1.* Communication path. Multiple channels can be multiplexed over a single cable in certain environments. *2.* In IBM, the specific path between large computers (such as mainframes) and attached peripheral devices.

channel-attached   Pertaining to attachment of devices directly by data channels (input/output channels) to a computer.

Channel Definition Format   See *CDF*.

Channel Interface Processor   See *CIP* in the "Cisco Systems Terms and Acronyms" section.

channel service unit   See *CSU*.

channelized E1   Access link operating at 2.048Mbps that is subdivided into 30 B-channels and 1 D-channel. Supports DDR, Frame Relay, and X.25. Compare to *channelized T1*.

channelized T1   Access link operating at 1.544Mbps that is subdivided into 24 channels (23 B-channels and 1 D-channel) of 64Kbps each. The individual channels or groups of channels connect to different destinations. Supports DDR, Frame Relay, and X.25. Also referred to as fractional T1. Compare to *channelized E1.*

CHAP   Challenge Handshake Authentication Protocol. Security feature supported on lines using PPP encapsulation that prevents unauthorized access. CHAP does not itself prevent unauthorized access; it merely identifies the remote end. The router or access server then determines whether that user is allowed access. Compare to *PAP.*

chat script   String of text that defines the login "conversation" that occurs between two systems. Consists of expect-send pairs that define the string that the local system expects to receive from the remote system and what the local system should send as a reply.

Cheapernet   Industry term used to refer to the IEEE 802.3 10Base2 standard or the cable specified in that standard. Compare to *Thinnet.* See also *10Base2, Ethernet,* and *IEEE 802.3.*

checksum   Method for checking the integrity of transmitted data. A checksum is an integer value computed from a sequence of octets taken through a series of arithmetic operations. The value is recomputed at the receiving end and compared for verification.

child peer group   Peer group for which another peer group is the parent peer group. See also *LGN, peer group,* and *parent peer group.*

choke packet   Packet sent to a transmitter to tell it that congestion exists and that it should reduce its sending rate.

CIA   Classical IP over ATM. Specification for running IP over ATM in a manner that takes full advantage of the features of ATM. Defined in RFC 1577.

CICNet   Regional network that connects academic, research, nonprofit, and commercial organizations in the Midwestern United States. Founded in 1988, CICNet was a part of the NSFNET and was funded by the NSF until the NSFNET dissolved in 1995. See also *NSFNET.*

CICS   Customer Information Control System. IBM application subsystem allowing transactions entered at remote terminals to be processed concurrently by user applications.

CID   Craft interface device. Terminal or PC-based interface that enables the performance of local maintenance operations.

CIDR   Classless interdomain routing. Technique supported by BGP4 and based on route aggregation. CIDR allows routers to group routes together in order to cut down on the quantity of routing information carried by the core routers. With CIDR, several IP networks appear to networks outside the group as a single, larger entity. With CIDR, IP addresses and their subnet masks are written as 4 octets, separated by periods, followed by a forward slash and a 2-digit number that represents the subnet mask. See also *BGP4.*

CIP   See *CIP* in the "Cisco Systems Terms and Acronyms" section.

CIR   Committed information rate. Rate at which a Frame Relay network agrees to transfer information under normal conditions, averaged over a minimum increment of time. CIR, measured in bits per second, is one of the key negotiated tariff metrics. See also *Bc.*

circuit   Communications path between two or more points.

circuit group   Grouping of associated serial lines that link two bridges. If one of the serial links in a circuit group is in the spanning tree for a network, any of the serial links in the circuit group can be used for load balancing. This load-balancing strategy avoids data ordering problems by assigning each destination address to a particular serial link.

circuit steering   Mechanism used by some ATM switches to eavesdrop on a virtual connection and copy its cells to another port where an ATM analyzer is attached. Also known as port snooping.

circuit switching   Switching system in which a dedicated physical circuit path must exist between sender and receiver for the duration of the "call." Used heavily in the telephone company network. Circuit switching can be contrasted with contention and token passing as a channel-access method, and with message switching and packet switching as a switching technique.

ciscoBus controller   See *SP* in the "Cisco Systems Terms and Acronyms" section.

Cisco Discovery Protocol   See *CDP* in the "Cisco Systems Terms and Acronyms" section.

Cisco FRAD   See *Cisco FRAD* in the "Cisco Systems Terms and Acronyms" section.

Cisco Frame Relay access device   See *Cisco FRAD* in the "Cisco Systems Terms and Acronyms" section.

CiscoFusion   See *CiscoFusion* in the "Cisco Systems Terms and Acronyms" section.

Cisco Internetwork Operating System software   See *Cisco IOS* in the "Cisco Systems Terms and Acronyms" section.

Cisco IOS   See *Cisco IOS* in the "Cisco Systems Terms and Acronyms" section.

Cisco Link Services   See *CLS* in the "Cisco Systems Terms and Acronyms" section.

Cisco Link Services Interface   See *CLSI* in the "Cisco Systems Terms and Acronyms" section.

CiscoView   See *CiscoView* in the "Cisco Systems Terms and Acronyms" section.

CIX   Commercial Internet Exchange. A connection point between the commercial Internet service providers (pronounced "kicks"). See *FIX* and *GIX*.

Class A station   See *DAS*.

Class B station   See *SAS (single attachment station)*.

classical IP over ATM   See *CIA*.

classless interdomain routing   See *CIDR*.

class of service   See *CoS*.

CLAW   Common Link Access for Workstations. Data Link layer protocol used by channel-attached RISC System/6000 series systems and by IBM 3172 devices running TCP/IP off-load. CLAW improves efficiency of channel use and allows the CIP to provide the unctionality of a 3172 in TCP/IP environments and support direct channel attachment. The output from TCP/IP mainframe processing is a series of IP datagrams that the router can switch without modifications.

Clear To Send   See *CTS*.

clear channel   Channel that uses out-of-band signaling (as opposed to in-band signaling), so the channel's entire bit rate is available.

CLEC   Competitive local exchange carrier. Company that builds and operates communication networks in metropolitan areas and provides its customers with an alternative to the local telephone company. See also *CAP*.

CLI   Command line interface. Interface that allows the user to interact with the operating system by entering commands and optional arguments. The UNIX operating system and DOS provide CLIs. Compare to *GUI*.

client   Node or software program (front-end device) that requests services from a server. See also *back end*, *front end*, and *server*.

client/server computing   Term used to describe distributed computing (processing) network systems in which transaction responsibilities are divided into two parts: client (front end) and server (back end). Both terms (client and server) can be applied to software programs or actual computing devices. Also called distributed computing (processing). Compare to *peer-to-peer computing*. See also *RPC*.

client-server model   Common way to describe network services and the model user processes (programs) of those services. Examples include the nameserver/ nameresolver paradigm of the DNS and fileserver/ file-client relationships such as NFS and diskless hosts.

CLNP   Connectionless Network Protocol. OSI Network layer protocol that does not require a circuit to be established before data is transmitted. See also *CLNS*.

CLNS   Connectionless Network Service. OSI Network layer service that does not require a circuit to be established before data is transmitted. CLNS routes messages to their destinations independently of any other messages. See also *CLNP*.

CLP   Cell loss priority. Field in the ATM cell header that determines the probability of a cell being dropped if the network becomes congested. Cells with CLP = 0 are insured traffic, which is unlikely to be dropped. Cells with CLP = 1 are best-effort traffic, which might be dropped in congested conditions in order to free up resources to handle insured traffic.

CLR   Cell loss ratio. In ATM, the ratio of discarded cells to cells that are successfully transmitted. CLR can be set as a QoS parameter when a connection is set up.

CLTP   Connectionless Transport Protocol. Provides for end-to-end Transport data addressing (via Transport selector) and error control (via checksum), but cannot guarantee delivery or provide flow control. The OSI equivalent of UDP.

cluster controller   *1.* Generally, an intelligent device that provides the connections for a cluster of terminals to a data link. *2.* In SNA, a programmable device that controls the input/output operations of attached devices. Typically, an IBM 3174 or 3274 device.

CMI   Coded mark inversion. ITU-T line coding technique specified for STS-3c transmissions. Also used in DS-1 systems. See also *DS-1* and *STS-3c*.

CMIP   Common Management Information Protocol. OSI network management protocol created and standardized by ISO for the monitoring and control of heterogeneous networks. See also *CMIS*.

CMIS   Common Management Information Services. OSI network management service interface created and standardized by ISO for the monitoring and control of heterogeneous networks. See also *CMIP*.

CMNS   Connection-Mode Network Service. Extends local X.25 switching to a variety of media (Ethernet, FDDI, Token Ring). See also *CONP*.

CMT   Connection management. FDDI process that handles the transition of the ring through its various states (off, active, connect, and so on), as defined by the ANSI X3T9.5 specification.

CO   Central office. Local telephone company office to which all local loops in a given area connect and in which circuit switching of subscriber lines occurs.

CO-IPX   Connection Oriented IPX. Native ATM protocol based on IPX under development by Novell.

coaxial cable   Cable consisting of a hollow outer cylindrical conductor that surrounds a single inner wire conductor. Two types of coaxial cable are currently used in LANs: 50-ohm cable, which is used for digital signaling, and 75-ohm cable, which is used for analog signaling and high-speed digital signaling.

CODEC   Coder-decoder. Device that typically uses pulse code modulation to transform analog signals into a digital bit stream and digital signals back into analog.

coded mark inversion   See *CMI*.

coder-decoder   See *CODEC*.

coding   Electrical techniques used to convey binary signals.

CO FRAD   Central office frame relay access device.

collapsed backbone Nondistributed backbone in which all network segments are interconnected by way of an internetworking device. A collapsed backbone might be a virtual network segment existing in a device such as a hub, a router, or a switch.

collision In Ethernet, the result of two nodes transmitting simultaneously. The frames from each device impact and are damaged when they meet on the physical media. See also *collision domain*.

collision detection See *CSMA/CD*.

collision domain In Ethernet, the network area within which frames that have collided are propagated. Repeaters and hubs propagate collisions; LAN switches, bridges and routers do not. See also *collision*.

command line interface See *CLI*.

Committed Burst See *Bc*.

committed information rate See *CIR*.

common carrier Licensed, private utility company that supplies communication services to the public at regulated prices.

common channel signaling See *CCS*.

Common Gateway Interface See *CGI*.

Common Link Access for Workstations See *CLAW*.

Common Management Information Protocol See *CMIP*.

Common Management Information Services See *CMIS*.

common part convergence sublayer See *CPCS*.

Common Programming Interface for Communications See *CPI-C*.

common transport semantic See *CTS*.

communication Transmission of information.

communication controller In SNA, a subarea node (such as an IBM 3745 device) that contains an NCP.

communication server Communications processor that connects asynchronous devices to a LAN or WAN through network and terminal emulation software. Performs only asynchronous routing of IP and IPX. Compare to *access server*.

communications line Physical link (such as wire or a telephone circuit) that connects one or more devices to one or more other devices.

community In SNMP, a logical group of managed devices and NMSs in the same administrative domain.

Community Antenna Television Now known as CATV. See *CATV*.

community name See *community string*.

community string Text string that acts as a password and is used to authenticate messages sent between a management station and a router containing an SNMP agent. The community string is sent in every packet between the manager and the agent. Also called a community name.

companding Contraction derived from the opposite processes of compression and expansion. Part of the PCM process whereby analog signal values are logically rounded to discrete scale-step values on a nonlinear scale. The decimal step number is then coded in its binary equivalent prior to transmission. The process is reversed at the receiving terminal using the same nonlinear scale. Compare to compression and expansion. See also *a-law* and *mu-law*.

complete sequence number PDU See *CSNP*.

Compressed Serial Link Internet Protocol See *CSLIP*.

compression The running of a data set through an algorithm that reduces the space required to store or the bandwidth required to transmit the data set. Compare to *companding* and *expansion*.

Computer Science Network See *CSNET*.

concentrator See *hub*.

Conference Europenne des Postes et des Telecommunications See *CEPT*.

configuration direct VCC In ATM, a bi-directional point-to-point VCC set up by a LEC to an LES. One of three control connections defined by Phase 1 LANE. Compare to *control distribute VCC* and *control direct VCC*.

configuration management One of five categories of network management defined by ISO for management of OSI networks. Configuration management subsystems are responsible for detecting and determining the state of a network. See also *accounting management, fault management, performance management,* and *security management*.

configuration register See *configuration register* in the "Cisco Systems Terms and Acronyms" section.

congestion Traffic in excess of network capacity.

congestion avoidance Mechanism by which an ATM network controls traffic entering the network to minimize delays. In order to use resources most efficiently, lower-priority traffic is discarded at the edge of the network if conditions indicate that it cannot be delivered.

congestion collapse Condition in which the retransmission of frames in an ATM network results in little or no traffic successfully arriving at the destination. Congestion collapse frequently occurs in ATM networks composed of switches that do not have adequate and effective buffering mechanisms complimented by intelligent packet discard or ABR congestion feedback mechanisms.

connection admission control See *CAC*.

connectionless Term used to describe data transfer without the existence of a virtual circuit. Compare to *connection-oriented*. See also *virtual circuit*.

Connectionless Broadband Data Service See *CBDS*.

Connectionless Network Protocol See *CLNP*.

Connectionless Network Service See *CLNS*.

connection management See *CMT*.

Connection-Mode Network Service See *CMNS*.

connection-oriented Term used to describe data transfer that requires the establishment of a virtual circuit. See also *connectionless* and *virtual circuit*.

Connection-Oriented Network Protocol See *CONP*.

CONP Connection-Oriented Network Protocol. OSI protocol providing connection-oriented operation to upper-layer protocols. See also *CMNS*.

CONS Connection-oriented network service.

console DTE through which commands are entered into a host.

constant bit rate See *CBR*.

Consultative Committee for International Telegraph and Telephone See *CCITT*.

content-addressable memory See *associative memory*.

contention Access method in which network devices compete for permission to access the physical medium. Compare to *circuit switching* and *token passing*.

Context-Based Access Control See *CBAC*.

control direct VCC In ATM, a bidirectional VCC set up by a LEC to a LES. One of three control connections defined by Phase 1 LANE. Compare to *configuration direct VCC* and *control distribute VCC*.

control distribute VCC In ATM, a unidirectional VCC set up from a LES to a LEC. One of three control connections defined by Phase 1 LANE. Typically, the VCC is a point-to-multipoint connection. Compare to *configuration direct VCC* and *control direct VCC*.

control point See *CP*.

convergence Speed and ability of a group of internetworking devices running a specific routing protocol to agree on the topology of an internetwork after a change in that topology.

convergence sublayer See *CS*.

conversation   In SNA, an LU 6.2 session between two transaction programs.

cookie   Piece of information sent by a Web server to a Web browser that the browser is expected to save and send back to the Web server whenever the browser makes additional requests of the Web server.

Cooperation for Open Systems Interconnection Networking in Europe   See *COSINE*.

Copper Distributed Data Interface   See *CDDI*.

COPS   Common Open Policy Service. Quality-of-service (QoS) policy exchange protocol proposed as an IETF standard for communicating network QoS policy information.

CORBA   Common Object Request Broker Architecture. OMG's answer to the need for interoperability among the rapidly proliferating number of hardware and software products available today. Simply stated, CORBA allows applications to communicate with one another no matter where they are located or who has designed them. See *IIOP*.

core gateway   Primary routers in the Internet.

core router   In a packet-switched star topology, a router that is part of the backbone and that serves as the single pipe through which all traffic from peripheral networks must pass on its way to other peripheral networks.

Corporation for Open Systems   See *COS*.

Corporation for Research and Educational Networking   See *CREN*.

CoS   Class of service. Indication of how an upper-layer protocol requires a lower-layer protocol to treat its messages. In SNA subarea routing, COS definitions are used by subarea nodes to determine the optimal route to establish a given session. A CoS definition comprises a virtual route number and a transmission priority field. Also called ToS.

COS   Corporation for Open Systems. Organization that promulgates the use of OSI protocols through conformance testing, certification, and related activities.

COSINE   Cooperation for Open Systems Interconnection Networking in Europe. European project financed by the EC to build a communication network between scientific and industrial entities in Europe. The project ended in 1994.

cost   Arbitrary value, typically based on hop count, media bandwidth, or other measures, that is assigned by a network administrator and used to compare various paths through an internetwork environment. Cost values are used by routing protocols to determine the most favorable path to a particular destination: the lower the cost, the better the path. Sometimes called path cost. See also *routing metric*.

count to infinity   Problem that can occur in routing algorithms that are slow to converge, in which routers continuously increment the hop count to particular networks. Typically, some arbitrary hop-count limit is imposed to prevent this problem.

CP   Control point. In SNA networks, element that identifies the APPN networking components of a PU 2.1 node, manages device resources, and provides services to other devices. In APPN, CPs are able to communicate with logically adjacent CPs by way of CP-to-CP sessions. See also *EN* and *NN*.

CPCS   Common part convergence sublayer. One of the two sublayers of any AAL. The CPCS is service-independent and is further divided into the CS and the SAR sublayers. The CPCS is responsible for preparing data for transport across the ATM network, including the creation of the 48-byte payload cells that are passed to the ATM layer. See also *AAL, ATM layer, CS, SAR,* and *SSCS*.

CPE   Customer premises equipment. Terminating equipment, such as terminals, telephones, and modems, supplied by the telephone company, installed at customer sites, and connected to the telephone company network.

CPI-C Common Programming Interface for Communications. Platform-independent API developed by IBM and used to provide portability in APPC applications. See also *APPC*.

CPP See *CPP (combinet proprietary protocol)* in the "Cisco Systems Terms and Acronyms" section.

cps Cells per second.

craft interface device See *CID*.

crankback A mechanism used by ATM networks when a connection setup request is blocked because a node along a selected path cannot accept the request. In this case, the path is rolled back to an intermediate node, which attempts to discover another path to the final destination using GCAC. See also *GCAC*.

CRC Cyclic redundancy check. Error-checking technique in which the frame recipient calculates a remainder by dividing frame contents by a prime binary divisor and compares the calculated remainder to a value stored in the frame by the sending node.

CREN Corporation for Research and Educational Networking. The result of a merger of BITNET and CSNET. CREN is devoted to providing Internet connectivity to its members, which include the alumni, students, faculty, and other affiliates of participating educational and research institutions, via BITNET III. See also *BITNET*, *BITNET III*, and *CSNET*.

CRM Cell rate margin. One of three link attributes exchanged using PTSPs to determine the available resources of an ATM network. CRM is a measure of the difference between the effective bandwidth allocation per traffic class as the allocation for sustainable cell rate.

cross talk Interfering energy transferred from one circuit to another.

CRV Call reference value. Number carried in all Q.931 (I.451) messages that provides an identifier for each ISDN call.

CS Convergence sublayer. One of the two sublayers of the AAL CPCS, which is responsible for padding and error checking. PDUs passed from the SSCS are appended with an 8-byte trailer (for error checking and other control information) and padded, if necessary, so that the length of the resulting PDU is divisible by 48. These PDUs are then passed to the SAR sublayer of the CPCS for further processing. See also *AAL*, *CPCS*, *SAR*, and *SSCS*.

CSA Canadian Standards Association. Agency within Canada that certifies products that conform to Canadian national safety standards.

CS-ACELP Conjugate Structure Algebraic Code Excited Linear Prediction. CELP voice compression algorithm providing 8Kbps, or 8:1 compression, standardized in ITU-T Recommendation G.729.

CSLIP Compressed Serial Link Internet Protocol. Extension of SLIP that, when appropriate, allows just header information to be sent across a SLIP connection, reducing overhead and increasing packet throughput on SLIP lines. See also *SLIP*.

CSMA/CD Carrier sense multiple access collision detect. Media-access mechanism wherein devices ready to transmit data first check the channel for a carrier. If no carrier is sensed for a specific period of time, a device can transmit. If two devices transmit at once, a collision occurs and is detected by all colliding devices. This collision subsequently delays retransmissions from those devices for some random length of time. CSMA/CD access is used by Ethernet and IEEE 802.3.

CSNET Computer Science Network. Large internetwork consisting primarily of universities, research institutions, and commercial concerns. CSNET merged with BITNET to form CREN. See also *BITNET* and *CREN*.

CSNP Complete sequence number PDU. PDU sent by the designated router in an OSPF network to maintain database synchronization.

CSU   Channel service unit. Digital interface device that connects end-user equipment to the local digital telephone loop. Often referred to together with DSU, as CSU/DSU. See also *DSU*.

CTD   Cell transfer delay. In ATM, the elapsed time between a cell exit event at the source UNI and the corresponding cell entry event at the destination UNI for a particular connection. The CTD between the two points is the sum of the total inter-ATM node transmission delay and the total ATM node processing delay.

CTI   Computer telephony integration. Name given to the merger of traditional telecommunications (PBX) equipment with computers and computer applications. The use of Caller ID to automatically retrieve customer information from a database is an example of a CTI application.

CTS   *1.* Clear To Send. Circuit in the EIA/TIA-232 specification that is activated when DCE is ready to accept data from DTE. *2.* Common transport semantic. Cornerstone of the IBM strategy to reduce the number of protocols on networks. CTS provides a single API for developers of network software and enables applications to run over APPN, OSI, or TCP/IP.

Customer Information Control System   See *CICS*.

customer premises equipment   See *CPE*.

cut-through packet switching   Packet switching approach that streams data through a switch so that the leading edge of a packet exits the switch at the output port before the packet finishes entering the input port. A device using cut-through packet switching reads, processes, and forwards packets as soon as the destination address is looked up and the outgoing port determined. Also known as on-the-fly packet switching. Compare to *store and forward packet switching*.

CxBus   See *CxBus* in the "Cisco Systems Terms and Acronyms" section.

Cyberspace   Term coined by William Gibson in his fantasy novel *Neuromancer* to describe the "world" of computers and the society that gathers around them.

Often used to refer to the Internet, the World Wide Web, or some combination thereof.

cycles per second   See *hertz*.

cyclic redundancy check   See *CRC*.

D

D4 framing   See *SF*.

DAC   Dual-attached concentrator. FDDI or CDDI concentrator capable of attaching to both rings of an FDDI or CDDI network. It can also be dual-homed from the master ports of other FDDI or CDDI concentrators.

DACS   Digital Access and Crossconnect System. AT&T's term for a digital crossconnect system.

DAP   Directory Access Protocol. Protocol used between a DUA and a DSA in an X.500 directory system. See also *LDAP*.

DARPA   Defense Advanced Research Projects Agency. U.S. Government agency that funded research for and experimentation with the Internet. Evolved from ARPA, and then, in 1994, back to ARPA. See also *ARPA*.

DARPA Internet   Obsolete term referring to the Internet. See *Internet*.

DAS   *1.* Dual attachment station. Device attached to both the primary and the secondary FDDI rings. Dual attachment provides redundancy for the FDDI ring: If the primary ring fails, the station can wrap the primary ring to the secondary ring, isolating the failure and retaining ring integrity. Also called a Class A station. Compare to *SAS*. *2.* Dynamically assigned socket. Socket that is dynamically assigned by DDP upon request by a client. In an AppleTalk network, the sockets numbered 128 to 254 are allocated as DASs.

DATABASE2   See *DB2*.

database object   Piece of information that is stored in a database.

data bus connector   See *DB connector.*

data channel   See *D channel.*

data circuit-terminating equipment   See *DCE.*

data communications equipment   See *DCE.*

Data Country Code   See *DCC.*

data direct VCC   In ATM, a bi-directional point-to-point VCC set up between two LECs. One of three data connections defined by Phase 1 LANE. Data direct VCCs do not offer any type of QOS guarantee, so they are typically used for UBR and ABR connections. Compare to *control distribute VCC* and *control direct VCC.*

Data Encryption Standard   See *DES.*

Data Exchange Interface   See *DXI.*

Data Flow Control layer   Layer 5 of the SNA architectural model. This layer determines and manages interactions between session partners, particularly data flow. Corresponds to the Session layer of the OSI model. See also *Data-Link Control layer, Path Control layer, Physical Control layer, Presentation Services layer, Transaction Services layer,* and *Transmission Control layer.*

datagram   Logical grouping of information sent as a Network layer unit over a transmission medium without prior establishment of a virtual circuit. IP datagrams are the primary information units in the Internet. The terms cell, frame, message, packet, and segment are also used to describe logical information groupings at various layers of the OSI reference model and in various technology circles.

Datagram Delivery Protocol   See *DDP.*

Datakit   AT&T proprietary packet switching system widely deployed by the RBOCs.

data-link connection identifier   See *DLCI.*

Data-Link Control layer   Layer 2 in the SNA architectural model. Responsible for the transmission of data over a particular physical link. Corresponds roughly to the Data-Link layer of the OSI model.

See also *Data Flow Control layer, Path Control layer, Physical Control layer, Presentation Services layer, Transaction Services layer,* and *Transmission Control layer.*

Data Link layer   Layer 2 of the OSI reference model. Provides reliable transit of data across a physical link. The Data Link layer is concerned with physical addressing, network topology, line discipline, error notification, ordered delivery of frames, and flow control. The IEEE divided this layer into two sublayers: the MAC sublayer and the LLC sublayer. Sometimes simply called Link layer. Roughly corresponds to the Data-Link Control layer of the SNA model. See also *Application layer, LLC, MAC, Network layer, Physical layer, Presentation layer, Session layer,* and *Transport layer.*

data-link switching   See *DLSw.*

data-link switching plus   See *DLSw+* in the "Cisco Systems Terms and Acronyms" section.

Data Movement Processor   See *DMP* in the "Cisco Systems Terms and Acronyms" section.

Data Network Identification Code   See *DNIC.*

data service unit   See *DSU.*

data set ready   See *DSR.*

data sink   Network equipment that accepts data transmissions.

data stream   All data transmitted through a communications line in a single read or write operation.

data terminal equipment   See *DTE.*

data terminal ready   See *DTR.*

DB2   IBM relational database management system.

dB   Decibels.

DB connector   Data bus connector. Type of connector used to connect serial and parallel cables to a data bus. DB connector names are in the format DB-x, where x represents the number of wires within the connector. Each line is connected to a pin on the connector, but in many cases, not all pins are assigned a function.

DB connectors are defined by various EIA/TIA standards.

DCA   Defense Communications Agency. U.S. Government organization responsible for DDN networks such as MILNET. Now called DISA. See also *DISA*.

DCC   Data Country Code. One of two ATM address formats developed by the ATM Forum for use by private networks. Adapted from the subnetwork model of addressing in which the ATM layer is responsible for mapping Network layer addresses to ATM addresses. Compare to *ICD*.

DCE   *1.* Data communications equipment (EIA expansion) *2.* Data circuit-terminating equipment (ITU-T expansion). Devices and connections of a communications network that comprise the network end of the user-to-network interface. The DCE provides a physical connection to the network, forwards traffic, and provides a clocking signal used to synchronize data transmission between DCE and DTE devices. Modems and interface cards are examples of DCE. Compare to *DTE*.

DCOM   Distributed Component Object Model. Protocol that enables software components to communicate directly over a network. Developed by Microsoft and previously called Network OLE, DCOM is designed for use across multiple network transports, including Internet protocols such as HTTP. See also *IIOP*.

DCS   Digital Crossconnect System. Network element providing automatic cross connection of a digital signal or its constituent parts.

D channel   *1.* Data channel. Full-duplex, 16Kbps (BRI) or 64Kbps (PRI) ISDN channel. Compare to *B channel*, *E channel*, and *H channel*. *2.* In SNA, a device that connects a processor and main storage with peripherals.

DCT   Discrete cosine transform.

DDM   Distributed data management. Software in an IBM SNA environment that provides peer-to-peer communication and file sharing. One of three SNA transaction services. See also *DIA* and *SNADS*.

DDN   Defense Data Network. U.S. military network composed of an unclassified network (MILNET) and various secret and top-secret networks. DDN is operated and maintained by DISA. See also *DISA* and *MILNET*.

DDP   Datagram Delivery Protocol. AppleTalk Network layer protocol that is responsible for the socket-to-socket delivery of datagrams over an AppleTalk internetwork.

DDR   Dial-on-demand routing. Technique whereby a router can automatically initiate and close a circuit-switched session as transmitting stations demand. The router spoofs keepalives so that end stations treat the session as active. DDR permits routing over ISDN or telephone lines using an external ISDN terminal adaptor or modem.

DE   Discard eligible. See also *tagged traffic*.

deadlock   *1.* Unresolved contention for the use of a resource. *2.* In APPN, when two elements of a process each wait for action by or a response from the other before they resume the process.

decibels   Abbreviated dB.

DECnet   Group of communications products (including a protocol suite) developed and supported by Digital Equipment Corporation. DECnet/OSI (also called DECnet Phase V) is the most recent iteration and supports both OSI protocols and proprietary Digital protocols. Phase IV Prime supports inherent MAC addresses that allow DECnet nodes to coexist with systems running other protocols that have MAC address restrictions. See also *DNA*.

DECnet routing   Proprietary routing scheme introduced by Digital Equipment Corporation in DECnet Phase III. In DECnet Phase V, DECnet completed its transition to OSI routing protocols (ES-IS and IS-IS).

decryption   Reverse application of an encryption algorithm to encrypted data, thereby restoring that data to its original, unencrypted state. See also *encryption*.

dedicated LAN   Network segment allocated to a single device. Used in LAN switched network topologies.

dedicated line   Communications line that is indefinitely reserved for transmissions, rather than switched as transmission is required. See also *leased line*.

de facto standard   Standard that exists by nature of its widespread use. Compare to *de jure standard*. See also *standard*.

default route   Routing table entry that is used to direct frames for which a next hop is not explicitly listed in the routing table.

Defense Advanced Research Projects Agency   See *DARPA*.

Defense Communications Agency   See *DCA*.

Defense Data Network   See *DDN*.

Defense Information Systems Agency   See *DISA*.

de jure standard   Standard that exists because of its approval by an official standards body. Compare to *de facto standard*. See also *standard*.

DEK   Data encryption key. Used for the encryption of message text and for the computation of message integrity checks (signatures).

delay   Time between the initiation of a transaction by a sender and the first response received by the sender. Also, the time required to move a packet from source to destination over a given path.

demand priority   Media access method used in 100VG-AnyLAN that uses a hub that can handle multiple transmission requests and can process traffic according to priority, making it useful for servicing time-sensitive traffic such as multimedia and video. Demand priority eliminates the overhead of packet collisions, collision recovery, and broadcast traffic typical in Ethernet networks. See also *100VG-AnyLAN*.

demarc   Demarcation point between carrier equipment and CPE.

demodulation   Process of returning a modulated signal to its original form. Modems perform demodulation by taking an analog signal and returning it to its original (digital) form. See also *modulation*.

demultiplexing   Separating of multiple input streams that were multiplexed into a common physical signal back into multiple output streams. See also *multiplexing*.

dense mode PIM   See *PIM dense mode*.

Department of Defense   See *DoD*.

Dependent LU   See *DLU*.

Dependent LU Requester   See *DLUR*.

Dependent LU Server   See *DLUS*.

DES   *1.* Data Encryption Standard. Standard cryptographic algorithm developed by the U.S. National Bureau of Standards. *2.* Destination end station.

designated bridge   Bridge that incurs the lowest path cost when forwarding a frame from a segment to the root bridge.

designated router   OSPF router that generates LSAs for a multiaccess network and has other special responsibilities in running OSPF. Each multiaccess OSPF network that has at least two attached routers has a designated router that is elected by the OSPF Hello protocol. The designated router enables a reduction in the number of adjacencies required on a multiaccess network, which in turn reduces the amount of routing protocol traffic and the size of the topological database.

destination address   Address of a network device that is receiving data. See also *source address*.

destination MAC   See *DMAC*.

destination service access point   See *DSAP*.

deterministic load distribution   Technique for distributing traffic between two bridges across a circuit group.

Guarantees packet ordering between source-destination pairs and always forwards traffic for a source-destination pair on the same segment in a circuit group for a given circuit-group configuration.

Deutsche Industrie Norm   See *DIN*.

Deutsche Industrie Norm connector   See *DIN connector*.

device   See *node*.

DHCP   Dynamic Host Configuration Protocol. Provides a mechanism for allocating IP addresses dynamically so that addresses can be reused when hosts no longer need them.

DIA   Document Interchange Architecture. Defines the protocols and data formats needed for the transparent interchange of documents in an SNA network. One of three SNA transaction services. See also *DDM* and *SNADS*.

dial backup   Feature that provides protection against WAN downtime by allowing the network administrator to configure a backup serial line through a circuit-switched connection.

dial-on-demand routing   See *DDR*.

dial-up line   Communications circuit that is established by a switched-circuit connection using the telephone company network.

differential encoding   Digital encoding technique whereby a binary value is denoted by a signal change rather than a particular signal level.

differential Manchester encoding   Digital coding scheme in which a mid-bit-time transition is used for clocking, and a transition at the beginning of each bit time denotes a zero. This coding scheme is used by IEEE 802.5 and Token Ring networks.

Diffusing Update Algorithm   See *DUAL* in the "Cisco Systems Terms and Acronyms" section.

Digital Network Architecture   See *DNA*.

digital signal level 0   See *DS-0*.

digital signal level 1   See *DS-1*.

digital signal level 3   See *DS-3*.

Dijkstra's algorithm   See *SPF*.

DIN   Deutsche Industrie Norm. German national standards organization.

DIN connector   Deutsche Industrie Norm connector. Multipin connector used in some Macintosh and IBM PC-compatible computers, and on some network processor panels.

directed search   Search request sent to a specific node known to contain a resource. A directed search is used to determine the continued existence of the resource and to obtain routing information specific to the node. See also *broadcast search*.

directed tree   Logical construct used to define data streams or flows. The origin of a data stream is the root. Data streams are unidirectional branches directed away from the root and toward targets, and targets are the leaves of the directed tree.

direct memory access   See *DMA*.

directory services   Services that help network devices locate service providers.

DISA   Defense Information Systems Agency. Formerly DCA. U.S. military organization responsible for implementing and operating military information systems, including the DDN. See also *DCA* and *DDN*.

discard eligible   See *tagged traffic*.

discovery architecture   APPN software that enables a machine configured as an APPN EN to automatically find primary and backup NNs when the machine is brought onto an APPN network.

discovery mode   Method by which an AppleTalk interface acquires information about an attached network from an operational node and then uses this information to configure itself. Also called dynamic configuration.

Distance Vector Multicast Routing Protocol   See *DVMRP*.

distance vector routing algorithm   Class of routing algorithms that iterate on the number of hops in a route to find a shortest-path spanning tree. Distance vector routing algorithms call for each router to send its entire routing table in each update, but only to its neighbors. Distance vector routing algorithms can be prone to routing loops, but are computationally simpler than link state routing algorithms. Also called Bellman-Ford routing algorithm. See also *link-state routing algorithm* and *SPF*.

distortion delay   Problem with a communication signal resulting from nonuniform transmission speeds of the components of a signal through a transmission medium. Also called group delay.

distributed computing (processing)   See *client/server computing*.

Distributed Data Management   See *DDM*.

Distributed Queue Dual Bus   See *DQDB*.

Distributed Relational Database Architecture   See *DRDA*.

DIT   Directory Information Tree. Global tree of entries corresponding to information objects in the OSI X.500 Directory.

DLCI   Data-link connection identifier. Value that specifies a PVC or SVC in a Frame Relay network. In the basic Frame Relay specification, DLCIs are locally significant (connected devices might use different values to specify the same connection). In the LMI extended specification, DLCIs are globally significant (DLCIs specify individual end devices). See also *LMI*.

DLSw   Data-link switching. Interoperability standard, described in RFC 1434, that provides a method for forwarding SNA and NetBIOS traffic over TCP/IP networks using Data Link layer switching and encapsulation.

DLSw uses SSP instead of SRB, eliminating the major limitations of SRB, including hop-count limits, broadcast and unnecessary traffic, timeouts, lack of flow control, and lack of prioritization schemes. See also *SRB* and *SSP (Switch-to-Switch Protocol)*.

DLSw+   See *DLSw+* in the "Cisco Systems Terms and Acronyms" section.

DLU   Dependent LU. LU that depends on the SSCP to provide services for establishing sessions with other LUs. See also *LU* and *SSCP*.

DLUR   Dependent LU Requester. Client half of the Dependent LU Requestor/Server enhancement to APPN. The DLUR component resides in APPN ENs and NNs that support adjacent DLUs by securing services from the DLUS. See also *APPN*, *DLU*, and *DLUS*.

DLUR node   In APPN networks, an EN or NN that implements the DLUR component. See also *DLUR*.

DLUS   Dependent LU Server. Server half of the Dependent LU Requestor/Server enhancement to APPN. The DLUS component provides SSCP services to DLUR nodes over an APPN network. See also *APPN*, *DLU*, and *DLUR*.

DLUS node   In APPN networks, a NN that implements the DLUS component. See also *DLUS*.

DMA   Direct memory access. Transfer of data from a peripheral device, such as a hard disk drive, into memory without that data passing through the microprocessor. DMA transfers data into memory at high speeds with no processor overhead.

DMAC   Destination MAC. The MAC address specified in the Destination Address field of a packet. Compare to *SMAC*. See also *MAC address*.

DMP   See *DMP* in the "Cisco Systems Terms and Acronyms" section.

DN   Distinguished Name. Global, authoritative name of an entry in the OSI Directory (X.500).

DNA Digital Network Architecture. Network architecture developed by Digital Equipment Corporation. The products that embody DNA (including communications protocols) are collectively referred to as DECnet. See also *DECnet*.

DNIC Data Network Identification Code. Part of an X.121 address. DNICs are divided into two parts: the first specifying the country in which the addressed PSN is located and the second specifying the PSN itself. See also *X.121*.

DNS Domain Name System. System used in the Internet for translating names of network nodes into addresses. See also *authority zone*.

DNSIX Department of Defense Intelligence Information System Network Security for Information Exchange. Collection of security requirements for networking defined by the U.S. Defense Intelligence Agency.

DOCSIS Data-over-Cable Service Interface Specifications. Defines technical specifications for equipment at both subscriber locations and cable operators' headends. Adoption of DOCSIS will accelerate deployment of data-over-cable services and ensure interoperability of equipment throughout system operators' infrastructures.

Document Interchange Architecture See *DIA*.

DoD Department of Defense. U.S. Government organization that is responsible for national defense. The DoD has frequently funded communication protocol development.

DoD Intelligence Information System Network Security for Information Exchange See *DNSIX*.

domain *1.* In the Internet, a portion of the naming hierarchy tree that refers to general groupings of networks based on organization-type or geography. *2.* In SNA, an SSCP and the resources it controls. *3.* In IS-IS, a logical set of networks.

Domain Networking system developed by Apollo Computer (now part of Hewlett-Packard) for use in its engineering workstations.

Domain Name System See *DNS*.

domain specific part See *DSP*.

dot address Refers to the common notation for IP addresses in the form n.n.n.n, where each number n represents, in decimal, 1 byte of the 4-byte IP address. Also called dotted notation or four-part dotted notation.

dotted decimal notation Syntactic representation for a 32-bit integer that consists of four 8-bit numbers written in base 10 with periods (dots) separating them. Used to represent IP addresses in the Internet as in 192.67.67.20. Also called dotted quad notation.

dotted notation See *dot address*.

downlink station See *ground station*.

downstream physical unit See *DSPU*.

DQDB Distributed Queue Dual Bus. Data Link layer communication protocol, specified in the IEEE 802.6 standard, designed for use in MANs. DQDB, which permits multiple systems to interconnect using two unidirectional logical buses, is an open standard that is designed for compatibility with carrier transmission standards, and is aligned with emerging standards for BISDN. SIP is based on DQDB. See also *MAN*.

DRAM Dynamic random-access memory. RAM that stores information in capacitors that must be periodically refreshed. Delays can occur because DRAMs are inaccessible to the processor when refreshing their contents. However, DRAMs are less complex and have greater capacity than SRAMs. See also *SRAM*.

DRDA Distributed Relational Database Architecture. IBM proprietary architecture.

drop Point on a multipoint channel where a connection to a networked device is made.

drop cable Cable that connects a network device (such as a computer) to a physical medium. A type of AUI. See also *AUI*.

DRP See *DRP* in the "Cisco Systems Terms and Acronyms" section.

DS-0 Digital signal level 0. Framing specification used in transmitting digital signals over a single channel at 64Kbps on a T1 facility. Compare to *DS-1* and *DS-3*.

DS-1 Digital signal level 1. Framing specification used in transmitting digital signals at 1.544Mbps on a T1 facility (in the United States) or at 2.108Mbps on an E1 facility (in Europe). Compare to *DS-0* and *DS-3*. See also *E1* and *T1*.

DS-1 domestic trunk interface See *DS-1/DTI*.

DS-1/DTI DS-1 domestic trunk interface. Interface circuit used for DS-1 applications with 24 trunks.

DS-3 Digital signal level 3. Framing specification used for transmitting digital signals at 44.736Mbps on a T3 facility. Compare to *DS-0* and *DS-1*. See also *E3* and *T3*.

DSA Directory System Agent. Software that provides the X.500 Directory Service for a portion of the directory information base. Generally, each DSA is responsible for the directory information for a single organization or organizational unit.

DSAP Destination service access point. SAP of the network node designated in the Destination field of a packet. Compare to *SSAP*. See also *SAP (service access point)*.

DSL Digital subscriber line. Public network technology that delivers high bandwidth over conventional copper wiring at limited distances. There are four types of DSL: ADSL, HDSL, SDSL, and VDSL. All are provisioned via modem pairs, with one modem located at a central office and the other at the customer site. Because most DSL technologies do not use the whole bandwidth of the twisted pair, there is room remaining for a voice channel. See also *ADSL, HDSL, SDSL,* and *VDSL*.

DSP Domain specific part. Part of an NSAP-format ATM address that contains an area identifier, a station identifier, and a selector byte. See also *NSAP*.

DSPU Downstream physical unit. In SNA, a PU that is located downstream from the host. See also *DSPU concentration* in the "Cisco Systems Terms and Acronyms" section.

DSPU concentration See *DSPU concentration* in the "Cisco Systems Terms and Acronyms" section.

DSR Data set ready. EIA/TIA-232 interface circuit that is activated when DCE is powered up and ready for use.

DSU Data service unit. Device used in digital transmission that adapts the physical interface on a DTE device to a transmission facility such as T1 or E1. The DSU is also responsible for such functions as signal timing. Often referred to together with CSU, as CSU/DSU. See also *CSU*.

DSX-1 Crossconnection point for DS-1 signals.

DTE Data terminal equipment. Device at the user end of a user-network interface that serves as a data source, destination, or both. DTE connects to a data network through a DCE device (for example, a modem) and typically uses clocking signals generated by the DCE. DTE includes such devices as computers, protocol translators, and multiplexers. Compare to *DCE*.

DTL Designated transit list. List of nodes and optional link IDs that completely specify a path across a single PNNI peer group.

DTMF Dual tone multifrequency. Use of two simultaneous voice-band tones for dialing (such as touch tone).

DTR Data terminal ready. EIA/TIA-232 circuit that is activated to let the DCE know when the DTE is ready to send and receive data.

DUA Directory User Agent. Software that accesses the X.500 Directory Service on behalf of the directory user. The directory user may be a person or another software element.

DUAL   See *DUAL* in the "Cisco Systems Terms and Acronyms" section.

dual-attached concentrator   See *DAC.*

dual attachment station   See *DAS.*

dual counter-rotating rings   Network topology in which two signal paths, whose directions are opposite each other, exist in a token-passing network. FDDI and CDDI are based on this concept.

dual-homed station   Device attached to multiple FDDI rings to provide redundancy.

dual homing   Network topology in which a device is connected to the network by way of two independent access points (points of attachment). One access point is the primary connection, and the other is a standby connection that is activated in the event of a failure of the primary connection.

Dual IS-IS   See *Integrated IS-IS.*

dual tone multifrequency   See *DTMF.*

DVMRP   Distance Vector Multicast Routing Protocol. Internetwork gateway protocol, largely based on RIP, that implements a typical dense mode IP multicast scheme. DVMRP uses IGMP to exchange routing datagrams with its neighbors. See also *IGMP.*

DXI   Data Exchange Interface. ATM Forum specification, described in RFC 1483, that defines how a network device such as a bridge, router, or hub can effectively act as an FEP to an ATM network by interfacing with a special DSU that performs packet segmentation and reassembly.

dynamic adaptive routing   Automatic rerouting of traffic based on a sensing and analysis of current actual network conditions, not including cases of routing decisions taken on predefined information.

dynamic address resolution   Use of an address resolution protocol to determine and store address information on demand.

Dynamic Buffer Management   Frame Relay and ATM service modules are equipped with large buffers and the patented Dynamic Buffer Management scheme for allocating and scaling traffic entering or leaving a node on a per-VC basis. The WAN switch dynamically assigns buffers to individual virtual circuits based upon the amount of traffic present and service-level agreements. This deep pool of available buffers readily accommodates large bursts of traffic into the node.

dynamic configuration   See *discovery mode.*

Dynamic IISP   Dynamic Interim-Interswitch Signaling Protocol. Basic call routing protocol that automatically reroutes ATM connections in the event of link failures. Dynamic IISP is an interim solution until PNNI Phase 1 is completed. Contrast with *IISP.*

dynamic random-access memory   See *DRAM.*

dynamic routing   Routing that adjusts automatically to network topology or traffic changes. Also called adaptive routing.

E

E1   Wide-area digital transmission scheme used predominantly in Europe that carries data at a rate of 2.048 Mbps. E1 lines can be leased for private use from common carriers. Compare to *T1.* See also *DS-1.*

E.164   *1.* ITU-T recommendation for international telecommunication numbering, especially in ISDN, BISDN, and SMDS. An evolution of standard telephone numbers. *2.* Name of the field in an ATM address that contains numbers in E.164 format.

E2A   Legacy protocols for providing OAM&P functions between a network element and an operations support system. See also *OAM&P.*

E3   Wide-area digital transmission scheme used predominantly in Europe that carries data at a rate of 34.368 Mbps. E3 lines can be leased for private use from common carriers. Compare to *T3.* See also *DS-3.*

early packet discard   See *EPD*.

early token release   Technique used in Token Ring networks that allows a station to release a new token onto the ring immediately after transmitting, instead of waiting for the first frame to return. This feature can increase the total bandwidth on the ring. See also *Token Ring*.

EARN   European Academic Research Network. European network connecting universities and research institutes. EARN merged with RARE to form TERENA. See also *RARE* and *TERENA*.

EBCDIC   Extended Binary Coded Decimal Interchange Code. Any of a number of coded character sets developed by IBM consisting of 8-bit coded characters. This character code is used by older IBM systems and telex machines. Compare to *ASCII*.

EBONE   European Backbone. Pan-European network backbone service.

EC   European Community.

E channel   Echo channel. 64Kbps ISDN circuit-switching control channel. The E channel was defined in the 1984 ITU-T ISDN specification, but was dropped in the 1988 specification. Compare to *B channel*, *D channel*, and *H channel*.

echo channel   See *E channel*.

echoplex   Mode in which keyboard characters are echoed on a terminal screen upon return of a signal from the other end of the line indicating that the characters were received correctly.

ECMA   European Computer Manufacturers Association. Group of European computer vendors who have done substantial OSI standardization work.

edge device   *1.* Physical device that is capable of forwarding packets between legacy interfaces (such as Ethernet and Token Ring) and ATM interfaces based on Data Link and Network layer information.

An edge device does not participate in the running of any Network layer routing protocol, but it obtains forwarding descriptions using the route distribution protocol. *2.* Any device that is not an ATM switch that can connect to an ATM switch.

EDI   Electronic data interchange. Electronic communication of operational data such as orders and invoices between organizations.

EDIFACT   Electronic Data Interchange for Administration, Commerce, and Transport. Data exchange standard administered by the United Nations to be a multi-industry EDI standard.

EEPROM   Electrically erasable programmable read-only memory. EPROM that can be erased using electrical signals applied to specific pins. See also *EPROM*.

EFCI   Explicit Forward Congestion Indication. In ATM, one of the congestion feedback modes allowed by ABR service. A network element in an impending congestion state or in a congested state can set the EFCI. The destination end-system can implement a protocol that adaptively lowers the cell rate of the connection based on the value of the EFCI. See also *ABR*.

EFF   Electronic Frontier Foundation. Foundation established to address social and legal issues arising from the impact on society of the increasingly pervasive use of computers as the means of communication and information distribution.

EGP   Exterior Gateway Protocol. Internet protocol for exchanging routing information between autonomous systems. Documented in RFC 904. Not to be confused with the general term exterior gateway protocol. EGP is an obsolete protocol that was replaced by BGP. See also *BGP*.

EIA   Electronic Industries Association. Group that specifies electrical transmission standards. The EIA and TIA have developed numerous well-known communications standards, including EIA/TIA-232 and EIA/TIA-449. See also *TIA*.

EIA-530 Refers to two electrical implementations of EIA/TIA-449: RS-422 (for balanced transmission) and RS-423 (for unbalanced transmission). See also *RS-422*, *RS-423*, and *EIA/TIA-449*.

EIA/TIA-232 Common Physical layer interface standard, developed by EIA and TIA, that supports unbalanced circuits at signal speeds of up to 64 Kbps. Closely resembles the V.24 specification. Formerly called as RS-232.

EIA/TIA-449 Popular Physical layer interface developed by EIA and TIA. Essentially, a faster (up to 2Mbps) version of EIA/TIA-232 capable of longer cable runs. Formerly called RS-449. See also *EIA-530*.

EIA/TIA-586 Standard that describes the characteristics and applications for various grades of UTP cabling. See also *Category 1 cabling*, *Category 2 cabling*, *Category 3 cabling*, *Category 4 cabling*, *Category 5 cabling*, and *UTC*.

EIGRP See *Enhanced IGRP* in the "Cisco Systems Terms and Acronyms" section.

EIP See *EIP* in the "Cisco Systems Terms and Acronyms" section.

EISA Extended Industry-Standard Architecture. 32-bit bus interface used in PCs, PC-based servers, and some UNIX workstations and servers. See also *ISA*.

ELAN Emulated LAN. ATM network in which an Ethernet or Token Ring LAN is emulated using a client-server model. ELANs are composed of an LEC, an LES, a BUS, and an LECS. Multiple ELANs can exist simultaneously on a single ATM network. ELANs are defined by the LANE specification. See also *BUS*, *LANE*, *LEC (LAN emulation client)*, *LECS*, and *LES*.

ELAP EtherTalk Link Access Protocol. Link-access protocol used in an EtherTalk network. ELAP is built on top of the standard Ethernet Data Link layer.

electrically erasable programmable read-only memory See *EEPROM*.

electromagnetic interference See *EMI*.

electromagnetic pulse See *EMP*.

electronic data interchange See *EDI*.

Electronic Data Interchange for Administration, Commerce, and Transport See *EDIFACT*.

Electronic Frontier Foundation See *EFF*.

Electronic Industries Association See *EIA*.

electronic mail See *email*.

Electronic Messaging Association See *EMA*.

electrostatic discharge See *ESD*.

ELMI Enhanced Local Management Interface.

EMA *1.* Enterprise Management Architecture. Digital Equipment Corporation network management architecture, based on the OSI network management model. *2.* Electronic Messaging Association. Forum devoted to standards and policy work, education, and development of electronic messaging systems such as email, voice mail, and facsimile.

email Electronic mail. Widely used network application in which text messages are transmitted electronically between end users over various types of networks using various network protocols.

EMI Electromagnetic interference. Interference by electromagnetic signals that can cause reduced data integrity and increased error rates on transmission channels.

EMIF ESCON Multiple Image Facility. Mainframe I/O software function that allows one ESCON channel to be shared among multiple logical partitions on the same mainframe. See also *ESCON*.

EMP Electromagnetic pulse. Caused by lightning and other high-energy phenomena. Capable of coupling enough energy into unshielded conductors to destroy electronic devices. See also *Tempest*.

emulated LAN See *ELAN*.

emulation mode Function of an NCP that enables it to perform activities equivalent to those performed by a transmission control unit.

EN End node. APPN end system that implements the PU 2.1, provides end-user services, and supports sessions between local and remote CPs. ENs are not capable of routing traffic and rely on an adjacent NN for APPN services. Compare to *NN*. See also *CP*.

encapsulation Wrapping of data in a particular protocol header. For example, Ethernet data is wrapped in a specific Ethernet header before network transit. Also, when bridging dissimilar networks, the entire frame from one network is simply placed in the header used by the Data Link layer protocol of the other network. See also *tunneling*.

encapsulation bridging Carries Ethernet frames from one router to another across disparate media, such as serial and FDDI lines. Contrast with *translational bridging*.

encoder Device that modifies information into the required transmission format.

encryption Application of a specific algorithm to data so as to alter the appearance of the data making it incomprehensible to those who are not authorized to see the information. See also *decryption*.

end node See *EN*.

end of transmission See *EOT*.

end point Device at which a virtual circuit or virtual path begins or ends.

end system See *ES*.

End System-to-Intermediate System See *ES-IS*.

Energy Sciences Network See *ESnet*.

Enhanced IGRP See *Enhanced IGRP* in the "Cisco Systems Terms and Acronyms" section.

Enhanced Interior Gateway Routing Protocol See *Enhanced IGRP* in the "Cisco Systems Terms and Acronyms" section.

Enhanced Monitoring Services See *Enhanced Monitoring Services* in the "Cisco Systems Terms and Acronyms" section.

Enterprise Management Architecture See *EMA*.

enterprise network Large and diverse network connecting most major points in a company or other organization. Differs from a WAN in that it is privately owned and maintained.

Enterprise System Connection See *ESCON*.

Enterprise System Connection channel See *ESCON channel*.

entity Generally, an individual, manageable network device. Sometimes called an alias.

entity identifier The unique address of an NVEs socket in a node on an AppleTalk network. The specific format of an entity identifier is network-dependent. See also *NVE*.

entity name Name that an NVE can assign to itself. Although not all NVEs have names, NVEs can possess several names (or aliases). An entity name is made up of three character strings: object, entity type, and zone. For example: Bldg 2 LaserJet 5:LaserWriter@Bldg 2 Zone. See also *NVE*.

entity type Part of an entity name that describes the entity's class. For example, LaserWriter or AFPServer. See also *entity name*.

EOM End of message. Indicator that identifies the last ATM cell containing information from a data packet that was segmented.

EOT End of transmission. Generally, a character that signifies the end of a logical group of characters or bits.

EPD Early packet discard. Mechanism used by some ATM switches for discarding a complete AAL5 frame when a threshold condition, such as imminent congestion, is met. EPD prevents congestion that would otherwise jeopardize the switch's ability to properly support existing connections with a guaranteed service. Compare to *TPD*.

EPROM   Erasable programmable read-only memory. Nonvolatile memory chips that are programmed after they are manufactured, and, if necessary, can be erased by some means and reprogrammed. Compare to *EEPROM* and *PROM*.

equalization   Technique used to compensate for communications channel distortions.

ER   Explicit rate. In ATM, an RM cell used to limit the ACR for a transmission to a specific value. Usually the source initially sets the ER initially to a requested rate, such as the PCR. Later, any network element in the path can reduce the ER to a value that the element can sustain. See also *ACR, PCR,* and *RM*.

erasable programmable read-only memory   See *EPROM*.

error control   Technique for detecting and correcting errors in data transmissions.

error-correcting code   Code having sufficient intelligence and incorporating sufficient signaling information to enable the detection and correction of many errors at the receiver.

error-detecting code   Code that can detect transmission errors through analysis of received data based on the adherence of the data to appropriate structural guidelines.

ES   End system. *1.* Generally, an end-user device on a network. *2.* Nonrouting host or node in an OSI network.

ESCON   Enterprise System Connection. IBM channel architecture that specifies a pair of fiber-optic cables, with either LEDs or lasers as transmitters, and a signaling rate of 200Mbps.

ESCON channel   IBM channel for attaching mainframes to peripherals such as storage devices, backup units, and network interfaces. This channel incorporates fiber channel technology. The ESCON channel replaces the bus and tag channel. Compare to *parallel channel.* See also *bus and tag channel.*

ESCON Multiple Image Facility   See *EMIF*.

ESD   Electrostatic discharge. Discharge of stored static electricity that can damage electronic equipment and impair electrical circuitry, resulting in complete or intermittent failures.

ESF   Extended Superframe Format. Framing type used on T1 circuits that consists of 24 frames of 192 bits each, with the 193rd bit providing timing and other functions. ESF is an enhanced version of SF. See also *SF*.

ESI   End system identifier. Identifier that distinguishes multiple nodes at the same level when the lower-level peer group is partitioned (usually an IEEE 802 address).

ES-IS   End System-to-Intermediate System. OSI protocol that defines how end systems (hosts) announce themselves to intermediate systems (routers). See also *IS-IS*.

ESnet   Energy Sciences Network. Data communications network managed and funded by the U.S. Department of Energy Office of Energy Research (DOE/OER). Interconnects the DOE to educational institutions and other research facilities.

ESP   Extended Services Processor.

ESS   Electronic Switching System. AT&T's term for an electronic central office switch. A 5ESS is AT&T's digital central office for end office applications. A 4ESS is its digital central office for toll center application.

Ethernet   Baseband LAN specification invented by Xerox Corporation and developed jointly by Xerox, Intel, and Digital Equipment Corporation. Ethernet networks use CSMA/CD and run over a variety of cable types at 10Mbps. Ethernet is similar to the IEEE 802.3 series of standards. See also *10Base2, 10Base5, 10BaseF, 10BaseT, 10Broad36, Fast Ethernet,* and *IEEE 802.3*.

Ethernet Interface Processor   See *EIP* in the "Cisco Systems Terms and Acronyms" section.

Ethernet meltdown   Event that causes saturation, or near saturation, on an Ethernet. It usually results from illegal or misrouted packets and typically lasts only a short time.

EtherTalk   Apple Computer's data-link product that allows an AppleTalk network to be connected by Ethernet cable.

EtherTalk Link Access Protocol   See *ELAP*.

ETSI   European Telecommunication Standards Institute. Organization created by the European PTTs and the EC to propose telecommunications standards for Europe.

EUnet   European Internet. European commercial Internet service provider. EUnet is designed to provide email, news, and other Internet services to European markets.

European Academic Research Network   See *EARN*.

European Computer Manufacturers Association See *ECMA*.

European Internet   See *EUnet*.

European Telecommunication Standards Institute See *ETSI*.

event   Network message indicating operational irregularities in physical elements of a network or a response to the occurrence of a significant task, typically the completion of a request for information. See also *alarm* and *trap*.

EWOS   European Workshop for Open Systems. The OSI Implementors Workshop for Europe.

Excess Burst   See *Be*.

excess rate   In ATM, traffic in excess of the insured rate for a given connection. Specifically, the excess rate equals the maximum rate minus the insured rate. Excess traffic is delivered only if network resources are available and can be discarded during periods of congestion. Compare to *insured rate* and *maximum rate*.

exchange identification   See *XID*.

EXEC   See *EXEC* in the "Cisco Systems Terms and Acronyms" section.

expansion   The process of running a compressed data set through an algorithm that restores the data set to its original size. Compare to *companding* and *compression*.

expedited delivery   Option set by a specific protocol layer telling other protocol layers (or the same protocol layer in another network device) to handle specific data more rapidly.

explicit forward congestion indication   See *EFCI*.

explicit rate   See *ER*.

explicit route   In SNA, a route from a source subarea to a destination subarea, as specified by a list of subarea nodes and transmission groups that connect the two.

explorer frame   Frame sent out by a networked device in a SRB environment to determine the optimal route to another networked device.

explorer packet   Generated by an end station trying to find its way through a SRB network. Gathers a hop-by-hop description of a path through the network by being marked (updated) by each bridge that it traverses, thereby creating a complete topological map. See also *all-routes explorer packet*, *local explorer packet*, and *spanning explorer packet*.

Extended Binary Coded Decimal Interchange Code See *EBCDIC*.

Extended Industry-Standard Architecture   See *EISA*.

Extended Services Processor   See *ESP* in the "Cisco Systems Terms and Acronyms" section.

Extended Superframe Format   See *ESF*.

exterior gateway protocol   Any internetwork protocol used to exchange routing information between autonomous systems. Not to be confused with Exterior Gateway Protocol (EGP), which is a particular instance of an exterior gateway protocol.

Exterior Gateway Protocol See *EGP.*

exterior router Router connected to an AURP tunnel, responsible for the encapsulation and deencapsulation of AppleTalk packets in a foreign protocol header (for example, IP). See also *AURP* and *AURP tunnel.*

EXZ excessive zeros.

F

failure domain Area in which a failure occurred in a Token Ring, defined by the information contained in a beacon. When a station detects a serious problem with the network (such as a cable break), it sends a beacon frame that includes the station reporting the failure, its NAUN, and everything in between. Beaconing in turn initiates a process called autoreconfiguration. See also *autoreconfiguration, beacon,* and *NAUN.*

fallback Mechanism used by ATM networks when rigorous path selection does not generate an acceptable path. The fallback mechanism attempts to determine a path by selectively relaxing certain attributes, such as delay, in order to find a path that meets some minimal set of desired attributes.

fan-out unit Device that allows multiple devices on a network to communicate using a single network attachment.

fantail Panel of I/O connectors that attaches to an equipment rack, providing easy access for data connections to a networking.

FAQ Frequently asked questions. Usually appears in the form of a "read-me" file in a variety of Internet forums. New users are expected to read the FAQ before participating in newsgroups, bulletin boards, video conferences, and so on.

FARNET Federation of American Research NETworks.

Fast Ethernet Any of a number of 100-Mbps Ethernet specifications. Fast Ethernet offers a speed increase ten times that of the 10BaseT Ethernet specification, while preserving such qualities as frame format, MAC mechanisms, and MTU. Such similarities allow the use of existing 10BaseT applications and network management tools on Fast Ethernet networks. Based on an extension to the IEEE 802.3 specification. Compare to *Ethernet.* See also *100BaseFX, 100BaseT, 100BaseT4, 100BaseTX, 100BaseX,* and *IEEE 802.3.*

Fast Ethernet Interface Processor See *FEIP* in the "Cisco Systems Terms and Acronyms" section.

Fast Sequenced Transport See *FST* in the "Cisco Systems Terms and Acronyms" section.

Fast Serial Interface Processor See *FSIP* in the "Cisco Systems Terms and Acronyms" section.

fast switching See *fast switching* in the "Cisco Systems Terms and Acronyms" section.

fault management One of five categories of network management defined by ISO for management of OSI networks. Fault management attempts to ensure that network faults are detected and controlled. See also *accounting management, configuration management, performance management,* and *security management.*

FCC Federal Communications Commission. U.S. Government agency that supervises, licenses, and controls electronic and electromagnetic transmission standards.

FCS Frame check sequence. Extra characters added to a frame for error control purposes. Used in HDLC, Frame Relay, and other Data Link layer protocols.

FDDI Fiber Distributed Data Interface. LAN standard, defined by ANSI X3T9.5, specifying a 100Mbps token-passing network using fiber-optic cable, with transmission distances of up to 2km. FDDI uses a dual-ring architecture to provide redundancy. Compare to *CDDI* and *FDDI II.*

FDDI II   ANSI standard that enhances FDDI. FDDI II provides isochronous transmission for connectionless data circuits and connection-oriented voice and video circuits. Compare to *FDDI.*

FDDI Interface Processor   See *FIP* in the "Cisco Systems Terms and Acronyms" section.

FDDITalk   Apple Computer's data-link product that allows an AppleTalk network to be connected by FDDI cable.

FDM   Frequency-division multiplexing. Technique whereby information from multiple channels can be allocated bandwidth on a single wire based on frequency. Compare to *ATDM, statistical multiplexing,* and *TDM.*

FECN   Forward explicit congestion notification. Bit set by a Frame Relay network to inform DTE receiving the frame that congestion was experienced in the path from source to destination. DTE receiving frames with the FECN bit set can request that higher-level protocols take flow-control action as appropriate. Compare to *BECN.*

Federal Communications Commission   See *FCC.*

Federal Networking Council   See *FNC.*

FEIP   See *FEIP (Fast Ethernet Interface Processor)* in the "Cisco Systems Terms and Acronyms" section.

FEP   Front-end processor. Device or board that provides network interface capabilities for a networked device. In SNA, typically an IBM 3745 device.

Fiber Distributed Data Interface   See *FDDI.*

fiber-optic cable   Physical medium capable of conducting modulated light transmission. Compared with other transmission media, fiber-optic cable is more expensive, but is not susceptible to electromagnetic interference, and is capable of higher data rates. Sometimes called optical fiber.

fiber-optic interrepeater link   See *FOIRL.*

FID0   Format indicator 0. One of several formats that an SNA TH can use. An FID0 TH is used for communication between an SNA node and a non-SNA node. See also *TH.*

FID1   Format indicator 1. One of several formats that an SNA TH can use. An FID1 TH encapsulates messages between two subarea nodes that do not support virtual and explicit routes. See also *TH.*

FID2   Format indicator 2. One of several formats that an SNA TH can use. An FID2 TH is used for transferring messages between a subarea node and a PU 2, using local addresses. See also *TH.*

FID3   Format indicator 3. One of several formats that an SNA TH can use. An FID3 TH is used for transferring messages between a subarea node and a PU 1, using local addresses. See also *TH.*

FID4   Format indicator 4. One of several formats that an SNA TH can use. An FID4 TH encapsulates messages between two subarea nodes that are capable of supporting virtual and explicit routes. See also *TH.*

field replaceable unit   Hardware component that can be removed and replaced on-site. Typical field-replaceable units include cards, power supplies, and chassis components.

file transfer   Category of popular network applications that allow files to be moved from one network device to another.

File Transfer, Access, and Management   See *FTAM.*

File Transfer Protocol   See *FTP.*

filter   Generally, a process or device that screens network traffic for certain characteristics, such as source address, destination address, or protocol, and determines whether to forward or discard that traffic based on the established criteria.

finger   Software tool for determining whether a person has an account at a particular Internet site. Many sites do not allow incoming finger requests.

FIP   See *FIP* in the "Cisco Systems Terms and Acronyms" section.

firewall   Router or access server, or several routers or access servers, designated as a buffer between any connected public networks and a private network. A firewall router uses access lists and other methods to ensure the security of the private network.

firmware   Software instructions set permanently or semipermanently in ROM.

FIX   Federal Internet Exchange. Connection point between the North American governmental internets and the Internet. The FIXs are named after their geographic regions, as in FIX West (Mountain View, California) and FIX East (College Park, Maryland). See *CIX*, *GIX*, and *MAE*.

flapping   Routing problem in which an advertised route between two nodes alternates (flaps) back and forth between two paths due to a network problem that causes intermittent interface failures.

Flash memory   Nonvolatile storage that can be electrically erased and reprogrammed so that software images can be stored, booted, and rewritten as necessary. Flash memory was developed by Intel and is licensed to other semiconductor companies.

flash update   Routing update sent asynchronously in response to a change in the network topology. Compare to *routing update*.

flat addressing   Scheme of addressing that does not use a logical hierarchy to determine location. For example, MAC addresses are flat, so bridging protocols must flood packets throughout the network to deliver the packet to the appropriate location. Compare to *hierarchical addressing*.

flooding   Traffic passing technique used by switches and bridges in which traffic received on an interface is sent out all of the interfaces of that device except the interface on which the information was originally received.

flow   Stream of data traveling between two endpoints across a network (for example, from one LAN station to another). Multiple flows can be transmitted on a single circuit.

flow control   Technique for ensuring that a transmitting entity, such as a modem, does not overwhelm a receiving entity with data. When the buffers on the receiving device are full, a message is sent to the sending device to suspend the transmission until the data in the buffers has been processed. In IBM networks, this technique is called pacing.

flowspec   In IPv6, the traffic parameters of a stream of IP packets between two applications. See also *IPv6*.

FLT   Full Line Terminal. Multiplexer that terminates a SONET span. See also *SONET*.

FM   Frequency modulation. Modulation technique in which signals of different frequencies represent different data values. Compare to *AM* and *PAM*. See also *modulation*.

FNC   Federal Networking Council. Group responsible for assessing and coordinating U.S. Federal agency networking policies and needs.

FOIRL   Fiber-optic interrepeater link. Fiber-optic signaling methodology based on the IEEE 802.3 fiber-optic specification. FOIRL is a precursor of the 10BaseFL specification, which is designed to replace it. See also *10BaseFL*.

format indicator 0   See *FID0*.

format indicator 1   See *FID1*.

format indicator 2   See *FID2*.

format indicator 3   See *FID3*.

format indicator 4   See *FID4*.

forward channel   Communications path carrying information from the call initiator to the called party.

forward delay interval   Amount of time an interface spends listening for topology change information after that interface has been activated for bridging and before forwarding actually begins.

forward explicit congestion notification   See *FECN*.

forwarding   Process of sending a frame toward its ultimate destination by way of an internetworking device.

FOTS   Fiber Optics Transmission Systems. Vendor-proprietary fiber-optic transmission equipment.

Fourier transform   Technique used to evaluate the importance of various frequency cycles in a time series pattern.

four-part dotted notation   See *dot address*.

FQDN   Fully qualified domain name. FQDN is the full name of a system, rather than just its host name. For example, aldebaran is a hostname and aldebaran.interop.com is an FQDN.

fractional T1   See *channelized T1*.

FRAD   Frame Relay access device. Any network device that provides a connection between a LAN and a Frame Relay WAN. See also *Cisco FRAD (Cisco Frame Relay access device)* and *FRAS (Frame Relay access support)* in the "Cisco Systems Terms and Acronyms" section.

fragment   Piece of a larger packet that has been broken down to smaller units.

fragmentation   Process of breaking a packet into smaller units when transmitting over a network medium that cannot support the original size of the packet. See also *reassembly*.

frame   Logical grouping of information sent as a Data Link layer unit over a transmission medium. Often refers to the header and trailer, used for synchronization and error control, that surround the user data contained in the unit. The terms cell, datagram, message, packet, and segment are also used to describe logical information groupings at various layers of the OSI reference model and in various technology circles.

frame check sequence   See *FCS*.

frame forwarding   Mechanism by which frame-based traffic, such as HDLC and SDLC, traverses an ATM network.

Frame Relay   Industry-standard, switched Data Link layer protocol that handles multiple virtual circuits using HDLC encapsulation between connected devices. Frame Relay is more efficient than X.25, the protocol for which it is generally considered a replacement. See also *X.25*.

Frame Relay access device   See *FRAD*.

Frame Relay access support   See *FRAS* in the "Cisco Systems Terms and Acronyms" section.

Frame Relay bridging   Bridging technique, described in RFC 1490, that uses the same spanning-tree algorithm as other bridging functions, but allows packets to be encapsulated for transmission across a Frame Relay network.

frame switch   See *LAN switch*.

FRAS   See *FRAS (Frame Relay access support)* in the "Cisco Systems Terms and Acronyms" section.

FRASM   Frame Relay access service module.

freenet   Community-based bulletin board system with email, information services, interactive communications, and conferencing.

free-trade zone   Part of an AppleTalk internetwork that is accessible by two other parts of the internetwork that are unable to directly access one another.

frequency   Number of cycles, measured in hertz, of an alternating current signal per unit time.

frequency-division multiplexing   See *FDM*.

frequency modulation   See *FM*.

front end   Node or software program that requests services of a back end. See also *back end*, *client*, and *server*.

front-end processor   See *FEP*.

FSIP   See *FSIP* in the "Cisco Systems Terms and Acronyms" section.

FST   See *FST* in the "Cisco Systems Terms and Acronyms" section.

FTAM   File Transfer, Access, and Management. In OSI, an Application layer protocol developed for network file exchange and management between diverse types of computers.

FTP   File Transfer Protocol. Application protocol, part of the TCP/IP protocol stack, used for transferring files between network nodes. FTP is defined in RFC 959.

full duplex   Capability for simultaneous data transmission between a sending station and a receiving station. Compare to *half duplex* and *simplex*.

full mesh   Term describing a network in which devices are organized in a mesh topology, with each network node having either a physical circuit or a virtual circuit connecting it to every other network node. A full mesh provides a great deal of redundancy, but because it can be prohibitively expensive to implement, it is usually reserved for network backbones. See also *mesh* and *partial mesh*.

fully qualified domain name   See *FQDN*.

Fuzzball   Digital Equipment Corporation LSI-11 computer system running IP gateway software. The NSFnet used these systems as backbone packet switches.

G

G.703/G.704   ITU-T electrical and mechanical specifications for connections between telephone company equipment and DTE using BNC connectors and operating at E1 data rates.

G.804   ITU-T framing standard that defines the mapping of ATM cells into the physical medium.

gateway   In the IP community, an older term referring to a routing device. Today, the term router is used to describe nodes that perform this function, and gateway refers to a special-purpose device that performs an Application layer conversion of information from one protocol stack to another. Compare to *router*.

Gateway Discovery Protocol   See *GDP* in the "Cisco Systems Terms and Acronyms" section.

gateway host   In SNA, a host node that contains a gateway SSCP.

gateway NCP   NCP that connects two or more SNA networks and performs address translation to allow cross-network session traffic.

Gateway-to-Gateway Protocol   See *GGP*.

GB   Gigabyte. Approximately 1,000,000,000 bytes.

GBps   Gigabytes per second.

Gb   Gigabit. Approximately 1,000,000,000 bits.

Gbps   Gigabits per second.

GCAC   Generic connection admission control. In ATM, a PNNI algorithm designed for CBR and VBR connections. Any node can use GCAC to calculate the expected CAC behavior of another node given than node's advertised link metrics and the QoS of a connection setup request. See also *CAC*.

GCRA   Generic cell rate algorithm. In ATM, an algorithm that defines conformance with respect to the traffic contract of the connection. For each cell arrival, the GCRA determines whether the cell conforms to the traffic contract.

GDP   See *GDP* in the "Cisco Systems Terms and Acronyms" section.

generic connection admission control See *GCAC*.

generic routing encapsulation See *GRE* in the "Cisco Systems Terms and Acronyms" section.

Get Nearest Server See *GNS*.

GGP Gateway-to-Gateway Protocol. MILNET protocol specifying how core routers (gateways) should exchange reachability and routing information. GGP uses a distributed shortest-path algorithm.

GHz Gigahertz.

gigabit Abbreviated Gb.

gigabits per second Abbreviated Gbps.

gigabyte Abbreviated GB.

gigabytes per second Abbreviated GBps.

gigahertz Abbreviated GHz.

GIX Global Internet eXchange. Common routing exchange point that allows pairs of networks to implement agreed-upon routing policies. The GIX is intended to allow maximum connectivity to the Internet for networks all over the world. See *CIX*, *FIX*, and *MAE*.

gleaning Process by which a router automatically derives AARP table entries from incoming packets. Gleaning speeds up the process of populating the AARP table. See also *AARP*.

GNS Get Nearest Server. Request packet sent by a client on an IPX network to locate the nearest active server of a particular type. An IPX network client issues a GNS request to solicit either a direct response from a connected server or a response from a router that tells it where on the internetwork the service can be located. GNS is part of the IPX SAP. See also *IPX* and *SAP (Service Advertising Protocol)*.

goodput Generally referring to the measurement of actual data successfully transmitted from the sender(s) to receiver(s). This is often a more useful measurement than the number of ATM cells per second throughput

of an ATM switch if that switch is experiencing cell loss that results in many incomplete, and therefore unusable, frames arriving at the recipient.

Gopher Distributed document delivery system. The Internet Gopher allows a neophyte user to access various types of data residing on multiple hosts in a seamless fashion.

GOSIP Government OSI Profile. U.S. Government procurement specification for OSI protocols. Through GOSIP, the government mandates that all federal agencies standardize on OSI and implement OSI-based systems as they become commercially available.

Government OSI Profile See *GOSIP*.

grade of service Measure of telephone service quality based on the probability that a call will encounter a busy signal during the busiest hours of the day.

graphical user interface See *GUI*.

GRE See *GRE* in the "Cisco Systems Terms and Acronyms" section.

ground station Collection of communications equipment designed to receive signals from (and usually transmit signals to) satellites. Also called a downlink station.

group address See *multicast address*.

group delay See *distortion delay*.

guard band Unused frequency band between two communications channels that provides separation of the channels to prevent mutual interference.

GUI Graphical user interface. User environment that uses pictorial as well as textual representations of the input and output of applications and the hierarchical or other data structure in which information is stored. Conventions such as buttons, icons, and windows are typical, and many actions are performed using a pointing device (such as a mouse). Microsoft Windows and the Apple Macintosh are prominent examples of platforms using a GUI.

H

H.320 Suite of ITU-T standard specifications for videoconferencing over circuit-switched media such as ISDN, fractional T-1, or switched-56 lines.

H.323 Extension of ITU-T standard H.320 that enables videoconferencing over LANs and other packet-switched networks, as well as video over the Internet.

half duplex Capability for data transmission in only one direction at a time between a sending station and a receiving station. BSC is an example of a half-duplex protocol. See also *BSC*. Compare to *full duplex* and *simplex*.

handshake Sequence of messages exchanged between two or more network devices to ensure transmission synchronization.

hardware address See *MAC address*.

HBD3 Line code type used on E1 circuits.

H channel high-speed channel. Full-duplex ISDN primary rate channel operating at 384Kbps. Compare to *B channel*, *D channel*, and *E channel*.

HDLC High-Level Data Link Control. Bit-oriented synchronous Data Link layer protocol developed by ISO. Derived from SDLC, HDLC specifies a data encapsulation method on synchronous serial links using frame characters and checksums. See also *SDLC*.

HDSL High-data-rate digital subscriber line. One of four DSL technologies. HDSL delivers 1.544Mbps of bandwidth each way over two copper twisted pairs. Because HDSL provides T1 speed, telephone companies have been using HDSL to provision local access to T1 services whenever possible. The operating range of HDSL is limited to 12,000 feet (3658.5 meters), so signal repeaters are installed to extend the service. HDSL requires two twisted pairs, so it is deployed primarily for PBX network connections, digital loop carrier systems, interexchange POPs, Internet servers,

and private data networks. Compare to *ADSL*, *SDSL*, and *VDSL*.

headend End point of a broadband network. All stations transmit toward the headend; the headend then transmits toward the destination stations.

header Control information placed before data when encapsulating that data for network transmission. Compare to *trailer*. See also *PCI*.

heartbeat See *SQE*.

HEC Header error control. Algorithm for checking and correcting an error in an ATM cell. Using the fifth octet in the ATM cell header, ATM equipment will check for an error and correct the contents of the header. The check character is calculated using a CRC algorithm allowing a single bit error in the header to be corrected or multiple errors to be detected.

HELLO Interior routing protocol used principally by NSFnet nodes. HELLO allows particular packet switches to discover minimal delay routes. Not to be confused with the Hello protocol.

hello packet Multicast packet that is used by routers for neighbor discovery and recovery. Hello packets also indicate that a client is still operating and network-ready.

Hello protocol Protocol used by OSPF systems for establishing and maintaining neighbor relationships. Not to be confused with HELLO.

HEPnet High-Energy Physics Network. Research network that originated in the United States, but that has spread to most places involved in high-energy physics. Well-known sites include Argonne National Laboratory, Brookhaven National Laboratory, Lawrence Berkeley Laboratory, and the SLAC.

hertz Measure of frequency. Abbreviated Hz. Synonymous with cycles per second.

heterogeneous network Network consisting of dissimilar devices that run dissimilar protocols and in many cases support dissimilar functions or applications.

HFC Hybrid fiber-coaxial. Technology being developed by the cable TV industry to provide two-way, high-speed data access to the home using a combination of fiber optics and traditional coaxial cable.

hierarchical addressing Scheme of addressing that uses a logical hierarchy to determine location. For example, IP addresses consist of network numbers, subnet numbers, and host numbers, which IP routing algorithms use to route the packet to the appropriate location. Compare to *flat addressing*.

hierarchical routing The complex problem of routing on large networks can be simplified by reducing the size of the networks. This is accomplished by breaking a network into a hierarchy of networks, where each level is responsible for its own routing.

High-Energy Physics Network See *HEPnet*.

High-Level Data Link Control See *HDLC*.

High-Performance Computing and Communications See *HPCC*.

High-Performance Computing Systems See *HPCS*.

High-Performance Parallel Interface See *HIPPI*.

High-Performance Routing See *HPR*.

High-Speed Communications Interface See *HSCI* in the "Cisco Systems Terms and Acronyms" section.

High-Speed Serial Interface See *HSSI*.

highway See *bus*.

HIP See *HIP* in the "Cisco Systems Terms and Acronyms" section.

HIPPI High-Performance Parallel Interface. High-performance interface standard defined by ANSI. HIPPI is typically used to connect supercomputers to peripherals and other devices.

holddown State into which a route is placed so that routers will neither advertise the route nor accept advertisements about the route for a specific length of time (the holddown period). Holddown is used to flush bad information about a route from all routers in the network. A route is typically placed in holddown when a link in that route fails.

homologation Conformity of a product or specification to international standards, such as ITU-T, CSA, TUV, UL, or VCCI. Enables portability across company and international boundaries.

hop Passage of a data packet between two network nodes (for example, between two routers). See also *hop count*.

hop count Routing metric used to measure the distance between a source and a destination. RIP uses hop count as its sole metric. See also *hop* and *RIP*.

host Computer system on a network. Similar to node, except that host usually implies a computer system, whereas node generally applies to any networked system, including access servers and routers. See also *node*.

host address See *host number*.

host name Name given to a machine. See also *FQDN*.

host node SNA subarea node that contains an SSCP. See also *SSCP*.

host number Part of an IP address that designates which node on the subnetwork is being addressed. Also called a host address.

Hot Standby Router Protocol See *HSRP* in the "Cisco Systems Terms and Acronyms" section.

hot swapping See *OIR* and *power-on servicing*.

HPCC High-Performance Computing and Communications. U.S. Government-funded program advocating advances in computing, communications, and related fields. The HPCC is designed to ensure U.S. leadership in these fields through education, research and development, industry collaboration, and implementation of high-performance technology.

See also the five components of the HPCC: *ASTA, BRHR, HPCS, IITA,* and *NREN.*

HPCS   High-Performance Computing Systems. Component of the HPCC program designed to ensure U.S. technological leadership in high-performance computing through research and development of computing systems and related software. See also *HPCC.*

HPR   High-Performance Routing. Second-generation routing algorithm for APPN. HPR provides a connectionless layer with nondisruptive routing of sessions around link failures, and a connection-oriented layer with end-to-end flow control, error control, and sequencing. Compare to *ISR.* See also *APPN.*

HSCI   See *HSCI* in the "Cisco Systems Terms and Acronyms" section.

HSRP   See *HSRP* in the "Cisco Systems Terms and Acronyms" section.

HSSI   High-Speed Serial Interface. Network standard for high-speed (up to 52Mbps) serial connections over WAN links.

HSSI Interface Processor   See *HIP* in the "Cisco Systems Terms and Acronyms" section.

HTML   Hypertext Markup Language. Simple hypertext document formatting language that uses tags to indicate how a given part of a document should be interpreted by a viewing application, such as a Web browser. See also *hypertext* and *browser.*

HTTP   Hypertext Transfer Protocol. The protocol used by Web browsers and Web servers to transfer files, such as text and graphic files.

hub   *1.* Generally, a term used to describe a device that serves as the center of a star-topology network. *2.* Hardware or software device that contains multiple independent but connected modules of network and internetwork equipment. Hubs can be active (where they repeat signals sent through them) or passive (where they do not repeat, but merely split, signals sent

through them). *3.* In Ethernet and IEEE 802.3, an Ethernet multiport repeater, sometimes called a concentrator.

hybrid network   Internetwork made up of more than one type of network technology, including LANs and WANs.

hyperlink   Pointer within a hypertext document that points (links) to another document, which may or may not also be a hypertext document.

hypertext   Electronically stored text that allows direct access to other texts by way of encoded links. Hypertext documents can be created using HTML, and often integrate images, sound, and other media that are commonly viewed using a browser. See also *HTML* and *browser.*

Hypertext Markup Language   See *HTML.*

Hypertext Transfer Protocol   See *HTTP.*

Hz   See *hertz.*

I

IAB   Internet Architecture Board. Board of internetwork researchers who discuss issues pertinent to Internet architecture. Responsible for appointing a variety of Internet-related groups such as the IANA, IESG, and IRSG. The IAB is appointed by the trustees of the ISOC. See also *IANA, IESG, IRSG,* and *ISOC.*

IAHC   Internet International Ad Hoc Committee. Coalition of participants from the broad Internet community, working to satisfy the requirement for enhancements to the Internet's global DNS. Organizations naming members to the committee include Internet Society (ISOC), Internet Assigned Numbers Authority (IANA), Internet Architecture Board (IAB), Federal Networking Council (FNC), International Telecommunication Union (ITU), International Trademark Association (INTA), and World Intellectual Property Organization (WIPO).

IANA Internet Assigned Numbers Authority. Organization operated under the auspices of the ISOC as a part of the IAB. IANA delegates authority for IP address-space allocation and domain-name assignment to the InterNIC and other organizations. IANA also maintains a database of assigned protocol identifiers used in the TCP/IP stack, including autonomous system numbers. See also *IAB, ISOC,* and *InterNIC.*

ICD International Code Designator. One of two ATM address formats developed by the ATM Forum for use by private networks. Adapted from the subnetwork model of addressing in which the ATM layer is responsible for mapping Network layer addresses to ATM addresses. Compare to *DCC.*

ICMP Internet Control Message Protocol. Network layer Internet protocol that reports errors and provides other information relevant to IP packet processing. Documented in RFC 792.

ICMP Router Discovery Protocol See *IRDP.*

ICR Initial cell rate.

I-D Internet-Draft. Working documents of the IETF, from its Areas and Working Groups. They are valid for a maximum of six months and might be updated, replaced, or obsoleted by other documents at any time. Very often, I-Ds are precursors to RFCs.

IDI Initial domain identifier. Portion of an NSAP or NSAP-format ATM address that specifies the address allocation and administration authority. See also *NSAP.*

IDN International Data Number. See also *X.121.*

IDP Initial domain part. Part of a CLNS address that contains an authority and format identifier, and a domain identifier.

IDPR Interdomain Policy Routing. Interdomain routing protocol that dynamically exchanges policies between autonomous systems. IDPR encapsulates inter-

autonomous system traffic and routes it according to the policies of each autonomous system along the path. IDPR is currently an IETF proposal. See also *policy routing.*

IDRP IS-IS Interdomain Routing Protocol. OSI protocol that specifies how routers communicate with routers in different domains.

IEC International Electrotechnical Commission. Industry group that writes and distributes standards for electrical products and components.

IEEE Institute of Electrical and Electronics Engineers. Professional organization whose activities include the development of communications and network standards. IEEE LAN standards are the predominant LAN standards today.

IEEE 802.1 IEEE specification that describes an algorithm that prevents bridging loops by creating a spanning tree. The algorithm was invented by Digital Equipment Corporation. The Digital algorithm and the IEEE 802.1 algorithm are not exactly the same, nor are they compatible. See also *spanning tree, spanning-tree algorithm,* and *Spanning-Tree Protocol.*

IEEE 802.12 IEEE LAN standard that specifies the Physical layer and the MAC sublayer of the Data Link layer. IEEE 802.12 uses the demand priority media-access scheme at 100Mbps over a variety of physical media. See also *100VG-AnyLAN.*

IEEE 802.2 IEEE LAN protocol that specifies an implementation of the LLC sublayer of the Data Link layer. IEEE 802.2 handles errors, framing, flow control, and the Network layer (Layer 3) service interface. Used in IEEE 802.3 and IEEE 802.5 LANs. See also *IEEE 802.3* and *IEEE 802.5.*

IEEE 802.3 IEEE LAN protocol that specifies an implementation of the Physical layer and the MAC sublayer of the Data Link layer. IEEE 802.3 uses CSMA/CD access at a variety of speeds over a variety of physical media. Extensions to the IEEE 802.3 standard specify implementations for Fast Ethernet. Physical variations of the original IEEE 802.3 specification include 10Base2, 10Base5, 10BaseF, 10BaseT, and 10Broad36. Physical variations for Fast Ethernet include 100BaseT, 100BaseT4, and 100BaseX.

IEEE 802.4 IEEE LAN protocol that specifies an implementation of the Physical layer and the MAC sublayer of the Data Link layer. IEEE 802.4 uses token-passing access over a bus topology and is based on the token bus LAN architecture. See also *token bus*.

IEEE 802.5 IEEE LAN protocol that specifies an implementation of the Physical layer and MAC sublayer of the Data Link layer. IEEE 802.5 uses token passing access at 4 or 16Mbps over STP cabling and is similar to IBM Token Ring. See also *Token Ring*.

IEEE 802.6 IEEE MAN specification based on DQDB technology. IEEE 802.6 supports data rates of 1.5 to 155Mbps. See also *DQDB*.

IEPG Internet Engineering Planning Group. Group, primarily composed of Internet service operators, whose goal is to promote a globally coordinated Internet operating environment. Membership is open to all.

IESG Internet Engineering Steering Group. Organization, appointed by the IAB, that manages the operation of the IETF. See also *IAB* and *IETF*.

IETF Internet Engineering Task Force. Task force consisting of over 80 working groups responsible for developing Internet standards. The IETF operates under the auspices of ISOC. See also *ISOC*.

IFIP International Federation for Information Processing. Research organization that performs OSI prestandardization work. Among other accomplishments, IFIP formalized the original MHS model. See also *MHS*.

I-frame Information frame. One of three SDLC frame formats. See also *S-frame* and *U-frame*.

IGMP Internet Group Management Protocol. Used by IP hosts to report their multicast group memberships to an adjacent multicast router. See also *multicast router*.

IGP Interior Gateway Protocol. Internet protocol used to exchange routing information within an autonomous system. Examples of common Internet IGPs include IGRP, OSPF, and RIP. See also *OSPF* and *RIP*, and *IGRP* in the "Cisco Systems Terms and Acronyms" section.

IGRP See *IGRP* in the "Cisco Systems Terms and Acronyms" section.

IIH IS-IS Hello. Message sent by all IS-IS systems to maintain adjacencies. See also *IS-IS*.

IINREN Interagency Interim National Research and Education Network. Evolving operating network system. Near term research and development activities will provide for the smooth evolution of this networking infrastructure into the future gigabit NREN.

IIOP Internet Inter-ORB Protocol. Protocol used in the CORBA framework for accessing objects across the Internet. See also *CORBA*.

IISP Interim-Interswitch Signaling Protocol. ATM signaling protocol for inter-switch communication using manually configured prefix tables. When a signaling request is received by a switch, the switch checks the destination ATM address against the prefix table and notes the port with the longest prefix match. It then forwards the signaling request across that port using UNI procedures. IISP is an interim solution until PNNI Phase 1 is completed. Formerly known as PNNI Phase 0. Contrast with *Dynamic IISP*.

IITA Information Infrastructure Technology and Applications. Component of the HPCC program intended to ensure U.S. leadership in the development of advanced information technologies. See also *HPCC*.

ILMI Interim Local Management Interface. Specification developed by the ATM Forum for incorporating network-management capabilities into the ATM UNI.

IMAP Internet Message Access Protocol. Method of accessing email or bulletin board messages kept on a mail server that can be shared. IMAP permits client electronic mail applications to access remote message stores as if they were local without actually transferring the message.

IMHO "In My Humble Opinion." One of many, many short-form phrases seen in email messages, newsgroups, and so on.

IMP Interface message processor. Old name for ARPANET packet switches. See also *ARPANET* and *packet switch*.

INA Information Networking Architecture. Bellcore object-oriented architecture for the management of ATM and SONET equipment and services in an operating company environment.

INASoft Bellcore implementation of INA. See also *INA*.

in-band signaling Transmission within a frequency range normally used for information transmission. Compare to *out-of-band signaling*.

Industry-Standard Architecture See *ISA*.

INE Intelligent Network Element. Network element that can be provisioned from a remote OSS.

information element In ATM, the portion of a signaling packet that carries information, such as addresses, used in the UNI specification. See also *UNI*.

Information Infrastructure Technology and Applications See *IITA*.

infrared Electromagnetic waves whose frequency range is above that of microwaves, but below that of the visible spectrum. LAN systems based on this technology represent an emerging technology.

initial domain identifier See *IDI*.

initial domain part See *IDP*.

INOC Internet Network Operations Center. BBN group that in the early days of the Internet monitored and controlled the Internet core gateways (routers). INOC no longer exists in this form.

Institute of Electrical and Electronics Engineers See *IEEE*.

insured burst In an ATM network, the largest burst of data above the insured rate that will be temporarily allowed on a PVC and not tagged by the traffic policing function for dropping in the case of network congestion. The insured burst is specified in bytes or cells. Compare to *maximum burst*. See also *insured rate*.

insured rate Long-term data throughput, in bits or cells per second, that an ATM network commits to support under normal network conditions. The insured rate is 100 percent allocated; the entire amount is deducted from the total trunk bandwidth along the path of the circuit. Compare to *excess rate* and *maximum rate*. See also *insured burst*.

insured traffic Traffic within the insured rate specified for an ATM PVC. This traffic should not be dropped by the network under normal network conditions. See also *CLP* and *insured rate*.

INTAP Interoperability Technology Association for Information Processing. Technical organization that has the official charter to develop Japanese OSI profiles and conformance tests.

Integrated IS-IS Routing protocol based on the OSI routing protocol IS-IS, but with support for IP and other protocols. Integrated IS-IS implementations send only one set of routing updates, making it more efficient than two separate implementations. Formerly called Dual IS-IS. Compare to *IS-IS*.

Integrated Services Digital Network See *ISDN*.

Integrated Services Internet IETF proposal for enhancing IP to allow it to support integrated or multimedia services, including traffic management mechanisms that closely match the traffic management mechanisms of ATM. An example is RSVP.

Intelligent QoS Management Suite Composed of Automatic Routing Management, Advanced CoS Management, Optimized Bandwidth Management, and Dynamic Buffer Management. Formerly called Advanced Networking Features.

interarea routing Term used to describe routing between two or more logical areas. Compare to *intra-area routing*.

Interdomain Policy Routing See *IDPR*.

interface *1.* Connection between two systems or devices. *2.* In routing terminology, a network connection. *3.* In telephony, a shared boundary defined by common physical interconnection characteristics, signal characteristics, and meanings of interchanged signals. *4.* Boundary between adjacent layers of the OSI model.

interface message processor See *IMP*.

interface processor See *interface processor* in the "Cisco Systems Terms and Acronyms" section.

interference Unwanted communication channel noise.

Interim Local Management Interface See *ILMI*.

Interior Gateway Protocol See *IGP*.

Interior Gateway Routing Protocol See *IGRP* in the "Cisco Systems Terms and Acronyms" section.

intermediate routing node See *IRN*.

Intermediate Session Routing See *ISR*.

intermediate system See *IS*.

Intermediate System-to-Intermediate System See *IS-IS*.

International Code Designator See *ICD*.

International Data Number See *X.121*.

International Electrotechnical Commission See *IEC*.

International Federation for Information Processing See *IFIP*.

International Organization for Standardization See *ISO*.

International Standards Organization Erroneous expansion of the acronym ISO. See *ISO*.

International Telecommunication Union Telecommunication Standardization Sector See *ITU-T*.

Internet Largest global internetwork, connecting tens of thousands of networks worldwide and having a "culture" that focuses on research and standardization based on real-life use. Many leading-edge network technologies come from the Internet community. The Internet evolved in part from ARPANET. At one time, called the DARPA Internet. Not to be confused with the general term internet. See also *ARPANET*.

internet Short for internetwork. Not to be confused with the Internet. See *internetwork*.

Internet address See *IP address*.

Internet Architecture Board See *IAB*.

Internet Assigned Numbers Authority See *IANA*.

Internet Control Message Protocol See *ICMP*.

Internet-Draft See *I-D*.

Internet Engineering Planning Group See *IEPG*.

Internet Engineering Steering Group See *IESG*.

Internet Engineering Task Force See *IETF*.

Internet Group Management Protocol See *IGMP*.

Internet Message Access Protocol See *IMAP*.

Internet Network Operations Center See *INOC*.

Internet protocol Any protocol that is part of the TCP/IP protocol stack. See also *IP* and *TCP/IP*.

Internet Protocol (IP, IPv4) Network layer for the TCP/IP protocol suite. Internet Protocol (version 4) is a connectionless, best-effort packet switching protocol. Defined in RFC 791.

Internet Protocol (IPng, IPv6) See *IPv6*.

Internet Registry See *IR*.

Internet Relay Chat See *IRC*.

Internet Research Steering Group See *IRSG*.

Internet Research Task Force See *IRTF*.

Internet service provider See *ISP*.

Internet Society See *ISOC*.

Internet telephony Generic term used to describe various approaches to running voice telephony over IP.

internetwork Collection of networks interconnected by routers and other devices that functions (generally) as a single network. Sometimes called an internet, which is not to be confused with the Internet.

internetworking General term used to refer to the industry devoted to connecting networks together. The term can refer to products, procedures, and technologies.

Internetwork Packet Exchange See *IPX*.

InterNIC Organization that serves the Internet community by supplying user assistance, documentation, training, registration service for Internet domain names, and other services. Formerly called NIC.

interoperability Capability of computing equipment manufactured by different vendors to communicate with one another successfully over a network.

Inter-Switching System Interface See *ISSI*.

Inter-Switch Link See *ISL* in the "Cisco Systems Terms and Acronyms" section.

intra-area routing Term used to describe routing within a logical area. Compare to *interarea routing*.

Inverse Address Resolution Protocol See *Inverse ARP*.

Inverse ARP Inverse Address Resolution Protocol. Method of building dynamic routes in a network. Allows an access server to discover the network address of a device associated with a virtual circuit.

I/O Input/output.

IOC Independent operating company. Independently owned company providing local telephone services to residential and business customers in a geographic area not served by an RBOC.

IONL Internal Organization of the Network Layer. OSI standard for the detailed architecture of the Network layer. Basically, it partitions the Network layer into subnetworks interconnected by convergence protocols (equivalent to internet working protocols), creating what the Internet community calls a catenet or internet.

IOS See *Cisco IOS* in the "Cisco Systems Terms and Acronyms" section.

IP Internet protocol. Network layer protocol in the TCP/IP stack offering a connectionless internetwork service. IP provides features for addressing, type-of-service specification, fragmentation and reassembly, and security. Defined in RFC 791.

IP address 32-bit address assigned to hosts using TCP/IP. An IP address belongs to one of five classes (A, B, C, D, or E) and is written as 4 octets separated by periods (dotted decimal format). Each address consists of a network number, an optional subnetwork number, and a host number. The network and subnetwork numbers together are used for routing; the host number is used to address an individual host within the network or subnetwork. A subnet mask is used to extract network and subnetwork information from the IP address. CIDR provides a new way of representing IP addresses and subnet masks. Also called an Internet address. See also *CIDR, IP,* and *subnet mask.*

IPCP   IP Control Protocol. Protocol that establishes and configures IP over PPP. See also *IP* and *PPP.*

IP datagram   Fundamental unit of information passed across the Internet. Contains source and destination addresses along with data and a number of fields that define such things as the length of the datagram, the header checksum, and flags to indicate whether the datagram can be (or was) fragmented.

IP multicast   Routing technique that allows IP traffic to be propagated from one source to a number of destinations or from many sources to many destinations. Rather than sending one packet to each destination, one packet is sent to a multicast group identified by a single IP destination group address.

IPng   See *IPv6.*

IP Security Option   See *IPSO.*

IPSO   IP Security Option. U.S. Government specification that defines an optional field in the IP packet header that defines hierarchical packet security levels on a per-interface basis.

IPv6   IP version 6. Replacement for the current version of IP (version 4). IPv6 includes support for flow ID in the packet header, which can be used to identify flows. Formerly called IPng (next generation).

IPX   Internetwork Packet Exchange. NetWare Network layer (Layer 3) protocol used for transferring data from servers to workstations. IPX is similar to IP and XNS.

IPXCP   IPX Control Protocol. Protocol that establishes and configures IPX over PPP. See also *IPX* and *PPP.*

IPXWAN   IPX wide-area network. Protocol that negotiates end-to-end options for new links. When a link comes up, the first IPX packets sent across are IPXWAN packets negotiating the options for the link. When the IPXWAN options are successfully determined, normal IPX transmission begins. Defined by RFC 1362.

IR   Internet Registry. IR was delegated the responsibility of network address and autonmuous system identifiers from the IANA which has the discretionary authority to delegate portions of its responsibility.

IRC   Internet Relay Chat. World-wide "party line" protocol that allows one to converse with others in real time. IRC is structured as a network of servers, each of which accepts connections from client programs, one per user.

IRDP   ICMP Router Discovery Protocol. Protocol that enables a host to determine the address of a router that it can use as a default gateway. Similar to ES-IS, but used with IP. See also *ES-IS.*

IRN   Intermediate routing node. In SNA, a subarea node with intermediate routing capability.

IRSG   Internet Research Steering Group. Group that is part of the IAB and oversees the activities of the IRTF. See also *IAB* and *IRTF.*

IRTF   Internet Research Task Force. Community of network experts that considers Internet-related research topics. The IRTF is governed by the IRSG and is considered a subsidiary of the IAB. See also *IAB* and *IRSG.*

IS   Intermediate system. Routing node in an OSI network.

ISA   Industry-Standard Architecture. 16-bit bus used for Intel-based personal computers. See also *EISA.*

isarithmic flow control   Flow control technique that permits travel through the network. Isarithmic flow control is not commonly implemented.

ISDN   Integrated Services Digital Network. Communication protocol, offered by telephone companies, that permits telephone networks to carry data, voice, and other source traffic. See also *BISDN*, *BRI*, *N-ISDN*, and *PRI*.

IS-IS   Intermediate System-to-Intermediate System. OSI link-state hierarchical routing protocol based on DECnet Phase V routing, whereby ISs (routers) exchange routing information based on a single metric, to determine network topology. Compare to *Integrated IS-IS*. See also *ES-IS* and *OSPF*.

IS-IS Hello   See *IIH*.

IS-IS Interdomain Routing Protocol   See *IDRP*.

ISL   See *ISL* in the "Cisco Systems Terms and Acronyms" section.

ISO   International Organization for Standardization. International organization that is responsible for a wide range of standards, including those relevant to networking. ISO developed the OSI reference model, a popular networking reference model.

ISO 3309   HDLC procedures developed by ISO. ISO 3309:1979 specifies the HDLC frame structure for use in synchronous environments. ISO 3309:1984 specifies proposed modifications to allow the use of HDLC in asynchronous environments as well.

ISO 9000   Set of international quality-management standards defined by ISO. The standards, which are not specific to any country, industry, or product, allow companies to demonstrate that they have specific processes in place to maintain an efficient quality system.

ISOC   Internet Society. International nonprofit organization, founded in 1992, that coordinates the evolution and use of the Internet. In addition, ISOC delegates authority to other groups related to the Internet, such as the IAB. ISOC is headquartered in Reston, Virginia, (United States). See also *IAB*.

isochronous transmission   Asynchronous transmission over a synchronous data link. Isochronous signals require a constant bit rate for reliable transport. Compare to *asynchronous transmission*, *plesiochronous transmission*, and *synchronous transmission*.

ISODE   ISO development environment. Large set of libraries and utilities used to develop upper-layer OSI protocols and applications.

ISO development environment   See *ISODE*.

ISP   Internet service provider. Company that provides Internet access to other companies and individuals.

ISR   Intermediate Session Routing. Initial routing algorithm used in APPN. ISR provides node-to-node connection-oriented routing. Network outages cause sessions to fail because ISR cannot provide nondisruptive rerouting around a failure. ISR was replaced by HPR. Compare to *HPR*. See also *APPN*.

ISSI   Inter-Switching System Interface. Standard interface between SMDS switches.

ITU-T   International Telecommunication Union Telecommunication Standardization Sector. International body that develops worldwide standards for telecommunications technologies. The ITU-T carries out the functions of the former CCITT. See also *CCITT*.

IVR   Interactive voice response. Term used to describe systems that provide information in the form of recorded messages over telephone lines in response to user input in the form of spoken words or more commonly DTMF signaling. Examples include banks that allow you to check your balance from any telephone and automated stock quote systems.

IXC   Inter-exchange carrier. Common carrier providing long distance connectivity between LATAs. The three major IXCs are AT&T, MCI, and Sprint, but several hundred IXCs offer long distance service in the United States.

J

jabber   *1.* Error condition in which a network device continually transmits random, meaningless data onto the network. *2.* In IEEE 802.3, a data packet whose length exceeds that prescribed in the standard.

JANET   Joint Academic Network. X.25 WAN connecting university and research institutions in the United Kingdom.

Japan UNIX Network   See *JUNET.*

Java   Object-oriented programming language developed at Sun Microsystems to solve a number of problems in modern programming practice. The Java language is used extensively on World Wide Web, particularly for applets.

JDBC   Java Database Connectivity. Java API that enables Java programs to execute SQL statements. This allows Java programs to interact with any SQL-compliant database. Because nearly all relational database management systems (DBMSs) support SQL, and because Java itself runs on most platforms, JDBC makes it possible to write a single database application that can run on different platforms and interact with different DBMSs. JDBC is similar to ODBC, but is designed specifically for Java programs, whereas ODBC is language-independent. JDBC was developed by JavaSoft, a subsidiary of Sun Microsystems. See *ODBC.*

jitter   Analog communication line distortion caused by the variation of a signal from its reference timing positions. Jitter can cause data loss, particularly at high speeds.

John von Neumann Computer Network   See *JvNCnet.*

Joint Academic Network   See *JANET.*

JPEG   Joint Photographics Expert Group. Graphic file format that was adopted as a standard by the ITU-T and the ISO. JPEG is most often used to compress still images using DCT analysis.

jumper   Electrical switch consisting of a number of pins and a connector that can be attached to the pins in a variety of different ways. Different circuits are created by attaching the connector to different pins.

JUNET   Japan UNIX Network. Nationwide, noncommercial network in Japan, designed to promote communication between Japanese and other researchers.

JvNCnet   John von Neumann Computer Network. Regional network, owned and operated by Global Enterprise Services, Inc., composed of T1 and slower serial links providing midlevel networking services to sites in the Northeastern United States.

K

KA9Q   Popular implementation of TCP/IP and associated protocols for amateur packet radio systems.

Karn's algorithm   Algorithm that improves round-trip time estimations by helping Transport layer protocols distinguish between good and bad round-trip time samples.

KB   Kilobyte. Approximately 1,000 bytes.

Kb   Kilobit. Approximately 1,000 bits.

KBps   Kilobytes per second.

Kbps   Kilobits per second.

keepalive interval   Period of time between each keepalive message sent by a network device.

keepalive message   Message sent by one network device to inform another network device that the virtual circuit between the two is still active.

Kerberos   Developing standard for authenticating network users. Kerberos offers two key benefits: It functions in a multivendor network, and it does not transmit passwords over the network.

Kermit   Popular file-transfer and terminal-emulation program.

kilobit   Abbreviated Kb.

kilobits per second   Abbreviated Kbps.

kilobyte   Abbreviated KB.

kilobytes per second   Abbreviated KBps.

L

L2F Protocol   Layer 2 Forwarding Protocol. Protocol that supports the creation of secure virtual private dial-up networks over the Internet.

label swapping   Routing algorithm used by APPN in which each router that a message passes through on its way to its destination independently determines the best path to the next router.

LAN   Local-area network. High-speed, low-error data network covering a relatively small geographic area (up to a few thousand meters). LANs connect workstations, peripherals, terminals, and other devices in a single building or other geographically limited area. LAN standards specify cabling and signaling at the Physical and Data Link layers of the OSI model. Ethernet, FDDI, and Token Ring are widely used LAN technologies. Compare to *MAN* and *WAN*.

LANE   LAN emulation. Technology that allows an ATM network to function as a LAN backbone. The ATM network must provide multicast and broadcast support, address mapping (MAC-to-ATM), SVC management, and a usable packet format. LANE also defines Ethernet and Token Ring ELANs. See also *ELAN*.

LAN emulation   See *LANE*.

LAN Emulation Client   See *LEC*.

LAN Emulation Configuration Server   See *LECS*.

LAN Emulation Server   See *LES*.

LANE UNI   LANE User-Network Interface.

LAN Manager   Distributed NOS, developed by Microsoft, that supports a variety of protocols and platforms. See also *NOS*.

LAN Manager for UNIX   See *LM/X*.

LAN Network Manager   See *LNM*.

LAN Server   Server-based NOS developed by IBM and derived from LNM. See also *LNM*.

LAN switch   High-speed switch that forwards packets between data-link segments. Most LAN switches forward traffic based on MAC addresses. This variety of LAN switch is sometimes called a frame switch. LAN switches are often categorized according to the method they use to forward traffic: cut-through packet switching or store-and-forward packet switching. Multilayer switches are an intelligent subset of LAN switches. Compare to *multilayer switch*. See also *cut-through packet switching* and *store and forward packet switching*.

LAPB   Link Access Procedure, Balanced. Data Link layer protocol in the X.25 protocol stack. LAPB is a bit-oriented protocol derived from HDLC. See also *HDLC* and *X.25*.

LAPD   Link Access Procedure on the D channel. ISDN Data Link layer protocol for the D channel. LAPD was derived from the LAPB protocol and is designed primarily to satisfy the signaling requirements of ISDN basic access. Defined by ITU-T Recommendations Q.920 and Q.921.

LAPM   Link Access Procedure for Modems. ARQ used by modems implementing the V.42 protocol for error correction. See also *ARQ* and *V.42.*

laser   Light amplification by stimulated emission of radiation. Analog transmission device in which a suitable active material is excited by an external stimulus to produce a narrow beam of coherent light that can be modulated into pulses to carry data. Networks based on laser technology are sometimes run over SONET.

LAT   Local-area transport. A network virtual terminal protocol developed by Digital Equipment Corporation.

LATA   Local access and transport area. Geographic telephone dialing area serviced by a single local telephone company. Calls within LATAs are called local calls. There are well over 100 LATAs in the United States.

latency   *1.* Delay between the time a device requests access to a network and the time it is granted permission to transmit. *2.* Delay between the time a device receives a frame and the time that frame is forwarded out the destination port.

Layer 3 Switching   Emerging Layer 3 switching technology that integrates routing with switching to yield very high routing throughput rates in the millions-of-packets- per-second range. The movement to Layer 3 switching is designed to address the downsides of the current generation of Layer 2 switches, which are functionally equivalent to bridges. These downsides for a large, flat network include being subject to broadcast storms, spanning tree loops, and address limitations.

LCI   Logical channel identifier.

LCN   Logical channel number.

LCP   Link Control Protocol. Protocol that establishes, configures, and tests data-link connections for use by PPP. See also *PPP.*

LCV   Line code violation. Occurrence of a BPV or EXZ error event.

LDAP   Lightweight Directory Access Protocol. Protocol that provides access for management and browser applications that provide read/write interactive access to the X.500 Directory.

LDCELP   Low-delay CELP. CELP voice compression algorithm providing 16Kbps, or 4:1 compression. Standardized in ITU-T Recommendation G.728.

leaf internetwork   In a star topology, an internetwork whose sole access to other internetworks in the star is through a core router.

leaky bucket   In ATM, a metaphor for the GCRA, which is used for conformance checking of cell flows from a user or network. The hole in the bucket represents the sustained rate at which cells can be accommodated, and the bucket depth represents the tolerance for cell bursts over a period of time. See also *GCRA.*

learning bridge   Bridge that performs MAC address learning to reduce traffic on the network. Learning bridges manage a database of MAC addresses and the interfaces associated with each address. See also *MAC address learning.*

LE_ARP   LAN Emulation Address Resolution Protocol. Protocol that provides the ATM address that corresponds to a MAC address.

leased line   Transmission line reserved by a communications carrier for the private use of a customer. A leased line is a type of dedicated line. See also *dedicated line.*

LEC   *1.* LAN Emulation Client. Entity in an end system that performs data forwarding, address resolution, and other control functions for a single ES within a single ELAN. An LEC also provides a standard LAN service interface to any higher-layer entity that interfaces to the LEC. Each LEC is identified by a unique ATM address, and is associated with one or more MAC addresses reachable through that ATM address. See also

ELAN and *LES*. *2.* Local exchange carrier. Local or regional telephone company that owns and operates a telephone network and the customer lines that connect to it.

LECS   LAN Emulation Configuration Server. Entity that assigns individual LANE clients to particular ELANs by directing them to the LES that corresponds to the ELAN. There is logically one LECS per administrative domain, and this serves all ELANs within that domain. See also *ELAN*.

LED   Light emitting diode. Semiconductor device that emits light produced by converting electrical energy. Status lights on hardware devices are typically LEDs.

LEN node   Low-entry networking node. In SNA, a PU 2.1 that supports LU protocols, but whose CP cannot communicate with other nodes. Because there is no CP-to-CP session between a LEN node and its NN, the LEN node must have a statically defined image of the APPN network.

LES   LAN Emulation Server. Entity that implements the control function for a particular ELAN. There is only one logical LES per ELAN, and it is identified by a unique ATM address. See also *ELAN*.

Level 1 router   Device that routes traffic within a single DECnet or OSI area.

Level 2 router   Device that routes traffic between DECnet or OSI areas. All Level 2 routers must form a contiguous network.

LGN   Logical group node. The node that represents its peer group in the peer group's parent peer group. See also *parent peer group* and *peer group*.

light amplification by stimulated emission of radiation   See *laser*.

light emitting diode   See *LED*.

limited resource link   Resource defined by a device operator to remain active only when being used.

limited-route explorer packet   See *spanning explorer packet*.

line   *1.* In SNA, a connection to the network. *2.* See *link*.

line card   Any I/O card that can be inserted in a modular chassis.

line code type   One of a number of coding schemes used on serial lines to maintain data integrity and reliability. The line code type used is determined by the carrier service provider. See also *AMI*, *B8ZS*, and *HBD3*.

line code violation   See *LCV*.

line conditioning   Use of equipment on leased voice-grade channels to improve analog characteristics, thereby allowing higher transmission rates.

line driver   Inexpensive amplifier and signal converter that conditions digital signals to ensure reliable transmissions over extended distances.

line of sight   Characteristic of certain transmission systems such as laser, microwave, and infrared systems in which no obstructions in a direct path between transmitter and receiver can exist.

line printer daemon   See *LPD*.

line turnaround   Time required to change data transmission direction on a telephone line.

link   Network communications channel consisting of a circuit or transmission path and all related equipment between a sender and a receiver. Most often used to refer to a WAN connection. Sometimes referred to as a line or a transmission link.

Link Access Procedure, Balanced   See *LAPB*.

Link Access Procedure for Modems   See *LAPM*.

Link Access Procedure on the D channel   See *LAPD*.

Link Control Protocol   See *LCP*.

Link layer   See *Data Link layer*.

Link-layer address   See *MAC address*.

link-state advertisement   See *LSA*.

link-state packet   See *LSA*.

link-state routing algorithm   Routing algorithm in which each router broadcasts or multicasts information regarding the cost of reaching each of its neighbors to all nodes in the internetwork. Link state algorithms create a consistent view of the network and are therefore not prone to routing loops, but they achieve this at the cost of relatively greater computational difficulty and more widespread traffic (compared with distance vector routing algorithms). Compare to *distance vector routing algorithm*. See also *Dijkstra's algorithm*.

LIS   Logical IP subnet. A group of IP nodes (such as hosts and routers) that connects to a single ATM network and belong to the same IP subnet.

listserv   Automated mailing list distribution system originally designed for the Bitnet/EARN network. Allows users to add or delete themselves from mailing lists without (other) human intervention.

little-endian   Method of storing or transmitting data in which the least significant bit or byte is presented first. Compare to *big-endian*.

LLAP   LocalTalk Link Access Protocol. Link-level protocol that manages node-to-node delivery of data on a LocalTalk network. LLAP manages bus access, provides a node-addressing mechanism, and controls data transmission and reception, ensuring packet length and integrity. See also *LocalTalk*.

LLC   Logical Link Control. Higher of the two Data Link layer sublayers defined by the IEEE. The LLC sublayer handles error control, flow control, framing, and MAC-sublayer addressing. The most prevalent LLC protocol is IEEE 802.2, which includes both con-nectionless and connection-oriented variants. See also *Data Link layer* and *MAC*.

LLC2   Logical Link Control, type 2. Connection-oriented OSI LLC-sublayer protocol. See also *LLC*.

LMI   Local Management Interface. Set of enhancements to the basic Frame Relay specification. LMI includes support for a keepalive mechanism, which verifies that data is flowing; a multicast mechanism, which provides the network server with its local DLCI and the multicast DLCI; global addressing, which gives DLCIs global rather than local significance in Frame Relay networks; and a status mechanism, which provides an on-going status report on the DLCIs known to the switch. Known as LMT in ANSI terminology.

LMT   See *LMI*.

LM/X   LAN Manager for UNIX. Monitors LAN devices in UNIX environments.

LNM   LAN Network Manager. SRB and Token Ring management package provided by IBM. Typically running on a PC, it monitors SRB and Token Ring devices, and can pass alerts up to NetView.

LNNI   LAN Emulation Network-to-Network Interface. Supports communication between the server components within a single ELAN. Phase 1 LANE protocols do not allow for the standard support of multiple LESs or BUSs within an ELAN. Phase 2 addresses these limitations.

load balancing   In routing, the ability of a router to distribute traffic over all its network ports that are the same distance from the destination address. Good load-balancing algorithms use both line speed and reliability information. Load balancing increases the use of network segments, thus increasing effective network bandwidth.

local access and transport area   See *LATA*.

local acknowledgment   Method whereby an intermediate network node, such as a router, responds to acknowledgments for a remote end host. Use of local acknowledgments reduces network overhead and, therefore, the risk of time-outs. Also known as local termination.

local adjacency   See *local adjacency* in the "Cisco Systems Terms and Acronyms" section.

local-area network   See *LAN*.

local-area transport   See *LAT*.

local bridge   Bridge that directly interconnects networks in the same geographic area.

local exchange carrier   See *LEC*.

local explorer packet   Packet generated by an end system in an SRB network to find a host connected to the local ring. If the local explorer packet fails to find a local host, the end system produces either a spanning explorer packet or an all-routes explorer packet. See also *all-routes explorer packet, explorer packet,* and *spanning explorer packet.*

local loop   Line from the premises of a telephone subscriber to the telephone company CO.

Local Management Interface   See *LMI*.

LocalTalk   Apple Computer's proprietary baseband protocol that operates at the Data Link and Physical layers of the OSI reference model. LocalTalk uses CSMA/CD and supports transmissions at speeds of 230.4Kbps.

LocalTalk Link Access Protocol   See *LLAP*.

local termination   See *local acknowledgment.*

local traffic filtering   Process by which a bridge filters out (drops) frames whose source and destination MAC addresses are located on the same interface on the bridge, thus preventing unnecessary traffic from being forwarded across the bridge. Defined in the IEEE 802.1 standard. See also *IEEE 802.1.*

logical address   See *network address.*

logical channel   Nondedicated, packet-switched communications path between two or more network nodes. Packet switching allows many logical channels to exist simultaneously on a single physical channel.

logical channel identifier   See *LCI*.

logical channel number   See *LCN*.

logical group node   See *LGN*.

Logical Link Control   See *LLC*.

Logical Link Control, type 2   See *LLC2*.

logical unit   See *LU*.

Logical Unit 6.2   See *LU 6.2.*

loop   Route where packets never reach their destination, but simply cycle repeatedly through a constant series of network nodes.

loopback test   Test in which signals are sent and then directed back toward their source from some point along the communications path. Loopback tests are often used to test network interface usability.

lossy   Characteristic of a network that is prone to lose packets when it becomes highly loaded.

low-entry networking node   See *LEN node*.

LPD   Line printer daemon. Protocol used to send print jobs between UNIX systems.

LSA   Link-state advertisement. Broadcast packet used by link-state protocols that contains information about neighbors and path costs. LSAs are used by the receiving routers to maintain their routing tables. Sometimes called an LSP.

LSP   Link-state packet. See *LSA*.

LU   Logical unit. Primary component of SNA, an NAU that enables end users to communicate with each other and gain access to SNA network resources.

LU 6.2   Logical Unit 6.2. In SNA, an LU that provides peer-to-peer communication between programs in a distributed computing environment. APPC runs on LU 6.2 devices. See also *APPC*.

LUNI   LAN Emulation User-to-Network Interface. The ATM Forum standard for LAN emulation on ATM networks. Defines the interface between the LEC and the LAN Emulation Server components. See also *BUS*, *LECS*, and *LES*.

M

MAC   Media Access Control. Lower of the two sublayers of the Data Link layer defined by the IEEE. The MAC sublayer handles access to shared media, such as whether token passing or contention will be used. See also *Data Link layer* and *LLC*.

MAC address   Standardized Data Link layer address that is required for every port or device that connects to a LAN. Other devices in the network use these addresses to locate specific ports in the network and to create and update routing tables and data structures. MAC addresses are 6 bytes long and are controlled by the IEEE. Also known as a hardware address, MAC-layer address, or physical address. Compare to *network address*.

MAC address learning   Service that characterizes a learning bridge, in which the source MAC address of each received packet is stored so that future packets destined for that address can be forwarded only to the bridge interface on which that address is located. Packets destined for unrecognized addresses are forwarded out every bridge interface. This scheme helps minimize traffic on the attached LANs. MAC address learning is defined in the IEEE 802.1 standard. See also *learning bridge* and *MAC address*.

MacIP   Network layer protocol that encapsulates IP packets in DDP packets for transmission over AppleTalk. MacIP also provides proxy ARP services. See also *DDP* and *proxy ARP*.

MAC-layer address   See *MAC address*.

MAE   Metropolitan Access Exchange. One of a number of Internet Exchange Points. Examples include MAE West and MAE East. See *CIX*, *FIX*, and *GIX*.

mail bridge   Mail gateway that forwards email between two or more networks while ensuring that the messages it forwards meet certain administrative criteria. A mail bridge is simply a specialized form of mail gateway that enforces an administrative policy with regard to what mail it forwards.

mail exchange record   See *MX record*.

mail exploder   Part of an email delivery system that allows a message to be delivered to a list of addressees. Mail exploders are used to implement mailing lists. Users send messages to a single address (for example, hacks@somehost.edu), and the mail exploder takes care of delivery to the individual mailboxes in the list.

mail gateway   Machine that connects two or more electronic mail systems (especially dissimilar mail systems on two different networks) and transfers messages between them. Sometimes the mapping and translation can be quite complex, and generally it requires a store-and-forward scheme whereby the message is received from one system completely before it is transmitted to the next system after suitable translations.

Maintenance Operation Protocol   See *MOP*.

MAN   Metropolitan-area network. Network that spans a metropolitan area. Generally, a MAN spans a larger geographic area than a LAN, but a smaller geographic area than a WAN. Compare to *LAN* and *WAN*.

managed object   In network management, a network device that can be managed by a network management protocol.

Management Information Base   See *MIB*.

management services SNA functions distributed among network components to manage and control an SNA network.

Manchester encoding Digital coding scheme, used by IEEE 802.3 and Ethernet, in which a mid-bit-time transition is used for clocking, and a 1 is denoted by a high level during the first half of the bit time.

Manufacturing Automation Protocol See *MAP*.

MAP Manufacturing Automation Protocol. Network architecture created by General Motors to meet the specific needs of the factory floor. MAP specifies a token-passing LAN similar to IEEE 802.4. See also *IEEE 802.4*.

MARS Multicast Address Resolution Server. Mechanism for supporting IP multicast. A MARS serves a group of nodes (known as a cluster); each node in the cluster is configured with the ATM address of the MARS. The MARS supports multicast through multicast messages of overlaid point-to-multipoint connections or through multicast servers.

Martian Humorous term applied to packets that turn up unexpectedly on the wrong network because of bogus routing entries. Also used as a name for a packet that has an altogether bogus (nonregistered or ill-formed) Internet address.

mask See *address mask* and *subnet mask*.

MAU Media attachment unit. Device used in Ethernet and IEEE 802.3 networks that provides the interface between the AUI port of a station and the common medium of the Ethernet. The MAU, which can be built into a station or can be a separate device, performs Physical layer functions including the conversion of digital data from the Ethernet interface, collision detection, and injection of bits onto the network. Sometimes referred to as a media access unit, also abbreviated MAU, or as a transceiver. In Token Ring, a MAU is known as a multistation access unit and is usually abbreviated MSAU to avoid confusion. See also *AUI* and *MSAU*.

maximum burst Specifies the largest burst of data above the insured rate that will be allowed temporarily on an ATM PVC, but will not be dropped at the edge by the traffic policing function, even if it exceeds the maximum rate. This amount of traffic will be allowed only temporarily; on average, the traffic source needs to be within the maximum rate. Specified in bytes or cells. Compare to *insured burst*. See also *maximum rate*.

maximum rate Maximum total data throughput allowed on a given virtual circuit, equal to the sum of the insured and uninsured traffic from the traffic source. The uninsured data might be dropped if the network becomes congested. The maximum rate, which cannot exceed the media rate, represents the highest data throughput the virtual circuit will ever deliver, measured in bits or cells per second. Compare to *excess rate* and *insured rate*. See also *maximum burst*.

maximum transmission unit See *MTU*.

MB Megabyte. Approximately 1,000,000 bytes.

Mb Megabit. Approximately 1,000,000 bits.

MBONE multicast backbone. Multicast backbone of the Internet. MBONE is a virtual multicast network composed of multicast LANs and the point-to-point tunnels that interconnect them.

Mbps Megabits per second.

MBS Maximum burst size. In an ATM signaling message, burst tolerance is conveyed through the MBS, which is coded as a number of cells. The burst tolerance together with the SCR and the GCRA determine the MBS that can be transmitted at the peak rate and still be in conformance with the GCRA. See also *GCRA* and *SCR*.

MCA Micro channel architecture. Bus interface commonly used in PCs and some UNIX workstations and servers.

MCDV   Maximum cell delay variation. In an ATM network, the maximum two-point CDV objective across a link or node for the specified service category. One of four link metrics exchanged using PTSPs to determine the available resources of an ATM network. There is one MCDV value for each traffic class. See also *CDV* and *PTSP*.

MCLR   Maximum cell loss ratio. In an ATM network, the maximum ratio of cells that do not successfully transit a link or node compared with the total number of cells that arrive at the link or node. One of four link metrics exchanged using PTSPs to determine the available resources of an ATM network. The MCLR applies to cells in the CBR and VBR traffic classes whose CLP bit is set to zero. See also *CBR, CLP, PTSP,* and *VBR*.

MCR   Minimum cell rate. Parameter defined by the ATM Forum for ATM traffic management. MCR is defined only for ABR transmissions, and specifies the minimum value for the ACR. See also *ABR (available bit rate), ACR,* and *PCR*.

MCTD   Maximum cell transfer delay. In an ATM network, the sum of the MCDV and the fixed delay component across the link or node. One of four link metrics exchanged using PTSPs to determine the available resources of an ATM network. There is one MCTD value for each traffic class. See also *MCDV* and *PTSP*.

MD   Mediation device. Device that provides protocol translation and concentration of telemetry information originating from multiple network elements and transport to an OSS. See also *OSS*.

MD5   Message Digest 5. Algorithm used for message authentication in SNMP v.2. MD5 verifies the integrity of the communication, authenticates the origin, and checks for timeliness. See also *SNMP2*.

media   Plural of medium. Various physical environments through which transmission signals pass. Common network media include twisted-pair, coaxial,

and fiber-optic cable, and the atmosphere (through which microwave, laser, and infrared transmission occurs). Sometimes called physical media.

Media Access Control   See *MAC*.

media access unit   See *MAU*.

media attachment unit   See *MAU*.

media interface connector   See *MIC*.

media rate   Maximum traffic throughput for a particular media type.

medium   See *media*.

megabit   Abbreviated Mb. Approximately 1,000,000 bits.

megabits per second   Abbreviated Mbps.

megabyte   Abbreviated MB. Approximately 1,000,000 bytes.

mesh   Network topology in which devices are organized in a manageable, segmented manner with many, often redundant, interconnections strategically placed between network nodes. See also *full mesh* and *partial mesh*.

message   Application layer (Layer 7) logical grouping of information, often composed of a number of lower-layer logical groupings such as packets. The terms datagram, frame, packet, and segment are also used to describe logical information groupings at various layers of the OSI reference model and in various technology circles.

Message Digest 5   See *MD5*.

message handling system   See *MHS*.

Message Queuing Interface   See *MQI*.

message switching   Switching technique involving transmission of messages from node to node through a network. The message is stored at each node until such time as a forwarding path is available. Contrast with *circuit switching* and *packet switching*.

message unit Unit of data processed by any Network layer.

metasignaling Process running at the ATM layer that manages signaling types and virtual circuits.

metering See *traffic shaping*.

metric See *routing metric*.

metropolitan-area network See *MAN*.

MHS message handling system. ITU-T X.400 recommmendations that provide message handling services for communications between distributed applications. NetWare MHS is a different (though similar) entity that also provides message-handling services. See also *IFIP*.

MIB Management Information Base. Database of network management information that is used and maintained by a network management protocol such as SNMP or CMIP. The value of a MIB object can be changed or retrieved using SNMP or CMIP commands, usually through a GUI network management system. MIB objects are organized in a tree structure that includes public (standard) and private (proprietary) branches.

MIC Media interface connector. FDDI de facto standard connector.

micro channel architecture See *MCA*.

microcode Translation layer between machine instructions and the elementary operations of a computer. Microcode is stored in ROM and allows the addition of new machine instructions without requiring that they be designed into electronic circuits when new instructions are needed.

microsegmentation Division of a network into smaller segments, usually with the intention of increasing aggregate bandwidth to network devices.

microwave Electromagnetic waves in the range 1 to 30 GHz. Microwave-based networks are an evolving technology gaining favor due to high bandwidth and relatively low cost.

MID Message identifier. In ATM, used to identify ATM cells that carry segments from the same higher-layer packet.

mid-level network mid-level networks (also referred to as regionals) make up the second level of the Internet hierarchy. They are the transit networks that connect the stub networks to the backbone networks.

midsplit Broadband cable system in which the available frequencies are split into two groups: one for transmission and one for reception.

MII Media Independent Interface. Standard specification for the interface between network controller chips and their associated media interface chip(s). The MII automatically senses 10- and 100-MHz Ethernet speeds.

Military Network See *MILNET*.

millions of instructions per second See *mips*.

MILNET Military Network. Unclassified portion of the DDN. Operated and maintained by the DISA. See also *DDN* and *DISA*.

MIME Multipurpose Internet Mail Extensions. An Internet message, as defined by RFC 822, consists of two parts: a header and a body. MIME defines a set of five extensions to RFC 822: a content type header field, a content transfer encoding header field, a MIME version header field, an optional content ID header field, and optional content descriptions header field. MIME has become the standard for attaching non-text files to email messages in a way that allows the attachment to be received intact over a network.

minimum cell rate See *MCR*.

MIP See *MIP* in the "Cisco Systems Terms and Acronyms" section.

mips Millions of instructions per second. Number of instructions executed by a processor per second.

MLP Multilink PPP. Method of splitting, recombining, and sequencing datagrams across multiple logical data links.

MMP Multichassis Multilink PPP. Extends MLP support across multiple routers and access servers. MMP enables multiple routers and access servers to operate as a single, large dial-up pool, with a single network address and ISDN access number. MMP correctly handles packet fragmenting and reassembly when a user connection is split between two physical access devices.

modem Modulator-demodulator. Device that converts digital and analog signals. At the source, a modem converts digital signals to a form suitable for transmission over analog communication facilities. At the destination, the analog signals are returned to their digital form. Modems allow data to be transmitted over voice-grade telephone lines.

modem eliminator Device allowing connection of two DTE devices without modems.

modulation Process by which the characteristics of electrical signals are transformed to represent information. Types of modulation include AM, FM, and PAM. See also AM, *FM*, and *PAM*.

modulator-demodulator See *modem*.

monomode fiber See *single-mode fiber*.

MOP Maintenance Operation Protocol. Digital Equipment Corporation protocol that provides a way to perform primitive maintenance operations on DECnet systems. For example, MOP can be used to download a system image to a diskless station.

Mosaic Public-domain WWW browser, developed at the NCSA. See also *browser*.

MOSPF Multicast OSPF. Intradomain multicast routing protocol used in OSPF networks. Extensions are applied to the base OSPF unicast protocol to support IP multicast routing.

MPEG Motion Picture Experts Group. Standard for compressing video. MPEG1 is a bit stream standard for compressed video and audio optimized to fit into a bandwidth of 1.5Mbps. MPEG2 is intended for higher quality video-on-demand applications and runs at data rates between 4 and 9Mbps. MPEG4 is a low-bit-rate compression algorithm intended for 64Kbps connections.

MPLS Multiprotocol Label Switching. Emerging industry standard upon which tag switching is based.

MPOA Multiprotocol over ATM. ATM Forum standardization effort specifying how existing and future Network layer protocols such as IP, IPv6, AppleTalk, and IPX run over an ATM network with directly attached hosts, routers, and multilayer LAN switches.

MQI Message Queuing Interface. International standard API that provides functionality similar to that of the RPC interface. In contrast to RPC, MQI is implemented strictly at the Application layer. See also *RPC*.

MSAU Multistation access unit. Wiring concentrator to which all end stations in a Token Ring network connect. The MSAU provides an interface between these devices and the Token Ring interface of a router. Sometimes abbreviated MAU.

MTA Message Transfer Agent. OSI application process used to store and forward messages in the X.400 Message Handling System. Equivalent to Internet mail agent.

MTU Maximum transmission unit. Maximum packet size, in bytes, that a particular interface can handle.

MUD Multi-user dungeon. Adventure, role playing games, or simulations played on the Internet. Players interact in real time and can change the "world" in the game as they play it. Most MUDs are based on the Telnet protocol.

mu-law North American companding standard used in conversion between analog and digital signals in PCM systems. Similar to the European a-law. See also *a-law* and *companding*.

multiaccess network Network that allows multiple devices to connect and communicate simultaneously.

multicast Single packets copied by the network and sent to a specific subset of network addresses. These addresses are specified in the Destination Address Field. Compare to *broadcast* and *unicast*.

multicast address Single address that refers to multiple network devices. Synonymous with group address. Compare to *broadcast address* and *unicast address*. See also *multicast*.

multicast backbone See *MBONE*.

multicast forward VCC VCC set up by the BUS to the LEC as a leaf in a point-to-multipoint connection. See also *BUS, LEC (LAN Emulation Client),* and *VCC*.

multicast group Dynamically determined group of IP hosts identified by a single IP multicast address.

Multicast OSPF See *MOSPF*.

multicast router Router used to send IGMP query messages on their attached local networks. Host members of a multicast group respond to a query by sending IGMP reports noting the multicast groups to which they belong. The multicast router takes responsibility for forwarding multicast datagrams from one multicast group to all other networks that have members in the group. See also *IGMP*.

multicast send VCC In an ATM network, a bi-directional point-to-point VCC set up by a LEC to a BUS. One of three data connections defined by Phase 1 LANE. Compare to *control direct VCC* and *control distribute VCC*. See also *BUS, LEC (LAN Emulation Client),* and *VCC*.

multicast server Establishes a one-to-many connection to each device in a VLAN, thus establishing a broadcast domain for each VLAN segment. The multicast server forwards incoming broadcasts only to the multicast address that maps to the broadcast address.

MultiChannel Interface Processor See *MIP* in the "Cisco Systems Terms and Acronyms" section.

multidrop line Communications line with multiple cable access points. Sometimes called a multipoint line.

multihomed host Host attached to multiple physical network segments in an OSI CLNS network.

multihoming Addressing scheme in IS-IS routing that supports assignment of multiple area addresses.

multilayer switch Switch that filters and forwards packets based on MAC addresses and network addresses. A subset of LAN switch. Compare to *LAN switch*.

multimode fiber Optical fiber supporting propagation of multiple frequencies of light. See also *single-mode fiber*.

multiple domain network SNA network with multiple SSCPs. See also *SSCP*.

multiplexing Scheme that allows multiple logical signals to be transmitted simultaneously across a single physical channel. Compare to *demultiplexing*.

multipoint line See *multidrop line*.

Multiprotocol over ATM See *MPOA*.

Multipurpose Internet Mail Extensions See *MIME*.

multistation access unit See *MSAU*.

multi-user dungeon See *MUD*.

multivendor network Network using equipment from more than one vendor. Multivendor networks pose many more compatibility problems than single-vendor networks. Compare to *single-vendor network*.

mux Multiplexing device. Combines multiple signals for transmission over a single line. The signals are demultiplexed, or separated, at the receiving end.

MX record   Mail exchange record. DNS resource record type indicating which host can handle email for a particular domain.

N

NACS   NetWare Asynchronous Communication Services. Novell software that supports Novell's AIO and NASI programming interfaces. NACS promotes the sharing of communications resources such as modems, asynchronous hosts, and X.25 network services.

NADF   North American Directory Forum. Collection of organizations that offer, or plan to offer, public directory services in North America, based on the CCITT X.500 Recommendations.

NADN   Nearest active downstream neighbor. In Token Ring or IEEE 802.5 networks, the closest downstream network device from any given device that is still active.

Nagle's algorithm   Actually two separate congestion control algorithms that can be used in TCP-based networks. One algorithm reduces the sending window; the other limits small datagrams.

NAK   Negative acknowledgment. Response sent from a receiving device to a sending device indicating that the information received contained errors. Compare to *acknowledgment*.

Name Binding Protocol   See *NBP*.

name caching   Method by which remotely discovered host names are stored by a router for use in future packet-forwarding decisions to allow quick access.

name resolution   Generally, the process of associating a name with a network location.

name server   Server connected to a network that resolves network names into network addresses.

namespace   Commonly distributed set of names in which all names are unique.

NANOG   North American Network Operator's Group. Primary forum for information exchange among U.S. exchange point participants, Internet service providers, and end users.

NAP   Network access point. Location for interconnection of Internet service providers in the United States for the exchange of packets.

NARP   NBMA Address Resolution Protocol. Functional subset of NHRP that returns only the address mappings of nodes that are directly connection the NBMA network. Compare to *NHRP*.

narrowband   See *baseband*.

Narrowband ISDN   See *N-ISDN*.

NAS   Network access server.

NASI   NetWare Asynchronous Support Interface.

NAT   Network Address Translation. Mechanism for reducing the need for globally unique IP addresses. NAT allows an organization with addresses that are not globally unique to connect to the Internet by translating those addresses into globally routable address space. Also known as Network Address Translator.

National Bureau of Standards   See *NBS*.

National Institute of Standards and Technology See *NIST*.

National Research and Education Network   See *NREN*.

National Science Foundation   See *NSF*.

National Science Foundation Network   See *NSFNET*.

native client interface architecture   See *NCIA* in the "Cisco Systems Terms and Acronyms" section.

NAU   Network addressable unit. SNA term for an addressable entity. Examples include LUs, PUs, and SSCPs. NAUs generally provide upper-level network services. Compare to *path control network*.

NAUN   Nearest active upstream neighbor. In Token Ring or IEEE 802.5 networks, the closest upstream network device from any given device that is still active.

NBFCP   NetBIOS Frames Control Protocol. Protocol that establishes and configures NetBIOS over PPP. See also *NetBIOS* and *PPP*.

NBMA   Nonbroadcast multiaccess. Term describing a multiaccess network that either does not support broadcasting (such as X.25) or in which broadcasting is not feasible (for example, an SMDS broadcast group or an extended Ethernet that is too large). See also *multiaccess network*.

NBP   Name Binding Protocol. AppleTalk transport-level protocol that translates a character string name into the DDP address of the corresponding socket client. NBP enables AppleTalk protocols to understand user-defined zones and device names by providing and maintaining translation tables that map names to their corresponding socket addresses.

NBS   National Bureau of Standards. Organization that was part of the U.S. Department of Commerce. Now known as NIST. See also *NIST*.

NCIA   See *NCIA* in the "Cisco Systems Terms and Acronyms" section.

NCP   *1.* Network Control Program. In SNA, a program that routes and controls the flow of data between a communications controller (in which it resides) and other network resources. *2.* Network Control Protocol. Series of protocols for establishing and configuring different Network layer protocols, such as for AppleTalk over PPP. See also *PPP*.

NCP/Token Ring Interconnection   See *NTRI*.

NCSA   National Center for Supercomputing Applications.

NDIS   Network driver interface specification. Microsoft specification for a generic, hardware- and protocol-independent device driver for NICs.

NE   Network element. In OSS, a single piece of telecommunications equipment used to perform a function or service integral to the underlying network.

nearest active upstream neighbor   See *NAUN*.

NEARNET   Regional network in New England (United States) that links Boston University, Harvard University, and MIT. Now part of BBN Planet. See also *BBN Planet*.

NEBS   Network Equipment Building Systems. In OSS, the Bellcore requirement for equipment deployed in a central office environment. Covers spatial, hardware, crafts person interface, thermal, fire resistance, handling and transportation, earthquake and vibration, airborne contaminants, grounding, acoustical noise, illumination, EMC, and ESD requirements.

negative acknowledgment   See *NAK*.

neighboring routers   In OSPF, two routers that have interfaces to a common network. On multiaccess networks, neighbors are dynamically discovered by the OSPF Hello protocol.

NET   Network entity title. Network addresses, defined by the ISO network architecture, and used in CLNS-based networks.

net   Short for network.

NetBEUI   NetBIOS Extended User Interface. Enhanced version of the NetBIOS protocol used by network operating systems such as LAN Manager, LAN Server, Windows for Workgroups, and Windows NT.

NetBEUI formalizes the transport frame and adds additional functions. NetBEUI implements the OSI LLC2 protocol. See also *LLC2* and *OSI*.

NetBIOS Network Basic Input/Output System. API used by applications on an IBM LAN to request services from lower-level network processes. These services might include session establishment and termination, and information transfer.

netiquette A pun on "etiquette" referring to proper behavior on a network.

NETscout See *NETscout* in the "Cisco Systems Terms and Acronyms" section.

NetView IBM network management architecture and related applications. NetView is a VTAM application used for managing mainframes in SNA networks. See also *VTAM*.

NetWare Popular distributed NOS developed by Novell. Provides transparent remote file access and numerous other distributed network services.

NetWare Link Services Protocol See *NLSP*.

NetWare Loadable Module See *NLM*.

network Collection of computers, printers, routers, switches, and other devices that are able to communicate with each other over some transmission medium.

network access point See *NAP*.

network access server See *access server* and *NAS*.

network address Network layer address referring to a logical, rather than a physical, network device. Also called a protocol address. Compare to *MAC address*.

network addressable unit See *NAU*.

Network Address Translation See *NAT*.

Network Address Translator See *NAT*.

network administrator Person responsible for the operation, maintenance, and management of a network. See also *network operator*.

network analyzer Hardware or software device offering various network troubleshooting features, including protocol-specific packet decodes, specific pre-programmed troubleshooting tests, packet filtering, and packet transmission.

Network Basic Input/Output System See *NetBIOS*.

network byte order Internet-standard ordering of the bytes corresponding to numeric values.

Network Control Program See *NCP*.

network driver interface specification See *NDIS*.

network entity title See *NET*.

Network File System See *NFS*.

Network Information Center See *InterNIC*.

Network Information Service See *NIS*.

network interface Boundary between a carrier network and a privately-owned installation.

network interface card See *NIC*.

Network layer Layer 3 of the OSI reference model. This layer provides connectivity and path selection between two end systems. The Network layer is the layer at which routing occurs. Corresponds roughly with the Path Control layer of the SNA model. See also *Application layer*, *Data Link layer*, *Physical layer*, *Presentation layer*, *Session layer*, and *Transport layer*.

network management Generic term used to describe systems or actions that help maintain, characterize, or troubleshoot a network.

Network Management Processor See *NMP* in the "Cisco Systems Terms and Acronyms" section.

network management system See *NMS*.

network management vector transport See *NMVT*.

network node See *NN*.

network node interface See *NNI*.

Network Node Server   SNA NN that provides resource location and route selection services for ENs, LEN nodes, and LUs that are in its domain.

network number   Part of an IP address that specifies the network to which the host belongs.

network operating system   See *NOS.*

Network Operations Center   See *NOC.*

network operator   Person who routinely monitors and controls a network, performing such tasks as reviewing and responding to traps, monitoring throughput, configuring new circuits, and resolving problems. See also *network administrator.*

network service access point   See *NSAP.*

network termination device 1   See *NT-1.*

Network Time Protocol   See *NTP.*

Network-to-Network Interface   See *NNI.*

network-visible entity   See *NVE.*

Next Hop Resolution Protocol   See *NHRP.*

NFS   Network File System. As commonly used, a distributed file system protocol suite developed by Sun Microsystems that allows remote file access across a network. In actuality, NFS is simply one protocol in the suite. NFS protocols include NFS, RPC, XDR, and others. These protocols are part of a larger architecture that Sun refers to as ONC. See also *ONC.*

NHRP   Next Hop Resolution Protocol. Protocol used by routers to dynamically discover the MAC address of other routers and hosts connected to a NBMA network. These systems can then directly communicate without requiring traffic to use an intermediate hop, increasing performance in ATM, Frame Relay, SMDS, and X.25 environments.

NHS   Next Hop Server. Server defined by the NHRP protocol that maintains next-hop resolution cache tables containing the IP-to-ATM address mappings of associated nodes and nodes that are reachable through routers served by the NHS.

NIC   *1.* Network interface card. Board that provides network communication capabilities to and from a computer system. Also called an adapter. See also *AUI.* *2.* Network Information Center. Organization whose functions have been assumed by the InterNIC. See also *InterNIC.*

NIS   Network Information Service. Protocol developed by Sun Microsystems for the administration of network-wide databases. The service essentially uses two programs: one for finding a NIS server and one for accessing the NIS databases.

N-ISDN   Narrowband ISDN. Communication standards developed by the ITU-T for baseband networks. Based on 64Kbps B channels and 16 or 64Kbps D channels. Contrast with *BISDN.* See also *BRI, ISDN,* and *PRI.*

NIST   National Institute of Standards and Technology. U.S. Government organization that supports and catalogs a variety of standards. Formerly the NBS. See also *NBS.*

NLM   NetWare Loadable Module. Individual program that can be loaded into memory and function as part of the NetWare NOS.

NLSP   NetWare Link Services Protocol. Link-state routing protocol based on IS-IS. See also *IS-IS.*

NMA   Network Management and Analysis. Bellcore OSS providing alarm surveillance and performance monitoring of intelligent network elements.

NMP   See *NMP (Network Management Processor)* in the "Cisco Systems Terms and Acronyms" section.

NMS   Network management system. System responsible for managing at least part of a network. An NMS is generally a reasonably powerful and well-equipped computer such as an engineering workstation.

NMSs communicate with agents to help keep track of network statistics and resources.

NMVT Network management vector transport. SNA message consisting of a series of vectors conveying network management specific information.

NN Network node. SNA intermediate node that provides connectivity, directory services, route selection, intermediate session routing, data transport, and network management services to LEN nodes and ENs. The NN contains a CP that manages the resources of both the NN itself and those of the ENs and LEN nodes in its domain. NNs provide intermediate routing services by implementing the APPN PU 2.1 extensions. Compare to *EN*. See also *CP*.

NNI *1.* Network-to-Network Interface. ATM Forum standard that defines the interface between two ATM switches that are both located in a private network or are both located in a public network. The interface between a public switch and private one is defined by the UNI standard. Also, the standard interface between two Frame Relay switches meeting the same criteria. Compare to *UNI*. *2.* Network node interface.

NOC Network Operations Center. Organization responsible for maintaining a network.

node *1.* Endpoint of a network connection or a junction common to two or more lines in a network. Nodes can be processors, controllers, or workstations. Nodes, which vary in routing and other functional capabilities, can be interconnected by links, and serve as control points in the network. Node is sometimes used generically to refer to any entity that can access a network, and is frequently used interchangeably with device. See also *host*. *2.* In SNA, the basic component of a network and the point at which one or more functional units connect channels or data circuits.

noise Undesirable communications channel signals.

nonbroadcast multiaccess See *NBMA*.

nonextended network AppleTalk Phase 2 network that supports addressing of up to 253 nodes and only 1 zone.

nonreturn to zero See *NRZ*.

nonreturn to zero inverted See *NRZI*.

nonseed router In AppleTalk, a router that must first obtain, and then verify, its configuration with a seed router before it can begin operation. See also *seed router*.

non-stub area Resource-intensive OSPF area that carries a default route, static routes, intra-area routes, interarea routes, and external routes. Nonstub areas are the only OSPF areas that can have virtual links configured across them, and are the only areas that can contain an ASBR. Compare to *stub area*. See also *ASBR* and *OSPF*.

nonvolatile random-access memory See *NVRAM*.

normal response mode See *NRM*.

Northwest Net NSF-funded regional network serving the Northwestern United States, Alaska, Montana, and North Dakota. Northwest Net connects all major universities in the region as well as many leading industrial concerns.

NOS Network operating system. Generic term used to refer to what are really distributed file systems. Examples of NOSs include LAN Manager, NetWare, NFS, and VINES.

Novell IPX See *IPX*.

NREN National Research and Education Network. Component of the HPCC program designed to ensure U.S. technical leadership in computer communications through research and development efforts in state-of-the-art telecommunications and networking technologies. See also *HPCC*.

NRM Normal response mode. HDLC mode for use on links with one primary station and one or more secondary stations. In this mode, secondary stations can transmit only if they first receive a poll from the primary station.

NRZ Nonreturn to zero. Signals that maintain constant voltage levels with no signal transitions (no return to a zero-voltage level) during a bit interval. Compare to *NRZI*.

NRZI Nonreturn to zero inverted. Signals that maintain constant voltage levels with no signal transitions (no return to a zero-voltage level), but interpret the presence of data at the beginning of a bit interval as a signal transition and the absence of data as no transition. Compare to *NRZ*.

NSAP Network service access point. Network addresses, as specified by ISO. An NSAP is the point at which OSI Network Service is made available to a Transport layer (Layer 4) entity.

NSF National Science Foundation. U.S. Government agency that funds scientific research in the United States. The now-defunct NSFNET was funded by the NSF. See also *NSFNET*.

NSFNET National Science Foundation Network. Large network that was controlled by the NSF and provided networking services in support of education and research in the United States, from 1986 to 1995. NSFNET is no longer in service.

NT-1 Network termination device 1. In ISDN, a device that provides the interface between customer premises equipment and central office switching equipment.

NTP Network Time Protocol. Protocol built on top of TCP that assures accurate local time-keeping with reference to radio and atomic clocks located on the Internet. This protocol is capable of synchronizing distributed clocks within milliseconds over long time periods.

NTRI NCP/Token Ring Interconnection. Function used by ACF/NCP to support Token Ring-attached

SNA devices. NTRI also provides translation from Token Ring-attached SNA devices (PUs) to switched (dial-up) devices.

null modem Small box or cable used to join computing devices directly, rather than over a network.

NVE Network-visible entity. Resource that is addressable through a network. Typically, an NVE is a socket client for a service available in a node.

NVRAM Nonvolatile RAM. RAM that retains its contents when a unit is powered off.

NYSERNet Network in New York (United States) with a T1 backbone connecting NSF, many universities, and several commercial concerns.

O

OAM cell Operation, Administration, and Maintenance cell. ATM Forum specification for cells used to monitor virtual circuits. OAM cells provide a virtual circuit-level loopback in which a router responds to the cells, demonstrating that the circuit is up, and the router is operational.

OAM&P Operations Administration Maintenance and Provisioning.

OARnet Ohio Academic Resources Network. Internet service provider that connects a number of U.S. sites, including the Ohio supercomputer center in Columbus, Ohio.

object instance Network management term referring to an instance of an object type that has been bound to a value.

OC Optical Carrier. Series of physical protocols (OC-1, OC-2, OC-3, and so forth) defined for SONET optical signal transmissions. OC signal levels put STS frames onto multimode fiber-optic line at a variety of speeds. The base rate is 51.84Mbps (OC-1);

each signal level thereafter operates at a speed divisible by that number (thus, OC-3 runs at 155.52Mbps). See also *SONET*, *STS-1*, and *STS-3c*.

OCLC Online Computer Library Catalog. Nonprofit membership organization offering computer-based services to libraries, educational organizations, and their users.

octet 8 bits. In networking, the term octet is often used (rather than byte) because some machine architectures employ bytes that are not 8 bits long.

ODA Open Document Architecture. ISO standard that specifies how documents are represented and transmitted electronically. Formerly called Office Document Architecture.

ODBC Open DataBase Connectivity. Standard application programming interface for accessing data in both relational and nonrelational database management systems. Using this application programming interface, database applications can access data stored in database management systems on a variety of computers even if each database management system uses a different data storage format and programming interface. ODBC is based on the call level interface specification of the X/Open SQL Access Group and was developed by Digitial Equipment Corporation, Lotus, Microsoft, and Sybase. Contrast with *JDBC*.

ODI Open Data-Link Interface. Novell specification providing a standardized interface for NICs (network interface cards) that allows multiple protocols to use a single NIC. See also *NIC*.

OEMI channel See *block multiplexer channel*.

Office Document Architecture See *ODA*.

Ohio Academic Resources Network See *OARnet*.

OIM OSI Internet Management. Group tasked with specifying ways in which OSI network management protocols can be used to manage TCP/IP networks.

OIR Online insertion and removal. Feature that permits the addition, replacement, or removal of cards without interrupting the system power, entering console commands, or causing other software or interfaces to shut down. Sometimes called hot swapping or power-on servicing.

OMG Object Management Group.

ONC Open Network Computing. Distributed applications architecture designed by Sun Microsystems, currently controlled by a consortium led by Sun. The NFS protocols are part of ONC. See also *NFS*.

ones density Scheme that allows a CSU/DSU to recover the data clock reliably. The CSU/DSU derives the data clock from the data that passes through it. In order to recover the clock, the CSU/DSU hardware must receive at least one 1 bit value for every 8 bits of data that pass through it. Also called pulse density.

online insertion and removal See *OIR*.

on-the-fly packet switching See *cut-through packet switching*.

open architecture Architecture with which third-party developers can legally develop products and for which public domain specifications exist.

open circuit Broken path along a transmission medium. Open circuits will usually prevent network communication.

Open Database Connectivity See *ODBC*.

Open Data-Link Interface See *ODI*.

Open Document Architecture See *ODA*.

Open Group Group formed in February 1996 by the consolidation of the two leading open systems consortia: X/Open Company Ltd (X/Open) and the Open Software Foundation (OSF).

Open Network Computing See *ONC*.

Open Shortest Path First See *OSPF*.

Open System Interconnection See *OSI.*

Open System Interconnection reference model See *OSI reference model.*

Operation, Administration, and Maintenance cell See *OAM cell.*

OPS/INE Operations Provisioning System/Intelligent Network Element. Bellcore OSS that provides provisioning services for intelligent network elements. See also *OSS.*

Optical Carrier See *OC.*

optical fiber See *fiber-optic cable.*

Optimized Bandwidth Management Cisco wide-area switches ensure fair and cost-efficient bandwidth utilization using various techniques. ABR and Optimized Banwidth Management are used for ATM and Frame Relay traffic. ABR is a standards-based ATM traffic management mechanism, and ForeSight is Cisco's implementation that mirrors ABR capabilities for Frame Relay traffic. ABR and Optimized Bandwidth Management optimize real-time traffic performance and throughput, and minimize data loss. Bandwidth management for voice is achieved through the use of standards-based voice compression and silence suppression mechanisms for circuit data services. Formerly called ForeSight.

Organizational Unique Identifier See *OUI.*

OSF Open Software Foundation. Group responsible for the Distributed Computing Environment (DCE) and the Distributed Management Environment (DME). See also *DCE.*

OSI Open System Interconnection. International standardization program created by ISO and ITU-T to develop standards for data networking that facilitate multivendor equipment interoperability.

OSI Internet Management See *OIM.*

OSINET International association designed to promote OSI in vendor architectures.

OSI Network Address Address, consisting of up to 20 octets, used to locate an OSI Transport entity. The address is formatted into two parts: an Initial Domain Part that is standardized for each of several addressing domains and a Domain Specific Part that is the responsibility of the addressing authority for that domain.

OSI Presentation Address Address used to locate an OSI Application entity. It consists of an OSI Network Address and up to three selectors, one each for use by the Transport, Session, and Presentation entities.

OSI reference model Open System Interconnection reference model. Network architectural model developed by ISO and ITU-T. The model consists of seven layers, each of which specifies particular network functions such as addressing, flow control, error control, encapsulation, and reliable message transfer. The lowest layer (the Physical layer) is closest to the media technology. The lower two layers are implemented in hardware and software, while the upper five layers are implemented only in software. The highest layer (the Application layer) is closest to the user. The OSI reference model is used universally as a method for teaching and understanding network functionality. Similar in some respects to SNA. See *Application layer, Data Link layer, Network layer, Physical layer, Presentation layer, Session layer,* and *Transport layer.*

OSPF Open Shortest Path First. Link-state, hierarchical IGP routing algorithm proposed as a successor to RIP in the Internet community. OSPF features include least-cost routing, multipath routing, and load balancing. OSPF was derived from an early version of the IS-IS protocol. See also *IGP, IS-IS,* and *RIP,* and *Enhanced IGRP* and *IGRP* in the "Cisco Systems Terms and Acronyms" section.

OSS Operations Support System. Network management system supporting a specific management function, such as alarm surveillance and provisioning, in a carrier network. Many OSSs are large centralized systems running on mainframes or minicomputers. Common OSSs used within an RBOC include NMA, OPS/INE, and TIRKS.

OUI   Organizational Unique Identifier. Three octets assigned by the IEEE in a block of 48-bit LAN addresses.

outframe   Maximum number of outstanding frames allowed in an SNA PU 2 server at any time.

out-of-band signaling   Transmission using frequencies or channels outside the frequencies or channels normally used for information transfer. Out-of-band signaling is often used for error reporting in situations in which in-band signaling can be affected by whatever problems the network might be experiencing. Contrast with *in-band signaling*.

P

PABX   Private Automatic Branch Exchange. Telephone switch for use inside a corporation. PABX is the preferred term in Europe, while PBX is used in the United States.

pacing   See *flow control*.

packet   Logical grouping of information that includes a header containing control information and (usually) user data. Packets are most often used to refer to Network layer units of data. The terms datagram, frame, message, and segment are also used to describe logical information groupings at various layers of the OSI reference model and in various technology circles. See also *PDU*.

packet assembler/disassembler   See *PAD*.

packet buffer   See *buffer*.

packet internet groper   See *ping*.

packet level protocol   See *PLP*.

packet switch   WAN device that routes packets along the most efficient path and allows a communications channel to be shared by multiple connections. Formerly called an IMP. See also *IMP*.

packet-switched data network   See *PSN*.

packet-switched network   See *PSN*.

packet switch exchange   See *PSE*.

packet switching   Networking method in which nodes share bandwidth with each other by sending packets. Compare to *circuit switching* and *message switching*. See also *PSN*.

packet-switching node   See *packet switch*.

PAD   Packet assembler/disassembler. Device used to connect simple devices (like character-mode terminals) that do not support the full functionality of a particular protocol to a network. PADs buffer data and assemble and disassemble packets sent to such end devices.

Palo Alto Research Center   See *PARC*.

PAM   Pulse amplitude modulation. Modulation scheme where the modulating wave is caused to modulate the amplitude of a pulse stream. Compare to *AM* and *FM*. See also *modulation*.

PAP   Password Authentication Protocol. Authentication protocol that allows PPP peers to authenticate one another. The remote router attempting to connect to the local router is required to send an authentication request. Unlike CHAP, PAP passes the password and host name or username in the clear (unencrypted). PAP does not itself prevent unauthorized access, but merely identifies the remote end. The router or access server then determines if that user is allowed access. PAP is supported only on PPP lines. Compare to *CHAP*.

parallel channel   Channel that uses bus and tag cables as a transmission medium. Compare to *ESCON channel*. See also *bus and tag channel*.

parallelism   Indicates that multiple paths exist between two points in a network. These paths might be of equal or unequal cost. Parallelism is often a network design goal: If one path fails, there is redundancy in the network to ensure that an alternate path to the same point exists.

parallel transmission   Method of data transmission in which the bits of a data character are transmitted simultaneously over a number of channels. Compare to *serial transmission.*

PARC   Palo Alto Research Center. Research and development center operated by XEROX. A number of widely used technologies were originally conceived at PARC, including the first personal computers and LANs.

PARC Universal Protocol   See *PUP.*

parent peer group   In ATM, a peer group that acts as a "parent" to a subordinate peer group. Organizing peer groups hierarchically reduces the exchange of PTSPs. See also *child peer group, peer group,* and *PTSP.*

parity check   Process for checking the integrity of a character. A parity check involves appending a bit that makes the total number of binary 1 digits in a character or word (excluding the parity bit) either odd (for odd parity) or even (for even parity).

partial mesh   Network in which devices are organized in a mesh topology, with some network nodes organized in a full mesh, but with others that are only connected to one or two other nodes in the network. A partial mesh does not provide the level of redundancy of a full mesh topology, but is less expensive to implement. Partial mesh topologies are generally used in the peripheral networks that connect to a fully meshed backbone. See also *full mesh* and *mesh.*

Password Authentication Protocol   See *PAP.*

Path Control layer   Layer 3 in the SNA architectural model. This layer performs sequencing services related

to proper data reassembly. The Path control layer is also responsible for routing. Corresponds roughly with the Network layer of the OSI model. See also *Data Flow Control layer, Data-Link Control layer, Physical Control layer, Presentation Services layer, Transaction Services layer,* and *Transmission Control layer.*

path control network   SNA concept that consists of lower-level components that control the routing and data flow through an SNA network and handle physical data transmission between SNA nodes. Compare to *NAU.*

path cost   See *cost.*

path name   Full name of a DOS, Mac OS, or UNIX file or directory, including all directory and subdirectory names. Consecutive names in a path name are typically separated by a backslash (\) for DOS, a colon (:) for Mac OS, and a forward slash (/) for UNIX.

payload   Portion of a cell, frame, or packet that contains upper-layer information (data).

payload type identifier   See *PTI.*

PBX   Private branch exchange. Digital or analog telephone switchboard located on the subscriber premises and used to connect private and public telephone networks.

PCI   Protocol control information. Control information added to user data to comprise an OSI packet. The OSI equivalent of the term header. See also *header.*

PCM   Pulse code modulation. Transmission of analog information in digital form through sampling and encoding the samples with a fixed number of bits.

PCR   Peak cell rate. Parameter defined by the ATM Forum for ATM traffic management. In CBR transmissions, PCR determines how often data samples are sent. In ABR transmissions, PCR determines the maximum value of the ACR. See also *ABR (available bit rate), ACR,* and *CBR.*

PCS   *1.* Personal Communications Service. Advanced network architecture that provides personal, terminal, and service mobility. In the United States, PCS spectrum has been allocated for broadband, narrowband, and unlicensed services. *2.* Port concentrator switch.

PDN   Public data network. Network operated either by a government (as in Europe) or by a private concern to provide computer communications to the public, usually for a fee. PDNs enable small organizations to create a WAN without all the equipment costs of long-distance circuits.

PDU   Protocol Data Unit. OSI term for packet. See also *BPDU* and *packet*.

peak cell rate   See *PCR*.

peak rate   Maximum rate, in kilobits per second, at which a virtual circuit can transmit.

peer group   Collection of ATM nodes that share identical topological databases and exchange full link state information with each other. Peer groups are arranged hierarchically to prevent excessive PTSP traffic. See also *parent peer group* and *PTSP*.

peer group leader   See *PGL*.

peer-to-peer computing   Calls for each network device to run both client and server portions of an application. Also describes communication between implementations of the same OSI reference model layer in two different network devices. Compare to *client/server computing*.

PEM   Privacy Enhanced Mail. Internet email that provides confidentiality, authentication, and message integrity using various encryption methods. Not widely deployed in the Internet.

performance management   One of five categories of network management defined by ISO for management of OSI networks. Performance management subsystems are responsible for analyzing and controlling network performance including network throughput and error

rates. See also *accounting management*, *configuration management*, *fault management*, and *security management*.

peripheral node   In SNA, a node that uses local addresses and is therefore not affected by changes to network addresses. Peripheral nodes require boundary function assistance from an adjacent subarea node.

permanent virtual circuit   See *PVC*.

permanent virtual connection   See *PVC*.

permanent virtual path   See *PVP*.

permit processing   See *traffic policing*.

Personal Communications Service   See *PCS*.

P/F   Poll/final bit. Bit in bit-synchronous Data Link layer protocols that indicates the function of a frame. If the frame is a command, a 1 in this bit indicates a poll. If the frame is a response, a 1 in this bit indicates that the current frame is the last frame in the response.

PGL   Peer group leader. In ATM, a node in a peer group that performs the functions of the LGN. Peer group leaders exchange PTSPs with peer nodes in the parent peer group to inform those nodes of the peer group's attributes and reachability and to propagate information about the parent group and the parent group's parents to the nodes in the peer group. See also *peer group* and *PTSP*.

PGP   Pretty Good Privacy. Public-key encryption application that allows secure file and message exchanges. There is some controversy over the development and use of this application, in part due to U.S. national security concerns.

phase   Location of a position on an alternating wave form.

phase shift   Situation in which the relative position in time between the clock and data signals of a transmission becomes unsynchronized. In systems using long cables at higher transmission speeds, slight variances in cable construction, temperature, and other factors can cause a phase shift, resulting in high error rates.

PHY   *1.* Physical sublayer. One of two sublayers of the FDDI Physical layer. See also *PMD.* *2.* Physical layer. In ATM, the Physical layer provides for the transmission of cells over a physical medium that connects two ATM devices. The PHY is comprised of two sublayers: PMD and TC. See also *PMD* and *TC.*

physical address   See *MAC address.*

Physical Control layer   Layer 1 in the SNA architectural model. This layer is responsible for the physical specifications for the physical links between end systems. Corresponds to the Physical layer of the OSI model. See also *Data Flow Control layer, Data-Link Control layer, Path Control layer, Presentation Services layer, Transaction Services layer,* and *Transmission Control layer.*

Physical layer   Layer 1 of the OSI reference model. The Physical layer defines the electrical, mechanical, procedural, and functional specifications for activating, maintaining, and deactivating the physical link between end systems. Corresponds with the Physical Control layer in the SNA model. See also *Application layer, Data Link layer, Network layer, Presentation layer, Session layer,* and *Transport layer.*

Physical layer convergence procedure   See *PLCP.*

Physical layer interface module   See *PLIM* in the "Cisco Systems Terms and Acronyms" section.

physical media   See *media.*

physical medium   See *media.*

physical medium dependent   See *PMD.*

Physical sublayer   See *PHY.*

physical unit   See *PU.*

Physical Unit 2   See *PU 2.*

Physical Unit 2.1   See *PU 2.1.*

Physical Unit 4   See *PU 4.*

Physical Unit 5   See *PU 5.*

Physics Network   See *PHYSNET.*

PHYSNET   Physics Network. Group of many DECnet-based physics research networks, including HEPnet. See also *HEPnet.*

piggybacking   Process of carrying acknowledgments within a data packet to save network bandwidth.

PIM   Protocol Independent Multicast. Multicast routing architecture that allows the addition of IP multicast routing on existing IP networks. PIM is unicast routing protocol independent and can be operated in two modes: dense and sparse. See also *PIM dense mode* and *PIM sparse mode.*

PIM dense mode   One of the two PIM operational modes. PIM dense mode is data-driven and resembles typical multicast routing protocols. Packets are forwarded on all outgoing interfaces until pruning and truncation occurs. In dense mode, receivers are densely populated, and it is assumed that the downstream networks want to receive and will probably use the datagrams that are forwarded to them. The cost of using dense mode is its default flooding behavior. Sometimes called dense mode PIM or PIM DM. Contrast with *PIM sparse mode.* See also *PIM.*

PIM DM   See *PIM dense mode.*

PIM SM   See *PIM sparse mode.*

PIM sparse mode   One of the two PIM operational modes. PIM sparse mode tries to constrain data distribution so that a minimal number of routers in the network receive it. Packets are sent only if they are explicitly requested at the RP (rendezvous point). In sparse mode, receivers are widely distributed, and the assumption is that downstream networks will not necessarily use the datagrams that are sent to them. The cost of using sparse mode is its reliance on the periodic refreshing of explicit join messages and its need for

RPs. Sometimes called sparse mode PIM or PIM SM. Contrast with *PIM dense mode*. See also *PIM* and *rendezvous point*.

ping   Packet Internet groper. ICMP echo message and its reply. Often used in IP networks to test the reachability of a network device.

ping-ponging   Phrase used to describe the actions of a packet in a two-node routing loop.

plain old telephone service   Abbreviated POTS. See *PSTN*.

PLCP   Physical layer convergence procedure. Specification that maps ATM cells into physical media, such as T3 or E3, and defines certain management information.

plesiochronous transmission   Term describing digital signals that are sourced from different clocks of comparable accuracy and stability. Compare to *asynchronous transmission, isochronous transmission*, and *synchronous transmission*.

PLIM   See *PLIM* in the "Cisco Systems Terms and Acronyms" section.

PLP   Packet level protocol. Network layer protocol in the X.25 protocol stack. Sometimes called X.25 Level 3 and X.25 Protocol. See also *X.25*.

PLSP   PNNI link state packets.

PLU   Primary Logical Unit. The LU that is initiating a session with another LU. See also *LU*.

PMD   Physical medium dependent. Sublayer of the FDDI Physical layer that interfaces directly with the physical medium and performs the most basic bit transmission functions of the network. See also *PHY*.

PNNI   *1*. Private Network-Network Interface. ATM Forum specification for distributing topology information between switches and clusters of switches that is used to compute paths through the network. The specification is based on well-known link-state routing

techniques and includes a mechanism for automatic configuration in networks in which the address structure reflects the topology. *2*. Private Network Node Interface. ATM Forum specification for signaling to establish point-to-point and point-to-multipoint connections across an ATM network. The protocol is based on the ATM Forum UNI specification with additional mechanisms for source routing, crankback, and alternate routing of call setup requests. *3*. Private Network-to-Network Interface.

PNNI Link State Packets   See *PLSP*.

PNNI topology state element   See *PTSE*.

PNO   Public Network Operator. See also *PTT*.

point of presence   See *POP*.

point-to-multipoint connection   One of two fundamental connection types. In ATM, a point-to-multipoint connection is a unidirectional connection in which a single source end-system (known as a root node) connects to multiple destination end-systems (known as leaves). Compare to *point-to-point connection*.

point-to-point connection   One of two fundamental connection types. In ATM, a point-to-point connection can be a unidirectional or bidirectional connection between two ATM end-systems. Compare to *point-to-multipoint connection*.

Point-to-Point Protocol   See *PPP*.

poison reverse updates   Routing updates that explicitly indicate that a network or subnet is unreachable, rather than implying that a network is unreachable by not including it in updates. Poison reverse updates are sent to defeat large routing loops.

policy-based routing   See *policy routing*.

policy routing   Routing scheme that forwards packets to specific interfaces based on user-configured policies. Such policies might specify that traffic sent from a particular network should be forwarded out one interface, whereas all other traffic should be forwarded out another interface.

poll/final bit See *P/F*.

polling Access method in which a primary network device inquires, in an orderly fashion, whether secondaries have data to transmit. The inquiry occurs in the form of a message to each secondary that gives the secondary the right to transmit.

POP *1.* Point of presence. In OSS, a physical location where an interexchange carrier installed equipment to interconnect with an LEC (local exchange carrier). *2.* Post Office Protocol. Protocol that client email applications use to retrieve mail from a mail server.

port *1.* Interface on an internetworking device (such as a router). *2.* In IP terminology, an upper-layer process that receives information from lower layers. Ports are numbered, and each numbered port is associated with a specific process. For example, SMTP is associated with port 25. A port number is also called a well-known address. *3.* To rewrite software or microcode so that it will run on a different hardware platform or in a different software environment than that for which it was originally designed.

port snooping See *circuit steering*.

POSI Promoting Conference for OSI. Group of executives from the six major Japanese computer manufacturers and Nippon Telephone and Telegraph that sets policies and commits resources to promote OSI.

POST Power-on self test. Set of hardware diagnostics that runs on a hardware device when that device is powered up.

Post Office Protocol See *POP*.

Post, Telephone, and Telegraph See *PTT*.

POTS Plain old telephone service. See *PSTN*.

power-on self test See *POST*.

power-on servicing Feature that allows faulty components to be diagnosed, removed, and replaced while the rest of the device continues to operate normally. Sometimes abbreviated POS. Sometimes called hot swapping. See also *OIR*.

PPP Point-to-Point Protocol. Successor to SLIP that provides router-to-router and host-to-network connections over synchronous and asynchronous circuits. Whereas SLIP was designed to work with IP, PPP was designed to work with several Network layer protocols, such as IP, IPX, and ARA. PPP also has built-in security mechanisms, such as CHAP and PAP. PPP relies on two protocols: LCP and NCP. See also *CHAP, LCP, NCP, PAP,* and *SLIP*.

Presentation layer Layer 6 of the OSI reference model. This layer ensures that information sent by the Application layer of one system will be readable by the Application layer of another. The Presentation layer is also concerned with the data structures used by programs and therefore negotiates data transfer syntax for the Application layer. Corresponds roughly with the Presentation Services layer of the SNA model. See also *Application layer, Data Link layer, Network layer, Physical layer, Session layer,* and *Transport layer*.

Presentation Services layer Layer 6 of the SNA architectural model. This layer provides network resource management, session presentation services, and some application management. Corresponds roughly with the Presentation layer of the OSI model. See also *Data Flow Control layer, Data-Link Control layer, Path Control layer, Physical Control layer, Transaction Services layer,* and *Transmission Control layer*.

Pretty Good Privacy See *PGP*.

PRI Primary Rate Interface. ISDN interface to primary rate access. Primary rate access consists of a single 64Kbps D channel plus 23 (T1) or 30 (E1) B channels for voice or data. Compare to *BRI*. See also *BISDN, ISDN,* and *N-ISDN*.

primary   See *primary station*.

Primary LU   See *PLU*.

Primary Rate Interface   See *PRI*.

primary ring   One of the two rings that make up an FDDI or CDDI ring. The primary ring is the default path for data transmissions. Compare to *secondary ring*.

primary station   In bit-synchronous Data Link layer protocols such as HDLC and SDLC, a station that controls the transmission activity of secondary stations and performs other management functions such as error control through polling or other means. Primary stations send commands to secondary stations and receive responses. Also called, simply, a primary. See also *secondary station*.

print server   Networked computer system that fields, manages, and executes (or sends for execution) print requests from other network devices.

priority queuing   Routing feature in which frames in an interface output queue are prioritized based on various characteristics such as packet size and interface type.

Privacy Enhanced Mail   See *PEM*.

private branch exchange   See *PBX*.

Private Network-Network Interface   See *PNNI*.

Private Network Node Interface   See *PNNI*.

PRMD   Private Management Domain. X.400 Message Handling System private organization mail system (for example, NASAmail).

process switching   See *process switching* in the "Cisco Systems Terms and Acronyms" section.

programmable read-only memory   See *PROM*.

PROM   Programmable read-only memory. ROM that can be programmed using special equipment. PROMs can be programmed only once. Compare to *EPROM*.

propagation delay   Time required for data to travel over a network, from its source to its ultimate destination.

protocol   Formal description of a set of rules and conventions that govern how devices on a network exchange information.

protocol address   See *network address*.

protocol control information   See *PCI*.

protocol converter   Enables equipment with different data formats to communicate by translating the data transmission code of one device to the data transmission code of another device.

Protocol Data Unit   See *PDU*.

Protocol Independent Multicast   See *PIM*.

protocol stack   Set of related communications protocols that operate together and, as a group, address communication at some or all of the seven layers of the OSI reference model. Not every protocol stack covers each layer of the model, and often a single protocol in the stack will address a number of layers at once. TCP/IP is a typical protocol stack.

protocol translator   Network device or software that converts one protocol into another similar protocol.

proxy   Entity that, in the interest of efficiency, essentially stands in for another entity.

proxy Address Resolution Protocol   See *proxy ARP*.

proxy ARP   Proxy Address Resolution Protocol. Variation of the ARP protocol in which an intermediate device (for example, a router) sends an ARP response on behalf of an end node to the requesting host. Proxy ARP can lessen bandwidth use on slow-speed WAN links. See also *ARP*.

proxy explorer   Technique that minimizes exploding explorer packet traffic propagating through an SRB network by creating an explorer packet reply cache, the entries of which are reused when subsequent explorer packets need to find the same host.

proxy polling See *proxy polling* in the "Cisco Systems Terms and Acronyms" section.

PSDN Packet-switched data network. See *PSN*.

PSE Packet switch exchange. Essentially, a switch. The term PSE is generally used in reference to a switch in an X.25 packet-switch. See also *switch*.

PSN Packet-switched network. Network that uses packet-switching technology for data transfer. Sometimes called a PSDN. See *packet switching*.

PSTN Public Switched Telephone Network. General term referring to the variety of telephone networks and services in place worldwide. Sometimes called POTS.

PTI Payload type identifier. 3-bit descriptor in the ATM cell header indicating the type of payload that the cell contains. Payload types include user and management cells; one combination indicates that the cell is the last cell of an AAL5 frame.

PTSE PNNI topology state element. Collection of PNNI information that is flooded among all logical nodes within a peer group. See also *peer group* and *PNNI*.

PTSP PNNI topology state packet. Type of PNNI routing packet used to exchange reachability and resource information among ATM switches to ensure that a connection request is routed to the destination along a path that has a high probability of meeting the requested QoS. Typically, PTSPs include bidirectional information about the transit behavior of particular nodes (based on entry and exit ports) and current internal state. See also *PNNI* and *QoS*.

PTT Post, Telephone, and Telegraph. Government agency that provides telephone services. PTTs exist in most areas outside North America and provide both local and long-distance telephone services.

PU Physical unit. SNA component that manages and monitors the resources of a node, as requested by an SSCP. There is one PU per node.

PU 2 Physical Unit 2. SNA peripheral node that can support only DLUs that require services from a VTAM host and that are only capable of performing the secondary LU role in SNA sessions.

PU 2.1 Physical Unit type 2.1. SNA network node used for connecting peer nodes in a peer-oriented network. PU 2.1 sessions do not require that one node reside on VTAM. APPN is based upon PU 2.1 nodes, which can also be connected to a traditional hierarchical SNA network.

PU 4 Physical Unit 4. Component of an IBM FEP capable of full-duplex data transfer. Each such SNA device employs a separate data and control path into the transmit and receive buffers of the control program.

PU 5 Physical Unit 5. Component of an IBM mainframe or host computer that manages an SNA network. PU 5 nodes are involved in routing within the SNA Path Control layer.

public data network See *PDN*.

Public Switched Telephone Network See *PSTN*.

pulse amplitude modulation See *PAM*.

pulse code modulation See *PCM*.

pulse density See *ones density*.

PUP PARC Universal Protocol. Protocol similar to IP developed at PARC.

PVC Permanent virtual circuit. Virtual circuit that is permanently established. PVCs save bandwidth associated with circuit establishment and tear down in situations where certain virtual circuits must exist all the time. In ATM terminology, called a permanent virtual connection. Compare to *SVC*. See also *virtual circuit*.

PVP Permanent virtual path. Virtual path that consists of PVCs. See also PVC and virtual path.

PVP tunneling   Permanent virtual path tunneling. Method of linking two private ATM networks across a public network using a virtual path. The public network transparently trunks the entire collection of virtual channels in the virtual path between the two private networks.

Q

Q.2931   ITU-T specification, based on Q.931, for establishing, maintaining, and clearing network connections at the B-ISDN user-network interface. The UNI 3.1 specification is based on Q.2931. See also *Q.931* and *UNI*.

Q.920/Q.921   ITU-T specifications for the ISDN UNI Data Link layer. See also *UNI*.

Q.922A   ITU-T specification for Frame Relay encapsulation.

Q.931   ITU-T specification for signaling to establish, maintain, and clear ISDN network connections. See also *Q.93B*.

Q.93B   ITU-T specification for signaling to establish, maintain, and clear BISDN network connections. An evolution of ITU-T recommendation Q.931. See also *Q.931*.

QLLC   Qualified Logical Link Control. Data Link layer protocol defined by IBM that allows SNA data to be transported across X.25 networks.

QoS   Quality of service. Measure of performance for a transmission system that reflects its transmission quality and service availability.

QoS parameters   Quality of service parameters. Parameters that control the amount of traffic the source in an ATM network sends over an SVC. If any switch along the path cannot accommodate the requested QoS parameters, the request is rejected, and a rejection message is forwarded back to the originator of the request.

QSIG   Q (point of the ISDN model) Signaling. Signaling standard.

Qualified Logical Link Control   See *QLLC*.

quality of service   See *QoS*.

quartet signaling   Signaling technique used in 100VG-AnyLAN networks that allows data transmission at 100Mbps over four pairs of UTP cable at the same frequencies used in 10BaseT networks. See also *100VG-AnyLAN*.

query   Message used to inquire about the value of some variable or set of variables.

queue   *1.* Generally, an ordered list of elements waiting to be processed. *2.* In routing, a backlog of packets waiting to be forwarded over a router interface.

queuing delay   Amount of time that data must wait before it can be transmitted onto a statistically multiplexed physical circuit.

queuing theory   Scientific principles governing the formation or lack of formation of congestion on a network or at an interface.

QUIPU   Pioneering software package developed to study the OSI Directory and provide extensive pilot capabilities.

R

RACE   Research on Advanced Communications in Europe. Project sponsored by the EC for the development of broadband networking capabilities.

radio frequency   See *RF*.

radio frequency interference   See *RFI*.

RADIUS   Database for authenticating modem and ISDN connections and for tracking connection time.

RAM Random-access memory. Volatile memory that can be read and written by a microprocessor.

random-access memory See *RAM*.

Rapid Transport Protocol See *RTP*.

RARE Ruseaux Associes pour la Recherche Europeenne. Association of European universities and research centers designed to promote an advanced telecommunications infrastructure in the European scientific community. RARE merged with EARN to form TERENA. See also *EARN* and *TERENA*.

RARP Reverse Address Resolution Protocol. Protocol in the TCP/IP stack that provides a method for finding IP addresses based on MAC addresses. Compare to *ARP*.

rate enforcement See *traffic policing*.

rate queue In ATM, a value associated with one or more virtual circuits that defines the speed at which an individual virtual circuit transmits data to the remote end. Each rate queue represents a portion of the overall bandwidth available on an ATM link. The combined bandwidth of all configured rate queues should not exceed the total available bandwidth.

RBHC Regional Bell holding company. One of seven regional telephone companies formed by the breakup of AT&T. RBHCs differ from RBOCs in that RBHCs cross state boundaries.

RBOC Regional Bell operating company. Seven regional telephone companies formed by the breakup of AT&T. RBOCs differ from RBHCs in that RBOCs do not cross state boundaries.

rcp Remote copy protocol. Protocol that allows users to copy files to and from a file system residing on a remote host or server on the network. The rcp protocol uses TCP to ensure the reliable delivery of data.

rcp server Router or other device that acts as a server for rcp. See also *rcp*.

RDI Remote defect identification. In ATM, when the Physical layer detects loss of signal or cell synchronization, RDI cells are used to report a VPC/VCC failure. RDI cells are sent upstream by a VPC/VCC endpoint to notify the source VPC/VCC endpoint of the downstream failure.

read-only memory See *ROM*.

Real Time Streaming Protocol See *RTSP*.

reassembly The putting back together of an IP datagram at the destination after it has been fragmented either at the source or at an intermediate node. See also *fragmentation*.

redirect Part of the ICMP and ES-IS protocols that allows a router to tell a host that using another router would be more effective.

redirector Software that intercepts requests for resources within a computer and analyzes them for remote access requirements. If remote access is required to satisfy the request, the redirector forms an RPC and sends the RPC to lower-layer protocol software for transmission through the network to the node that can satisfy the request.

redistribution Allowing routing information discovered through one routing protocol to be distributed in the update messages of another routing protocol. Sometimes called route redistribution.

redundancy *1.* In internetworking, the duplication of devices, services, or connections so that, in the event of a failure, the redundant devices, services, or connections can perform the work of those that failed. See also *redundant system. 2.* In telephony, the portion of the total information contained in a message that can be eliminated without loss of essential information or meaning.

redundant system Computer, router, switch, or other system that contains two or more of each of the most important subsystems, such as two disk drives, two CPUs, or two power supplies.

regional Bell holding company See *RBHC.*

regional Bell operating company See *RBOC.*

registered jack connector See *RJ connector.*

relative rate See *RR.*

relay OSI terminology for a device that connects two or more networks or network systems. A Data Link layer (Layer 2) relay is a bridge; a Network layer (Layer 3) relay is a router. See also *bridge* and *router.*

reliability Ratio of expected to received keepalives from a link. If the ratio is high, the line is reliable. Used as a routing metric.

Reliable SAP Update Protocol See *RSUP* in the "Cisco Systems Terms and Acronyms" section.

reload The event of a Cisco router rebooting, or the command that causes the router to reboot.

remote bridge Bridge that connects physically disparate network segments via WAN links.

remote copy protocol See *rcp.*

remote defect identification See *RDI.*

remote job entry See *RJE.*

remote login See *rlogin.*

Remote Monitoring See *RMON.*

Remote Operations Service Element See *ROSE.*

remote-procedure call See *RPC.*

remote shell protocol See *rsh.*

remote source-route bridging See *RSRB.*

rendezvous point Router specified in PIM sparse mode implementations to track membership in multicast groups and to forward messages to known multicast group addresses. See also *PIM sparse mode.*

repeater Device that regenerates and propagates electrical signals between two network segments. See also *segment.*

replication Process of keeping a copy of data, either through shadowing or caching. See also *caching* and *shadowing.*

Request For Comments See *RFC.*

request/response unit See *RU.*

Request To Send See *RTS.*

Research on Advanced Communications in Europe See *RACE.*

Reseaux Associes pour la Recherche Europeenne See *RARE.*

Resource Reservation Protocol See *RSVP.*

Reverse Address Resolution Protocol See *RARP.*

Reverse Path Forwarding See *RPF.*

RF Radio frequency. Generic term referring to frequencies that correspond to radio transmissions. Cable TV and broadband networks use RF technology.

RFC Request For Comments. Document series used as the primary means for communicating information about the Internet. Some RFCs are designated by the IAB as Internet standards. Most RFCs document protocol specifications such as Telnet and FTP, but some are humorous or historical. RFCs are available online from numerous sources.

RFI Radio frequency interference. Radio frequencies that create noise that interferes with information being transmitted across unshielded copper cable.

RFS Remote File System. Distributed file system, similar to NFS, developed by AT&T and distributed with their UNIX System V operating system.

RHC Regional holding company.

RIF Routing Information Field. Field in the IEEE 802.5 header that is used by a source-route bridge to determine through which Token Ring network segments a packet must transit. A RIF is made up of ring and bridge numbers as well as other information.

RII   Routing Information Identifier. Bit used by SRT bridges to distinguish between frames that should be transparently bridged and frames that should be passed to the SRB module for handling.

ring   Connection of two or more stations in a logically circular topology. Information is passed sequentially between active stations. Token Ring, FDDI, and CDDI are based on this topology.

ring group   Collection of Token Ring interfaces on one or more routers that is part of a one-bridge Token Ring network.

ring latency   Time required for a signal to propagate once around a ring in a Token Ring or IEEE 802.5 network.

ring monitor   Centralized management tool for Token Ring networks based on the IEEE 802.5 specification. See also active monitor and standby monitor.

ring topology   Network topology that consists of a series of repeaters connected to one another by unidirectional transmission links to form a single closed loop. Each station on the network connects to the network at a repeater. While logically a ring, ring topologies are most often organized in a closed-loop star. Compare to *bus topology*, *star topology*, and *tree topology*.

RIP   Routing Information Protocol. IGP supplied with UNIX BSD systems. The most common IGP in the Internet. RIP uses hop count as a routing metric. See also *hop count*, *IGP*, and *OSPF*, and *Enhanced IGRP* and *IGRP* in the "Cisco Systems Terms and Acronyms" section.

RIPE   Reseaux IP Europeennes. Group formed to coordinate and promote TCP/IP-based networks in Europe.

RJ connector   Registered jack connector. Standard connectors originally used to connect telephone lines. RJ connectors are now used for telephone connections and for 10BaseT and other types of network connections.

RJ-11, RJ-12, and RJ-45 are popular types of RJ connectors.

RJE   Remote job entry. Application that is batch-oriented, as opposed to interactive. In RJE environments, jobs are submitted to a computing facility, and output is received later.

rlogin   Remote login. Terminal emulation program, similar to Telnet, offered in most UNIX implementations.

RM   Resource management. Management of critical resources in an ATM network. Two critical resources are buffer space and trunk bandwidth. Provisioning can be used to allocate network resources in order to separate traffic flows according to service characteristics.

RMON   Remote monitoring. MIB agent specification described in RFC 1271 that defines functions for the remote monitoring of networked devices. The RMON specification provides numerous monitoring, problem detection, and reporting capabilities.

ROLC   Routing over large clouds. Working group in IETF created to analyze and propose solutions to problems that arise when performing IP routing over large, shared media networks such as ATM, Frame Relay, SMDS, and X.25.

ROM   Read-only memory. Nonvolatile memory that can be read, but not written, by the microprocessor.

root account   Privileged account on UNIX systems used exclusively by network or system administrators.

root bridge   Exchanges topology information with designated bridges in a spanning-tree implementation in order to notify all other bridges in the network when topology changes are required. This prevents loops and provides a measure of defense against link failure.

ROSE   Remote Operations Service Element. OSI RPC mechanism used by various OSI network application protocols.

round-trip time   See *RTT*.

route   Path through an internetwork.

routed protocol   Protocol that can be routed by a router. A router must be able to interpret the logical internetwork as specified by that routed protocol. Examples of routed protocols include AppleTalk, DECnet, and IP.

route extension   In SNA, a path from the destination subarea node through peripheral equipment to a NAU.

route map   Method of controlling the redistribution of routes between routing domains.

Route Processor   See *RP* in the "Cisco Systems Terms and Acronyms" section.

router   Network layer device that uses one or more metrics to determine the optimal path along which network traffic should be forwarded. Routers forward packets from one network to another based on Network layer information. Occasionally called a gateway (although this definition of gateway is becoming increasingly outdated). Compare to *gateway*. See also *relay*.

route redistribution   See *redistribution*.

route summarization   Consolidation of advertised addresses in OSPF and IS-IS. In OSPF, this causes a single summary route to be advertised to other areas by an area border router.

Route/Switch Processor   See *RSP* in the "Cisco Systems Terms and Acronyms" section.

routing   Process of finding a path to a destination host. Routing is very complex in large networks because of the many potential intermediate destinations a packet might traverse before reaching its destination host.

routing domain   Group of end systems and intermediate systems operating under the same set of administrative rules. Within each routing domain is one or more areas, each uniquely identified by an area address.

Routing Information Field   See *RIF*.

Routing Information Identifier   See *RII*.

Routing Information Protocol   See *RIP*.

routing metric   Method by which a routing algorithm determines that one route is better than another. This information is stored in routing tables. Metrics include bandwidth, communication cost, delay, hop count, load, MTU, path cost, and reliability. Sometimes referred to simply as a metric. See also *cost*.

routing over large clouds   See *ROLC*.

routing protocol   Protocol that accomplishes routing through the implementation of a specific routing algorithm. Examples of routing protocols include IGRP, OSPF, and RIP.

routing table   Table stored in a router or some other internetworking device that keeps track of routes to particular network destinations and, in some cases, metrics associated with those routes.

Routing Table Maintenance Protocol   See *RTMP*.

Routing Table Protocol   See *RTP*.

routing update   Message sent from a router to indicate network reachability and associated cost information. Routing updates are typically sent at regular intervals and after a change in network topology. Compare to *flash update*.

RP   See *RP* in the "Cisco Systems Terms and Acronyms" section.

RPC   Remote-procedure call. Technological foundation of client-server computing. RPCs are procedure calls that are built or specified by clients and executed on servers, with the results returned over the network to the clients. See also *client/server computing*.

RPF   Reverse Path Forwarding. Multicasting technique in which a multicast datagram is forwarded out of all but the receiving interface if the receiving interface is the one used to forward unicast datagrams to the source of the multicast datagram.

RR Relative rate. In ATM, one of the congestion feedback modes provided by ABR service. In RR mode, switches set a bit in forward and backward RM cells to indicate congestion. See also *ABR (available bit rate)* and *RM*.

RS-232 Popular Physical layer interface. Now known as EIA/TIA-232. See also *EIA/TIA-232*.

RS-422 Balanced electrical implementation of EIA/TIA-449 for high-speed data transmission. Now referred to collectively with RS-423 as EIA-530. See also *EIA-530* and *RS-423*.

RS-423 Unbalanced electrical implementation of EIA/TIA-449 for EIA/TIA-232 compatibility. Now referred to collectively with RS-422 as EIA-530. See also *EIA-530* and *RS-422*.

RS-449 Popular Physical layer interface. Now known as EIA/TIA-449. See *EIA/TIA-449*.

RSA Acronym stands for Rivest, Shamir, and Adelman, the inventors of the technique. Public-key cryptographic system which may be used for encryption and authentication.

rsh Remote shell protocol. Protocol that allows a user to execute commands on a remote system without having to log in to the system. For example, rsh can be used to remotely examine the status of a number of access servers without connecting to each communication server, executing the command, and then disconnecting from the communication server.

RSP See *RSP* in the "Cisco Systems Terms and Acronyms" section.

RSRB Remote source-route bridging. SRB over WAN links. See also *SRB*.

RSUP See *RSUP* in the "Cisco Systems Terms and Acronyms" section.

RSVP Resource Reservation Protocol. Protocol that supports the reservation of resources across an IP network. Applications running on IP end systems can use RSVP to indicate to other nodes the nature (bandwidth, jitter, maximum burst, and so forth) of the packet streams they want to receive. RSVP depends on IPv6. Also known as Resource Reservation Setup Protocol. See also *IPv6*.

RTCP RTP Control Protocol. Protocol that monitors the QOS of an IPv6 RTP connection and conveys information about the on-going session. See also *RTP (Real-Time Transport Protocol)*.

RTFM "Read the fantastic manual." Acronym often used when someone asks a simple or common question.

RTMP Routing Table Maintenance Protocol. Apple Computer's proprietary routing protocol. RTMP establishes and maintains the routing information that is required to route datagrams from any source socket to any destination socket in an AppleTalk network. Using RTMP, routers dynamically maintain routing tables to reflect changes in topology. RTMP was derived from RIP. See also *RTP (Routing Table Protocol)*.

RTP *1.* Routing Table Protocol. VINES routing protocol based on RIP. Distributes network topology information and aids VINES servers in finding neighboring clients, servers, and routers. Uses delay as a routing metric. See also *SRTP*. *2.* Rapid Transport Protocol. Provides pacing and error recovery for APPN data as it crosses the APPN network. With RTP, error recovery and flow control are done end-to-end rather than at every node. RTP prevents congestion rather than reacts to it. *3.* Real-Time Transport Protocol. One of the IPv6 protocols. RTP is designed to provide end-to-end network transport functions for applications transmitting real-time data, such as audio, video, or simulation data, over multicast or unicast network services. RTP provides services such as payload type identification, sequence numbering, timestamping, and delivery monitoring to real-time applications.

RTP Control Protocol   See *RTCP*.

RTS   Request To Send. EIA/TIA-232 control signal that requests a data transmission on a communications line.

RTSC   "Read the source code." One of many short-hand phrases used in chat sessions and email conversations.

RTSP   Real Time Streaming Protocol. Enables the controlled delivery of real-time data, such as audio and video. Sources of data can include both live data feeds, such live audio and video, and stored content, such as pre-recorded events. RTSP is designed to work with established protocols, such as RTP and HTTP.

RTT   Round-trip time. Time required for a network communication to travel from the source to the destination and back. RTT includes the time required for the destination to process the message from the source and generate a reply. RTT is used by some routing algorithms to aid in calculating optimal routes.

RU   Request/response unit. Request and response messages exchanged between NAUs in an SNA network.

run-time memory   Memory accessed while a program runs.

RVI   Required visual inspection.

S

SAC   Single-attached concentrator. FDDI or CDDI concentrator that connects to the network by being cascaded from the master port of another FDDI or CDDI concentrator.

sampling rate   Rate at which samples of a particular waveform amplitude are taken.

SAP   *1.* Service access point. Field defined by the IEEE 802.2 specification that is part of an address specification. Thus, the destination plus the DSAP define

the recipient of a packet. The same applies to the SSAP. See also *DSAP* and *SSAP*. *2.* Service Advertising Protocol. IPX protocol that provides a means of informing network clients, via routers and servers, of available network resources and services. See also *IPX*.

SAR   Segmentation and reassembly. One of the two sublayers of the AAL CPCS, responsible for dividing (at the source) and reassembling (at the destination) the PDUs passed from the CS. The SAR sublayer takes the PDUs processed by the CS and, after dividing them into 48-byte pieces of payload data, passes them to the ATM layer for further processing. See also *AAL, ATM layer, CPCS, CS,* and *SSCS*.

SAS   *1.* Single attachment station. Device attached only to the primary ring of an FDDI ring. Also known as a Class B station. Compare to *DAS*. See also FDDI. *2.* Statically assigned socket. Socket that is permanently reserved for use by a designated process. In an AppleTalk network, SASs are numbered 1 to 127; they are reserved for use by specific socket clients and for low-level built-in network services.

satellite communication   Use of orbiting satellites to relay data between multiple earth-based stations. Satellite communications offer high bandwidth and a cost that is not related to distance between earth stations, long propagation delays, or broadcast capability.

SBus   Bus technology used in Sun SPARC-based workstations and servers. The SBus specification was adopted by the IEEE as a new bus standard.

SCR   Sustainable cell rate. Parameter defined by the ATM Forum for ATM traffic management. For VBR connections, SCR determines the long-term average cell rate that can be transmitted. See also *VBR*.

SCTE   Serial clock transmit external. Timing signal that DTE echoes to DCE to maintain clocking. SCTE is designed to compensate for clock phase shift on long cables. When the DCE device uses SCTE instead of its internal clock to sample data from the DTE, it is better able to sample the data without error even if there is a phase shift in the cable. See also *phase shift*.

SDH Synchronous Digital Hierarchy. European standard that defines a set of rate and format standards that are transmitted using optical signals over fiber. SDH is similar to SONET, with a basic SDH rate of 155.52Mbps, designated at STM-1. See also *SONET* and *STM-1*.

SDLC Synchronous Data Link Control. SNA Data-Link Control layer communications protocol. SDLC is a bit-oriented, full-duplex serial protocol that has spawned numerous similar protocols, including HDLC and LAPB. See also *HDLC* and *LAPB*.

SDLC broadcast See *SDLC broadcast* in the "Cisco Systems Terms and Acronyms" section.

SDLC Transport See *SDLC Transport* in the "Cisco Systems Terms and Acronyms" section.

SDLLC See *SDLLC* in the "Cisco Systems Terms and Acronyms" section.

SDSL Single-line digital subscriber line. One of four DSL technologies. SDSL delivers 1.544Mbps both downstream and upstream over a single copper twisted pair. The use of a single twisted pair limits the operating range of SDSL to 10,000 feet (3048.8 meters). Compare to *ADSL*, *HDSL*, and *VDSL*.

SDSU SMDS DSU. DSU for access to SMDS via HSSIs and other serial interfaces.

SDU Service data unit. Unit of information from an upper-layer protocol that defines a service request to a lower-layer protocol.

SEAL Simple and efficient AAL. Scheme used by AAL5 in which the SAR sublayer segments CS PDUs without adding additional fields. See also *AAL*, *AAL5*, *CS*, and *SAR*.

secondary See *secondary station*.

secondary ring One of the two rings making up an FDDI or CDDI ring. The secondary ring is usually reserved for use in the event of a failure of the primary ring. Compare to *primary ring*.

secondary station In bit-synchronous Data Link layer protocols such as HDLC, a station that responds to commands from a primary station. Sometimes referred to simply as a secondary. See also *primary station*.

Section DCC Section Data Communications Channel. In OSS, a 192-Kbps data communications channel embedded in the section overhead for OAM&P traffic between two SONET network elements. See also *OAM&P* and *SONET*.

security management One of five categories of network management defined by ISO for management of OSI networks. Security management subsystems are responsible for controlling access to network resources. See also *accounting management*, *configuration management*, *fault management*, and *performance management*.

seed router Router in an AppleTalk network that has the network number or cable range built in to its port descriptor. The seed router defines the network number or cable range for other routers in that network segment and responds to configuration queries from non-seed routers on its connected AppleTalk network, allowing those routers to confirm or modify their configurations accordingly. Each AppleTalk network must have at least one seed router. See also *nonseed router*.

segment *1*. Section of a network that is bounded by bridges, routers, or switches. *2*. In a LAN using a bus topology, a segment is a continuous electrical circuit that is often connected to other such segments with repeaters. *3*. Term used in the TCP specification to describe a single Transport layer unit of information. The terms datagram, frame, message, and packet are also used to describe logical information groupings at various layers of the OSI reference model and in various technology circles.

segmentation and reassembly   See *SAR*.

selector   Identifier (octet string) used by an OSI entity to distinguish among multiple SAPs at which it provides services to the layer above.

Sequenced Packet Exchange   See *SPX*.

Sequenced Packet Protocol   See *SPP*.

Sequenced Routing Update Protocol   See *SRTP*.

serial clock transmit external   See *SCTE*.

Serial Line Internet Protocol   See *SLIP*.

serial transmission   Method of data transmission in which the bits of a data character are transmitted sequentially over a single channel. Compare to *parallel transmission*.

serial tunnel   See *STUN* in the "Cisco Systems Terms and Acronyms" section.

server   Node or software program that provides services to clients. See also *back end*, *client*, and *front end*.

Server Message Block   See *SMB*.

service access point   See *SAP*.

Service Advertising Protocol   See *SAP*.

service data unit   See *SDU*.

service point   Interface between non-SNA devices and NetView that sends alerts from equipment unknown to the SNA environment.

service profile identifier   See *SPID*.

Service Specific Connection Oriented Protocol   See *SSCOP*.

Service Specific Convergence sublayer   See *SSCS*.

session   *1.* Related set of communications transactions between two or more network devices. *2.* In SNA, a logical connection enabling two NAUs to communicate.

Session layer   Layer 5 of the OSI reference model. This layer establishes, manages, and terminates sessions between applications and manages data exchange between presentation layer entities. Corresponds to the Data Flow control layer of the SNA model. See also *Application layer*, *Data Link layer*, *Network layer*, *Physical layer*, *Presentation layer*, and *Transport layer*.

SET   Secure Electronic Transactions. SET specification developed to allow for secure credit card and off-line debit card (check card) transactions over the World Wide Web.

SF   Super Frame. Common framing type used on T1 circuits. SF consists of 12 frames of 192 bits each, with the 193rd bit providing error checking and other functions. SF is superseded by ESF, but is still widely used. Also called D4 framing. See also *ESF*.

S-frame   Supervisory frame. One of three SDLC frame formats. See also *I-frame* and *U-frame*.

SGML   Standardized Generalized Markup Language. International standard for the definition of system-independent, device-independent methods of representing text in electronic form.

SGMP   Simple Gateway Monitoring Protocol. Network management protocol that was considered for Internet standardization and later evolved into SNMP. Documented in RFC 1028. See also *SNMP*.

shadowing   Form of replication in which well-defined units of information are copied to several DSAs.

shaping   See *traffic shaping*.

shielded cable   Cable that has a layer of shielded insulation to reduce EMI.

shielded twisted-pair   See *STP*.

shortest path first algorithm   See *SPF*.

shortest-path routing   Routing that minimizes distance or path cost through application of an algorithm.

signaling Process of sending a transmission signal over a physical medium for purposes of communication.

signaling packet Generated by an ATM-connected device that wants to establish a connection with another such device. The signaling packet contains the ATM NSAP address of the desired ATM endpoint, as well as any QoS parameters required for the connection. If the endpoint can support the desired QoS, it responds with an accept message, and the connection is opened. See also *QoS*.

Signaling System 7 See *SS7*.

signal quality error See *SQE*.

silicon switching See *silicon switching* in the "Cisco Systems Terms and Acronyms" section.

silicon switching engine See *SSE* in the "Cisco Systems Terms and Acronyms" section.

Silicon Switch Processor See *SSP* in the "Cisco Systems Terms and Acronyms" section.

simple and efficient AAL See *SEAL*.

Simple Gateway Monitoring Protocol See *SGMP*.

Simple Mail Transfer Protocol See *SMTP*.

Simple Multicast Routing Protocol See *SMRP*.

Simple Network Management Protocol See *SNMP*.

simplex Capability for transmission in only one direction between a sending station and a receiving station. Broadcast television is an example of a simplex technology. Compare to *full duplex* and *half duplex*.

single-attached concentrator See *SAC*.

single attachment station See *SAS*.

single-mode fiber Fiber-optic cabling with a narrow core that allows light to enter only at a single angle. Such cabling has higher bandwidth than multimode fiber, but requires a light source with a narrow spectral width (for example, a laser). Also called monomode fiber. See also *multimode fiber*.

single-route explorer packet See *spanning explorer packet*.

single-vendor network Network using equipment from only one vendor. Single-vendor networks rarely suffer compatibility problems. See also *multivendor network*.

SIP *1.* SMDS Interface Protocol. Used in communications between CPE and SMDS network equipment. Allows the CPE to use SMDS service for high-speed WAN internetworking. Based on the IEEE 802.6 DQDB standard. See also *DQDB*. *2.* Serial Interface Processor.

SLAC Stanford Linear Accelerator Center.

sliding window flow control Method of flow control in which a receiver gives transmitter permission to transmit data until a window is full. When the window is full, the transmitter must stop transmitting until the receiver advertises a larger window. TCP, other transport protocols, and several Data Link layer protocols use this method of flow control.

SLIP Serial Line Internet Protocol. Standard protocol for point-to-point serial connections using a variation of TCP/IP. Predecessor of PPP. See also *CSLIP* and *PPP*.

slotted ring LAN architecture based on a ring topology in which the ring is divided into slots that circulate continuously. Slots can be either empty or full, and transmissions must start at the beginning of a slot.

SMAC Source MAC. MAC address specified in the Source Address field of a packet. Compare to DMAC. See also *MAC address*.

SMB Server Message Block. File-system protocol used in LAN manager and similar NOSs to package data and exchange information with other systems.

SMDS   Switched Multimegabit Data Service. High-speed, packet-switched, datagram-based WAN networking technology offered by the telephone companies. See also *CBDS*.

SMDS Interface Protocol   See *SIP*.

SMF   Single-mode fiber.

SMI   Structure of Management Information. Document (RFC 1155) specifying rules used to define managed objects in the MIB. See also *MIB*.

smoothing   See *traffic shaping*.

SMRP   Simple Multicast Routing Protocol. Specialized multicast network protocol for routing multimedia data streams on enterprise networks. SMRP works in conjunction with multicast extensions to the AppleTalk protocol.

SMT   Station Management. ANSI FDDI specification that defines how ring stations are managed.

SMTP   Simple Mail Transfer Protocol. Internet protocol providing email services.

SNA   Systems Network Architecture. Large, complex, feature-rich network architecture developed in the 1970s by IBM. Similar in some respects to the OSI reference model, but with a number of differences. SNA is essentially composed of seven layers. See also *Data Flow Control layer*, *Data-Link Control layer*, *Path Control layer*, *Physical Control layer*, *Presentation Services layer*, *Transaction Services layer*, and *Transmission Control layer*.

SNA Distribution Services   See *SNADS*.

SNA Network Interconnection   See *SNI*.

SNADS   SNA Distribution Services. Consists of a set of SNA transaction programs that interconnect and cooperate to provide asynchronous distribution of information between end users. One of three SNA transaction services. See also *DDM* and *DIA*.

SNAP   Subnetwork Access Protocol. Internet protocol that operates between a network entity in the subnetwork and a network entity in the end system. SNAP specifies a standard method of encapsulating IP datagrams and ARP messages on IEEE networks. The SNAP entity in the end system makes use of the services of the subnetwork and performs three key functions: data transfer, connection management, and QoS selection.

SNI   *1.* Subscriber Network Interface. Interface for SMDS-based networks that connects CPE and an SMDS switch. See also *UNI*. *2.* SNA Network Interconnection. IBM gateway connecting multiple SNA networks.

SNMP   Simple Network Management Protocol. Network management protocol used almost exclusively in TCP/IP networks. SNMP provides a means to monitor and control network devices, and to manage configurations, statistics collection, performance, and security. See also *SGMP* and *SNMP2*.

SNMP2   SNMP Version 2. Version 2 of the popular network management protocol. SNMP2 supports centralized as well as distributed network management strategies, and includes improvements in the SMI, protocol operations, management architecture, and security. See also *SNMP*.

SNMP communities   Authentication scheme that enables an intelligent network device to validate SNMP requests.

SNP   Sequence number protection.

SNPA   Subnetwork point of attachment. Data Link layer address (such as an Ethernet address, X.25 address, or Frame Relay DLCI address). SNPA addresses are used to configure a CLNS route for an interface.

socket   *1.* Software structure operating as a communications end point within a network device. *2.* Addressable entity within a node connected to an

AppleTalk network; sockets are owned by software processes known as socket clients. AppleTalk sockets are divided into two groups: SASs, which are reserved for clients such as AppleTalk core protocols, and DASs, which are assigned dynamically by DDP upon request from clients in the node. An AppleTalk socket is similar in concept to a TCP/IP port.

socket client   Software process or function implemented in an AppleTalk network node.

socket listener   Software provided by a socket client to receive datagrams addressed to the socket. See also *socket client.*

socket number   8-bit number that identifies a socket. A maximum of 254 different socket numbers can be assigned in an AppleTalk node.

SOHO   Small office, home office. Networking solutions and access technologies for offices that are not directly connected to large corporate networks.

SONET   Synchronous Optical Network. High-speed (up to 2.5Gbps) synchronous network specification developed by Bellcore and designed to run on optical fiber. STS-1 is the basic building block of SONET. Approved as an international standard in 1988. See also *SDH, STS-1,* and *STS-3c.*

source address   Address of a network device that is sending data. See also *destination address.*

source MAC   See *SMAC.*

source-route bridging   See *SRB.*

source-route translational bridging   See *SR/TLB.*

source-route transparent bridging   See *SRT.*

source service access point   See *SSAP.*

Southeastern Universities Research Association Network   See *SURAnet.*

SP   See *SP* in the "Cisco Systems Terms and Acronyms" section.

SPAG   Standards Promotion and Application Group. Group of European OSI manufacturers that chooses option subsets and publishes these in the "Guide to the Use of Standards" (GUS).

spam   Term used to describe unsolicited email or newsgroup posts, often in the form of commercial announcements. The act of sending a spam is called, naturally, spamming.

span   Full-duplex digital transmission line between two digital facilities.

SPAN   See *SPAN* in the "Cisco Systems Terms and Acronyms" section.

spanning explorer packet   Follows a statically configured spanning tree when looking for paths in an SRB network. Also known as a limited-route explorer packet or a single-route explorer packet. See also *all-routes explorer packet, explorer packet,* and *local explorer packet.*

Spanning Tree   Loop-free subset of a network topology. See also *spanning-tree algorithm* and *Spanning-Tree Protocol.*

Spanning Tree algorithm   Algorithm used by the Spanning-Tree Protocol to create a spanning tree. Sometimes abbreviated as STA. See also *spanning tree* and *Spanning-Tree Protocol.*

Spanning Tree Protocol   Bridge protocol that uses the spanning-tree algorithm, enabling a learning bridge to dynamically work around loops in a network topology by creating a spanning tree. Bridges exchange BPDU messages with other bridges to detect loops, and then remove the loops by shutting down selected bridge interfaces. Refers to both the IEEE 802.1 Spanning-Tree Protocol standard and the earlier Digital Equipment Corporation Spanning-Tree Protocol upon which it is based. The IEEE version supports bridge domains and allows the bridge to construct a loop-free topology across an extended LAN. The IEEE version is generally preferred over the Digital version. Sometimes abbreviated as

STP. See also *BPDU, learning bridge, MAC address learning, spanning tree,* and *spanning-tree algorithm.*

sparse mode PIM   See *PIM sparse mode.*

speed matching   Feature that provides sufficient buffering capability in a destination device to allow a high-speed source to transmit data at its maximum rate, even if the destination device is a lower-speed device.

SPF   Shortest path first algorithm. Routing algorithm that iterates on length of path to determine a shortest-path spanning tree. Commonly used in link-state routing algorithms. Sometimes called Dijkstra's algorithm. See also *link-state routing algorithm.*

SPID   Service profile identifier. Number that some service providers use to define the services to which an ISDN device subscribes. The ISDN device uses the SPID when accessing the switch that initializes the connection to a service provider.

split-horizon updates   Routing technique in which information about routes is prevented from exiting the router interface through which that information was received. Split-horizon updates are useful in preventing routing loops.

SPNNI connection   See *SPNNI connection* in the "Cisco Systems Terms and Acronyms" section.

spoofing   *1.* Scheme used by routers to cause a host to treat an interface as if it were up and supporting a session. The router spoofs replies to keepalive messages from the host in order to convince that host that the session still exists. Spoofing is useful in routing environments such as DDR, in which a circuit-switched link is taken down when there is no traffic to be sent across it in order to save toll charges. See also *DDR. 2.* The act of a packet illegally claiming to be from an address from which it was not actually sent. Spoofing is designed to foil network security mechanisms such as filters and access lists.

spooler   Application that manages requests or jobs submitted to it for execution. Spoolers process the submitted requests in an orderly fashion from a queue. A print spooler is a common example of a spooler.

SPP   Sequenced Packet Protocol. Provides reliable, connection-based, flow-controlled packet transmission on behalf of client processes. Part of the XNS protocol suite.

SPX   Sequenced Packet Exchange. Reliable, connection-oriented protocol that supplements the datagram service provided by Network layer (Layer 3) protocols. Novell derived this commonly used NetWare transport protocol from the SPP of the XNS protocol suite.

SQE   Signal quality error. Transmission sent by a transceiver back to the controller to let the controller know whether the collision circuitry is functional. Also called heartbeat.

SQL   Structured Query Language. International standard language for defining and accessing relational databases.

SRAM   Type of RAM that retains its contents for as long as power is supplied. SRAM does not require constant refreshing, as does DRAM. Compare to *DRAM.*

SRB   Source-route bridging. Method of bridging originated by IBM and popular in Token Ring networks. In an SRB network, the entire route to a destination is predetermined, in real time, prior to the sending of data to the destination. Contrast with *transparent bridging.*

SRT   Source-route transparent bridging. IBM bridging scheme that merges the two most prevalent bridging strategies: SRB and transparent bridging. SRT employs both technologies in one device to satisfy the needs of all ENs. No translation between bridging protocols is necessary. Compare to *SR/TLB.*

SR/TLB   Source-route translational bridging. Method of bridging where source-route stations can communicate with transparent bridge stations with the help of an intermediate bridge that translates between the two bridge protocols. Compare to *SRT*.

SRTP Sequenced Routing Update Protocol. Protocol that assists VINES servers in finding neighboring clients, servers, and routers. See also *RTP (Routing Table Protocol)*.

SS7 Signaling System 7. Standard CCS system used with BISDN and ISDN. Developed by Bellcore. See also *CCS*.

SSAP Source service access point. SAP of the network node designated in the Source field of a packet. Compare to *DSAP*. See also *SAP (service access point)*.

SSCOP Service Specific Connection Oriented Protocol. Data link protocol that guarantees delivery of ATM signaling packets.

SSCP System services control points. Focal points within an SNA network for managing network configuration, coordinating network operator and problem determination requests, and providing directory services and other session services for network end users.

SSCP-PU session Session used by SNA to allow an SSCP to manage the resources of a node through the PU. SSCPs can send requests to, and receive replies from, individual nodes in order to control the network configuration.

SSCS Service Specific Convergence sublayer. One of the two sublayers of any AAL. SSCS, which is service dependent, offers assured data transmission. The SSCS can be null as well, in classical IP over ATM or LAN emulation implementations. See also *AAL, ATM layer, CPCS, CS,* and *SAR*.

SSE See *SSE* in the "Cisco Systems Terms and Acronyms" section.

SSL Secure Socket Layer. Encryption technology for the Web used to provide secure transactions such as the transmission of credit card numbers for e-commerce.

SSP 1. Switch-to-Switch Protocol. Protocol specified in the DLSw standard that routers use to establish DLSw connections, locate resources, forward data, and handle flow control and error recovery. See also *DLSw*. 2. Silicon Switch Processor. See *SSP* in the "Cisco Systems Terms and Acronyms" section.

STA See *spanning-tree algorithm*.

stack See *protocol stack*.

standard Set of rules or procedures that are either widely used or officially specified. See also *de facto standard* and *de jure standard*.

standby monitor Device placed in standby mode on a Token Ring network in case an active monitor fails. See also *active monitor* and *ring monitor*.

StarLAN CSMA/CD LAN, based on IEEE 802.3, developed by AT&T.

star topology LAN topology in which end points on a network are connected to a common central switch by point-to-point links. A ring topology that is organized as a star implements a unidirectional closed-loop star, rather than point-to-point links. Compare to *bus topology, ring topology,* and *tree topology*.

start-stop transmission See *asynchronous transmission*.

startup range Range of values (from 65280 to 65534) from which an AppleTalk node selects the network number part of its provisional address if it has not saved another network number.

statically assigned socket See *SAS*.

static route Route that is explicitly configured and entered into the routing table. Static routes take precedence over routes chosen by dynamic routing protocols.

Station Management See *SMT*.

statistical multiplexing Technique whereby information from multiple logical channels can be transmitted across a single physical channel. Statistical multiplexing dynamically allocates bandwidth only to active input channels, making better use of available bandwidth and allowing more devices to be connected than with other multiplexing techniques. Also referred to as statistical time-division multiplexing or stat mux. Compare to *ATDM*, *FDM*, and *TDM*.

statistical time-division multiplexing See *statistical multiplexing*.

stat mux See *statistical multiplexing*.

STD Subseries of RFCs that specify Internet standards. The official list of Internet standards is in STD 1.

STM-1 Synchronous Transport Module level 1. One of a number of SDH formats that specifies the frame structure for the 155.52-Mbps lines used to carry ATM cells. See also *SDH*.

store and forward packet switching Packet-switching technique in which frames are completely processed before being forwarded out the appropriate port. This processing includes calculating the CRC and checking the destination address. In addition, frames must be temporarily stored until network resources (such as an unused link) are available to forward the message. Contrast with *cut-through packet switching*.

STP *1.* Shielded twisted-pair. Two-pair wiring medium used in a variety of network implementations. STP cabling has a layer of shielded insulation to reduce EMI. Compare to *UTP*. See also twisted pair. *2.* See *Spanning-Tree Protocol*.

stream-oriented Type of transport service that allows its client to send data in a continuous stream. The transport service will guarantee that all data will be delivered to the other end in the same order as sent and without duplicates.

Structure of Management Information See *SMI*.

STS-1 Synchronous Transport Signal level 1. Basic building block signal of SONET, operating at

51.84Mbps. Faster SONET rates are defined as STS-*n*, where *n* is a multiple of 51.84Mbps. See also *SONET*.

STS-3c Synchronous Transport Signal level 3, con-catenated. SONET format that specifies the frame structure for the 155.52-Mbps lines used to carry ATM cells. See also *SONET*.

stub area OSPF area that carries a default route, intra-area routes, and interarea routes, but does not carry external routes. Virtual links cannot be configured across a stub area, and they cannot contain an ASBR. Compare to *non-stub area*. See also *ASBR* and *OSPF*.

stub network Network that has only a single connection to a router.

STUN See *STUN* in the "Cisco Systems Terms and Acronyms" section.

subarea Portion of an SNA network that consists of a subarea node and any attached links and peripheral nodes.

subarea node SNA communication controller or host that handles complete network addresses.

subchannel In broadband terminology, a frequency-based subdivision creating a separate communications channel.

subinterface One of a number of virtual interfaces on a single physical interface.

subnet See *subnetwork*.

subnet address Portion of an IP address that is speci-fied as the subnetwork by the subnet mask. See also *IP address*, *subnet mask*, and *subnetwork*.

subnet mask 32-bit address mask used in IP to indi-cate the bits of an IP address that are being used for the subnet address. Sometimes referred to simply as mask. See also *address mask* and *IP address*.

subnetwork *1.* In IP networks, a network sharing a particular subnet address. Subnetworks are networks arbitrarily segmented by a network administrator in order to provide a multilevel, hierarchical routing structure while shielding the subnetwork from the addressing complexity of attached networks. Sometimes called a subnet. See also *IP address, subnet address,* and *subnet mask. 2.* In OSI networks, a collection of ESs and ISs under the control of a single administrative domain and using a single network access protocol.

Subnetwork Access Protocol   See *SNAP.*

subnetwork point of attachment   See *SNPA.*

Subscriber Network Interface   See *SNI.*

subvector   Data segment of a vector in an SNA message. A subvector consists of a length field, a key that describes the subvector type, and subvector specific data.

Super Frame   See *SF.*

Super-JANET   Latest phase in the development of JANET, the UK educational and research network run by UKERNA. It uses SMDS and ATM to provide multiservice network facilities for many new applications including multimedia conferencing.

supernet   Aggregation of IP network addresses advertised as a single classless network address. For example, given four Class C IP networks—192.0.8.0, 192.0.9.0, 192.0.10.0 and 192.0.11.0—each having the intrinsic network mask of 255.255.255.0, one can advertise the address 192.0.8.0 with a subnet mask of 255.255.252.0.

supervisory processor   See *RP* in the "Cisco Systems Terms and Acronyms" section.

SURAnet   Southeastern Universities Research Association Network. Network connecting universities and other organizations in the Southeastern United States. SURAnet, originally funded by the NSF and a part of the NSFNET, is now part of BBN Planet. See also *BBN Planet, NSF,* and *NSFNET.*

sustainable cell rate   See *SCR.*

SVC   Switched virtual circuit. Virtual circuit that is dynamically established on demand and is torn down when transmission is complete. SVCs are used in situations where data transmission is sporadic. Called a switched virtual connection in ATM terminology. Compare to *PVC.*

switch   *1.* Network device that filters, forwards, and floods frames based on the destination address of each frame. The switch operates at the Data Link layer of the OSI model. *2.* General term applied to an electronic or mechanical device that allows a connection to be established as necessary and terminated when there is no longer a session to support.

switched LAN   LAN implemented with LAN switches. See *LAN switch.*

Switched Multimegabit Data Service   See *SMDS.*

Switched Port Analyzer   See *span.*

switched virtual circuit   See *SVC.*

switched virtual connection   See *SVC.*

Switch Processor   See *SP* in the "Cisco Systems Terms and Acronyms" section.

Switch-to-Switch Protocol   See *SSP.*

synchronization   Establishment of common timing between sender and receiver.

Synchronous Data Link Control   See *SDLC.*

Synchronous Digital Hierarchy   See *SDH.*

Synchronous Optical Network   See *SONET.*

synchronous transmission   Term describing digital signals that are transmitted with precise clocking. Such signals have the same frequency, with individual characters encapsulated in control bits (called start bits and stop bits) that designate the beginning and end of each character. Compare to *asynchronous transmission, isochronous transmission,* and *plesiochronous transmission.*

Synchronous Transport Module level 1   See *STM-1*.

Synchronous Transport Signal level 1   See *STS-1*.

Synchronous Transport Signal level 3, concatenated   See *STS-3c*.

sysgen   System generation. Process of defining network resources in a network.

system generation   See *sysgen*.

system services control points   See *SSCP*.

Systems Network Architecture   See *SNA*.

T

T1   Digital WAN carrier facility. T1 transmits DS-1-formatted data at 1.544Mbps through the telephone-switching network, using AMI or B8ZS coding. Compare to *E1*. See also *AMI*, *B8ZS*, and *DS-1*.

T3   Digital WAN carrier facility. T3 transmits DS-3-formatted data at 44.736Mbps through the telephone switching network. Compare to *E3*. See also *DS-3*.

TABS   Telemetry Asynchronous Block Serial. AT&T polled point-to-point or multipoint communication protocol that supports moderate data transfer rates over intra-office wire pairs.

TAC   Terminal Access Controller. Internet host that accepts terminal connections from dial-up lines.

TACACS   Terminal Access Controller Access Control System. Authentication protocol, developed by the DDN community, that provides remote access authentication and related services, such as event logging. User passwords are administered in a central database rather than in individual routers, providing an easily scalable network security solution. See also *TACACS+* in the "Cisco Systems Terms and Acronyms" section.

TACACS+   See *TACACS+* in the "Cisco Systems Terms and Acronyms" section.

tagged traffic   ATM cells that have their CLP bit set to 1. If the network is congested, tagged traffic can be dropped to ensure delivery of higher-priority traffic. Sometimes called DE traffic. See also *CLP*.

tag switching   High-performance, packet-forwarding technology that integrates Network layer (Layer 3) routing and Data Link layer (Layer 2) switching and provides scalable, high-speed switching in the network core. Tag switching is based on the concept of label swapping, in which packets or cells are assigned short, fixed-length labels that tell switching nodes how data should be forwarded.

TARP   TID Address Resolution Protocol. In OSS, a protocol that resolves a TL-1 TID to a CLNP address (NSAP).

TAXI 4B/5B   Transparent Asynchronous Transmitter/Receiver Interface 4-byte/5-byte. Encoding scheme used for FDDI LANs as well as for ATM. Supports speeds of up to 100Mbps over multimode fiber. TAXI is the chipset that generates 4B/5B encoding on multimode fiber. See also *4B/5B local fiber*.

TBOS protocol   Telemetry Byte Oriented Serial protocol. Protocol that transmits alarm, status, and control points between NE and OSS. TBOS defines one physical interface for direct connection between the telemetry equipment and the monitored equipment.

TC   Transmission convergence. Sublayer of the ATM Physical layer that transforms the flow of cells into a steady flow of bits for transmission over the physical medium. When transmitting, the TC sublayer maps the cells into the frame format, generates the HEC, and sends idle cells when there is nothing to send. When receiving, the TC sublayer delineates individual cells in the received bit stream and uses HEC to detect and correct errors. See also *HEC* and *PHY*.

T-carrier   TDM transmission method usually referring to a line or cable carrying a DS-1 signal.

TCP   Transmission Control Protocol. Connection-oriented Transport layer protocol that provides reliable full-duplex data transmission. TCP is part of the TCP/IP protocol stack. See also *TCP/IP*.

TCP and UDP over Lightweight IP   See *TULIP*.

TCP and UDP over Nonexistent IP   See *TUNIP*.

TCP/IP   Transmission Control Protocol/Internet Protocol. Common name for the suite of protocols developed by the U.S. DoD in the 1970s to support the construction of worldwide internetworks. TCP and IP are the two best-known protocols in the suite. See also *IP* and *TCP*.

TCU   Trunk coupling unit. In Token Ring networks, a physical device that enables a station to connect to the trunk cable.

TDM   Time-division multiplexing. Technique in which information from multiple channels can be allocated bandwidth on a single wire based on preassigned time slots. Bandwidth is allocated to each channel regardless of whether the station has data to transmit. Compare to *ATDM*, *FDM*, and *statistical multiplexing*.

TDR   Time domain reflectometer. Device capable of sending signals through a network medium to check cable continuity and other attributes. TDRs are used to find Physical layer network problems.

TE   Terminal equipment. Any ISDN-compatible device that can be attached to the network, such as a telephone, fax, or computer.

Technical Office Protocol   See *TOP*.

TEI   Terminal endpoint identifier. Field in the LAPD address that identifies a device on an ISDN interface. See also *TE*.

telco   Abbreviation for telephone company.

Telecommunication Management Network   See *TMN*.

telecommunications   Term referring to communications (usually involving computer systems) over the telephone network.

Telecommunications Industry Association   See *TIA*.

telemetry   Capability of transmitting or retrieving data over long distance communication links, such as satellite or telephone.

Telemetry Asynchronous Block Serial   See *TABS*.

telephony   Science of converting sound to electrical signals and transmitting it between widely removed points.

telex   Teletypewriter service allowing subscribers to send messages over the PSTN.

Telnet   Standard terminal emulation protocol in the TCP/IP protocol stack. Telnet is used for remote terminal connection, enabling users to log in to remote systems and use resources as if they were connected to a local system. Telnet is defined in RFC 854.

Tempest   U.S. military standard. Electronic products adhering to the Tempest specification are designed to withstand EMP. See also *EMP*.

TERENA   Trans-European Research and Education Networking Association. Organization that promotes information and telecommunications technologies development in Europe. Formed by the merger of EARN and RARE. See also *EARN* and *RARE*.

termid   SNA cluster controller identification for switched lines only. Also called Xid.

terminal   Simple device at which data can be entered or retrieved from a network. Generally, terminals have a monitor and a keyboard, but no processor or local disk drive.

Terminal Access Controller   See *TAC*.

Terminal Access Controller Access Control System
See *TACACS.*

terminal adapter   Device used to connect ISDN BRI
connections to existing interfaces such as EIA/TIA-232.
Essentially, an ISDN modem.

terminal emulation   Network application in which a
computer runs software that makes it appear to a
remote host as a directly attached terminal.

terminal endpoint identifier   See *TEI.*

terminal equipment   See *TE.*

terminal server   Communications processor that connects asynchronous devices such as terminals, printers,
hosts, and modems to any LAN or WAN that uses
TCP/IP, X.25, or LAT protocols. Terminal servers provide the internetwork intelligence that is not available
in the connected devices.

terminator   Device that provides electrical resistance
at the end of a transmission line to absorb signals on
the line, thereby keeping them from bouncing back
and being received again by network stations.

Texas Higher Education Network   See *THEnet.*

TFTP   Trivial File Transfer Protocol. Simplified version of FTP that allows files to be transferred from one
computer to another over a network.

TH   Transmission header. SNA header that is
appended to the SNA basic information unit (BIU).
The TH uses one of a number of available SNA header
formats. See also *FID0, FID1, FID2, FID3,* and *FID4.*

THC over X.25   See *THC over X.25* in the "Cisco
Systems Terms and Acronyms" section.

THEnet   Texas Higher Education Network. Regional
network comprising over 60 academic and research
institutions in the Texas (United States) area.

Thinnet   Term used to define a thinner, less expensive
version of the cable specified in the IEEE 802.3

10Base2 standard. Compare to *Cheapernet.* See also
10Base2, Ethernet, and *IEEE 802.3.*

three-way handshake   Process whereby two protocol
entities synchronize during connection establishment.

throughput   Rate of information arriving at, and
possibly passing through, a particular point in a network system.

TIA   Telecommunications Industry Association.
Organization that develops standards relating to
telecommunications technologies. Together, the TIA
and the EIA have formalized standards, such as
EIA/TIA-232, for the electrical characteristics of data
transmission. See also *EIA.*

TIC   Token Ring interface coupler. Controller
through which an FEP connects to a Token Ring.

TID   Terminal Identifier.

time-division multiplexing   See *TDM.*

time domain reflectometer   See *TDR.*

Time Notify   See *TNotify.*

timeout   Event that occurs when one network device
expects to hear from another network device within a
specified period of time, but does not. The resulting
timeout usually results in a retransmission of information or the dissolving of the session between the two
devices.

Time To Live   See *TTL.*

TIRKS   Trunk Information Record Keeping System.
Bellcore OSS that provides record keeping for interof-
fice trunk facilities. See also *OSS.*

TL-1   Transaction Language One. Bellcore term for
intelligent network elements.

TLAP   TokenTalk Link Access Protocol. Link-access
protocol used in a TokenTalk network. TLAP is built
on top of the standard Token Ring Data Link layer.

TM   See *traffic management.*

TMN   Telecommunication Management Network. ITU-T generic model for transporting and processing OAM&P information for a telecommunications network. See also *OAM&P.*

TN3270   Terminal emulation software that allows a terminal to appear to an IBM host as a 3278 Model 2 terminal.

TNotify   Time Notify. Specifies how often SMT initiates neighbor notification broadcasts. See also *SMT.*

token   Frame that contains control information. Possession of the token allows a network device to transmit data onto the network. See also *token passing.*

token bus   LAN architecture using token passing access over a bus topology. This LAN architecture is the basis for the IEEE 802.4 LAN specification. See also *IEEE 802.4.*

token passing   Method by which network devices access the physical medium in an orderly fashion based on possession of a small frame called a token. Contrast with *circuit switching* and *contention*. See also *token.*

Token Ring   Token-passing LAN developed and supported by IBM. Token Ring runs at 4 or 16Mbps over a ring topology. Similar to IEEE 802.5. See also *IEEE 802.5*, *ring topology*, and *token passing.*

Token Ring interface coupler   See *TIC.*

TokenTalk   Apple Computer's data-link product that allows an AppleTalk network to be connected by Token Ring cables.

TokenTalk Link Access Protocol   See *TLAP.*

TOP   Technical Office Protocol. OSI-based architecture developed for office communications.

topology   Physical arrangement of network nodes and media within an enterprise networking structure.

ToS   Type of service. See *CoS.*

TP0   Transport Protocol Class 0. OSI connectionless transport protocol for use over reliable subnetworks. Defined by ISO 8073.

TP4   Transport Protocol Class 4. OSI connection-based transport protocol. Defined by ISO 8073.

TPD   Trailing packet discard. Mechanism used by some ATM switches that allows the remaining cells supporting an AAL5 frame to be discarded when one or more cells of that AAL5 frame are dropped. This avoids sending partial AAL5 frames through the ATM network when they will have to be retransmitted by the sender. Compare to *EPD.*

TPPMD   Twisted-pair physical medium dependent.

traceroute   Program available on many systems that traces the path a packet takes to a destination. It is mostly used to debug routing problems between hosts. There is also a traceroute protocol defined in RFC 1393.

traffic management   Techniques for avoiding congestion and shaping and policing traffic, Allows links to operate at high levels of utilization by scaling back lower-priority, delay-tolerant traffic at the edge of the network when congestion begins to occur.

traffic policing   Process used to measure the actual traffic flow across a given connection and compare it to the total admissible traffic flow for that connection. Traffic beyond the agreed-upon flow can be tagged (where the CLP bit is set to 1) and can be discarded en route if congestion develops. Traffic policing is used in ATM, Frame Relay, and other types of networks. Also known as admission control, permit processing, rate enforcement, and UPC. See also *tagged traffic.*

traffic profile   Set of CoS attribute values assigned to a given port on an ATM switch. The profile affects numerous parameters for data transmitted from the port including rate, cell drop eligibility, transmit priority, and inactivity timer. See also *CoS.*

traffic shaping   Use of queues to limit surges that can congest a network. Data is buffered and then sent into the network in regulated amounts to ensure that the traffic will fit within the promised traffic envelope for the particular connection. Traffic shaping is used in ATM, Frame Relay, and other types of networks. Also known as metering, shaping, and smoothing.

trailer   Control information appended to data when encapsulating the data for network transmission. Compare to *header*.

trailing packet discard   See *TPD*.

transaction   Result-oriented unit of communication processing.

Transaction Services layer   Layer 7 in the SNA architectural model. Represents user application functions, such as spreadsheets, word-processing, or email, by which users interact with the network. Corresponds roughly with the Application layer of the OSI reference model. See also *Data Flow Control layer*, *Data-Link Control layer*, *Path Control layer*, *Physical Control layer*, *Presentation Services layer*, and *Transaction Services layer*.

transceiver   See *MAU*.

transceiver cable   See *AUI*.

Trans-European Research and Education Networking Association   See *TERENA*.

transfer syntax   Description on an instance of a data type that is expressed as a string of bits.

transit bridging   Bridging that uses encapsulation to send a frame between two similar networks over a dissimilar network.

translational bridging   Bridging between networks with dissimilar MAC sublayer protocols. MAC information is translated into the format of the destination network at the bridge. Contrast with *encapsulation bridging*.

Transmission Control layer   Layer 4 in the SNA architectural model. This layer is responsible for establishing, maintaining, and terminating SNA sessions, sequencing data messages, and controlling session level flow. Corresponds to the Transport layer of the OSI model. See also *Data Flow Control layer*, *Data-Link Control layer*, *Path Control layer*, *Physical Control layer*, *Presentation Services layer*, and *Transaction Services layer*.

Transmission Control Protocol   See *TCP*.

Transmission Control Protocol/Internet Protocol   See *TCP/IP*.

transmission convergence   See *TC*.

transmission group   In SNA routing, one or more parallel communications link treated as one communications facility.

transmission header   See *TH*.

transmission link   See *link*.

TRANSPAC   Major packet data network run by France Telecom.

Transparent Asynchronous Transmitter/Receiver Interface 4-byte/5-byte   See *TAXI 4B/5B*.

transparent bridging   Bridging scheme often used in Ethernet and IEEE 802.3 networks in which bridges pass frames along one hop at a time based on tables associating end nodes with bridge ports. Transparent bridging is so named because the presence of bridges is transparent to network end nodes. Contrast with *SRB*.

Transport layer   Layer 4 of the OSI reference model. This layer is responsible for reliable network communication between end nodes. The Transport layer provides mechanisms for the establishment, maintenance, and termination of virtual circuits, transport fault detection and recovery, and information flow control. Corresponds to the Transmission Control layer of the SNA model. See also *Application layer*, *Data Link layer*, *Network layer*, *Physical layer*, *Presentation layer*, and *Session layer*.

Transport Protocol Class 0   See *TP0*.

Transport Protocol Class 4   See *TP4*.

trap   Message sent by an SNMP agent to an NMS, console, or terminal to indicate the occurrence of a significant event, such as a specifically defined condition or a threshold that was reached. See also *alarm* and *event*.

tree topology   LAN topology similar to a bus topology, except that tree networks can contain branches with multiple nodes. Transmissions from a station propagate the length of the medium and are received by all other stations. Compare to *bus topology*, *ring topology*, and *star topology*.

TRIP   See *TRIP* in the "Cisco Systems Terms and Acronyms" section.

Trivial File Transfer Protocol   See *TFTP*.

trunk   Physical and logical connection between two switches across which network traffic travels. A backbone is composed of a number of trunks.

trunk coupling unit   See *TCU*.

trunk up-down   See *TUD*.

TTL   Time To Live. Field in an IP header that indicates how long a packet is considered valid.

TUD   Trunk up-down. Protocol used in ATM networks that monitors trunks and detects when one goes down or comes up. ATM switches send regular test messages from each trunk port to test trunk line quality. If a trunk misses a given number of these messages, TUD declares the trunk down. When a trunk comes back up, TUD recognizes that the trunk is up, declares the trunk up, and returns it to service. See also *trunk*.

TULIP   TCP and UDP over Lightweight IP. Proposed protocol for running TCP and UDP applications over ATM.

TUNIP   TCP and UDP over Nonexistent IP. Proposed protocol for running TCP and UPD applications over ATM.

tunneling   Architecture that is designed to provide the services necessary to implement any standard point-to-point encapsulation scheme. See also *encapsulation*.

TUV   German test agency that certifies products to European safety standards.

twisted pair   Relatively low-speed transmission medium consisting of two insulated wires arranged in a regular spiral pattern. The wires can be shielded or unshielded. Twisted pair is common in telephony applications and is increasingly common in data networks. See also *STP* and *UTP*.

two-way simultaneous   See *TWS* in the "Cisco Systems Terms and Acronyms" section.

TYMNET   See *XStream*.

Type 1 operation   IEEE 802.2 (LLC) connectionless operation.

Type 2 operation   IEEE 802.2 (LLC) connection-oriented operation.

type of service   See *ToS*.

U

UART   Universal Asynchronous Receiver/Transmitter. Integrated circuit, attached to the parallel bus of a computer, used for serial communications. The UART translates between serial and parallel signals, provides transmission clocking, and buffers data sent to or from the computer.

UB Net/One   Ungermann-Bass Net/One. Routing protocol, developed by UB Networks, that uses hello packets and a path-delay metric, with end nodes communicating using the XNS protocol. There are a number of differences between the manner in which Net/One uses the XNS protocol and the usage common among other XNS nodes.

UBR Unspecified bit rate. QoS class defined by the ATM Forum for ATM networks. UBR allows any amount of data up to a specified maximum to be sent across the network, but there are no guarantees in terms of cell loss rate and delay. Compare to *ABR*, *CBR*, and *VBR*.

UBR+ Unspecified bit rate plus. UBR service complemented by ATM switches that use intelligent packet discard mechanisms such as EPD or TPD. See also *EPD* and *TPD*.

UDLP UniDirectional Link Protocol. Protocol used by inexpensive, receive-only antennas to receive data via satellite.

UDP User Datagram Protocol. Connectionless Transport layer protocol in the TCP/IP protocol stack. UDP is a simple protocol that exchanges datagrams without acknowledgments or guaranteed delivery, requiring that error processing and retransmission be handled by other protocols. UDP is defined in RFC 768.

U-frame Unnumbered frame. One of three SDLC frame formats. See also *I-frame* and *S-frame*.

UKERNA UK Education and Research Networking Association.

UL Underwriters Laboratories. Independent agency within the United States that tests product safety.

ULP Upper-layer protocol. Protocol that operates at a higher layer in the OSI reference model, relative to other layers. ULP is sometimes used to refer to the next-highest protocol (relative to a particular protocol) in a protocol stack.

unbalanced configuration HDLC configuration with one primary station and multiple secondary stations.

Underwriters Laboratories See *UL*.

Ungermann-Bass Net/One See *UB Net/One*.

UNI User-Network Interface. ATM Forum specification that defines an interoperability standard for the interface between ATM-based products (a router or an ATM switch) located in a private network and the ATM switches located within the public carrier networks. Also used to describe similar connections in Frame Relay networks. See also *NNI*, *Q.920/Q.921*, and *SNI (Subscriber Network Interface)*.

unicast Message sent to a single network destination. Compare to *broadcast* and *multicast*.

unicast address Address specifying a single network device. Compare to *broadcast address* and *multicast address*. See also *unicast*.

UniDirectional Link Protocol See *UDLP*.

uninsured traffic Traffic within the excess rate (the difference between the insured rate and maximum rate) for an ATM VCC. This traffic can be dropped by the network if congestion occurs. See also *CLP*, *insured rate*, and *maximum rate*.

unipolar Literally meaning one polarity, the fundamental electrical characteristic of internal signals in digital communications equipment. Contrast with *bipolar*.

unity gain In broadband networks, the balance between signal loss and signal gain through amplifiers.

Universal Asynchronous Receiver/Transmitter See *UART*.

Universal Resource Locator See *URL*.

UNIX Operating system developed in 1969 at Bell Laboratories. UNIX has gone through several iterations since its inception. These include UNIX 4.3 BSD (Berkeley Standard Distribution), developed at the University of California at Berkeley, and UNIX System V, Release 4.0, developed by AT&T.

UNIX-to-UNIX Copy Program   See *UUCP*.

unnumbered frames   HDLC frames used for various control and management purposes, including link startup and shutdown, and mode specification.

unshielded twisted-pair   See *UTP*.

unspecified bit rate   See *UBR*.

UPC   Usage parameter control. See *traffic policing*.

upper-layer protocol   See *ULP*.

urban legend   Story, which may start with a grain of truth, that has been retold and ends up on the Internet. Some legends that periodically make their rounds include "The Infamous Modem Tax," "Craig Shergold/Brain Tumor/Get Well Cards," and "The $250 Cookie Recipe." Urban legends are conceptually similar to space junk that stays in orbit for years.

URL   Universal Resource Locator. Standardized addressing scheme for accessing hypertext documents and other services using a browser. See also *browser*.

usage parameter control   See *traffic policing*.

USENET   Initiated in 1979, one of the oldest and largest cooperative networks, with over 10,000 hosts and a quarter of a million users. Its primary service is a distributed conferencing service called News.

User Datagram Protocol   See *UDP*.

User-Network Interface   See *UNI*.

UTC   Coordinated Universal Time. Time zone at zero degrees longitude. Formerly called Greenwich Mean Time (GMT) and Zulu time.

UTP   Unshielded twisted-pair. Four-pair wire medium used in a variety of networks. UTP does not require the fixed spacing between connections that is necessary with coaxial-type connections. There are five types of UTP cabling commonly used: Category 1 cabling, Category 2 cabling, Category 3 cabling, Category 4 cabling, and Category 5 cabling. Compare to *STP*. See also *EIA/TIA-586* and *twisted pair*.

UUCP   UNIX-to-UNIX Copy Program. Protocol stack used for point-to-point communication between UNIX systems.

uudecode   UNIX-to-UNIX decode. Method of decoding ASCII files that were encoded using uuencode. See also *uuencode*.

uuencode   UNIX-to-UNIX encoding. Method of converting binary files to ASCII so that they can be sent over the Internet via email. The name comes from its use by the UNIX operating system's uuencode command. See also *uudecode*.

UVM   Universal Voice Module.

UVM-C   Universal Voice Module-Channelized.

UVM-U   Universal Voice Module-Unchannelized.

V

V.24   ITU-T standard for a Physical layer interface between DTE and DCE. V.24 is essentially the same as the EIA/TIA-232 standard. See also *EIA/TIA-232*.

V.25bis   ITU-T specification describing procedures for call setup and teardown over the DTE-DCE interface in a PSDN.

V.32   ITU-T standard serial line protocol for bidirectional data transmissions at speeds of 4.8 or 9.6Kbps. See also *V.32bis*.

V.32bis   ITU-T standard that extends V.32 to speeds up to 14.4Kbps. See also *V.32*.

V.34   ITU-T standard that specifies a serial line protocol. V.34 offers improvements to the V.32 standard, including higher transmission rates (28.8Kbps) and enhanced data compression. Compare to *V.32*.

V.35 ITU-T standard describing a synchronous, Physical layer protocol used for communications between a network access device and a packet network. V.35 is most commonly used in the United States and in Europe, and is recommended for speeds up to 48Kbps.

V.42 ITU-T standard protocol for error correction using LAPM. See also *LAPM*.

variable bit rate See *VBR*.

variable-length subnet mask See *VLSM*.

VBR Variable bit rate. QoS class defined by the ATM Forum for ATM networks. VBR is subdivided into a real time (RT) class and non-real time (NRT) class. VBR (RT) is used for connections in which there is a fixed timing relationship between samples. VBR (NRT) is used for connections in which there is no fixed timing relationship between samples, but that still need a guaranteed QoS. Compare to *ABR*, *CBR*, and *UBR*.

VC See *virtual circuit*.

VCC Virtual channel connection. Logical circuit, made up of VCLs, that carries data between two end points in an ATM network. Sometimes called a virtual circuit connection. See also *VCI*, *VCL*, and *VPI*.

VCI Virtual channel identifier. 16-bit field in the header of an ATM cell. The VCI, together with the VPI, is used to identify the next destination of a cell as it passes through a series of ATM switches on its way to its destination. ATM switches use the VPI/VCI fields to identify the next network VCL that a cell needs to transit on its way to its final destination. The function of the VCI is similar to that of the DLCI in Frame Relay. Compare to *DLCI*. See also *VCL* and *VPI*.

VCL Virtual channel link. Connection between two ATM devices. A VCC is made up of one or more VCLs. See also *VCC*.

VCN Virtual circuit number. 12-bit field in an X.25 PLP header that identifies an X.25 virtual circuit.

Allows DCE to determine how to route a packet through the X.25 network.

VDSL Very-high-data-rate digital subscriber line. One of four DSL technologies. VDSL delivers 13 to 52Mbps downstream and 1.5 to 2.3Mbps upstream over a single twisted copper pair. The operating range of VDSL is limited to 1,000 to 4,500 feet (304.8 to 1,372 meters). Compare to *ADSL*, *HDSL*, and *SDSL*.

vector Data segment of an SNA message. A vector consists of a length field, a key that describes the vector type, and vector-specific data.

Veronica Very Easy Rodent Oriented Netwide Index to Computer Archives. Gopher utility that effectively searches Gopher servers based on a user's list of keywords.

Versatile Interface Processor See *VIP* in the "Cisco Systems Terms and Acronyms" section.

VF Variance factor. One of three link attributes exchanged using PTSPs to determine the available resources of an ATM network. VF is a relative measure of CRM normalized by the variance of the aggregate cell rate on the link. See also *CRM*.

VINES Virtual Integrated Network Service. NOS developed and marketed by Banyan Systems.

VIP See *VIP* in the "Cisco Systems Terms and Acronyms" section.

virtual address See *network address*.

virtual channel See *virtual circuit*.

virtual channel connection See *VCC*.

virtual channel identifier See *VCI*.

virtual channel link See *VCL*.

virtual circuit Logical circuit created to ensure reliable communication between two network devices. A virtual circuit is defined by a VPI/VCI pair, and can be either permanent (PVC) or switched (SVC). Virtual circuits are used in Frame Relay and X.25. In ATM, a virtual circuit is called a virtual channel. Sometimes abbreviated VC. See also *PVC, SVC, VCI, virtual route,* and *VPI.*

virtual circuit connection   See *VCC.*

virtual circuit number   See *VCN.*

virtual connection   In ATM, a connection between end users that has a defined route and endpoints. See also *PVC* and *SVC.*

Virtual Integrated Network Service   See *VINES.*

virtual IP   See *VIP* in the "Cisco Systems Terms and Acronyms" section.

virtualization   Process of implementing a network based on virtual network segments. Devices are connected to virtual segments independent of their physical location and their physical connection to the network.

virtual LAN   See *VLAN.*

virtual LAN internetwork   See *VLI.*

Virtual Networking Services   See *Virtual Networking Services* in the "Cisco Systems Terms and Acronyms" section.

virtual path   Logical grouping of virtual circuits that connect two sites. See also *virtual circuit.*

virtual path connection   See *VPC.*

virtual path identifier   See *VPI.*

virtual path identifier/virtual channel identifier   Abbreviated VPI/VCI. See *VCI* and *VPI.*

virtual path link   See *VPL.*

virtual ring   Entity in an SRB network that logically connects two or more physical rings together either locally or remotely. The concept of virtual rings can be expanded across router boundaries.

virtual route   In SNA, a logical connection between subarea nodes that is physically realized as a particular explicit route. SNA terminology for virtual circuit. See also *virtual circuit.*

virtual subnet   Logical grouping of devices that share a common Layer 3 subnet.

virtual telecommunications access method   See *VTAM.*

Virtual Terminal Protocol   See *VTP.*

VLAN   Virtual LAN. Group of devices on one or more LANs that are configured (using management software) so that they can communicate as if they were attached to the same wire, when in fact they are located on a number of different LAN segments. Because VLANs are based on logical rather than physical connections, they are extremely flexible.

VLI   Virtual LAN internetwork. Internetwork composed of VLANs. See also *VLAN.*

VLSM   Variable-length subnet mask. Ability to specify a different subnet mask for the same network number on different subnets. VLSM can help optimize available address space.

VNS   See *Virtual Networking Services* in the "Cisco Systems Terms and Acronyms" section.

VP   Virtual path. One of two types of ATM circuits identified by a VPI. A virtual path is a bundle of virtual channels, all of which are switched transparently across an ATM network based on a common VPI. See also *VPI.*

VPC   Virtual path connection. Grouping of VCCs that share one or more contiguous VPLs. See also *VCC* and *VPL.*

VPDN   Virtual private dial-up network. See also *VPN.*

VPI   Virtual path identifier. 8-bit field in the header of an ATM cell. The VPI, together with the VCI, is used to identify the next destination of a cell as it passes through a series of ATM switches on its way to its destination. ATM switches use the VPI/VCI fields to identify the next VCL that a cell needs to transit on its way to its final destination. The function of the VPI is similar to that of the DLCI in Frame Relay. Compare to *DLCI*. See also *VCI* and *VCL*.

VPI/VCI   See *VCI* and *VPI*.

VPL   Virtual path link. Within a virtual path, a group of unidirectional VCLs with the same end points. Grouping VCLs into VPLs reduces the number of connections to be managed, thereby decreasing network control overhead and cost. A VPC is made up of one or more VPLs.

VPN   Virtual Private Network. Enables IP traffic to travel securely over a public TCP/IP network by encrypting all traffic from one network to another. A VPN uses "tunneling" to encrypt all information at the IP level.

VRML   Virtual Reality Modeling Language. Specification for displaying three-dimensional objects on the World Wide Web. Think of it as the 3-D equivalent of HTML.

VS/VD   Virtual source/virtual destination.

VTAM   Virtual telecommunications access method. Set of programs that control communication between LUs. VTAM controls data transmission between channel-attached devices and performs routing functions. See also *LU*.

VT-*n*   Virtual Tributary level *n*. SONET format for mapping a lower-rate signal into a SONET payload. For example, VT-1.5 is used to transport a DS-1 signal. See also *DS-1* and *SONET*.

VTP   Virtual Terminal Protocol. ISO application for establishing a virtual terminal connection across a network.

W

WAIS   Wide Area Information Server. Distributed database protocol developed to search for information over a network. WAIS supports full-text databases, which allow an entire document to be searched for a match (as opposed to other technologies that only allow an index of key words to be searched).

WAN   Wide-area network. Data communications network that serves users across a broad geographic area and often uses transmission devices provided by common carriers. Frame Relay, SMDS, and X.25 are examples of WANs. Compare to *LAN* and *MAN*.

watchdog packet   Used to ensure that a client is still connected to a NetWare server. If the server has not received a packet from a client for a certain period of time, it sends that client a series of watchdog packets. If the station fails to respond to a predefined number of watchdog packets, the server concludes that the station is no longer connected and clears the connection for that station.

watchdog spoofing   Subset of spoofing that refers specifically to a router acting for a NetWare client by sending watchdog packets to a NetWare server to keep the session between client and server active. See also *spoofing*.

watchdog timer   *1*. Hardware or software mechanism that is used to trigger an event or an escape from a process unless the timer is periodically reset. *2*. In NetWare, a timer that indicates the maximum period of time that a server will wait for a client to respond to a watchdog packet. If the timer expires, the server sends another watchdog packet (up to a set maximum). See also *watchdog packet*.

waveform coding   Electrical techniques used to convey binary signals.

W-DCS Wideband Digital Crossconnect System. SONET DCS capable of crossconnecting DS-1 and VT1.5 signals. See also *DCS*, *DS-1*, *SONET*, and *VT-n*.

Web browser See *browser*.

WFQ Weighted fair queuing. Congestion management algorithm that identifies conversations (in the form of traffic streams), separates packets that belong to each conversation, and ensures that capacity is shared fairly between these individual conversations. WFQ is an automatic way of stabilizing network behavior during congestion and results in increased performance and reduced retransmission.

wide-area network See *WAN*.

wideband See *broadband*.

wildcard mask 32-bit quantity used in conjunction with an IP address to determine which bits in an IP address should be ignored when comparing that address with another IP address. A wildcard mask is specified when setting up access lists.

WinSock Windows Socket Interface. Software interface that allows a wide variety of applications to use and share an Internet connection. WinSock is implemented as dynamic link library (DLL) with some supporting programs, such as a dialer program that initiates the connection.

wiring closet Specially designed room used for wiring a data or voice network. Wiring closets serve as a central junction point for the wiring and wiring equipment that is used for interconnecting devices.

WISCNET TCP/IP network in Wisconsin (United States) connecting University of Wisconsin campuses and a number of private colleges. Links are 56Kbps and T1.

workgroup Collection of workstations and servers on a LAN that are designed to communicate and exchange data with one another.

Workgroup Director See *WorkGroup Director* in the "Cisco Systems Terms and Acronyms" section.

workgroup switching Method of switching that provides high-speed (100Mbps) transparent bridging between Ethernet networks and high-speed translational bridging between Ethernet and CDDI or FDDI.

World Wide Web See *WWW*.

wrap Action taken by an FDDI or CDDI network to recover in the event of a failure. The stations on each side of the failure reconfigure themselves, creating a single logical ring out of the primary and secondary rings.

WWW World Wide Web. Large network of Internet servers providing hypertext and other services to terminals running client applications such as a browser. See also *browser*.

X

X.121 ITU-T standard describing an addressing scheme used in X.25 networks. X.121 addresses are sometimes called IDNs.

X.21 ITU-T standard for serial communications over synchronous digital lines. The X.21 protocol is used primarily in Europe and Japan.

X.21bis ITU-T standard that defines the Physical layer protocol for communication between DCE and DTE in an X.25 network. Virtually equivalent to EIA/TIA-232. See also *EIA/TIA-232* and *X.25*.

X.25 ITU-T standard that defines how connections between DTE and DCE are maintained for remote terminal access and computer communications in PDNs. X.25 specifies LAPB, a Data Link layer protocol, and PLP, a Network layer protocol. Frame Relay has to some degree superseded X.25. See also *Frame Relay*, *LAPB*, and *PLP*.

X.25 Level 3   See *PLP*.

X.25 Protocol   See *PLP*.

X.28   ITU-T recommendation that defines the terminal-to-PAD interface in X.25 networks. See also *PAD* and *X.25*.

X.29   ITU-T recommendation that defines the form for control information in the terminal-to-PAD interface used in X.25 networks. See also *PAD* and *X.25*.

X.3   ITU-T recommendation that defines various PAD parameters used in X.25 networks. See also *PAD* and *X.25*.

X3T9.5   Number assigned to the ANSI Task Group of Accredited Standards Committee for their internal, working document describing FDDI.

X.400   ITU-T recommendation specifying a standard for email transfer.

X.500   ITU-T recommendation specifying a standard for distributed maintenance of files and directories.

X.75   ITU-T specification that defines the signalling system between two PDNs. X.75 is essentially an NNI. See also *NNI*.

X Display Manager Control Protocol   See *XDMCP*.

XDMCP   X Display Manager Control Protocol. Protocol used to communicate between X terminals and workstations running the UNIX operating system.

XDR   eXternal Data Representation. Standard for machine-independent data structures developed by Sun Microsystems. Similar to BER.

xDSL   Group term used to refer to ADSL, HDSL, SDSL and VDSL. All are emerging digital technologies using the existing copper infrastructure provided by the telephone companies. xDSL is a high-speed alternative to ISDN.

Xerox Network Systems   See *XNS*.

XID   Exchange identification. Request and response packets exchanged prior to a session between a router and a Token Ring host. If the parameters of the serial device contained in the XID packet do not match the configuration of the host, the session is dropped.

Xid   See *termid*.

XML   eXtensible Markup Language. Designed to enable the use of SGML on the World Wide Web. XML allows you to define your own customized markup language.

XNS   Xerox Network Systems. Protocol suite originally designed by PARC. Many PC networking companies, such as 3Com, Banyan, Novell, and UB Networks used or currently use a variation of XNS as their primary transport protocol. See also *X Window System*.

X Recommendations   CCITT documents that describe data communication network standards. Well-known ones include X.25 Packet Switching standard, X.400 Message Handling System, and X.500 Directory Services.

XRemote   Protocol developed specifically to optimize support for the X Window System over a serial communications link.

XStream   Major public PSN in the United States operated by MCI. Formerly called TYMNET.

X terminal   Terminal that allows a user simultaneous access to several different applications and resources in a multivendor environment through implementation of X Windows. See also *X Window System*.

X Window System   Distributed, network-transparent, device-independent, multitasking windowing and graphics system originally developed by MIT for communication between X terminals and UNIX workstations. See also *X terminal*.

Z

zero code suppression   Line coding scheme used for transmission clocking. Zero line suppression substitutes a one in the seventh bit of a string of eight consecutive zeros. See also *ones density*.

ZIP   Zone Information Protocol. AppleTalk Session layer protocol that maps network numbers to zone names. ZIP is used by NBP to determine which networks contain nodes that belong to a zone. See also *ZIP storm* and *zone*.

ZIP storm   Broadcast storm that occurs when a router running AppleTalk propagates a route for which it currently has no corresponding zone name. The route is then forwarded by downstream routers, and a ZIP storm ensues. See also *ZIP*.

zone   In AppleTalk, a logical group of network devices. See also *ZIP*.

Zone Information Protocol   See *ZIP*.

zone multicast address   Data-link-dependent multicast address at which a node receives the NBP broadcasts directed to its zone. See also *NBP*.

Overview of the Cisco Certification Process

Cisco certification is achieved by passing one or more certification exams. Cisco certification exams are designed to evaluate your knowledge of Cisco routers and switches as well as internetworking theory. These exams are conducted at authorized Prometric Testing Centers, making them available in over 1,400 locations world wide. Contact Sylvan Prometric at www.sylvan-prometric.com to locate the testing center nearest you.

Cisco's certification exams are based upon information provided in training courses available through Cisco Authorized Training Partners. Although the courses are not required for certification, attendance in the courses can provide valuable information and hands-on experience to assist in your preparation for the certification exams. A list of the current Authorized Training Partners is available at www.cisco.com/pcgi-bin/front.x/wwtraining/listAllTP.pl.

INTRODUCTION

Cisco currently offers six degrees of certification in three different tracks or fields of expertise, for a total of 18 possible certifications available.

The three certification tracks are Routing/Switching, WAN Switching, and ISP Dial. The Routing/Switching and WAN Switching tracks are each broken into Network Support and Network Design tracks. See Figure B.1

Routing/Switching		WAN Switching		ISP Dial
Network Support	Network Design	Network Support	Network Design	
CCNA CCNP Specialties: •Security •Voice Access •Network Management •LAN ATM •SNA Solutions CCIE	CCDA CCDP	CCNA CCNP CCIE	CCDD	CCIE

FIGURE B.1
Cisco certification flowchart.

The rest of the chapter discusses the requirements to achieve each of these certifications in detail, broken down by the three main certification tracks.

> **NOTE**
>
> **Classes Available**   Cisco offers courses to assist in preparation for all exams, with the exception of CCIE exams. The course names are the same as the exam names.

ROUTING/SWITCHING TRACK

Routing/Switching professionals must have the following abilities:

◆ Install and configure a network to increase bandwidth, improve response times, and enhance reliability and quality of service.

◆ Maximize performance and improve network security.

◆ Create a global intranet.

◆ Provide a range of application-oriented solutions.

Network Support

In the Network Support track, Cisco offers Cisco Certified Network Associate (CCNA), Cisco Certified Network Professional (CCNP), and Cisco Certified Internet Expert (CCIE). In addition, Cisco's Routing/Switching Network Support track offers five specialty areas: Security, Voice Access, Network Management, LAN ATM, and SNA Solutions.

CCNA

This certification is designed for management of small internetworks with limited interconnection.

CCNA certification is awarded to networking professionals who pass CCNA exam #640-407.

To prepare for this exam, Cisco recommends either of the two tracks, shown in table B.1. These tracks are a combination of instructor-led and self-study courses. Both ITM and HPSDC are self paced courses available through Cisco training partners as are the instructor-led CRLS and ICRC courses.

TABLE B.1

CCNA EXAM PREPARATION TRACKS

Track 1	Track 2
Internetworking Technologies (ITM)	Internetworking Technologies (ITM)
Cisco Routing and LAN Switching (CRLS)	Introduction to Cisco Router Configuration (ICRC)
	High-Performance Solutions for Desktop Connectivity (HPSDC)

CCNP

This certification focuses on the ability of the candidate to design, install, and manage larger internetworks.

CCNP certification requires CCNA certification followed by one of two test tracks as outlined in Table B.2. Track 1 focuses on the fundamentals of routed and switched networks, including installation and configuration of routers and switches. Track 2 provides more in-depth knowledge of advanced routing protocols and interconnectivity, including dial up services. Both tracks include Cisco's troubleshooting course (CIT).

TABLE B.2

REQUIREMENTS FOR CCNP CERTIFICATION

Track 1	Track 2
CCNA status	CCNA status
Foundation Routing/ Switching (FRS) Exam #640-406	Advanced Cisco Router Configuration (ACRC) Exam #604-403
Cisco Internetwork Troubleshooting (CIT) Exam #604-406	Cisco LAN Switch Configuration (CLSC) Exam #604-404
	Configuring Monitoring and Troubleshooting Dial up Services (CMTD) Exam #604-405
	Cisco Internetwork Troubleshooting (CIT) Exam #604-406

CCNP Specialties

To keep up with the changing demands of internetworking, Cisco provides five areas of specialization with the CCNP certification. These specializations allow the candidate to focus on a specific field of technological expertise. This provides customers and employers with the ability to locate a professional with the skills to fill their internetworking needs.

Cisco's fields of specialization are Security, Voice Access, Network Management, LAN ATM, and SNA Solutions. The requirements for the specializations are outlined in the following sections.

Security

The Security Specialist certification expands upon CCNP with a focus on internetwork security, including standalone firewall products and Cisco IOS software.

Security Specialist certification requires the following:

◆ CCNP certification

◆ Managing Cisco Network Security (MCNS) Exam #640-442

Voice Access

Voice Access specialization focuses on the skills required for implementing and managing voice and data integration of IP, ATM, and Frame Relay networks.

The requirements for this specialty are as follows:

◆ CCNP certification

◆ Cisco Voice Essentials, Cisco Voice over Frame Relay, ATM, and IP (CVOICE) Exam #640-447

Network Management

Cisco's Network Management Specialist certification expands upon CCNP with a focus on network management solutions for routed and switched internetworks.

Network Management Specialist requires the following:

◆ CCNP certification

◆ Managing Cisco Routed Internetworks (MCRI) Exam #640-443

◆ Managing Cisco Switched Internetworks (MCSI) Exam #640-444

LAN ATM

The focus of LAN ATM specialization is building and maintaining ATM networks in a campus environment.

LAN ATM Specialist certification requires the following:

◆ CCNP certification

◆ Cisco Campus ATM Solutions (CATM) Exam #640-446

SNA Solutions

Cisco's SNA Solution Specialist certification includes a focus on installation, configuration, and troubleshooting Cisco routers in SNA environments.

SNA Solutions certification requires the following:

◆ CCNP certification

◆ SNA Configuration for Multiprotocol Administrators (SNAM) Exam #640-445

◆ Cisco Data Link Switching Plus (DLSWP) Exam #640-450

CCIE

CCIE is Cisco's highest certification available. Although CCNP status is not required to achieve CCIE certification, it is recommended to use the CCNP track as a stepping stone to help prepare the candidate to succeed in pursuit of CCIE. In addition to CCNP training, the candidate should also be familiar with the information provided in Installing and Maintaining Cisco Routers (IMCR), Cisco Data Link Switching Plus (DLSWP), and Cisco Internetwork Design (CID), as well as having significant hands-on experience. When following these recommendations, you should be aware that SNAM is a prerequisite to DLSWP.

Recommended prerequisites to taking the CCIE exam are as follows:

- ◆ CCNP training
- ◆ Installing and Maintaining Cisco Routers (IMCR)
- ◆ Cisco Data Link Switching Plus (DLSWP)
- ◆ Cisco Internetwork Design (CID)
- ◆ Significant hands-on experience

Requirements of CCIE certification are as follows:

- ◆ Cisco's CCIE-Routing/Switching Qualification Exam #350-001
- ◆ CCIE-Routing/Switching Certification Laboratory

The CCIE Routing/Switching lab is an intense two-day, hands-on, practical exam. The first day of the lab consists of a session in which the candidate is presented with a scenario to implement using Cisco Routing/Switching equipment. Other connectivity equipment may be included. On the second day, the candidate is presented with faults that have been added to the first day's implementation. The candidate is to diagnose, isolate, and remove the faults.

Network Design

The Network Design Certification track is designed for professionals who need the skills required to design complex internetwork systems, including routed LAN and WAN systems as well as switched LAN networks. Network Design candidates should already have the ability to install, configure, and operate internetworking systems including routers, LAN switches, and WAN switches.

CCDA

No previous certification is required for CCDA status.

The self-paced course Designing Cisco Networks (CDN) is recommended to adequately prepare for CCDA certification. This course will provide you with a working knowledge of design strategies for small networks and a good foundation for building toward CCDP status. CCNA Certification is granted for passing the associated Exam #640-441.

Requirements for CCDA status are as follows:

- ◆ Designing Cisco Networks (CDN) Exam #640-441

CCDP

CCDP is Cisco's highest level of design certification. It is designed to bring together all the phases of internetwork design using Cisco routers and switches.

A candidate for CCDP must have attained both CCDA and CCNA status. In addition, Cisco requires the candidate to follow one of two certification tracks (see Table B.3). Track 1 includes Foundation Routing/Switching (FRS) Exam #640-409 and Cisco Internetwork Design (CID) Exam #640-025. This track provides a strong working knowledge of installing and configuring routers and switches in addition to more advanced design concepts.

Track 2 covers Advanced Cisco Router Configuration (ACRC) Exam #640-403, Cisco LAN Switch Configuration (CLSC) Exam #640-404, Configuring, Monitoring, Troubleshooting Dial up services (CMTD) Exam #640-405, and Cisco Internetwork Design (CID) Exam #640-025. This track is designed for the professional who needs more specific information on routing, switching, and dial-up systems.

TABLE B.3

REQUIREMENTS FOR CCDP STATUS

Track1	Track 2
CCNA status	CCNA status
CCDA status	CCDA status
Foundation Routing/ Switching (FRS) Exam #640-409	Advanced Cisco Router Configuration (ACRC) Exam #640-403
Cisco Internetwork Design (CID) Exam #640-025(CLSC)	Cisco LAN Switch Configuration Exam #640-404
	Configuring, Monitoring, Troubleshooting Dial up services (CMTD) Exam #640-405
	Cisco Internetwork Design (CID) Exam #640-025

WAN Switching

Network professionals who achieve WAN Switching certification will have proven expertise in the following:

◆ Media and telephony transmission techniques, error detection, and Time Division Multiplexing (TDM)

◆ Knowledge of Frame Relay and ATM

◆ Knowledge of Cisco-specific technologies, including WAN switch platforms, applications, architectures, and interfaces

◆ Knowledge of service provider technology, including packet encapsulation and network-to-network interconnections

Network Support

Like the Routing/Switching category, WAN Switching has similarly separated tracks within it. In the Network Support track, Cisco offers Cisco Certified Network Associate (CCNA), Cisco Certified Network Professional (CCNP), and Cisco Certified Internet Expert (CCIE). However, there are no specialties within the CCNP status offered for the WAN Switching category.

CCNA

This certification is designed for management of small internetworks with limited interconnection. CCNA certification is awarded to networking professionals who pass CCNA-WAN Switching exam #640-410.

Recommended training for the CCNA WAN-Switching certification is as follows:

◆ WAN Quick Start Self-paced CD-ROM

◆ Installation of Cisco WAN Switches course (ICWS)

CCNP

This certification focuses on the ability of the candidate to design, install, and manage larger internetworks.

CCNP certification requires CCNA certification followed by a series of courses and associated exams.

WAN-Switching CCNP certification requirements are as follows:

◆ CCNA-WAN Switching status

◆ Multiband Switch and Service Configuration (MSSC) Exam #640-419

◆ BPX Switch and Service Configuration (BSSC) Exam #640-425

◆ MGX ATM Concentrator Configuration (MACC) Exam #640-411

◆ Cisco Strataview Plus Installation and Operations (SVIO) Exam #640-451

CCIE

The CCIE WAN Switching lab is an intense two-day, hands-on, practical exam. The first day of the lab consists of a session in which the candidate is presented with a scenario to implement using Cisco WAN Switching equipment. Other connectivity equipment may be included. On the second day, the candidate is presented with faults that have been added to the first day's implementation. The candidate is to diagnose, isolate, and remove the faults.

Recommended training for CCIE includes the following:

◆ CCNP-WAN Switching status

◆ Project Management Network Implementation Services (PMNIS) Self-Paced CD-ROM

◆ Significant hands-on experience

The requirements for CCIE-WAN Switching Certification are as follows:

◆ CCIE-WAN Switching Qualification Exam #350-007

◆ CCIE-WAN Switching Certification Laboratory

Network Design

For candidates who need the ability to design switched WAN networks with a high degree of efficiency and reliability, Cisco offers WAN Switching Network Design certification. This certification's focus is on creating ATM and Frame Relay networks with the ability to manage traffic and voice services.

Network Design candidates should already have the ability to install, configure, and operate internetworking systems including routers, LAN switches, and WAN switches.

> **NOTE**
>
> **No CCDA Certification** Cisco has no CCDA certification in its WAN Switching Design track.

CCDP

CCDP is Cisco's highest level of design certification. It is designed to bring together all phases of internetwork design using Cisco routers and switches in a WAN environment.

A candidate for CCDP must have attained both CCNA and CCNP status. In addition, Cisco requires Designing Switched WAN and Voice Solutions (DSWVS) Exam #640-413.

Requirements for CCDP in the WAN-Switching segment are as follows:

◆ CCNA-WAN Switching status

◆ CCNP-WAN Switching status

◆ Designing Switched WAN and Voice Solutions (DSWVS) Exam #640-413

ISP Dial

ISP services have become a world-wide business. These providers need well-trained professionals who can install, configure, and maintain their complex networking systems. Cisco's ISP Dial certification gives a candidate the ability to stand out from the crowd as a proven expert in all facets of Internet Provider technology.

CCIE

The only certification available in the ISP Dial track, CCIE status requires significant training and experience in the field of dial up and WAN internetworking. With the tremendous growth in Internet access, proven professionals are needed to design and implement reliable and efficient connectivity methods. CCIE in ISP Dial certification allows providers to select the best candidates to implement these solutions.

Recommended training for the CCIE-ISP Dial certification is as follows:

◆ CCNP training

◆ Installing and Maintaining Cisco Routers (IMCR)

◆ Cisco Internetwork Design (CID)

◆ Managing Cisco Network Security (MCNS)

◆ Cisco AS5200 Universal Access Server (AS5200)

◆ Significant hands-on experience

Requirements of CCIE certification are Cisco's CCIE-ISP Dial Qualification Exam #350-004 and CCIE-ISP Dial Certification Laboratory. The CCIE ISP Dial lab is an intense two-day, hands-on, practical exam. The first day of the lab consists of a session in which the candidate is presented with a scenario to implement using Cisco ISP Dial equipment. Other connectivity equipment may be included. On the second day, the candidate is presented with faults that have been added to the first day's implementation. The candidate is to diagnose, isolate, and remove the faults.

Requirements for CCIE-ISP Dial are as follows:

◆ CCIE-ISP Dial Qualification Exam #350-004

◆ CCIE-ISP Dial Certification Laboratory

HOW TO BECOME A CERTIFIED CISCO SYSTEMS INSTRUCTOR

Cisco maintains very strict policies regarding CCSI candidates. Prerequisites include a strong working knowledge of computer systems, significant hands-on experience with routing/switching and/or WAN environments, and previous teaching experience. Each CCSI is certified on a per course basis and must be sponsored by a Cisco Training Partner. To achieve certification, the candidate must sign a partner agreement, attend the standard course (for which certification is desired) presented by a CCSI, pass the exam for the course, and pass Cisco's Instructor Certification Process (ICP).

The ICP is an intensive two-day session in which the instructor candidate is evaluated by Cisco for presentation skills, technical knowledge, and hands-on lab capabilities. This evaluation is performed at Cisco's facilities.

To become certified to teach additional courses, the CCSI is required to attend the course at any of Cisco's Training Partners, pass the appropriate exam, and submit a Request for Additional Certification Form to Cisco.

CONCLUSION

Many IT employers require certification as a condition of hire. Certification is much more than just a reward for learning a particular topic. It provides candidates with the ability to quickly and easily prove a working knowledge of IT systems and integration.

Cisco certification goes beyond most professional certifications in the networking industry by requiring more
than simply memorizing facts and theories. To achieve
these certifications, the candidate should have significant practical working knowledge of the equipment
and systems discussed. In this way, Cisco helps to eliminate the well-known problem of "certified" professionals who have book knowledge but little, if any, ability
to apply that knowledge. The CCIE lab is deliberately
designed to prevent this type of situation. This helps to
make Cisco certified candidates much more valuable to
potential employers and customers.

Thank you for choosing New Riders' *CCNA Training
Guide.* Good luck in pursuing your Cisco certifications!

What's On the CD-ROM

This appendix offers a brief rundown of what you'll find on the CD-ROM that comes with this book. For a more detailed description of the newly developed Top Score test engine, exclusive to New Riders Publishing, please see Appendix D, "How to Use the Top Score Software Suite."

TOP SCORE

Top Score is a test engine developed exclusively for New Riders Publishing. In addition to providing a means of evaluating your knowledge of the exam material, Top Score features several innovations that help you to improve your mastery of the subject matter. For example, the practice tests allow you to check your score according to exam area or category, which helps you determine which topics you need to study further. Other modes allow you to obtain immediate feedback on your response to a question, explanation of the correct answer, and even hyperlinks to the chapter in an electronic version of the book where the topic of the question is covered. Again, for a complete description of the benefits of Top Score, see Appendix D.

Before you attempt to run the Top Score software, make sure that autorun is enabled. If you prefer not to use autorun, you can run the application from the CD-ROM by double-clicking the START.EXE file from within Explorer.

EXCLUSIVE ELECTRONIC VERSION OF TEXT

As alluded to above, the CD-ROM also contains the electronic version of this book in Portable Document Format (PDF). In addition to the links to the book that are built into the Top Score engine, you can use this version to help search for terms you need to study or other book elements. The electronic version comes complete with all figures as they appear in the book.

COPYRIGHT INFORMATION AND DISCLAIMER

Macmillan Computer Publishing's Top Score test engine: Copyright 1999 New Riders Publishing. All rights reserved. Made in U.S.A.

How to Use the Top Score Software Suite

GETTING STARTED

The installation procedure is very simple. Put the CD into the CD-ROM drive. The auto-run function starts and after a moment, you will see the opening screen. Click Exit to quit, or click Learn to proceed. If you click Learn, you will see a window offering you the choice of launching any of the three Top Score applications.

> **NOTE**
>
> **Getting Started Without Autorun** If you have disabled the autorun function, you can start the Top Score Test Simulation Software Suite by viewing the contents of the CD-ROM in Explorer and double-clicking START.EXE.

At this point you are ready to use the Top Score Test Simulation Software Suite.

INSTRUCTIONS ON USING THE TOP SCORE TEST SIMULATION SOFTWARE SUITE

Top Score Software consists of the following three applications:

◆ Practice Exams

◆ Study Cards

◆ Flash Cards

The Practice Exams application provides exams that simulate the test center certification exams. The Study Cards serve as a study aid organized around specific exam objectives. Both are in multiple-choice format. Flash Cards, another study aid, requires responses to open-ended questions that test your knowledge of the material at a level deeper than that of recognition memory.

To start the Study Cards, Practice Exams, or Flash Cards application, follow these steps:

1. Begin from the overview of the CD contents (double-click the CD-ROM Contents icon). The left window provides you with options for obtaining further information about any of the Top Score applications as well as a way to launch them.

2. Click a book icon, and a listing of related topics appears below it in Explorer fashion.

3. Click an application name. This displays more detailed information for that application in the right window.

4. To start an application, click its book icon. Then click on the Starting the Program option. Do this for Practice Exams, for example. Information appears in the right window. Click on the button for the exam, and the opening screens of the application appear.

Further details about using each of the applications follow.

Using the Top Score Practice Exams

The Practice Exams interface is simple and straightforward. To begin a practice exam, click the button for the exam name. After a moment, you see an opening screen similar to the one shown in Figure D.1.

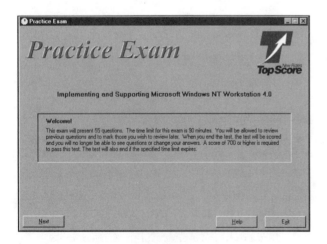

FIGURE D.1
Top Score Practice Exams opening screen.

Click on the Next button to see a disclaimer and copyright screen. Read the information, and then click Top Score's Start button. A notice appears indicating that the program is randomly selecting questions for the practice exam from the exam database (see Figure D.2.)

The items are selected from a larger set of 150–900 questions. The random selection of questions from the database takes some time to retrieve. Don't reboot; your machine is not hung!

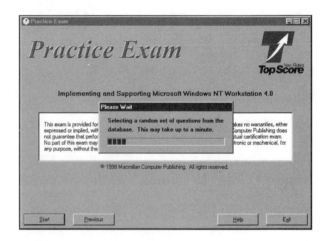

FIGURE D.2
Top Score's Please Wait notice.

After the questions have been selected, the first test item appears. See Figure D.3 for an example of a test item screen.

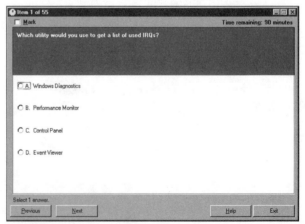

FIGURE D.3
A Top Score test item requiring a single response.

Notice several important features of this window. The question number and the total number of retrieved questions appears in the top-left corner of the window in the control bar. Immediately below that is a check box labeled Mark, which enables you to mark any exam item as one you would like to return to later. Across the screen from the Mark check box, you see the total time remaining for the exam.

The test question is located in a colored section (it's gray in the figure). Directly below the test question, in the white area, are response choices. Be sure to note that immediately below the responses are instructions about how to respond, including the number of responses required. You will notice that question items requiring a single response, such as that shown in Figure D.3, have option buttons. Items requiring multiple responses have check boxes (see Figure D.4).

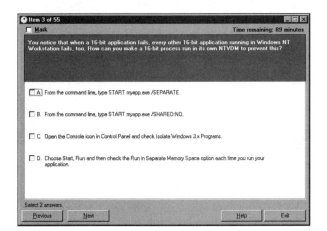

FIGURE D.4
A Top Score test item requiring multiple responses.

Some questions and some responses do not appear on the screen in their entirety. You will recognize such items because a scroll bar appears to the right of the question item or response. Use the scroll bar to reveal the rest of the question or response item.

The buttons at the bottom of a window enable you to move back to a previous test item, proceed to the next test item, or exit Top Score Practice Exams.

Some items require you to examine additional information referred to as *Exhibits*. These screens typically include graphs, diagrams, or other types of visual information that you must refer to in order to respond to the test question. You can access Exhibits by clicking the Exhibit button, also located at the bottom of the window.

After you complete the practice test by moving through all of the test questions for your exam, you arrive at a summary screen titled Item Review (see Figure D.5).

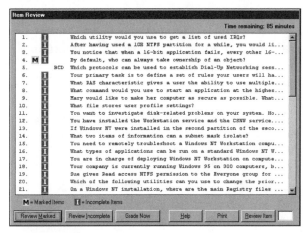

FIGURE D.5
The Top Score Item Review window.

This window enables you to see all the question numbers, your response(s) to each item, any questions you have marked, and any you've left incomplete. The buttons at the bottom of the screen enable you to review all the marked items and incomplete items in numeric order.

If you want to review a specific marked or incomplete item, simply type the desired item number in the box in the lower-right corner of the window and click the Review Item button. This takes you to that particular item. After you review the item, you can respond to the question. Notice that this window also offers the Next and Previous options. You can also select the Item Review button to return to the Item Review window.

> **NOTE**
>
> **Your Time Is Limited**   If you exceed the time allotted for the test, you do not have the opportunity to review any marked or incomplete items. The program will move on to the next screen.

After you complete your review of the practice test questions, click the Grade Now button to find out how you did. An Examination Score Report is generated for your practice test (see Figure D.6). This report displays the required score for this particular certification exam, and provides your score on the practice test, and a grade. The report also breaks down your performance on the practice test by the specific objectives for the exam. Click the Print button to print out the results of your performance.

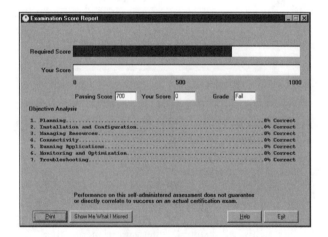

FIGURE D.6
The Top Score Examination Score Report window.

You also have the option of reviewing those items that you answered incorrectly. Click the Show Me What I Missed button to view a summary of those items. You can print out that information if you need further practice or review; such printouts can be used to guide your use of Study Cards and Flash Cards.

Using Top Score Study Cards

To start the software, begin from the overview of the CD contents. Click the Study Cards icon to see a listing of topics. Clicking Study Cards brings up more detailed information for this application in the right window.

To launch Study Cards, click on Starting the Program. In the right window, click on the button for the exam in which you are interested. After a moment, an initial screen similar to that of the Practice Exams appears.

Click on the Next button to see the first Study Cards screen (see Figure D.7).

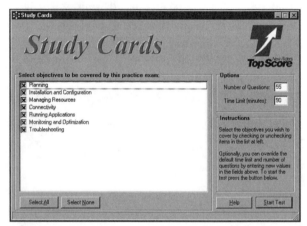

FIGURE D.7
The first Study Cards screen.

The interface for Study Cards is very similar to that of Practice Exams. However, several important options enable you to prepare for an exam. The Study Cards material is organized according to the specific objectives for each exam. You can opt to receive questions on all the objectives, or you can use the check boxes to request questions on a limited set of objectives. For example, if you have already completed a Practice Exam and your score report indicates that you need work on Planning, you can choose to cover only the Planning objectives for your Study Cards session.

You can also determine the number of questions presented by typing the number of questions you want into the option box at the right of the screen. You can control the amount of time you will be allowed for a review by typing the number of minutes into the Time Limit option box immediately below the one for the number of questions.

When you're ready, click the Start Test button, and Study Cards randomly selects the indicated number of questions from the question database. A dialog box appears, informing you that this process could take some time. After the questions are selected, the first item appears, in a format similar to that in Figure D.8.

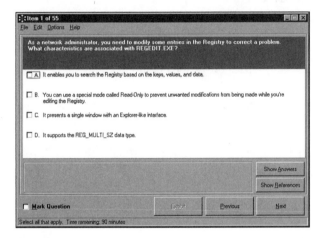

FIGURE D.8
A Study Cards item.

Respond to the questions in the same manner you did for Practice Exam questions. Option buttons signify that a single answer is required, whereas check boxes indicate that multiple answers are expected.

Notice the menu options at the top of the window. You can pull down the File menu to exit from the program. The Edit menu contains commands for the copy function and even allows you to copy questions to the Windows clipboard.

Should you feel the urge to take some notes on a particular question, you can do so via the Options menu. When you pull it down, choose Open Notes, and Notepad opens. Type any notes you want to save for later reference. The Options menu also allows you to start over with another exam.

The Study Cards application provides you with immediate feedback of whether you answered the question correctly. Click the Show Answers button to highlight the correct answer(s)on the screen, as shown in Figure D.9.

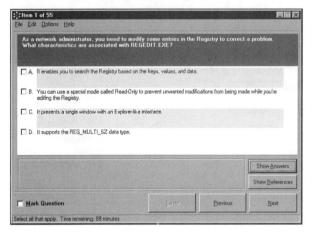

FIGURE D.9
The correct answer is highlighted.

Study Cards also includes Item Review, Score Report, and Show Me What I Missed features that function the same as those in the Practice Exams application.

Using Top Score Flash Cards

Flash Cards offers a third way to use the exam question database. The Flash Cards items do not offer you multiple-choice answers to choose from; instead, they require you to respond in a short answer/essay format. Flash Cards is intended to help you learn the material well enough to respond with the correct answers in your own words, rather than just by recognizing the correct answer.

If you have the depth of knowledge to answer questions without prompting, you should certainly be prepared to pass a multiple-choice exam.

Start the Flash Cards application in the same way you did Practice Exams and Study Cards. Click the Flash Cards icon, and then click Start the Program. Click the button for the exam in which you are interested, and the opening screen appears. It looks similar to the example shown in Figure D.10.

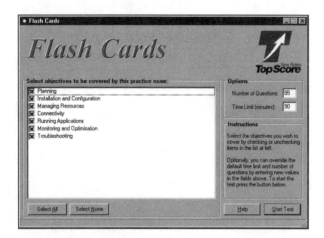

FIGURE D.10
The Flash Cards opening screen.

You can choose Flash Cards according to the various objectives, as you did Study Cards. Simply select the objectives you want to cover, enter the number of questions you want, and enter the amount of time you want to limit yourself to. Click the Start Test button to start the Flash Cards session, and you see a dialog box notifying you that questions are being selected.

The Flash Cards items appear in an interface similar to that of Practice Exams and Study Cards (see Figure D.11).

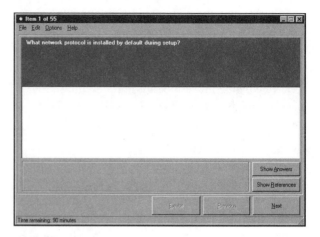

FIGURE D.11
A Flash Cards item.

Notice, however, that although a question is presented, no possible answers appear. You type your answer in the white space below the question (see Figure D.12).

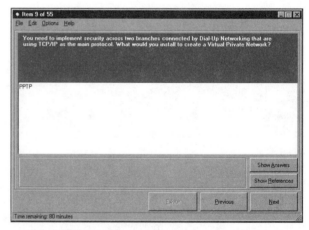

FIGURE D.12
A typed answer in Flash Cards.

Compare your answer to the correct answer by clicking the Show Answers button (see Figure D.13).

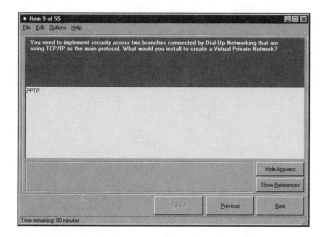

FIGURE D.13
The correct answer is shown.

You can also use the Show Reference button in the same manner as described earlier in the Study Cards section.

The pull-down menus provide nearly the same functionality as those in Study Cards, with the exception of a Paste command on the Edit menu instead of the Copy Question command.

Flash Cards provide simple feedback; they do not include an Item Review or Score Report. They are intended to provide you with an alternative way of assessing your level of knowledge that will encourage you to learn the information more thoroughly than other methods do.

SUMMARY

The Top Score Test Simulation Software Suite's applications provide you with several approaches to exam preparation. Use Practice Exams to do just that—practice taking exams, not only to assess your learning, but also to prepare yourself for the test-taking situation. Use Study Cards and Flash Cards as tools for more focused assessment and review, and to reinforce the knowledge you are gaining. You will find that these three applications are the perfect way to finish off your exam preparation.

Symbols

A

B

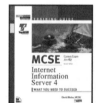

NEW RIDERS CERTIFICATION TITLES

FAST TRACKS

The Accelerated Path to Certification Success

Fast Tracks provide an easy way to review the key elements of each certification technology without being bogged down with elementary-level information.

These guides are perfect for when you already have real-world, hands-on experience. They're the ideal enhancement to training courses, test simulators, and comprehensive training guides.

No fluff—simply what you really need to pass the exam!

MCSE Fast Track:
Networking Essentials
1-56205-939-4,
$19.99, 9/98

MCSE Fast Track:
Windows 98
0-7357-0016-8,
$19.99, 12/98

MCSE Fast Track:
TCP/IP
1-56205-937-8,
$19.99, 9/98

MCSE Fast Track:
Windows NT Server 4
1-56205-935-1,
$19.99, 9/98

MCSE Fast Track: Windows
NT Server 4 Enterprise
1-56205-940-8,
$19.99, 9/98

MCSE Fast Track: Windows
NT Workstation 4
1-56205-938-6,
$19.99, 9/98

A+ Fast Track:
Core/Hardware Exam &
DOS/Windows Exam
0-7357-0028-1,
$34.99, 3/99

MCSE Fast Track: Internet
Information Server 4
1-56205-936-X
$19.99, 9/98

MCSE Fast Track: SQL
Server 7 Administration
0-7357-0041-9,
$29.99, Q2/99

MCSE/MCSD Fast Track:
SQL Server 7 Database Design
0-7357-0040-0,
$29.99, 2/99

MCSD Fast Track: Visual
Basic 6 Exam 70-175
0-7357-0018-4,
$19.99, 12/98

MCSD Fast Track: Visual
Basic 6 Exam 70-176
0-7357-0019-2,
$19.99, 12/98

MCSD Fast Track:
Solution Architectures
0-7357-0029-X,
$29.99, Q3/99

New Riders Certification Titles

TestPreps

PRACTICE, CHECK, PASS!

Questions. Questions. And more questions. That's what you'll find in our New Riders *TestPreps*. They're great practice books when you reach the final stage of studying for the exam. We recommend them as supplements to our *Training Guides*.

What makes these study tools unique is that the questions are the primary focus of each book. All the text in these books support and explain the answers to the questions.

✓ **Scenario-based questions** challenge your experience.

✓ **Multiple-choice questions** prep you for the exam.

✓ **Fact-based questions** test your product knowledge.

✓ **Exam strategies** assist you in test preparation.

✓ **Complete yet concise explanations of answers** make for better retention.

✓ **Two practice exams** prepare you for the real thing.

✓ **Fast Facts** offer you everything you need to review in the testing center parking lot.

Practice, practice, practice—pass with New Riders TestPreps!

MCSE TestPrep: Networking Essentials, Second Edition

0-7357-0010-9, $19.99, 12/98

MCSE TestPrep: Windows 98

1-56205-922-X, $19.99, 11/98

MCSE TestPrep: Windows 95, Second Edition

0-7357-0011-7, $29.99, 12/98

MCSE TestPrep: Windows NT Server 4, Second Edition

0-7357-0012-5, $19.99, 12/98

MCSE TestPrep: Windows NT Server 4 Enterprise, Second Edition

0-7357-0009-5, $19.99, 11/98

MCSE TestPrep: Windows NT Workstation 4, Second Edition

0-7357-0008-7, $19.99, 12/98

MCSE TestPrep: TCP/IP, Second Edition

0-7357-0025-7, $19.99, 12/98

A+ Certification TestPrep

1-56205-892-4, $19.99, 12/98

MCSD TestPrep: Visual Basic 6 Exams

0-7357-0032-X, $29.99, 1/99

Test Preps

FIRST EDITIONS

MCSE TestPrep: SQL Server 6.5 Administration, 0-7897-1597-X

MCSE TestPrep: SQL Server 6.5 Design and Implementation, 1-56205-915-7

MCSE TestPrep: Windows 95 70-64 Exam, 0-7897-1609-7

MCSE TestPrep: Internet Explorer 4, 0-7897-1654-2

MCSE TestPrep: Exchange Server 5.5, 0-7897-1611-9

MCSE TestPrep: IIS 4.0, 0-7897-1610-0

How to Contact Us

IF YOU NEED THE LATEST UPDATES ON A TITLE THAT YOU'VE PURCHASED:

1) Visit our Web site at www.newriders.com.

2) Click on the Product Support link, and enter your book's ISBN number, which is located on the back cover in the bottom right-hand corner.

3) There you'll find available updates for your title.

IF YOU ARE HAVING TECHNICAL PROBLEMS WITH THE BOOK OR THE CD THAT IS INCLUDED:

1) Check the book's information page on our Web site according to the instructions listed above, or

2) Email us at support@mcp.com, or

3) Fax us at (317) 817-7488 attn: Tech Support.

IF YOU HAVE COMMENTS ABOUT ANY OF OUR CERTIFICATION PRODUCTS THAT ARE NON-SUPPORT RELATED:

1) Email us at certification@mcp.com, or

2) Write to us at New Riders, 201 W. 103rd St., Indianapolis, IN 46290-1097, or

3) Fax us at (317) 581-4663.

IF YOU ARE OUTSIDE THE UNITED STATES AND NEED TO FIND A DISTRIBUTOR IN YOUR AREA:

Please contact our international department at international@mcp.com.

IF YOU WISH TO PREVIEW ANY OF OUR CERTIFICATION BOOKS FOR CLASSROOM USE:

Email us at pr@mcp.com. Your message should include your name, title, training company or school, department, address, phone number, office days/hours, text in use, and enrollment. Send these details along with your request for desk/examination copies and/or additional information.

WE WANT TO KNOW WHAT YOU THINK

To better serve you, we would like your opinion on the content and quality of this book. Please complete this card and mail it to us or fax it to 317-581-4663.

Name _____

Address _____

City _____ State _____ Zip _____

Phone _____ Email Address _____

Occupation _____

Which certification exams have you already passed? _____
_____
_____
_____

Which certification exams do you plan to take? _____
_____
_____
_____

What influenced your purchase of this book?
❑ Recommendation ❑ Cover Design
❑ Table of Contents ❑ Index
❑ Magazine Review ❑ Advertisement
❑ Reputation of New Riders ❑ Author Name

How would you rate the contents of this book?
❑ Excellent ❑ Very Good
❑ Good ❑ Fair
❑ Below Average ❑ Poor

What other types of certification products will you buy/have you bought to help you prepare for the exam?
❑ Quick reference books ❑ Testing software
❑ Study guides ❑ Other

What do you like most about this book? Check all that apply.
❑ Content ❑ Writing Style
❑ Accuracy ❑ Examples
❑ Listings ❑ Design
❑ Index ❑ Page Count
❑ Price ❑ Illustrations

What do you like least about this book? Check all that apply.
❑ Content ❑ Writing Style
❑ Accuracy ❑ Examples
❑ Listings ❑ Design
❑ Index ❑ Page Count
❑ Price ❑ Illustrations

What would be a useful follow-up book to this one for you?_____
Where did you purchase this book? _____
Can you name a similar book that you like better than this one, or one that is as good? Why?_____
_____
_____

How many New Riders books do you own? _____
What are your favorite certification or general computer book titles? _____
_____

What other titles would you like to see us develop?_____
_____

Any comments for us? _____
_____
_____

Fold here and tape to mail

- -

New Riders
201 W. 103rd St.
Indianapolis, IN 46290

NEW RIDERS TOP SCORE TEST SIMULATION SOFTWARE SUITE

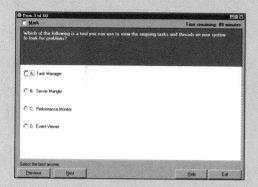

Practice Exams simulate the actual Cisco exams. Option buttons and check boxes indicate whether there is one or more than one correct answer. All test questions are presented randomly to create a unique exam each time you practice—the ideal way to prepare.

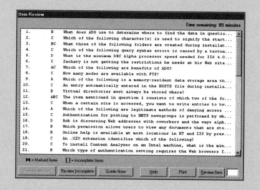

The Item Review shows you the answers you've already selected and the questions you need to revisit before grading the exam.

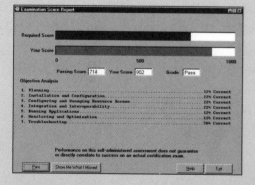

The Score Report displays your score for each objective category, helping you to define which objectives you need to study more. It also shows you what score you need to pass and your total score.

Study Cards allow you to test yourself and receive immediate feedback and an answer explanation. Link to the text for more in-depth explanations.

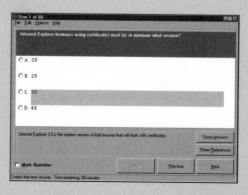